# Handbook of Individual Differences in Reading

D1710128

The central unifying theme of this state-of-the-art contribution to research on literacy is its rethinking and reconceptualization of individual differences in reading. Previous research, focused on cognitive components of reading, signaled the need for ongoing work to identify relevant individual differences in reading, to determine the relationship(s) of individual differences to reading development, and to account for interactions among individual differences. Addressing developments in each of these areas, this volume also describes affective individual differences, and the environments in which individual differences in reading may emerge, operate, interact, and change.

The scant comprehensive accounting of individual differences in reading is reflected in the nature of reading instruction programs today, the outcomes that are expected from successful teaching and learning, and the manner in which reading development is assessed. An important contribution of this volume is to provide *prima facie* evidence of the benefits of broad conceptualization of the ways in which readers differ. The *Handbook of Individual Differences in Reading* moves the field forward by encompassing cognitive, non-cognitive, contextual, and methodological concerns. Its breadth of coverage serves as both a useful summary of the current state of knowledge and a guide for future work in this area.

**Peter Afflerbach** is Professor of Reading in the Department of Teaching and Learning, Policy and Leadership at the University of Maryland, USA.

# Handbook of Individual Differences in Reading

## Reader, Text, and Context

*Edited by*
*Peter Afflerbach*

NEW YORK AND LONDON

First published 2016
by Routledge
711 Third Avenue, New York, NY 10017

and by Routledge
2 Park Square, Milton Park, Abingdon, Oxon OX14 4RN

*Routledge is an imprint of the Taylor & Francis Group, an informa business*

*Library of Congress Cataloging in Publication Data*
  Handbook of individual differences in reading : reader, text, and context / edited by Peter Afflerbach.
  pages cm
  Includes bibliographical references and index.
  1. Individualized reading instruction—Handbooks, manuals, etc.
  I. Afflerbach, Peter, editor of compilation.
  LB1050.38.H36 2015
  372.41'7—dc23
  2015001048

ISBN: 978–0-415–65887–4 (hbk)
ISBN: 978–0-415–65888–1 (pbk)
ISBN: 978–0-203–07556–2 (ebk)

Typeset in Bembo and Stone Sans
by Florence Production Ltd, Stoodleigh, Devon, UK

Printed and bound in the United States of America
by Edwards Brothers Malloy

*This volume is dedicated to the memory of two wonderful people:*

*Joan Kelly Afflerbach, Librarian, New York City Public Schools, and*

*Lois Grimes Afflerbach, Librarian, Queens College, City University of New York.*

# Contents

Contents

# Foreword

Perusing the chapters in the *Handbook of Individual Differences in Reading: Reader, Text and Context* got us in a historical state of mind as this book's appearance will mark thirty-five years since the present two writers embarked on our own studies of individual differences in reading development. Work in the field was extremely sparse then, not interdisciplinary at all, and fairly narrowly focused. This wonderful volume edited by Peter Afflerbach certainly demonstrates that we have come a long way since then and that all three of these deficiencies have been largely remedied. Areas that had just been opened up in the 1980s are now dense with detailed findings and important theoretical developments. Areas of study that barely existed in the 1980s are now fields with strong momentum. All are represented in the volume.

In a volume of such diversity and such quality it is hard to think of "value added" comments that might have some generality as opposed to being applicable to only a couple of selected chapters. Two generic points do come to mind though. They represent two issues that we discussed over thirty years ago that at the time were largely unrecognized in reading theory. The two interrelated issues do in fact receive more attention now, although perhaps *still* not as much as they should.

One of our oldest admonitions to the field was that models of reading development must be used to constrain theories of individual differences, and must be used in addition to constrain models of reading disability. That is, speculations about the causes of individual differences in reading acquisition need to be constrained by a specified model of the reading acquisition process itself. Confusion reigned in our field throughout the 1970s and 1980s because studies of individual differences had uncovered a plethora of information processing tasks on which the performance of skilled and less skilled readers differ. However, the field was not allowing any of these to be "killed off" in a Popperian sense because they were not convergent with an emerging consensus on a developmental model of reading. Byrne (1992) articulated the problem very cogently:

> One thing that could be said about this rather long list of possible causes of reading problems is that it is needed, because reading is multifaceted and because there are many kinds of problems. This is a standard line of reasoning . . . [but] given the uncertainty about a typology of reading difficulties and given that fewer explanatory constructs than reading problems may be needed, there may well be too much explanatory power for the job at hand. A way is needed to constrain the power. Economy of explanation characterizes the scientific endeavor and should be invoked in this branch of science. It is possible that the explanatory power available could be constrained if it were required that each of the many hypothetical causes of reading problems fits a well-worked-out account of the acquisition procedure (p. 3).

At the time Byrne wrote, few papers in the reading literature had attempted the type of integration that he recommended: fitting the empirical research on individual differences into a model of the acquisition process. Most investigators had either focused on developing generic developmental models of stages that all children traverse, or they had concentrated on looking for patterns of correlations in studies of individual differences. The field gradually spawned more of the type of synthesis that Byrne recommended, and the fruitful results can be seen in this volume (see Afflerbach, Chapter 1, for a discussion of the evolution of conceptualizations of individual differences in reading, and Loughlin & Alexander, Chapter 27, for a discussion of the complex relations and interactions of individual differences).

Our own early sporadic attempts at this type of synthesis (Cunningham, 1990; Stanovich, 1986; Stanovich, Cunningham, & Cramer, 1984) proved to us how difficult this type of comprehensively convergent theory was to execute. The 1986 Matthew effects paper did receive flattering attention, but even it confused some readers by moving back and forth between issues of development and issues of individual differences. A decade later, Bast and Reitsma (1998) still thought it was necessary to clarify things. They made a very useful distinction between the *Matthew effect* and the *Matthew effect model*. The former refers to the fan-spread effect on variability with time—that over time, the variability in reading and reading-related cognitive skills increases. The term "fan spread" is not a technical term, but rather a jargon term used in this literature to refer to situations where the variability in a performance metric increases with age. In contrast, as Bast and Reitsma pointed out, a Matthew effect model

> attempts to account for these fan-spread effects. The fan spread is, however, simply one component of the Matthew effect phenomenon. The most important feature of the model as proposed by Stanovich (1986) is the underlying developmental pattern that causes the outcome. The phenomenon of increasing achievement differences is hypothesized to be caused by a specific developmental pattern of interrelations between reading skills and other variables.
>
> (Bast & Reitsma, 1998, p. 1373)

The distinction made by Bast and Reitsma (1998) is useful because much of the attention subsequent to the Matthew paper had focused on the fan-spread effect itself, whereas we were always equally concerned with the developmental model, regardless of whether a fan-spread exists for certain skills or not. In short, the issue of reciprocal causation involving reading experience is not totally coextensive with the issue of the fan-spread effect. It is possible for reading experience to be a causal factor in cognitive growth whether or not it is a cause of a fan-spread. For instance, if a student is motivated to read, they will read more frequently. Reading volume is a major factor for the development of vocabulary, facilitating reading comprehension and hence as reading becomes more efficient, levels of print exposure should further increase. In another example highlighting the social emotional aspects of reading, when learning to read comes easily, students often enter into a positive feedback loop leading to feelings of success and competence. This sense of self-efficacy fosters increased interest to explore the worlds of books independently, yielding affective identification as a reader that leads to increased persistence in the face of difficult text. The reminder by Bast and Reitsma to clarify the distinction between the *Matthew effect* and the *Matthew effect model* leads to the second, and related, point of context for the present volume: that the factors affecting the variability in a skill are not necessarily the same factors related to its mean level, as will be discussed below.

Of course, this point is often a caveat to heritability studies of reading and reading-related cognitive skills. It is important to remember that heritability (an individual difference concept) does not imply lack of malleability (a concept referring to the absolute level of performance). The sometimes confusing difference between when a study is addressing variability in a skill and when a study is discussing the absolute performance level for a particular task can make our literature difficult to read. Being sure to keep the implications drawn from these studies consistent can be a difficult task. Consider an example related to Matthew effects.

Schools create opportunities for learning and for acquiring critical skills and knowledge. But children then proceed to *use* those skills outside of school. The differential reading skills thus acquired enable differential bootstrapping of further vocabulary, knowledge, and cognitive structures outside of school (one of the key points from the 1986 paper). These bootstrapped knowledge bases then create further individual differences that become manifest in differential performance as children grapple with subsequent in-school content and skills. For example, Stanovich (2000) discussed studies finding that the summer period, when the children are not in school, accounts for more of the gap between the high-achieving and low-achieving students than does the period when the children are actually in school. It is important to note though, that this research (showing fan spread over the summer) does not at all contradict the research showing unique effects of the school year on cognitive development (Frazier & Morrison, 1998; Morrison, Alberts, & Griffith, 1997). The latter is focused on the *mean levels* of cognitive skills, whereas the former concerned changes in the *variability*. It is perfectly possible for mean levels of skills to be more affected during the school year rather than the summer and for the summer to be the main cause of the variability in those skills.

One can easily imagine a (simplified) Matthew-like model that could account for such an effect. If during school the cognitive growth of all children is occurring and during the summer the growth for only a subset of children is occurring, then mean levels will be increasing to a greater extent during the school year. However, if the particular children who are displaying growth during the summer are precisely those children who are already reading voraciously (and hence continue to read during the summer) and whose achievement is already at the top of the distribution, then the further growth spawned by the summer reading that these children do will increase overall variance.

In short, when deriving policy implications from studies of reading acquisition and studies of reading difficulties, it is important to keep the domains that we have discussed here clearly differentiated. That is, it is important to be clear when a study has implications for generic models of reading development and when a study has implications for individual differences. Relatedly, many nontargeted educational interventions may be generically efficacious in that they raise the absolute level of performance, but the same educational interventions might well increase the variability among children. In fact, this is the most common finding in educational research (Ceci & Papierno, 2005).

Things that raise everyone's level of performance also tend to be things that make the rich richer—they are generally efficacious in the sense that they help everyone, but they help the advantaged even more than the less advantaged. This is an inconvenient truth of educational psychology. We would like, in fact, to have the opposite. We would like to raise everyone's level but at the same time close achievement gaps, that is, reduce variance in achievement. There are profound philosophical questions raised by the fact that absolute levels of performance and variability are most often positively correlated (Ceci & Papierno, 2005). We will not begin to grapple with these questions until we are clear about the fact that developmental models and absolute levels are conceptually distinct from variability and models of individual differences.

Fortunately, the chapters in this wonderful volume grapple with and begin to address these issues. An impressive array of international scholars have identified and discuss the complex nature of individual differences and their impact on reading and its development in this volume.

The reconceptualization of individual differences in reading has broad implications for the field ranging from how we regard the constructs of reading and reading development, the nature of reading curriculum and instruction, the outcomes of effective reading instruction, and assessment and evaluation of students' reading growth and levels of achievement.

Anne E. Cunningham
University of California, Berkeley

Keith E. Stanovich
University of Toronto

## References

Bast, J., & Reitsma, P. (1998). Analyzing the development of individual differences in terms of Matthew effects in reading: Results from a Dutch longitudinal study. *Developmental Psychology, 34,* 1373–1399.

Byrne, B. (1992). Studies in the acquisition procedure for reading: Rationale, hypotheses, and data. In P. B. Gough, L. C. Ehri, & R. Treiman (Eds.), *Reading acquisition* (pp. 1–34). Hillsdale, NJ: Erlbaum.

Ceci, S. J., & Papierno, P. B. (2005). The rhetoric and reality of gap closing: When the "have-nots" gain but the "haves" gain even more. *American Psychologist, 60,* 149–160.

Cunningham, A. E. (1990). Explicit versus implicit instruction in phonemic awareness. *Journal of Experimental Child Psychology, 50,* 429–444.

Frazier, J. A., & Morrison, F. J. (1998). The influence of extended-year schooling on growth of achievement and perceived competence in early elementary school. *Child Development, 69*(2), 495–517.

Morrison, F. J., Alberts, D. M., & Griffith, E. M. (1997). Nature–nurture in the classroom: Entrance age, school readiness, and learning in children. *Developmental Psychology, 33*(2), 254–262.

Stanovich, K. E. (1986). Matthew effects in reading: Some consequences of individual differences in the acquisition of literacy. *Reading Research Quarterly, 21,* 360–407.

Stanovich, K. E. (2000). *Progress in understanding reading: Scientific foundations and new frontiers.* New York: Guilford Press.

Stanovich, K. E., Cunningham, A. E., & Cramer, B. (1984). Assessing phonological awareness in kindergarten children: Issues of task comparability. *Journal of Experimental Child Psychology, 38,* 175–190.

# Preface

Individual differences in reading are of interest for research, policy, and practice: the examination of difference across the history of reading research provides a compelling account of how readers vary, and a compelling warrant for continued inquiry. Well over a century ago, William James (1890) notes that individual differences are a key to understanding how people vary in their ability at the same task:

> An unlearned carpenter of my acquaintance once said in my hearing: "There is very little difference between one man and another; but what little there is, *is very important*." This distinction seems to me to go to the root of the matter (p. 24).

This volume is developed in the spirit of honoring the notion that individual differences are, indeed, very important.

There are several purposes to this volume. First, it is intended to provide a representative, state-of-the-art account of the diverse individual differences that are involved in acts of reading, and in students' reading development. Thirty years ago, Stanovich (1986) proposed the Matthew effect—an explanation of the rapid, even exponential growth exhibited by accomplished student readers. While Stanovich focused on cognitive components of reading, including comprehension and vocabulary, he noted the need for ongoing research to (1) continue to identify relevant individual differences in reading; (2) determine the relationship(s) of individual differences to reading development; and (3) account for interactions among individual differences. The chapters in this volume address developments in each of these areas. The volume also describes the environments in which individual differences in reading may emerge, operate, interact, and change.

The volume is also intended to provide *prima facie* evidence of the benefit of broad conceptualization of the ways in which readers differ. Recent educational policy, influenced by the Report of the National Reading Panel, embodied in the No Child Left Behind legislation, and realized in the Reading First program, focuses narrowly on the cognitive strategies and skills associated with reading. Similarly, high stakes tests at state, national, and international levels reinforce the primacy of reading strategies and skills. While these skills and strategies are requisite for reading development and success (Stanovich, 1986), they do not represent all of readers' consequential individual differences. Nor do strategy and skill fully explain developing readers' success or failure. For example, attending to individual differences in students' self-efficacy or motivation to read can have significant, positive effect.

The lack of comprehensive accounting of individual differences in reading is reflected in the nature of reading programs, the outcomes that are expected from successful teaching and learning, and the manner in which reading development is assessed. It is my hope that this volume contributes to a fuller accounting and appreciation of individual differences in reading, and better understanding of how individual differences matter in students' reading development.

## References

James, W. (1890). The importance of individuals. *The Open Court, 4,* 24–37; reprinted in *The will to believe and other essays in popular philosophy* (1897; reprinted, New York: Dover, 1956).

Stanovich, K. (1986). Matthew effects in reading: Some consequences of individual differences in the acquisition of literacy. *Reading Research Quarterly, 21,* 360–407.

# Acknowledgments

This volume owes much to my many colleagues in reading. I am particularly grateful to Peter Johnston and Dick Allington—at the beginning of my formal study of reading at the University of Albany, both influenced my thinking about readers who struggle and excel, and the individual differences that feature. At the University of Maryland, my work with Michael Pressley examined the necessity of strategies, and the essential of positive affect for reading success. John Guthrie created compelling instruction at the intersection of cognitive strategies, and motivation and engagement. Patricia Alexander's model of domain learning allowed for conceptualizing reading development on several trajectories, including the cognitive and affective. Pat also provided important counsel and advice as I developed the prospectus for this volume. P. David Pearson and I presented several research sessions on evolving understandings of individual differences in reading, and these sessions directly informed the development of this volume. The questions, discussions, and projects of undergraduate and graduate students at the University of Maryland have had a beneficial influence on my thinking. Naomi Silverman provided ongoing encouragement, insight, and enthusiasm as the volume progressed. Lastly, I thank each of the authors involved in this project. They undertook this task with insight and vigor that are palpable in each chapter. Their work was a pleasure to read, and to learn from.

# 1

# An Overview of Individual Differences in Reading

## Research, Policy, and Practice

*Peter Afflerbach*

In this chapter I describe the promise and challenge related to individual differences in reading. The promise emanates from a continuing interest in identifying individual differences and their origins, and in describing their influence on reading development. The challenge relates to the fact that individual differences in reading are narrowly conceptualized in reading education policy, and in related testing and reading instruction programs. This chapter has two main sections. In the first, I overview central and historic themes in theory and practice related to students' individual differences in reading. I begin with a brief overview of a century's worth of interest in individual differences. I examine attributions made to nature, nurture, or both as sources of difference, and the influence of environments on readers' individual differences. Following, I focus on the distinction between cognitive and affective aspects of individual differences. I then turn to the dynamic nature of individual differences—how they interact, how they influence acts of reading, and how they are influenced by acts of reading. The second section of the chapter describes the disconnection between current understanding of individual differences in reading, and educational policy, testing, and classroom instruction. I describe how individual differences in reading are narrowly conceptualized in consequential legislation and reading curriculum, and the influence of testing on reading policy and practice.

Throughout the chapter, I liberally sample from original sources: I believe the manner in which individual differences have been described across the past century adds to our understanding of the evolution of conceptualizations of these differences. These sources also illustrate the critical links between research and practice that are necessary for identifying and addressing developing student readers' differences.

## Ongoing Development of Our Understanding of Individual Differences

Individual differences in how people do things have been a focus of psychology for centuries, and accounts of variation in human behavior are richly told with an individual differences narrative. In 1868, Peirce investigated factors that are shared by "great men," and that influence individual's development. Peirce identifies individuals' ancestry and birth order, family background and childhood, physical stature, peculiarities, general health, levels of education, precociousness, work habits, and motivation and drive. He uses the resulting data to theorize the relationships of individuals' differences with their accomplishments. Peirce's work focuses on specific individual differences, including those from the physical, cognitive, affective and social realms. Peirce presages the interest on how individual differences develop, as well as future investigations of their often-complex interactions.

In one of the first investigations of students' individual differences in reading, Theisen (1920) reviews the use of reading test scores to identify differences:

> The results of standardized tests have everywhere revealed wide differences in reading ability. They have shown decided variations in such factors as rate of reading, knowledge of vocabulary, ability to gather thought from the printed page, and ability to read orally (p. 560).

With the above observation, Theisen frames students' individual differences in relation to factors that contribute to reading ability. From this perspective, it is possible to designate a student as different, and to specify the difference. Theisen's observation anticipates that across the history of the construct, the conceptualization of individual differences will skew strongly towards reading strategies and skills. Following, Moore (1938) situates individual differences in the classroom, focusing on students' reading development, specifically reading readiness:

> readiness involves many different factors in which a typical pupil is unevenly advanced. At the present time we do not know what weight to give to each and every characteristic . . . There are certain causes of individual differences which have received less attention than they seem to deserve. These causes briefly are: (1) variation in intelligence, (2) in sensory equipment, (3) in physical equipment, (4) in language ability, (5) in rate of learning, (6) in response to motivation, (7) in sex, and (8) emotional control (p. 164).

The above list reflects Moore's deconstruction of the reader and identification of areas in which individual differences exist. It is a preliminary proposition that individual differences in reading may result from nature, or nurture, or an interaction of the two. Moore notes that certain "causes" of individual differences receive less attention than others. His list of differences leans decidedly towards organic, "born with" differences such as sensory equipment, physical equipment, and gender. Importantly, Moore notes that individual differences may reside in both cognitive and affective realms.

Moore (1938) is also one of the first to acknowledge that as the identification of individual differences continues, and as descriptions of the array of individual differences in reading are elaborated, this knowledge should be accompanied by a theory of how to "weight" the differences. Determining the role and value of individual differences, and their centrality to reading and reading development, is a work in progress. Moore notes that the lack of theory of how to assign importance to individual differences creates challenge in conceptualizing classroom practice that effectively addresses the differences:

> All teachers realize to some degree the range of abilities found in every class group. We know that we can expect to find a range of reading ability of at least three grades from the first to the third and at least five or more grades for pupils in the grades from the third through the eighth grade. Despite these general facts few of us have a definite guiding philosophy as to what should be our attitude towards the differences we know to exist (p. 165).

Attention to individual differences continues. Consider Cunningham and Stanovich's (1998) questions, reflecting decades of inquiry into how readers develop, and how individual differences impact that development:

> Given that life-long reading habits are such strong predictors of verbal cognitive growth, what is it that predicts these habits? We've been looking at reading volume as a predictor of reading comprehension and cognitive ability, but what predicts reading volume or avid reading? (p. 146).

The above excerpt reminds that there are many possible relationships between the particular individual differences. Cunningham and Stanovich (1998) further describe how individual differences are situated in and impacted by the instructional environment:

> Further exacerbating the problem is the fact that less-skilled readers often find themselves in materials that are too difficult for them . . . The combination of deficient decoding skills, lack of practice, and difficult materials results in unrewarding early reading experiences that lead to less involvement in reading-related activities. . . unrewarding reading experiences multiply; and practice is avoided or merely tolerated without real cognitive involvement (p. 137).

Thus, the study of individual differences and the determination of their obvious or subtle influences on reading are enhanced by consideration of the environments and contexts in which individual differences develop.

## The Influences of Nature and Nurture on Individual Differences

How individual differences develop, and their influence on reading, are key questions for research and practice. Artley (1981) suggests that reading development is impacted by a mixture of individual differences emanating from both nature and nurture: they are "inherited and acquired." He describes the need for reading instruction to address these individual differences, as opposed to focusing on imaginary and elusive mean performance targets among children of the same age:

> In fact, the history of elementary education during the last 75 years has been concerned in one way or another with ways to cope with the multitude of issues growing out of the fact that children of the same chronological age are different by virtue of their inherited and acquired characteristics (p. 142).

Strang (1961) shares this sentiment, suggesting that individual differences in reading derive from nature and nurture, and from the interactions of students with their reading environments. She introduces a broad array of reader characteristics that can influence both single acts of reading, and an individual's overall reading development. In doing so, she establishes categories for inquiry into individual differences that remain valid to this day:

> getting meaning from the printed page is a biopsychological process that is influenced by the individual's ability, his experiences, his needs, his attitudes, his values, and his self-concept. Each individual interacts with the total reading situation in accord with his unique pattern of characteristics. His memory of each experience with reading further influences his perception of, and his response to, each new situation (p. 414).

Peter Afflerbach

Strang anticipates the paradigmatic movement from behaviorism to information processing and cognition. She even suggests that students' metacognition (a concept not yet so-named) influences individual differences, with memory of past reading experiences influencing current and future reading acts. She also proposes the mutability of individual differences based on interactions between organisms and their environments (e.g., students in classrooms and in reading groups; Bronfenbrenner, 1979):

> Thus, the psychology of reading has become more complex since the early days of the stimulus-response theory. The influence of the individual, his abilities and background, has been inserted between the stimulus and the response; the S-R bond has become the S-O-R bond, or the stimulus-organism-response bond. Moreover, we recognize that the individual does not learn in isolation but is influenced by the complex social network in which he lives and learns (p. 414).

Going forward, an important focus for research is the individual differences that are stable within individuals, and those that are influenced by factors in the reading environment. The dynamics of these differences, how they operate to influence reading and how they influence reading, are deserving of researchers' attention. In addition, the environments in which reading occurs figure largely in how inherent individual differences are accommodated, and in how reading skills and attitudes are nurtured.

## Cognition and Affect in the Conceptualization of Individual Differences

Throughout the history of research on individual differences in reading there is a focus on the cognitive (see Cunningham and Stanovich, this volume). Many studies examine individual differences in the systems that support cognition, such as attention, memory and vision. There is also considerable research on individual differences in readers' strategies and skills that are supported by these systems, including phonemic awareness, sound–symbol correspondences, fluency, vocabulary, and comprehension.

In contrast, the study of affect as an individual difference in reading is more recent, and less prevalent in the research literature. Motivation and engagement and self-efficacy are examples of individual differences where thick threads of affect are woven through cognitive operations. In addition, metacognition interacts with affect in reading, as readers build understandings not only of their cognitive operations, but also of their emotional states before, during, and after reading.

Moore (1938) focuses on both cognitive and affective phenomena involved in children's reading test-taking. The following description is notable for the attention given individual differences in affect that are interwoven into the students' experience, and the perennial concerns with the influence of testing on children:

> "In testing children in this study the examiners were impressed with the intense effort put forth by most of the children in trying to name or to write letters. The efforts were often painful to observe: sustained frowning, alternate squirming and rigidity of body, pointing tensely, labored breathing, grunting, whispering, and even weeping." Can you not visualize the great variation, the marked difference in the children studied?
>
> (Wilson, cited in Moore, 1938, pp. 163–164)

Hunt also catalogs difference, and student attitude is considered a key individual difference. However, he maintains the focus on cognitive individual differences:

> Actually, from the first day of Grade 1, the teacher meets an ever widening range of ability and background. First-grade children differ greatly in their language facility, knowledge of stories, experiences with materials, visual discrimination, general information, and attitudes towards reading and school.
>
> (Hunt, 1952, p. 417)

The skewing of attention towards cognitive individual differences continues to this day. The long-running conversation about the roles, power, and relationships of cognition and affect in learning is often dominated by cognition (e.g., Lazarus, 1984; Zajonc, 1984). This imbalance is reflected in contemporary reading curriculum, instruction, and assessment. Thus, determining and addressing students' individual differences in strategy and skill are common targets of educational policy and reading programs. For example, reading instructional programs contain detailed approaches to teaching sound–symbol correspondences, but lack detailed approaches to helping students develop self-efficacy as readers. Individual differences in student affect often receive less "official" notice, although attending to them is a hallmark of successful teaching (Dolezal Welsh, Pressley, & Vincent, 2003). While research on individual differences in affect is less common than research on cognitive differences, it is rarer still that affect-related research results inform reading policy and large-scale curriculum initiatives.

## Individual Differences in Readers Interact and Influence Reading

Individual differences can interact, and their effects can be pronounced or muted.

Strang (1961) describes the intertwining of differences during reading diagnosis, and how these differences may interact to further influence a student's reading development:

> The child's responses may be influenced by his anxiety in a strange situation, by his having to say "I don't know" to many questions, and by the depressing sense of failure as the items become harder. Lapses in attention may lower the child's score. Emotional situations and associations may throw him off the track. If he wants very much to read better immediately, he may feel annoyed at not being given instruction in reading. Other interests and sheer fatigue may also influence his responses unfavorably (p. 418).

Strang reminds us that it is not sufficient to identify and address isolate individual differences. Better to best understand how differences interact within the individual. Betts' (1940) observations of student readers experiencing reading frustration are strikingly similar to those noted by Strang, and signal that acts of reading are influenced by affect:

> as the typical pupil becomes increasingly frustrated, he may exhibit tension, movements of the body, hands, and feet, he may frown and squint, and he may exhibit other types of emotional behavior characteristic of a frustrated individual (p. 741).

The interaction of readers' individual differences and their influence on reading achievement are famously accounted for in Stanovich's portrayal of Matthew effects in reading (1986; see also Merton, 1968). Conducting a synthesis of research on the development of young readers' cognitive strategies and skills, Stanovich attributes superior reading development to "reciprocal relationships—situations where the causal connection between reading ability and the efficiency of a cognitive process is bidirectional" (p. 360). When the Matthew effect is operating, the rich get richer. Initial success with reading begets ongoing success: increased reading experience provides more practice with strategies and skills, and prior knowledge accrues as readers encounter new information. All contribute to future reading performance. However, struggling readers experience a related phenomenon: the poor stay poor. We might call this a "reverse Matthew effect." Initial, and then ongoing, lack of success at reading is related to different individual differences, and can lead students to a cognitive and affective crossroads, with struggles to construct meaning and little or no inclination to try to read:

> Readers of differing skill soon diverge in the amount of practice they receive at reading and writing activities. They also have different histories of success, failure, and reward in the context of academic tasks. The long-term effects of such differing histories could act to create other cognitive and behavioral differences between readers of varying skill . . . There is already some evidence suggesting that differences in self-esteem, rather than being the cause of achievement variability, are actually consequences of ability and achievement (p. 373).

Stanovich anchors the Matthew effect to individual differences in cognitive strategies and skills, and domain knowledge. However, the above account acknowledges the influence of differences in affect on students' reading development, including motivation and self-esteem, and suggests that future investigations focus on both cognition and affect.

Ongoing research contributes to our understanding of the interactions between readers' individual differences. Consider, for example, research related to readers' self-efficacy that indicates that an increase in readers' self-efficacy is often paired with an increase in motivation (McCrudden, Perkins, & Putney, 2005). Higher self-efficacy is related to enhanced reading comprehension and achievement (Solheim, 2011). High achieving students possess high self-efficacy; they make fewer attributions for their performance to external causes that include task difficulty, luck, and teacher help (Shell, Colvin, & Bruning, 1995). Correlational evidence charts the relationship between self-efficacy and epistemic beliefs (Phan, 2008). Following the thread from self-efficacy, epistemic beliefs influence achievement, as they can promote engagement in learning and persistence at challenging tasks (Afflerbach, Cho, & Kim, 2014; Schommer, 1994). Metacognition involves monitoring and evaluating processes that can influence students' epistemic understanding (Richter & Schmid, 2010), and sophisticated epistemic beliefs lead readers to engage in elaborated metacognitive processes (Pieschl, Stallmann, & Bromme, 2014).

To summarize, there is an ongoing evolution in our understanding of individual differences in reading, and their influences on acts of reading and reading development. Differences exist within individual readers; the provenance of difference may be traced to nature, nurture, or both. Individual differences may be shaped by reading environments, including those in homes and classrooms. Individual differences are evinced in both the cognitive and affective realms of reading, although the historic narrative of readers' individual differences is dominated by cognition. The dynamic nature of individual differences, their developmental trajectories, and their interactions, are increasingly comprehended. These differences can interact in a manner that is beneficial, or detrimental to reading. As we learn more about the nature and origin of individual differences, we better understand their role in acts of reading, and in reading development. Given this wealth of knowledge about readers' individual differences, I next focus on how, and if, they are a focus of educational policy and practice.

## The Disconnection between Current Understanding of Individual Differences and Reading Policy, Testing, and Instruction

Copious research describes the range and importance of individual differences in reading. Yet, the past decades have witnessed a narrowing of the conceptualization of what is central to students' reading development, as reflected in policy, curriculum, and testing. That this diminution is occurring as our understanding of individual differences in reading expands is not anticipated by a theory of sensible use of research findings. Particular individual differences may be acknowledged, while others are ignored. There are several explanations for the disjuncture between policy and practice, and the research and theory related to individual differences.

## The Conceptualization of Individual Differences as Strategy and Skill

Cognitive strategies and skills enjoy privileged status as the most consequential individual differences for students' reading development. The focus on cognitive strategy and skill is ongoing (Afflerbach, Pearson, & Paris, 2008), and is itself influenced by a series of reciprocal relationships. Education policy, reading tests, and reading instruction programs interact to reinforce one another. These interactions result in the maintenance of belief that individual differences in readers' strategies and skills are, at a minimum, the most important differences. In the extreme, strategy and skill are positioned as all that matters for students' reading development and achievement. This contributes to a concomitant lack of attention to other individual differences that influence students' reading development.

## The National Reading Panel Report and Individual Differences

In the United States, reading instruction is heavily influenced by the Federal government, and Federal government policy in reading continues to be heavily influenced by the National Reading Panel Report (NRP; National Institute of Child Health and Human Development, 2000). The NRP Report identifies five cognitive strategy and skill areas in which students vary, and a selective synthesis of research leads the NRP to conclude that phonemic awareness, phonics, fluency, vocabulary, and comprehension must be the focus of reading instruction. The NRP describes the five strategies and skills identified as:

> instructional topics of widespread interest in the field of reading education that have been articulated in a wide range of theories, research studies, instructional programs, curricula, assessments, and educational policies. The Panel elected to examine these and subordinate questions because *they currently reflect the central issues in reading instruction and reading achievement.*
>
> (Retrieved from http://www.nichd.nih.gov/publications/nrp/upload/ smallbook_pdf.pdf, p. 3; italics added)

The corollary conclusion of the NRP Report for reading policy, instruction, and assessment is this: individual differences in reading strategies and skills explain the differences between successful and struggling readers.

This conclusion could be anticipated by the criteria for reading research used for inclusion in the NRP Report:

> To be included in the database, studies had to measure reading as an outcome. Reading was defined to include several behaviors such as the following: reading real words in isolation or in context, reading pseudowords that can be pronounced but have no meaning, reading text aloud or silently, and comprehending text that is read silently or orally (p. 5).

The above "measure of reading as an outcome" has exclusive focus on cognitive strategies and skills, and is accomplished using tests. Reading research that is included in the NRP features tests for statistically significant differences that derive from comparisons of treatment and control groups' test scores. The test scores are a measure of students' cognitive strategies and skills, such as oral reading fluency or reading comprehension.

Thus, consideration of readers and their individual differences by the NRP is restricted by the nature of the outcomes assessed: Research studies that examine a student's performance at pronouncing pseudowords and real words in isolation are included, but other outcomes that are demonstrably powerful and necessary for successful reading, such as the development and maintenance of student readers' self-efficacy and motivation, are ignored. Research on reading development and related individual differences that does not include tests of cognitive strategy and skill is not included in the report of the NRP.

In effect, the NRP approach to research synthesis eliminates from consideration a considerable amount of reading research. Among the "un-included" research is that which focuses on individual differences other than strategy and skill. The NRP did express concerns with how the NRP Report might be interpreted. In particular, the NRP did not want "missing" aspects of reading to be assigned secondary or tertiary importance, in policy or practice. Thus, it included the following caveat: "The Panel's silence on other topics should not be interpreted as indicating that other topics have no importance or that improvement in those areas would not lead to greater reading achievement" (p. 3). However, this is just what transpires as the US Department of Education uses the NRP Report to develop reading education policy. As often happens when research syntheses migrate to policy makers' desks, there is a loss in translation. The naming of five sets of cognitive strategies and skills has the result of significantly reduced attention to other aspects of reading development and achievement, and their related individual differences.

## Reading Instruction and Student Reading Development Based on "Scientific Evidence"

In accordance with No Child Left Behind and Reading First initiatives, states applying for Reading First grants are required to purchase reading instruction materials that are based on "scientific evidence" from reading research. Few would argue against reading programs being based on proven instructional approaches that address students' specific reading needs. However, Federal law guarantees that the "scientific evidence" undergirding effective reading programs is reading test scores. Reading programs are determined to be effective when they are based on research that finds statistically significant differences between experimental treatment and control group learning outcomes. The dependent variables in this research are reading test scores—a proxy for students' cognitive strategy and skill use. The use of test scores to deem particular reading instruction programs acceptable mimics the NRP's use of test scores to certify cognitive strategy and skill research as the guide to fostering students' reading development.

"Acceptable" reading instruction programs focus on the "big 5" of phonemic awareness, phonics, fluency, vocabulary, and comprehension, and individual differences in student growth in these strategies and skills is measured by tests.

In addition to being the basis for privileging particular individual differences within reading programs, tests of cognitive strategy and skill are the primary measure of school-wide achievement. In the United States, whether or not students and schools are making adequate yearly progress (AYP) is determined each year in grades 3 through 8 using test scores. Again, these scores represent reading progress as strategy and skill development. There are no standardized tests scores for positive student reading affect, effective metacognition, higher order thinking, growth in self-efficacy, or for a student's turn towards intrinsic, positive motivation to read. To reiterate, test scores are the currency that buy reading research and reading programs using the labels "important" and "evidence based," respectively. Under this regime, individual differences that are not tested are considered less salient to reading development than the cognitive strategies and skills that are tested.

This phenomenon is not restricted to a particular country—international comparisons of students' reading and literacy achievement, including the Program for International Student Assessment (PISA; Organization for Economic Cooperation and Development, 2014) and Progress in International Reading Literacy Study (PIRLS; International Association for the Evaluation of Educational Achievement, 2011) also employ tests whose items predominantly sample the strategy and skill domain of reading.

However, there may be cause for cautious optimism. PIRLS (2011) includes a questionnaire that focuses on differences in students' habits and emotions related to reading. In the following, students rate on a continuum from "Agree a lot" to "Disagree a lot":

- I read only if I have to
- I like talking about what I read with other people
- I would be happy if someone gave me a book as a present
- I think reading is boring
- I would like to have more time for reading
- I enjoy reading

(Retrieved from: http://nces.ed.gov/Surveys/PIRLS/pdf/
P11_Student%20Q_USA_final.pdf)

The results from such questionnaires and rating tasks are classified as "background information," but it is encouraging that high stakes, international tests are acknowledging the importance of these aspects of reading development. In the meantime, as students are compared across countries, test scores focus on strategy and skill, and describe a nation's educational standing, school accountability, teacher quality, and student growth (Afflerbach, 2002). That test scores represent a narrow range of both learning outcomes and students' individual differences in reading should be incentive to change current assessments.

A recent initiative with major influence on both curriculum and assessment is the Common Core State Standards. The English/Language Arts Standards (ELA: National Governors Association Center for Best Practices & Council of Chief State School Officers, 2010) describe increasingly complex cognitive outcomes that are expected from students as they matriculate across grades. The affiliated assessment consortia, Smarter Balanced Assessment Consortium (SBAC) and Partnership for Assessment of Readiness for College and Careers (PARCC), produce tests with exclusive focus on cognitive strategy, skill, and content area knowledge gain.

Thus, testing practices continue to reinforce the idea that cognitive strategy and skill are the individual differences that matter most, often to the exclusion of other individual differences, which related research describes as powerful.

Additional factors operate to bolster a narrow conceptualization of individual differences in reading. Economists use the term *path dependence* to describe how particular social and educational practices maintain, even in the face of suitable, valid alternatives. McDonnell (2008) defines path dependence as follows: "Major social policies create networks of vested interests that benefit from a policy and that develop operational rules and structures to protect it from political attacks and attempts to alter it" (p. 52). There are vested interests that are content with maintaining the status quo focus on strategies and skills as the individual differences that matter. Education publishing companies and testing companies are examples of these "vested interests": their profits within the current system amount to billions of dollars each year. Robust sales of reading programs and reading tests depend on reading development, and attending individual differences, being conceptualized as strategy and skill building.

A final example of the pervasive influence of testing on how learning, educational outcomes, and individual differences may be conceptualized comes from Alexander, James, and Glaser (1987). In reviewing the results of the National Assessment of Educational Progress, they observe the following: "And so, unfortunately, we are apt to measure what we can, and eventually come to value what is measured over what is left unmeasured. The shift is subtle and occurs gradually" (p. 23). If the above proposal of coming "to value what is measured over what is left unmeasured" is accurate, then advocating for changes in reading tests to include a more realistic array of students' individual differences is a considerable challenge going forward.

## Individual Differences in Reading: Looking Ahead

Research continues to inform us of the diversity of individual differences in reading, their importance to reading theory, and their contributions to students' reading development. In 1986, Stanovich commented on his preliminary account of individual differences: "The review is not so much a complete model of the development of individual differences as an outline to be filled in by future research" (p. 395). This volume demonstrates that considerable work is being done to "fill in" our understanding, in terms of the range of individual differences that impact reading development, and the detailed descriptions of these differences. While Stanovich focuses on the cognitive work that readers do, we are now privy to research that describes a range of cognitive and affective individual differences. In addition, we have growing understanding of the provenance of individual differences, their interactions, and the relationship between instruction and reading environments and the development of these differences. The chapters that follow describe how individual differences "fit" with reading theory, and have important implications for theory and practice. In addition, the volume describes the social milieu in which classes of individual differences are created and valued.

It is one thing to build and test detailed theories of individual differences, and another to implement practice based on these details. A reconceptualization of individual differences in reading is not worth much to children who lack phonics skills and motivation to read, but whose related classroom experience is limited to skill instruction. Addressing an increased array of individual differences in reading complexifies teaching. Consider zones of proximal development (Vygotsky, 1978), across which a talented teacher guides students. Scaffolded reading strategy instruction commonly helps students in one such traverse. What else matters in a student's reading development? What is the equivalent of strategy instruction for crucial aspects of an individual student's reading growth, including the development of a student's self-efficacy, motivation and engagement, and higher order thinking? Research of the individual differences in reading helps answer these questions.

Understanding the broad array of individual differences that exist in every reader, and learning how they operate for each of our students is critical work. Strang (1961) notes: "In view of the complexity of the reading process and in view of individual differences in response to teaching methods, should we not be more concerned with the flexible use of methods and the combination of the best features of several methods?" (p. 427).

The scholars cited throughout this chapter provide insights that demonstrate that awareness of individual differences, and suitably addressing them in the classroom is ongoing work. Returning to Moore (1938), we consider the perennial conflict of broadly conceptualizing individual readers and their differences, while being restricted by narrowly-bounded instructional systems: "The significance of individual differences challenges as never before the best efforts of all teachers in this day of inadequately developed averages, norms, and standards" (p. 166). The breadth of theory of individual differences that is now explicated might be a pleasant surprise for Moore, but he would be fully familiar with the need to move from research-based theory to effective reading instruction practice.

In closing, I trust that the chapters in this volume represent progress based on Stanovich's (1986) forward-looking observation for research and theory on individual differences in reading: "Many of the hypotheses to be advanced are quite tentative, as the empirical evidence relating to several of them is far from definitive" (p. 365). Over the last 30 years, tentative hypotheses regarding individual differences in reading have been tested, challenged, and revised. Additional areas of difference have been identified, accompanied by efforts to determine their central or ancillary influence on reading development. The needed work of reconceptualizing individual differences in reading and considering their implications for practice continues, as informed by the reading research presented in this volume.

# References

Afflerbach, P. (2002). The road to folly and redemption: Perspectives on the legitimacy of high stakes testing. *Reading Research Quarterlyv*, 37, 348–360.

Afflerbach, P., Cho, B., & Kim, J. (2014). Inaccuracy and reading in multiple text and Internet/hypertext environments. In D. Rapp & J. Braasch (Eds.), *Processing inaccurate information: Theoretical and applied perspectives from cognitive science and the educational sciences*. Cambridge, MA: MIT Press, pp. 403–424.

Afflerbach, P., Pearson, D., & Paris, S. (2008). Clarifying differences between reading skills and reading strategies. *Reading Teacher, 61*, 364–373.

Alexander, L., James, T., & Glaser, R. (1987). *The nation's report card: Improving the assessment of student achievement*. Cambridge, MA: National Academy of Education.

Artley, S. (1981). Individual differences and reading instruction. *Elementary School Journal, 82*, 142–151.

Betts, E. (1940). Reading problems at the intermediate-grade level. *Elementary School Journal*, 40, 737–746.

Bronfenbrenner, U. (1979). *The ecology of human development: Experiments by nature and design*. Cambridge, MA: Harvard University Press.

Cunningham, A., & Stanovich, K. (1998). What reading does for the mind. *Journal of Direct Instruction, 1*, 137–149.

Dolezal, S., Welsh, L., Pressley, M., & Vincent, M. (2003). How nine third-grade teachers motivate student academic engagement. *Elementary School Journal, 103*, 239–267.

Hunt, J. (1952). What high school teachers should know about individual differences in reading. *School Review, 60*, 417–423.

International Association for the Evaluation of Educational Achievement (2011). Progress in International Reading Literacy Study 2011. Retrieved from: http://www.iea.nl/pirls_2011.htm.

Lazarus, R. (1984). On the primacy of cognition. *American Psychologist, 39*, 124–129.

McCrudden, M., Perkins, P., & Putney, L. (2005) Self-efficacy and interest in the use of reading strategies. *Journal of Research in Childhood Education, 20*, 119–132.

McDonnell, L. (2008). The politics of educational accountability: Can the clock be turned back? In Ryan, K. & Shepard, L. (Eds.), *The future of test-based accountability*. New York: Routledge, pp. 47–68.

Merton, R. (1968). The Matthew effect in science. *Science, 159*, 56–63.

Moore, J. (1938). The significance of individual differences in relation to reading. *Peabody Journal of Education, 16*, 162–166.

National Governors Association Center for Best Practices & Council of Chief State School Officers (2010). *Common Core State Standards for English language arts and literacy in history/social studies, science, and technical subjects*. Washington, DC: NGA.

National Institute of Child Health and Human Development (2000). *Report of the National Reading Panel. Teaching children to read: An evidence-based assessment of the scientific research literature on reading and its implications for reading instruction* (NIH Publication No. 00-4769). Washington, DC: US Government Printing Office.

Organization for Economic Cooperation and Development (2014). PISA 2012 results in focus: What 15-year-olds know and what they can do with what they know. Retrieved from: http://www.oecd.org/pisa/keyfindings/pisa-2012-results-overview.pdf.

Peirce, C. (1868). *Collected papers*. Cambridge, MA: Harvard University Press.

Phan, H. (2008). Unifying different theories of learning: Theoretical framework and empirical evidence. *Educational Psychology, 28*, 325–340.

Pieschl, S., Stallmann, F., & Bromme, R. (2014). High school students' adaptation of task definitions, goals and plans to task complexity: The impact of epistemic beliefs. *Psychological Topics, 23*, 31–52.

Richter, T., & Schmid, S. (2010). Epistemological beliefs and epistemic strategies in self-regulated learning. *Metacognition and Learning, 5*, 47–65.

Schommer, M. (1994). An emerging conceptualization of epistemological beliefs and their role in learning. In R. Garner & P. Alexander (Eds.), *Beliefs about text instruction,* Hillsdale, NJ: Erlbaum, pp. 25–39.

Shell, D., Colvin, C., & Bruning, R. (1995). Self-efficacy, attributions, and outcome expectancy mechanisms in reading and writing achievement: Grade-level and achievement-level differences. *Journal of Educational Psychology, 87*, 386–398.

Solheim, J. (2011). The impact of reading self-efficacy and task value on reading comprehension scores in different item formats. *Reading Psychology, 32*, 1–27.

Stanovich, K. (1986). Matthew effects in reading: Some consequences of individual differences in the acquisition of literacy. *Reading Research Quarterly, 21*, 360–407.

Strang, R. (1961). Controversial programs and procedures in reading. *School Review, 69*, 413–428.

Theisen, W. (1920). Provisions for individual differences in the teaching of reading. *Journal of Educational Research, 2*, 560–571.

Vygotsky, L. S. (1978). *Mind in society: The development of higher psychological processes*. Cambridge, MA: Harvard University Press.

Zajonc, R. (1984). On the primacy of affect. *American Psychologist, 39*, 117–123.

# 2

# Identifying Individual Differences in Reading

## What Are We Looking For?

*Emily Fox and Liliana Maggioni*

## Statement of the Problem

The aim of this chapter is to encourage a conversation about what we as a field are looking for in investigating individual differences in reading. Initiating such a conversation requires somewhat of a bird's-eye view of what has been done and is being done in the way of research. However, the research on individual differences in reading has been tremendously prolific—as shown by the need for an entire handbook devoted to discussing such research. Therefore, we will use examples to illustrate what we see as important patterns and influences related to individual differences, but do not here carry out a systematic review or analysis.

We initially consider the investigation of individual differences by psychologists and educational researchers on a broad scale as a way to lay out the basics of the general territory within which we will be operating and to establish a context within which to explore the possibilities for reading research. How, in general, are researchers' aims structured when investigating individual differences, and from what fundamental assumptions do they originate? We turned to disciplinary reference works in order to get a general sense of the possible approaches to research on individual differences, specifically, to the entries on "Individual Differences" in encyclopedias of psychology and behavioral science (Breslin, 2004), education (Corno, 2003; Ho, Tomlinson, & Whipple, 2003; Kyllonen & Gitomer, 2003), human development (Reeve, 2006), cognitive science (Lubinski & Webb, 2005), industrial and organizational psychology (Webb & Lubinski, 2007), social psychology (McCrae, 2007), and educational psychology (Magliano & Perry, 2008).

In general, the study of individual differences is interested in understanding how differences in human characteristics are related to important differences in human behaviors and life outcomes. From the social psychologist's point of view, for example, individual differences are "enduring psychological features that contribute to the shaping of behavior and to each individual's sense of self" (McCrae, 2007). The larger purpose of studying individual differences is typically seen as being able to optimize the potential of the individual through being able to predict key life outcomes, such as job satisfaction, and through meeting the educational, occupational, or therapeutic needs of the individual so far as possible, by providing appropriate training, remediation, or opportunities. For educational and developmental purposes, there tends to be more emphasis on remediation and addressing issues of inequity, with the goal of achieving "a shared standard of excellence" (Ho et al., 2003) or providing "equal rights and opportunities" (Reeve, 2006) for all students, rather than fulfillment of individual potential.

With regard to fundamental assumptions that appear to shape studies of individual differences in general, the characteristics considered of interest are usually classified under three broad areas of human functioning: cognition (primarily intelligence); affect/ personality/ temperament; and conation (motivation and volition). Some diversity is found in the characterizations of these realms, particularly for the affective and conative areas, and particularly with regard to the role of interests or preferences, beliefs, and values.

At the same time, however, in the overviews of individual difference research presented in the various encyclopedias, a consistent point of emphasis is the fundamental overlap and interdependency among these constructs, so that, for example, "For some purposes, affective and conative processes have proven to be so interconnected that it makes little sense even to psychologists to separate them" (Corno, 2003, p. 1119). These interconnections produce profiles and patterns in the relations of characteristics and behaviors seen:

> Although each of the major classes of individual differences—cognitive abilities, preferences, and personality—has traditionally been examined in isolation from the other two, these classes are not independent. Cognitive abilities, preferences, and personality traits tend to covary systematically to create constellations of personal attributes, and these complexes have interdependent developmental implications.
>
> (Webb & Lubinski, 2007)

The viewpoint regarding the stability of individual differences is twofold. On the one hand, they are considered as relatively stable abilities, traits, or dispositions inherent in the person (who is typically assumed to be an adult); on the other hand, particularly when considering human development and education, certain types of individual differences are viewed as more potentially malleable, arising from or interacting significantly with environmental features or influences. In general, though, the need to consider the contribution of the interaction of the individual and the situation is also acknowledged when measuring individual differences and interpreting their likely meaning or impact with regard to outcomes of interest. In general, it is also emphasized that most people fall somewhere in the middle of the range for typical individual difference variables—true outliers on most individual difference characteristics of interest (intellect, personality, temperament, motivation, volition) are rare.

Now, having briefly overviewed the territory covered in investigations of individual differences with regard to their aims and assumptions, what do we see as the possibilities that are open to us for thinking about individual differences in relation to reading? We would like to be able to understand how and why readers differ in terms of the entire range of aspects—cognitive, affective, and conative—that matter for what they do in the way of reading. We would like to have a better understanding of how individuals develop as readers, from the earliest stages of acquisition on up to being able to read to accomplish valued and self-chosen goals as adults, and to get a better grasp on what would help us to predict their different developmental paths. We are also interested in investigating the differential success of different individuals in accomplishing particular reading-related tasks and how they may respond in particular reading situations. It would be important to be able get a sense of why different individuals choose to engage in different reading behaviors, for which we will also need to know about how they think of themselves as readers and what they think reading is. Finally, we would like to know how reading itself helps shape development and can itself become a source of individuation and variability in the characteristics and identity of the individual reader.

The investigation of individual differences enables us to go after such understandings, which should then support our being able to intervene in appropriate and helpful ways, whether we are aiming at fulfilling potential or equalizing opportunities. However, how do we know which individual differences and constellations of individual differences will provide productive explanatory avenues for investigation? And how well do the various avenues that have been taken in the research so far come together into a story about readers and how they may differ in ways that matter?

## Investigating Individual Differences in Reading

Investigations of individual differences in reading have primarily been based on a few overarching models of reading processes and early reading development. They have addressed how such individual differences influence the (primarily cognitive) processes and products of reading, as well as differences in the development of the skills and capabilities required for executing those reading processes. The guiding purpose has been, on the whole, to gain understandings that can allow us to help struggling readers (Magliano & Perry, 2008).

Because of this focus on struggling readers, considerable attention has been given to individual differences related to entry-level reading processes and reading acquisition. This line of research has relied on a few key stories and motifs about what matters in learning to read, including Stanovich's highly influential review on Matthew effects in reading (1986), the simple view of reading forwarded by Gough and Tunmer (1986), and Perfetti's body of work on word identification and lexical quality (2007). Its major aim has been to parse out the contributions of various individual difference variables in predicting initial success in word reading, and sometimes also later success in reading comprehension. Potential variables of interest have typically included general cognitive ability, verbal ability (including receptive vocabulary), working memory, phonological awareness and skills, speech perception and production, knowledge of letter names, and rapid automatized naming (Bowey, 2005). Another intersecting line of research has considered the role of early environmental influences in children's differential literacy development, building upon such work as Clay's (1989) on the importance of young children's concepts of print that develop from their initial contacts with books, and Hart and Risley's (1995) foundational work on the role of the language use in the home environment in young children's vocabulary development.

Beyond these inquiries into individual differences and their relation to students' entry-level reading, the field has also taken up the investigation of differences in reading at the level of text comprehension and learning from text (e.g., Johnston, Barnes, & Desrochers, 2008). Among the important stories about individual differences in reading processes and products at this level are Kintsch's construction–integration model of reading comprehension (1998) and van den Broek's landscape model (van den Broek, Risden, Fletcher, & Thurlow, 1996). These are both information-processing based accounts of what goes on during and results from reading, and in both of them the reader is assumed to be constructing a mental representation of what the text "says." In these models, crucial individual difference variables related to reading processes and products at the level of text comprehension include relevant background knowledge for text topic(s), attentional resources, reading strategies or language skills, decoding skills, and, for the landscape model, the reader's own standards for coherence of the mental representation constructed. Guthrie and Wigfield (1999) built upon this view of reading comprehension as involving the construction of mental representations in their motivational–cognitive model of reading, incorporating additional motivational processes as well as the primarily cognitive aspects identified in the information-processing accounts. With motivation and engagement in the picture, additional potential individual difference variables related to reading processes and outcomes at the level of text comprehension emerge, among them interest in the text and in the activity of reading, task mastery goals, self-efficacy, and beliefs about the nature of reading (e.g., Anmarkrud & Bråten, 2009).

At the level of text comprehension, it appears that some of the potential individual difference variables being considered (such as working memory or vocabulary size) are more inherent in the person, while others (such as relevant background knowledge or topic interest) involve the interaction of the person's characteristics and the features of the reading situation. A highly influential report from the RAND Reading Study Group (RRSG, 2002) on reading comprehension characterized interaction as an essential attribute of reading comprehension, identifying the interacting components as reader, text, and activity, all nested within and interacting as well with the surrounding sociocultural context. Individual differences thought to be important sources of variability within this more comprehensive account of reading comprehension are wider ranging. They include fluency of word recognition, vocabulary and linguistic knowledge, a suite of non-linguistic cognitive abilities and processes (e.g., attention, working memory, visualization), engagement and motivation, understanding of the purposes of reading, discourse knowledge, domain knowledge related to the text, level of cognitive and metacognitive strategy development, and beliefs about personal reading competence (RRSG, 2002, p. 22). In keeping with their interactive view of reading comprehension, the RRSG also noted that these conjoined variables may operate differently in different reading situations:

> Thus, patterns of strength or weakness in the domains of word-reading accuracy, fluency, comprehension strategies, vocabulary, domain knowledge, interest, and motivation can lead to performances that vary as a function of the text and of the task being engaged in. (p. 24)

The RAND report (RRSG, 2002) laid out an ambitious program of research on reading comprehension, including research on the general and situation-specific roles of the entire set of cognitive, affective, and conative individual difference variables outlined. The purpose was to develop reading instruction and reading assessments that can foster proficient (adult) reading by supporting the progress of at-risk (young) readers, where proficient reading is precisely that reading that is cross-situationally successful and does not falter with different tasks or in different situations. However, the developmental trajectory from beginning to proficient reading is not entirely clear, and the bulk of the emphasis remained on getting the young reader successfully started with comprehending and learning from texts, both in and out of school.

Lifespan models of reading development support a more integrated understanding of the different pathways that different types of readers take as they progress beyond beginning reading, or of why they respond in different ways in different reading situations. Chall (1983) outlined stages of reading development, each with their particular demands on the developing reader in terms of the nature of the reading being done, and therefore entailing the consideration of both inter- and intra-individual differences across time. Because her story was a normative one, her focus was not on identifying key ways that individuals can vary inter-individually, and she tended to speak rather generally of cognitive and language abilities as underpinning differences between individual readers. However, in identifying the critical shifts in the type of reading being done, she also mapped out the additional critical variables expected to contribute to success at each new type of reading.

The aspect of her story that has received the most attention and has been taken up into the discourse is the transition in elementary school from "learning to read" to "reading to learn," which is thought to be a major potential stumbling-block for struggling readers of a variety of types. This idea that "learning to read" is finished in elementary school is an unfortunate legacy of Chall's account of the stages of reading development. In fact, her developmental story goes well beyond that point. By Stage 5 (which she was not sure that many people could achieve), the type of reading being done demands "synthesis, reorganization, and critical reaction to what is being read in often difficult and contradictory texts" (1983, p. 51). Such reading requires "broad knowledge of the content that one will be reading at Stage 5, high efficiency in reading, personal courage, daring, confidence, and humility" (p. 52), as well as a full understanding and acceptance of what is at stake in reading in this way.

Another lifespan developmental model centers directly on individual difference variables, considering the contributions they make to success at reading at different stages of reading development. Alexander's (2006) model of reading development maps out the trajectory of reading development in terms of linked changes in the reader's knowledge, interest, and strategic processing, with these variables considered in relation to both the domain of reading and also the academic domains within which reading in academic contexts occurs. In her model, the reader's approach to reading, engagement in reading, and ability to construct coherent meaning and build knowledge from text will vary depending on where the reader is positioned with regard to these key variables. Efficiency in basic reading processes such as word identification, referent matching, and drawing of local bridging inferences (and the supporting reader characteristics or abilities required for this) is encompassed primarily in the strategic processing variable, where strategic processing is effortful, deliberate, and consumes attentional resources, whereas automated, efficient processing is not. Work at higher-level meaning-building processing is better able to happen when lower-level processing such as word identification or grasp of literal meaning occurs automatically (and therefore not via strategic processing). Different reader profiles associated with differential likelihood of success across reading situations are generated by different combinations of strengths or weaknesses in knowledge, interest, and strategic processing (e.g., Fox, Dinsmore, Maggioni, & Alexander, 2009).

## Focusing on Cognitive Processes

These lifespan models and the scope of the research program outlined in the RAND report, along with the expansion into motivational territory with the motivational–cognitive model of Guthrie and Wigfield (1999), seem to open up at least the potential for investigation of many of our questions of interest regarding individual differences in reading. However, although the lifespan models and the view of reading comprehension presented in the RAND report do open up space for investigation of individual differences in affective and conative characteristics as important for reading, the research has concentrated primarily on cognitive processes and the proficiencies they require. For example, the entry on "Individual Differences" in the *Encyclopedia of Educational Psychology* (Magliano & Perry, 2008) presents an information-processing-based discussion of the reading process that addresses exclusively cognitive and cognition-related contributors to reading processes and products. Stanovich (2009) has distinguished reflective, algorithmic, and autonomous processes in thinking and called for more attention to incorporating measurement of the reflective processes into our investigations of important differences in human intelligence. In considering the research on individual differences in reading, it appears that just as with the research on intelligence, the bulk of the attention has gone to potential individual differences in the relatively impersonal autonomous and algorithmic processes, and much less to those in which it matters who the person is as well as what his or her processing capabilities and proficiencies are.

Research on individual differences in reading has a strong focus on reading acquisition and the move into reading to learn, as well as, understandably, an emphasis on identification of factors contributing to or associated with reading difficulties and disabilities (Magliano & Perry, 2008). Although it is acknowledged that just getting children started successfully with reading does not guarantee their later success in the types of reading they will need to do in school or in their lives, the developmental and contextual range of much of the individual difference research in reading is quite constricted, especially for the research on reading development (Fox & Alexander, 2011). We seem to be very far from a view of reading as a necessary and valued part of people's lives at all ages, a behavior in which they can choose to engage in a wide variety of situations, for a wide variety of purposes, and with a wide variety of types of texts.

In general, the story that has been told in the research also relies upon a somewhat artificial compartmentalization of various more or less theoretically distinct (but certainly not independent) categories of possible differences between (or more rarely, within) readers. Each separate category tends to become its own center of gravity, and variations in how to operationalize its possible aspects and in which readers to measure them for which level of reading become important issues (e.g., Melby-Lervag, Lyster, & Hulme, 2012). As a consequence, there is more than enough material to justify separate chapters in this handbook on the contributions to individual differences in reading performance for each of these types of variables: memory; perception; attention; phonemic awareness; word identification; fluency; vocabulary; prior knowledge; metacognition; engagement and motivation; self-efficacy, agency, and volition; self-esteem and self-concept; epistemic beliefs; and higher-order thinking.

The story about individual differences in reading at this point has become an almost wholly quantitative story about different inputs into or modulators of the reading process (e.g., Savage, Pillay, & Melidona, 2007; Warmington & Hulme, 2012; Was, 2010). When the process and its development become the core concern, the reader's characteristics or proficiencies become disconnected from the reader and become objects of study in their own right; we are investigating individual differences in the reading process, but disembodied, in a sense, from the individual readers.

Finally, there is often a sense of sampling from a menu of possible factors and types of reading-related proficiencies, but without a strong underlying coherence or shape to the story that is being told across studies. The individual differences that are being singled out and then brought together to determine their relative value as predictors or contributors to development of a particular form of reading performance (typically a standardized assessment of comprehension, word identification, or both) can have a somewhat arbitrary and generic character, plugging in one or more verbal ability variables, one or more phonetic processing-related or decoding-related variables (occasionally a motivation- or volition-related variable), and so forth, in order to account for the different types of processing thought to make up reading. It is typical to see a battery of assessments, such as in the study by Berninger and colleagues (2006), of different possible paths for development of reading comprehension by at-risk young readers. They measured children's verbal IQ, word identification, word attack, passage comprehension (cloze, recall, and inferential tasks), oral reading fluency, oral reading accuracy, sentence comprehension, working memory span, and rapid automatized naming of letters. It becomes difficult to bring together what is learned about individual differences in reading across studies because of variations in what is measured and how it is measured (Johnston et al., 2008).

Our stories about even just the cognitive-processing aspects of the multiple levels of the reading process have become so involved that adding on additional layers presents an extremely difficult methodological, analytic, and theoretical challenge (Fox & Alexander, 2009). This means that the interactive and layered nature of the processing-related, motivational, and contextual contributors to what a given reader does in a given situation is often not taken into account. As Schatschneider and Petscher (2011) noted in their chapter on statistical modeling in literacy research:

> In studying literacy, it would be almost impossible for a researcher to collect observations on all the biological, cognitive, social, emotional, and environmental influences on reading behavior, even though most literacy researchers would acknowledge the importance of all these areas. (p. 63)

The meanings of the constructs that we do choose to measure do not, therefore, always have a happy home within a clearly articulated theoretical framework binding together the different roles these multiple types of variables play in contributing to individual differences in reading for the different kinds of readers and reading we want to know about.

## Centering Consideration of Individual Differences on the Reader

Given the identified possibilities for research on individual differences in reading and our framing of the current situation, we now consider what we could be doing differently. In our view, there are many interesting and relevant questions that are not being addressed, and the ways in which other questions are being addressed may not be building effectively toward a coherent and satisfying understanding of how individual readers differ in important reading-related ways. In a famous essay on Tolstoy, Isaiah Berlin (1951/2013) gave us the contrast between the hedgehog and the fox as a way to represent important differences in how to understand the world, with the hedgehog knowing one big thing, while the fox knows many things:

> For there exists a great chasm between those, on one side, who relate everything to a single central vision, one system, less or more coherent or articulate, in terms of which they understand, think and feel—a single, universal, organising principle in terms of which alone all that they are and say has significance—and on the other side, those who pursue many ends, often unrelated and even contradictory, connected, if at all, only in some de facto way, for some psychological or physiological cause, related to no moral or aesthetic principle (p. 2).

This dichotomy seems highly relevant for the situation we have described with regard to how individual differences in reading are conceptualized for investigation. We are looking for knowledge of many things, which means that we are missing perhaps the larger story within which they all make sense.

Our intuition is that one way to unify the work that is being done on individual differences in reading and to be able to get at important questions that are now put aside or seem out of reach is for us to re-position ourselves more on the side of the hedgehog than the fox. And our suggestion along these lines is to re-cast this enterprise as essentially one of understanding individual differences in *readers*, rather than in the reading process. We suggest that the reader should be at the center of the story, as the binding construct from which our investigations and questions should begin and to which they should return. Taking reading as the essentially complex communicative behavior of a person interacting with a text rather than as a disassembled set of processes or forces (motivational, affective, psycho-physical, cognitive, contextual, and so forth) means that we begin from an undeniably unified phenomenon, in the person of the reader who is incorporating the activity of reading into his or her life (Fox & Alexander, 2011). Such a unified view would support the articulation of a coherent theoretical rationale for which aspects of the reader to foreground in a particular investigation, as well as providing a home for the findings of each investigation within a well-structured and continually more fleshed-out story about interesting differences between and within readers.

An excellent example of framing a story about the nature of reading around the reader as its center and the type of insights and possibilities such a stance can generate is provided in the lifelong work of William Gray. From his earliest forays into outlining a theory of reading development (e.g., Gray, 1925), he included reading attitudes, habits, skills, and tastes as relevant to reading development, along with readers' awareness of different reading purposes. He highlighted the linking in reading of cognition, motivation, communicativeness, purposefulness, and transformative power, as well as the role of reading in the larger social context. In a later work, Gray (1951) explicitly incorporated cognitive, physical, developmental, attitudinal, and motivational factors, along with environment and context, as affecting growth in reading, all as bound up together in the person of the reader:

> In the final analysis, progress in reading is determined by the interests and needs of the individual learner. Here many factors are involved: the reader's background; his capacity to learn; his physical, mental, and emotional status; his interests, motives, and drives; his immediate and oncoming developmental needs; his biases, prejudices, and preconceptions; and his home and community environment . . . In other words, growth in reading is influenced by the total development of a child and by all the factors that promote it. (p. 434)

Gray did not consider just the childhood aspect of reading development, but also thought it crucial to understand what later stages of reading development would involve for the reader. In their study of maturity in reading, Gray and Rogers (1956) worked to identify the specific characteristics of the fully mature reader from a theoretical and empirical standpoint. They found that mature readers find reading to be an essential part of their daily lives, they are strongly aware of the contribution of reading to their personal growth as individuals, as learners, and as socially aware citizens, and they choose reading material that supports growth in these aspects.

In looking back to Gray's work as an example of what we see as the viability and potential of centering on the reader, we are not seeking to be regressive or reactionary, and we are not inspired by nostalgia. We do not advocate dismissal of what has been learned so far by focusing on the reading process, but at the same time we would suggest that it could be quite profitable to take into account in addition what had been learned before that by focusing on the reader. One way to consider what it means to have developed a better understanding of a phenomenon is to look at the degree to which a previously undifferentiated and inclusive whole has become complex and specific (Marton & Booth, 1997). The proposed shift in perspective on studying individual differences in reading is a return to a view of reading as a whole, that is, as the behavior of a reader. However, it can be seen as a whole that is becoming increasingly differentiated through the efforts of researchers who have concentrated on parts or aspects of that whole

(Alexander & Fox, 2013; Fox & Alexander, 2009). We do not necessarily need to let go of the many things we know, as long as we can understand them as embedded in and radiating from the core phenomenon that gives them their meaning; that is, the reader and what the reader does. In one of their early articles on the construction–integration model, Kintsch and van Dijk (1978) argued that only the decomposition of the comprehension process would enable us to study it effectively:

> If it were not possible to separate aspects of the total comprehension process for study, our enterprise would be futile. We believe, however, that the comprehension process can be decomposed into components, some of which may be manageable at present, while others can be put aside until later. (p. 364)

We are suggesting that perhaps now the time has come to recompose the comprehension process (and the other levels of reading) by putting it back within the reader.

Our argument so far has been that one important benefit of centering on the reader is unification; another important shift that this entails is that what is at the center of our stories is now a person. This person, the reader, reads as part of what he or she does, in the consciousness of who he or she is, as an expression of his or her values, beliefs, and goals. Being a reader can be a significant thread in an individual's identity and lifelong project of identity development (Athey, 1985). Identity as a reader also includes knowledge of one's own tastes and interests, and possibly also of the limits of one's knowledge, tastes, and interests; the mature reader, in Gray's description, is "keenly aware of his own dominant interests, beliefs, hopes, and biases" (1954, p. 397). These aspects of the individual's sense of identity as a reader play a role in the types of reading situations entered into and in the stance the reader takes within those situations (e.g., Schutte & Malouff, 2007).

Centering on the reader and considering reading as a complex communicative behavior not only brings the person of the reader into the spotlight, it means that we must look and see the other person involved here, the one with whom the reader is communicating. Bringing the reader into the heart of our story also entails acknowledging the presence of the author. Just as we do not have a reading process operating on its own, we similarly do not have texts that occur spontaneously and present themselves to be processed. The reader chooses to read in a certain way and for a certain purpose what the author has chosen to write in a certain way and for a certain purpose. Orienting our understanding of what the reader is doing in reading around this idea of an interaction with the text as the product of an author gives us a very different place to stand, and a much more powerful story about what different readers do and understand than that provided by the machinery of text processing (Alexander et al., 2011).

This perspective thus positions our thinking as beginning with the reader and acknowledging the author, positioning reading as a fundamentally human act, a complex and integrated phenomenon within which particular perceptual, physiological, cognitive, motivational, social, contextual strands or combinations thereof might then be foregrounded and traced. We anticipate that starting from the reader and taking reading as the reader's intentional, complex, communicative behavior involving derivation of meaning from presented text (Fox & Alexander, 2011) will construct a space for discourse within which it is appropriate to consider both observational and experiential orientations toward the reader and to use both quantitative and qualitative descriptions. Such a stance should support conceptualization of what readers do in reading as both context-specific and consistent, permit aiming both at discovering relations between variables and at determining the meanings of the variables, and enable direction of research toward both explanatory and emancipatory applications (Marton & Svensson, 1979).

We will then be looking essentially at what the reader does when reading, and our stories about the individual differences involved can radiate out from that center in many different directions without losing their ability to connect to each other.

At the same time, once the reader is placed at the center of our inquiries, the essential complexity of the phenomenon observed cannot be dismissed nor disguised. In other words, putting the reading process back into the reader cannot be likened to linking together the pieces of a jigsaw, because the very shape of each piece now comes to be defined only in relation to the other parts and to the whole. Perhaps this is why following in the footsteps of the fox and trying to address the complexity by dissolving it into an assembly of discrete factors does not seem to have produced satisfying explanations of differences in reading. Far from being an issue relevant only to the topic of this chapter, this problem affects most social sciences inquiries, so much so that we have found the reflections of a well-known economist very relevant to the shift in perspective we are advocating here.

In his speech accepting the 1974 Nobel Prize for economics, von Hayek observed that the complexity that characterizes most of the structures studied by the social sciences is not limited to the quantifiable characteristics of the individual elements that compose them or to the frequency of their manifestation; rather, their complexity essentially derives from the relations among these individual factors. As Gray observed in regard to reading, "its growth is influenced by the total development of a child and by all the factors that promote it" (1951, p. 434).

The consequence of such a state of affairs is the impossibility of predicting specific outcomes without knowing the values of *all* of the relevant factors characterizing the complex phenomenon. If this were the case, what would be the value of trying to study individual components of the reading process? From a predictive perspective, such an attempt would necessarily be inadequate and might well produce results that do not reflect the individual experiences of diverse readers. Our other option is to follow von Hayek and let go of the idea that only the quantitatively measurable factors are scientifically important in what constitutes our object of study. We argue that this would put us in a position to better understand the phenomenon at hand, free to use what has been gained through the study of individual factors to deepen the comprehension of the complex structure that characterizes our inquiry, the reader. But such a shift does not come cheap. As hinted above, it forces us to admit that our models may at best predict how, in general, individual readers' situations will likely evolve under specific conditions, conditions that we will never be able to fully determine and quantify. Such an outcome may fall short of the far-reaching expectations of policy makers and other stakeholders, which are less likely to be fully informed by consideration of such issues.

Yet we find the "true but imperfect knowledge" advocated by von Hayek theoretically preferable to and pragmatically more useful than the appearance of exact knowledge produced by abstracting the study of individual factors from their personal context. The former form of knowledge, though humbling, may at least indicate what conditions may, in general, foster growth and what conditions will likely stifle it, leaving the ultimate determination of the outcome to the still mostly unknown interplay of personal and social factors. The latter risks granting the scientific stamp of approval to specific interventions based on simplifications that are likely false (and thus not scientific), yet proposed (or imposed) as *the* way to growth.

We also propose two key instruction-related implications of this shift to a perspective on individual differences in reading that centers on the reader. The first is that it is critical that reading be approached in the classroom as communicative, as one person's interaction with the ideas of another; the reader's interaction with the text as the product of an author. Although it is encouraging to see this aspect of the reading–writing connection acknowledged in the Common Core State Standards in relation to writing, awareness of the author is only minimally present in the language describing the standards for reading (Common Core State Standards Initiative, 2010), which is concerning. The other implication is that taking into account the reader as an individual leads to the conclusion that reading itself should not be split apart into in-school and out-of-school reading; the same reader is doing both. Presenting school reading as a tool providing access to instructional material and out-of-school reading as an immersive form of recreation can lead to the dichotomization of reading into pleasurable leisure reading for escape and entertainment on the one hand, and effortful, unpleasant, difficult reading to learn on the other. Such a divorce of enjoyment and learning from text has clear negative consequences in terms of development as a reader and learner.

In conclusion, we would like to point out that the set of questions about individual differences in readers that we introduced at the beginning of our chapter is itself premised on having already made the shift to centering on the reader. The very framing of our enterprise in investigating individual differences as one in which these are the key questions to answer means that we are already focusing on the reader. We hope that raising these questions has begun some of the work of opening up a space for further conversation about where we want to go in our research and theorizing about individual differences that are important for what readers do and who they can be. We have offered our own suggestion of a new orientation for our stories, investigations, and conclusions about individual differences, one that is centered on the reader. As a field, we do need to consider our aims and the directions we are taking to fulfill them. Ultimately, this means that we do need to think about why reading matters and about why differences between individual readers are something we need to understand.

## References

Alexander, P. A. (2006). The path to competence: A lifespan developmental perspective on reading. *Journal of Literacy Research*, *37*, 413–436.

Alexander, P. A., Dinsmore, D. L., Fox, E., Grossnickle, E. M., Loughlin, S. M., Maggioni, L., . . . Winters, F. I. (2011). Higher-order thinking and knowledge: Domain-general and domain-specific trends and future directions. In G. Schraw (Ed.), *Assessment of higher order thinking skills* (pp. 47–88). Charlotte, NC: Information Age Publishers.

Alexander, P. A., & Fox, E. (2013). A historical perspective on reading research and practice, redux. In D. E. Alvermann, N. J. Unrau, & R. B. Ruddell, (Eds.), *Theoretical models and processes of reading* (6th ed., pp. 3–46). Newark, DE: International Reading Association.

Anmarkrud, Ø., & Bråten, I. (2009). Motivation for reading comprehension. *Learning and Individual Differences*, *19*, 252–256.

Athey, I. (1985). Reading research in the affective domain. In H. Singer & R. B. Ruddell (Eds.), *Theoretical models and processes of reading* (3rd ed., pp. 527–557). Newark, DE: International Reading Association.

Berlin, I. (2013). *The hedgehog and the fox* (2nd ed.). Princeton, NJ: Princeton University Press. (Original work published 1951.)

Berninger, V. W., Abbott, R. D., Vermeulen, K., & Fulton, C. M. (2006). Paths to reading comprehension in at-risk second graders. *Journal of Learning Disabilities*, *39*(4), 334–351.

Bowey, J. A. (2005). Predicting individual differences in learning to read. In M. J. Snowling & C. Hulme (Eds.), *The science of reading: A handbook* (pp. 155–172). Malden, MA: Blackwell.

Breslin, F. D. (2004). Individual differences. In *The concise Corsini encyclopedia of psychology and behavioral science*. Retrieved from http://proxy-um.researchport.umd.edu/login?qurl=http%3A%2F%2Fwww.credoreference.com/entry/wileypsych/individual_differences

Clay, M. M. (1989). Concepts about print in English and other languages. *Reading Teacher*, *42*(4), 268–276.

Common Core State Standards Initiative (2010). *Common Core State Standards for English language arts and literacy in history/social studies, science, and technical subjects*. Washington, DC: Council of Chief State School Officers and National Governors Association. Retrieved from http://www.corestandards.org/

Corno, L. (2003). Individual differences: Affective and conative processes. In J. M. Guthrie (Ed.), *Encyclopedia of education* (pp. 1118–1121). New York: Macmillan.

Fox, E., & Alexander, P. A. (2009). Text comprehension: A retrospective, perspective, and prospective. In S. E. Israel & G. G. Duffy (Eds.), *Handbook of research on reading comprehension* (pp. 227–239). New York: Routledge.

Fox, E., & Alexander, P. A. (2011). Learning to read. In R. Mayer & P. A. Alexander (Eds.), *Handbook of research on learning and instruction* (pp. 7–31). New York: Routledge.

Fox, E., Dinsmore, D. L., Maggioni, L., & Alexander, P. A. (2009, April). *Factors associated with undergraduates' success in reading and learning from course texts.* Paper presented at the annual meeting of the American Educational Research Association, San Diego.

Gough, P. B., & Tunmer, W. E. (1986). Decoding, reading, and reading disability. *Remedial and Special Education, 7,* 6–10.

Gray, W. S. (1925). A modern program of reading instruction for the grades and the high school. In G. W. Whipple (Ed.), *Report of the National Committee on Reading: 24th yearbook of the National Society for the Study of Education* (pp. 21–73). Chicago, IL: NSSE.

Gray, W. S. (1951). Foundation stones in the road to better reading. *Elementary School Journal, 51,* 427–435.

Gray, W. S. (1954). The nature of mature reading. *School Review, 62,* 393–398.

Gray, W. S., & Rogers, B. (1956). *Maturity in reading, its nature and appraisal.* Chicago, IL: University of Chicago Press.

Guthrie, J. T., & Wigfield, A. (1999). How motivation fits into a science of reading. *Scientific Studies of Reading, 3*(3), 199–205.

Hart, B., & Risley, T. R. (1995). *Meaningful differences in the everyday lives of young American children.* Baltimore, MD: Paul H. Brookes.

Ho, H., Tomlinson, H. A., & Whipple, A. D. (2003). Individual differences: Gender equity and schooling. In J. M. Guthrie (Ed.), *Encyclopedia of education* (pp. 1125–1129). New York: Macmillan.

Johnston, A. M., Barnes, M. A., & Desrochers, A. (2008). Reading comprehension: Developmental processes, individual differences, and interventions. *Canadian Psychology, 49*(2), 125–132.

Kintsch, W. A. (1998). *Comprehension: A paradigm for cognition.* New York: Cambridge University Press.

Kintsch, W., & van Dijk, T. A. (1978). Toward a model of text comprehension and production. *Psychological Review, 85,* 363–394.

Kyllonen, D. C., & Gitomer, G. H. (2003). Individual differences: Abilities and aptitudes. In J. M. Guthrie (Ed.), *Encyclopedia of education* (pp. 1112–1118). New York: Macmillan.

Lubinski, D., & Webb, R. M. (2005). Individual differences. In *Encyclopedia of cognitive science.* Retrieved from http://proxy-um.researchport.umd.edu/login?qurl=http%3A%2F%2Fwww.credoreference.com/entry/wileycs/individual_differences

McCrae, R. R. (2007). Individual differences. In *Encyclopedia of social psychology.* Retrieved from http://proxy-um.researchport.umd.edu/login?qurl=http%3A%2F%2Fwww.credoreference.com/entry/sagesocpsyc/individual_differences

Magliano, J., & Perry, P. (2008). Individual differences. In N. Salkind (Ed.), *Encyclopedia of educational psychology* (pp. 512–518). Thousand Oaks, CA: SAGE. doi:10.4135/9781412963848.n137

Marton, F., & Booth, S. (1997). *Learning and awareness.* Mahwah, NJ: Lawrence Erlbaum Associates.

Marton, F., & Svensson, L. (1979). Conceptions of research in human learning. *Higher Education, 8,* 471–496.

Melby-Lervag, M., Lyster, S. H., & Hulme, C. (2012). Phonological skills and their role in learning to read: A meta-analytic review. *Psychological Bulletin, 138*(2), 322–352.

Perfetti, C. (2007). Reading ability: Lexical quality to comprehension. *Scientific Studies of Reading, 11*(4), 357–383.

RAND Reading Study Group (2002). *Reading for understanding: Toward an R&D program in reading comprehension.* Santa Monica, CA: RAND.

Reeve, C. L. (2006). Individual differences. In *Encyclopedia of human development.* Retrieved from http://proxy-um.researchport.umd.edu/login?qurl=http%3A%2F%2Fwww.credoreference.com/entry/sagehd/individual_differences

Savage, R., Pillay, V., & Melidona, S. (2007). Deconstructing rapid automatized naming: Component processes and the prediction of individual differences. *Learning and Individual Differences, 17,* 129–146.

Schatschneider, C., & Petscher, Y. (2011). Statistical modeling in literacy research. In M. L. Kamil, P. D. Pearson, E. B. Moje, & P. P. Afflerbach (Eds.), *Handbook of reading research, Volume IV* (pp. 54–65). New York: Routledge.

Schutte, N. S., & Malouff, J. M. (2007). Dimensions of reading motivation: Development of an adult reading motivation scale. *Reading Psychology, 28,* 469–489.

Stanovich, K. E. (1986). Matthew effects in reading: Some consequences of individual differences in the acquisition of literacy. *Reading Research Quarterly, 21*(4), 360–407.

Stanovich, K. E. (2009). *What intelligence tests miss.* New Haven, CT: Yale University Press.

van den Broek, P., Risden, K., Fletcher, C. R., & Thurlow, R. (1996). A "landscape" view of reading: Fluctuating patterns of activation and the construction of a stable memory representation. In B. K. Britton & A. C. Graesser (Eds.), Models of understanding text (pp. 165–187). Mahwah, NJ: Erlbaum.

von Hayek, F. A. (1974). *The pretence of knowledge* (Nobel Prize Lecture). Retrieved from http://www.nobelprize.org/nobel_prizes/economic-sciences/laureates/1974/hayek-lecture.html

Warmington, M., & Hulme, C. (2012). Phoneme awareness, visual-verbal paired associate learning, and rapid automatized naming as predictors of individual differences in reading ability. *Scientific Studies of Reading, 16*(1), 45–62.

Was, C. A. (2010). Individual differences in reading are more than just working memory: The case for available long-term memory. *Individual Differences Research, 8*(3), 132–139.

Webb, R. M., & Lubinski, D. (2007). Individual differences. In *Encyclopedia of industrial and organizational psychology.* Retrieved from http://proxy-um.researchport.umd.edu/login?qurl=http%3A%2F%2Fwww.credoreference.com/entry/sageindorg/individual_differences

# 3

# Metacognition

*Marcel V. J. Veenman*

## Introduction

Metacognition refers to the descriptive knowledge of, and the regulatory control over one's cognitive system (Veenman, van Hout-Wolters, & Afflerbach, 2006). The relevance of metacognition for reading has been recognized early on (Baker & Brown, 1984). Reading not only pertains to studying texts and textbooks, as reading activities are omnipresent in various school tasks. When writing a paper, students have to search for information in the library or on the Internet. Even problem solving in physics or mathematics requires thorough reading of the problem statement. Many students, however, fail to exert adequate metacognitive control while reading (Veenman, 2013a). A literature review by Wang, Haertel, and Walberg (1990) revealed that metacognition is the most important predictor of learning outcomes, surpassing other cognitive and motivational characteristics of students. In an overview of studies with students (9–26 years) performing different tasks in various school domains, Veenman (2008) estimated that metacognitive skillfulness accounted for 40 percent of learning outcomes. The impact of individual differences in metacognition is also acknowledged in reading research (Baker, 2005; Pressley & Afflerbach, 1995; Veenman & Beishuizen, 2004).

The concept of metacognition has its roots in developmental psychology with Piaget and Flavell as progenitors. Metacognition initially focused on the developing person's thinking about cognition. In particular, metamemory research addressed children's increasing knowledge of how memory operates (Flavell & Wellman, 1977). Brown (1978; Brown & DeLoache, 1978) added self-regulation to the conceptualization of metacognition. Metacognitive strategies and skills for goal setting, planning, monitoring, and evaluation coordinate the execution of cognitive processes. This distinction between metacognitive declarative knowledge about one's cognitive system on the one hand, and metacognitive skills for regulating cognitive processes on the other, is recurrent in definitions of metacognition (Schraw & Moshman, 1995; Veenman et al., 2006).

## Metacognitive Knowledge

Metacognitive knowledge refers to one's declarative knowledge about the interplay between person, task, and strategy characteristics (Flavell, 1979). For instance, a student may think that s/he (person) has difficulties with reading complex texts (task) and, consequently, that s/he should invest more effort in thoroughly reading a scientific article (strategy). Conversely, another student may positively evaluate his/her reading proficiency, thus putting less effort into reading the same article. Some researchers presume that metacognitive knowledge only refers to correct knowledge, derived from earlier experiences (Schraw & Moshman, 1995). The assumption is that only accurate and flawless knowledge can be truly metacognitive by nature. Metacognitive knowledge, however, may be incorrect when learners overestimate or underestimate their competences, relative to the subjectively perceived task complexity (Veenman et al., 2006). For instance, students sometimes erroneously think that they only have to read a textbook once in preparation for an exam, even after repeatedly failing on earlier exams. Such flawed self-knowledge may prove resistant to change, especially when students misattribute their failure to external causes such as poor teachers or unfair exams. Even correct metacognitive knowledge does not guarantee an adequate execution of appropriate skills, as students may lack the motivation or capability to do so. Alexander, Carr, and Schwanenflugel (1995) found a discrepancy between children's knowledge about monitoring and their application of monitoring skills. Winne (1996) argued that knowledge has no effect on behavior until that knowledge is actually used. Consequently, metacognitive knowledge often poorly predicts learning outcomes (Veenman, 2005). Metacognitive knowledge is part of a person's belief system, which contains broad, often tacit ideas about the nature and functioning of the cognitive system (Flavell, 1979). Individual beliefs are personal and subjective by nature, and so remains metacognitive knowledge when it is not put to the test by the actual execution of strategies or skills. The proof of the pudding is in the eating, not in the recipe.

## Metamemory

Metamemory initially referred to the declarative knowledge about one's memory capabilities and about strategies that affect memory processes (Flavell & Wellman, 1977). It was assumed that knowledge of memory processes would affect memory performance, although mediated by memory strategies such as selective attention and rehearsal. Indeed, moderate correlations between declarative metamemory and reading comprehension have been reported (Van Kraayenoord, Beinicke, Slagmüller, & Schneider, 2012). Later, the focus shifted from declarative metamemory to procedural metamemory with monitoring as a key process (Schneider, 2008). Judgment of Learning (JOL) and Feeling of Knowing (FOK) refer to a person's predictions of future test performance, either on items that have been learned (JOL), or on items that are to be studied (FOK). Accuracy of predictions is calculated from the discrepancy between predictions and actual performance on items of a memory test, such as vocabulary tests (Nelson & Narens, 1990). As FOKs and JOLs are the result of monitoring item difficulty and evaluating memory content, procedural metamemory is part of metacognitive skillfulness, instead of metacognitive knowledge (Veenman, 2011a).

## Conditional Knowledge

A noteworthy component of metacognitive knowledge is conditional knowledge (Schraw & Dennison, 1994; Veenman, 2011a). Conditional knowledge pertains to declarative knowledge about when a particular metacognitive strategy should be applied and to what purpose. Poor readers often are not aware of *what* strategy should be deployed *when* during reading, or *why* the strategy should be used. Adequate conditional knowledge, however, does not warrant actual strategy use because students may lack the procedural knowledge for *how* to enact the strategy. It is like taking your first driving lesson, when you know many useful things about a car but you still have to learn how to drive one. In fact, conditional knowledge provides an entry to the first stage of skill acquisition, where a metacognitive strategy has to be built from the available conditional knowledge. This strategy is then consciously applied step by step and gradually transformed into a skill (Afflerbach, Pearson, & Paris, 2008; Veenman, 2011a). Thus, conditional knowledge is a prerequisite, yet insufficient condition for the acquisition of metacognitive strategies and skills.

## Metacognitive Strategies and Skills

Metacognitive strategies and skills pertain to the acquired repertoire of procedural knowledge for monitoring and controlling one's learning behavior (Veenman, 2011a). The essential difference between a strategy and a skill is that strategies require deliberate, conscious effort, whereas the execution of skills is (partly) automatized (Afflerbach, Pearson, & Paris, 2008; Alexander & Jetton, 2000). Pressley and Afflerbach (1995) discerned some 150 different activities in detail for constructively responsive reading, most of which are representative of metacognitive strategies and skills. They based their taxonomy on an exhaustive analysis of thinking aloud protocols from expert readers. Such an extensive taxonomy, however, may be too sophisticated for analyzing the metacognitive reading behavior of secondary-school students (Meijer, Veenman, & van Hout-Wolters, 2006) or university students (Veenman & Beishuizen, 2004). These students enact metacognitive strategies and skills on a more global level while studying a text, leaving out many detailed activities from Pressley and Afflerbach's taxonomy. Therefore, a global description of metacognitive strategies and skills is presented here. A distinction is made between metacognitive activities at the onset of a reading task, during the reading task, and at the end of the reading task (Pressley & Afflerbach, 1995; Veenman, 2013a; Zimmerman, 2000).

### *Orientation and Planning at the Onset of Reading*

At the onset of a task, orienting activities are preparatory to reading or studying a text. First, students should properly read the assignment, if any, to understand what is expected from the reading task. The assignment could provide vital information for later goal setting. Next, students should read the title of the text, which contains essential information about the topic of the text. They should read the abstract, whenever available, to get an overview of the text. Once the topic of the text is known, students can activate prior knowledge about the subject matter from memory. Activating prior knowledge is helpful in understanding the text while reading, but it also facilitates storage of new information in long-term memory. Then students may scan the text for subheadings, paragraph structure, and text length to get an impression of the reading task that lies ahead of them, and to estimate the text difficulty and time needed for reading the text. Students ought to set reading goals, depending on the nature of the reading task. It makes a difference whether one is reading a text in preparation for an exam, whether one is looking for specific information needed for writing a paper, or whether one is reading a novel for leisure. Such reading goals should specify what kind of information in the text is relevant to the student, which is the point of departure for planning one's reading activities. Reading plans pertain to focusing on relevant parts of the text, the allocation of reading time, and selecting methods for processing the content (e.g., by making schemas or concept maps). Students may diverge in reading goals and plans. For instance, when reading a history text, some students are devoted to memorizing dates and events, whereas others emphasize the causes and consequences of historical events (Van der Stel & Veenman, 2010). Armed with such a reading plan, students may enter the arena of reading.

A participant from the study of Van der Stel and Veenman (2010) may illustrate the orientation behavior of metacognitive proficient readers. This participant first read the title of a history text on the American civil war to grasp the major theme and used this information to recollect prior knowledge about the topic. Thus, concepts like North versus South, slavery, and the assassination of Lincoln were activated. Next, he skimmed the text for subtitles and paragraphs to get an overview of the text structure. Then, he deliberately turned to reading the conclusion, because he wanted "to know what the text is heading for." After reading the conclusion paragraph, he noticed that he did not understand all of it, but he had a global idea of directions for reading the text. For instance, he wanted to know more precisely how slavery affected the civil war. In fact, this is an expression of goal setting. Subsequently, he returned to the first page and devised a reading plan for mapping particular concepts and their relations, before actually starting to read. In contrast, poor metacognitive readers tend to skip the title of the text and immediately start reading linearly, from beginning to end (Van der Stel & Veenman, 2010; Veenman & Beishuizen, 2004).

## Monitoring and Selecting Methods for Processing Text During Reading

During reading, metacognitive proficient readers keep a close watch on their reading behavior. They monitor their comprehension of words, sentences, and paragraphs (Baker & Brown, 1984; Markman, 1985). Whenever they encounter confusions or miscomprehensions, they take actions to remedy their lack of understanding by consulting a dictionary, by backtracking and rereading the text carefully, or by purposefully navigating through the text in search of information (Pressley & Afflerbach, 1995; Puntambekar & Stylianou, 2005; Veenman & Beishuizen, 2004). Students with poor monitoring skills, on the other hand, either do not detect miscomprehension or they do not take action to resolve the problem. For instance, they may replace an unknown word with an incorrect familiar one without noticing, even when the familiar word does not fit in with the context (Veenman, 2013a). Monitoring also refers to whether progress is made towards reading goals (Veenman, 2013a). During reading, metacognitive proficient students keep track of whether their understanding of the text brings them closer to what they want to know. If not, they may decide to change their reading plan, to reset reading goals, or to abandon reading when the required information is absent.

Metacognitive proficient students also select methods for actively processing text during reading. They close read and paraphrase difficult text parts, they generate self-questions, they draw conclusions and make inferences, they relate new information to prior knowledge, they take notes and selectively highlight or underline text, and they draw up schemas or concept maps (Pressley & Afflerbach 1995; Veenman, 2013a). Poor metacognitive students, on the other hand, do not actively process the text or they do so ineffectively. For instance, when first-year psychology students at Leiden University open their books, many pages appear to be entirely colored yellow with a marking pen. This unselective marking of pages indicates an inability to distinguish relevant from irrelevant information, partly due to a lack of content knowledge, but ultimately due to deficient metacognition (Veenman & Beishuizen, 2004). Metacognitive proficient readers only highlight main concepts, definitions, and findings, leaving most of the page unmarked (Veenman, 2013a).

## Evaluation and Recapitulation After Reading

After reading, metacognitive proficient students evaluate their comprehension of the text against their reading goals. For instance, they consider whether the text was sufficiently studied to pass the exam, or whether they obtained the required information. They may generate "end-of-the-chapter" questions to test the consistency and completeness of their comprehension (Pressley & Afflerbach, 1995). If not, they may reread certain parts of the text or review their notes. Moreover, they often make a concise summary of the text, recapitulating the central theme, arguments pro and con, evidence or decisive events, and important conclusions drawn (Pressley & Afflerbach, 1995; Veenman, 2013a). Finally, they may reflect on the reading process to improve their reading for future occasions (Veenman, 2013a). Poor metacognitive students, especially younger students, tend to adhere to the full stop after reading the last word of the text by saying "ready."

The execution of metacognitive strategies and skills before, during, and after reading is a cyclic process, rather than being strictly linear (Veenman, 2013a; Zimmerman, 2000). While reading, students may come to the conclusion that the text content is not corresponding to their prior expectations. This may lead to reorientation on the reading task, and to adjusting or fine-tuning reading goals and plans. Moreover, students may already draw conclusions and summarize paragraphs while reading, in advance of later recapitulation. After reading, evaluation of text comprehension may result in reorientation on the task assignment or reading goals, or in rereading text parts.

## Model of Metacognitive Skills as Self-Instructions

In a process model of metacognitive skills, cognitive activity should be distinguished from metacognitive activity. When students are thinking aloud during reading, this distinction becomes manifest as they may express their intention to apply a particular metacognitive skill while enacting the cognitive behavioral consequences of that skill. During silent reading, however, metacognitive skills remain covert mechanisms that have to be inferred from their behavioral consequences (Veenman et al., 2006). For instance, when a student consults a dictionary, it is assumed that a preceding monitoring process has made the student aware of an unfamiliar word or phrase, and that a local planning process resulted in looking for a dictionary. Thus, higher-order metacognitive skills draw on lower-order cognitive processes. Metaphorically speaking, metacognitive skills represent the driver, while cognitive processes make up the vehicle for employing those skills (Veenman, 2011a).

In his model of metacognition, Nelson distinguished an "object-level" from a "meta-level" in the cognitive system (Nelson & Narens, 1990). At the object-level, lower-order cognitive processes are executed, such as decoding, parsing, and lexical access for reading. In addition, component processes of more complex reading skills, such as relating, comparing, and making inferences, are located at the object-level. Higher-order processes of evaluation and planning at the meta-level govern the object-level. Nelson postulated two flows of information linking the meta-level to the object-level. Information about the state of the object-level is conveyed to the meta-level through monitoring processes, while directions from the meta-level are transferred to the object-level through control processes. Thus, if an error occurs on the object-level, a monitoring process will alert the meta-level and control processes will be activated to resolve the problem. Nelson's model can be metaphorically conceived as the production unit of a company, where the shop floor symbolizes the object-level and the manager overlooking the shop floor personifies the meta-level. The manager monitors activity on the shop floor to detect errors that may obstruct the production process, upon which the manager's instructions restore production at the shop floor. Basically, this is a bottom–up model because metacognitive control is triggered by anomalies in cognitive activity (Veenman, 2011a).

Veenman (2011a) extended Nelson's bottom–up model with a top–down approach in which metacognitive skills are conceived as an acquired program of self-instructions for initiating and regulating cognitive processes at the object-level. This program of self-instructions is activated whenever the learner is faced with performing a task. Self-instructions can be represented by a production system of condition–action rules (Anderson, 1996), which contains conditional knowledge about when to apply a particular metacognitive skill and procedural instructions for how to implement the skill at the object-level. For instance, activating prior knowledge after reading the title of the text can be represented by the rule: "IF you have inferred the topic or theme from the title of the text, THEN retrieve all that you know about the topic from memory." In contrast with Nelson's view, self-instructions from the meta-level are self-induced, that is, they need not necessarily be triggered by anomalies in task performance. The monitoring flow serves to identify which conditions are satisfied for activating self-instructions. Metacognitive skilled students have an orderly set of self-instructions available that will help them work through the task. The output of an implemented self-instruction will subsequently satisfy conditions for the next self-instruction.

Such a program of self-instructions is acquired through experience and training, much in the same way as cognitive skills are learned (Veenman, 2011a). According to ACT-R theory (Anderson, 1996), skill acquisition passes through three successive stages. In the cognitive stage, *declarative* knowledge of condition and actions is interpreted and arranged in order to allow for a verbal description of a strategy (*What* to do, *When*, *Why*, and *How*; Veenman et al., 2006). Metacognitive knowledge, in particular conditional knowledge, is incorporated in this verbal description. In fact, conditional knowledge of the *Why* and *When* define the IF-side of a production rule. The *What* and *How* constitute the THEN-side of a production rule. Initially, the metacognitive strategy needs to be consciously performed step-by-step, while being prone to error. Conscious execution of a strategy at this stage requires extra effort, which may temporarily interfere with cognitive performance (Puntambekar & Stylianou, 2005; Veenman et al., 2006). During the second, associative stage, verbal descriptions of the strategy are transformed into a procedural representation. Errors are eliminated and separate procedures are assembled into an organized set. Gradually, strategies turn into more fluent and accurate skills. Finally, the execution of skills is fine-tuned and automated in the autonomous stage. Some metacognitive skills will not entirely pass through this last stage, as they need to be consciously applied and tuned to the task at hand. For instance, goal setting remains strategic, that is, intentionally and deliberately employed contingent on task characteristics (Afflerbach et al., 2008; Alexander & Jetton, 2000). Monitoring processes, on the other hand, may run in the background until an error or anomaly is detected (Samuels, Ediger, Willcutt, & Palumbo, 2005). Consciously checking the meaning of every word or phrase would interfere with reading fluency. Yet, proficient readers are alerted whenever they encounter unknown words or inconsistencies in the text. In the same vein, some planning processes may become automated or habitual (Borkowski, Carr, & Pressley, 1987), such as skimming a text before reading, or rereading a sentence when one does not grasp its meaning. In fact, the repertoire of metacognitive self-instructions should become good practice, albeit adaptively applied.

## Development of Metacognition

Many students spontaneously acquire a repertoire of self-instructions, either by themselves through reading practice, or by observing good reading models (parents, teachers, etc.). Skill acquisition, however, is constrained by the developmental trajectory of metacognition. In a nutshell, the development of metacognition can be characterized by the emergence of metamemory at the age of 5 to 6 years, followed by an expansion of metacognitive knowledge in early childhood, and the incremental use of strategies and skills from late childhood into adolescence (Veenman, 2011a). Earlier developmental processes of Theory of Mind (ToM) and Executive Functions (EF), however, pave the way for metacognitive development.

## Precursors of Metacognition

Theory of Mind (ToM) pertains to children's knowledge about the mind and, in particular, knowledge about mental states such as beliefs, desires, and intentions. Crucial to the development of ToM is the perception of a child older than 4 years that another person may not know what the child knows. A longitudinal study of Lockl and Schneider (2006) evidenced that ToM at the age of 4 to 5 years is a precursor of later metamemory performance at the age of 5 to 6 years. According to Flavell (2004), ToM is prerequisite to thinking about mental states. Thus, ToM is a stepping-stone for readers to take different perspectives, to understand the different positions of protagonists in a story, and to differentiate between fact, belief, and fiction.

Executive functions (EF) refer to processes of inhibition, selective attention, working memory efficiency, and elementary forms of planning. EF capacity is related to the maturation of the prefrontal cortex from early childhood throughout adolescence. Blair and Razza (2007) established that especially inhibitory control is a strong predictor of early literacy in children of 3 to 5 years old. Inhibition may prevent readers from rushing through a text while ignoring relevant features. In general, EF processes could be conceived as basic building blocks for later development of metacognitive skills, such as planning ahead and monitoring one's reading activities.

## Development of Metacognitive Knowledge

The acquisition of declarative metamemory sets the stage for the development of metacognitive knowledge (Flavell & Wellman, 1977; Schneider, 2008). Preschool children already experience that they sometimes forget or inaccurately recollect knowledge or events. Once in primary school, children become aware of task demands and memory strategies, such as rereading or rehearsing difficult materials. Children, however, do not effectively use strategies for restudying materials before the age of 10 (Metcalfe & Finn, 2013). Metamemory rapidly increases with age until it reaches a peak in late adolescence (Schneider, 2008). A longitudinal study by Kurtz and Borkowski (1987) indicated that metamemory of children in the age of 7 to 9 years facilitates the acquisition of summarization skills for reading comprehension at the age of 10 to 12 years. Thus, declarative metamemory indirectly affects later memory performance through the acquisition of strategies.

During the early school years, the scope of metacognitive knowledge is gradually broadened to other aspects of cognitive functioning. Children learn to differentiate tasks and demands, they become aware of their own capacities and limitations, and they increasingly recognize conditions for strategic behavior. Studies have shown that metacognitive knowledge of reading strategies increases with age, and that this knowledge is predictive of later reading comprehension (Paris & Flukes, 2005). This conditional knowledge is the overture to the development of metacognitive reading-comprehension skills in successive years. Strategic behavior, however, is initially obstructed or frustrated by the inadequacy of conditional knowledge (Annevirta & Vauras, 2006). Moreover, the educational focus on technical reading during early primary-school years

(Chall, 1979) draws less on higher-order strategy use. Once children have learned to read more or less fluently, a shift from technical to comprehensive reading calls for the actual application of metacognitive strategies.

## Development of Metacognitive Strategies and Skills

Children younger than 8 years are not entirely devoid of metacognitive strategies or skills if tasks are made appropriate to their interest and level of understanding. Even 5-year-old children may demonstrate rudimentary forms of planning and self-correction in playful situations, such as distributing dolls over a limited number of chairs (Whitebread et al., 2009). In the same vein, children of 6 to 8 years may occasionally notice that they do not understand task instructions and ask for clarification, provided that they possess an adequate level of metacognitive knowledge (Annevirta & Vauras, 2006). Furthermore, children may engage in comprehension-monitoring activities before they are fluent readers, when prompted to do so (Baker, 2005). Apparently, metacognitive skills already develop at a basic level alongside metacognitive knowledge during preschool or early primary-school years, but they become more sophisticated and academically oriented when formal educational requires the utilization of a metacognitive repertoire (Veenman, 2011a). From the age of 8 years on, children give evidence of a steep increase in frequency and quality of metacognitive skills (Alexander et al., 1995; Schmitt & Sha, 2009; Van der Stel & Veenman, 2010; Veenman & Spaans, 2005). This development of metacognitive skills continues well into adulthood (Veenman, Wilhelm, & Beishuizen, 2004; Weil et al., 2013). At all ages, however, profound individual differences in the execution of metacognitive skills can be observed, indicating a differential developmental pace of metacognitive skills among students (Veenman et al., 2004; Van der Stel & Veenman, 2014). Without further instruction, some students hardly acquire or learn to produce metacognitive skills, while others spontaneously expand and refine their repertoire over time.

## Domain-Specificity Versus Generality of Metacognitive Skills

Until the age of 14, the metacognitive skills of children have a substantial domain- or task-specific orientation. The same students may vary in metacognitive skills applied to reading, problem-solving, or discovery-learning tasks (Van der Stel & Veenman, 2010; Veenman & Spaans, 2005). Veenman and Spaans (2005, p. 172) concluded that "metacognitive skills may initially develop on separate islands of tasks and domains that are very much alike." Between the age of 14 and 15 years, however, metacognitive skills generalize across tasks and domains. In a longitudinal study, Van der Stel and Veenman (2014) followed 12-year-olds for three successive years while they performed a reading task in history and a problem-solving task in mathematics each year. Principal-component analysis on metacognitive-skill measures for both tasks extracted a general component accounting for 44 percent and 41 percent of variance in the first two years, and a weaker domain-specific component, fading out from 22 percent down to 17 percent of variance accounted for. At the age of 15 years, however, only a general component remained with 48 percent of variance accounted for. Apparently, the partially separate repertoires for the two tasks and domains were merged into one general repertoire. More evidence for the domain-general nature of metacognitive skills beyond the age of 15 has been obtained in other studies (cf., Veenman & Beishuizen, 2004; Veenman & Spaans, 2005; Veenman et al., 2004). Around the age of 15, students have attained a personal repertoire of self-instructions at the meta-level that they tend to apply whenever they encounter a new task. Obviously, the implementation of generalized self-instructions at the object-level requires an adaptation to constraints of the task and domain at hand (Veenman, 2011a). Tuning metacognitive skills to task constraints characterizes expert reading. This notion of generalized metacognitive skills has implications for the instruction, training, and transfer of metacognitive skills across tasks and domains.

## Assessment of Metacognitive Reading Strategies and Skills

### Off-line Versus On-line Assessments

When assessing metacognitive skills, off-line methods should be distinguished from on-line methods that are administered concurrent to task performance (Veenman, 2005, 2011b). Off-line methods pertain to self-report instruments, such as questionnaires and interviews, administered either prior or retrospective to reading. Frequently used questionnaires for strategy use in reading or text studying are the MSLQ (Pintrich & De Groot, 1990) and the MAI (Schraw & Dennison, 1994). Students have to answer questions about their strategy use and skill application on a Likert-type scale. Off-line self-reports, however, suffer from validity problems. When answering questions, students have to consult their memory to reconstruct earlier strategic processes in reading, a reconstruction process which is susceptible to memory failure and distortions (Veenman, 2011a). Moreover, questions may prompt the recall of strategy use that never occurred (Veenman, 2011b). Questions may evoke an illusion of familiarity with strategies that are inquired for and students may respond by labeling their behavior accordingly. Finally, when rating their strategy use on Likert-type scales, students have to compare themselves with others (peers or teachers). Individual reference points may vary between students, yielding disparate data (Veenman, 2011a).

On-line methods, on the other hand, register metacognitive strategies and skills that are actually employed while reading, according to a standardized coding system. The essential difference between off-line and on-line methods is that off-line measures merely rely on subjective self-reports, whereas on-line measures entail the coding of actual reading behavior on externally defined criteria. Typical on-line methods for reading tasks are thinking aloud, eye-movement registration, and computer-logfile registrations (Veenman, 2013b). Thinking aloud means that students merely verbalize the content of working memory while performing a reading task, such verbalization does not distort the ongoing cognitive processes (Ericsson & Simon, 1993). Thinking aloud is used for analyzing reading processes, for assessing metacognitive skills of participants in reading research, as well as for diagnosing metacognitive deficiencies in readers (Veenman, 2013a).

Recently, computers allow for unobtrusive on-line registration of reading activities in logfiles. In *gStudy*, a hypermedia environment with logfile registration (Hadwin, Nesbit, Jamieson-Noel, Code, & Winne, 2007), readers are provided with tools for making notes, highlighting text, and making links across concepts during reading. Trace data of study events are stored in a logfile, from which frequencies and patterns of study activities over time can be produced. Logfile registration, however, only collects concrete reader activities at the object level, which implies that self-instructions at the meta-level need to be inferred by the researcher without verbal accounts from readers. Consequently, logfile measures should be triangulated with other on-line measures (Veenman, 2013b).

### Validity of Metacognitive Assessments

When considering measurement validity, many researchers only address internal consistency (Veenman, 2005). A more relevant criterion, however, is construct validity, which is supported when different methods yield converging data (Baker & Brown, 1984; Veenman, 2011b). Studies with multi-method designs have shown that off-line measures hardly correlate with on-line measures of metacognitive skills in reading (Veenman, 2005; Winne & Jamieson-Noel, 2002). Moreover, correlations among similar off-line measures are low, in contrast with high correlations among on-line measures (Veenman, 2005). In conclusion, perceived strategy use in off-line self-reports does not adequately represent actual strategy use while reading. Therefore, on-line methods are indispensable to assessing metacognitive strategies and skills for reading.

## Instruction and Training of Metacognitive Skills

Given the impact of metacognitive skills for reading and the huge individual differences that persist over the course of development, metacognitive poor readers need to be explicitly instructed and trained. There are three principles for effective instruction of metacognitive skills (Veenman et al., 2006). According to the principle of *embedded instruction*, metacognitive instruction should be integrated within the context of a reading task. Embedded instruction enables the student to connect conditional knowledge of which skill to apply when (the IF-side of production rules) to the procedural knowledge of how the skill is applied (the THEN-side) in a concrete task setting. According to the principle of *informed instruction*, students should be informed about the benefit of applying metacognitive skills in order to make them exert the extra effort that instructed skills initially require. In fact, reading performance may be temporarily impaired due to the effort expenditure needed for skill acquisition (Magliano, Trabasso, & Graesser, 1999; Puntambekar & Stylianou, 2005). Students may be inclined to abandon the instructed skills, unless they appreciate why metacognitive skills eventually facilitate reading. The third principle of *prolonged training* aims at a smooth and sustained application of metacognitive skills. As a rule, a longer duration yields better training results (Dignath & Büttner, 2008). Required duration of instruction, however, may vary with the number and complexity of skills instructed, and the reading competency of individual students (Veenman, 2011a). Veenman et al. (2006) referred to these three principles as the *WWW&H* rule for extensive metacognitive instruction. Students should be instructed, modeled, and trained *when* to apply *what* skill, *why* and *how* in the context of a task (Borkowski et al., 1987; Brown, 1978). In the same vein, Veenman (2013a) provides a step-by-step action plan for training a sequence of concrete metacognitive activities for reading.

### Examples of Metacognitive Instruction and Training Programs

A groundbreaking example of a metacognitive training program for reading comprehension is Reciprocal Teaching (Brown & Palincsar, 1987). During 20 training sessions, students with poor reading-comprehension skills collaboratively read texts in small groups with a teacher. In the first sessions, the teacher modeled four metacognitive strategies for reading comprehension (questioning, summarizing, clarifying, and predicting) according to the informed-training principle. Next, the teacher provided adaptive support to the students, contingent on their mastery of strategies. Support was gradually reduced over time as students took over responsibility for group discussions. Due to this scaffolding, students eventually could apply the four strategies independent of the teacher. Moreover, pre and post-test comparisons revealed that Reciprocal Teaching substantially improved the students' reading comprehension. Later researchers have fruitfully adopted Reciprocal Teaching in training studies.

Pressley and Gaskins (2006) developed a teaching method on a special school for students with low reading abilities. Throughout the day, teachers of all school disciplines addressed students with metacognitive reading instructions. Teachers incessantly explained, modeled, and stimulated the use of metacognitive strategies, such as establishing the purpose for reading, grasping the theme and main ideas of the text, predicting further developments in the text, relating new information to prior knowledge, monitoring understanding through self-questioning, resolving incomprehension by rereading, summarizing the text, and reviewing the reading process. After spending several years at this special school, students returned to regular education with above average reading scores, compared to same-age students.

Azevedo, Greene, and Moos (2007) asked students to study a complex hypermedia text about the blood circulatory system. Half of the students received metacognitive prompts from a human tutor, instigating them to set goals, activate prior knowledge, plan time and effort allocation, monitor comprehension and progress, and to apply strategies such as summarizing, hypothesizing, and drawing diagrams. Prompted students employed more self-regulatory activities and attained higher levels of reading comprehension, relative to control students without prompts.

These successful studies have in common that they advance the execution of metacognitive strategies and skills in line with the aforementioned three principles and the WWW&H rule. Many training studies, however, suffer from an incomplete design. They only present instructional effects on reading comprehension, but they fail to report effects on metacognitive behavior. Instructional effectiveness is accounted for by the causal chain of instruction leading to improved strategy use and, thus, to enhanced reading comprehension (Veenman, 2013a). Otherwise, instructional effects on comprehension measures could equally be attributed to, for instance, extended time on task due to compliance with instructions. To ensure that lasting effects are attained in reading research and practice, it is imperative that both dependent measures of metacognitive skillfulness and reading comprehension are assessed subsequent to training.

## Availability versus Production Deficiencies

Not all students are alike in their need for instruction. Students who display poor metacognitive behavior may suffer from availability or production deficiencies (Veenman, Kerseboom, & Imthorn, 2000). Students with an availability deficiency do not have metacognitive skills at their disposal. They lack the conditional and procedural knowledge of metacognitive self-instructions and, consequently, they need to be fully instructed according to the WWW&H rule. Students with a production deficiency, on the other hand, have metacognitive skills available, but they do not spontaneously apply self-instructions for some reason (Brown & DeLoache, 1978). For instance, they do not recognize the relevance of metacognitive skills for a particular task, or test anxiety obstructs the execution of skills (Veenman et al., 2000). Production deficiencies may arise, for instance, when difficult texts are read under time pressure (Veenman & Beishuizen, 2004). These students need not be fully trained in *how* to employ metacognitive skills as they are capable of producing the skills on familiar tasks or when relieved of performance pressure. Prompting or cueing will remind production-deficient students of applying metacognitive skills, but it will leave the metacognitive behavior of availability-deficient students unaffected (Veenman et al., 2000).

## Concluding Remarks

Reading is a basic intellectual function in school learning and in everyday life. In order to become proficient readers, students not only need to acquire lower-order skills for fluent reading, they also have to adopt metacognitive skills for reading comprehension. A theoretical framework of metacognitive self-instructions accounted for how metacognitive skills are acquired and employed by students. Metacognitive self-instructions make up a well-organized repertoire of strategies and skills at the meta-level that actively controls and regulates cognitive reading activities at the object-level. From a developmental perspective, it was depicted how declarative metacognitive knowledge of reading strategies contributes to the formation of self-instructions. Thus, declarative metacognitive knowledge only indirectly affects reading comprehension through the application of metacognitive strategies and skills. Moreover, task-specific metacognitive skills merge into a general repertoire of metacognitive self-instructions across tasks and domains.

These notions have implications for the assessment and training of metacognitive strategies and skills. Off-line self-reports, such as questionnaires and interviews, suffer from validity problems and they do not reflect the students' actual metacognitive behavior during reading. Consequently, the assessment of metacognitive strategies and skills should resort to on-line methods. Thinking aloud provides direct access to both metacognitive self-instructions at the meta-level and their implementation on the object-level. On-line measures that only assess behavior at the object-level, which may or may not be instigated by metacognitive self-instructions, ought to be validated before they are used for assessing metacognitive reading behavior (Veenman, 2013b).

In order to be successful, metacognitive instruction and training should follow the principles of embedded, informed, and prolonged instruction. Instruction should explicitly address the *what*, *when*, *why*, and *how* that constitute a metacognitive self-instruction. An additional challenge to instruction is that task- and domain-specific metacognitive skills merge into a general repertoire of self-instructions in the course of development. Therefore, instruction and training of metacognitive strategies and skills should be extended to reading for multiple tasks and disciplines (Pressley & Gaskins, 2006; Veenman et al., 2004). Diversity of reading tasks would allow for "high-road transfer," that is, bridging and synchronizing the conditions and actions of skills across tasks and disciplines (Salomon & Perkins, 1989). Especially for students of 13 to 15 years, variety in reading tasks during instruction may foster the generalization of metacognitive self-instructions. Such a general repertoire of metacognitive reading skills is a powerful tool for managing new reading tasks when entering academic education or when applying for a new job.

Finally, the notion of availability versus production deficiencies stresses an individual approach to instruction and training of metacognitive skills. It is not just a matter of educational efficiency that instruction should be attuned to the individual needs of students. Production-deficient students may get bored or frustrated by extensive instruction and, consequently, they may adversely abandon the use of strategies and skills. Therefore, individualized assessments of metacognitive deficiencies are prerequisite to adaptive instruction. After all, the ultimate goal is to make students metacognitively proficient, constructively responsive readers.

## References

Afflerbach, P., Pearson, P. D., & Paris, S. G. (2008). Clarifying differences between reading skills and reading strategies. *Reading Teacher*, *61*, 364–373.

Alexander, J. M., Carr, M., & Schwanenflugel, P. J. (1995). Development of metacognition in gifted children: Directions for future research. *Developmental Review*, *15*, 1–37.

Alexander, P. A., & Jetton, T. L. (2000). Learning from text: A multidimensional and developmental perspective. In M. L. Kamil, P. B. Mosenthal, P. D. Pearson, & R. Barr (Eds.), *Handbook of reading research. Volume III* (pp. 285–310). Mahwah, NJ: Erlbaum.

Anderson, J. R. (1996). *The architecture of cognition*. Mahwah, NJ: Erlbaum.

Annevirta, T., & Vauras, M. (2006). Developmental changes of metacognitive skill in elementary school children. *Journal of Experimental Education*, *74*, 197–225.

Azevedo, R., Greene, J. A., & Moos, D. C. (2007). The effect of a human agent's external regulation upon college students' hypermedia learning. *Metacognition and Learning*, *2*, 67–87.

Baker, L. (2005). Developmental differences in metacognition: Implications for metacognitively oriented reading instruction. In S. E. Israel, C. C. Block, K. L. Bauserman, & K. Kinnucan-Welsch (Eds.), *Metacognition in literacy learning* (pp. 641–679). Mahwah, NJ: Erlbaum.

Baker, L., & Brown, A. L. (1984). Metacognitive skills and reading. In P. D. Pearson (Ed.), *Handbook of reading research* (pp. 353–394). New York: Longman.

Blair, C., & Razza, R. P. (2007). Relating effortful control, executive function, and false belief understanding to emerging math and literacy ability in Kindergarten. *Child Development, 78*, 647–663.

Borkowski, J. G., Carr, M., & Pressley, M. (1987). "Spontaneous" strategy use: Perspectives from metacognitive theory. *Intelligence, 11*, 61–75.

Brown, A. (1978). Knowing when, where, and how to remember: A problem of metacognition. In R. Glaser (Ed.), *Advances in instructional psychology, Vol. 1* (pp. 77–165). Hillsdale, NJ: Erlbaum.

Brown, A. L., & DeLoache, J. S. (1978). Skills, plans, and self-regulation. In R. S. Siegel (Ed.), *Children's thinking: What develops?* (pp. 3–35). Hillsdale, NJ: Erlbaum.

Brown, A. L., & Palincsar, A. S. (1987). Reciprocal teaching of comprehension skills: A natural history of one program for enhancing learning. In J. D. Day & J. G. Borkowski (Eds.), *Intelligence and exceptionality: New directions for theory, assessment, and instructional practices* (pp. 81–131). Norwood, NJ: Ablex.

Chall, J. S. (1979). The great debate: Ten years later, with a modest proposal for reading stages. In L. B. Resnick & P. A. Weaver (Eds.), *Theory and practice of early reading, Vol. 1* (pp. 29–55). Mahwah, NJ: Erlbaum.

Dignath, C., & Büttner, G. (2008). Components of fostering self-regulated learning among students. A meta-analysis on intervention studies at primary and secondary school level. *Metacognition and Learning, 3*, 231–264.

Ericsson, K. A., & Simon, H. A. (1993). *Protocol analysis*. Cambridge: MIT Press.

Flavell, J. H. (1979). Metacognition and cognitive monitoring: A new area of cognitive-developmental inquiry. *American Psychologist, 34*, 906–911.

Flavell, J. H. (2004). Theory-of-Mind development: Retrospect and prospect. *Merrill-Palmer Quarterly, 50*, 274–290.

Flavell, J. H., & Wellman, H. M. (1977). Metamemory. In R. V. Kail & J. W. Hagen (Eds.), *Perspectives on the development of memory and cognition* (pp. 3–33). Hillsdale, NJ: Erlbaum.

Hadwin, A. F., Nesbit, J. C., Jamieson-Noel, D., Code, J., & Winne, P. H. (2007). Examining trace data to explore self-regulated learning. *Metacognition and Learning, 2*, 107–124.

Kurtz, B. E., & Borkowski, J. G. (1987). Development of strategic skills in impulsive and reflective children: A longitudinal study of metacognition. *Journal of Experimental Child Psychology, 43*, 129–148.

Lockl, K., & Schneider, W. (2006). Precursors of metamemory in young children: The role of theory of mind and metacognitive vocabulary. *Metacognition and Learning, 1*, 15–31.

Magliano, J. P., Trabasso, T., & Graesser, A. C. (1999). Strategic processing during comprehension. *Journal of Educational Psychology, 91*, 615–629.

Markman, E. M. (1985). Comprehension monitoring: Developmental and educational issues. In S. J. Chipman, J. W. Segal, & R. Glaser (Eds.), *Thinking and learning skills: Research and open questions, Vol. 2* (pp. 275–291). Hillsdale, NJ: Erlbaum.

Meijer, J., Veenman, M. V. J., & van Hout-Wolters, B. H. A. M. (2006). Metacognitive activities in text-studying and problem-solving: Development of a taxonomy. *Educational Research and Evaluation, 12*, 209–237.

Metcalfe, J., & Finn, B. (2013). Metacognition and control of study choice in children. *Metacognition and Learning, 8*, 19–46.

Nelson, T. O., & Narens, L. (1990). Metamemory: A theoretical framework and new findings. In G. Bower (Ed.), *The psychology of learning and motivation, Vol. 26*, pp. 125–173.

Paris, J. G., & Flukes, J. (2005). Assessing children's metacognition about strategic reading. In S. E. Israel, C. C. Block, K. L. Bauserman, & K. Kinnucan-Welsch (Eds.), *Metacognition in literacy learning* (pp. 121–139). Mahwah, NJ: Erlbaum.

Pintrich, P. R., & De Groot, E. V. (1990). Motivational and self-regulated leaning components of classroom academic performance. *Journal of Educational Psychology, 82*, 33–40.

Pressley, M., & Afflerbach, P. (1995). *Verbal protocols of reading: The nature of constructively responsive reading*. Hillsdale, NJ: Erlbaum.

Pressley, M., & Gaskins, I. (2006). Metacognitive competent reading is constructively responsive reading: How can such reading be developed in students? *Metacognition and Learning, 1*, 99–113.

Puntambekar, S., & Stylianou, A. (2005). Designing navigation support in hypertext systems based on navigation patterns. *Instructional Science, 33*, 451–481.

Salomon, G., & Perkins, D. N. (1989). Rocky roads to transfer: Rethinking mechanisms of a neglected phenomenon. *Educational Psychologist, 24*, 113–142.

Samuels, S. J., Ediger, K. M., Willcutt, J. R., & Palumbo, T. J. (2005). Role of automaticity in metacognition and literacy instruction. In S. E. Israel, C. C. Block, K. L. Bauserman, & K. Kinnucan-Welsch (Eds.), *Metacognition in literacy learning* (pp. 41–59). Mahwah, NJ: Erlbaum.

Schmitt, M. C., & Sha, S. (2009). The developmental nature of meta-cognition and the relationship between knowledge and control over time. *Journal of Research in Reading, 32*, 254–271.

Schneider, W. (2008). The development of metacognitive knowledge in children and adolescents: Major trends and implications for education. *Mind, Brain, and Education, 2*, 114–121.

Schraw, G., & Dennison, R. S. (1994). Assessing metacognitive awareness. *Contemporary Educational Psychology, 19*, 460–475.

Schraw, G., & Moshman, D. (1995). Metacognitive theories. *Educational Psychology Review, 7*, 351–371.

Van der Stel, M., & Veenman, M. V. J. (2010). Development of metacognitive skillfulness: A longitudinal study. *Learning and Individual Differences, 20*, 220–224.

Van der Stel, M., & Veenman, M. V. J. (2014). Metacognitive skills and intellectual ability of young adolescents: A longitudinal study from a developmental perspective. *European Journal of Psychology of Education, 29*, 117–137. doi:10.1007/s10212–013–0190–5.

Van Kraayenoord, C. E., Beinicke, A., Slagmüller, M., & Schneider, W. (2012). Word identification, metacognitive knowledge, motivation, and reading comprehension: An Australian study of grade 3 and 4 pupils. *Australian Journal of Language and Literacy, 35*, 51–68.

Veenman, M. V. J. (2005). The assessment of metacognitive skills: What can be learned from multi-method designs? In C. Artelt & B. Moschner (Eds.), *Lernstrategien und Metakognition: Implikationen für Forschung und Praxis* (pp. 75–97). Berlin: Waxmann.

Veenman, M. V. J. (2008). Giftedness: Predicting the speed of expertise acquisition by intellectual ability and metacognitive skillfulness of novices. In M. F. Shaughnessy, M. V. J. Veenman, & C. Kleyn-Kennedy (Eds.), *Meta-cognition: A recent review of research, theory, and perspectives* (pp. 207–220). Hauppage: Nova Science Publishers.

Veenman, M. V. J. (2011a). Learning to self-monitor and self-regulate. In R. Mayer & P. Alexander (Eds.), *Handbook of research on learning and instruction* (pp. 197–218). New York: Routledge.

Veenman, M. V. J. (2011b). Alternative assessment of strategy use with self-report instruments: A discussion. *Metacognition and Learning, 6*, 205–211.

Veenman, M. V. J. (2013a). Training metacognitive skills in students with availability and production deficiencies. In H. Bembenutty, T. Cleary, & A. Kitsantas (Eds.), *Applications of self-regulated learning across diverse disciplines: A tribute to Barry J. Zimmerman* (pp. 299–324). Charlotte, NC: Information Age Publishing.

Veenman, M. V. J. (2013b). Assessing metacognitive skills in computerized learning environments. In R. Azevedo & V. Aleven (Eds.), *International handbook of metacognition and learning technologies* (pp. 157–168). New York: Springer.

Veenman, M. V. J., & Beishuizen, J. J. (2004). Intellectual and metacognitive skills of novices while studying texts under conditions of text difficulty and time constraint. *Learning and Instruction, 14*, 619–638.

Veenman, M. V. J., Kerseboom, L., & Imthorn, C. (2000). Test anxiety and metacognitive skillfulness: Availability versus production deficiencies. *Anxiety, Stress, and Coping, 13*, 391–412.

Veenman, M. V. J., & Spaans, M. A. (2005). Relation between intellectual and metacognitive skills: Age and task differences. *Learning and Individual Differences, 15*, 159–176.

Veenman, M. V. J., Wilhelm, P., & Beishuizen, J. J. (2004). The relation between intellectual and metacognitive skills from a developmental perspective. *Learning and Instruction, 14*, 89–109.

Veenman, M. V. J., van Hout-Wolters, B. H. A. M., & Afflerbach, P. (2006). Metacognition and learning: Conceptual and methodological considerations. *Metacognition and Learning, 1*, 3–14.

Wang, M. C., Haertel, G. D., & Walberg, H. J. (1990). What influences learning? A content analysis of review literature. *Journal of Educational Research, 84*, 30–43.

Weil, L. G., Fleming, S. M., Dumontheil, I., Kilford, E. J., Weil, R. S., Rees, D. G. . . . Blakemore, S. (2013). The development of metacognitive ability in adolescence. *Consciousness and Cognition, 22*, 264–271.

Whitebread, D., Coltman, P., Pasternak, D. P., Sangster, C., Grau, V., Bingham, S. . . . Demetriou, D. (2009). The development of two observational tools for assessing metacognition and self-regulated learning in young children. *Metacognition and Learning, 4*, 63–85.

Winne, P. H. (1996). A metacognitive view of individual differences in self-regulated learning. *Learning and Individual Differences, 8*, 327–353.

Winne, P. H., & Jamieson-Noel, D. (2002). Exploring students' calibrations of self reports about study tactics and achievement. *Contemporary Educational Psychology, 27*, 551–572.

Zimmerman, B. J. (2000). Attainment of self-regulation: A social cognitive perspective. In M. Boekaerts, P. Pintrich, & M. Zeidner (Eds.), *Handbook of self-regulation, research, and applications* (pp. 13–39). Orlando, FL: Academic Press.

# 4

# Engagement and Motivational Processes in Reading

*John T. Guthrie and Susan Lutz Klauda*

In reading research and educational psychology, engagement and motivation are increasingly prominent issues. This chapter aims to chart the relations among achievement, engagement, motivation, and cognitive processes in reading with relevance to classroom contexts and attention to individual differences. Because these constructs all are deeply researched, they can be characterized and connected in various ways. Drawing on well-established research findings, we seek to represent the linkages that hold particular promise for reading educators. In doing so, we use a mid level of complexity. We steer a middle course between the highest refinement of constructs that is needed for research and the distillation of the constructs to simpler versions of multi-faceted factors which are more accessible for policy and education leaders.

Individual differences in motivation and engagement take several forms. First, there are global differences in level of motivation. For the most motivated students, reading is a highly valued, enjoyable activity that is central to their identity. The least motivated students find reading impossibly difficult, distasteful, and unimportant in their lives. This variable is positively associated with amount of reading. Students with relatively high intrinsic motivation (reading enjoyment) read three times more than students with relatively low intrinsic motivation (Wigfield & Guthrie, 1997). Second, different motivations typify different individuals. Some students are high in self-efficacy, believing they are very proficient readers, but do not value reading very much. Other students are keenly devoted to grades and incentives (i.e., have high extrinsic motivation) but are not interested in reading for enjoyment (i.e., have low intrinsic motivation). That is, students vary not only in global level of motivation, but in the profile of their multiple specific motivations. Third, connections between specific motivations and achievement vary among students. For example, self-efficacy correlates with achievement more highly for European American than African American students (McRae, 2011). Despite individual diversity in the strengths and relations of different motivations, there are patterns; motivation links systematically with other reading variables, although exceptions are inevitable. This chapter charts those patterns.

## General Relations among the Factors of Motivation, Engagement, and Achievement

In the ambitious *Handbook of Research on Student Engagement*, Eccles and Wang (2012) write a commentary entitled "So what is student engagement anyway?" They adopt the definition provided by Skinner and Pitzer (2012) that "engagement is the visible manifestation of motivation" (p. 135) while expressing the traditional view that motivation refers to the internal processes that energize and direct behavior. Emphasizing the importance of distinguishing crisply between constructs, Eccles and Wang embrace the traditional framework that motivation influences behavior, which in turn influences various outcomes, such as learning. In other words, A → B → C, where A = motivation, B = behavior, and C = learning and achievement.

Reeve's (2012) definitions of motivation and engagement agree with those of Eccles and Wang (2012) conceptually, but depart from them operationally. Reeve concurs that "motivation is a force that energizes and directs behavior" (p. 150), and that "engagement refers to the extent of students' active involvement in a learning activity" (p. 150). He proposes and measures four aspects of engagement, but he does not measure motivation extensively. In his framework, behavioral engagement comprises attention, effort, and persistence in tasks; emotional engagement includes interest and enthusiasm; cognitive engagement involves deep mental processing and self-regulation; and agentic engagement refers to proactive, intentional forms of learning. Although his measures of these four engagement constructs predict achievement well (Reeve, 2012), we believe that the roles of motivation are underrepresented in his system.

## Predictors and Outcomes of Reading Engagement: A Proposed Heuristic Model

### Model Overview

This model is intended to depict patterns of individual differences in motivation and engagement as they are associated with reading achievement. In a review of the contributions of classroom contexts to various engagement-related outcomes, Guthrie, Wigfield, and You (2012) proposed the following model: Classroom contexts → Motivations → Behavioral engagement → Reading achievement. This model concurs substantively with the Eccles and Wang (2012) perspective. Our position, in accord with both Eccles and Wang (2012) and Reeve (2012), is that behavioral engagement refers to active participation as typified by effort, time, and persistence. However, in contrast to Reeve (2012), we believe that motivations such as intrinsic motivation and self-efficacy influence behavioral engagement. For example, when students participate in reading for personal interest (intrinsic motivation) and believe in their capacity (self-efficacy), their behavioral engagement becomes more enthusiastic, confident, and cognitively sophisticated. In this model, and in contrast to Reeve's (2012) engagement framework, the indicators (measures) of engagement are distinguished from the precursors (antecedents) of engagement.

In the heuristic model in Figure 4.1 we propose that classroom contexts influence multiple motivations and cognitions are all important contributors to engagement, and they generate myriad qualities of behavioral engagement. Behavioral engagement will vary widely in observable effort, time, persistence, enthusiasm, and cognitive involvement that underlie the behaviors. In turn, higher qualities of engagement will generate higher qualities of reading achievement as manifested in fluency, vocabulary, literal comprehension, and reasoning (higher-order comprehension) performance.

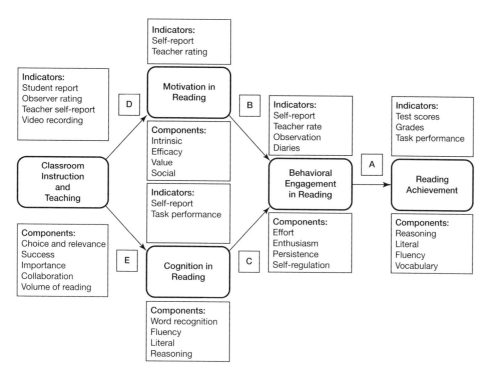

*Figure 4.1* In the "Indicators" box with Reading Achievement, can you spell out "Task performance"? Success in classroom tasks.

## Behavioral Engagement Processes in the Heuristic Model

Our research suggests that engagement may be indicated by positive qualities such as a student's enthusiasm and devotion of effort that correlate positively with achievement. In contrast, a different form of engagement may consist of active avoidance of reading, including rejecting, evading, minimizing effort, and disconnecting from reading tasks (Guthrie, Klauda, & Ho, 2013). We refer to the former, positive aspects of engagement as *dedication* and the latter, negative, aspects as *avoidance*. This view is similar to that of Skinner, Kindermann, and Furrer (2009) who use the terms *engagement* and *disaffection* to represent similarly distinct forms. The advantage of this duality is that the constructs authentically characterize students' varieties of engagement, and they simultaneously contribute to predicting achievement (Guthrie et al., 2013).

## Motivations in the Heuristic Model

Motivations in reading were examined in a detailed review by Schiefele, Schaffner, Moller, and Wigfield (2012). One of their conclusions was that the intrinsic–extrinsic differentiation of motivation is quite legitimate, conceptually and empirically. Intrinsic motivation includes curiosity, or seeking new experiences or information, and involvement, or deep immersion in text. In our proposed heuristic model, we include intrinsic motivation due to its prominent role in predicting acquisition of reading, reading competence, and reading engagement in the forms of effort, time spent, and amount of reading (Guthrie, Wigfield, Metsala, & Cox, 1999).

Schiefele and colleagues proposed that self-efficacy and value represent preconditions of intrinsic motivation rather than actual motivations (Schiefele et al., 2012). Although conceivable, there is little empirical support for this notion. In our heuristic model we include the motivational construct of self-efficacy, or one's belief in her capacity to perform reading tasks. Self-efficacy is conceptually relevant because it energizes behavior and is highly correlated with achievement from grades K–12 , suggesting its integral role in reading development. Similarly, we incorporate the motivation of value in reading, which refers to belief in the importance of reading because it is useful or interesting. Beyond its self-evident relevance, value correlates with reading competence increasingly as students progress through grades K–8 (Ho & Guthrie, 2013). Finally in this heuristic model, we embrace a social construct, which refers to positive behaviors toward peers and sharing favorable beliefs with classmates about reading. This construct is rooted in socialization theories of education that propose that fostering social relationships among students and between teachers and students is central to students' acquisition of academic dispositions and competencies (Eccles, & Wang, 2012). We have not included the widely researched construct of extrinsic motivation due to its typically negative correlations with achievement, nor the constructs from goal theory, such as mastery goals, which have been studied mainly with secondary students (Pintrich, 2000).

### Cognitive Processes in the Heuristic Model

At the K–3 grade level, reading competencies are usually conceptualized and measured in three forms: letter and simple word recognition, word attack and deliberate decoding, sentence and passage comprehension. To investigate these, researchers often use measures such as the Woodcock-Johnson subtests of letter–word, word attack, passage comprehension, and spelling (Foorman et al., 2006). In addition, Foorman et al. found that primary-level instruction often focused on phonemic awareness, structural analysis of words, vocabulary, and grammar. At the intermediate and secondary levels, more complex self-regulation processes are also at play. In a model highly predictive of school reading for ninth-grade students, factors correlating with comprehension included background knowledge, strategies (such as questioning), word reading, vocabulary, and inference (Cromley & Azevedo, 2007). While most factors directly predict comprehension, the effects of strategies on comprehension are often mediated by inference. Because these cognitive systems receive the overwhelming attention of teachers and researchers in reading, we propose that the powers of motivation and engagement variables must be addressed in their typical context of individual differences in reading. The unique benefits of motivation and engagement will be described in a later section, as will classroom contexts that support motivation and engagement.

## Connections of Reading Engagement, Motivation, Cognitive Processes, and Achievement

### Engagement and Achievement (Path A)

At all levels of schooling, engagement has been correlated with reading achievement. This proposition is depicted as Path A in the heuristic model (Figure 4.1). For primary students, behavioral engagement as indicated by teachers' observations of students' active participation, enthusiasm for reading, and effort in overcoming difficulties predicts cognitive reading competencies, both within a grade level and across grades (Hughes, Lou, Kwok, & Loyd, 2008). Among elementary students, behavioral engagement in the form of students' amount of reading predicted standardized reading comprehension scores highly (De Naeghel, Van Keer, Vansteenskiste, & Rosseel, 2012). Using a similar measure of behavioral engagement, Guthrie et al. (1999) showed that a nationally representative sample of secondary students' reading engagement predicted standardized reading achievement when socioeconomic status was controlled. In a meta-analysis of students from K–12, yet another indicator of behavioral engagement in reading consisting of print exposure was shown to predict reading comprehension substantially. Print exposure also predicted word recognition and oral language skills for younger children (Mol, & Bus, 2011).

Most broadly, the 2009 Program for International Student Assessment (PISA) survey of 15-year-olds in more than 40 countries showed that reading engagement predicted reading-literacy achievement substantially (OECD, 2010). Not only was engagement nearly equal to reading strategies in its prediction of achievement, but engagement mediated a substantial amount of the effect of socioeconomic status and gender on achievement. That is, when lower income students were engaged readers, their achievement nearly matched the achievement of higher income students, and reading engagement nearly closed the gender gap between the boys and girls in most countries (OECD, 2010). It is abundantly evident that many indicators manifest the association of behavioral engagement and reading achievement across a variety of cultures and social conditions. This is good news for education policy because engagement can be increased in classrooms by teachers who use engagement-generating instructional practices, as described later in this chapter. Furthermore, it is interesting that individual differences in engagement were so strongly associated with achievement that the apparent influence on achievement of another form of individual difference (variation in socioeconomic background) diminished. This finding suggests that it may be particularly powerful for teachers of students from weaker socioeconomic backgrounds to systematically implement practices known to foster engagement.

## Motivations and Engagement (Path B)

In the heuristic model, we propose that the effects of motivation on engagement are especially important; that is, motivation does not automatically or magically translate into increased achievement. Rather, in line with our general frame, Motivation → Engagement → Achievement, we suspect that motivation exerts its power to increase achievement through increasing students' amount of cognitively intense, personally significant reading activity; motivation fuels sustained, self-regulated reading activity, of which one consequence is relatively high reading test scores or teacher-awarded grades. Empirically, the pathway is well supported. For elementary students, Becker, McElvany, and Kortenbruck (2010) showed that intrinsic motivation linked strongly with students' behavioral engagement in the form of amount of reading (as rated by students and parents). For middle-schoolers, Guthrie et al. (2013) found that self-reported motivations of intrinsic motivation, self-efficacy, value, and prosocial behaviors were positively correlated with positive behavioral engagement, termed dedication, whereas motivations of perceived difficulty, devaluing, and antisocial behaviors were correlated with avoidance.

## Cognitive Processes and Engagement (Path C)

It is equally plausible that students who possess an abundance of well-formed reading competencies might be more behaviorally engaged readers than those who do not. It is difficult to conceive of a student investing high amounts of time and persistence in reading if the student does not have an established cognitive system for reading. Although struggling readers may often work assiduously, they are rarely voracious consumers of text. Empirical studies confirm the strength of Path C in the heuristic model. For instance, among primary students, teachers' ratings of students' behavioral engagement in the form of active, enthusiastic participation in learning was well predicted by students' reading achievement on standardized tests in the same time period (Hughes et al., 2008). Highly engaged readers were high achievers, and vice versa. In this case the cognitive process of reading and reading achievement were quite similar. More studies at the primary level should be directed to the relations of specific cognitive processes and engagement. At the elementary level, students who were capable of deeply comprehending and integrating multiple texts were likely to be frequent readers of lengthy books (Guthrie et al., 1999). This association of cognitive competence and behavioral engagement was highly significant even when individual difference factors of background knowledge, socioeconomic status, and motivation were controlled statistically. In sum, cognitive competencies in reading – themselves another aspect of individual differences in reading — are connected to reading behavioral engagement according to diverse measures of both reading engagement and achievement, suggesting that Path C is well established.

## Unique Contributions of Motivation and Cognition to Engagement

In the previous section, we suggested that reading motivations and cognitive processes are associated with reading engagement; they may in fact be considered sources of individual differences in engagement. However, the evidence was limited to simple correlations. Thus it is possible that because cognitively able students are also motivated, the correlation of motivation and engagement may be an artifact of the power of cognition. This issue is crucial, because if motivation is an artifact, we need not emphasize it in education, although it may be a valuable contributor to a configuration of individual differences. Regrettably, most motivation theories do not test whether their motivational variables influence achievement in the context of relevant cognitions. For this discussion, we propose that motivation and cognition each have distinctive, unique effects on achievement.

At all grade levels investigators have examined whether individual differences in motivation and cognitive reading competencies have distinct effects on achievement. For elementary grade students, Becker et al. (2010) showed that students' intrinsic motivation increased their behavioral engagement, as measured by amount of reading, when prior reading achievement and extrinsic motivation were controlled. The association of motivation and engagement was quite strong. Cohering with this finding, Guthrie et al. (1999) found that elementary students' behavioral engagement in the form of reading amount was predicted by intrinsic motivation even when previous achievement and background knowledge were statistically controlled. Whatever their achievement level, more intrinsically motivated students were more likely to read widely and deeply than less intrinsically motivated ones.

For middle school students, Jang, Kim, and Reeve (2012) found that behavioral engagement as represented by students' self-ratings of their active involvement in learning was predicted by their perceived autonomy, a construct closely related to intrinsic motivation. The association was sustained when grades from a range of classes were controlled. Among secondary students, Guthrie et al. (1999) reported that the motivation of interest in English/Language Arts increased behavioral engagement as measured by reading amount when standardized reading achievement and socioeconomic status were controlled. According to Jang (2008), college students who concentrated intensely understood unfamiliar, difficult text more deeply than students who were less behaviorally engaged. In this investigation students were randomly assigned to a treatment that would increase their engagement vs. a treatment not expected to influence engagement.

Thus prior cognitive reading competencies were controlled experimentally rather than through multiple regression procedures. Several investigators have reported that motivation variables of task value or self-reported 'grit' predict reading achievement even when strong cognitive variables such as IQ and the use of self-regulated strategies are statistically controlled (Bråten, Ferguson, Anmarkrud, & Strømsø, 2013).

Finally, for primary students, Hughes et al. (2008) found in a three-year longitudinal study that motivation influenced students' engagement even when their level of reading performance was controlled statistically. Higher performing students were more engaged based on teacher ratings than lower performing students, irrespective of their motivation level. In interpreting this study, we consider the authors' measure of the quality of teacher–student relationships to reflect students' motivation levels, in line with our conception of social motivation. This assumption is warranted, moreover, from extensive evidence that many qualities of the teacher–student relationship are positively connected to classroom literacy engagement (Pianta, Hamre, & Allen, 2012). Thus, it appears in the Hughes et al. study that both motivation and reading cognition had effects on students' engagement levels. Altogether, however, evidence of the unique associations of individual differences in motivation and cognition with engagement for primary students is weaker than other grade levels, and more direct tests of their unique effects are needed.

## Motivation and Engagement Spur Growth of Achievement Over Time

To this point, connections among reading engagement, motivation, and achievement, as shown in the heuristic model, have been made within discreet acts in a limited time period. However, motivations also energize achievement growth over time. Students who are highly motivated in the fall of an academic year will surpass their less motivated peers the following spring even when they begin at the same achievement level. It is reasonable to question how this occurs, and research has not explored this dynamic fully. Research reviewed here shows, however, that motivation increases behavioral engagement, including time, effort, concentration, and a high volume of reading. In addition, being a highly engaged reader is associated with proficient reading. Reading proficiency depends on automaticity of many cognitive processes including decoding print to language, use of background knowledge for comprehension, and rapid inferencing at local and global levels (Kintsch & Kintsch, 2005). Automaticity is known to accelerate from frequency of meaningful activity. Consequently, we believe it is reasonable to suggest that motivation and engagement build achievement growth by fostering automaticity of processes fundamental to reading expertise.

Evidence that reading motivation fuels achievement growth is plentiful. Creating a growth model over three years of middle school, Retelsdorf, Koller, and Moller (2011) showed that reading comprehension (reasoning with text) in year 3 was predicted by the motivations of interest and curiosity in year 1 when reading comprehension in year 1 was controlled. Interest spurred comprehension growth irrespective of prior comprehension levels. The more basic cognitive process of decoding speed showed the same result. Working with elementary students, Taboada, Tonks, Wigfield, and Guthrie (2009) reported that internal reading motivation based on teachers' ratings predicted growth of achievement over three months according to two reading measures, a standardized comprehension test and a task requiring integrating information from and reasoning with multiple texts. Because the students' motivations were inferred from teacher ratings of enthusiasm, interests, and voluntary reading, it is more consistent with our current distinction of motivation and engagement to refer to the teachers' ratings as a measure of behavioral engagement rather than internal motivation. Accepting that reformulation, the finding is that behavioral engagement predicted reading growth in two achievement measures.

To describe the strength of these motivation effects, Guthrie, Hoa, Wigfield, Tonks, Humenick, and Littles (2007) reported growth of reading comprehension grade equivalence scores for fourth graders. Holding prior achievement constant, students who were highly interested in reading in the fall gained 3 years in reading grade equivalent in the 3 months until winter. Moreover, students who increased in interest and involvement during the same 3 months gained 1 year of reading grade equivalence. Notably, students with low interest showed no reading comprehension growth in the same period, which indicates an achievement decline relative to their improving peers. These findings confirm that the benefits of motivation for achievement growth are not a mere marginal luxury. Reading motivation may stand as the strongest psychological variable influencing achievement.

## Classroom Practices and Contexts Influence Motivations (Path D)

***Providing choices and relevance increase intrinsic motivation.*** Grounded in self-determination theory (Ryan & Deci, 2009), autonomy support in the classroom refers to shared control between the teacher and students. When teachers afford students input and choices in their learning, their interests and participation increase (Zhou, Ma & Deci, 2009), which enhances achievement (Reeve, 2012). Experimental studies have shown that 'intrinsic framing' is stronger than 'extrinsic framing' for facilitating conceptual learning from text (Vansteenkiste, Simons, Lens, Soenens, & Matos, 2005). In these experiments, emphasizing personal interest or relevance (intrinsic framing) rather than task proficiency (extrinsic framing) as a basis for reading consistently leads to deeper text comprehension among young adolescents. Classroom autonomy support has been shown to increase students' intrinsic motivation (enjoyment and enthusiasm) as well as engagement (active participation and sustained work) reciprocally at multiple grade levels (Skinner & Belmont, 1993). In our model, we use both choices and relevance to represent autonomy support.

***Examples of providing choice and relevance.*** Giving choices in the classroom is often misunderstood. It is not merely a trip to the media center to select books or extended free reading with no instruction. We encourage many mini-choices during instruction. Teachers can give students a mini-choice of which character to focus on in a story. They read about all characters while becoming an expert on one. In a book on civil war history, students can choose which battles to learn about most deeply. Then in class discussion, they learn about all battles in the war and their relations to each other.

Choice of texts is important, but choice of task also can be powerful. Suppose a teacher has taught students to make predictions and also to write their own questions about a text before reading. In learning about the early explorers, students can be given a choice of whether to write two questions related to an explorer's goals or personality, or make two predictions about the outcome of an expedition described in text. Later the teacher may ask students to use the opposite strategy. While having the opportunity for input, students nevertheless cover the reading curriculum comprehensively.

Turning to the importance of providing relevance, consider that texts that are remote from students' experience and knowledge base are usually boring. Teachers can foster interest in any text, however, by increasing its relevance through related media. A brief, 5-minute video depicting a lion hunting a gazelle in the Serengeti Plain will pique students' interest in reading a text on predation. With newfound interest, students will read more avidly about predation and survival in various biomes.

In science, hands on activities, such as looking at a leaf through a magnifying glass, or observing life in an aquarium will focus, sustain, and deepen reading about biology. In history, brief videos of historical enactments can launch a class discussion of politics (such as those related to slavery) and foster penetrating analysis of related texts (such as the emancipation proclamation). Offering students choices within texts and providing real world activities related to texts generate intrinsic motivation for reading.

*Assuring success increases self-efficacy.* From the viewpoint of Bandura's social cognitive theory, competence support during reading instruction has been investigated experimentally (Schunk & Mullen, 2009). Studies of competence support in the form of providing feedback on progress and helping students set realistic goals in a specific reading task increases self-efficacy for the particular academic domain of the activity (Schunk & Zimmerman, 2007). Competence support may also appear in the form of using content domain texts, such as science trade books, that are readily decodable and enable students to derive meaning related to their observations and knowledge of the world while learning reading skills (Guthrie, McRae, & Klauda, 2007).

*Examples of assuring success.* An obvious but profound act is to provide students text they can read successfully; or, in other words, that addresses individual differences in reading proficiency. No motivation is more debilitating than dread of difficulty. When a low achieving student faces a daunting text, she will take steps to avoid it within a few minutes. The alternative is humiliation, which she has learned to minimize. Although comprehensive academic standards such as the Common Core state that students should read on-grade or more challenging texts, not all students should begin there. To build self-confidence, effective teachers locate texts that students can read aloud fluently and understand literally. Instruction can then be devoted to deeper comprehension with manageable text. Gaining proficiency and self-efficacy occur together.

*Emphasizing the importance of reading increases students' valuing.* Drawing on expectancy-value theory (Eccles & Wigfield, 2002), evidence shows that there is a significant association between teachers' expectations for students and students' growth in reading achievement. As students internalize the expectations of significant others for a specific domain such as English, their value for that domain and selections of courses in that domain increase (Durik, Vida, & Eccles, 2006). Several studies have reported the benefits of providing a 'valuing rationale' for reading an uninteresting text. In two studies, for example, the valuing rationale described how information in the text would provide immediate professional benefit for prospective teachers. Groups receiving a valuing rationale showed enhanced behavioral engagement (close attention to reading) and increased conceptual comprehension of information text compared to no-rationale groups (Jang, 2008). In another study, asking students to find usefulness and applicability in text increased students' comprehension in both laboratory and classroom settings compared to control conditions (Hulleman, Godes, Hendricks, & Harackiewicz, 2010). We use the phrase 'emphasizing importance' to represent the instructional practice of providing a valuing rationale.

*Examples of emphasizing importance.* For older students in secondary school, teachers can use the very technique employed in several studies. Teachers can request students to write a statement explaining how a text will benefit them in some way. The text may improve their competence as a professional; it may be crucial to performing well in the next course; it may afford them a memorable literary experience that influences their understanding of themselves.

For younger adolescents in CORI, we foster recognition of the importance of text through concrete activities. For instance, in a day, students view a brief video, record their observations, read extensively on the same topic, and share their learning with a partner. After 60 minutes the teacher asks students to reflect on which activity they learned the most from. Inevitably they realize that reading the text was most informative. Teachers emphasize the importance of text in other ways, too. After reading a complex text, they ask students to identify the sentences that most helped them understand, and explain why. After a debate, teachers ask students to show the textual sources of their best points. Gradually students realize that texts help them to speak, write, and explain new things to their friends. Broader, more general discussion of which texts were most informative, interesting, or provocative also will enrich the perceptions that text is valuable.

*Arranging collaboration fosters prosocial goals*. Collaborative activity in the classroom is often viewed as a driver of literacy engagement. Our conception of this construct is grounded in activity theory (Leontiev, 1981; Scribner & Cole, 1981) and its extension to classrooms by Gutiérrez and Lee (2009). When the more expert teacher and less expert student collaborate in culturally valued literate practices, students acquire the literate action scenarios (Scribner & Cole, 1981). Successful student uptake of literacy practices generates increased academic proficiencies. An equally abundant research literature related to collaboration examines teacher–student relationships that support students' social and emotional well-being during learning (Martin, & Dowson, 2009). Furthermore, favorable relationships with teachers and peers foster active participation in school activities among secondary school students (Juvonen, Espinoza, & Knifsend, 2009). In the absence of these personal connections, students' engagement declines, leading disproportionately to disengagement (Griffiths, Lilles, Furlong, & Sidhwa, 2009) and dropping out (Rumberger, 2011). Thus teacher–student collaboration and emotional relationships are expected to influence students' academic and reading engagement directly without necessarily being mediated through a motivational construct.

*Examples of arranging collaboration*. Reading is often a solo, silent activity. In contrast, students are social creatures. Most simply, teachers can harness students' desires to interact by fostering reading as a social pursuit. Teachers can ask students of any age to read together. For the youngest, this may be partners reading aloud simultaneously. For older elementary aged students, partner reading can consist of individuals reading a passage silently and sharing the most salient points. Partners can each write a challenging question for the other to answer, and the outcomes can be discussed. If partners in upper elementary school write a summary of a chapter, they can then compare which summary elements in their chapters are common and which ones are distinct. Such partnerships can be short and simple, consisting of 5 minutes of reading and 1 minute of sharing. They can become as long and complex as the students can successfully perform.

Student-led discussion groups are exciting for class members. If they are well-organized, they can increase the depth of students' reading comprehension. In CORI for grade 7, teachers use an adaptation of the 'collaborative reasoning' approach (Chinn, Anderson, & Waggoner, 2001). After every member of a group reads a complex text for 10–15 minutes silently, the discussion begins. One team member states a key point; the next person adds a new, relevant point; each person contributes new information. At the end, the last person states a summary of what the members said, and the group discusses whether the summary was complete or should be extended. To be successful, teachers must set a few rules for groups regarding such aspects as the number of students per group, turn-taking, active listening, full participation of all members, and accountability for staying on task (which, for instance, could be demonstrated through writing or explaining the final synthesis).

*Roles of motivation practices*. The practices of motivation support are designed to increase engaged reading. The point of affording choice, for example, is not to teach students how to make good choices, although that may be necessary. The point is to motivate more and deeper reading. If the time required to make a choice consumes 20 minutes out of a 30 minute learning activity, very little reading was accomplished. In a 30 minute time slot, 3 minutes should be given for the choice and 27 minutes for the reading. The cost of time taken for the motivational activity is justified only if it increases the total time spent reading within an instructional unit. If 10 minutes is given to discussion on one day, the activity was successful only if it generates more than 10 additional minutes reading within a few days. Because learning from text socially is powerful, well-organized discussion builds deeper and longer reading capacities. This criterion applies to each motivation practice, including support for choice, relevance, success, importance, and collaboration. Motivation activities should accelerate amount and depth of reading by 200%–500%. That is how the heuristic model works. Classroom contexts energize motivations (Path D); motivations energize engagement behaviors (Path B); and engagement fuels achievement (Path A). Quantity of engaged reading is a vitally important individual difference variable, with some students much higher than others. When classroom contexts foster it for everyone, the associated factor of achievement is likely to increase for all students.

## Discussion of the Heuristic Model and Its Implications

*Limitations*. A substantial issue related to the multiple pathways and potential pathways in the heuristic model remains to be addressed. It is possible to draw additional connective ties within the model to achievement. For example, motivation may directly increase achievement; that is, it is possible that engagement does not mediate all of the effects of motivation on achievement (Becker, MacElvany & Kortenbuck, 2010). Further, the relationships may all be reciprocal; in other words, each arrow could be bidirectional. Space does not allow us to describe or defend the presence or absence of every possible path in a completely saturated version of the heuristic model. However, we argue that there is evidence favoring each of the lettered paths in the model. Due to space limits, we have not presented evidence supporting Path E which links classroom instruction to cognitive processes in reading. Many other reviews and chapters address this vital link. Furthermore, space does not permit the presentation of the substantial body of experimental data that more strongly suggest causal links in the model. A single, accurate model enjoying the concurrence of all behavioral scientists does not yet exist. In its absence, we propose that under typical conditions of measurement and modeling, each of the paths A–E in the current model can be empirically justified.

*Implications*. Following the heuristic model, classroom teaching should be designed to include a fusion of motivation and cognitive support for reading engagement, from the primary grades through higher education. Without motivation, children cannot become engaged readers who devote the time and manifest the self-regulation needed to become proficient readers. A cognitively capable reader is only half a reader. Dependent on engagement, reading expertise emerges only when both the cognitive and motivational halves of reading are deliberately nurtured by teachers and administrators. To build literacy, classroom excellence can be fostered by following this foundation for richer literacy learning experiences for all students. Although students vary dramatically in their reading motivation and engagement, classroom contexts can raise the aspirations and commitments of all.

## References

Becker, M., McElvany, N., & Kortenbruck, M. (2010). Intrinsic and extrinsic reading motivation aspredictors of reading literacy: A longitudinal study. *Journal of Educational Psychology*, *102*, 773–786.

Bråten, I., Ferguson, L., Anmarkrud, O., & Strømsø, H. (2013). Prediction of learning and comprehension when adolescents read multiple texts: The roles of word-level processing, strategic approach and reading motivation. *Reading and Writing*, *26*, 321–348.

Chinn, C. A., Anderson, R. C., & Waggoner, M. A. (2001). Patterns of discourse in two kinds of literature discussion. *Reading Research Quarterly*, *36*(4), 378–411.

Cromley, J., & Azevedo, R. (2007). Testing and refining the direct and indirect inferential mediation model of reading comprehension. *Journal of Educational Psychology*, *99*, 311–325.

De Naeghel, J., Van Keer, H., Vansteenkiste, M., & Rosseel, Y. (2012). The relation between elementary students' recreational and academic reading motivation, reading frequency, engagement and comprehension: A self-determination theory perspective. *Journal of Educational Psychology*, *104*, 1006–1021.

Durik, A. M., Vida, M., & Eccles, J. S. (2006). Task values and ability beliefs as predictors of high school literacy choices: A developmental analysis. *Journal of Educational Psychology*, *98*, 382–393.

Eccles, J., & Wang, M. (2012). Part I Commentary: So what is student engagement anyway? In S. Christensen, A. Reschly, & C. Wylie (Eds.), *Handbook of research on student engagement* (pp. 133–145). New York: Springer Science.

Eccles, J. S., & Wigfield, A. (2002). Motivational beliefs, values, and goals. *Annual Review of Psychology*, *53*, 109–132.

Foorman, B., Schatschneider, C., Eakin, M., Fletcher, J., Moats, L., & Francis, D. (2006). The impact of instructional practices in Grades 1 and 2 on reading and spelling achievement in high poverty schools. *Contemporary Educational Psychology*, *31*, 1–29.

Griffiths, A., Lilles, E., Furlong, M., & Sidhwa, J. (2009). The relations of adolescent student engagement with troubling and high-risk behaviors. In K. R. Wenzel & A. Wigfield (Eds.), *Handbook of motivation at school* (pp. 563–585). New York: Routledge/Taylor & Francis Group.

Guthrie, J. T., Hoa, A. L. W., Wigfield, A., Tonks, S. M., Humenick, N. M., & Littles, E. (2007). Reading motivation and reading comprehension growth in the later elementary years. *Contemporary Educational Psychology*, *32*, 282–313.

Guthrie, J. T., Wigfield, A., & You, W. (2012). Instructional contexts for engagement and achievement in reading. In S. Christensen, A. Reschly, & C. Wylie (Eds.), *Handbook of research on student engagement* (pp. 601–634). New York: Springer Science.

Guthrie, J. T., Klauda, S. L., & Ho, A. (2013). Modeling the relationships among reading instruction, motivation, engagement, and achievement for adolescents. *Reading Research Quarterly*, *48*, 9–26.

Guthrie, J. T., McRae, A. C., & Klauda, S. L. (2007). Contributions of Concept-Oriented Reading Instruction to knowledge about interventions for motivations in reading. *Educational Psychologist*, *42*,237–250.

Guthrie, J. T., Wigfield, A., Metsala, J. L., & Cox, K. E. (1999). Motivational and cognitive predictors of text comprehension and reading amount. *Scientific Studies of Reading*, *3*(3), 231–257.

Gutiérrez, K., & Lee, C. D. (2009). Robust informal learning environments for youth from non-dominant groups: Implications for literacy learning in formal schooling. In L. M. Morrow, R. Rueda, & D. Lapp (Eds.), *Handbook of research on literacy and diversity* (pp. 216–232). New York: Guilford Press.

Ho, A. N., & Guthrie, J. T. (2013). Patterns of association among multiple motivations and aspects of achievement in reading. *Reading Psychology*, *34*, 101–147.

Hughes, J., Lou, W., Kwok, O., & Loyd, L. (2008). Teacher–student support effortful, engagement, and achievement: A 3-year longitudinal study. *Journal of Educational Psychology*, *100*, 1–14.

Hulleman, C. S., Godes, O., Hendricks, B. L., & Harackiewicz, J. M. (2010). Enhancing interest and performance with a utility value intervention. *Journal of Educational Psychology*, *102,* 880–895.

Jang, H. (2008). Supporting students' motivation, engagement, and learning during an uninteresting activity. *Journal of Educational Psychology*, *100,* 798–811.

Jang, H., Kim, E., & Reeve, J. (2012). Longitudinal test of self-determination theory's motivation mediation model in a naturally occurring classroom context. *Journal of Educational Psychology*, *104*, 1175–1188.

Kintsch, W., & Kintsch, E. (2005). Comprehension. In S. G. Paris & S. A. Stahl (Eds.), *Children's reading comprehension and assessment* (pp. 71–92). Mahwah, NJ: Erlbaum.

Leontiev, A. A. (1981). *Psychology and the language learning process*. Oxford: Pergamon.

McRae, A. (2011). *Teacher competence support for reading in middle school*. Doctoral Dissertation, University of Maryland, College Park, MD.

Martin, A. J., & Dowson, M. (2009). Interpersonal relationships, motivation, engagement, and achievement: Yields for theory, current issues, and educational practice. *Review of Educational Research, 79,* 327–365.

Mol, S., & Bus, A. (2011). To read or not to read: A meta-analysis of print exposure from infancy to early adulthood. *Psychological Bulletin, 137,* 267–296.

OECD (2010). PISA 2009 Results: Learning to Learn – Student Engagement, Strategies and Practices (Volume III) http://dx.doi.org/10.1787/9789264083943-en

Pianta, R., Hamre, B., & Allen, J. (2012). Teacher-student relationships and engagement; Conceptualizing, measuring, and improving the capacity of classroom interactions. In S. Christensen, A. Reschly, & C. Wylie (Eds.), *Handbook of research on student engagement* (pp. 365–386). New York: Springer Science.

Pintrich, P. R. (2000). Multiple goals, multiple pathways: The role of goal orientation in learning and achievement. *Journal of Educational Psychology, 92,* 544–555.

Reeve, J. (2012). A self-determination theory perspective on student engagement. In S. Christensen, A. Reschly, & C. Wylie (Eds.), *Handbook of research on student engagement* (pp. 149–173). New York: Springer Science.

Retelsdorf, J., Koller, O., & Moller, J. (2011). On the effects of motivation on reading performance growth in secondary school. *Learning and Instruction, 21,* 550–559.

Rumberger, R. (2011). *Dropping out: Why students quit school and what can be done about it*. Cambridge, MA: Harvard University Press.

Ryan, R. M., & Deci, E. L. (2009). Promoting self-determined school engagement: Motivation, learning, and well-being. In K. R. Wenzel & A. Wigfield (Eds.), *Handbook of motivation at school* (pp. 171–195). New York: Routledge/Taylor & Francis Group.

Schiefele, U., Schaffner, E., Moller, J., & Wigfield, A. (2012). Dimensions of reading motivation and their relation to reading behavior and competence. *Reading Research Quarterly, 47,* 427–463.

Schunk, D., & Mullen, C. (2009). Self-efficacy as an engaged learner. In K. R. Wenzel & A. Wigfield (Eds.), *Handbook of motivation at school* (pp. 291–237). New York: Routledge/Taylor & Francis Group.

Schunk, D., & Zimmerman, B. (2007). Influencing children's self-efficacy and self-regulation of reading and writing through modeling. *Reading & Writing Quarterly, 23,* 7–25.

Scribner, S., & Cole, M. (1981). *The psychology of literacy*. Cambridge, MA: Harvard University Press.

Skinner, E. A., & Belmont, M. J. (1993). Motivation in the classroom: Reciprocal effects of teacher behavior and student engagement across the school year. *Journal of Educational Psychology, 85,* 571–581.

Skinner, E. A., Kindermann, T. A., & Furrer, C. J. (2009). A motivational perspective on engagement and disaffection: Conceptualization and assessment of children's behavioral and emotional participation in academic activities in the classroom. *Educational and Psychological Measurement, 69,* 493–525.

Skinner, E., & Pitzer, J. (2012). Developmental dynamics of student engagement, coping, and everyday resilience. In S. Christensen, A. Reschly, & C. Wylie (Eds.), *Handbook of research on student engagement* (pp. 21–45). New York: Springer Science.

Taboada, A., Tonks, S., Wigfield, A., & Guthrie, J. (2009). Effects of motivational and cognitive variables on reading comprehension. *Reading and Writing, 22,* 85–106.

Vansteenkiste, M., Simons, J., Lens, W., Soenens, B., & Matos, L. (2005). Examining the motivational impact of intrinsic versus extrinsic goal framing and autonomy-supportive versus internally controlling communication style on early adolescents' academic achievement. *Child Development, 76,* 483–501.

Wigfield, A., & Guthrie, J. T. (1997). Relations of children's motivation for reading to the amount and breadth of their reading. *Journal of Educational Psychology, 89,* 420–432.

Zhou, M., Ma, W. J., & Deci, E. L. (2009). The importance of autonomy for rural Chinese children's motivation for learning. *Learning and Individual Differences, 19,* 492–498.

# 5

# Self-Efficacy, Agency, and Volition

## Student Beliefs and Reading Motivation

*Dale H. Schunk and William D. Bursuck*

Reading is a fundamental human skill. As children develop their reading skills, they increase their likelihood of succeeding in multiple areas of the school's curriculum. Reading extends beyond schooling; it is critical for success in careers and brings much knowledge and pleasure for persons across their life spans (Bruning, Schraw, & Norby, 2011).

Reading often is viewed as a coordinated series of cognitive-linguistic skills, such as decoding and comprehending. In recent years, however, researchers have begun to examine the role of motivation in reading because focusing only on cognitive and linguistic skills fails to account for the wide individual differences found in children's success in acquiring and applying reading skills (Guthrie & McRae, 2011).

In this chapter we review theory and research on three types of student motivational beliefs that can affect reading: self-efficacy, agency, and volition. As used in this chapter, *self-efficacy* refers to one's perceived capabilities for learning or performing actions at designated levels; *agency* is the belief that one can exert a large degree of control over important events in one's life; and *volition* refers to the belief that one can successfully implement strategies to attain important goals. As applied to reading, students' motivation is apt to be higher when they believe that they are capable of performing well, can control their success in reading, and can implement strategies that help keep them engaged.

We provide a theoretical overview of self-efficacy, agency, and volition, describing how they differ and complement one another to enhance student motivation. Next, we briefly review several theories of reading, providing the situational milieu for self-efficacy, agency, and volition. Key research studies on the roles of these three variables in reading motivation are then reviewed. The chapter concludes with a discussion of the implications of the theory and research for ongoing theory development, future research, and classroom practice related to individual differences in reading.

## Theoretical Background

### *Self-Efficacy*

Self-efficacy is grounded in Bandura's (1986) social cognitive theory, which postulates reciprocal interactions among three sets of influences: personal (e.g., cognitions, beliefs, skills, affects), behavioral (i.e., one's actions), and social/environmental (e.g., peers, teachers, sounds, objects). The nature of these reciprocal interactions can be illustrated using self-efficacy, a personal factor. Research shows that self-efficacy influences achievement behaviors, such as task choice, effort, persistence, and use of effective learning strategies (Schunk & Pajares, 2009). In turn, these behaviors affect self-efficacy. When learners work on tasks and observe their progress, their self-efficacy for continued learning is enhanced.

The link between personal and social/environmental factors can be illustrated with students with learning disabilities, many of whom hold low self-efficacy for learning (Licht & Kistner, 1986). Those who work with such students may react to the students based on perceived common attributes, such as low skills, rather than based on their actual capabilities. Social/environmental feedback can affect self-efficacy. When teachers tell students, "I know you can do this," students may experience heightened self-efficacy due to the expressed confidence.

The link between behavioral and social/environmental factors often is seen in instructional sequences. Social/environmental factors can direct behaviors. For example, when teachers call students' attention to a display (e.g., "Look at this"), students may attend with varied deliberation. The influence of behavior on the social environment occurs when teachers ask questions and particular students' answers convey a lack of understanding. Teachers are likely to reteach the material rather than continue with the lesson.

Self-efficacy is hypothesized to influence behaviors and environments and in turn be affected by them (Bandura, 1986, 1997; Schunk, 2012). Students with high self-efficacy for learning are apt to be motivated to learn and engage in self-regulated learning by setting goals, using effective learning strategies, monitoring their comprehension, and evaluating their goal progress. Such students also are likely to create effective environments for learning, such as by eliminating or minimizing distractions and by finding effective study partners. In turn, self-efficacy can be influenced by the outcomes of behaviors such as goal progress and achievement, as well as by inputs from the environment such as feedback from teachers and social comparisons with peers.

Bandura (1997) postulated that people acquire information to gauge their self-efficacy from their performance accomplishments, vicarious experiences (i.e., verbalizations and actions by others), forms of social persuasion, and physiological indexes. One's performances provide the most reliable information for assessing self-efficacy because they are tangible indicators of one's capabilities. Successful performances raise self-efficacy whereas failures can lower it, although an occasional failure or success after many successes or failures may not have much impact.

Individuals acquire much information about their capabilities through knowledge of how others perform (Bandura, 1997). Similarity to others is a cue for gauging self-efficacy (Schunk, 2012). Observing similar others succeed can raise observers' self-efficacy and motivate them to engage in the task because they may believe that if others can succeed they can as well; however, a vicarious increase in self-efficacy can be negated by subsequent performance failure. Students who observe similar peers fail or have difficulty with a task, such as comprehending a written passage, may believe they lack the competence to succeed, which may not motivate them to attempt the task.

Individuals also develop self-efficacy from social persuasions they receive from others (Bandura, 1997), such as when a teacher tells a student, "I know you can do this."

Social persuasions must be credible to cultivate people's beliefs in their capabilities for successfully attaining outcomes. Although positive feedback can raise self-efficacy, the increase will not endure if students subsequently perform poorly (Schunk, 2012). Conversely, negative persuasions can lower self-efficacy.

Individuals acquire self-efficacy information from physiological and emotional states such as anxiety and stress (Bandura, 1997). Strong emotional reactions to a task provide cues about anticipated success or failure. When students experience negative thoughts and fears about their capabilities such as feeling nervous thinking about reading aloud, those reactions can lower self-efficacy and trigger additional stress that contributes to the feared inadequate performance. Learners should be more efficacious when they feel less anxious about academic outcomes.

Self-efficacy can influence the choices people make and the actions they pursue (Schunk & Pajares, 2009). Individuals tend to select tasks and activities in which they feel competent and avoid those in which they do not. Unless people believe that their actions will produce the desired consequences, they have little incentive to engage in those actions.

Self-efficacy also helps determine how much effort students expend, how long they persist when confronting obstacles, and how resilient they are in the face of adversity (Schunk & Pajares, 2009). With respect to reading, students with a strong sense of self-efficacy approach reading tasks as challenges to be addressed rather than as threats to be avoided. They set challenging goals and maintain strong commitment to them, heighten and sustain their efforts in the face of difficulties, and quickly recover their sense of self-efficacy after setbacks.

## Agency

The concept of agency is grounded in social cognitive theory and in self-determination theory. Social cognitive theory reflects the idea of agency because it contends that individuals seek to exert a large degree of control over the outcomes of their actions (Bandura, 1997). They hold beliefs that allow them to influence their thoughts, feelings, actions, social interactions, and aspects of their environments. Thus, students who want to improve their reading comprehension strategies may seek teachers' assistance to do so. At the same time, individuals are influenced by their actions and aspects of their social environments. Students are apt to change their behaviors in response to feedback from their teachers and coaches.

According to social cognitive theory, strategies for increasing agency can be aimed at promoting emotional, cognitive, or motivational processes, increasing behavioral competencies, or improving aspects of one's environments. Teachers are responsible for their students' learning. Using social cognitive theory as a framework, teachers can seek to improve their students' emotional states and correct their faulty beliefs and habits of thinking (personal factors) by providing feedback conveying that students have made progress in learning. Teachers also can help raise students' reading skills, strategies, and self-regulation (behaviors) through their teaching and by giving students opportunities for self-regulated practice. And teachers can alter classroom features and social interactions (social/environmental factors) by creating a positive classroom climate conducive to enhancing students' reading motivation and competencies.

Self-determination theory also stresses the concept of agency. This theory assumes that people are inherently motivated to learn and postulates that individuals have three fundamental needs: competence, autonomy, and relatedness (Ryan & Deci, 2009). The need for competence refers to people's desire to feel capable of learning and developing their talents. The need for autonomy reflects the idea of agency in that it involves the belief that one has control over one's actions and that these actions reflect one's desires. The need for relatedness denotes wanting to feel attached or connected with others.

In this perspective, autonomy is represented as a continuum ranging from low to high. At the lower end, behavior is externally regulated; for example, doing something to earn a reward or avoid a punishment. Students at this level believe that their behaviors are externally controlled. Slightly farther along the continuum, learners still feel externally controlled although they are more active in controlling or regulating themselves to behave in a certain fashion. Subsequently they may fully accept the target behavior as their own and thus feel a sense of autonomy for acting in accordance with their values. At the next level, students accept the behavior, value it as their own, and seek to make it consistent with other aspects of their sense of self. Finally at the highest level of autonomy, learners feel intrinsically motivated and engage in actions because they find them interesting and engaging.

Thus, autonomy develops as people increasingly internalize external motivators into their value systems and believe that they are engaging in behaviors relatively free of external constraints. With respect to reading motivation, students are apt to feel more autonomous when they enjoy reading and want to read to improve their skills and learn more about the world in which they live.

## Volition

The study of volition has a long history. Nineteenth-century psychologists such as William James and Wilhelm Wundt defined it as the act of using one's will (Hunt, 1993). Interest in volition was revived by contemporary psychologists who redefined it as the capability to maintain focus and effort directed toward goals, especially in the face of distractions (Corno, 1994).

Psychologists who study volition differentiate it from motivation. From a volitional perspective, motivation comprises the cognitive processes involved in planning and setting goals whereas volition comes into play once people begin their efforts toward goal implementation (Heckhausen, 1991; Kuhl, 1984, 2000). In this chapter, volition beliefs refer to learners' perceived capabilities to sustain their motivation directed toward goal attainment.

There are wide individual differences in learners' volitional efforts (Corno, 1994). Some students set goals, plan and implement strategies for accomplishing them, and make goal progress in spite of competing goals, distractions, and interruptions. Other students may be good planners but often become sidetracked from their goal plans.

The conceptual basis of volition is found in action control theory (Heckhausen & Gollwitzer, 1987; Kuhl, 1984), which construes volition as the capability to use available resources to manage one's maintenance of intentions (Corno, 1994). Volition involves self-regulation since it helps to protect goals and keep persons on track, even when it may be in individuals' best interests to change or adapt goals.

In reading, volition helps keep students engaged in tasks to accomplish their reading goals in the face of competing goals and distractions including social and emotional factors. Volition may be enhanced when learners' perceive certain conditions, such as tasks that are difficult or tedious, or the potential distractions are numerous. In these cases, students may implement strategies that they believe will help them, such as finding a conducive environment (e.g., quiet place) in which to read, setting goals for when and how long to read, and building in study breaks.

Although self-efficacy, agency, and volition have distinct meanings, they share points of overlap. In general, students who believe they are capable of reading well also are likely to believe that they can control their reading outcomes and use strategies that will help them accomplish their reading goals. In turn, successful reading should strengthen students' self-efficacy, agency, and volition beliefs. Collectively these three types of student beliefs should help students remain productively engaged in reading and continue to develop their reading skills.

## Reading

Hoover and Gough (1990) describe what they call the *simple view of reading*. In this model, reading comprehension is seen as the product of word reading and language comprehension. Word reading involves decoding, or the ability to translate written letters into spoken words. Language comprehension refers to the ability to understand linguistic information, be it oral (listening) or written (reading). According to this model, good readers have both adequate word reading and language comprehension skills. Problem readers, or those who cannot understand what they read, are of three types: adequate linguistic comprehension but inadequate decoding; adequate decoding but inadequate linguistic comprehension; and both inadequate decoding and limited linguistic comprehension (Adloff, Perfetti, & Catts, 2011).

While most reading instruction includes both decoding and comprehension instruction (Bruning et al., 2011), approaches differ in how skills within these reading areas are stressed and taught. Bottom-up processing models stress explicit, systematic instruction, in which both decoding and comprehension skills are analyzed, sequenced, and taught directly (Bursuck & Damer, 2014; Carnine, Silbert, Kameenui, & Tarver, 2010). Top-down approaches emphasize students learning by doing; students are guided (more than directly taught) as they construct rules for decoding and linguistic understandings (Fountas & Pinnell, 1996).

Both types of reading models have their strengths and drawbacks. What is clear is that skilled reading requires that learners be able to decode and comprehend. It is also clear that successful comprehension requires language/conceptual understanding and automated basic skills. Nonetheless, studies on the simple model of reading have revealed that reading is not quite that simple. Indeed, evidence suggests that a large amount of the variance in reading comprehension scores is due to factors other than decoding or language comprehension (Adloff et al., 2011). Two such factors are cognitive strategies (e.g., information processing, metacognition) and motivation (Byrnes, 1996; Guthrie & McRae, 2011; Mayer, 1999).

Information processing strategies involve top-down and bottom-up processing on the part of the learner. For example, the construction-integration model (Kintsch, 1988, 1998) postulates that readers build a text microstructure from its propositions (i.e., the smallest pieces of information that can be judged true or false). Readers link these propositions with the prior knowledge in their memories, a type of bottom-up processing. For example, with a passage about baseball readers activate their "playing baseball" schema and link new information with knowledge in the schema. At the same time, readers build a macrostructure, or the overall meaning of the text. The macrostructure is hierarchical and comprises main ideas, or higher-level propositions developed from the microstructure. Kintsch's model is highly interactive, where processes of constructing and integrating information can occur rather automatically while being integrated into a schema-driven overall text structure.

Effective metacognitive reading strategies involve the deliberate conscious control of one's mental activities (Paris, Wixson, & Palincsar, 1986). Metacognition is involved when learners set goals, evaluate goal progress, and make necessary adaptations in their strategies to ensure success. Thus, as learners develop skills they become more adept at determining their goal in reading (e.g., find main ideas, read for details), selecting a strategy that they believe will help them accomplish the goal, checking their progress while reading, and adapting their strategy if they are not being as successful as they should be.

Most traditional and current models of reading, including the simple view of reading and the construction-integration model described herein, do not emphasize motivational aspects such as self-efficacy, agency, and volition. A model of reading comprehension that does include motivational variables was proposed by the RAND Reading Study Group (2002).

In this model, comprehension entails three elements—the reader, text, and activity—that occur within a larger sociocultural context that affects and is affected by the reader and that interacts with each element.

Readers bring individual competencies to reading, which include differences in cognitive competencies (e.g., attention, memory), knowledge (e.g., vocabulary, topic knowledge), and motivational beliefs (e.g., self-efficacy, goals). While engaged in reading, readers' competencies may change and especially as a result of instruction. Motivational factors can change in a positive or negative way, depending on readers' successes and perceived progress in reading.

Features of the text affect comprehension. These features include the surface code (exact wording), text base (idea units denoting meaning), and a cognitive representation of the mental models in the text. The difficulty of the text also can affect the relationship between text and reader as more difficult texts will be tougher to comprehend. Students may or may not be motivated to read difficult text, depending on their skills and reading experience.

The activity refers to the purpose for reading such as learning material for a test or reading for enjoyment. The purpose can be affected by motivational variables such as interest and self-efficacy. Readers also may have more than one purpose in reading, such as learning material for a test and advancing one's understanding of a topic. Consequences of reading are part of the activity and may include increased knowledge, applications, or enjoyment, all of which may motivate readers to read more.

Reader, text, and activity are dynamically related across the phases of reading: pre-reading, reading, and post-reading. They also occur within a larger sociocultural context. In schooling, contexts include classrooms and schools, but children's capacities are influenced by factors outside of schools such as their experiences in homes and communities. There are wide individual differences in the experiences children have outside and inside schools. For example, those from higher socioeconomic families will have greater access to resources that can influence reading, as will those who attend better-funded schools. A host of contextual and sociocultural factors can influence how reading is taught, the resources available, and the content of reading materials, all of which affect the development of children's reading skills and motivation.

## Motivationally Relevant Reading Research

This section discusses some representative reading research studies in which the motivation constructs of self-efficacy, agency, and volition were explored. Although separate sub-headings are used, the studies show some overlap in the constructs, given their close relationship.

### Self-Efficacy

Schunk and Rice (1985, 1987, 1992, 1993) conducted a series of studies that investigated how teaching children to use reading comprehension strategies influenced their self-efficacy, comprehension skill, and other achievement outcomes. The participants in these studies were elementary schoolchildren with reading disabilities. In one study (Schunk & Rice, 1985), children in grades 4 to 5 were pretested on self-efficacy and comprehension. They then received instruction and practice in reading comprehension strategies over 20 sessions. For the instruction, an adult verbalized and applied a six-step comprehension strategy to sample stories: What do I have to do? (1) Read the question, (2) Read the story, and (3) Look for key words. (4) Reread each question, and (5) Answer that question. (6) Reread the story if I don't know the answer. After the teacher modeled and demonstrated the strategy, children in the strategy verbalization condition verbalized aloud the strategies prior to applying them to stories, whereas children in the no strategy verbalization condition did not verbalize the strategies aloud prior to applying them. Children received a post-test following the last instructional session.

The results showed that children who had verbalized the strategies aloud demonstrated higher comprehension self-efficacy and achievement compared with children who had not verbalized aloud. These results suggest that verbalizing aloud the strategies may have created in children a sense of personal agency that they could control their reading outcomes, which can raise self-efficacy and performance. Such strategy verbalization also can help focus and maintain children's attention on important task aspects, and verbalization, as a form of rehearsal, can promote strategy encoding and retention and thus facilitate subsequent use.

A similar procedure was employed by Schunk and Rice (1992). In the first study, children were assigned to one of three conditions: strategy verbalization, strategy verbalization plus strategy value feedback, instructional control. The strategy value feedback consisted of the teacher periodically attributing individual children's success in comprehension to their use of the strategy's steps (e.g., "You got it right because you followed the steps in the right order"). Children in the instructional control condition received reading comprehension instruction and practice but were not taught the strategy. A post-test followed the instructional sessions, and a maintenance test was given six weeks later.

The results showed that on the post-test and maintenance test, strategy value feedback children demonstrated higher self-efficacy and achievement than did children in the other two conditions. Providing strategy value feedback is likely to boost children's perception of control over their reading outcomes. The feedback linked children's success to use of the strategy, which should help build their self-efficacy and maintain use of the strategy, as suggested by the maintenance test results.

In the second study, children received ten instructional sessions on finding main ideas followed by ten sessions on locating details. The five-step strategy taught for finding main ideas had as one of the steps, "Think about what the details have in common and what would make a good title." It was modified for use with details by replacing this step with, "Look for key words." Children in the strategy modification condition were taught to modify the strategy for use with details by making this step substitution. Children assigned to the strategy instruction and the instructional control conditions received instruction on locating details during the second half of the training program but they were not taught to modify the strategy.

The results showed that strategy modification students judged self-efficacy higher and demonstrated higher achievement than did students in the other two conditions on the post-test and maintenance test. During the skill post-test and maintenance assessment, children verbalized aloud as they read and answered questions. Strategy modification students verbalized more strategic steps than did children in the other two conditions.

The superiority of the strategy modification condition suggests that it gave children a sense of greater control over their reading outcomes. Children who understand how to use a strategy and modify it for use on different tasks are apt to feel in control of outcomes, which can raise their self-efficacy and motivate them to perform better. Instructing them how to modify it is helpful, because they may not automatically maintain its use or modify it to fit other tasks.

## Agency

The Concept-Oriented Reading Instruction (CORI) program is designed to enhance students' sense of agency involving their reading success (Guthrie, Wigfield, & Perencevich, 2004). The CORI program combines multiple cognitive strategies with motivational practices, and is grounded in research showing that: (1) strategy training can increase students' reading comprehension (National Reading Panel, 2000), and (2) motivational components help raise students' engagement in reading (Guthrie & Wigfield, 2000).

CORI includes instruction in the following cognitive strategies designed to improve reading comprehension: activating background knowledge, questioning, searching for information, summarizing, organizing graphically, and identifying story structure. The motivational components emphasized are: using content goals, providing hands-on activities, affording students choices, using interesting texts, and promoting collaboration. The cognitive strategy and motivational components collectively can raise students' sense of agency because these components help students learn ways to read successfully while actively engaged in contexts that allow them choices and interactions (Guthrie, Wigfield, & VonSecker, 2000).

Guthrie, Wigfield, Barbosa et al. (2004) implemented the CORI program with third graders who were assigned to either a CORI or strategy instruction condition. The program ran for 12 weeks, 90 minutes per day. The reading comprehension context was science (ecology in life science). Within CORI, each of the six strategy instruction components was taught for one week and then for the next six weeks strategies were systematically integrated with one another. Strategy instruction included teacher modeling with scaffolding provided according to students' needs, along with student practice, practices consistent with those described by the National Reading Panel (2000).

The five CORI motivational components were addressed as follows. Content goals were incorporated in science instruction, which helped to motivate students because the goals for learning were directly linked with content they were to learn. Students were given choices about which birds or animals to study in depth and which books to read on the topic. The unit included many hands-on experiences such as experiments and in-depth investigations. Trade books were used to promote interest in the texts. Collaboration was evident in several activities including students' discussing issues and questions with others and sharing information and texts.

In the strategy instruction only condition, teachers taught the same content in the same fashion but without the preceding motivational components. However, some motivational aspects were present as teachers used a variety of instructional practices and addressed students' self-efficacy by helping them gain proficiency in using comprehension strategies.

Students were pretested and post-tested on various cognitive and motivational variables. The results showed that compared with the strategy instruction group, CORI led to higher comprehension, strategy use, and motivation. In a second study, a third group was included (traditional instruction), in which students received regular reading instruction differentiated to individual needs. The post-test results showed that CORI students demonstrated higher reading comprehension performance than students in the other two conditions and also surpassed the strategy instruction students in reading motivation.

Taken together, these results show that successful reading requires more than teaching children to use effective strategies. The motivational aspects are postulated to enhance children's reading engagement, which should promote better comprehension. The motivational components, as a group, are designed to facilitate children developing a sense of agency that they can control their reading outcomes.

## Volition

*Self-Regulated Strategy Development* (SRSD) is an instructional approach that combines strategy instruction with motivational components (Harris, Graham, & Santangelo, 2013). The strategy instruction is designed to enhance students' self-regulation as they engage in reading comprehension. It also addresses volition because students learn a strategy that helps them stay focussed on the task and become increasingly independent readers. Students who believe they understand and can successfully apply a strategy that improves their comprehension are apt to feel a sense of agency that they can control their reading outcomes, as well as a heightened sense of self-efficacy, both of which help keep them motivated to engage in the task.

Although SRSD has been applied primarily to writing (Harris, Graham, & Mason, 2006), Mason (2004) adapted and applied the approach to reading comprehension with struggling readers. Students received instruction and practice in an SRSD instructional strategy, *TWA*: *Think* before reading, think *While* reading, think *After* reading. Other students received a comparison instructional strategy known as reciprocal questioning (RQ), in which students learn how to develop and answer questions about text.

Students were tested before and after instruction, as well as three weeks following instruction to gauge maintenance. Measures assessed reading comprehension, motivation, self-efficacy, and perceived effectiveness of TWA and RQ. For both instructional conditions, students received collaborative and scaffolded instruction in six stages for strategy acquisition: pre-skill development, discuss the strategy, model the strategy, memorize the strategy, guided practice, independent practice. Initially students practiced the strategy collaboratively with the instructor who applied the strategy to science and social studies topics. Students then practiced in pairs until independent practice was achieved, and then received instruction as needed until they could individually produce main idea summaries, or retell or ask or answer questions suitably.

Each TWA phase included three steps: think before reading (think about the author's purpose, what you know, what you want to learn), think while reading (think about reading speed, linking knowledge, rereading parts), and think after reading (think about the main idea, summarizing information, what you learned). Students received between 11 and 15 instructional sessions. The instructor verbalized and modeled application of each of the nine steps in the TWA strategy. The instructor ensured that students learned the steps in the strategy and then read a passage to the students while modeling the strategy before, during, and after reading. Students and teachers worked collaboratively applying the strategy to passages, after which students worked in pairs. While working together students self-monitored their performance with a strategy checklist and self-recorded their performance. Lessons were continued until each student demonstrated independence in using the strategy.

TWA reflected the SRSD program goal of providing students with strategies for self-regulating their performances. This program enhances volition beliefs because the strategies help to prevent students from being distracted from their goal of successful comprehension before, during, and after reading. This program also can raise self-efficacy and agency; students who successfully apply the strategy feel more in control of their comprehension outcomes and efficacious about being successful.

The RQ treatment provided students with examples of good types of comprehension questions to ask. Although the teacher modeled the use of this treatment, the teacher did not model the self-instructions contained in TWA. The format of RQ instructional sessions was otherwise similar to that of TWA sessions.

The results showed that on measures of oral reading comprehension, TWA students outperformed RQ students. There were, however, no significant differences between groups on measures of written reading comprehension or motivation measures (self-efficacy, intrinsic motivation). On the post-test, there was evidence that about half of the TWA students used parts or all of the strategy, although fewer displayed maintenance on the follow-up test.

## Implications for Theory Development, Research, and Practice

The preceding sections support the idea that self-efficacy, agency, and volition are key motivational variables that can affect students' reading engagement and skill development. Although we have distinguished these three variables, they are interlinked. Students who feel efficacious about learning and performing well in reading also are apt to believe that they can exert a large degree of control over their reading outcomes and that they can effectively deploy methods to keep themselves productively engaged and goal directed. In turn, successful reading can strengthen students' self-efficacy, agency, and volition beliefs and motivate them to stay engaged.

Theory and research suggest some implications for theory development, research, and educational practice. Given the importance of these student beliefs for reading, we recommend that theories of reading acquisition incorporate motivational beliefs and explain how they interact with cognitive variables to affect students' reading engagement and skill development. The RAND Reading Study Group (2002) paradigm for reading comprehension offers a model for theoretical development, because student motivational beliefs constitute a core aspect of variables associated with the reader. Information processing theories of learning have increasingly incorporated motivational variables (e.g., Winne & Hadwin, 2008), and we recommend that theories of reading follow suit.

With respect to research, we recommend that researchers investigate how students' motivational beliefs operate with learners at different age and developmental levels. All of the interventions described herein were done with elementary-age students. More research needs to be conducted with middle and high school students, who face reading demands much different from those of younger students and whose issues related to self-efficacy may be increasingly pronounced (Slavin, Cheung, Groff, & Lake, 2008).

There are also wide individual differences in students' acquisition of reading skills with corresponding variability in their motivational beliefs. Struggling readers have qualitatively and quantitatively different skill sets than do proficient readers, and the frequent difficulties they experience are apt to result in less-adaptive self-efficacy, agency, and volitional beliefs. For example, students who struggle mainly with decoding may display different motivational beliefs than students who can decode but have language deficiencies. Both of these groups may, in turn, differ from students experiencing problems in both areas. Regardless, to develop reading skills among struggling readers requires addressing both cognitive and motivational factors. Researchers might investigate how well changes in cognitive and motivational factors correspond with one another. For example, as struggling readers develop skills, their past difficulties may outweigh their present successes and lead to them continuing to hold less adaptive beliefs. Thus, motivational and cognitive influences can be tailored to individual differences among students as they gain competency.

A final recommendation is that practitioners ensure that reading instruction helps to build students' beliefs about their learning capabilities, control over reading, and capabilities to keep themselves productively engaged in reading. Successful reading instruction will serve to teach students skills and strategies and give them opportunities to practice and refine them. As students apply skills and strategies and observe their learning progress, their self-efficacy for continued learning is strengthened, along with their agency and volition beliefs.

Teachers may be tempted to assist students so that they can be successful. Assistance often is necessary in the early stages of learning as teachers provide corrective instruction, scaffolding, and feedback. But success gained with much help does not build strong self-efficacy, agency, or volition beliefs, because students are likely to attribute their success to the help they have received. Allowing students to succeed on their own exerts stronger effects on motivational outcomes. While teacher supports are necessary for initial skill acquisition, research on reciprocal teaching shows that the most robust increases in reading comprehension occur when teachers gradually reduce their level of support (Englert & Mariage, 1991; Palincsar & Brown, 1984).

In line with this suggestion we recommend that instruction be individualized as much as possible. Students do not learn in the same way or at the same rate. When assignments are not individualized, some students will succeed but others will have difficulty. When those in the latter group socially compare their performances to those of students who have done well, they are apt to doubt their capabilities for learning. Individualizing instruction minimizes opportunities for social comparisons. Teachers can point out to individual students the progress they have made in learning (e.g., "See how much better you're doing on these now?"), and the perception of progress by learners helps to strengthen their self-efficacy, agency, and volition beliefs.

## Conclusion

Self-efficacy, agency, and volition beliefs contribute importantly to students' learning and academic success. Reading research has identified programs that successfully help build students' skills and motivational beliefs. Further theory development and research will clarify how individual differences in cognitive and motivational variables interact to produce successful reading. Educators should take into account the potential effects of instructional conditions not only on students' reading skills and strategies but also on their individual differences in self-efficacy, agency, and volition beliefs. Enhancing these beliefs among students should improve their motivation and learning and produce classrooms that are more enjoyable to learn in.

## References

Adloff, S. M., Perfetti, C. A., & Catts, H. (2011). Developmental changes in reading comprehension: Implications for assessment and instruction. In S. Samuels & A. Farstrup (Eds.), *Reading instruction: What research has to say* (pp. 186–214). Newark, DE: International Reading Association.

Bandura, A. (1986). *Social foundations of thought and action: A social cognitive theory.* Englewood Cliffs, NJ: Prentice Hall.

Bandura, A. (1997). *Self-efficacy: The exercise of control.* New York: Freeman.

Bruning, R. H., Schraw, G. J., & Norby, M. M. (2011). *Cognitive psychology and instruction* (5th ed.). Boston: Pearson Education.

Bursuck, W. D., & Damer, M. (2014). *Teaching reading to students who are at-risk or have disabilities* (3rd ed.). Boston: Pearson Education.

Byrnes, J. P. (1996). *Cognitive development and learning in instructional contexts.* Boston: Allyn & Bacon.

Carnine, D. W., Silbert, J., Kameenui, E. J., & Tarver, S. (2010). *Direct instruction reading* (5th ed.). Englewood Cliffs, NJ: Merrill/Prentice Hall.

Corno, L. (1994). Student volition and education: Outcomes, influences, and practices. In D. H. Schunk & B. J. Zimmerman (Eds.), *Self-regulation of learning and performance: Issues and educational applications* (pp. 229–251). Hillsdale, NJ: Erlbaum.

Englert, C., & Mariage, T. (1991). Making students partners in the comprehension process: Organizing the reading "POSSE." *Learning Disability Quarterly, 14,* 123–138.

Fountas, I., & Pinnell, G. S. (1996). *Guided reading: Good first teaching for all children.* Portsmouth, NH: Heinemann.

Guthrie, J. T., & McRae, A. (2011). Reading engagement among African American and European American students. In S. Samuels & A. Farstrup (Eds.), *Reading instruction: What research has to say* (pp. 115–142). Newark, DE: International Reading Association.

Guthrie, J. T., & Wigfield, A. (2000). Engagement and motivation in reading. In M. L. Kamil, P. B. Mosenthal, P. D. Pearson, & R. Barr (Eds.), *Reading research handbook* (Vol. 3, pp. 403–424). Mahwah, NJ: Erlbaum.

Guthrie, J. T., Wigfield, A., Barbosa, P., Perencevich, K. C., Taboada, A., Davis, M. H., . . . Tonks, S. (2004). Increasing reading comprehension and engagement through concept-oriented reading instruction. *Journal of Educational Psychology*, *96*, 403–423.

Guthrie, J. T., Wigfield, A., & Perencevich, K. C. (Eds.) (2004). *Motivating reading comprehension: Concept-oriented reading instruction*. Mahwah, NJ: Erlbaum.

Guthrie, J. T., Wigfield, A., & VonSecker, C. (2000). Effects of integrated instruction on motivation and strategy use in reading. *Journal of Educational Psychology*, *92*, 331–341.

Harris, K. R., Graham, S., & Mason, L. H. (2006). Improving the writing, knowledge, and motivation of struggling young writers: Effects of self-regulated strategy development with and without peer support. *American Educational Research Journal*, *43*, 295–340.

Harris, K. R., Graham, S., & Santangelo, T. (2013). Self-regulated strategies development in writing: Development, implementation, and scaling up. In H. Bembenutty, T. J. Cleary, & A. Kitsantas (Eds.), *Applications of self-regulated learning across diverse disciplines: A tribute to Barry J. Zimmerman* (pp. 59–87). Charlotte, NC: Information Age Publishing.

Heckhausen, H. (1991). *Motivation and action*. Berlin: Springer-Verlag.

Heckhausen, H., & Gollwitzer, P. (1987). Thought contents and cognitive functioning in motivational vs. volitional states of mind. *Motivation and Emotion*, *11*, 101–120.

Hoover, W. A., & Gough, P. B. (1990). The simple view of reading. *Reading and Writing: An Interdisciplinary Journal*, *2*, 127–160.

Hunt, M. (1993). *The story of psychology*. New York: Doubleday.

Kintsch. W. (1988). The role of knowledge in discourse comprehension: A construction-integration model. *Psychological Review*, *95*, 163–182.

Kintsch, W. (1998).*Comprehension: A paradigm for cognition*. Cambridge, UK: Cambridge University Press.

Kuhl, J. (1984). Volitional aspects of achievement motivation and learned helplessness: Toward a comprehensive theory of action control. In B. A. Maher (Ed.), *Progress in experimental personality research* (Vol. 13, pp. 99–171). New York: Academic Press.

Kuhl, J. (2000). A functional-design approach to motivation and self-regulation: The dynamics of personality systems interactions. In M. Boekaerts, P. R. Pintrich, & M. Zeidner (Eds.), *Handbook of self-regulation* (pp. 111–169). San Diego, CA: Academic Press.

Licht, B. G., & Kistner, J. A. (1986). Motivational problems of learning-disabled children: Individual differences and their implications for treatment. In J. K. Torgesen & B. W. L. Wong (Eds.), *Psychological and educational perspectives on learning disabilities* (pp. 225–255). Orlando, FL: Academic Press.

Mason, L. (2004). Explicit Self-Regulated Strategy Development versus reciprocal questioning: Effects on expository reading comprehension among struggling readers. *Journal of Educational Psychology*, *96*, 283–296.

Mayer, R. E. (1999). *The promise of educational psychology: Learning in the content areas*. Upper Saddle River, NJ: Merrill/Prentice Hall.

National Reading Panel (2000). *Teaching children to read: An evidence-based assessment of the scientific research literature on reading and its implications for reading instruction*. Washington, DC: National Institute of Child Health and Human Development.

Palincsar, A. S., & Brown, A. L. (1984). Reciprocal teaching of comprehension-fostering and comprehension-monitoring activities. *Cognition and Instruction*, *1*, 117–175.

Paris, S. G., Wixson, K. K., & Palincsar, A. S. (1986). Instructional approaches to reading comprehension. In E. Z. Rothkopf (Ed.), *Review of research in education* (Vol. 13, pp. 91–128). Washington, DC: American Educational Research Association.

RAND Reading Study Group (2002). *Reading for understanding: Toward an R & D program in reading comprehension*. Santa Monica, CA: RAND.

Ryan, R. M., & Deci, E. L. (2009). Promoting self-determined school engagement: Motivation, learning, and well-being. In K. R. Wentzel & A. Wigfield (Eds.), *Handbook of motivation at school* (pp. 171–195). New York: Routledge.

Schunk, D. H. (2012). Social cognitive theory. In K. R. Harris, S. Graham, & T. Urdan (Eds.), *APA educational psychology handbook: Vol. 1. Theories, constructs, and critical issues* (pp. 101–123). Washington, DC: American Psychological Association.

Schunk, D. H., & Pajares, F. (2009). Self-efficacy theory. In K. R. Wentzel & A. Wigfield (Eds.), *Handbook of motivation at school* (pp. 35–53). New York: Routledge.

Schunk, D. H., & Rice, J. M. (1985). Verbalization of comprehension strategies: Effects on children's achievement outcomes. *Human Learning*, *4*, 1–10.

65

Schunk, D. H., & Rice, J. M. (1987). Enhancing comprehension skill and self-efficacy with strategy value information. *Journal of Reading Behavior, 19*, 285–302.

Schunk, D. H., & Rice, J. M. (1992). Influence of reading comprehension strategy information on children's achievement outcomes. *Learning Disability Quarterly, 15*, 51–64.

Schunk, D. H., & Rice, J. M. (1993). Strategy fading and progress feedback: Effects on self-efficacy and comprehension among students receiving remedial reading services. *Journal of Special Education, 27*, 257–276.

Slavin, R., Cheung, A., Groff, C., & Lake, C. (2008). Effective reading programs for middle and high schools: A best evidence synthesis. *Reading Research Quarterly, 43*, 290–322.

Winne, P. H., & Hadwin, A. F. (2008). The weave of motivation and self-regulated learning. In D. H. Schunk & B. J. Zimmerman (Eds.), *Motivation and self-regulated learning: Theory, research, and applications* (pp. 297–314). New York: Taylor & Francis.

# 6

# The Role of Epistemic Beliefs in the Comprehension of Single and Multiple Texts

*Ivar Bråten, Helge I. Strømsø, and Leila E. Ferguson*

## Introduction

The purpose of this chapter is to review theory and research on the role of epistemic beliefs in text comprehension and discuss implications for educational research and practice. While "beliefs" refer to what individuals accept as or want to be true (Murphy & Mason, 2006), "epistemic beliefs", in particular, refer to what individuals believe knowledge is like and how they believe people come to know (Hofer & Bendixen, 2012). A growing body of research indicates that epistemic beliefs may guide readers' goals, processing activities, and comprehension. Take, for example, a student believing that knowledge in a domain is absolute and unchanging and consists of isolated facts. When this student encounters an expository text in that domain that deals with a complex issue for which there is no clear-cut, accurate answer, his or her reading goals (e.g., to gather pieces of factual information and identify the correct answer) and processing activities (e.g., rehearsing unrelated facts and searching for the "truth" about the issue) may be out of step with the task at hand and result in frustration and confusion on part of the student, as well as a superficial understanding that does not reflect the tentativeness and complexity of the issue.

Presumably, the problems become even more salient when this student tries to understand an issue by reading multiple texts that discuss the issue from different perspectives, which is the rule rather than the exception in the information-saturated contexts facing twenty-first-century readers (Alexander, 2012; Rouet, 2006). Essentially, comprehension of multiple texts differs from comprehension of single texts because the former requires that readers integrate information from textual entities expressing diverse and even contradictory viewpoints while they also keep sources apart (i.e., note and remember "who says what") (Perfetti, Rouet, & Britt, 1999).

The remainder of this chapter is divided into three main sections. In the first, we provide a theoretical background by discussing different conceptualizations of epistemic beliefs as well as conceptualizations of the comprehension of single and multiple texts that address the role of epistemic beliefs. In the second, we review research linking individual differences in epistemic beliefs to the comprehension of single and multiple texts, including web-based texts, with this research primarily framed by the epistemic belief conceptualizations of Hofer and Pintrich (1997) and Greene, Azevedo, and Torney-Purta (2008). Finally, in the third main section, we summarize research regarding individual differences in epistemic beliefs in relation to text comprehension and discuss the implications of this work for future research and instructional practice.

## Theoretical Background

### Epistemic Beliefs

Epistemic beliefs can be considered a form of personal epistemology, which concerns lay persons' (as opposed to trained philosophers') views about knowledge and knowing (i.e., about the epistemic) (Bråten, 2011). Most educational and psychological work on personal epistemology has been rooted in Perry's (1970) longitudinal research, suggesting that college students start out believing that knowledge consists of simple, unchanging facts handed down by authority, and then progress toward a conception of knowledge as consisting of complex, tentative concepts based on reasoning. Several researchers have continued Perry's effort to identify developmental trajectories in students' personal epistemology, mostly through the use of interviewing methodology (e.g., Baxter Magolda, 1992; King & Kitchener, 1994; Kuhn, 1991). Typically, this line of research describes a trajectory starting with an absolutist or dualist view where knowledge is viewed as either right or wrong and where it is possible to know what is right with certainty. This is followed by a period of multiplicity where multiple conflicting views are acknowledged as equally valid. Finally, a more evaluativistic perspective develops where individuals acknowledge that there is no absolute certain knowledge but still consider it possible to evaluate knowledge claims and justify claims through the use of supporting evidence.

Schommer (1990) departed from the developmental approach and introduced the belief system approach, using quantitative assessment to examine relationships between dimensions of epistemic beliefs and other academic constructs, including text comprehension. In her conceptualization, individuals hold more or less independent epistemic beliefs about the certainty, simplicity, and source of knowledge, as well as related beliefs about learning and intelligence (which were originally conceived of as epistemic beliefs by Schommer). Refining Schommer's (1990) conceptualization on the basis of an extensive review of the personal epistemology literature, Hofer and Pintrich (1997) proposed two dimensions concerning the nature of knowledge (how one defines knowledge) and two dimensions concerning the nature of knowing (how one comes to know), with each dimension reflecting a continuum from naïve to sophisticated beliefs. The two dimensions concerning the nature of knowledge are *certainty of knowledge*, ranging from the belief that knowledge is absolute and unchanging to the belief that knowledge is tentative and evolving, and *simplicity of knowledge*, ranging from the belief that knowledge consists of an accumulation of more or less isolated facts to the belief that knowledge consists of highly interrelated concepts. The two dimensions concerning the nature of knowing are *source of knowledge*, ranging from the conception that knowledge originates outside the self and resides in external authority, from which it may be transmitted, to the conception that knowledge is actively constructed by the person in interaction with others, and *justification for knowing*, ranging from justification of knowledge claims through observation and authority, or on the basis of what feels right, to the use of rules of inquiry and the evaluation and integration of different sources.

More recently, Greene et al. (2008) argued that because philosophical epistemology centers on how claims can be justified as knowledge, only one of the dimensions described by Hofer and Pintrich (1997), the one concerning justification for knowing, deserves to be labeled epistemic. In addition, they proposed that justification for knowing should be differentiated into more than one dimension, especially highlighting separate dimensions of justification by authority and personal justification. According to Greene et al. (2008), a multidimensional perspective on justification beliefs also follows from philosophical epistemology, which identifies a number of sources, both external and internal to the individual, that can legitimately be used to justify knowledge claims (see also, Chinn, Buckland, & Samarapungavan, 2011). Building on Greene et al. (2008), Ferguson and colleagues used think-aloud (Ferguson, Bråten, & Strømsø, 2012) and questionnaire data (Ferguson, Bråten, Strømsø, & Anmarkrud, 2013) to differentiate three types of sources that students draw on in their effort to justify knowledge claims. Along with justification by an external authoritative source and justification by personal opinion, these authors included a third dimension reflecting that students consider which claims to believe on the basis of cross-checking, comparing, and corroborating across several sources of information (termed "justification by multiple sources").

Although most research on epistemic beliefs in relation to text comprehension has been framed by the multidimensional models of Schommer (1990) and Hofer and Pintrich (1997) and, more recently, by the multidimensional justification belief frameworks of Greene et al. (2008) and Ferguson et al. (2012, 2013), some recent work has also built on the multidimensional model of Royce (1978). This model describes individuals' beliefs about how knowledge is justified along the dimensions of empiricism (i.e., by direct observation), rationalism (i.e., by logic and reason), and metaphorism (i.e., by symbolically derived universal insight).

Of note is that early conceptualizations assumed that epistemic beliefs were independent of content domain, implying, for example, that students would hold the same beliefs about knowledge in history as in natural science, with this assumption reflected in attempts to assess epistemic beliefs at a domain-general level (Schommer, 1990). Because of a growing consensus that epistemic beliefs may vary across content domains (Muis, Bendixen, & Haerle, 2006), general measures have been supplemented with questionnaires targeting epistemic beliefs in specific domains (Conley, Pintrich, Vekiri, & Harrison, 2004; Hofer, 2000). Moreover, recent evidence indicates that epistemic beliefs may vary across specific topics within content domains, with this reflected in questionnaires devised to measure topic-specific epistemic beliefs (Bråten, Gil, Strømsø, & Vidal-Abarca, 2009; Stahl & Bromme, 2007). Notably, topic-specific epistemic beliefs have also been studied by means of think-aloud methodology (Hofer 2004; Ferguson et al., 2012; Mason, Ariasi, & Boldrin, 2011). Accordingly, extant research on the role of epistemic beliefs in text comprehension has linked epistemic beliefs at different levels of specificity to the comprehension of single and multiple texts.

The increased emphasis on contextual factors is not only reflected in more specific measures. Although epistemic belief dimensions were originally considered to range from naïve (lower level) to sophisticated (higher level) beliefs (Hofer & Pintrich, 1997; Schommer, 1990), this notion is problematic because beliefs that are adaptive in one context may not necessarily be adaptive in another context (Bråten, Strømsø, & Samuelstuen, 2008). Rather than considering particular beliefs to be generally more sophisticated than others, this speaks for the contextualization of belief–comprehension relationships, with the effectiveness of particular beliefs presumably varying with reading-task context and level of reader expertise.

## Comprehension of Single and Multiple Texts: Including Epistemic Beliefs

In Kintsch's (1988) influential construction-integration model, content area prior knowledge is the *sine qua non* of deeper-level text comprehension. That is, to get underneath the more superficial text-internal meaning of the text (i.e., the textbase) and interpret the situation described in the text (i.e., construct a situation model), information residing in the text itself needs to be integrated with information residing in long-term memory (i.e., prior knowledge). Besides prior knowledge, reading motivation and cognitive and metacognitive strategies are considered to play prominent roles in text comprehension. For example, in the constructionist framework proposed by Graesser, Singer, and Trabasso (1994), strategies are important because readers use them to construct coherent mental representations and explanations of situations described in the texts, and in the engagement model of Guthrie and Wigfield (2000) and the model of domain learning of Alexander (2005), not only strategic processing but also motivational constructs, in particular intrinsic motivation and interest, feature on a par with content knowledge as contributors to good text comprehension.

Recently, Afflerbach, Cho, Kim, Crassas, and Doyle (2013) called for an expansion of existing conceptualizations of successful reading to include epistemic beliefs, arguing that epistemic beliefs "influence students' approaches to learning in the classroom, the cognitive skills and strategies that students use, and the stances readers take toward text" (p. 444). In particular, those authors highlight the importance of epistemic beliefs for facilitating or constraining the use of critical thinking strategies in reading to evaluate text content as well as source credibility.

Accordingly, Alexander's (2012) most recent view on reading competence is strongly influenced by theory and research in not only expertise development but also in epistemic beliefs. While the literature on expertise suggests that competent readers display a configuration of principled content domain knowledge, deep-processing strategies, and personal interest for the domain or topic of the text, the current literature on epistemic beliefs indicates that competent readers are also more likely to believe that knowledge is contextualized and complex and that, given the authored and potentially biased nature of text, textual claims need to be justified by considering the credentials of the author as well as the evidence that he or she provides.

Finally, because epistemic beliefs may be particularly important when people work on complex learning tasks (Spiro, Feltovich, & Coulson, 1996), and because the comprehension of multiple texts can be described as a more complex task than the comprehension of one single text (Wineburg, 1998), the role of epistemic beliefs, in general, may be greater in multiple-text than in single-text comprehension. The documents model of multiple-text comprehension introduced by Perfetti et al. (1999) extends Kintsch's (1988) construction-integration model by describing two additional representational structures needed to comprehend multiple texts: a representation of the integrated content across texts (i.e., a situations model) and a representation including information about the sources of the most important information in the situations model as well as information about how the various sources are related (i.e., an intertextual model). Bråten, Britt, Strømsø, and Rouet's (2011) integrated model of epistemic beliefs and multiple-text comprehension specifies how each of the four epistemic belief dimensions described by Hofer and Pintrich (1997) may influence multiple-text comprehension, with beliefs falling on the simplicity and justification dimensions, in particular, facilitating or constraining situations model construction and beliefs falling on the certainty and source dimensions, in particular, facilitating or constraining intertext model construction. For example, viewing knowledge as complex rather than simple is supposed to facilitate situations model construction because readers define the task as integration, aim at a coherent representation, engage in overview generation, cross-text elaboration, and corroboration, and accept a coherent, integrated understanding. Moreover, viewing knowledge as tentative and evolving rather than certain is supposed to facilitate intertext model construction because readers define the task as exploring different sources, aim at understanding different perspectives, pay attention to uncertainties, establish source–content and source–source links, accept understanding of breadth and diversity, and use an argument schema.

In the following section, we review research that provides the empirical foundation for expanding current conceptualization to include epistemic beliefs among the individual differences underlying text comprehension.

## Research on Epistemic Beliefs and Text Comprehension

### Epistemic Beliefs and Single-Text Comprehension

There is a considerable body of research showing that beliefs in tentative and evolving rather than certain knowledge, as well as in interrelated conceptual rather than isolated factual knowledge, are related to more adaptive processing and better text-based learning and comprehension when students read single expository texts (Kardash & Scholes, 1996, 2000; Kendeou, Muis, & Fulton, 2011; Mason, Gava, & Boldrin, 2008; Schommer, 1990; Schommer, Crouse, & Rhodes, 1992; Schraw, Bendixen, & Dunkle, 2002). For example, Schommer (1990) initially found that for students who read a passage in which the concluding paragraph was removed, belief in certain knowledge was related to inappropriate absolute conclusions. Later, research by Kardash and Scholes (1996) confirmed that students believing in certain knowledge tend to avoid inconclusive or tentative interpretations of complex textual information, with additional studies (Kendeou et al., 2011; Mason et al., 2008) linking beliefs in tentative and evolving rather than certain knowledge to students' text-based learning of science concepts that contradict their initial understandings (i.e., conceptual change learning). With respect to the simplicity dimension, Schommer et al. (1992) initially found that the less students believed knowledge to consist of isolated facts, the better they comprehended statistical text, with similar findings reported by Schraw et al. (2002).

There is also some evidence to suggest that relationships between beliefs about knowledge and performance may be mediated by strategic text processing. For example, students believing more in uncertain and complex knowledge seem more likely to engage in comprehension monitoring and bridging inferences (Kardash & Howell, 2000) as well as in conceptual change processes (Kendeou et al., 2011).

In comparison, the research base relating beliefs about knowing to single-text comprehension is more inconsistent and meager. Concerning beliefs about the source of knowledge, Schraw and Bruning (1996) compared two types of beliefs that readers may bring to a reading task: the belief that meaning is actively constructed by the reader and the belief that reading is to extract the author's intended meaning and translate the text's meaning in an objective manner. They found that for undergraduates reading an expository text, viewing reading as active meaning construction positively affected personal engagement and recall of text information but was unrelated to text-based inferences. However, Schraw (2000), using a narrative text, found that holding the belief that reading involves active meaning construction rather than transmission of meaning from author or text positively affected text-based (thematic) inferences as well as holistic text interpretation but was unrelated to the comprehension of main ideas. Somewhat later, Mason, Scirica, and Salvi (2006) tried to replicate Schraw's (2000) findings in two studies with Italian middle- and high-school students reading narrative text. In the first study, belief in personal meaning construction was unrelated to both the comprehension of main ideas and the production of text (thematic) inferences while it positively affected holistic text interpretation. In the second study, the comprehension of main ideas, the production of text inferences, and holistic text interpretation all seemed to be positively affected by the belief that the reader is an important constructor of knowledge. Thus, although the research base regarding a relation between beliefs about the source of knowledge and single-text comprehension is small and somewhat inconsistent, there is some evidence to suggest that beliefs in personal construction of knowledge may facilitate text processing and comprehension when reading narrative text. Viewing the process of knowing as inherently subjective may not be equally beneficial when trying to comprehend challenging expository text, however.

Regarding beliefs about justification for knowing, Mason and colleagues (Mason & Boscolo, 2004; Mason & Scirica, 2006) used a questionnaire developed by Kuhn, Cheney, and Weinstock (2000) to assess personal epistemology in terms of absolutist, multiplist, and evaluativist stances and related those stances to performance. Of note is that these stances essentially describe the development of beliefs about justification for knowing: Individuals start at an absolutist stage where no justification is needed and progress through a multiplist stage where justification is mainly personal, to an evaluativist stage where awareness of rules of inquiry and what counts as evidence in the domain makes them realize that some claims are better justified as knowledge than others. In brief, Mason's work indicates that more developed beliefs concerning justification for knowing are linked to deeper-level comprehension, as reflected in students' argumentative reasoning after reading expository (i.e., science) text.

Of note is that most of the studies examining epistemic beliefs in relation to single-text comprehension assessed beliefs about knowledge and knowing in general as opposed to in specific domains or topics within domains. Also, all studies referred to above used questionnaires to assess epistemic beliefs.

## Epistemic Beliefs and Multiple-Text Comprehension

Bråten et al. (2011) recently summarized empirical links established between the dimensions figuring in Hofer and Pintrich's (1997) framework and multiple-text comprehension. With respect to beliefs concerning the certainty of knowledge, Strømsø, Bråten, and Samuelstuen (2008) initially found that such beliefs may uniquely predict multiple-text comprehension, with readers believing knowledge about the issue dealt with in the texts to be tentative and evolving more likely to perform well on an intertextual comprehension task than were readers believing knowledge about the issue to be absolute and unchanging. Later, Bråten and Strømsø (2010a) demonstrated that beliefs in tentative and evolving rather than certain knowledge play a particularly important role when students are trying to construct arguments based on what they read. In addition, research by Pieschl, Stahl, and Bromme (2008) indicates that readers believing more in tentative and evolving knowledge may be more likely to study the materials in full breadth and dig into even the more problematic and controversial aspects of the issue they read about in multiple texts.

Regarding the simplicity dimension, findings consistently indicate that believing knowledge to be complex rather than simple may be facilitative when readers try to build an integrated understanding across expository texts (Barzilai & Zohar, 2012; Bråten & Strømsø, 2010a, 2010b; Pieschl et al., 2008; Strømsø et al., 2008). For example, Strømsø et al. (2008) reported that beliefs in complex and theoretical rather than isolated and factual knowledge uniquely predicted students' deeper-level, intertextual understanding after variance associated with gender, study experience, word decoding, and prior knowledge was accounted for. Moreover, there is some evidence that beliefs in complex knowledge may be related to self-regulated and deeper-level processing in the form of overview generation and cross-text elaboration when students read multiple texts (Pieschl et al., 2008). Further, students believing knowledge in an area to be complex may be less likely to rely on information from sources that often simplify rather than elaborate upon complex issues, such as a newspaper (Strømsø, Bråten, & Britt, 2011).

Regarding the source of knowledge dimension, there is currently some evidence that viewing knowledge to be transmitted by authorities and expert authors rather than constructed by the self may be adaptive when students read multiple expository texts on a relatively unfamiliar topic (Bråten et al., 2008; Strømsø et al., 2008). In such contexts, viewing knowledge as personal construction rather than transmitted from experts may be maladaptive because readers concentrate too much on subjective interpretation at the expense of figuring out precisely what the authors and texts say. In corroboration of this, Strømsø et al. (2011) found that viewing knowledge to be transmitted by expert authors was related to more trust in information encountered in external sources, less emphasis on personal opinion as a criterion for judging the trustworthiness of sources, and more attention to content when judging the trustworthiness of presumably reliable sources, such as a well-known and highly respected research center.

Finally, with respect to the justification for knowing dimension, believing that knowledge claims need to be justified through reason, rules of inquiry, and the evaluation and integration of multiple sources has been found to uniquely predict multiple-text comprehension (Bråten, & Strømsø, 2010b; Strømsø, & Bråten, 2009). Likewise, in a study focussing on Internet-specific epistemic beliefs (i.e., beliefs concerning what knowledge and knowing are like on the Internet), Kammerer, Bråten, Gerjets, and Stømsø, (2013) found that the more students believed that web-based knowledge claims need to be checked against other information sources, reason, and prior knowledge, the more likely they were to avoid one-sidedness and construct a balanced representation of the different arguments presented on multiple websites. Also focussing on Internet-specific epistemic beliefs, Strømsø and Bråten (2010) and Chiu, Liang, and Tsai (2013) found that beliefs related to the justification for knowing uniquely predicted the use of metacognitive strategies among Norwegian and Taiwanese students, respectively, with students tending to believe that Internet-based knowledge claims need to be checked against other information sources also more likely to use strategies such planning, monitoring, and regulating when dealing with course-related information on the Internet. Additionally, the belief that knowledge claims should be based on reason, scientific inquiry, and the evaluation and integration of multiple sources has been linked to trust in research-based sources and attention to different source characteristics when evaluating such sources (Strømsø et al., 2011).

Recently, the different types of justification beliefs figuring in the trichotomous justification belief framework of Ferguson and colleagues (Ferguson et al., 2012, 2013), including personal justification, justification by authority, and justification by multiple sources, have also been examined in relation to multiple-text comprehension. For example, Bråten, Ferguson, Strømsø, and Anmarkrud (2013) found that beliefs in personal justification were a unique negative predictor of multiple-text comprehension when prior knowledge was controlled for, whereas beliefs in justification by multiple sources were a unique positive predictor. Facilitative effects of beliefs in justification by multiple sources were also suggested by Bråten, Anmarkrud, Brandmo, and Strømsø (2014), who found that both effort and the use of deeper-level intertextual strategies mediated the positive effect of such beliefs on multiple-text comprehension.

## Examining Profiles of Epistemic Beliefs in Relation to Text Comprehension

While the predominant approach in research on epistemic beliefs in relation to both single- and multiple-text comprehension has been to try to link beliefs on individual dimensions (e.g., beliefs concerning the certainty of knowledge or justification by multiple sources) to performance through variable-centered approaches such as analysis of variance and multiple regression analysis, some studies have used a person-centered approach, profiling students on the basis of several dimensions of epistemic beliefs and examining profile differences in text-based learning and comprehension (Bråten et al., 2008; Buehl & Alexander, 2005; Ferguson & Bråten, 2013; Franco et al., 2012; Mason et al., 2011). For example, Franco et al. (2012) used a domain-general epistemic profiles questionnaire based on Royce's (1978) framework to profile students as higher on justification by metaphorical means (i.e., universal insight) than on justification by rational means (i.e., logic and reason) and empirical means (i.e., direct observation) or as higher on rational means than on justification by metaphorical and empirical means. The findings indicated that students used more deeper-level strategies and gained more conceptual knowledge from a science text when the text explained the concept in question in a way that was consistent with students' epistemic belief profiles (i.e., in a metaphorical or rational way), with this also highlighting the contextual nature of belief–comprehension relationships.

Also targeting single-text reading, Buehl and Alexander (2005) cluster analyzed questionnaire data to identify distinct epistemic belief profiles within the domain of history, finding that students who held low beliefs in certain and isolated history knowledge, in combination with either low or moderate beliefs in authority as the source of history knowledge, learned more from a history text that students with other belief profiles.

Focussing on multiple-text comprehension, Bråten et al. (2008) found that in the context of reading multiple expository texts on a relatively unfamiliar topic, the most adaptive epistemic belief profile combined high beliefs in knowledge transmitted from experts with high beliefs in complex knowledge. In accordance with Buehl and Alexander (2005), Bråten et al. (2008) also found that low beliefs in expertise/authority as the source of knowledge are not necessarily maladaptive when combined with high beliefs in the interrelated and complex nature of knowledge.

Further, in the context of web search on a controversial scientific issue, Mason et al. (2011) identified two epistemic belief profiles through cluster analysis of online think-aloud data—one likely to believe in authority as a source of knowledge as well as in justification of knowledge claims through scientific evidence; the other only likely to believe in authority as a source of knowledge. With respect to learning about the topic from multiple web-based sources, students in the former profile group outperformed students in the latter.

Finally, in a sample of tenth graders, Ferguson and Bråten (2013) profiled individual differences on the basis of the three types of justification beliefs included in their trichotomous framework as well on the basis of students' knowledge about the subject dealt with in the texts, finding that a subgroup characterized by relatively high level of knowledge and relatively low level of personal justification in combination with strong beliefs in justification by multiple sources performed best on a multiple-text comprehension measure.

## Towards Context-Specificity and Complexity

Compared to research on epistemic beliefs in relation to single-text-based learning and comprehension, research targeting multiple-text reading has put more emphasis on the context-specificity of epistemic beliefs by typically using not only domain-specific (Bråten et al., 2013, 2014; Ferguson & Bråten, 2013; Kammerer et al., 2013; Strømsø & Bråten, 2010) but also topic-specific (Bråten et al., 2008; Bråten & Strømsø, 2010a, 2010b; Strømsø et al., 2008, 2011) epistemic belief questionnaires, as well as other methodologies (e.g., verbal protocols; Barzilai & Zohar, 2012; Mason et al., 2011) to assess topic-specific epistemic beliefs. Moreover, research on epistemic beliefs and multiple-text comprehension has contributed to a clarification of the context-specific nature of belief–comprehension relationships by showing that beliefs that are productive in one reading-task setting may not necessarily be so in another, as exemplified by different findings regarding the source of knowledge dimension in single- and multiple-text-reading settings (Bråten et al., 2008). In addition, research within a multiple-text paradigm has identified epistemic beliefs and combinations of beliefs that may be particularly adaptive in the context of working with multiple expository texts on complex and controversial issues (Bråten et al., 2013, 2014; Ferguson & Bråten, 2013). Finally, studying epistemic beliefs in relation to multiple-text comprehension has broadened the research agenda to include more complex reading tasks (Bråten et al., 2011). In this line of research, increased complexity is also reflected in a more complex dimensionality of epistemic beliefs, especially as a unidimensional approach to justification for knowing has been replaced with a multidimensional approach to this construct that has provided new knowledge on the role of epistemic beliefs in text processing and comprehension (Ferguson & Bråten, 2013).

## Summary and Future Directions

Research within the single-text paradigm has generally indicated that beliefs in tentative and evolving rather than certain knowledge, as well as in complex rather than simple knowledge, are related to more adaptive text processing and better comprehension. Additionally, there is some evidence that readers may profitably believe in the self as a source of knowledge when reading narrative text, and that beliefs in evidence-based justification of knowledge claims may facilitate deeper-level comprehension of science text. Research within the multiple-text paradigm, on the other hand, has documented that viewing knowledge as tentative and evolving rather than certain, complex rather than simple, originating in expert authors rather than the reader, and justified by rules of inquiry and cross-checking of knowledge sources rather than own opinion and experience may predict students' abilities to synthesize information from expository texts expressing diverse and even contradictory viewpoints on a particular topic.

Research on both single- and multiple-text comprehension suggests, moreover, that relationships between adaptive epistemic beliefs and comprehension are mediated by deeper-level cognitive and metacognitive strategies such as inference generation, conceptual change processing, cross-text elaboration, and planning, monitoring, and regulating. Finally, general trends that were discovered in our review included increased emphasis on contextualization (of beliefs and belief-comprehension relationships), complexity (of comprehension tasks and belief dimensionality), and justification (as a central and multidimensional epistemic belief construct).

Although researchers have begun to study interactions between different epistemic belief dimensions, there is still little work on how epistemic beliefs relate to and interact with other relevant individual difference variables, such as prior knowledge and motivation (see, however, Ferguson & Bråten, 2013). According to Bromme, Kienhues, and Stahl (2008), interactions between knowledge and epistemic beliefs may be complex and context-sensitive, with higher knowledge sometimes, but not always, associated with stronger endorsement of particular epistemic beliefs and, at the same time, weaker endorsement of other epistemic beliefs. One possibility is, for example, that higher knowledge relates positively to beliefs in personal justification of knowledge and negatively to beliefs in certain knowledge in one context (e.g., when reading poetry), while higher knowledge may be associated with more reliance on external authority (rather than the self) as a source of knowledge, as well as with stronger beliefs in certain knowledge, in another context (e.g., when reading human anatomy). Such complex, context-sensitive interactions between epistemic beliefs and other components of text comprehension, including prior knowledge, should be further studied through person-centered as well as variable-centered approaches to provide a more solid empirical grounding for including epistemic beliefs in a network of individual difference variables underlying successful single- and multiple-text comprehension. For example, in a recent attempt to flesh out a more comprehensive model of what it takes to build integrated understandings from multiple conflicting texts, Bråten et al. (2014) suggested that epistemic beliefs concerning the justification for knowing, together with personality dispositions, motivational orientations, and prior knowledge, underlie processes related to effort, deeper-level strategies, and text-based interest, which, in turn, may influence multiple-text comprehension directly. Much future empirical work with different readers in different reading-task situations is needed to further specify relationships between both distal and proximal contributors to comprehension performance, however.

Another issue where more work is needed concerns the possibility that relationships between epistemic beliefs and text comprehension may be bidirectional rather than unidirectional. In particular, it has been theoretically assumed that when readers try to make sense of complex and ill-structured problems by working with multiple perspectives that challenge their current epistemic beliefs, belief changes may occur (Bråten et al., 2011; Greene, Muis, & Pieschl, 2010; Tsai, 2004). There is also some empirical evidence that students may, indeed, change their epistemic beliefs as a result of working with complex reading tasks where they encounter conflicting views on unsettled issues (Barzilai & Zohar, 2012; Ferguson et al., 2013; Kienhues, Stadtler, & Bromme, 2011; Porsch & Bromme, 2011). For example, Kienhues et al. (2011) presented undergraduates with websites containing either conflicting or consistent information on a controversial medical topic, finding that participants studying conflicting sites believed less in a single correct and straightforward answer to the issue than those studying consistent sites. Although this research has typically not investigated whether resulting changes in epistemic beliefs are accompanied by improved text comprehension, Ferguson et al. (2013) recently found that students changing their epistemic beliefs after reading multiple conflicting texts on a science issue also scored higher on a measure of multiple-text comprehension than students reading multiple consistent texts on the same issue.

Albeit preliminary, the above-mentioned research suggests that a curricular approach where multiple texts are used to provide different perspectives on an event, phenomenon, or issue may provide a hotbed for epistemic change (see also, Afflerbach et al., 2013). It seems important, however, that rather than having students read and reflect on multiple conflicting texts independently, their work with such texts should be embedded in a broader instructional context, including a constructivist epistemic climate (Muis & Duffy, 2013). For example, to facilitate the development of adaptive epistemic beliefs, students' independent, unguided work with multiple conflicting texts may profitably be supplemented with scaffolded support in the form of an explicit discourse concerning both text content and the epistemic implications of that content (Sandoval & Morrison, 2003). Following recent work on contrasting cases by Braasch, Bråten, Strømsø, Anmarkrud, and Ferguson (2013), one possibility is to have students compare and contrast more and less adaptive epistemic cognition (i.e., beliefs in action) displayed by two hypothetical students and embed such individual work with multiple conflicting texts within dyadic and instructor-led whole-class discussions organized to promote explanation and application of productive epistemic beliefs in text comprehension. In any case, it is essential that future intervention work attempting to promote epistemic belief change through text-based approaches not only evaluate their success in terms of more adaptive epistemic beliefs but also in terms of accompanying improvements in text comprehension, with such work also allowing for firmer conclusions regarding cause-and-effect relationships between epistemic beliefs and text comprehension. Notably, evidence-based instruction in classrooms to facilitate the development of adaptive epistemic beliefs as well as text comprehension should be regarded as a task not only for reading teachers. Given the importance of advanced literacy competencies across the school subjects, it is equally pertinent that future research in this area provides teachers with a solid grounding for addressing and challenging students' beliefs about knowledge and knowing as part of their subject matter teaching.

## References

Afflerbach, P., Cho, B.-Y., Kim, J.-Y., Crassas, M. E., & Doyle, B. (2013). Reading: What else matters besides strategies and skills? *The Reading Teacher, 66,* 440–448.

Alexander, P. A. (2005). The path to competence: A lifespan development perspective on reading. *Journal of Literacy Research, 37,* 413–436.

Alexander, P. A. (2012). Reading into the future: Competence for the 21st century. *Educational Psychologist, 47,* 259–280.

Barzilai, S., & Zohar, A. (2012). Epistemic thinking in action: Evaluating and integrating online sources. *Cognition and Instruction, 30,* 39–85.

Baxter Magolda, M. B. (1992). *Knowing and reasoning in college: Gender-related patterns in students' intellectual development.* San Francisco, CA: Jossey-Bass.

Braasch, J. L. G., Bråten, I., Strømsø, H. I., Anmarkrud, Ø., & Ferguson, L. E. (2013). Promoting secondary school students' evaluation of source features of multiple documents. *Contemporary Educational Psychology, 38,* 180–195.

Bråten, I. (2011). Personal epistemology in education. In V. G. Aukrust (Ed.), *Learning and cognition in education* (pp. 52–58). Oxford: Elsevier.

Bråten, I., Anmarkrud, Ø., Brandmo, C., & Strømsø, H. I. (2014). Developing and testing a model of direct and indirect relationships between individual differences, processing, and multiple-text comprehension. *Learning and Instruction, 30,* 9–24.

Bråten, I., Britt, M. A., Strømsø, H. I., & Rouet, J. F. (2011). The role of epistemic beliefs in the comprehension of multiple expository texts: Toward an integrated model. *Educational Psychologist, 46,* 48–70.

Bråten, I., Ferguson, L. E., Strømsø, H. I., & Anmarkrud, Ø. (2013). Justification beliefs and multiple-documents comprehension. *European Journal of Psychology of Education, 28,* 879–902.

Bråten, I., Gil, L., Strømsø, H. I., & Vidal-Abarca, E. (2009). Personal epistemology across cultures: Exploring Norwegian and Spanish university students' epistemic beliefs about climate change. *Social Psychology of Education, 12,* 529–560.

Bråten, I., & Strømsø, H. I. (2010a). Effects of task instruction and personal epistemology on the understanding of multiple texts about climate change. *Discourse Processes, 47,* 1–31.

Bråten, I., & Strømsø, H. I. (2010b). When law students read multiple documents about global warming: Examining the role of topic-specific beliefs about the nature of knowledge and knowing. *Instructional Science, 38,* 635–657.

Bråten, I., Strømsø, H. I., & Samuelstuen, M. S. (2008). Are sophisticated students always better? The role of topic-specific personal epistemology in the understanding of multiple expository texts. *Contemporary Educational Psychology, 33,* 814–840.

Bromme, R., Kienhues, D., & Stahl, E. (2008). Knowledge and epistemological beliefs: An intimate but complicate relationship. In M. S. Khine (Ed.), *Knowing, knowledge, and beliefs: Epistemological studies across diverse cultures* (pp. 423–441). New York: Springer.

Buehl, M. M., & Alexander, P. A. (2005). Motivation and performance differences in students' domain-specific epistemological belief profiles. *American Educational Research Journal, 42,* 697–726.

Chinn, C. A., Buckland, L. A., & Samarapungavan, A. (2011). Expanding the dimensions of epistemic cognition: Arguments from philosophy and psychology. *Educational Psychologist, 46,* 141–167.

Chiu, Y.-L., Liang, J.-C., & Tsai., C.-C. (2013). Internet-specific beliefs and self-regulated learning in online academic information searching. *Metacognition and Learning, 8,* 235–260.

Conley, A. M., Pintrich, P. R., Vekiri, I., & Harrison, D. (2004). Changes in epistemological beliefs in elementary science students. *Contemporary Educational Psychology, 29,* 186–204.

Ferguson, L. E., & Bråten, I. (2013). Student profiles of knowledge and epistemic beliefs: Changes and relations to multiple-text comprehension. *Learning and Instruction, 25,* 49–61.

Ferguson, L. E., Bråten, I., & Strømsø, H. I. (2012). Epistemic cognition when students read multiple documents containing conflicting scientific evidence: A think-aloud study. *Learning and Instruction, 22,* 103–120.

Ferguson, L. E., Bråten, I., Strømsø, H. I., & Anmarkrud, Ø. (2013). Epistemic beliefs and comprehension in the context of reading multiple documents: Examining the role of conflict. *International Journal of Educational Research, 62*, 100–114.

Franco, G. M., Muis, K. R., Kendeou, P., Ranellucci, J., Sampasivam, L., & Wang, X. (2012). Examining the influences of epistemic beliefs and knowledge representations on cognitive processing and conceptual change when learning physics. *Learning and Instruction, 22*, 62–77.

Graesser, A. C., Singer, M., & Trabasso, T. (1994). Constructing inferences during narrative text comprehension. *Psychological Review, 101*, 371–395.

Greene, J. A., Azevedo, R., & Torney-Purta, J. (2008). Modeling epistemic and ontological cognition: Philosophical perspectives and methodological directions. *Educational Psychologist, 43*, 142–160.

Greene, J. A., Muis, K. R., & Pieschl, S. (2010). The role of epistemic beliefs in students' self-regulated learning with computer-based learning environments: Conceptual and methodological issues. *Educational Psychologist, 45*, 245–257.

Guthrie, J. T., & Wigfield, A. (2000). Engagement and motivation in reading. In M. L. Kamil, P. B. Mosenthal, P. D. Pearson, & R. Barr (Eds.), *Handbook of reading research* (Vol. 3, pp. 403–422). Mahwah, NJ: Erlbaum.

Hofer, B. K. (2000). Dimensionality and disciplinary differences in personal epistemology. *Contemporary Educational Psychology, 25*, 378–405.

Hofer, B. K. (2004). Epistemological understanding as a metacognitive process: Thinking aloud during online searching. *Educational Psychologist, 39*, 43–55.

Hofer, B. K., & Bendixen, L. D. (2012). Personal epistemology: Theory, research, and future directions. In K. R. Harris, S. Graham, & T. Urdan (Eds.), *APA educational psychology handbook: Vol. 1. Theories, constructs, and critical issues* (pp. 227–256). Washington, DC: American Psychological Association.

Hofer, B. K., & Pintrich, P. R. (1997). The development of epistemological theories: Beliefs about knowledge and knowing and their relation to learning. *Review of Educational Research, 67*, 88–140.

Kammerer, Y., Bråten, I., Gerjets, P., & Strømsø, H. I. (2013). The role of Internet-specific epistemic beliefs in laypersons' source evaluations and decisions during Web search on a medical issue. *Computers in Human Behavior, 29*, 1193–1203.

Kardash, C. M., & Howell, K. L. (2000). Effects of epistemological beliefs and topic-specific beliefs on undergraduates' cognitive and strategic processing of dual-positional text. *Journal of Educational Psychology, 92*, 524–535.

Kardash, C. M., & Scholes, R. J. (1996). Effects of preexisting beliefs, epistemological beliefs, and need for cognition on interpretation of controversial issues. *Journal of Educational Psychology, 88*, 260–271.

Kendeou, P., Muis, K. R., & Fulton, S. (2011). Reader and text factors in reading comprehension processes. *Journal of Research in Reading, 34*, 365–383.

Kienhues, D., Stadtler, M., & Bromme, R. (2011). Dealing with conflicting or consistent medical information on the web: When expert information breeds laypersons' doubts about experts. *Learning and Instruction, 21*, 193–204.

King, P. M., & Kitchener, K. S. (1994) *Developing reflective judgment: Understanding and promoting intellectual growth and critical thinking in adolescents and adults.* San Francisco, CA: Jossey-Bass.

Kintsch, W. (1988). The role of knowledge in discourse comprehension: A construction-integration model. *Psychological Review, 95*, 163–182.

Kuhn, D. (1991). *The skills of argument.* Cambridge, UK: Cambridge University Press.

Kuhn, D., Cheney, R., & Weinstock, M. (2000). The development of epistemological understanding. *Cognitive Development, 15*, 309–328.

Mason, L., Ariasi, N., & Boldrin, A. (2011). Epistemic beliefs in action: Spontaneous reflections about knowledge and knowing during online information searching and their influence on learning. *Learning and Instruction, 21*, 137–151.

Mason, L., & Boscolo, P. (2004). Role of epistemological understanding and interest in interpreting a controversy and in topic-specific belief change. *Contemporary Educational Psychology, 29*, 103–128.

Mason, L., Gava, M., & Boldrin, A. (2008). On warm conceptual change: The interplay of text, epistemological beliefs, and topic interest. *Journal of Educational Psychology, 100*, 291–309.

Mason, L., & Scirica, F. (2006). Prediction of students' argumentation skills about controversial topics by epistemological understanding. *Learning and Instruction, 16*, 492–509.

Mason, L., Scirica, F., & Salvi, L. (2006). Effects of beliefs about meaning construction and task instructions on interpretation of narrative text. *Contemporary Educational Psychology, 31*, 411–437.

Muis, K. R., Bendixen, L. D., & Haerle, F. C. (2006). Domain-generality and domain-specificity in personal epistemology research: Philosophical and empirical reflections in the development of a theoretical framework. *Educational Psychology Review*, *18*, 3–54.

Muis, K. R., & Duffy, M. C. (2013). Epistemic climate and epistemic change: Instruction designed to change students' beliefs and learning strategies and improve achievement. *Journal of Educational Psychology*, *105*, 213–225.

Murphy, P. K., & Mason, L. (2006). Changing knowledge and beliefs. In P. A. Alexander & P. H. Winne (Eds.), *Handbook of educational psychology* (2nd ed., pp. 305–324). Mahwah, NJ: Erlbaum.

Perfetti, C. A., Rouet, J. F., & Britt, M. A. (1999). Toward a theory of documents representation. In H. van Oostendorp & S. R. Goldman (Eds.), *The construction of mental representation during reading* (pp. 99–122). Mahwah, NJ: Erlbaum.

Perry, W. G. (1970). *Forms of intellectual and ethical development in the college years: A scheme*. New York: Holt, Rinehart, & Winston.

Pieschl, S., Stahl, E., & Bromme, R. (2008). Epistemological beliefs and self-regulated learning with hypertext. *Metacognition and Learning*, *3*, 17–37.

Porsch, T., & Bromme, R. (2011). Effects of epistemological sensitization on source choices. *Instructional Science*, *39*, 805–819.

Rouet, J. F. (2006). *The skills of document use: From text comprehension to Web-based learning*. Mahwah, NJ: Erlbaum.

Royce, J. R. (1978). Three ways of knowing and the scientific world view. *Methodology and Science*, *11*, 146–164.

Sandoval, W. A., & Morrison, K. (2003). High school students' ideas about theories and theory change after a biological inquiry unit. *Journal of Research in Science Teaching*, *40*, 369–392.

Schommer, M. (1990). Effects of beliefs about the nature of knowledge on comprehension. *Journal of Educational Psychology*, *82*, 498–504.

Schommer, M., Crouse, A., & Rhodes, N. (1992). Epistemological beliefs and mathematical text comprehension: Believing it is simple does not make it so. *Journal of Educational Psychology*, *84*, 435–443.

Schraw, G. (2000). Reader beliefs and meaning construction in narrative text. *Journal of Educational Psychology*, *92*, 96–106.

Schraw, G., Bendixen, L. D., & Dunkle, M. E. (2002). Development and validation of the Epistemic Belief Inventory (EBI). In B. K. Hofer & P. R. Pintrich (Eds.), *Personal epistemology: The psychology of beliefs about knowledge and knowing* (pp. 261–275). Mahwah, NJ: Erlbaum.

Schraw, G., & Bruning, R. (1996). Readers' implicit models of reading. *Reading Research Quarterly*, *31*, 290–305.

Spiro, R. J., Feltovich, P. J., & Coulson, R. L. (1996). Two epistemic world-views: Prefigurative schemas and learning in complex domains. *Applied Cognitive Psychology*, *10*, S51–S61.

Stahl, E., & Bromme, R. (2007). The CAEB: An instrument for measuring connotative aspects of epistemological beliefs. *Learning and Instruction*, *17*, 773–785.

Strømsø, H. I., & Bråten, I. (2009). Beliefs about knowledge and knowing and multiple-text comprehension among upper secondary students. *Educational Psychology*, *29*, 425–445.

Strømsø, H. I., & Bråten, I. (2010). The role of personal epistemology in the self-regulation of Internet-based learning. *Metacognition and Learning*, *5*, 91–111.

Strømsø, H. I., Bråten, I., & Britt, M. A. (2011). Do students' beliefs about knowledge and knowing predict their judgment of texts' trustworthiness? *Educational Psychology*, *31*, 177–206.

Strømsø, H. I., Bråten, I., & Samuelstuen, M. S. (2008). Dimensions of topic-specific epistemological beliefs as predictors of multiple text understanding. *Learning and Instruction*, *18*, 513–527.

Tsai, C.-C. (2004). Beyond cognitive and metacognitive tools: The use of the Internet as an "epistemological" tool for instruction. *British Journal of Educational Technology*, *35*, 525–536.

Wineburg, S. (1998). Reading Abraham Lincoln: An expert/expert study in the interpretation of historical texts. *Cognitive Science*, *22*, 319–346.

# 7

# Individual Differences in Phonological Awareness and Their Role in Learning to Read

*Jamie M. Quinn, Mercedes Spencer, and Richard K. Wagner*

Phonological awareness is one of the most important predictors of reading in normally developing children (McBride-Chang & Kail, 2002; Schatschneider, Fletcher, Francis, Carlson, & Foorman, 2004; Vloedgraven & Verhoeven, 2009; Wagner & Torgesen, 1987). In addition, deficits in phonological processing are a hallmark of individuals with reading problems (Al Otaiba & Fuchs, 2002; Olson, Forsberg, & Rack, 1994; Stanovich, 1988; Vellutino, Fletcher, Snowling, & Scanlon, 2004).

By way of organization, this chapter is divided into three sections. In the first section, we introduce the topic of individual differences in phonological awareness by considering common conceptualizations, dimensionality of the construct, the development of phonological awareness, and common predictors of individual differences in phonological awareness. In the second section, we consider potentially causal influences of individual differences in phonological awareness on the acquisition of beginning reading skills, and conversely, the effects of learning to read on the subsequent development of phonological awareness. In the third and final section, we draw some conclusions about the nature of individual differences in phonological awareness and their relations with reading, and consider some implications for practice.

## Individual Differences in Phonological Awareness

### Common Conceptualizations

*Phonological awareness* broadly refers to awareness of and access to the sound structure of oral language (Vloedgraven & Verhoeven, 2009; Wagner & Torgesen, 1987). This term encompasses awareness of all the sound structure of oral language, ranging from awareness of rhyme to the awareness of an individual sound in a consonant cluster (e.g., string). The commonly used term *phonemic awareness* refers to a specific kind of phonological awareness, namely, awareness of phonemes, a phonological unit that roughly corresponds to the sounds of the letters in an alphabetic writing system. The term *phonological sensitivity* was introduced to refer to early, rudimentary forms of full-blown phonological awareness (Bowey, 2002; Stanovich, 1992).

Wagner and Torgesen (1987) conceptualized phonological awareness as one of three key reading-related phonological processes. The second key reading-related phonological process is phonological recoding in lexical access, which refers to recoding written symbols into sounds as a means of accessing lexical entries in long-term memory for words. The final key reading-related phonological process is phonetic recoding in working memory (also called phonological memory), which refers to using phonological codes for short-term storage of linguistic information. Each of these kinds of phonological processing is related to individual differences in early reading (Bradley & Bryant, 1983; Siegel, 1993; Treiman, Freyd, & Baron, 1983).

## Dimensionality of Phonological Awareness

The dimensionality of phonological awareness has been subject to considerable investigation. Carroll, Snowling, Hulme, and Stevenson (2003) reported a two-factor structure in their longitudinal study, with rhyming and phoneme tasks representing separable though correlated abilities. Wagner, Torgesen, Laughon, Simmons, and Rashotte (1993) found the best fitting confirmatory factor analysis model for seven phonological awareness tasks was a two-factor correlated model: phonological synthesis (the three blending tasks: onset and rime, blending phonemes into words, and blending phonemes into nonwords) and phonological analysis (the four analysis tasks: phoneme elision, sound categorization, first sound comparison, and phoneme segmentation). The synthesis tasks measured how well children could blend isolated onsets, rimes, and phonemes together to create words or nonwords, whereas the analysis tasks measured how well children could remove, categorize, separate, and compare phonemes in real words.

In contrast, three early investigations of dimensionality provided evidence that phonological awareness is a unidimensional construct (Stahl & Murray, 1994; Stanovich, Cunningham, & Cramer, 1984; Yopp, 1988). However, these studies had limited sample sizes and restricted age ranges (Schatschneider et al., 2004). Wagner and colleagues (1997) reported good fit for a model that specified phonological awareness as a second-order factor with analysis and synthesis representing first-order factors that differed primarily in task requirements as opposed to more fundamental aspects of phonological awareness. Schatschneider et al. (1999) investigated the factor structure of seven phonological awareness tasks using an item response theory model and the results supported phonological awareness as a unidimensional factor. A second item response theory modeling study also supported a unidimensional factor for phonological awareness (Vloedgraven & Verhoeven, 2009).

Overall, the results suggest that the dimensionality of phonological awareness is largely characterized by a single, underlying dimension, with method variance associated with task differences as a likely explanation for results that suggest more than one dimension. Phonological awareness tasks differ in required strategies and processing requirements such as working memory. For example, blending phonemes, which refers to blending the segments associated with the sound of the letters "p," "o," "t," and "s" into the word "pots," requires a different strategy and less working memory than does phoneme reversal, which refers to reversing the order of the sounds in "pots" to get "stop."

# Development of Phonological Awareness

## Prelinguistic Developmental Trends

Acquisition of rudimentary forms of phonological awareness occurs rapidly in the first few years of life (Torgesen, & Mathes, 2000). Within the first year, infants are readily acquiring knowledge about common speech sounds present in their native language and are capable of prelinguistic forms of communication (e.g., crying, laughing, gesturing, reaching; Jusczyk, Luce, & Charles-Luce, 1994). Although actions such as crying or gesturing are not considered forms of meaningful language, they tend to be effective in regulating the behaviors of others and give rise to cooing and other vocalizations (Stoel-Gammon, 2011). Children as young as eight months old are capable of understanding word boundaries within speech (Saffran, Aslin, & Newport, 1996). This understanding appears to support word learning and the potential for phonological sensitivity (Aslin, Woodward, LaMendola, & Bever, 1996). Around this time, infants also begin to engage in more intentional vocalizations (i.e., babbling) that eventually give rise to meaningful verbalizations, and typically developing infants tend to exhibit fairly regular patterns of simple words and syllables (e.g., CVC, CVCV) that can be understood by adults (Coplan & Gleason, 1988).

By two years of age, children's vocabularies expand to 300 words on average (Lee, 2011). Children at this age display a working knowledge of several lexical characteristics, including basic word structures, syllables, and sound classes (Stoel-Gammon, 1987). Additionally, young children's capacity to create representations for words that are presented to them only one or two times indicates they are using various kinds of word-level information—including phonological information—to assist their early linguistic acquisition (Carey, 1978).

## The Emergence of Phonological Awareness

Children develop phonological awareness by the time they are three or four years old (Wagner et al., 1987), with some reporting awareness as early as two years of age (Lonigan, Burgess, Anthony, & Barker, 1998). At the start of kindergarten, most children already show word awareness, should be able to isolate words from a stream of speech, and display awareness for rhyming words (Torgesen & Mathes, 1998). Further, a child should be able to segment simple consonant–vowel–consonant syllables into the onset, which refers to any consonants before a vowel within a syllable, and rime, which refers to the vowel and remaining consonants within a syllable (Liberman, Shankweiler, Fischer, & Carter, 1974). For example, for the multisyllabic word *baseball*, the first syllable contains the onset *b* and rime *ase* while the second syllable contains the onset *b* and rime *all*. Towards the end of kindergarten, children should be able to isolate beginning sounds in words, such as the /k/ in *cat* and engage in phoneme blending, such that they should understand the isolated sounds of /b/ /oi/ can be blended to make the word *boy* (Anthony, Lonigan, Driscoll, Phillips, & Burgess, 2003; Fowler, 1991; Lonigan, Burgess, & Anthony, 2000). Liberman et al. (1974) found that only about 50 percent of 4- and 5-year-old children were able to tap out the number of syllables within a multisyllabic word whereas 90 percent of 6-year-old children were able to successfully complete this task. Similarly, Treiman and Zukowski (1991, 1996) reported that children as young as 4 years old can perform onset-rime tasks correctly as much as 56 percent of the time. Performance increases to 100 percent in 6-year-old children, indicating children are continuously improving upon their phonological skills well beyond preschool and kindergarten.

Phonological awareness has a fairly stable and predictable developmental trajectory in typically developing children (see Anthony, & Francis, 2005). For instance, children cannot detect or manipulate phonemes prior to being able to detect or manipulate rimes or onsets, and children cannot detect or manipulate rimes or onsets prior to being able to detect syllables (Goswami, & Bryant, 1990; Liberman & Shankweiler, 1985; Liberman et al., 1974). Further, children's ability to detect phonologically similar or dissimilar words develops prior to their ability to phonologically manipulate or segment words (e.g., Anthony et al., 2003; Carroll et al., 2003).

What underlies this fairly steady developmental progression of children's phonological awareness is not known definitively. One plausible explanation is the lexical restructuring hypothesis (Fowler, 1991; Walley, 1993). Infants and toddlers process words in a whole-unit fashion and very rarely engage in active phonetic decomposition (Fowler, 1991). This holistic approach most likely occurs because very young children tend to have only a few words within their lexicon, many of which are phonemically distinct (e.g., *bye* and *stop*), making it relatively unnecessary for them to have more detailed word representations.

However, as children mature, sensitivity to within-word information becomes more refined due to an expanding vocabulary that includes similar sounding words (Nagy, Anderson, & Herman, 1987). Developing children must engage in lexical restructuring and refine their phonological sensitivity because they need to distinguish between words that have increased phonetic similarity (e.g., *met* and *mat*) (Locke, 1988; Walley, Metsala, & Garlock, 2003). Yet, lexical restructuring does not happen all at once and depends on a number of factors, including lexical neighborhood density and word frequency and familiarity (for a review, see Walley et al., 2003).

## Predictors of Individual Differences in Phonological Awareness

Individual differences in phonological awareness are pronounced and measurable. What predicts individual differences in phonological awareness has been a topic of great research interest. Beginning with rudimentary forms of phonological awareness, an analysis of babbling determined that infants whose babbling contained greater percentages of true consonants were more likely to achieve greater phonological proficiency by age 3 (Vihman & Greenlee, 1987). Certain pre-speech tendencies have also been identified as potentially influential to early phonological development (e.g., Vihman, Ferguson, & Elbert, 1986).

The age at which words are acquired and the relative neighborhood density of known words (i.e., the number of words that are phonologically similar to a target word) are predictors of individual differences in phonological awareness (De Cara & Goswami, 2003; Gerhand & Barry, 1999; Walley & Metsala, 1992). For example, Garlock, Walley, and Metsala (2001) examined the effect of word frequency, age of acquisition, and neighborhood density in 64 preschool and kindergarten children, 64 elementary-aged children, and 64 adults. They found that the age of acquisition and lexical neighborhood density affected all groups' spoken word recognition ability. Further, for the children in their sample, recognizing early-acquired words from sparse neighborhoods contributed to their phonological awareness.

One potentially important source of individual differences in phonological awareness is individual differences in the quality of underlying phonological representations (Boada & Pennington, 2006; Elbro, Borstrøm, & Petersen, 1998; Elbro & Pallesen, 2002). The quality of underlying phonological representations refers to the accuracy with which individual sounds and strings of sounds are stored in long-term memory. Individuals with poorer representations (i.e., inaccurate or incomplete) tend to have weaker phonological skills as well as weaknesses in other literacy-related skills (Carroll & Snowling, 2004; Elbro & Jensen, 2005; Fowler, 1991; Swan & Goswami, 1997).

Oral language exposure, the simplicity of syllable structures, and the saliency and complexity of onsets have also been identified as factors that are related to performance on phonological awareness measures (Cooper, Roth, Speece, & Schatschneider, 2002; Cossu, Shankweiler,

Liberman, Katz, & Tola, 1988). Acquisition of phonological skills is affected by vowel and consonant harmony, which are phonological constraints that require vowels or consonants to belong to particular classes. For example, Durgunoğlu and Öney (1999) investigated the effect of vowel and consonant harmony on the phonological development in 138 Turkish- and English-speaking kindergarten students. Results indicated that the Turkish-speaking students were better at syllable manipulation and phoneme deletion tasks. Because the Turkish language requires vowel harmony when multiple affixes are linked, this suggests that harmony affects phonological awareness.

Children whose languages are orthographically transparent (e.g., Italian) are better at phonological awareness tasks than children whose languages are less transparent (e.g., English) (Cossu et al., 1988; Tyler & Burnham, 2006). Further, certain types of text-based pre-reading skills have been found to influence the acquisition of phonological awareness. For example, Burgess and Lonigan (1998) investigated the longitudinal effects of letter knowledge on phonological sensitivity of 97 children aged 4 and 5. Results suggested potential bidirectional relations: Phonological sensitivity uniquely contributed to letter name and letter sound knowledge; letter knowledge in turn was found to significantly predict future acquisition of phonological sensitivity. Furthermore, previous experience with letters and words can affect phonological representations (e.g., Byrne & Liberman, 1999).

Finally, several studies have examined relations between working memory or short-term memory and phonological awareness, on the basis of the fact that processing of phonological information should theoretically occur within the phonological loop of working memory (see Baddeley & Hitch, 1974; Leather & Henry, 1994; Rohl & Pratt, 1995). Strong correlations are typically found between measures of phonological awareness and short-term, phonological memory, especially when multiple indicators are used to allow the creation of more reliable latent variables. For example, the Comprehensive Test of Phonological Processing (Wagner, Torgesen, Rashotte, & Pearson, 2013) has subtests that measure both phonological awareness and phonological memory. Confirmatory factor analyses of data from a nationally representative normative sample resulted in correlations between phonological awareness and phonological memory of .73 for the 4-to-6-year-old version and .67 for the 7-to-21-year-old version. When both phonological awareness and phonological memory are used as simultaneous predictors of reading, phonological memory does not typically account for variance independent of phonological awareness because they are highly correlated constructs and because phonological awareness tends to be more strongly related to early reading than is phonological memory (Oakhill & Kyle, 2000; Snowling, Hulme, Smith, & Thomas, 1994).

## Causal Relations between the Development of Phonological Awareness and Reading

A reason for the extraordinary interest shown in the construct of phonological awareness is a belief that it is related to the acquisition of beginning reading skills and that it may also be a cause of reading disability (Brady, Braze, & Fowler, 2011). We know that performance on measures of phonological awareness is correlated with performance on measures of decoding, but what underlies this correlation? Three alternative hypotheses will be considered in turn.

### Phonological Awareness Plays a Causal Role in Learning to Read

The first hypothesis is that individual differences in phonological awareness play a causal role in learning to read. Consider the English spoken words "cat," "rat," and "hat." A child with a well-developed level of phonological awareness is likely to be able to hear that these three words have different sounds in the beginning and roughly the same sounds in the middle and end. The similarities and differences between these spoken words are reflected in their English spellings: They have different initial letters and identical medial and final letters. Consequently, a child with a well-developed level of phonological awareness is likely to find alphabetic writing systems to be a sensible way to represent speech by print. Conversely, a child lacking phonological awareness is likely to find the writing system to be quite arbitrary.

Stanovich (1993) argued that phonological awareness is a "good predictor not just because it is an incidental correlate of something else," but that it is fundamental to understanding letter–sound relations (Stanovich, 1993, p. 28). Evidence that phonological processing enables or facilitates acquisition of early spelling and reading abilities comes from a number of longitudinal studies in which structural equation modeling was used to demonstrate that early phonological awareness is related to later reading independently of the autoregressive effect of early reading on later reading (e.g., Aarnoutse, van Leeuwe, & Verhoeven, 2005; de Jong & van der Leij, 2002; Wagner, Torgesen, & Rashotte, 1994; Wagner et al., 1997). Complementing the evidence of causal relations between the development of phonological awareness and learning to read from longitudinal correlational studies is evidence from experimental studies that training in phonological awareness facilitates the development of reading (Bradley, & Bryant, 1983; Carroll et al., 2003).

Castles and Coltheart (2004) reviewed the evidence from longitudinal correlational studies and training studies to determine the extent to which the literature supported the conclusion that phonological awareness played a causal role in the acquisition of early reading skills. Beginning with longitudinal correlational studies, they concluded that any causal role phonological awareness plays in learning to read and write is likely due to phonemic awareness (e.g., Hulme et al., 2002; Perfetti, Beck, Bell, & Hughes, 1987; Stuart, 1995). They did not find evidence in the literature to support syllabic awareness as playing a causal role in the acquisition of reading. They reached the same conclusion about rhyme awareness despite mixed results. They cited methodological limitations in two studies that were supportive of causal relations between rhyme awareness and learning to read (Bryant, MacLean, Bradley, & Crossland, 1990; Muter, Hulme, Snowling, & Taylor, 1998), and they cited other studies that reported null effects (e.g., Duncan, Seymour, & Hill, 1997; Stuart, 1995). However, other studies did support a role for rhyme awareness in learning to read (Bowey, 2002).

Turning to training and intervention studies, Castles and Coltheart (2004) imposed relatively strict criteria on what constitutes evidence that training in phonological awareness improves reading. For example, the training program could only include training in phonological awareness, and participants were required to have no preexisting letter-sound knowledge. These criteria were imposed to rule out the possibility that what was really being trained was phonics (i.e., knowledge of letter–sound correspondences), which is known to be an effective way to teach early reading, as opposed to phonological awareness per se. Unfortunately, most of the literature consists of studies with participants who were old enough (i.e., kindergarten and beyond) to have some letter knowledge, and combining phonological awareness training activities with activities designed to foster letter sound knowledge is common. After adopting their exclusionary criteria, they concluded that there is no substantial evidence of a causal role for phonemic awareness in early reading and spelling acquisition. Hulme, Snowling, Caravolas, and Carroll (2005) criticized the exclusionary criteria Castles and Coltheart used as unnecessary and as hindering their ability to detect causal relations. Hulme et al. argued that there is plenty of evidence available for establishing a causal influence of phonological awareness on early reading, particularly when mediating pathways are considered.

Most of the research on potentially causal influences of phonological awareness on learning to read reviewed so far has been limited to studies of young children learning to read alphabetic languages, primarily English. Given this state of affairs, it is not surprising that explanations for a causal influence of phonological awareness on learning to read have focused on characteristics of learning to read an alphabet.

All English words can be pronounced by stringing together members from a set of from 35 to 45 phonemes or basic sounds that make a difference in meaning. The range in phoneme set size reflects different systems of classification. There is a rough correspondence between phonemes and letters of the alphabet. Given this correspondence, learning to read an alphabetic language such as English takes off when children begin to recognize the alphabetical principle that describes relations between phonemes and letters (Adams, 1990; Snow, Burns, & Griffin, 1998).

This explanation of why phonological awareness influences the acquisition of beginning reading skills has been challenged by the fact that phonological awareness remains a good predictor of early reading acquisition in non-alphabetic languages such as Chinese (e.g., Ho & Bryant, 1997; McBride-Chang & Kail, 2002). There do appear to be differences in which aspects of phonological awareness are related to reading acquisition and when, depending on the kind of written script that must be learned and whether the relation between spoken and written language is relatively transparent or opaque (Öney & Durgunoğlu, 1997; McBride-Chang et al., 2002; Treiman & Zukowski, 1991). But the basic fact that phonological awareness is universally related to learning to read regardless of the nature of the written script suggests that an explanation grounded in the alphabetic principle is wrong. Perhaps the explanation of the universal relation between phonological awareness and learning to read reflects the fact that all written scripts convey information about pronunciation as well as meaning, and that it is the link between phonological awareness and pronunciation that underlies the observed relation.

## Learning to Read Facilitates Development of Phonological Awareness

The second hypothesis about the basis for the observed correlation between measures of phonological awareness and decoding is that the early development of reading and writing skills has a causal influence on the subsequent development of phonological awareness (Ehri, 1987). The rationale for this hypothesis assumes an alphabetic writing system and applies to phonemic awareness, which refers to phonological awareness that involves phonemes as the linguistic unit. If letters in an alphabet roughly correspond to phonemes in an oral language, and phonemes are abstract units rather than something that can be observed directly in the acoustic spectrum, learning letters and their sounds provides a concrete representation of phonemes and thereby enhances phonological awareness. Support for this hypothesis comes from a number of sources. First, phonemic awareness typically does not develop until children are taught to read and write (see Goswami, & Bryant, 1990, for an overview). This fact was first noted in a seminal study by Liberman et al. (1974), who found that no child in pre-kindergarten could segment words into phonemes whereas almost half (46 percent) could segment words into syllables. Relatedly, Morais, Cary, Alegria, and Bertelsons (1979) reported that illiterate Portuguese adults performed worse on measures of phonological awareness than did formerly illiterate Portuguese adults who had been taught to read. A second source of support for this hypothesis comes from the observation that some children use spelling strategies on some measures of phonological awareness. This is readily apparent on the phoneme reversal task, a measure of phonological awareness that requires reversing the order of sounds in a spoken word. For example, if the target word is "tab," the correct response would be "bat," which is "tab" with the phonemes put in reverse order. Phoneme reversal is more difficult for items that have silent letters (e.g., "knead" becomes "dean"), presumably because this penalizes use of spelling strategies. Finally, Chinese readers who learned pinyin, which is an alphabetic transcription of Chinese, perform better on measures of phonological awareness than do Chinese readers who do not learn pinyin (Read, Yun-Fei, Hong-Yin, & Bao-Qing, 1986).

## Bidirectional and Reciprocal Influences of Phonological Awareness and Reading

A third hypothesis about the basis for the observed correlation between measures of phonological awareness and decoding represents a combination of the first two hypotheses, namely, that bidirectional causal influences exist. Direct support for this hypothesis comes from causal modeling of longitudinal data from studies that were designed to test for causal influences from phonological awareness to decoding and from decoding to phonological awareness (Burgess & Lonigan, 1998; Perfetti et al., 1987; Wagner et al., 1994). Indirect support for this hypothesis comes from the evidence that supported each of the first two hypotheses.

# Conclusions

Phonological awareness is an oral language skill that refers to one's awareness of and access to the sounds of one's oral language. Results from a number of confirmatory factor analyses and also from item response theory modeling of phonological awareness item sets suggest that the construct of phonological awareness is characterized by a single, underlying dimension, with differences in what is measured by various phonological awareness tasks being attributable to method variance rather than multiple forms of phonological awareness.

The development of phonological awareness has been investigated extensively. A clear developmental progression in phonological awareness is well established, characterized by awareness of successively smaller phonological units (i.e., compound words, syllables, onsets and rime, individual phonemes, and phonemes in consonant clusters). It is not known with certainty what drives this developmental progression. One plausible candidate is that as vocabulary increases in size with development, the lexicon or internal dictionary is restructured to accommodate the need to access individual entries from an expanding universe of similar sounding words.

Individual differences in phonological awareness may be pronounced and can be measured reliably. A number of predictors of individual differences in phonological awareness have been investigated. It is clear that differences in phonological awareness are associated with differences in both oral language development and perhaps also with differences in the nature of the written script that has been learned. Individual differences in the quality of underlying phonological representations have been proposed as an explanation for observed individual differences in phonological awareness.

Phonological awareness is of particular interest because it appears to be related to the normal acquisition of beginning reading skills and because a deficit in phonological awareness is a hallmark of reading disability. Substantial evidence exists that individual differences in phonological awareness exert a causal influence on the development of early reading skills. Conversely, learning to read appears to exert a causal influence on the subsequent development of phonological awareness, particularly phonemic awareness. Individuals with reading disability perform more poorly on measures of phonological awareness than do normal readers.

Regarding implications for practice, knowledge about phonological awareness and its role in the development of reading skills has been translated into changes in assessment practices used with individuals who are suspected of having reading problems and in how reading is taught. Beginning with assessment practices, tests of phonological awareness are commonly administered to individuals who are reported to have reading- or language-related problems. For example, the Comprehensive Test of Phonological Processing (CTOPP-2) (Wagner et al., 2013) contains six subtests that measure phonological awareness. Elision requires saying a word after dropping out a phonological segment (e.g., Say cat. Now say cat without saying /k/). Blending Words requires combining phonological segments that are presented separately into a whole word (e.g., What word do these sounds make? r-e-d). Blending Nonwords is identical to blending words except that the stimuli are nonwords. Sound Matching involves presenting a target word and then identifying which response item has the same first or last sound as the target word. Phoneme Isolation requires identifying a target sound in a word (e.g., What is the middle sound in the word take?). Finally, Segmenting Nonwords requires segmenting a nonword into its separate sounds (e.g., Say frab one sound at a time).

Turning to instruction, the major reading series used in the United States all include instruction and practice in phonological awareness activities. The importance of phonological awareness to reading instruction appears to be greater during the initial years of reading instruction relative to later years (Snowling, 1987). In their meta-analyses, moderate-to-strong overall effect sizes were found for reading instruction that includes explicit instruction in phonological awareness relative to comparable instruction that does not include phonological awareness instruction (Bus & Van Ijzendoorn, 1999; National Reading Panel, 2000).

Whereas most children seem to develop sufficient levels of phonological awareness to facilitate beginning reading, some children do not. Instruction that helps children with poor phonological awareness identify the sounds in their oral language can improve both phonological awareness and early reading, particularly when letters are used as a concrete representation of sounds (National Reading Panel, 2000).

In summary, growth in our understanding of individual differences in phonological awareness and their relations with the development of reading and of reading problems has happened at a remarkable pace over the past 30 years. Our increased understanding has been translated into profound changes in the nature of reading instruction and in the kind of assessments that are done when individuals appear to have a reading problem.

## Acknowledgments

Support for writing this chapter was provided by grant number P50 HD052120 from the *Eunice Kennedy Shriver* National Institute of Child Health and Human Development and by Predoctoral Interdisciplinary Research Training Fellowships R305B04074 and R305B090021 from the Institute for Education Sciences to the first two authors.

## References

Aarnoutse, C., van Leeuwe, J., & Verhoeven, L. (2005). Early literacy from a longitudinal perspective. *Educational Research and Evaluation: An International Journal on Theory and Practice, 11*, 253–275.

Adams, M. J. (1990). *Beginning to read: Thinking and learning about print*. Cambridge, MA: MIT Press.

Al Otaiba, S., & Fuchs, D. (2002). Characteristics of children who are unresponsive to early literacy intervention: A review of the literature. *Remedial and Special Education, 23*, 300–316.

Anthony, J. L., & Francis, D. J. (2005). Development of phonological awareness. *Current Directions in Psychological Science, 14*(5), 255–259. doi:http://dx.doi.org/10.1111/j.0963–7214.2005.00376.x

Anthony, J. L., Lonigan, C. J., Driscoll, K., Phillips, B. M., & Burgess, S. R. (2003). Phonological sensitivity: A quasi-parallel progression of word structure units and cognitive operations. *Reading Research Quarterly*, *38*(4), 470–487. doi:http://dx.doi.org/10.1598/RRQ.38.4.3

Aslin, R. N., Woodward, J. Z., LaMendola, N. P., & Bever, T. G. (1996). Models of word segmentation in fluent maternal speech to infants. In J. L. Morgan & K. Demuth (Eds.), *Signal to syntax: Bootstrapping from speech to grammar in early acquisition* (pp. 117–134). Hillsdale, NJ: Lawrence Erlbaum Associates.

Baddeley, A. D., & Hitch, G. J. (1974). Working memory. In G. H. Bower (Ed.), *The psychology of learning and motivation* (Vol. 8, pp. 47–89). New York: Academic Press.

Boada, R., & Pennington, B. F. (2006). Deficient implicit phonological representations in children with dyslexia. *Journal of Experimental Child Psychology*, *95*(3), 153–193. doi:http://dx.doi.org/ 10.1016/ j.jecp.2006.04.003

Bowey, J. A. (2002). Reflections on onset-rime and phoneme sensitivity as predictors of beginning word reading. *Journal of Experimental Child Psychology*, *82*, 29–40. doi:http://dx.doi.org/ 10.1006/jecp. 2002.2671

Brady, S. A., Braze, D., & Fowler, C. A. (Eds.) (2011). *Explaining individual differences in reading*. New York: Psychology Press.

Bradley, L., & Bryant, P. E. (1983). Categorising sounds and learning to read: A causal connection. *Nature*, *310*, 419–421. doi:http://dx.doi.org/10.1038/301419a0

Bryant, P. E., MacLean, M., Bradley, L. L., & Crossland, J. (1990). Rhyme, alliteration, phoneme detection, and learning to read. *Developmental Psychology*, *26*, 429–438. doi:http://dx.doi.org/10.1037/0012-1649.26.3.429

Burgess, S. R., & Lonigan, C. J. (1998). Bidirectional relations of phonological sensitivity and prereading abilities: Evidence from a preschool sample. *Journal of Experimental Child Psychology*, *70*(2), 117–141. doi:http://dx.doi.org/10.1006/jecp.1998.2450

Bus, A. G., & Van Ijzendoorn, M. H. (1999). Phonological awareness and early reading: A meta-analysis of experimental training studies. *Journal of Educational Psychology*, *91*, 403–414. doi:http://dx.doi.org//0022-0663.91.3.403

Byrne, B., & Liberman, A. M. (1999). Meaninglessness, productivity and reading: Some observations about the relation between the alphabet and speech. In J. Oakhill & R. Beard (Eds.), *Reading development and the teaching of reading: A psychological perspective* (pp. 157–173). Oxford: Blackwell Science.

Carey, S. (1978). The child as word learner. In J. Bresnan, G. Miller, & M. Halle (Eds.), *Linguistic theory and psychological reality* (pp. 264–293). Cambridge, MA: MIT Press.

Carroll, J. M., Snowling, M. J., Hulme, C., & Stevenson, J. (2003). The development of phonological awareness in preschool children. *Developmental Psychology*, *39*, 913–923. doi:http://dx.doi.org/10.1037/0012-1649.39.5.913

Carroll, J. M., & Snowling, M. J. (2004). Language and phonological skills in children at high risk of reading difficulties. *Journal of Child Psychology and Psychiatry*, *45*(3), 631–640. doi:http://dx.doi.org/10.1111/j.1469-7610.2004.00252.x

Castles, A., & Coltheart, M. (2004). Is there a causal link from phonological awareness to success in learning to read? *Cognition*, *91*(1), 77–111. doi:http://dx.doi.org/10.1016/S0010-0277(03)00164-1

Cooper, D. H., Roth, F. P., Speece, D. L., & Schatschneider, C. (2002). The contribution of oral language skills to the development of phonological awareness. *Applied Psycholinguistics*, *23*(3), 399–416. doi:http://dx.doi.org/10.1017/S0142716402003053

Coplan, J., & Gleason, J. R. (1988). Unclear speech: Recognition and significance of unintelligible speech in preschool children. *Pediatrics*, *82*, 447–452.

Cossu, G., Shankweiler, D., Liberman, I. Y., Katz, L., & Tola, G. (1988). Awareness of phonological segments and reading ability in Italian children. *Applied Psycholinguistics*, *9*, 1–16. doi:http://dx.doi.org/10.1017/S0142716400000424

De Cara, B., & Goswami, U. (2003). Phonological neighbourhood density: Effects in a rhyme awareness task in five-year-old children. *Journal of Child Language*, *30*, 695–710. doi:http://dx.doi.org/10.1017/S0305000903005725

de Jong, P. F., & van der Leij, A. (2002). Effects of phonological abilities and linguistic comprehension on the development of reading. *Scientific Studies of Reading*, *6*, 51–77. doi:http://dx.doi.org/10.1207/S1532799XSSR0601_03

Duncan, L. G., Seymour, P. H. K., & Hill, S. (1997). How important are rhyme and analogy in beginning reading? *Cognition*, *63*, 171–208. doi:http://dx.doi.org/10.1016/S0010-0277(97)00001-2

Durgunoğlu, A. Y., & Öney, B. (1999). A cross-linguistic comparison of phonological awareness and word recognition. *Reading and Writing*, *11*(4), 281–299. doi: http://dx.doi.org/10.1023/A:1008093232622

Ehri, L. C. (1987). Learning to read and spell words. *Journal of Reading Behavior*, *19*, 5–31. doi:http://dx.doi.org/ 10.1080/10862968709547585

Elbro, C., Borstrøm, I., & Petersen, D. K. (1998). Predicting dyslexia from kindergarten: The importance of distinctness of phonological representations of lexical items. *Reading Research Quarterly*, *33*(1), 36–60. doi:http://dx.doi.org/10.1598/RRQ.33.1.3

Elbro, C., & Jensen, M. N. (2005). Quality of phonological representations, verbal learning, and phoneme awareness in dyslexic and normal readers. *Scandinavian Journal of Psychology*, *46*(4), 375–384. doi:http://dx.doi.org/10.1111/j.1467-9450.2005.00468.x

Elbro, C., & Pallesen, B. R. (2002). The quality of phonological representations and phonological awareness: A causal link? In L. Verhoeven, C. Elbro, & P. Reitsma (Eds.), *Precursors of Functional Literacy* (pp. 17–31). Philadelphia, PA: John Benjamins North America.

Fowler, A. E. (1991). How early phonological development might set the stage for phoneme awareness. In S. Brady & D. Shankweiler (Eds.), *Phonological processes in literacy: A tribute to Isabelle Y. Liberman* (pp. 97–118). Hillsdale, NJ: Lawrence Erlbaum Associates.

Garlock, V. M., Walley, A. C., & Metsala, J. L. (2001). Age-of-acquisition, word frequency, and neighborhood density effects on spoken word recognition by children and adults. *Journal of Memory and Language*, *45*, 468–492. doi:http://dx.doi.org/10.1006/jmla.2000.2784

Gerhand, S., & Barry, C. (1999). Age of acquisition, word frequency, and the role of phonology in the lexical decision task. *Memory & Cognition*, *27*(4), 592–602. doi:http://dx.doi.org/10.3758/BF03211553

Goswami, U., & Bryant, P. (1990). *Phonological skills and learning to read*. Hove, UK: Erlbaum.

Ho, C. S. H., & Bryant, P. (1997). Phonological skills are important in learning to read Chinese. *Developmental Psychology*, *33*(6), 946–951. doi:http://dx.doi.org/10.1037/0012-1649.33.6.946

Hulme, C., Hatcher, P. J., Nation, K., Brown, A., Adams, J., & Stuart, G. (2002). Phoneme awareness is a better predictor of early reading skill than onset-rime awareness. *Journal of Experimental Child Psychology*, *82*, 2–28. doi:http://dx.doi.org/10.1006/jecp.2002.2670

Hulme, C., Snowling, M., Caravolas, M., & Carroll, J. (2005). Phonological skills are (probably) one cause of success in learning to read: A comment on Castles and Coltheart. *Scientific Studies of Reading*, *9*, 351–365. doi:http://dx.doi.org/10.1207/s1532799xssr0904_2

Jusczyk, P. W., Luce, P. A., & Charles-Luce, J. (1994). Infants' sensitivity to phonotactic patterns in the native language. *Journal of Memory and Language*, *33*, 630–645. doi:http://dx.doi.org/10.1006/jmla.1994.1030

Leather, C. V., & Henry, L. A. (1994). Working memory span and phonological awareness tasks as predictors of early reading ability. *Journal of Experimental Child Psychology*, *58*, 88–111. doi:http://dx.doi.org/10.1006/jecp.1994.1027

Lee, J. (2011). Size matters: Early vocabulary as a predictor of language and literacy competence. *Applied Psycholinguistics*, *32*(1), 69–92. doi:http://dx.doi.org/10.1017/S0142716410000299

Liberman, I. Y., & Shankweiler, D. (1985). Phonology and the problems of learning to read and write. *Remedial and Special Education*, *6*(6), 8–17. doi:http://dx.doi.org/10.1177/074193258500600604

Liberman, I.Y., Shankweiler, D., Fischer, F. W., & Carter, B. (1974). Explicit syllable and phoneme segmentation in the young child. *Journal of Experimental Child Psychology*, *18*, 201–212. doi:http://dx.doi.org/10.1016/0022-0965(74)90101-5

Locke, J. L. (1988). The sound shape of early lexical representations. In M. D. Smith & J. L. Locke (Eds.), *The emergent lexicon: The child's development of a linguistic vocabulary* (pp. 3–18). New York: Academic Press.

Lonigan, C. J., Burgess, S. R., & Anthony, J. L. (2000). Development of emergent literacy and early reading skills in preschool children: Evidence from a latent-variable longitudinal study. *Developmental Psychology*, *36*(5), 596–613. doi:http://dx.doi.org/10.1037/0012-1649.36.5.596

Lonigan, C. J., Burgess, S. R., Anthony, J. L., & Barker, T. A. (1998). Development of phonological sensitivity in 2- to 5-year-old children. *Journal of Educational Psychology*, *90*, 294–311. doi:http://dx.doi.org/10.1037/0022-0663.90.2.294-613

McBride-Chang, C., & Kail, R. (2002). Cross-cultural similarities in the predictors of reading acquisition. *Child Development*, *73*, 1392–1407. doi:http://dx.doi.org/10.1111/1467-8624.00479

Morais, J., Cary, L., Alegria, J., & Bertelson, P. (1979). Does awareness of speech as a sequence of phones arise spontaneously? *Cognition*, *7*, 323–331.doi: http://dx.doi.org/10.1016/0010-0277(79)90020-9

Muter, V., Hulme, C., Snowling, M., & Taylor, S. (1998). Segmentation, not rhyming, predicts early progress in learning to read. *Journal of Experimental Child Psychology*, *71*, 3–27. doi:http://dx.doi.org/10.1006/jecp.1998.2453

Nagy, W. E., Anderson, R. C., & Herman, P. A. (1987). Learning word meanings from context during normal reading. *American Educational Research Journal*, *24*, 237–270. doi:10.3102/00028312024002237

National Reading Panel (2000). *Report of the National Reading Panel teaching children to read: An evidence-based assessment of the scientific research literature on reading and its implications for reading instruction.* Washington, DC: National Institute of Child Health and Human Development.

Oakhill, J., & Kyle, F. (2000). The relation between phonological awareness and working memory. *Journal of Experimental Child Psychology*, *75*(2), 152–164. doi:http://dx.doi.org/10.1006/jecp.1999.2529

Olson, R., Forsberg, H., Wise, B., & Rack, J. (1994). Measurement of word recognition, orthographic, and phonological skills. In G. R. Lyon (Ed.), *Frames of reference for the assessment of learning disabilities: New views on measurement issues* (pp. 243–277). Baltimore, MD: Paul H. Brookes.

Öney, B., & Durgunoğlu, A.-Y. (1997). Beginning to read in Turkish: A phonologically transparent orthography. *Applied Psycholinguistics*, *18*, 1–15. http://dx.doi.org/10.1017/S014271640000984X

Perfetti, C. A., Beck, I., Bell, L. C., & Hughes, C. (1987). Phonemic knowledge and learning to read are reciprocal: A longitudinal study of first grade children. *Merrill-Palmer Quarterly*, *33*, 283–320.

Read, C., Yun-Fei, Z., Hong-Yin, N., & Bao-Qing, D. (1986). The ability to manipulate speech sounds depends on knowing alphabetic writing. *Cognition*, *24*(1), 31–44. doi:http://dx.doi.org/10.1016/0010-0277(86)90003-X

Rohl, M., & Pratt, C. (1995). Phonological awareness, verbal working memory and the acquisition of literacy. *Reading and Writing*, *7*, 327–360. doi:http://dx.doi.org/10.1007/BF01027723

Saffran, J. R., Aslin, R. N., & Newport, E. L. (1996). Statistical learning by 8-month-old infants. *Science*, *274*(5294), 1926–1928. doi:http://dx.doi.org/10.1126/science.274.5294.192

Schatschneider C., Fletcher J. M., Francis D. J., Carlson C. D., & Foorman B. R. (2004). Kindergarten prediction of reading skills: A longitudinal comparative analysis. *Journal of Educational Psychology*, *96*, 265–282. doi: http://dx.doi.org/10.1037/0022-0663.96.2.265

Siegel, L. S. (1993). Phonological processing deficits as the basis of a reading disability. *Developmental Review*, *13*, 246–257. doi:http://dx.doi.org/10.1006/drev.1993.1011

Snow, C. E., Burns, M. S., & Griffin, P. (Eds.) (1998). *Preventing reading difficulties in young children.* Washington, DC: National Academy Press.

Snowling, M. J. (1987). *Dyslexia: A cognitive developmental perspective.* Oxford, UK: Blackwell.

Snowling, M. J., Hulme, C., Smith, A., & Thomas, J. (1994). The effects of phonetic similarity and list length on children's sound categorization performance. *Journal of Experimental Child Psychology*, *58*, 160–180. doi:http://dx.doi.org/10.1006/jecp.1994.1030

Stahl, S. A., & Murray, B. A. (1994). Defining phonological awareness and its relationship to early reading. *Journal of Educational Psychology*, *86*(2), 221–234. doi:http://dx.doi.org/10.1037/0022-0663.86.2.221

Stanovich, K. E. (1988). Explaining the differences between the dyslexic and the garden-variety poor reader: The phonological-core variable-difference model. *Journal of Learning Disabilities*, *21*, 590–604. doi:http://dx.doi.org/ 10.1177/002221948802101003

Stanovich, K. E. (1992). Speculations on the causes and consequences of individual differences in early reading acquisition. In P. Gough, L. Ehri, & R. Treiman (Eds.), *Reading acquisition* (pp. 307–342). Hillsdale, NJ: Erlbaum.

Stanovich, K. E. (1993). Romance and reality. In Consortium on Reading Excellence, *Reading research anthology: The why? of reading instruction* (pp. 24–35). Novato, CA: Arena Press.

Stanovich, K. E., Cunningham, A. E., & Cramer, B. B. (1984). Assessing phonological awareness in kindergarten children: Issues of task comparability. *Journal of Experimental Child Psychology*, *38*, 175–190. doi:http://dx.doi.org/10.1016/0022-0965(84)90120-6

Stuart, M. (1995). Prediction and qualitative assessment of five- and six-year-old children's reading: A longitudinal study. *British Journal of Educational Psychology*, *65*, 287–296. doi:http://dx.doi.org/10.1111/j.2044-8279.1995.tb01150.x

Stoel-Gammon, C. (1987). Phonological skills of 2-year-olds. *Language, Speech, and Hearing Services in Schools*, *18*, 323–329. doi:http://dx.doi.org/10.1044/0161-1461.1804.323

Stoel-Gammon, C. (2011). Relationships between lexical and phonological development in young children. *Journal of Child Language*, *38*, 1–34. doi:http://dx.doi.org/10.1017/S0305000910000425

Swan, D., & Goswami, U. (1997). Phonological awareness deficits in developmental dyslexia and the phonological representations hypothesis. *Journal of Experimental Child Psychology*, *66*(1), 18–41. doi:http://dx.doi.org/10.1006/jecp.1997.2375

Torgesen, J. K., & Mathes, P. G. (1998). *What every teacher should know about phonological awareness.* Tallahassee, FL: Florida Department of Education.

Torgesen, J. K., & Mathes, P. G. (2000). *A basic guide to understanding, assessing, and teaching phonological awareness.* Austin, TX: Pro-Ed.

Treiman, R., Freyd, J. J., & Baron, J. (1983). Phonological recoding and use of spelling-sound rules in reading of sentences. *The Journal of Verbal Learning and Verbal Behavior, 22,* 682–700. doi:http://dx.doi.org/10.1016/S0022-5371(83)90405-X

Treiman, R., & Zukowski, A. (1991). Levels of phonological awareness. In S. A. Brady & D. P. Shankweiler (Eds.), *Phonological processes in literacy: A tribute to Isabelle Y. Liberman* (pp. 67–83). Hillsdale, NJ: Lawrence Erlbaum Associates.

Treiman, R., & Zukowski, A. (1996). Children's sensitivity to syllables, onsets, rimes, and phonemes. *Journal of Experimental Child Psychology, 61,* 193–215. doi:http://dx.doi.org/10.1006/jecp.1996.0014

Tyler, M. D., & Burnham, D. K. (2006). Orthographic influences on phoneme deletion response times. *Quarterly Journal of Experimental Psychology, 59,* 2010–2031. doi:http://dx.doi.org/10.1080/17470210500521828

Vellutino, F. R., Fletcher, J. M., Snowling, M. J., & Scanlon, D. M. (2004). Specific reading disability (dyslexia): What have we learned in the past four decades? *Journal of Child Psychology and Psychiatry, 45,* 2–40. doi:http://dx.doi.org/10.1046/j.0021-9630.2003.00305.x

Vihman, M. M., Ferguson, C. A., & Elbert, M. (1986). Phonological development from babbling to speech: Common tendencies and individual differences. *Applied Psycholinguistics, 7,* 3–40. doi:http://dx.doi.org/10.1017/S0142716400007165

Vihman, M. M., & Greenlee, M. (1987). Individual differences in phonological development: Ages one and three years. *Journal of Speech, Language & Hearing Research, 30*(4), 503–521. doi:http://dx.doi.org/10.1044/jshr.3004.503

Vloedgraven, J., & Verhoeven, L. (2009). The nature of phonological awareness throughout the elementary grades: An item response theory perspective. *Learning and Individual Differences, 19,* 161–169. doi:http://dx.doi.org/10.1016/j.lindif.2008.09.005

Wagner, R. K., Balthazor, M., Hurley, S., Morgan, S., Rashotte, C, Shaner, R. . . . Stage, S. (1987). The nature of prereaders' phonological processing abilities. *Cognitive Development, 2,* 355–373. doi:http://dx.doi.org/10.1016/S0885-2014(87)80013-8

Wagner, R. K., & Torgesen, J. K. (1987). The nature of phonological processing and its causal role in the acquisition of reading skills. *Psychological Bulletin, 101,* 192–212. doi:http://dx.doi.org/10.1037/0033-2909.101.2.192

Wagner, R. K., Torgesen, J. K., Laughon, P., Simmons, K., & Rashotte, C. A. (1993). Development of young readers' phonological processing abilities. *Journal of Educational Psychology, 85,* 83–103. doi:http://dx.doi.org/10.1037/0022-0663.85.1.83

Wagner, R. K., Torgesen, J. K., & Rashotte, C. A. (1994). Development of reading-related phonological processing abilities: New evidence of bidirectional causality from a latent variable longitudinal study. *Developmental Psychology, 30,* 73–87. doi:http://dx.doi.org/10.1037/0012-1649.30.1.73

Wagner, R. K., Torgesen, J. K., Rashotte, C. A., Hecht, S. A., Barker, T. A., Burgess, S. R., . . . Garon, T. (1997). Changing relations between phonological processing abilities and word-level reading as children develop from beginning to skilled readers: A 5-year longitudinal study. *Developmental Psychology, 33,* 468–479. doi:http://dx.doi.org/10.1037/0012-1649.33.3.468

Wagner, R. K., Torgesen, J. K., Rashotte, C. A., & Pearson, N. (2013). *The Comprehensive Test of Phonological Processing* (2nd ed.). Austin, TX: Pro-Ed.

Walley, A. C. (1993). The role of vocabulary development in children's spoken word recognition and segmentation ability. *Developmental Review, 13,* 286–350. doi:http://dx.doi.org/10.1006/drev.1993.1015

Walley, A. C., & Metsala, J. L. (1992). Young children's age-of-acquisition estimates for spoken words. *Memory & Cognition, 20,* 171–182. doi:http://dx.doi.org/10.3758/BF03197166

Walley, A. C., Metsala, J. L., & Garlock, V. M. (2003). Spoken vocabulary growth: Its role in the development of phoneme awareness and early reading ability. *Reading and Writing, 16,* 5–20.

Yopp, H. K. (1988). The validity and reliability of phonemic awareness tests. *Reading Research Quarterly, 23*(2), 159–177. doi:http://dx.doi.org/10.2307/747800

# 8

# Individual Differences in Word Recognition

## Reading Acquisition and Reading Disabilities

*Jamie L. Metsala and Margaret D. David*

As skilled readers, our purposes for reading include gaining knowledge and understanding through texts, interpreting and critically evaluating perspectives put forth in texts, and many other aspects of reading comprehension and reading enjoyment. It is within the context of becoming a skilled reader that the current chapter examines individual differences in word recognition. Expert readers recognize words quickly and effortlessly, freeing cognitive resources for the higher-level goals of reading (Perfetti, 2007). The critical role of word recognition in higher-level cognitive aspects of reading has been well established. Individual differences in word recognition are the strongest predictor of reading comprehension in grades 1–3 (e.g., Vellutino, Tunmer, Jaccard, & Chen, 2007; National Reading Panel, 2000), and account for variance in comprehension throughout later schooling (e.g., Cunningham & Stanovich, 1998; Scarborough, Ehri, Olson, & Fowler, 1998). In the English language, there are substantial individual differences in children's achievement of both word recognition accuracy and speed (Jenkins, Fuchs, van den Broek, Espin, & Deno, 2003), each of which contribute to reading fluency and comprehension (Jenkins et al., 2003; Torgesen, 2006).

Not only is there a need to acquire accurate and quick word recognition, but becoming proficient in these skills early in the acquisition process is important to later reading achievement (e.g., Juel, 1988) and to becoming a more avid reader (Cunningham & Stanovich, 1998). Furthermore, word recognition deficits are the defining feature of reading disabilities/dyslexia, and are most often attributed to difficulties acquiring the alphabetic principle (for reviews see Lovett, 1992; Siegel, 1998; Stanovich, 2000). While individual differences in word recognition are most strongly associated with reading comprehension in the early elementary grades (Vellutino et al., 2007), for those who fail to become proficient in this skill, the effects on comprehension remain extensive (Gersten, Fuchs, Williams, & Baker, 2001).

Given that proficient word recognition is a necessary component of skilled reading, it has been an area of sustained research activity. The goals of this research have included: understanding how word recognition accuracy and automaticity are acquired; delineating what variables at genetic, neurobiological, cognitive, and environmental levels of analyses cause individual differences in word recognition and contribute to reading disabilities; and understanding components of effective reading programs that enable most/all children to become proficient in word reading. In this chapter, we highlight several aspects of two developmental frameworks of word recognition. We then briefly review research related to cognitive correlates of reading, including phonological awareness, orthographic processing, rapid automatized naming, and morphological awareness. We end the chapter with an examination of environmental factors related to word reading achievement, focusing on prevention and intervention studies in this area.

## Developmental Frameworks

Two influential frameworks of reading acquisition help to identify factors in the reading process that may cause individual differences in word recognition. Essential to Ehri's (1998, 2005, 2014) phase model is the child's progression from a pre-reader, to strategically decoding words based on the application of grapheme–phoneme correspondences, through to recognizing words by "sight." This means that words are recognized automatically, without consciously applying a decoding routine, and with simultaneous activation and constraints from words' pronunciations and meanings. While sight word recognition is often assumed to access whole-word or lexical-level internal orthographic-representations, the "connection-forming process" (Ehri, 2005) between orthographic and phonological units likely reflects learning regularities between English phonology and orthography at multiple levels of mappings (e.g., individual and positional grapheme–phoneme units, as well as rime, syllabic, morphemic, and lexical sound-to-spelling correspondences). The levels of mappings that are most consistent or regular within a given orthography may be most readily acquired by the developing reader (Ziegler & Goswami, 2005).

Consistent in many respects with Ehri's phase model, Share's (1995, 2008) self-teaching framework asserts that it is the strategic, left-to-right, letter-by-letter sounding-out process that provides the level of fine-grained analysis required by the developing reader to build the detailed orthographic representations that support "sight" word reading. Even beginning readers may require only a few accurate decoding trials with a word before acquiring a functional orthographic representation (e.g., Ehri & Saltmarsh, 1995). Individual differences in the rate of acquisition and the quality of orthographic representations will impact a reader's word recognition skills. Share (2008) proposed that the "phonology first/orthography second" hypothesis arises from the mechanics of self-teaching. Since phonological recoding (decoding a word based on sound–spelling correspondences) is the process through which higher-level orthographic representations are formed, variation in these representations will depend primarily upon the efficiency of the learner's phonological recoding skills. In addition to phonological skills, there may be other factors that contribute to the acquisition and quality of orthographic representations (Share, 2008). Consistent with these two developmental frameworks, phonological and orthographic processing and factors that may contribute to variation in these domains have been major foci for research concerning acquisition and individual differences in word recognition.

## Factors Related to Individual Differences in Word Recognition Acquisition and Achievement

### Phonological Awareness and Vocabulary

The role of phonological awareness in word recognition development and reading disabilities has been well documented over recent decades (Quinn et al., Chapter 7). Phonological awareness (PA) can be thought of as skill at making judgments about and manipulating sublexical units of oral language (i.e., levels of sound units that make up words; e.g., syllables, onsets, rimes, phonemes). In particular, the ability to access and manipulate individual phonemes (phonemic awareness) is most strongly associated with concurrent and future word reading achievement (Ehri et al., 2001). Furthermore, individuals with word recognition deficits have persistent difficulties with phonemic awareness (e.g., Stanovich & Siegel, 1994) and phonemic awareness training improves word reading abilities (Ehri et al., 2001). The later finding most strongly supports the proposed causal role of PA in word recognition (for review see Stanovich, 2000; Quinn et al., Chapter 7). Given this critical role in the development of word recognition and reading disabilities, an ancillary goal has been to delineate the developmental processes underlying the origins and growth of PA (e.g., Elbro & Jensen, 2005; Metsala 1999, 2011; Swan & Goswami, 1997). This seems particularly appropriate given the consensus that PA "is a skill that is acquired during the preschool (early childhood) period, prior to formal reading instruction" (Lonigan, 2007, p. 21). Over this early childhood period, PA is a stable individual difference trait (Lonigan, Burgess, & Anthony, 2000); is separable from other phonological constructs (Lonigan et al., 2009); and is consistently a front runner amongst cognitive and linguistic skills predicting later word recognition achievement (e.g., Lonigan et al., 2000, 2009; for review see the National Early Literacy Panel Report, 2008).

Vocabulary knowledge is strongly associated with PA in this early childhood period. We have proposed that vocabulary growth impacts the structure and neighborhood organization of spoken word representations in the mental dictionary, and this "lexical restructuring" gives rise to access of segmental information in words' phonological representations (i.e., phonemic awareness; Metsala, 1997, 1999, 2011; Metsala & Walley, 1998; see also Storkel, 2002). Regardless of the underlying mechanisms, research has found unique contributions of early vocabulary knowledge to PA. For example, vocabulary measures of Finnish 3-year-olds predicted variance in later PA, beyond that accounted for by letter knowledge; the home literacy environment affected PA indirectly through its impact on vocabulary (Torppa et al., 2007; see also Silvén, Niemi, & Voeten, 2002). Vocabulary has been found to contribute unique variance to PA beyond other speech and cognitive variables in young typically developing children (e.g., McDowell, Lonigan, & Goldstein, 2007), in young children with speech disorders (Rvachew & Grawburg, 2006), in samples of young children from middle and lower socioeconomic backgrounds (Burgess & Lonigan, 1998; McDowell et al., 2007), and in a sample of older grade 2 and 3 children with reading disabilities (Wise, Sevcik, Morris, Lovett, & Wolf, 2007). Lonigan (2007) found that a group of children who received an oral language/vocabulary intervention were higher than a comparison group on vocabulary and PA; on the other hand, the group that received a PA-only intervention scored higher on PA but not on vocabulary. Within the context of largely correlational studies, Lonigan's findings more strongly support a causal role for vocabulary growth on PA skills.

Vocabulary also asserts a more direct impact on reading, as knowledge of words' pronunciations and meanings facilitates word recognition and comprehension (Biemiller, 2003; Snow, Burns, & Griffin, 1998). These multiple pathways from early vocabulary to reading achievement may help to illuminate some of the mechanisms responsible for the observed relationship between families' socioeconomic status (SES) and reading achievement. Preschoolers from economically disadvantaged backgrounds have less well developed vocabulary knowledge (e.g., Lonigan, 2007), and standard mean vocabulary scores may be more than one standard deviation below the normative mean (e.g., Lonigan, 2007; McDowell et al., 2007). Early language experience likely accounts for a substantial amount of this variance. For example, for one sample it was estimated that while children from high-SES backgrounds heard roughly 11,000 utterances per day, children from low-SES backgrounds heard around 700 utterances per day (Hart & Risley, 1995). Such differences in amount and style of child-directed speech are related to variation in vocabulary knowledge in toddlers and young children (Pan, Rowe, Singer, & Snow, 2005; Rowe, 2008). To continue with this causal link, a relationship between vocabulary knowledge at 12 and 24 months and later PA at 3 and 4 years of age has been demonstrated (Silvén et al., 2002). Indeed, studies in the US have shown that children from disadvantaged backgrounds start school with lower vocabulary knowledge (e.g., Lee & Burkam, 2002); and by the beginning of fourth grade, one-half of children from economically disadvantaged homes in the US were not able to read at the basic level, as measured by the NAEP (Lee, Grigg, & Donahue, 2007). In summary, variance in SES will be related to vocabulary, which in turn, has direct and indirect influences on word recognition and comprehension. Although critical to later reading achievement, it has proven difficult to impact general vocabulary knowledge in samples of young, at-risk preschoolers (for reviews see Neuman, 2011; Wasik & Hindman, 2011).

## Orthographic Processing

As referenced in the developmental frameworks, orthographic representations are proposed to be instrumental to acquiring automatic word recognition, which in turn has been found to be critical to text-reading fluency and comprehension (Torgesen, 2006). Indeed, a strong association has been found between processing visual-orthographic information and word recognition achievement (for review see Cunningham, Nathan, & Raher, 2011). Orthographic processing (OP) has been measured by tasks that tap word-specific knowledge (e.g., the Homophone Choice Task in which the correct word spelling is chosen from pairs of stimuli; "rain–rane"; Olson, Forsberg, Wise, & Rack, 1994) and tasks that assess word-general or language-specific knowledge (e.g., the Letter-String Choice Task in which the one item with a more "word-like" spelling is chosen: filv–filk, jull–jukk; Treiman, 1993). Research has confirmed that the various measures of OP are tapping a single construct which is reliably separable from other reading-related factors such as PA (e.g., Cunningham, Perry, & Stanovich, 2001; Gayán & Olson, 2003; Hagiliassis, Pratt, & Johnston, 2006; but see Conrad, Harris, & Williams, 2013). Cunningham et al. (2011) recommend an encompassing definition of OP:

> Orthographic processing is the ability to form, store, and access orthographic representations, which a) specify the allowable order of letters within the orthography of a specific language, and b) are themselves tightly linked to phonological, semantic, morphological, and syntactic information within the language system within which they operate (p. 263).

Measures of OP have been found to predict concurrent and future word recognition beyond phonological measures (e.g., Roman, Kirby, Parrila, Wade-Woolley, & Deacon, 2009). Furthermore, studies on children's learning of new orthographic representations support the self-teaching hypothesis: first, individual differences in reading new words (i.e., phonological recoding) is related to acquisition of orthographic representations; and, second, OP accounts for variance in learning new orthographic representations beyond that accounted for by phonological recoding (e.g., Bowey & Muller, 2005; Cunningham, 2006; Cunningham et al., 2001). Taken together, these studies reinforce the importance of instruction that targets proficiency in beginning readers' phonological recoding skills, and highlight the need for increased understanding of additional factors influencing orthographic processing.

Reading experience is one variable that has a strong association with orthographic processing skills (see Cunningham et al., 2011), and varies greatly amongst readers. One estimate was that skilled middle-school readers read 1–50 million words per year while poor readers read about 100,000 words per year (Nagy & Anderson, 1984). This skill level by reading amount interaction is seen as early as grade 1 (Biemiller, 1999). OP is one of the many reading-related and broader cognitive skills that are impacted by these differences in print exposure (for review, see Stanovich, 2000). Measures of print exposure have been shown to account for variance in OP after variance accounted for by phonological skills (e.g., Cunningham et al., 2001), strengthening the argument that print exposure facilitates acquisition of orthographic representations. Furthermore, children with reading disabilities who sometimes perform better on OP tasks than younger children reading at the same level (e.g., Olson, Wise, Connors, & Rack, 1990; Stanovich & Siegel, 1994) may do so because they have a greater amount of print experience. The implications are that frequent and wide reading will facilitate efficiency in word recognition, and thus needs to be one goal of reading instruction.

Rapid automatized naming is a second variable that has been found to have a strong association with OP (e.g., Bowers, & Wolf, 1993; Roman et al., 2009) and with reading rate (for review see Norton & Wolf, 2012). Rapid automatized naming (RAN) is an individual's speed at sequentially naming rows of individual letters or numbers (or sometimes pictured objects). Recent research suggests that while RAN is related to typical measures of OP, it may not be as strongly associated with learning new orthographic representations (Powell, Stainthorp, & Stuart, 2014). It has been proposed that RAN constitutes a second core deficit in reading disabilities, and may be related to reading rate deficits in particular (Norton & Wolf, 2012). Samples of readers with this "double deficit" have been found to have poorer reading achievement than groups with a single deficit in PA or in RAN alone (for review see Norton & Wolf, 2012); however, these greater reading impairments may be due to a "statistical artifact" related to categorizing children based on "two correlated, continuous variables" (p. 245; Schatschneider, Carlson, Francis, Foorman, & Fletcher, 2002; see also, Pennington, Cardoso-Martins, Green, & Lefly, 2001). In a review of the research, it was suggested that evidence to date did not support two separate constructs underlying reading disabilities (Vukovic & Siegel, 2006). The mechanisms accounting for the relationships between RAN, OP, and word recognition need to be better understood; currently, there does not appear to be a direct role for RAN in reading instruction.

One criticism of research in the area of orthographic processing has been that individual differences in OP measures may be a result, rather than a cause, of skill in word recognition (e.g., Burt, 2006; Castles & Nation, 2006). In a study following children from grades 1 to 3, OP did not predict later unique variance in word reading; however, word reading did quite consistently predict later OP skills (Deacon, Benere, & Castles, 2012). Further investigation is warranted to settle the direction of causality in OP's association with word recognition. Another issue that we suggest confounds findings in this area is that phonological recoding becomes increasingly parasitic upon previous orthographic learning as larger sublexical orthographic-mappings are relied upon to recode unfamiliar words (e.g., frequent bigram and trigram spellings, rimes, morphemes, syllables; Brown & Deavers, 1999; Share, 2008). Relatively early in the acquisition process, recoding will become confounded by past learning of orthographic representations; therefore, decoding pseudowords is not a pure measure of "phonological recoding efficiency" as often used in these OP learning studies. In their behavior-genetic analysis, Byrne et al. (2008) found that shared genes were responsible for the covariation in heritability of phonological recoding and orthographic learning, and suggested that there doesn't need to be a causal direction proposed between these two factors (see also Gayán & Olson, 2003). We suggest that the primacy of the association between phonological awareness and word recognition may, in part, be due to the relative difficulty and variation in processing the phonological versus orthographic perceptual fields (although a fuller discussion is beyond the scope of this chapter, see Dahan & Magnuson, 2011, for a review of spoken word recognition development).

## Morphological Awareness

A considerable amount of research has found that morphological awareness (MA) contributes to aspects of reading ability (for review, see Bowers, Kirby, & Deacon, 2010), and suggests that children with reading disabilities may have deficits in this area (e.g., Shankweiler et al., 1995). Morphemes are the smallest units of meaning in a language and morphological awareness (MA) refers to one's understanding of, and ability to manipulate, the morphological structure of words (Deacon, 2012). The concept of MA is illustrated by word analogy tasks that are frequently used to measure this skill, requiring the participant to supply the missing word (e.g., i) paint: painter; bake:_____ ii) Today I will swim: Yesterday I _____). In concurrent and longitudinal studies, MA has been shown to contribute unique variance to word recognition (e.g., Kirby et al., 2012); however, this may not be the case when variance due to earlier reading skill is taken into account (e.g., Deacon & Kirby, 2004).

Studies examining the impact of MA training on reading have the potential to test the causal role of MA on word recognition skills. MA interventions frequently focus on children "identifying morphemes within words, building words from morphemes, learning root or affix meanings, and highlighting morpheme patterns or rules" (Goodwin & Ahn, 2013). Goodwin and Ahn's recent meta-analysis revealed positive effects of programs including MA training on word decoding, PA, and morphological knowledge, but not for reading fluency and comprehension. Overall, larger effect sizes were found for younger children, quasi-experimental methodologies, and experimental measures; there were no differences in effect sizes found in terms of the scope of the intervention (i.e., MA alone versus more encompassing reading interventions). In contrast, from a similar analysis it was concluded that MA interventions were more effective when combined with other aspects of reading instruction and for weaker readers (Bowers et al., 2010). These authors also noted significant variability across study outcomes and some tenuous effects. In this relatively new area of research, the unique contribution of MA training to word recognition is not yet well delineated; however, the general findings from research thus far suggest that instruction in MA in the classroom may benefit children's word reading and/or comprehension (Carlisle, 2000).

## Teaching All Children to Read

In this chapter, we have largely focused on proximal, cognitive causes of individual differences in word recognition. More distal associations to variation in word recognition, and thus risk status for reading disabilities, have been linked to socioeconomic backgrounds, early language and literacy environments, and early reading instruction (D'Angiulli, Siegel, & Hertzman, 2004; D'Angiulli, Siegel, & Maggi, 2004; Molfese, Modglin, & Molfese, 2003). This section of the chapter focuses on the impact of instruction on individual differences in word recognition and the interaction between interventions and factors that have traditionally placed children at greater risk for reading disabilities. Early prevention programs have sought to bring all young children into the average range for word recognition accuracy and speed, given the serious negative impact of failure in these skills on later reading achievement. One focus has been on general classroom instruction as, frequently, too many children are not acquiring proficient basic reading skills and large numbers can overwhelm remedial education systems (Foorman, &

Al Otaiba, 2009). For example, in the 2012–2013 academic year, it was reported that 63 percent of grade 2 children were meeting expectations for accuracy and fluency in leveled readers for the largest school board in Nova Scotia (HRSB, 2013; see Lee et al., 2007 for similar grade 4 assessment results across the United States).

Classroom approaches that include explicit and systematic phonics and PA instruction as components of a complete early literacy program benefit young normally-achieving readers and at-risk readers (Foorman, Francis, Fletcher, Schatschneider, & Mehta 1998; National Reading Panel, 2000; for review of post-NRP data see Brady, 2011; and see Moats, 2000, 2007 concerning the necessary integrity of PA and phonics instruction). From studies on classroom Peer-Assisted Learning Strategies (PALS) it has been estimated that all but 4–6 percent of the grade 1 population would be achieving within average levels on word recognition with this low-intensity approach to including PA and phonics in the classroom (Al Otaiba & Fuchs, 2006; for review see Al Otaiba & Torgesen, 2007). In the PALS settings, teachers provide structured reading lessons which are followed by pairs of higher and lower achieving students practicing PA and phonics skills. Foorman and colleagues (1998) similarly estimated that only 5–6 percent of the grade 1 student population would continue to have word reading deficits given the classroom instruction from the most effective condition in their study, direct and systematic instruction in letter–sound correspondences, and reading practice in decodable books (Open Court Reading, 1995). Significantly fewer students would need tertiary level interventions for word recognition deficits given these approaches to classroom instruction. For children who do remain below average on word recognition, initial measures of PA are frequently poorer (e.g., Foorman et al., 1998), as has sometimes also been found on initial measures of vocabulary, RAN, and difficult behavior (Al Otaiba & Fuchs, 2006).

Early reading interventions have focused on providing explicit and systematic instruction in PA and phonics to those most severely impaired in these skills in Kindergarten and grade 1 (e.g., Chard et al., 2008). Studies have found that an intensive intervention focusing on these components in grade 1 may be adequate to bring most students deemed "at-risk" into the average range on reading measures, with intervention continuing in grade 2 for the remaining students (e.g., Vellutino et al., 1996; Vellutino, Scanlon, & Jaccard, 2003; Vaughn et al., 2009). Many of these studies found that initial PA and RAN scores characterize the group in need of continued intervention; however, these relationships to pre-intervention abilities are attenuated by intervention (e.g., Mathes et al., 2005). Similar to studies with older children (Lovett et al., 2000), grade 1 students have not responded differentially to the type of intervention based on their cognitive profiles (Mathes et al., 2005). Given such effective multi-tiered interventions, it has been estimated that approximately 1–4 percent of the population would continue to have deficits in word reading (Al Otaiba & Torgesen, 2007).

Studies have also examined interactions between reading instruction and factors traditionally associated with increased rates of reading failure. English Language Learning-status and SES-status were no longer related to reading achievement by grade 2 and 3 within the context of a strong play-based PA and alphabet-learning Kindergarten program, alongside elementary programs rich in oral language instruction, children's literature, direct instruction in comprehension strategies, and targeted Tier II interventions (NVSD, 2013); furthermore, only 2–4 percent of the population had reading disabilities in grade 2 and grade 4 (D'Anguilli et al., 2004; Lesaux & Siegel, 2003). Results from a similar RTI approach showed steady increases in reading scores for each of four years of implementation (reported in McIntosh, Bennett, & Price, 2011). In the fourth year, 92 percent of students were meeting or exceeding grade-level expectations on grade 4 provincial tests (compared to 68 percent provincially) as were 94 percent of Aboriginal students (compared to 51 percent of Aboriginal students provincially). These research studies demonstrate necessary components of language arts programs that can help all children learn to read and minimize, or even eliminate, the impact of traditional risk factors on reading achievement. These components include explicit and systematic phonemic awareness and phonics instruction, multi-tiered interventions, targeted oral language learning, and direct instruction in reading-comprehension strategies. Furthermore, these components need to take place within the context of a language and literature-rich classroom setting. While a discussion of the observed malleability of skills that have large heritable components (i.e., phonological and orthographic processing) is beyond the scope of this chapter, the interested reader is referred to Olson, Byrne, and Samuelsson (2009).

Students with word recognition deficits in grades 2 and above also show significant gains from interventions similar to those described for younger children (i.e., with systematic and explicit instruction in PA, phonics, and fluency; for review see Torgesen, 2006); however, interventions for older students may need to be more intense and lengthier, and do not consistently bring performance on standardized reading measures into the average range (Lovett et al., 2000; Torgesen, 2006). Research with samples of older students with reading disabilities also does not support the differentiation of readers based on overall cognitive ability nor on more distal factors traditionally related to children's early risk status (e.g., Morris et al., 2012; Stuebing et al., 2002). In their intervention with older students with reading disabilities, IQ, SES, and race were not related to students' responses to intervention (Morris et al., 2012).

Even within the context of intensive interventions that normalize word reading accuracy and comprehension, fluency scores remain far below average levels (e.g., Torgesen et al., 2001). While participants in Torgesen et al.'s (2001) study significantly improved in the number of words read per minute, their status on fluency measures relative to same-age normally achieving peers remained well below average. Another study demonstrated that even an intensive intervention that brought the mean reading fluency scores close the average range for children in grades 1 and 2 did not do so for the students in grades 3–6; word recognition and comprehension scores did come into the average range for all age groups (Rashotte, MacPhee, & Torgesen, 2001). Word reading rate has been argued to be the most important factor on text reading fluency (Torgesen & Hudson, 2006) and was found to be more strongly associated with reading comprehension than rate of connected text reading for groups of students with both average and below average reading comprehension achievement (Wise et al., 2010). Torgesen (2006) proposed that a substantial deficit in reading amount over prolonged years of schooling amongst students with reading disabilities (i.e., 9 to 12 years and older) may explain why fluency has remained an area of difficulty, as opposed to problems with the reading interventions per se. Whether students in one study spent 5 percent or 50 percent of the intervention time on continuous text reading, fluency standard scores remained well below average (Torgesen et al., 2001).

The effect of reading amount on orthographic processing reviewed earlier in this chapter is consistent with Torgesen's (2006) causal explanation of the continued fluency deficits in students with reading disabilities (see also, Torgesen & Hudson, 2006). As well as possible ways to "make-up" lost reading time, a critical question for intervention researchers may be whether there is a targeted skill that, if exercised, could mimic the effects of print exposure on building orthographic representations and facilitating word recognition efficiency. For example, a component of the SpellRead™ (2009) program is on speeded practice with sublexical sound-spelling patterns (e.g., pa_; ame; soo). As students master a targeted time for a collection of sound-spelling patterns, they progress through increasingly more difficult collections of patterns (known as "card packs" to the students). This speeded practice with sublexical patterns was built into the program to facilitate word recognition rate or automaticity (MacPhee, personal communication, April 18, 2013). In a recent study, although mean fluency standard scores did not come into the average range, for 7–18-year-olds with reading disabilities these were increased reliably and practically, alongside mean outcome scores in the average range for word reading and reading comprehension (Metsala & Steele, 2013). There was also a unique contribution of individual students' mastery of these sublexical sound-spelling patterns to outcome fluency scores after 40 and 80 hours of the SpellRead intervention. Through research that further illuminates the relationships between components of reading interventions and word reading speed, the field may soon be in a position to better remediate fluency deficits in children with reading disabilities.

## Summary

This chapter examined research concerning cognitive and environmental factors that have been demonstrated or proposed to cause individual differences in word recognition. Research on phonological awareness and grapheme–phoneme correspondence knowledge have had very practical implications for reading programs. Continuing research addressing orthographic processing, rapid automatized naming, and morphological awareness may also be informative for classroom instruction. Currently we understand that reading amount will impact automaticity in word recognition and therefore should be one goal of reading programs. A better understanding of the complex network of knowledge and sources of variation underlying word processing automaticity may advance interventions aimed at increasing reading fluency, possibly providing an avenue to compensate for years of lost reading experience in students with reading disabilities. In addition, it appears that including instruction in morphological awareness will positively impact achievement in word recognition and/or reading comprehension (e.g., Carlisle, 2000).

As discussed, current understandings of word recognition acquisition and variation have informed classroom instruction, as well as reading intervention programs. Early programs aimed at preventing later word recognition difficulties have done so successfully in all but a small proportion of children. Examples of the practical impact of this research have been seen in reports of district-wide program implementations such as that in North Vancouver (NVSD, 2014). Intervention research for children with reading disabilities has also led to increased efficacy at normalizing word recognition and reading comprehension for these students and has impacted practice in school systems. The long-term research program of Lovett and colleagues has led to the EMPOWER™ Reading program (Lovett, Lacerenza, & Borden, 2006), used as part of a tiered intervention approach in many Ontario school boards. Similarly, the SpellRead™ (2009) program is evidence-based and is used in many US school boards and private reading clinics across North America. Despite advances in the science of word reading acquisition and instruction, too many children in our education systems are not receiving adequate instruction to support early acquisition of proficient word recognition. It would seem the complexities of current social and political contexts will need to be interwoven with the scientific studies of reading to fully explain the current state of reading instruction, even in as delimited a domain as word recognition.

## Acknowledgments

The preparation of this chapter was supported by Natural Sciences and Engineering Research Council of Canada Discovery Grant 341588–2008 (to JLM).

## References

Al Otaiba, S., & Fuchs, D. (2006). Who are the young children for whom best practices in reading are ineffective? An experimental and longitudinal study. *Journal of Learning Disabilities*, *39*(5), 414–431.

Al Otaiba, S., & Torgesen, J. (2007). Effects from intensive standardized kindergarten and first-grade interventions for the prevention of reading difficulties. In S. R. Jimerson, M. K. Burns, & A. M. VanDerHayden (Eds.), *Handbook of response to intervention* (pp. 212–222). New York: Springer US.

Biemiller, A. (1999). *Language and literacy success*. Cambridge, MA: Brookline Books.

Biemiller, A. (2003). Vocabulary: Needed if more children are to read well. *Reading Psychology*, *24*(3–4), 323–335.

Bowers, P. G., & Wolf, M. (1993). Theoretical links among naming speed, precise timing mechanisms and orthographic skill in dyslexia. *Reading and Writing*, *5*(1), 69–85.

Bowers, P. N., Kirby, J. R., & Deacon, S. H. (2010). The effects of morphological instruction on literacy skills: A systematic review of the literature. *Review of Educational Research*, *80*(2), 144–179.

Bowey, J. A., & Muller, D. (2005). Phonological recoding and rapid orthographic learning in third-graders' silent reading: A critical test of the self-teaching hypothesis. *Journal of Experimental Child Psychology*, *92*(3), 203–219.

Brady, S. A. (2011). Efficacy of phonics teaching for reading outcomes: Indications from post-NRP research. In S. Brady, D. Braze, & C. Fowler (Eds.), *Explaining individual differences in reading: Theory and evidence* (pp. 69–96). Hoboken, NJ: Psychology Press.

Brown, G. D., & Deavers, R. P. (1999). Units of analysis in nonword reading: Evidence from children and adults. *Journal of Experimental Child Psychology*, *73*(3), 208–242.

Burgess, S. R., & Lonigan, C. J. (1998). Bidirectional relations of phonological sensitivity and pre-reading abilities: Evidence from a preschool sample. *Journal of Experimental Child Psychology*, *70*(2), 117–141.

Burt, J. S. (2006). What is orthographic processing skill and how does it relate to word identification in reading? *Journal of Research in Reading*, *29*(4), 400–417.

Byrne, B., Coventry, W. L., Olson, R. K., Hulslander, J., Wadsworth, S., DeFries, J. C., . . . Samuelsson, S. (2008). A behavior genetic analysis of orthographic learning, spelling and decoding. *Journal of Research in Reading*, *31*(1), 8–21.

Carlisle, J. F. (2000). Awareness of the structure and meaning of morphologically complex words: Impact on reading. *Reading and Writing*, *12*(3), 169–190.

Castles, A., & Nation, K. (2006). How does orthographic learning happen? In S. Andrews (Ed.), *From inkmarks to ideas: Current issues in lexical processing* (pp. 151–179). New York: Psychology Press.

CBC News (2013, December 17). Dartmouth parents want change to keep kids in school. *CBC News*. Retrieved from http://www.cbc.ca/news/canada/nova-scotia/dartmouth-parents-want-change-to-keep-kids-in-school-1.2467004.

Chard, D. J., Stoolmiller, M., Harn, B. A., Wanzek, J., Vaughn, S., Linan-Thompson, S., & Kame'enui, E. J. (2008). Predicting reading success in a multilevel schoolwide reading model: A retrospective analysis. *Journal of Learning Disabilities*, *41*(2), 174–188.

Conrad, N., Harris, N., & Williams, J. (2013). Individual differences in children's literacy development: The contribution of orthographic knowledge. *Reading and Writing*, *26*(8), 1223–1239.

Cunningham, A. E. (2006). Accounting for children's orthographic learning while reading text: Do children self-teach? *Journal of Experimental Child Psychology*, *95*(1), 56–77.

Cunningham, A. E., Nathan, R. G., & Raher, K. (2011). Orthographic processing in models of word recognition. In M. L. Kamil, P. D. Pearson, E. Birr Moje, & P. P. Afflerblach (Eds.), *Handbook of reading research* (Vol. 4, pp. 259–285). New York: Routledge.

Cunningham, A. E., Perry, K. E., & Stanovich, K. E. (2001). Converging evidence for the concept of orthographic processing. *Reading and Writing*, *14*(5–6), 549–568.

Cunningham, A. E., & Stanovich, K. E. (1998). The impact of print exposure on word recognition. In J. L. Metsala & L. C. Ehri (Eds.), *Word recognition in beginning literacy* (pp. 235–262). Hoboken, NJ: Taylor & Francis.

Dahan, D., & Magnuson, J. (2011). Spoken word recognition. In M. Traxler & M. A. Gernsbacher (Eds.), *Handbook of psycholinguistics* (2nd ed., pp. 249–284). San Diego, CA: Academic Press.

D'Angiulli, A., Siegel, L. S., & Hertzman, C. (2004). Schooling, socioeconomic context and literacy development. *Educational Psychology*, *24*(6), 867–883.

D'Angiulli, A., Siegel, L. S., & Maggi, S. (2004). Literacy instruction, SES, and word-reading achievement in English-language learners and children with English as a first language: A longitudinal study. *Learning Disabilities Research & Practice*, *19*(4), 202–213.

Deacon, S. H. (2012). Sounds, letters and meanings: The independent influences of phonological, morphological and orthographic skills on early word reading accuracy. *Journal of Research in Reading*, *35*(4), 456–475.

Deacon, S. H., Benere, J., & Castles, A. (2012). Chicken or egg? Untangling the relationship between orthographic processing skill and reading accuracy. *Cognition*, *122*(1), 110–117.

Deacon, S. H., & Kirby, J. R. (2004). Morphological awareness: Just "more phonological"? The roles of morphological and phonological awareness in reading development. *Applied Psycholinguistics*, *25*(2), 223–238.

Ehri, L. C. (1998). Grapheme–phoneme knowledge is essential for learning to read words in English. In J. L. Metsala & L. C. Ehri (Eds.), *Word recognition in beginning literacy* (pp. 3–40). Hoboken, NJ: Taylor & Francis.

Ehri, L. C. (2005). Development of sight word reading: Phases and findings. In M. J. Snowling & C. Hulme (Eds.), *The science of reading: A handbook* (pp. 135–154). Malden, MA: Blackwell Publishing.

Ehri, L. C. (2014). Orthographic mapping in the acquisition of sight word reading, spelling memory, and vocabulary learning. *Scientific Studies of Reading*, *18*(1), 5–21.

Ehri, L. C., Nunes, S. R., Willows, D. M., Schuster, B. V., Yaghoub-Zadeh, Z., & Shanahan, T. (2001). Phonemic awareness instruction helps children learn to read: Evidence from the National Reading Panel's meta-analysis. *Reading Research Quarterly*, *36*(3), 250–287.

Ehri, L. C., & Saltmarsh, J. (1995). Beginning readers outperform older disabled readers in learning to read words by sight. *Reading and Writing*, *7*(3), 295–326.

Elbro, C., & Jensen, M. N. (2005). Quality of phonological representations, verbal learning, and phoneme awareness in dyslexic and normal readers. *Scandinavian Journal of Psychology*, *46*(4), 375–384.

Foorman, B. R., Francis, D. J., Fletcher, J. M., Schatschneider, C., & Mehta, P. (1998). The role of instruction in learning to read: Preventing reading failure in at-risk children. *Journal of Educational Psychology*, *90*(1), 37–55.

Foorman, B. R., & Al Otaiba, S. (2009). Reading remediation: State of the art. In K. Pugh & P. McCardle (Eds.), *How children learn to read: Current issues and new directions in the integration of cognition, neurobiology, and genetics of reading and dyslexia research and practice* (pp. 257–274). New York: Psychology Press.

Gayán, J., & Olson, R. K. (2003). Genetic and environmental influences on individual differences in printed word recognition. *Journal of Experimental Child Psychology*, *84*(2), 97–123.

Gersten, R., Fuchs, L. S., Williams, J. P., & Baker, S. (2001). Teaching reading comprehension strategies to students with learning disabilities: A review of research. *Review of Educational Research*, *71*(2), 279–320.

Goodwin, A. P., & Ahn, S. (2013). A meta-analysis of morphological interventions in English: Effects on literacy outcomes for school-age children. *Scientific Studies of Reading*, *17*(4), 257–285.

Hagiliassis, N., Pratt, C., & Johnston, M. (2006). Orthographic and phonological processes in reading. *Reading and Writing*, *19*(3), 235–263.

Hart, B., & Risley, T. R. (1995). *Meaningful differences in the everyday experience of young American children*. Baltimore, MD: Paul H. Brookes.

HRSB (Halifax Regional School Board) (2013). *Getting to great: Annual Report to the community: September 2012–June 2014*. Retrieved December 10, 2013 from http://www.hrsb.ns.ca/tools/schoolfinder/communityreports/GVW2012.pdf.

Jenkins, J. R., Fuchs, L. S., van den Broek, P., Espin, C., & Deno, S. L. (2003). Sources of individual differences in reading comprehension and reading fluency. *Journal of Educational Psychology*, *95*(4), 719–729.

Juel, C. (1988). Learning to read and write: A longitudinal study of 54 children from first through fourth grades. *Journal of Educational Psychology*, *80*(4), 437–447.

Kirby, J. R., Deacon, S. H., Bowers, P. N., Izenberg, L., Wade-Woolley, L., & Parrila, R. (2012). Children's morphological awareness and reading ability. *Reading and Writing*, *25*(2), 389–410.

Lee, J., Grigg, W. S., & Donahue, P. (2007). *The nation's report card: Reading, 2007*. Retrieved January 11, 2014 from http://nces.ed.gov/pubsearch/pubsinfo.asp?pubid=2007496.

Lee, V. E., & Burkam, D. T. (2002). *Inequality at the starting gate: Social background differences in achievement as children begin school*. Washington, DC: Economic Policy Institute.

Lesaux, N. K., & Siegel, L. S. (2003). The development of reading in children who speak English as a second language. *Developmental Psychology*, *39*(6), 1005–1019.

**Jamie L. Metsala and Margaret D. David**

Lonigan, C. J. (2007). Vocabulary development and the development of phonological awareness skills in preschool children. In R. K. Wagner, A. E. Muse, & K. R. Tannenbaum (Eds.), *Vocabulary acquisition: Implications for reading comprehension* (pp. 15–31). New York: Guilford Press.

Lonigan, C. J., Anthony, J. L., Phillips, B. M., Purpura, D. J., Wilson, S. B., & McQueen, J. D. (2009). The nature of preschool phonological processing abilities and their relations to vocabulary, general cognitive abilities, and print knowledge. *Journal of Educational Psychology, 101*(2), 345–358.

Lonigan, C. J., Burgess, S. R., & Anthony, J. L. (2000). Development of emergent literacy and early reading skills in preschool children: Evidence from a latent-variable longitudinal study. *Developmental Psychology, 36*(5), 59–613.

Lovett, M. W. (1992). Developmental dyslexia. In S. J. Segalowitz & I. Rapin (Eds.), *Handbook of neuropsychology* (Vol. 7, pp. 163–185). New York: Elsevier Science.

Lovett, M. W., Lacerenza, L., & Borden, S. (2006). *Empower™ Reading.* Toronto, ON: Hospital for Sick Children.

Lovett, M. W., Lacerenza, L., Borden, S. L., Frijters, J. C., Steinbach, K. A., & De Palma, M. (2000). Components of effective remediation for developmental reading disabilities: Combining phonological and strategy-based instruction to improve outcomes. *Journal of Educational Psychology, 92*(2), 263–283.

McDowell, K. D., Lonigan, C. J., & Goldstein, H. (2007). Relations among socioeconomic status, age, and predictors of phonological awareness. *Journal of Speech, Language, and Hearing Research, 50*(4), 1079–1092.

McIntosh, K., Bennett, J. L., & Price, K. (2011). Evaluation of social and academic effects of School-wide Positive Behaviour Support in a Canadian school district. *Exceptionality Education International, 21*(1), 46–60.

Mathes, P. G., Denton, C. A., Fletcher, J. M., Anthony, J. L., Francis, D. J., & Schatschneider, C. (2005). The effects of theoretically different instruction and student characteristics on the skills of struggling readers. *Reading Research Quarterly, 40*(2), 148–182.

Metsala, J. L. & David, M. D. (2015). Response to an Intensive Reading Intervention as a Function of Age and Sublexical Sound-Spelling Automaticity. Manuscript submitted for publication.

Metsala, J. L. (1999). Young children's phonological awareness and nonword repetition as a function of vocabulary development. *Journal of Educational Psychology, 91*(1), 3–19.

Metsala, J. L. (2011). Lexical reorganization and the emergence of phonological awareness. In S. B. Neuman & D. K. Dickinson (Eds.), *Handbook of early literacy research* (Vol. 3, pp. 66–84). New York: Guilford Press.

Metsala, J. L., Arnold, E., & Steele, E. (2013). *Response to an intensive intervention as a function of age, phonological processing, and sublexical sound-spelling automaticity.* Paper presented at the 4th All-European Dyslexia Conference, Växjö, Sweden, September.

Metsala, J. L., & Walley, A. C. (1998). Spoken vocabulary growth and the segmental restructuring of lexical representations: Precursors to phonemic awareness and early reading ability. In J. L. Metsala & L. C. Ehri (Eds.), *Word recognition in beginning literacy* (pp. 89–120). Mahwah, NJ: Lawrence Erlbaum and Associates.

Moats, L. C. (2000). *Every child reading: A professional development guide.* Washington, DC: Learning First Alliance.

Moats, L. C. (2007*). Whole language high jinks.* Washington, DC: Thomas Fordham Foundation.

Molfese, V. J., Modglin, A., & Molfese, D. L. (2003). The role of environment in the development of reading skills: A longitudinal study of preschool and school-age measures. *Journal of Learning Disabilities, 36*(1), 59–67.

Morris, R. D., Lovett, M. W., Wolf, M., Sevcik, R. A., Steinbach, K. A., Fritjers, J. C., & Shapiro, M. B. (2012). Multiple-component remediation for developmental reading disabilities: IQ, socioeconomic status, and race as factors in remedial outcome. *Journal of Learning Disabilities, 45*(2), 99–127.

Nagy, W. E., & Anderson, R. C. (1984). How many words are there in printed school English? *Reading Research Quarterly, 19*, 304–330.

National Early Literacy Panel (2008). *Developing early literacy: Report of the National Early Literacy Panel.* Washington, DC: National Institute for Literacy.

National Reading Panel (2000). Teaching children to read. (NIH Publication No. 00–4769). Bethesda, MD: National Institute of Child Health and Human Development.

Neuman, S. B. (2011). The challenge of teaching vocabulary in early education. In S. B. Neuman & D. K. Dickinson (Eds.), *Handbook of early literacy research*, (Vol. 3, pp. 358–373). New York: Guilford Press.

Norton, E. S., & Wolf, M. (2012). Rapid automatized naming (RAN) and reading fluency: Implications for understanding and treatment of reading disabilities. *Annual Review of Psychology*, *63*, 427–452.

NVSD (North Vancouver School District) (2013). *District literacy plan 2013*. Retrieved January. 14, 2014 from http://www.sd44.ca/Board/Literacy/Documents/DistrictLiteracyPlan2013_14.pdf.

Olson, R. K., Byrne, B., & Samuelsson, S. (2009). Reconciling strong genetic and strong environmental influences on individual differences and deficits in reading ability. In K. Pugh & P. McCardle (Eds.), *How children learn to read: Current issues and new directions in the integration of cognition, neurobiology and genetics of reading and dyslexia research and practice* (pp. 215–233). New York: Psychology Press.

Olson, R., Forsberg, H., Wise, B., & Rack, J. (1994). Measurement of word recognition, orthographic, and phonological skills. In G. R. Lyon (Ed.), *Frames of reference for the assessment of learning disabilities: New views on measurement issues* (pp. 243–277). Baltimore, MD: Paul H. Brookes Publishing.

Olson, R. K., Wise, B., Connors, F., & Rack, J. (1990). Organization, heritability, and remediation of component word recognition and language skills in disabled readers. In T. H. Carr & B. A. Levy (Eds.), *Reading and its development: Component skills approaches* (pp. 261–322). San Diego, CA: Academic Press.

Open Court Reading (1995). *Collections for young scholars*. Chicago, IL: SRA/McGraw-Hill.

Pan, B. A., Rowe, M. L., Singer, J. D., & Snow, C. E. (2005). Maternal correlates of growth in toddler vocabulary production in low-income families. *Child Development*, *76*(4), 763–782.

Pennington, B. F., Cardoso-Martins, C., Green, P. A., & Lefly, D. L. (2001). Comparing the phonological and double deficit hypotheses for developmental dyslexia. *Reading and Writing*, *14*(7–8), 707–755.

Perfetti, C. (2007). Reading ability: Lexical quality to comprehension. *Scientific Studies of Reading*, *11*(4), 357–383.

Powell, D., Stainthorp, R., & Stuart, M. (2014). Deficits in orthographic knowledge in children poor at rapid automatized naming (RAN) tasks? *Scientific Studies of Reading*, *18*(3), 192–207.

Rashotte, C. A., MacPhee, K., & Torgesen, J. K. (2001). The effectiveness of a group reading instruction program with poor readers in multiple grades. *Learning Disability Quarterly*, *24*(2), 119–134.

Roman, A. A., Kirby, J. R., Parrila, R. K., Wade-Woolley, L., & Deacon, S. H. (2009). Toward a comprehensive view of the skills involved in word reading in Grades 4, 6, and 8. *Journal of Experimental Child Psychology*, *102*(1), 96–113.

Rowe, D. W. (2008). Social contracts for writing: Negotiating shared understandings about text in the preschool years. *Reading Research Quarterly*, *43*(1), 66–95.

Rvachew, S., & Grawburg, M. (2006). Correlates of phonological awareness in preschoolers with speech sound disorders. *Journal of Speech, Language, and Hearing Research*, *49*(1), 74–87.

Scarborough, H. S., Ehri, L. C., Olson, R. K., & Fowler, A. E. (1998). The fate of phonemic awareness beyond the elementary school years. *Scientific Studies of Reading*, *2*(2), 115–142.

Schatschneider, C., Carlson, C. D., Francis, D. J., Foorman, B. R., & Fletcher, J. M. (2002). Relationship of rapid automatized naming and phonological awareness in early reading development: Implications for the double-deficit hypothesis. *Journal of Learning Disabilities*, *35*(3), 245–256.

Shankweiler, D., Crain, S., Katz, L., Fowler, A. E., Liberman, A. M., Brady, S. A., . . . Shaywitz, B. A. (1995). Cognitive profiles of reading-disabled children: Comparison of language skills in phonology, morphology, and syntax. *Psychological Science*, *6*(3), 149–156.

Share, D. L. (1995). Phonological recoding and self-teaching: Sine qua non of reading acquisition. *Cognition*, *55*(2), 151–218.

Share, D. L. (1999). Phonological recoding and orthographic learning: A direct test of the self-teaching hypothesis. *Journal of Experimental Child Psychology*, *72*(2), 95–129.

Share, D. L. (2008). Orthographic learning, phonological recoding, and self-teaching. In R. V. Kail (Ed.), *Advances in child development and behavior* (Vol. 36, pp. 31–82). San Diego, CA: Elsevier Academic Press.

Siegel, L. S. (1998). Phonological processing deficits and reading disabilities. In J. L. Metsala & L. C. Ehri (Eds.), *Word recognition in beginning literacy* (pp. 141–161). Mahwah, NJ: Lawrence Erlbaum Associates.

Silvén, M., Niemi, P., & Voeten, M. J. (2002). Do maternal interaction and early language predict phonological awareness in 3-to 4-year-olds? *Cognitive Development*, *17*(1), 1133–1155.

Snow, C. E., Burns, M. S., & Griffin, P. (Eds.) (1998). *Preventing reading difficulties in young children*. Washington, DC: National Academy Press.

SpellRead™ Program (2009). Austin, TX: PCI-Education.

Stanovich, K. E. (2000). *Progress in understanding reading: Scientific foundations and new frontiers*. New York: Guilford Press.

Stanovich, K. E., & Siegel, L. S. (1994). Phenotypic performance profile of children with reading disabilities: A regression-based test of the phonological-core variable-difference model. *Journal of Educational Psychology*, *86*(1), 24–53.

Storkel, H. L. (2002). Restructuring of similarity neighborhoods in the developing mental lexicon. *Journal of Child Language*, *29*(2), 251–274.

Stuebing, K. K., Fletcher, J. M., LeDoux, J. M., Lyon, G. R., Shaywitz, S. E., & Shaywitz, B. A. (2002). Validity of IQ-discrepancy classifications of reading disabilities: A meta-analysis. *American Educational Research Journal*, *39*(2), 469–518.

Swan, D., & Goswami, U. (1997). Phonological awareness deficits in developmental dyslexia and the phonological representations hypothesis. *Journal of Experimental Child Psychology*, *66*(1), 18–41.

Torgesen, J. K. (2006). Recent discoveries from research on remedial interventions for children with dyslexia. In M. Snowling & C. Hulme (Eds.), *The science of reading: A handbook* (pp. 521–537). Oxford: Blackwell.

Torgesen, J. K., Alexander, A. W., Wagner, R. K., Rashotte, C. A., Voeller, K. K., & Conway, T. (2001). Intensive remedial instruction for children with severe reading disabilities. *Journal of Learning Disabilities*, *34*(1), 33–58.

Torgesen, J. K., & Hudson, R. (2006). Reading fluency: Critical issues for struggling readers. In S. J. Samuels & A. Farstrup (Eds.), *Reading fluency: The forgotten dimension of reading success* (pp.130–158). Newark, DE: International Reading Association.

Torppa, M., Poikkeus, A.-M., Laasko, M.-L., Tolvanen, A., Leskinen, E., Leppanen, P. H. T., . . . Lyytinen, H. (2007). Modeling the early paths of phonological awareness and factors supporting its development in children with and without familial risk of dyslexia. *Scientific Studies of Reading*, *11*(2), 73–103.

Treiman, R. (1993). *Beginning to spell: A study of first-grade children*. New York: Oxford University Press.

Vaughn, S., Wanzek, J., Murray, C. S., Scammacca, N., Linan-Thompson, S., & Woodruff, A. L. (2009). Response to early reading intervention examining higher and lower responders. *Exceptional Children*, *75*(2), 165–183.

Vellutino, F. R., Scanlon, D. M., & Jaccard, J. (2003). Toward distinguishing between cognitive and experiential deficits as primary sources of difficulty in learning to read: A two year follow-up of difficult to remediate and readily remediated poor readers. In B. R. Foorman (Ed.), *Preventing and remediating reading difficulties: Bringing science to scale* (pp. 73–120). Baltimore, MD: York Press.

Vellutino, F. R., Scanlon, D. M., Sipay, E. R., Small, S. G., Pratt, A., Chen, R., & Denckla, M. B. (1996). Cognitive profiles of difficult-to-remediate and readily remediated poor readers: Early intervention as a vehicle for distinguishing between cognitive and experiential deficits as basic causes of specific reading disability. *Journal of Educational Psychology*, *88*(4), 601–638.

Vellutino, F. R., Tunmer, W. E., Jaccard, J. J., & Chen, R. (2007). Components of reading ability: Multivariate evidence for a convergent skills model of reading development. *Scientific Studies of Reading*, *11*(1), 3–32.

Vukovic, R. K., & Siegel, L. S. (2006). The double-deficit hypothesis: A comprehensive analysis of the evidence. *Journal of Learning Disabilities*, *39*(1), 25–47.

Warmington, M., & Hulme, C. (2012). Phoneme awareness, visual-verbal paired-associate learning, and rapid automatized naming as predictors of individual differences in reading ability. *Scientific Studies of Reading*, *16*(1), 45–62.

Wasik, B. A., & Hindman, A. H. (2011). Identifying critical components of an effective preschool language and literacy coaching intervention model. In S. B. Neuman, & D. K. Dickinson (Eds.), *Handbook of early literacy research* (Vol. 3, pp. 322–336). New York: Guilford Press.

Wise, J. C., Sevcik, R. A., Morris, R. D., Lovett, M. W., & Wolf, M. (2007). The relationship among receptive and expressive vocabulary, listening comprehension, pre-reading skills, word identification skills, and reading comprehension by children with reading disabilities. *Journal of Speech, Language, and Hearing Research*, *50*(4), 1093–1109.

Wise, J. C., Sevcik, R. A., Morris, R. D., Lovett, M. W., Wolf, M., Kuhn, M., . . . Schwanenflugel, P. (2010). The relationship between different measures of oral reading fluency and reading comprehension in second-grade students who evidence different oral reading fluency difficulties. *Language, Speech, and Hearing Services in Schools*, *41*(3), 340–348.

Wolf, M., & Bowers, P. G. (1999). The double-deficit hypothesis for the developmental dyslexias. *Journal of Educational Psychology*, *91*(3), 415–438.

Ziegler, J. C., & Goswami, U. (2005). Reading acquisition, developmental dyslexia, and skilled reading across languages: A psycholinguistic grain size theory. *Psychological Bulletin*, *131*(1), 3–29.

# 9

# Reading Fluency

*Paula J. Schwanenflugel and Melanie R. Kuhn*

In this chapter, we provide a description of the components of reading fluency and discuss the development of individual differences in fluency, including the development of fluency in English learners. While the focus of the chapter will be oral reading fluency, we will also address the transition from oral to silent reading.

## Definitions of Reading Fluency

Despite the dominance of certain definitions of fluency in the classroom, there is a lack of consensus among researchers as to which elements of the reading process should be included in a definition of fluency and which should be relegated to another aspect of skilled reading. Some definitions are very expansive in scope. For example, Wolf and Katzir-Cohen (2001) state:

> reading fluency involves every process and subskill involved in reading . . . unlike reading accuracy, which can be executed without utilizing some important reading components like semantic processes, we argue that fluency is influenced by the development of rapid rates of processing in all the components of reading (p. 220).

Others are more circumscribed, emphasizing only those processes involved in accurate and automatic word recognition (e.g., Hudson, Pullen, Lane, & Torgesen, 2009). A third definition eschews automaticity and accuracy in favor of those prosodic processes involved in good oral reading performance (Daane, Campbell, Grigg, Goodman, & Oranje, 2005; Rasinski, Rikli, & Johnston, 2009). Yet another describes fluent reading as the ability to decode and comprehend text simultaneously (Samuels, 2006). After examining the evidence associated with fluency, Kuhn, Schwanenflugel, and Meisinger (2010) suggest that reading fluency should be defined as:

> Fluency combines accuracy, automaticity, and oral reading prosody, which, taken together, facilitate the reader's construction of meaning. It is demonstrated during oral reading through ease of word recognition, appropriate pacing, phrasing, and intonation. It is a factor in both oral and silent reading that can limit or support comprehension (p. 242).

This definition recognizes fluency's foundational relationship with comprehension, while focusing attention on the accurate, automatic, and prosodic reading characteristics of fluent reading. In our view, good comprehension includes processes that develop over an individual's lifetime, long after most of us would be considered fluent (Paris, 2005). Importantly, while poor fluency often interferes with comprehension, good fluency does not necessarily guarantee good comprehension. In fact, if individuals are limited by their vocabulary, topic knowledge, knowledge of the language, or ability to draw sensible inferences while reading, they will experience difficulty comprehending a selection despite fluent reading.

## Fluency and Automaticity

The key features of fluency discussed by Kuhn et al. (2010) are accuracy, automaticity, and prosody. Automaticity in this case refers to the accurate, quick, and effortless execution of processes connected with reading text. Automaticity and accuracy develop concurrently as young readers engage in practice. Indeed, an emphasis on reading accuracy in instruction has the effect of increasing reading speed as well, regardless of whether or not speed has been targeted (Hudson, Isakson, Richman, Lane, & Arriaza-Allen, 2011).

Typically, the automaticity aspect of fluency is measured by calculating words correct per minute (*wcpm*) for connected text reading. This automatic processing of text is thought to free up cognitive resources for comprehension and it is the element of reading fluency that is most often measured. In fact, increases in automaticity with a given text accrue rather quickly early in practice and begin to diminish at a certain point, despite further practice; this process is reflective of the so-called *power law of learning* (Logan, 1997). Evidence for this power law can be seen in the cumulative effects of practice over the long term. For example, between 2nd and 4th grade, children gain an average of 34 wcpm in terms of their reading rate, but gain only 1 wcpm between 6th and 8th grade (Hasbrouck & Tindal, 2006).

Benefits of practice are derived at the sub-lexical, lexical, phrasal, and, possibly, sentence levels. Children begin to read by using smaller chunks such as simple letter–sound correspondences, move to larger units such as syllables and morphemes (Nunes, Bryant, & Barros, 2012), and, eventually, read whole words. This collapsing of steps, called *unitization*, along with the speeding up of sub-processes allows reading to become effortless and quick. Oft-repeated words and phrases shift from being read using slow, arduous, word-by-word processing to smooth and natural readings. Unfortunately, children who have difficulty converting letter decoding into multi-letter units for naming have poorer oral reading fluency growth later (Harn, Stoolmiller, & Chard, 2008).

## Fluency and Reading Prosody

Reading aloud with good prosody (used here interchangeably with the term *reading expression*) is also an important marker in the development of reading fluency (Kuhn et al., 2010). Reading prosody is determined by variations in pitch (traditionally, fundamental frequency, $F_0$), stress and intensity (amplitude) placed on certain words and phrases, and pausing that may interrupt or contribute to the rhythm and flow of the reading. Good reading prosody has been theorized to emerge when children acquire automatic decoding and sight word recognition skills that free up resources for expression and comprehension (Schwanenflugel, Hamilton, Kuhn, Wisenbaker, & Stahl 2004).

Fluent children show substantial pitch variability and pitch distinctions that are adult-like (Benjamin & Schwanenflugel, 2010; Miller & Schwanenflugel, 2006). They show falling pitch at the ends of declarative sentences and distinct pitch rises as they read yes–no questions (Miller, & Schwanenflugel, 2006). When fluent children pause within the reading, they do so at grammatically relevant junctures within a sentence (Benjamin & Schwanenflugel, 2010). They assign appropriate stress patterns to syllables within words (Gutierrez-Palma & Palma-Reyes, 2007). They also highlight linguistically focused text elements prosodically through increased pitch and amplitude (Schwanenflugel, Westmoreland, & Benjamin, 2013). Essentially, as children become fluent, their reading begins to incorporate many of the prosodic features we find in spontaneous speech.

As children develop good reading prosody, it becomes possible for listeners to rate them reliably as sounding more expressive (Benjamin et al., 2013; Rasinski et al., 2009). Currently, ratings schemes that measure reading expression vary in the number of dimensions that are rated, ranging from one (NAEP fluency scale; Daane et al., 2005) or two (Comprehensive Oral Reading Scale; Benjamin et al., 2013) to four (Multidimensional Fluency Scale; Paige, Rasinski, & Magpuri-Lavell, 2012). Since poor oral reading prosody can remain a problem for struggling readers from childhood through adulthood (Binder et al., 2013; Paige et al., 2012), it is important that we determine which students are experiencing difficulty with this component of their fluency development.

In sum, fluent oral reading sounds much like regular speech, whereas disfluent reading is often monotone, hesitant and fails to encode the communicative intent of the author. While we include studies in this review that exclude prosody measures in favor of wcpm alone, from a validity standpoint doing so de-emphasizes expression in our understanding of reading fluency (Kuhn et al., 2010; Schwanenflugel, & Benjamin, 2012).

## Fluency and Comprehension

A key point in our definition of reading fluency is that it can limit or support reading comprehension. This understanding is backed up by strong correlations found between reading fluency and comprehension. As elementary school children are building fluency, these correlations are usually between .50 and .85, whether measured by wcpm or prosody-linking metrics (Lai, Benjamin, Schwanenflugel, & Kuhn, 2013; Valencia et al., 2010). Further, the correlations are strong across reading comprehension assessment methods such as CBM maze tests, group administered comprehension tests, and end-of-year state tests, although the correlations are somewhat higher when tests are administered individually (Reschly, Busch, Betts, Deno, & Long, 2009). Oral reading fluency, measured as wcpm, is often used for reading benchmark assessment; these are periodic assessments administered throughout the school year to evaluate children's progress toward long-term reading goals (Deno, Fuchs, Marston, & Shin, 2001). Fluency benchmark assessments are seen as particularly effective since, unlike comprehension passages, they are relatively free of racial or socioeconomic status bias (Hintze, Callahan, Matthews, Williams, & Tobin, 2002). Finally, in terms of development, students' growth rates in oral reading fluency help predict later comprehension (Kim, Petscher, Schatschneider, & Foorman, 2010).

However, it is worth noting that when all aspects of fluency are measured, the ability to predict reading comprehension improves. Adding measures of expression to wcpm allows us to account for an additional 3–20 percent over the variance accounted for by wcpm alone (Benjamin & Schwanenflugel, 2010; Benjamin et al., 2013; Valencia et al., 2010). This is important since, children who read with acceptable reading rates but poor expression comprehend less well.

Some research finds that the correlation between fluency and comprehension gradually weakens to the .50–.60 mark over elementary school and into middle school (Denton et al.,

2011; Silberglitt, Burns, Madyun, & Lail, 2006), whereas other researchers have not observed this downward trend (Reschly et al., 2009; Valencia et al., 2010). However, if the downward trend is real, the cause may be attributed to changes in the reading materials themselves. These materials become more complex, requiring greater topic knowledge, vocabulary, and inferencing abilities as children proceed through school (Paris, 2005). Despite this, disfluency remains a barrier to comprehension for a subset of adolescent struggling readers (Brasseur-Hock, Hock, Kieffer, Biancarosa, & Deshler, 2011; Rasinski et al., 2009). Bearing this in mind, fluency's relationship to comprehension remains strong enough to serve as a general proxy for reading skills as a whole, although we caution that these evaluations only provide a snapshot of a student's reading.

## Word Callers and Comprehension

The *word caller* concept is often used for children who show good reading fluency but minimal comprehension. This point of view is described eloquently in the article, "She's my best reader, she just can't comprehend" (Applegate, Applegate, & Modla, 2009). Indeed, in one study, teachers nominated nearly a quarter of their students as word callers (Meisinger, Bradley, Schwanenflugel, & Kuhn, 2010). However, if fluency is foundational to comprehension and there is strong correlation between the two, how can there be so many word callers?

It turns out that not that many elementary children qualify as true word callers. A true word caller should have at least average fluency, but substantially below average reading comprehension skills. Of all the students Meisinger, Bradley, Schwanenflugel, and Kuhn (2009) looked at, they identified only 2 percent of elementary children as true word callers. In a second study, Hamilton and Shinn (2003) identified *no* true word callers among teacher-identified word callers. However, Quirk and Beem (2012) were able to identify many true word callers among English learners.

Exactly how teachers identify word callers is unclear, but they often nominate children who are *neither* particularly fluent nor good at comprehension (Meisinger et al., 2009; Hamilton & Shinn, 2003). Intriguingly, Meisinger et al. (2010) did find that, according to one criterion, the number of true word callers increased to nearly 10 percent by 5th grade. Whether this percentage continues to increase through middle school we cannot say. However, this increase makes sense if the correlation between reading fluency and comprehension weakens around that time, as other factors such as topic knowledge, vocabulary, and inferencing abilities become more important.

## Directionality of the Influence Between Fluency and Comprehension

Up to this point, we have described reading fluency as a foundational skill for comprehension. This suggests that fluency supports comprehension as a bottom-up, data-driven process. However, it has been argued that the relationship between fluency and comprehension is bi-directional: both reciprocal and interactive. This reciprocity view holds that expectations driven from memory may provide influences above and beyond bottom-up processes. In this view, context speeds up the recognition of upcoming words through expectancies generated from discourse features, collocations accrued from prior knowledge, and the general priming operations of the lexicon. Thus, having good comprehension of ongoing text might affect the speed, accuracy, and prosody involved in reading text as well.

Evidence for reciprocal effects of comprehension on fluency has been difficult to establish. It is relatively easy to show that reading comprehension predicts reading fluency, even after controlling for various fluency-related factors measured concurrently (Berninger et al., 2010).

In fact, several studies have used a longitudinal design to evaluate whether there is a reciprocal relationship between fluency and comprehension. In these designs, researchers assess children's reading fluency and comprehension skills over several time points to determine whether changes in one skill lead to changes in the other skill later on. Klauda and Guthrie (2008) examined changes in reading fluency and comprehension in 5th graders over a 12-week period. Fluency at the earlier time point significantly predicted later comprehension after controlling for earlier comprehension skills, although the effect was very small. Similarly, Lai et al. (2014) followed 2nd grade children over an eight-month period but failed to find evidence of reciprocity.

Priebe, Keenan, and Miller (2012) started with the premise that, if comprehension skills were to enhance word recognition and fluency skills, it would do so primarily on passages for which children had topic knowledge. They selected children who had similar fluency, reading comprehension, and vocabulary skills, but who varied on topic knowledge. They then asked the children to read passages for which they did or did not have topic knowledge. Having topic knowledge significantly increased fluency (and improved comprehension) for poor decoders, but made no difference for average readers in terms of either fluency or comprehension. Thus, poor decoders used topic knowledge as a compensatory mechanism to help them read more fluently whereas skilled readers did not (Stanovich, West, & Feeman, 1981).

The issue of directionality of effects between fluency and comprehension remains a somewhat open question. Indeed, individual differences in this directionality may enable us to understand the role that fluency plays in reading. The directional relationship from fluency to comprehension is not in doubt and seems to apply to most readers. Indeed, having accurate, automatic, and expressive reading seems to assist in the construction of meaning for all readers. But using ongoing comprehension to identify upcoming words, and influence fluency, may be relegated to very poor readers.

## Fluency in Developmental Context

In Chall's (1996) stage model of reading, fluency is said to emerge during the third in a series of stages describing reading development. In the first two stages, children have: (1) gained familiarity with emergent literacy skills such as an ability to manipulate phonemes, book-handling knowledge, and a few sight words; and (2) learned how to link phonemes to basic letter patterns, and blend them to decode basic words. It is only after children become adept at these skills that they begin to develop fluency. According to Chall, once children can read most texts with some fluency, they can begin to use their cognitive resources to learn from text. Chall described the distinction between the first three stages and later ones as the transition between "learning to read" and "reading as a tool for learning, as texts begin to contain new words and ideas beyond their own language and their knowledge of the world" (Chall, & Jacobs, 2003, p. 15).

This view of reading has been critiqued as depicting a hard and fast distinction between developmental periods. The dichotomy from learning to read to reading to learn may not be based in the changing structure of reading skills, however, and changing instructional emphasis away from decoding after a certain point is not only beneficial to reading outcomes, but, we would argue, it is also essential (Sonnenschein, Stapleton, & Benson, 2010). We might also point out that learning to read construed in a broader sense does not end after children begin to acquire fluency. However, the existence of the theoretical dichotomy that occurs before and after fluency remains an open question.

Some would further argue that Chall's model implies comprehension instruction should be put off until after children become fluent (Houck & Ross, 2012). However, we view this as a misreading of her work. Indeed, comprehension instruction can ensue while maintaining an effective classroom focus on fluency (Kuhn et al., 2006; Schwanenflugel et al., 2009; Stahl, 2008). Integrating both types of instruction is especially important for struggling readers who might not receive comprehension instruction otherwise. Once children become fundamentally fluent, however, the curricular balance should shift away from decoding and fluency, as the Chall model suggests.

A third critique is directed at the emphasis on using texts with familiar settings and concepts in the learning to read phase. Certainly, the Common Core State Standards, with its emphasis on informational text, will introduce children early to the idea that reading can serve as a means to learn new things. At a basic level, some findings suggest that fourth graders can read informational text as fluently as narratives without negative impact on comprehension (Cervetti, Bravo, Hiebert, Pearson, & Jaynes, 2009). Finally, there is no evidence that using texts containing unfamiliar materials instructionally for fluency practice is particularly problematic for building fluency (Hiebert, 2005).

## Transition to Silent Reading

To a large extent, oral reading has been viewed as a transitional period on the way to silent reading. Oral reading may boost the phonological code for young children, helping them maintain information in working memory. This use of oral reading can be seen when adults switch to an oral mode upon encountering difficult text (Hardyck & Petrinovich, 1970). Further, oral reading may assist children by providing them with an external self-regulating function until the reading process has become fully internalized (Prior et al., 2011). Oral reading is also used in early elementary school to provide teachers with information about students' reading proficiency

It is also important to note that low-skilled and beginning readers understand what they are reading better in the oral mode than silent mode (Holmes & Allison, 1985; Miller & Smith, 1985). Prior et al. (2011) showed that, in general, oral reading comprehension was superior in 1st through 5th grades, but silent reading was superior by 7th grade. Silent reading fluency becomes uniquely related to comprehension above and beyond the effects of oral reading fluency as reading skills develop (Kim, Wagner, & Lopez, 2012) and fluent readers make the transition to good comprehension during silent reading sooner (Kim et al., 2012). Thus, oral reading is a transitional mode of reading that helps children make the most of their developing reading skills.

## Developmental Precursors to Fluency

Because of the impact of reading fluency on later reading skills, it is important to be able to discern which children will and will not have difficulties acquiring appropriate levels of fluency. A goal of research on reading precursors is to discern factors that will enable us to identify children who will later have reading problems. As we have moved away from IQ-achievement discrepancy formulas to identify reading disabilities (Fletcher et al., 1994), it becomes increasingly important to determine the correct precursors to measure. A second benefit of identifying precursors is to recognize which skills can be targeted instructionally to improve children's fluency over the long haul.

### Letter Naming Automaticity

Letter naming automaticity, often called letter name fluency, refers to the number of randomly presented letters that kindergarten or first grade children can name in one minute. Letter naming automaticity may help children to integrate the connections between phonemes and letters, setting the stage for fast and accurate decoding later (Treiman, Tincoff, Rodriguez, Mouzaki, & Francis, 1998). Speece, Mills, Ritchey, and Hillman (2003) determined that letter name automaticity showed the greatest sensitivity and specificity out of eight literacy measures in distinguishing kindergarteners who would fall below the 25th percentile on reading fluency assessments at the end of 1st grade. Stage, Sheppard, Davidson, and Browning (2001) also found that kindergarteners' letter name automaticity predicted which children would show limited fluency growth later. Thus, children having slow letter naming skills are likely to display reading fluency difficulties later.

These findings would suggest that interventions focused on increasing letter automaticity might be warranted. Unfortunately, the only intervention we are aware of on this topic carried out intensive letter training intervention over 12 school days and had very transient effects on reading fluency, disappearing after only seven weeks (Fugate, 1997).

## Rapid Automatized Naming (RAN)

Rapid automatized naming refers to the speed with which a student is able to identify numbers, letters, colors, or pictures of objects presented sequentially from left to right. RAN is predictive of reading fluency, although the effect size may be small when other factors are controlled for (Hudson, Torgesen, Lane, & Turner, 2012; Schwanenflugel et al., 2006). Taub and Szente (2012) showed that RAN scores (letter and digit naming) predicted reading fluency in grades 1–4, but that its effects were mediated by the development of phonological awareness. Georgiou, Parrila, and Papadopoulous (2008) found 1st-grade digit naming to be predictive of reading fluency in 1st and 2nd-grade English readers, but only in 1st-grade Greek children. Slow RAN is associated with a small number of Finnish children (5.6 percent) having particularly slow fluency later (Lyytinen et al., 2006). It is also possible that RAN is more important for learning to read in nontransparent orthographies such as English, and logographic languages such as Chinese (Pan et al., 2011). Therefore, the function of RAN might be to capture arbitrary mappings between orthography and phonology.

Unfortunately, there are a variety of interpretations of RAN ranging from its possible measurement of automaticity of access to phonological or orthographic representations (Bowers, 1995; Torgesen, Wagner, Rashotte, Burgess, & Hecht, 1997) to its reflection of common processes with reading "from eye saccades to working memory to the connecting of orthographic and phonological representations" (Norton, & Wolf, 2012, p. 430). Without a good understanding of the meaning of RAN for the development of reading fluency, it is difficult to determine how to use information related to RAN instructionally to prevent fluency problems later (Kirby, Georgiou, Martinussen, & Parrila, 2010). Not many reading researchers would advocate the training of generalized naming speed as a way of improving struggling readers' later fluency.

## Phonological/Phonemic Awareness

Phonological awareness refers to children's developing knowledge regarding the sound system of language, particularly in reference to syllables, onsets, rimes, and phonemes, and children's ability to manipulate them. Phonological awareness is a good predictor of later reading fluency, even after controlling for a variety of other factors (Georgiou et al., 2008; Speece et al., 2003; Taub & Szente, 2012). Lei et al. (2011) identified a specific group of children with poor reading fluency who had poor phonological awareness (as well as poor RAN and morphological awareness) early on. Phonological awareness probably has its greatest impact on learning to read words fluently (Ehri, 1995; Eldridge, 2005; Roman, Kirby, Parrila, Wade-Woolley, & Deacon, 2009; Vassen & Blomert, 2010). Presumably, then, having intensive classroom instruction on phonological awareness during the period of emergent literacy should impact later reading fluency by increasing children's word recognition automaticity. Yet, Reading and Van Deuren (2007) found that a classroom emphasis on phonological awareness skills in kindergarten had no effects on reading fluency by the end of 1st grade.

## Bilingualism and Reading Fluency

The impact of second language literacy on reading skills and their development is an important research focus. We have discussed how reading fluency is highly indicative of the general state of reading skills among young readers. Less clear, however, is the role that reading fluency plays among children whose dominant language is not English. Other linguistic skills surely have a role to play, and studying this topic will help us better understand the factors involved in learning to read. We will focus here on what we know about the development of reading fluency in English learners (ELs) living in the US.

As noted earlier, one reason that reading fluency has been emphasized in both assessment and instruction is its strong correlation with reading comprehension. As with native speakers, there is a good, although weaker, correlation between reading fluency and reading comprehension in EL children (.40–.60 for ELs compared to .50–.85 for non-ELs; Crosson & Lesaux, 2010; Quirk & Beem, 2012). The impact of oral reading fluency on reading comprehension is reasonably moderated by English oral language competencies such as vocabulary and listening comprehension (Crosson & Lesaux, 2010). For example, Quirk and Beem (2012) noted a distinct gap between EL children's normative reading fluency and their comprehension skills. They identified as many as 55.5 percent of 2nd and 3rd-grade ELs as word callers (normative fluency > 2/3 SD reading comprehension scores). These findings support the view that oral language is an important foundation that allows fluency to serve as the bridge to comprehension.

Identifying which EL students need special education services can be particularly problematic and oral reading fluency assessment can be an important component when determining whether a particular child needs such services. Al Otaiba et al. (2009) found that both EL children who never qualified for English language services and those who graduated from ESL programs read below grade level and both groups showed slower growth when compared to national norms; this pattern was even more evident among children currently receiving ESL programming. Linan-Thompson, Cirino, and Vaughn (2007) suggest that this discrepancy between ELs and the normative growth rate may be particularly useful in specifying which ELs will and will not need special education services later. While we would argue that this area needs additional exploration, what is clear is that national norms for fluency that fail to take language status into account are not as valid for use with English learners.

## Implications of Individual Differences in Reading Fluency for Theories of Reading Fluency

Our understanding of the importance of reading fluency has been built on the study of individual differences. To a great extent, the dominant methodology has been correlations and related techniques. We have described the central role of reading fluency in determining the general status of reading skills in young readers. Reading fluency, as described by wcpm and reading expression, are good, reliable indicators of later reading ability. Slow, inaccurate, inexpressive readers tend to do poorly on assessments of later reading comprehension whereas fluent readers tend to do well. Theoretically, this suggests that poor fluency impedes access to higher levels of comprehension because the children lack a veridical account of the text and the cognitive resources to engage comprehension processes. However, findings with EL children have shown us that fluency by itself is not enough to support good comprehension. Without the language foundation to support comprehension, comprehension will be limited.

We have also described a distinct role for reading expression in fluency. Children who read in a monotone fashion with inappropriate and long pause breaks are unlikely to have good comprehension. The precise mechanisms by which oral reading prosody may assist in comprehension are unclear, but we do know that good expression marks much that is important to comprehension, including attention to syntactic structures, topicality, and informational focus. More work is needed to discern how much emphasis to place on expression in fluency instruction (Ardoin, Morena, Binder, & Foster, 2013).

Children who are not automatic with the precursors of reading fluency (letter naming, RAN, and phonological awareness) are likely to have fluency problems later. Letter naming and phonological awareness seem to us to be *true* precursors (i.e., a skill that precedes another and that often leads to its development). RAN, on the other hand, strikes us as more of a predictor than a precursor. What is lacking with all of these precursors, however, is an understanding of whether, how, and how much to intervene instructionally with them to support later reading fluency.

We have also discussed oral reading as a transitional phase in learning to read. Research suggests that children who do not have good oral reading skills may experience difficulty comprehending what they read when reading silently. It is also the case that we have yet to determine exactly how fluent children need to be to make the transition to silent reading. Finally, we need to understand how long disfluent children should continue in the oral reading mode and how their transition to silent reading can be best fostered.

Reading fluency has moved from being among the most neglected topics in our understanding of reading development to a highly developed one. As shown in this chapter, our developing understanding of individual differences in reading fluency will provide us with a fuller understanding of how reading fluency provides a bridge to comprehension.

## References

Al Otaiba, S., Petscher, Y., Pappamihiel, N. E., Williams, R. S., Dyrlund, A. K., & Connor, C. (2009). Modeling oral reading fluency and development in Latino students: A longitudinal study across second and third grade. *Journal of Educational Psychology, 101*(2), 315–329.

Applegate, M. D., Applegate, A. J., & Modla, V. B. (2009). "She's my best reader; she just can't comprehend": Studying the relationship between fluency and comprehension. *Reading Teacher, 62*(6), 512–521.

Ardoin, S. P., Morena, L. S., Binder, K. S., & Foster, T. E. (2013). Examining the impact of feedback and repeated readings on oral reading fluency: Let's not forget prosody. *School Psychology Quarterly, 28*(4), 391–404. doi:10.1037/spq0000027

Benjamin, R. G., & Schwanenflugel, P. J. (2010). Text complexity and oral reading prosody in young readers. *Reading Research Quarterly, 45*(4), 388–404.

Benjamin, R. G., Schwanenflugel, P. J., Meisinger, E. B., Groff, C., Kuhn, M. R., & Steiner, L. (2013). A spectrographically grounded scale for evaluating reading expressiveness. *Reading Research Quarterly, 48*(2), 105–133.

Berninger, V. W., Abbott, R. D., Trivedi, P., Olson, E., Gould, L., Hiramatsu, S., . . . York Westhaggen, S. (2010). Applying the multiple dimensions of reading fluency to assessment and instruction. *Journal of Psychoeducational Assessment, 28*(1), 3–18.

Binder, K. S., Tighe, E., Jiang, Y., Kaftanski, K., Qi, C., & Ardoin, S. P. (2013). Reading expressively and understanding thoroughly: An examination of prosody in adults with low literacy skills. *Reading and Writing*, *26*(5), 665–680.

Bowers, P. G. (1995). Tracing symbol naming speed's unique contributions to reading disability over time. *Reading and Writing: An Interdisciplinary Journal*, *7*(2), 189–216.

Brasseur-Hock, I. F., Hock, M. F., Kieffer, M. J., Biancarosa, G., & Deshler, D. D. (2011). Adolescent struggling readers in urban schools: Results of a latent class analysis. *Learning and Individual Differences*, *21*, 438–452.

Cervetti, G. N., Bravo, M. A., Hiebert, E. H., Pearson, P. D., & Jaynes, C. A. (2009). Text genre and science content: Ease of reading, comprehension, and reader preference. *Reading Psychology*, *30*, 487–511.

Chall, J. S. (1996). *Stages of reading development* (2nd ed.). Fort Worth, TX: Harcourt-Brace.

Chall, J. S., & Jacobs, V. A. ( 2003). The classic study on poor children's fourth grade slump. *American Educator*, *27*(1), 14–15.

Crosson, A. C., & Lesaux, N. K. (2010). Revisiting assumptions about the relationship of fluent reading to comprehension: Spanish-speaker's text-reading fluency in English. *Reading and Writing*, *23*, 475–494.

Daane, M. C., Campbell, J. R., Grigg, W. S., Goodman, M. J., & Oranje, A. (2005). *Fourth-grade students reading aloud: NAEP 2002 special study of oral reading. The nation's report card (NCES 2006469)*. Washington, DC: US Department of Education, Institute of Education Sciences.

Deno, S. L., Fuchs, L. S., Marston, D. B., & Shin, J. (2001). Using curriculum-based measurement to establish growth standards for students with learning disabilities. *School Psychology Review*, *30*, 507–524.

Denton, C. A., Barth, A. E., Fletcher, A. E., Wexler, J., Vaughn, S., Cirino, P. T., . . . Francis, D. J. (2011). The relations among oral and silent reading fluency and comprehension in middle school: Implications for identification and instruction of students with reading difficulties. *Scientific Studies of Reading*, *15*(2), 109–135.

Ehri, L. C. (1995). Phases of development in learning to read words by sight. *Journal of Research in Reading*, *18*, 116–125.

Eldridge, J. L. (2005). Foundations of fluency: An exploration. *Reading Psychology*, *26*, 161–181.

Fletcher, J. M., Shaywitz, S. E., Shankweiler, D. P., Katz, L., Liberman, I. Y., Stuebing, K. K., . . . Shaywitz, B. A. (1994). Cognitive proviles of reading disability: Comparisons of discrepancy and low achievement definitions. *Journal of Educational Psychology*, *86*, 6–23.

Fugate, M. H. (1997). Letter training and its effect on the development of beginning reading skills. *School Psychology Quarterly*, *12*(2), 170–192.

Georgiou, G. K., Parrila, R., & Papadopoulos, T. C. (2008). Predictors of word decoding and reading fluency in English and Greek: A cross-linguistic comparison. *Journal of Educational Psychology*, *100*, 566–580.

Gutierrez-Palma, N., & Palma-Reyes, A. (2007). Stress sensitivity and reading performance in Spanish: A study with children. *Journal of Research in Reading*, *30*(2), 157–168.

Hamilton, C., & Shinn, M. R. (2003). Characteristics of word callers: An investigation of the accuracy of teachers' judgments of reading comprehension and oral reading skills. *School Psychology Review*, *32*(2), 228–240.

Hardyck, C. D., & Petrinovich, L F. (1970). Subvocal speech comprehension level as a function of the difficulty level of reading material. *Journal of Verbal Learning and Verbal Behavior*, *9*, 647–652.

Harn, B. A., Stoolmiller, M., & Chard, D. J. (2008). Measuring the dimensions of alphabetic principle on the reading development of first graders: The role of automaticity and unitization. *Journal of Learning Disabilities*, *41*(2), 143–157.

Hasbrouck, J., & Tindal, G. A. (2006). Oral reading fluency norms: A valuable assessment tool for reading teachers. *Reading Teacher*, *59*, 636–644.

Hiebert, E. H. (2005). The effects of text difficulty on second graders' fluency development. *Reading Psychology*, *26*, 183–209.

Hintze, J. M., Callahan, J. E., Matthews, M. J., Williams, S. A. S., & Tobin, K. G. (2002). Oral reading fluency and prediction of reading comprehension in African American and Caucasian elementary school children. *School Psychology Review*, *31*(4), 540–553.

Holmes, B. C., & Allison, R. W. (1985). The effect of four modes of reading on children's reading comprehension. *Reading Research and Instruction*, *25*, 9–20.

Houck, B. D., & Ross, K. (2012). Dismantling the myth of learning to read and reading to learn. *ASCD Express*, *7*(11). Retrieved from http://www.ascd.org/ascd-express/vol7/711-houck.aspx.

Hudson, R. F., Isakson, C., Richman, T., Lane, H. B., & Arriaza-Allen, S. (2011). An examination of a small-group decoding intervention for struggling readers: Comparing accuracy and automaticity criteria. *Learning Disabilities Research & Practice, 26*(1), 15–27.

Hudson, R. F., Pullen, P. C., Lane, H. B., & Torgesen, J. K. (2009). The complex nature of reading fluency: A multidimensional view. *Reading & Writing Quarterly, 25*, 4–32.

Hudson, R. F., Torgesen, J. K., Lane, H. B., & Turner, S. J (2012). Relations among reading skills and sub-skills and text-level reading proficiency in developing readers. *Reading and Writing, 25*(2), 483–507.

Kim, Y.-S., Petscher, Y., Schatschneider, C., & Foorman, B. (2010). Does growth rate in oral reading fluency matter in predicting reading comprehension achievement? *Journal of Educational Psychology, 102*(3), 652–667.

Kim, Y.-S., Wagner, R. K., & Lopez, D. (2012). Developmental relations between reading fluency and reading comprehension: A longitudinal study from grade one to grade two. *Journal of Experimental Child Psychology, 113*, 93–111.

Kirby, J. R., Georgiou, G. K., Martinussen, R., & Parrila, R. (2010). Naming speed and reading: From prediction to instruction. *Reading Research Quarterly, 45*(3), 341–362.

Klauda, S. L., & Guthrie, J. T. (2008). Relationships of three components of reading fluency to reading comprehension. *Journal of Educational Psychology, 100*(2), 310–321.

Kuhn, M. R. (2005). A comparative study of small group fluency instruction. *Reading Psychology, 26*(2), 127–146.

Kuhn, M. R., Schwanenflugel, P. J., & Meisinger, E. B. (2010). Aligning theory and assessment of reading fluency: Automaticity, prosody, and definitions of fluency. *Reading Research Quarterly, 45*(2), 232–253.

Kuhn, M. R., Schwanenflugel, P. J., Morris, R. D., Morrow, L. M., Bradley, B. A., Meisinger, E., . . . Stahl, S. A. (2006). Teaching children to become fluent and automatic readers. *Journal of Literacy Research, 38*, 357–387.

Lai, S. A., Benjamin, R. G., Schwanenflugel, P. J., & Kuhn, M. R. (2014). The longitudinal relationship between reading fluency and reading comprehension skills in second grade children. *Reading & Writing Quarterly, 30*, 116–138. doi:10.1080/10573569.2013.789785

Lei, L., Pan, J., Liu, H., McBride-Chang, C., Li, H., Zhang, Y. . . . Shu, H. (2011). Developmental trajectories of reading development and impairment from ages 3 to 8 years in Chinese children. *Journal of Child Psychology and Psychiatry, 52*(2), 212–220.

Linan-Thompson, S., Cirino, P. T., & Vaughn, S. (2007). Determining English Language Learners' response to intervention: Questions and some answers. *Learning Disability Quarterly, 30*, 185–195.

Logan, G. D. (1997). Automaticity and reading: Perspectives from the instance theory of automatization. *Reading & Writing Quarterly, 13*(2), 123–146.

Lyytinen, H., Erskine, J., Tolvanen, A., Torppa, M., Poikkeus, A., & Lyytinen, P. (2006). Trajectories of reading development: A follow-up from birth to school age of children with and without risk for dyslexia. *Merrill-Palmer Quarterly, 52*(3), 514–546.

Meisinger, E. B., Bradley, B. A., Schwanenflugel, P. J., & Kuhn, M. R. (2009). Myth and reality of the word caller: The relationship between teacher nominations and prevalence among elementary school children. *School Psychology Quarterly, 24*, 147–159.

Meisinger, E. B., Bradley, B. A., Schwanenflugel, P. J., & Kuhn, M. R. (2010). Teachers' perception of word callers and related literacy concepts. *School Psychology Review, 39*(1), 54–68.

Miller, J., & Schwanenflugel, P. J. (2006). Prosody of syntactically complex sentences in the oral reading of young children. *Journal of Educational Psychology, 98*, 839–853.

Miller, S. D., & Smith, D. E. (1985). Differences in literal and inferential comprehension after reading orally and silently. *Journal of Educational Psychology, 77*, 341–348.

Norton, E. S., & Wolf, M. (2012). Rapid automatized naming (RAN) and reading fluency: Implications for understanding and treatment of reading disabilities. *Annual Review of Psychology, 63*, 427–452.

Nunes, T., Bryant, P., & Barros, R. (2012). The development of word recognition and its significance for comprehension and fluency. *Journal of Educational Psychology, 104*(4), 959–972.

Paige, D. D., Rasinski, T. B., & Magpuri-Lavell, T. (2012). Is fluent, expressive reading important for high school readers? *Journal of Adolescent & Adult Literacy, 56*(1), 67–76.

Pan, J., McBride-Chang, C., Shu, H., Liu, H., Zhang, Y., & Li, H. (2011). What is in the naming? A 5-year longitudinal study of early rapid naming and phonological sensitivity in relation to subsequent reading skills in both native Chinese and English as a second language. *Journal of Educational Psychology, 103*(4), 897–908.

Paris, S. G. (2005). Reinterpreting the development of reading skills. *Reading Research Quarterly*, *40*(2), 184–202.

Priebe, S. J., Keenan, J. M., & Miller, A. C. (2012). How prior knowledge affects word identification and comprehension. *Reading and Writing*, *25*, 131–149.

Prior, S. M., Fenwick, K. D., Saunders, K. S., Ouellette, R., O'Quinn, C., & Harvey, S. (2011). Comprehension after oral and silent reading: Does grade level matter? *Literacy Research and Instruction*, *50*, 183–194.

Quirk, M., & Beem, S. (2012). Examining the relations between reading fluency and reading comprehension for English Language learners. *Psychology in the Schools*, *49*(6), 539–553.

Rasinski, T. V., Rikli, A., & Johnston, S. (2009). Reading fluency: More than automaticity? More than a concern for the primary grades? *Literacy Research and Instruction*, *48*(4), 350–361.

Reading, S., & Van Deuren, D. (2007). Phonemic awareness: When and how much to teach? *Reading Research and Instruction*, *46*(3), 267–282.

Reschly, A. L., Busch, T. W., Betts, J., Deno, S. L., & Long, J. D. (2009). Curriculum-based measurement oral reading as an indicator of reading achievement: A meta-analysis of the correlational evidence. *Journal of School Psychology*, *47*, 427–469.

Roman, A. A., Kirby, J. R., Parrila, R. K., Wade-Woolley, L., & Deacon, S. H. (2009). Toward a comprehensive view of the skills involved in word reading in Grades 4, 6, and 8. *Journal of Experimental Child Psychology*, *102*, 96–113.

Samuels, S. J. (2006). Reading fluency: Its past, present, and future. In T. Rasinski, C. Blachowicz, & K. Lems (Eds.), *Fluency instruction: Research-based best practices* (pp. 7–20). New York: Guilford.

Schwanenflugel, P. J., & Benjamin, R. G. (2012). Reading expressiveness: The neglected aspect of reading fluency. In T. Rasinski, C. Blachowicz, & K. Lems (Eds.), *Fluency instruction, second edition: Research-based best practices* (pp. 35–54). New York: Guilford.

Schwanenflugel, P. J., Hamilton, A. M., Kuhn, M. R., Wisenbaker, J. & Stahl, S. A. (2004). Becoming a fluent reader: Reading skill and prosodic features in the oral reading of young readers. *Journal of Educational Psychology*, *96*, 119–129.

Schwanenflugel, P. J., Kuhn, M. R., Morris, R. D., Morrow, L. M., Meisinger, E. B., Woo, D. G., & Quirk, M. (2009). Insights into fluency instruction: Short- and long-term effects of two reading programs. *Literacy Research and Instruction*, *48*, 318–336.

Schwanenflugel, P. J., Meisinger, E., Wisenbaker, J. M., Kuhn, M. R., Strauss, G. P. & Morris, R. D. (2006). Becoming a fluent and automatic reader in the early elementary school years. *Reading Research Quarterly*, *41*, 496–522.

Schwanenflugel, P. J., Westmoreland, M. R., & Benjamin, R. G. (2013). Reading fluency skill and the prosodic marking of linguistic focus. *Reading and Writing*, *28*(1), 9–30. doi:10.1007/s11145–013–9456–1.

Silberglitt, B., Burns, M. K., Madyun, N. H., & Lail, K. E. (2006). Relationship of reading fluency assessment data with state accountability test scores: A longitudinal comparison of grade levels. *Psychology in the Schools*, *43*, 527–535.

Sonnenschein, S., Stapleton, L. M., & Benson, A. (2010). The relation between the type and amount of instruction and growth in children's reading competencies. *American Educational Research Journal*, *47*(2), 358–389.

Speece, D. L., Mills, C., Ritchey, K. D., & Hillman, E. (2003). Initial evidence that letter fluency tasks are valid indicators of early reading skill. *Journal of Special Education*, *36*(4), 223–233.

Stage, S. A., Sheppard, J., Davidson, M. M., & Browning, M. M. (2001). Prediction of first-graders' growth in oral reading fluency using kindergarten letter fluency. *Journal of School Psychology*, *39*(3), 225–237.

Stahl, K. A. D. (2008). Creating opportunities for comprehension instruction within fluency-oriented reading. In M. R. Kuhn & P. J. Schwanenflugel (Eds.), *Fluency in the classroom* (pp. 55–74). New York: Guilford.

Stanovich, K. E., West, R. F., & Feeman, D. J. (1981). A longitudinal study of sentence context effects in second-grade children: Tests of an interactive-compensatory model. *Journal of Experimental Child Psychology*, *32*, 185–199.

Taub, G. E., & Szente, J. (2012). The impact of rapid automatized naming and phonological awareness on the reading fluency of a minority student population. *Journal of Research in Childhood Education*, *26*(4), 359–370.

Torgesen, J. K., Wagner, R. K., Rashotte, C. A., Burgess, S., & Hecht, S. (1997). Contributions of phonological awareness and rapid automatic naming ability to the growth of word-reading skills in second- to fifth-grade children. *Scientific Studies of Reading*, *1*, 161–185.

Treiman, R., Tincoff, R., Rodriguez, K., Mouzaki, A., & Francis, D. J. (1998). The foundations of literacy: Learning the sounds of letters. *Child Development*, *69*(6), 1524–1540.

Wolf, M., & Katzir-Cohen, T. (2001). Reading fluency and its intervention. *Scientific Studies of Reading*, *5*(3), 211–229.

Valencia, S. W., Smith, A. T., Reece, A. M., Li, M., Wixson, K. K., & Newman, H. (2010). Oral reading fluency assessment: Issues of construct, criterion, and consequential validity. *Reading Research Quarterly*, *45*(3), 270–291.

Vassen, A., & Blomert, L. (2010). Long-term cognitive dynamics of fluent reding development. *Journal of Experimental Child Psychology*, *105*, 213–231.

# 10

# Complexities of Individual Differences in Vocabulary Knowledge

## Implications for Research, Assessment, and Instruction

*Michael J. Kieffer and Katherine D. Stahl*

Since the 1980s, researchers have recognized the importance of vocabulary knowledge for individual differences in reading comprehension (Anderson & Freebody, 1981; Beck, Perfetti, & McKeown, 1982; S. A. Stahl & Fairbanks, 1986; Stanovich, 1986). Over the last few decades, some consensus has emerged regarding the multifaceted nature of individual differences in vocabulary, relations between vocabulary and reading comprehension ability, and principles that guide effective vocabulary instruction. Although several questions remain unanswered about how to conceptualize, assess, and teach word meanings, enough is known about vocabulary that some useful principles can be offered to educators.

However, vocabulary has received more attention from reading researchers than from classroom teachers—both historically (Durkin, 1978/1979) and currently (e.g., Gamse, Jacob, Horst, Boulay, & Unlu, 2008; Lesaux, Kieffer, Faller, & Kelley, 2010). Recent large-scale studies in primary-grade classrooms have demonstrated that vocabulary instruction is typically limited in both quantity (e.g., comprising only 8–12 minutes of a typical reading block; Gamse et al., 2008) and in quality (Carlisle, Kelcey, & Berebitsky, 2013), despite increased emphasis placed on vocabulary in recent years. Drawing on recommendations from the National Reading Panel Report (NICHD, 2000), the 2001 Reading First initiative prioritized vocabulary as one of the "Big Five" pillars of reading instruction. Yet Gamse and colleagues (2008) found that the initiative led to only small increases in time spent on vocabulary. Word meanings tend to receive superficial and incidental attention, whereas phonics skills often receive intensive and systematic treatment. Upper-elementary and middle-school grades neglect vocabulary instruction as well (e.g., Lesaux et al., 2010). Based on recent research and our experiences as teacher educators, we believe that educators neglect vocabulary not simply because they lack an appreciation for its importance, but also because vocabulary is a complex domain to understand, to assess, and to teach.

In this chapter, we highlight some complexities of individual differences in vocabulary that make this domain particularly challenging to assess and to teach, and we recommend methods for improving research, assessment, and instruction in light of those complexities. In so doing, we explain points of consensus among researchers (drawing heavily on seminal reviews, rather than providing our own comprehensive review of original studies). We also aim to move beyond summarizing what we know to emphasize important open questions and emerging evidence regarding the nature of vocabulary knowledge, new directions for assessment, and the relations between vocabulary and other, less commonly studied individual differences implicated in reading.

## Complexities of Vocabulary Knowledge

Researchers have long agreed that knowledge of word meanings is a complex domain (e.g., Nagy & Scott, 2000). Contrary to the reductive notions of vocabulary that sometimes influence instruction, knowing a word means more than simply being able to recite a definition or identify a synonym. Similarly, development of vocabulary involves more than adding new words to one's lexicon. However, despite agreement that vocabulary knowledge is complex, researchers have differed in their conceptions of these complexities.

### Vocabulary as an Unconstrained Skill

Unlike some other commonly studied reading-related domains, vocabulary is an unconstrained skill. Paris (2005) contrasts reading skills that are constrained to small sets of knowledge and mastered in relatively brief periods of development with other skills that are unconstrained in terms of knowledge and developmental period. Paris suggests that skills may be constrained conceptually, developmentally, and by measurement.

Constrained skills include word pronunciations and related phonological representations, which rely on a finite set of sound–symbol correspondences that apply across contexts. This consistency makes constrained skills like phonics easy to assess. If a reader knows the sound of the orthographic pattern *ate*, it does not matter whether she is reading a poem or a medical journal; the pronunciation remains the same. Learning to apply this set of sound–symbol correspondences accurately is also constrained developmentally (at least for most typically developing readers). Most children learn to decode words in the primary grades and then reach a plateau when they have enough skill to accurately decode the majority of words in any text. Skill levels vary widely between individuals as they learn to decode, but once most readers have mastered decoding, those differences in skill level narrow considerably and contribute far less to individual differences in reading comprehension ability, at least for typically developing readers (e.g., Hoover & Gough, 1990).

By contrast, vocabulary knowledge is unconstrained both conceptually and developmentally. Conceptually, the use of vocabulary knowledge to construct meaning during reading is influenced by text, context, and reader characteristics. For example, the words *temple* and *observe* have the potential to yield different mental representations depending on the reader and the reading situation. The word *temple* might conjure up a synagogue or a Buddhist temple depending upon the prior experience of the listener. In a scientific context, *to observe* can mean to use all the senses to learn about a phenomenon, whereas the everyday usage simply means to use sight. Such variations by text, context, reading purposes, and reader characteristics mean that teaching and assessing vocabulary are more complex tasks than teaching and assessing more constrained sets of knowledge that can be applied more widely and consistently. Relatedly, vocabulary knowledge is unconstrained developmentally—it develops throughout the lifespan as readers encounter new words and refine their understandings of familiar ones.

121

Related to Paris' distinction between constrained and unconstrained skills, Snow and Kim (2007) make the point that vocabulary is a larger "problem space" than those presented by other foundational reading-related skills. For instance, if the goal is to comprehend common 12th-grade-level texts by the end of high school, students must learn 26 letters, 44 phonemes, and a couple hundred spelling rules to decode most words in English texts, but they must learn as many as 75,000 words to comprehend those texts (Snow & Kim, 2007). Moreover, successful comprehension requires knowing not only one definition for each of these words, but also knowing their multiple meanings, variations in shades of meaning by context, connotations, etc.

Further explaining why vocabulary is a difficult domain to teach and assess, Nagy and Scott (2000) identify five specific aspects of vocabulary that make it complex: (1) Incrementality: Knowledge of a given word varies along a continuum from no knowledge through partial knowledge to full, productive command of the word's meanings, connotations, and uses. (2) Multidimensionality: Knowledge about a given word includes several different types of knowledge (e.g., knowledge of the word's semantic and morphological relationships to other words, appropriateness to specific contexts, connotations, and metaphorical uses). (3) Polysemy: Many words have multiple meanings and shades of meaning that vary by context. (4) Interrelatedness: Word meanings are not independent from each other but intricately related and interdependent. (5) Heterogeneity: Different types of words are known in different ways and vary in their utility. Since Nagy and Scott (2000), new research has enriched our understanding of these complexities and raised additional questions, as we describe below.

## Incrementality

Individuals vary—between one another and over the course of development—not only in how many words they know, but also in how well they know those words. Incremental vocabulary growth refers to how knowledge expands with one's ability to understand any given word receptively and one's ability to use it productively in both speech and writing across situations (e.g., Bravo & Cervetti, 2008). There is general consensus that growth in word knowledge progresses along a continuum that ranges from having no knowledge of a word to passive knowledge (abilities to recognize its meaning in a specific context, then to recognize it across varying contexts), to more active knowledge that includes the ability to use the word appropriately in oral and written communication and extend the word to metaphorical applications (e.g., Beck, McKeown, & Kucan, 2002; Bravo & Cervetti, 2008).

Incrementality has implications for thinking about assessing and addressing individual differences in classrooms. Educators often think of grade-level vocabulary words as either known or unknown by their students, but students often have some level of exposure to them and vary in how well they know them. Assessment, then, needs to be sensitive to students' positions along the continuum of knowledge of words targeted for instruction. Likewise, vocabulary instruction should consider how to create opportunities for students to gain new knowledge of targeted words, regardless of where they start along this continuum.

## Multidimensionality

Although vocabulary is most often assessed by having students match words and single definitions, synonyms, or pictures, researchers have become interested in other aspects of word knowledge, including awareness and knowledge of semantic and morphological relations, stylistic register, connotations, and collocational behavior (i.e., what other words a given word commonly occurs with). Researchers have theorized that these other aspects of word meaning knowledge can be characterized as depth of vocabulary as opposed to breadth of vocabulary (Anderson & Freebody, 1981; Stahl & Nagy, 2006).

Among aspects of word knowledge beyond definitions, perhaps the most studied in recent years is morphological awareness, i.e., understanding how word parts such as roots and affixes form complex words (Carlisle, 1995). Growing evidence suggests the importance of morphological awareness to reading comprehension, above and beyond the contributions of synonym or definitional knowledge (e.g., Carlisle, 2000; Nagy, Berninger, & Abbott, 2006). Morphological awareness may be particularly important to the domain of academic vocabulary (see discussion below), because this domain demonstrates greater morphological complexity than the vocabulary used in everyday conversation (e.g., Nagy & Townsend, 2012).

Although theories of vocabulary's multidimensionality have had wide influence in research, there is a surprisingly limited empirical basis for identifying distinct aspects of vocabulary knowledge as measurably separable dimensions of individual differences. Recently, Kieffer and Lesaux (2012) used confirmatory factor analysis (CFA) with data from sixth graders from linguistically diverse backgrounds on 13 vocabulary measures to empirically test some theoretical distinctions between dimensions of vocabulary. Although they found evidence for the distinction between word-specific linguistic knowledge (e.g., definitions, synonyms) and word-general metalinguistic knowledge (e.g., morphological awareness, contextual sensitivity), they found less evidence for the common distinction between breadth and depth of word knowledge. By contrast, Tannenbaum, Torgensen, and Wagner (2006), using similar analyses but different measures, found evidence for a distinction between depth and breadth in a third-grade sample. A similarly unsettled question is whether morphological awareness can be measured independently from other aspects of vocabulary knowledge. Wagner, Muse, and Tannenbaum (2007), using CFA with data from fourth graders, found that morphological awareness could not be distinguished reliably from vocabulary knowledge, whereas Kieffer and Lesaux (2012) have found evidence for separating these dimensions among sixth graders from linguistically diverse backgrounds. There is a clear need for more empirical tests of various hypotheses about the dimensions of individual differences in vocabulary knowledge.

These questions have implications not only for psychometric research, but also instructional research; if outcomes of an intervention are not measurably separable, we cannot trust claims that the intervention has effects on one aspect of vocabulary, but no effects on another. Similarly, if dimensions of vocabulary are so closely intertwined that they cannot be separated in assessment, it raises the question of whether they can—or should—be separated in instruction. Theoretical distinctions among vocabulary dimensions may be useful for linguistics and reading researchers, but that does not mean that isolating these dimensions into separate lessons is warranted; for instance, evidence suggests that integrating morphology instruction into other types of vocabulary instruction is more effective than providing it in isolation (Bowers, Kirby, & Deacon, 2010). Further research comparing different instructional approaches is needed to provide more definitive answers about how teachers should account for multidimensionality.

## Polysemy

Vocabulary instruction and assessment is made more complex by the fact that words not only can have completely unrelated meanings (e.g., *can* of worms and *can* as a verb), but also can have distinct, yet related, shades of meaning (e.g., *analyzing* a poem and *analyzing* data) that depend on texts, purposes for reading, and contexts. Nagy and Scott (2000) point out that polysemy makes using a dictionary difficult, since readers need to integrate information from a given text and context to select the appropriate definition. As noted above, polysemy is also part of what makes vocabulary a particularly large and unconstrained problem space—new meanings for existing words are constantly being created (consider recently developed meanings for *web* or the new verb form *to text*).

Assessment can be sensitive to polysemy by being more specific about the meanings and shades of meaning that are targeted for assessment (e.g., by providing more context when assessing word meanings; see discussion of assessment below). Assessing students' metalinguistic sensitivity to how word meanings change by context may also be valuable, given evidence that this sensitivity differs across readers, somewhat independently of the number of words that they can define (e.g., Kieffer & Lesaux, 2012). Researchers likewise recommend giving explicit attention to polysemy during instruction (e.g., Stahl & Nagy, 2006; Graves, 2006), in the interest of developing readers who are prepared to navigate this complexity during reading.

## Interrelatedness

Computer technology can now demonstrate the interrelatedness of words and word learning (e.g., Landauer & Dumais, 1997). Clusters of words tend to be learned together and reflect more general conceptual knowledge links or networks of mental representations. Based on differences in language and world experience, two individuals may have different networks of knowledge surrounding the same word. For example, two young children may both use the word *moon* in the classroom and reflect a basic understanding of the word as it is used during a read-aloud such as *Goodnight Moon*. However, given their differences in prior knowledge, the two children may have very different networks of knowledge surrounding the word *moon* (see Figure 10.1).

Interrelatedness has important implications for intervention research and efforts to improve instruction. One basic implication is that semantically related words should be taught together (Stahl & Nagy, 2006). A broader implication, though, is that vocabulary instruction cannot be divorced from conceptual development and content instruction. Recent vocabulary interventions have embedded explicit teaching of word meanings into rich discussions of sophisticated content (e.g., Lesaux et al., 2010; Neuman, Newman, & Dwyer, 2011; Snow, Lawrence, & White, 2009). In our estimation, these approaches are promising, not only because they provide rich contexts in which to learn the word meanings (Beck et al., 2002; Stahl & Fairbanks, 1986), but also because they position vocabulary teaching as central to teachers' natural inclinations and professional obligations to give students access to conceptually rich content. The contrast to this orientation, which we see all too often in schools, is teaching vocabulary in isolation, as a constrained list of words and definitions to memorize.

## Heterogeneity

Another complexity of vocabulary is heterogeneity—the fact that not all words are created equal. Some domains of word meanings are more necessary than others for comprehension of school texts. Given that reading comprehension involves an interaction between a specific reader, a specific text, and a specific activity, all situated within a certain sociocultural context (RAND Reading Study Group, 2002), the vocabulary that readers need to understand depends on what they are reading, why they are reading, what they will do with the information gained from reading, and the context in which they are reading. Out-of-school leisure reading is likely to require different domains of vocabulary than academic school reading. Given the huge number of possible word meanings to teach and the time involved in teaching targeted words in depth, selecting which words to teach is an important instructional decision.

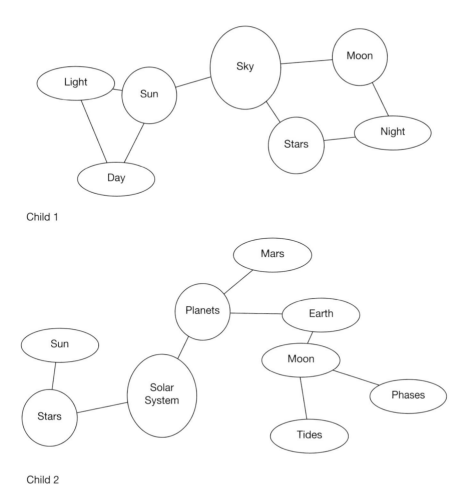

Child 1

Child 2

*Figure 10.1* Mental representations for the word *moon*

Researchers have begun to define academic vocabulary as a specialized domain that is important to comprehending school texts, including both literature and informational texts in the content areas. They have established several sets of guidelines for prioritizing which words to teach (e.g., Beck et al., 2002; Coxhead, 2002; Nagy & Hiebert, 2010; Nagy & Townsend, 2012; Stahl & Nagy, 2006). Perhaps the best-known and most influential guideline among educators is Beck and colleagues' (2002) three tiers of words, which draw on their seminal instructional research (e.g., Beck et al., 1982). In this approach, Tier One consists of basic words (e.g., *clock, baby*) rarely requiring instruction in school, Tier Three includes low-frequency words that are often limited to specific content domains (e.g., *isotope, peninsula*), and Tier Two includes the "high-frequency words for mature language users" (e.g., *coincidence, absurd, industrious*) that are most important to teach (pp. 15–16). Beck and colleagues further clarify that Tier Two words are words for which "students already have ways to express the concepts represented by the words" (p. 16). Therefore, their instructional protocol for teaching Tier Two words consists of providing synonyms and child-friendly definitions, and ensuring opportunities for extensive use of the new word in a range of contexts.

Beck and colleagues do not negate the importance of teaching new concepts, but seem to allocate this instruction only to Tier Three words. Although we agree that many new concepts are specific to content domains (so are appropriately classified in Tier Three), we would point out that other cross-domain academic concepts (e.g., *evidence, influence*) will be new to some students and thus appropriate for teaching as general academic vocabulary.

Stahl and Nagy (2006) recommend two criteria for choosing words to teach: *importance* to the literature or informational text that students are reading and *utility*, which includes usefulness to future reading and usefulness at the time it is taught. Nagy and Hiebert (2011) expand on these criteria by suggesting educators consider the roles that the word plays in the language (i.e., frequency, dispersion), in the lexicon (i.e., morphological and semantic relations), in students' existing knowledge (i.e., familiarity, conceptual difficulty), and in the lesson (i.e., for the particular text and larger curriculum).

One influential operationalization of the utility criterion is Coxhead's (2000) Academic Word List (AWL), a list of 570 word families (3,000 words total) that appear most frequently across several disciplines in college textbooks, but do not appear among the 2,000 most frequent words in English. Educators can be confident that the list contains words that students will frequently encounter later. However, the danger with any *a priori* word list is that it can encourage isolated vocabulary instruction, when teachers take up lists of words and definitions to be memorized (based on their own judgments or because of mandates from their schools or districts). To protect against this, Graves (2006) recommends that teachers compare words in their current texts with existing word lists, such as the AWL, and prioritize those that appear in both, an approach that recent vocabulary interventions have implemented effectively (e.g., Lesaux et al., 2010; Snow et al., 2009).

In addition to general academic vocabulary that cuts across disciplines (i.e., Tier Two and AWL words), Nagy and Townsend (2012) point out the importance of discipline-specific academic word meanings. These include both concepts that are unique to individual academic disciplines (e.g., *photosynthesis, industrialization, fraction*) and discipline-specific meanings of polysemous words (e.g., the differing definitions of *revolution* in science and history).

Choosing words to teach is a complex endeavor and an area that requires further study. The dangers of choosing an inappropriate set of words are clear. In addition to wasting instructional time, teaching unimportant words can actually hurt students' comprehension of key ideas in a text (Wixson, 1986). Nonetheless, no studies to our knowledge have investigated the effects of teaching different types of potentially important words (e.g., Tier Two words selected by teachers compared to AWL words) on comprehension—such investigations could help validate proposed definitions of academic vocabulary and identify the most useful approach for selecting words to teach.

Taken together, these five aspects of complexity—each related to vocabulary's nature as an unconstrained domain—inform our claims about individual differences in vocabulary knowledge. When we say that some readers' vocabularies are "well-developed" and others are "under-developed," we risk ignoring these complexities. A more nuanced conception of individual differences in vocabulary knowledge would consider where students' knowledge of important and useful word meanings lies along a continuum of knowledge. It would also consider readers' differing semantic networks of related words, rather than just their knowledge of isolated words, and recognize that individual differences might be wider or narrower based on the aspect of vocabulary knowledge being targeted.

## Vocabulary and Individual Differences in Reading Comprehension

Since the 1980s, reading researchers have recognized that individual differences in vocabulary knowledge and individual differences in reading comprehension ability are highly correlated. Anderson and Freebody (1981) proposed three hypotheses to explain this relationship. Although their hypotheses are not mutually exclusive, their implications for assessment and instruction differ. The *Instrumentalist* hypothesis, perhaps intuitively, suggests that students with larger and deeper vocabularies have more information about the words they encounter in texts and can use that information to understand those texts. This hypothesis draws support from meta-analytic evidence that effects of vocabulary instruction are much larger for comprehension of texts, including the words targeted by the instruction, than for comprehension of other texts on global, standardized measures (Elleman, Lindo, Morphy, & Compton, 2009; Stahl & Fairbanks, 1986). This finding implies that direct vocabulary instruction in specific words will be useful, but also that its usefulness may be limited by the utility of the words taught, i.e., how often students will encounter the targeted words later.

The second explanation, the *Aptitude* hypothesis, suggests that students who score higher on vocabulary tests have learned more word meanings from exposure to oral and written language, because they have higher levels of generalized verbal aptitude. This aptitude, in turn, contributes to their development of reading comprehension skills, independently of knowledge of specific word meanings. This hypothesis underlies the use of vocabulary assessments as indicators of generalized intelligence, both historically (e.g., Terman, Kohs, Chamberlain, Anderson, & Henry, 1918) and in contemporary studies in developmental psychology (e.g., NICHD Early Child Care Research Network, 2005). A corollary of this hypothesis is that teaching students more word meanings does not improve verbal aptitude, thus providing an argument against the use of explicit instruction in specific words to improve general reading comprehension ability. However, even a strong version of this hypothesis may not invalidate all vocabulary instruction, if one conceptualizes verbal aptitude as multidimensional and not simply a function of inherited generalized intelligence. Nagy (2007) refined the *Aptitude* hypothesis with his *Metalinguistic* hypothesis—individual differences in vocabulary represent underlying differences in specific metalinguistic abilities (e.g., morphological awareness, sensitivity to context) needed for reading comprehension. Given evidence that metalinguistic abilities can be taught (especially in the case of morphological awareness; e.g., Bowers et al., 2010), Nagy's hypothesis supports vocabulary instruction that targets metalinguistic skills over instruction in specific word meanings.

The third explanation, the *Knowledge* hypothesis, suggests that individual differences in vocabulary primarily capture differences in exposure to and familiarity with the conceptual knowledge that is important to a given context. In our reading, this hypothesis does not negate the importance of direct vocabulary instruction, but it does suggest that vocabulary instruction should attend less to teaching new labels and attend more to concept development and disciplinary content (e.g., Lesaux et al., 2010; Neuman et al., 2011; Snow et al., 2009).

Another (potentially compatible) hypothesis about vocabulary development comes from Stanovich's (1986) *Matthew effects* hypothesis, which posits reciprocal developmental relations between reading ability and cognitive skills (including vocabulary). Under this hypothesis, individual strengths in early reading ability facilitate later vocabulary development by providing more opportunities (and more motivation) to read and comprehend text successfully; broader and deeper vocabularies, in turn, facilitate other aspects of reading comprehension development, creating an upward spiral for students with early success in reading acquisition. By contrast, students who struggle with early reading acquisition read less, succeed less when they do, and may have fewer opportunities to read (e.g., when tracked into classes that expect less frequent reading). With fewer opportunities to grow their vocabularies, they fall further behind other students in reading comprehension over time. Regarding instruction, the *Matthew effects* hypothesis supports more independent reading of a variety of texts. Many vocabulary researchers consider wide reading compatible with explicit instruction in specific words, concepts, and metalinguistic word-learning strategies (e.g., Graves, 2006; Stahl & Nagy, 2006), but it can be difficult to fit all this instruction into the school day.

In 1981, Anderson and Freebody concluded that neither theory nor data at the time was sufficient to conclude which of their three hypotheses was most tenable. It is not clear to us that we have made enough progress since then to favor one hypothesis or to reconcile them fully with the *Matthew effects* and *Metalinguistic* hypotheses. Moreover, instructional applications based on these various hypotheses have not been tested against one another, in part because most instructional intervention studies compare one theoretically driven approach with a "business-as-usual" condition, rather than comparing approaches with differing theoretical bases. Nonetheless, given the potential compatibility of these hypotheses, we tend to emphasize the consensus regarding instruction that can be found, even as these theoretical issues remain unsettled.

## Principles for Effective Vocabulary Instruction

We have already foreshadowed much of the consensus on the *content* of vocabulary instruction— it should address multiple dimensions of vocabulary knowledge (notably combining instruction in deep knowledge of specific word meanings with teaching of metalinguistic word-learning skills), it should emphasize instruction in new concepts as well as new labels, and it should supplement direct teaching with rich language exposure through opportunities to listen to and read a wide variety of texts. Stahl and Nagy (2006) illustrate one such multifaceted approach well with their "vocabulary growth pyramid" (see Figure 10.2), a heuristic to help educators combine multiple components of vocabulary instruction and allocate their efforts efficiently.

In addition, there is solid consensus among researchers regarding effective *methods* for teaching specific word meanings. Stahl and Fairbanks' (1986) seminal meta-analysis identified three principles that guided effective vocabulary instructional approaches: (1) provide both definitional and contextual information about words; (2) engage students in deep processing of the words' meanings and uses (i.e., increasing levels of semantic processing and mental effort by requiring students to generate novel responses using the words, rather than just recognizing associations or comprehending uses of the words); and (3) provide multiple, meaningful exposures to the words. As McKeown and Beck (2006) pointed out, no studies since Stahl and Fairbanks' meta-analysis have provided evidence to contradict these three principles. There is perhaps less consensus on how to integrate the teaching of word-learning strategies (e.g., using morphology, using definitions, and using context) and balance it with instruction in specific words, despite wide recognition that learning such strategies is essential.

There is also less consensus (and less evidence) about how to accommodate wide individual differences among students in the course of vocabulary instruction. Most intervention studies estimate a treatment effect for an average participant. Such estimates often provide scant information about (1) how effective the approach is for students with differing instructional profiles and (2) how to modify the approach for different students. Some recent studies address the first question by investigating how treatment effects differ by students' individual differences. For instance, Lesaux and colleagues (in press) found evidence that their multi-componential approach to academic vocabulary instruction in sixth grade was most effective for students with standardized vocabulary scores below the 25th percentile. Such evidence suggests that their

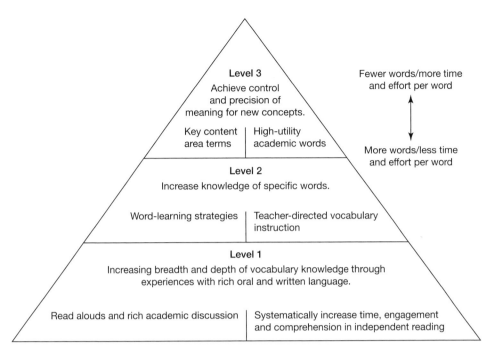

*Figure 10.2* The Vocabulary Growth Pyramid (Stahl & Nagy, 2006)

approach might be most appropriate for sixth graders with underdeveloped vocabulary breadth. By contrast, Penno, Wilkinson, and Moore (2002) found that kindergarteners with the highest initial vocabulary levels benefitted the most from their intervention, which involved listening to stories and teachers' explanations of target word meanings. As such evidence accumulates, we may be able to determine better which approaches suit particular instructional profiles.

More research is needed to inform vocabulary instruction that accommodates individual differences. Selecting which words to teach and deciding on the intensity and duration of instruction should ideally be informed by individual students' strengths and needs. Recently, Loftus and Coyne (2013) called for integrating vocabulary instruction into multi-tiered intervention efforts within a response-to-intervention framework. They argue that whole-class, Tier One vocabulary instruction may be insufficient for those students with lower initial vocabulary scores, and that small-group, Tier Two supplemental interventions can be effective for narrowing individual differences in vocabulary. Their Tier Two intervention was characterized by increased instructional intensity (i.e., additional review, repetition, and deep processing activities). They found that this supplemental intervention narrowed vocabulary differences among students, whereas Tier One alone did not.

As we have described, several research-based principles for the content and methods of effective vocabulary instruction have been articulated and operationalized in curricula and interventions. Nonetheless, if the goal of vocabulary instruction is to narrow individual differences, which all too often follow along lines of socioeconomic class, race, language background, and other structural inequalities (Hart & Risley, 1995; Snow, Burns, & Griffin, 1998), we have more to learn about how to implement these principles in heterogeneous classrooms. We must also find ways to measure individual differences in vocabulary levels and growth.

## Vocabulary Assessment

If we want to know what someone knows about a word, then the assessment must be capable of capturing the five complexities of word knowledge described earlier (Nagy & Scott, 2000). A single assessment is unlikely to capture both quantity and quality of vocabulary knowledge or growth. This complexity can be offputting in schools that value tests of constrained skills that develop along linear trajectories. Measuring automatic recognition of high-frequency words is relatively simple. By contrast, measuring multiple dimensions of word knowledge requires that receptive and productive tasks be administered in multiple contexts. Despite the difficulty, an attempt at vocabulary assessment is essential in order to identify individual differences in children's word knowledge and to monitor and support ongoing vocabulary development.

### Assessment Dimensions

Read (2000) developed three continua for designing and evaluating vocabulary assessments. Although originally designed for assessments for English language learners, they are useful tools for appraising most vocabulary assessments and interpreting assessment results. These dimensions influence how sensitive different assessments may be in identifying and tracing individual differences in vocabulary knowledge.

#### Discrete Embedded

This dimension focuses on how the assessment positions vocabulary as either distinct from or embedded within other reading and language competencies. Both the Peabody Picture Vocabulary Test, Fourth Edition (PPVT-4) and the Expressive Vocabulary Test, Second Edition (EVT-2) measure vocabulary as a discrete skill. Further along the continuum, the Qualitative Reading Inventory 5 asks vocabulary questions following text reading as part of a comprehension construct. Finally, the most embedded vocabulary assessment tasks call for evaluators to mine the vocabulary from a written or spoken product, often in authentic contexts. For example, in a study of young children's learning during integrated science and literacy lessons, students demonstrated improvement in both the quantity and quality of conceptual vocabulary included in the constructed response portion of post-tests intended to test science knowledge (Bravo, Cervetti, Hiebert, & Pearson, 2008). Assessments such as these provide a lens for viewing individual differences in generative and receptive vocabulary, and display ways that individual learners situate vocabulary within personal networks of knowledge.

#### Comprehensive Selective

This dimension refers to the size of the corpus of words sampled for the assessment. Most standardized, norm-referenced tests like the PPVT-4 and the EVT-2 lie on the comprehensive end of the continuum because they select words from a universal corpus of the English language, though their user manuals do not state how their word-selection process considered meaning networks, word frequency, morphology, or decodability (Pearson, Hiebert, & Kamil, 2007). The primary function of these norm-referenced tests is to psychometrically differentiate students without considering individual differences in word learning (NICHD, 2000; Pearson et al., 2007; Scott, Hoover, Flinspach, & Vevea, 2008). These tests often lack sensitivity to measure growth on instructionally targeted vocabulary, so their results can make instruction seem overwhelming to teachers if they view the goal as improvement on such comprehensive measures. In an era that ties teacher accountability to student test scores, the absence of assessments that can sensitively demonstrate student vocabulary growth may contribute to vocabulary instruction's low priority (Gamse et al., 2008).

Alternatively, if a test consists of a sample of words drawn from a single disciplinary content unit, the test is highly selective. The selectivity somewhat constrains an unconstrained skill (Stahl & Bravo, 2010), which may be conceptually problematic, but also practically beneficial. Tests based on highly selective vocabulary samples can identify individual student differences, inform instruction of semantic clusters, and detect student growth, including lexical nuances.

## Context-independent/Context-dependent

This dimension is defined by how much identification of the word meaning depends on the context. The most context-independent assessments present words in isolation. The new National Assessment of Educational Progress reading vocabulary measure is context-dependent. The items are polysemous words found within the reading passages. Multiple-choice items call for the reader to select the word's meaning as used within the passage, while the multiple-choice distractors are the word's other meanings. (See Pearson et al., 2007 for a description of how this framework relates to current research.)

## *New Directions in Vocabulary Assessment*

The most commonly used vocabulary assessments tend to measure receptive knowledge rather than productive abilities. In order to get a comprehensive view of a student's functional word knowledge, it seems likely that measures are needed of both isolated word knowledge and the student's facility (in reading, writing, and speaking) with academic vocabulary in authentic contexts (Nagy &Townsend, 2012; NICHD, 2000).

## Informal Measures of Vocabulary Knowledge

Current norm-referenced, vocabulary assessments lack instructional sensitivity and only serve as a baseline indicator of global vocabulary (Scott et al., 2008; NICHD, 2000). As an alternative, the National Reading Panel recommended teacher-generated assessments that match the instructional context. Researchers have justified the design of their own vocabulary assessments for similar reasons. K. A. D. Stahl and Bravo (2010) identified three assessments that were validated in empirical studies, adaptable to classrooms, and appropriate for native English speakers and English learners: (1) the Vocabulary Knowledge Rating Scale (Wesche & Paribakht, 1996); (2) the Vocabulary Recognition Task (Stahl, 2008); and the Vocabulary Assessment Magazine (Bravo et al., 2008). Stahl and Bravo recommended that these tasks be used to assess both the disciplinary vocabulary and academic vocabulary situated within a unit of study. The advantages of these formative measures are their sensitivity to individual differences, sensitivity to growth, item interrelatedness, potential for showing both receptive and productive facility, and clear connections to instruction.

## Technology and Vocabulary Assessment

Computer technology is changing the formats and delivery of assessments as well as the selection of vocabulary for assessment and teaching. Researchers are increasingly using computer technology to identify word and morphological frequency data, to analyze the interrelatedness of words, and to generate random sets of test items.

One example is the Vocabulary Innovation in Education (VINE) assessment that uses computer technology for vocabulary selection and score interpretation (Scott et al., 2008). The VINE test is built on principles of incrementality, heterogeneity, interrelatedness, and curriculum connection. It is a discrete, decontextualized fourth-grade assessment that consists of two 15-minute subtests, one testing vocabulary in fiction and one testing vocabulary in nonfiction that are drawn from California's curriculum. Vocabulary items were selected and weighted based on the degree that incremental knowledge of each word discriminated between respondents with different abilities, including differing proficiency levels of English learners. Such computerized vocabulary assessments provide many of the advantages of informal assessments, but are more time efficient and can provide norm-referenced information. However, more research is needed on the feasibility of using adaptations of these assessments in classrooms.

## Vocabulary and Less Commonly Studied Individual Differences

Vocabulary is also interrelated with many of the individual differences discussed in other chapters in this handbook. In particular, many dimensions of individual differences may be implicated in promoting vocabulary growth and/or may be consequences of vocabulary growth, as we have mentioned above. Although one could argue for relations between nearly every topic in this volume and vocabulary, we focus here on three individual differences that have been the topic of recent emerging research: executive functioning, meta-cognition, and motivation.

### Executive Functioning

Executive functioning (EF) is an umbrella term for a set of higher-order, cognitive processes that facilitate planning, problem solving, and the initiation and maintenance of goal-directed behavior (Pennington & Ozonoff, 1996). EF is thought to include three related, yet distinct, core cognitive dimensions: attention shifting, inhibitory control, and working memory/updating (e.g., Miyake, Friedman, Emerson, Witzki, & Howerter, 2000). Working memory has been long recognized as important to reading (e.g., Swanson & Siegel, 2001), but emerging evidence highlights additional, unique roles for attention shifting and inhibitory control in reading comprehension. EF skills have been implicated in the development of foundational skills related to word reading in early childhood (e.g., Blair & Razza, 2007) and a few studies have linked EF skills to reading comprehension in middle childhood (e.g., Cutting, Materek, Cole, Levine, & Mahone, 2009; Kieffer, Vukovic, & Berry, 2013).

There are also good theoretical reasons to believe the EF skills have a bidirectional, reciprocal relation with vocabulary growth. On one hand, students who are better able to regulate their attention, inhibit distracting information, and hold more information in working memory are likely to be better equipped to learn new vocabulary from oral and written contexts. Consider a fourth grader with well-developed decoding skills reading an informational text that includes several new word meanings which are surrounded by rich, supportive contexts; to decipher the meaning of a novel word, she would need to purposefully shift her attention from the gist of the passage to the contextual and morphological clues surrounding this word. Similarly, paying close attention during a read-aloud or during direct instruction on vocabulary requires more precise attention to the language heard than is typically required to follow the flow of a conversation.

On the other hand, vocabulary growth may facilitate the development of EF skills, particularly in early childhood. From a Vygotskian perspective, language provides tools for regulating one's conscious activity (Vygotsky, 1978), so it follows that children with broader and deeper vocabularies may have more sophisticated tools with which to regulate their attention. For instance, parents of toddlers who encourage them to "use their words" to regulate their emotions and behaviors as they interact with the world have an intuition about this relation between language and EF skills.

The empirical evidence on this reciprocal relation is still limited. Although several studies have demonstrated a correlation between vocabulary scores and scores on EF tasks (e.g., Blair & Razza, 2007; Cutting et al., 2009), these studies typically treat vocabulary as a control or a matching variable (generally treating vocabulary as a proxy for verbal intelligence) rather than as a cause or effect of EF development. Recently, Kieffer and colleagues (2013) investigated whether the relation between EF skills and reading comprehension was mediated by oral language comprehension. They found that language comprehension partially mediated the relation between attention shifting and reading comprehension, suggesting that one mechanism by which EF facilitates reading comprehension may be via language development. Similarly, there is some evidence in the language acquisition literature that the ability to avoid perserveration (i.e., repetition of a particular response after receiving feedback that it is no longer appropriate), an ability closely linked to attention shifting and inhibitory control, differentiates mature adult language users from "less developed" child language users (for a review, see Mazuka, Jincho, & Oishi, 2009). Because of their cross-sectional, observational designs, these studies cannot shed light on the temporal or causal relation between EF skills and language skills. Future research on the role of EF skills in new vocabulary learning—including both intentional learning in the context of instruction and implicit learning from oral and written contexts—is needed. Similarly, research on the potential benefits of language development for EF development would be valuable to understand this potentially reciprocal relation.

## Meta-cognition

Meta-cognition, or thinking about one's cognitive processes (e.g., Flavell, 1979), is also likely to be involved in vocabulary development. In particular, metalinguistic awareness, a subset of meta-cognition defined as the ability to reflect on and manipulate the structural features of spoken and written language (Tunmer, Herriman, & Nesdale, 1988; Nagy, 2007) may be essential to successful learning of new word meanings. Nagy (2007) highlights several aspects of metalinguistic awareness that have been implicated in vocabulary learning, including understanding and navigating definitions (e.g., Scott & Nagy, 1997), using subtle syntactic clues to extract the most important information from a sentence's context (e.g., Goerss, Beck, & McKeown, 1999), using broader context clues and constraints on word meanings from prior text, prior knowledge, situational context (i.e., pragmatic awareness; Snow, 1994; Tunmer et al., 1988), and the aforementioned morphological awareness.

Growing evidence suggests that these features of metalinguistic awareness as they apply to vocabulary learning can be enhanced through instruction that explicitly teaches word-learning strategies. For morphological awareness, in particular, recent meta-analytic (Bowers et al., 2010) and qualitative reviews (Carlisle, 2010) highlight the value of teaching students to use word parts to decipher and learn the meanings of new complex words. The evidence is more equivocal for the efficacy of teaching students to infer word meanings from context; Fukkink and de Glopper's (1998) meta-analysis found that relatively short-term interventions (as short as 90 minutes and no longer than eight hours) could improve this ability, whereas Kuhn and Stahl (1998) suggest that the effects of instruction in using context are not greater than the effects of simple practice.

## Motivation

Developing a rich academic vocabulary, like many other academic pursuits, requires motivation on the part of the child or adolescent involved. Clearly, students must be engaged for direct teaching of word meanings to be successful, a reality that has led designers of recent vocabulary interventions with adolescents to integrate vocabulary teaching into rich discussions about controversial topics that are relevant to young people, such as Internet bullying, single-gender classrooms, or academic tracking (Lesaux et al., 2010; Snow et al., 2009).

Beyond engagement during direct instruction, motivation is also important in the extensive independent word learning that a student must engage in to acquire a deep and broad vocabulary. Scott and Nagy (2004) link motivation explicitly to word consciousness, which they define as "the knowledge and dispositions necessary to learn, appreciate, and effectively use words" (p. 201). Although word consciousness certainly involves metalinguistic awareness of the types described above, it also includes affective dispositions including an interest in words and a willingness to take risks in speaking and writing with new words. One of the early efforts to promote word consciousness was Beck and colleagues' (1982) Word Wizard activity, which encourages students to use target vocabulary in their conversations and writing and to notice when target words are used in a new text or conversation outside of their regular vocabulary lessons. A more recent research effort is under way to collaborate with teachers in developing an intervention to promote word consciousness with emphasis on its affective aspects (Miller, Gage-Serio, & Scott, 2010). Because word consciousness is theorized to have effects outside of a given intervention period, more research on the long-term effects of promoting word consciousness is needed.

## Conclusion

In this chapter, we aimed to describe some of the complexities of individual differences in vocabulary knowledge as they relate to reading comprehension, to explore the implications of these complexities for assessment and instruction, and to raise some hypotheses about how vocabulary relates to less commonly studied individual differences in reading-related skills. As we have described, the multifaceted nature of vocabulary—as it differs within and between students—makes it a domain that is challenging to conceptualize, assess, and teach. Although research in recent years has made substantial progress in highlighting some of these complexities, their implications for understanding individual differences in reading have yet to be fully explored.

We have identified some new avenues for such exploration throughout this chapter. Specifically, given questions about the dimensionality of vocabulary knowledge, we need additional studies that examine how and when hypothesized distinctions among subskills can and cannot be operationalized as measurable separable constructs. Similarly, in light of competing hypotheses for the role of vocabulary in reading comprehension, we need research comparing instructional approaches with different theoretical bases (e.g., contrasting approaches that target new conceptual knowledge with approaches that teach new labels for familiar concepts). Regarding assessment to shed light on individual differences, we need innovative design and research efforts to develop vocabulary assessments that capture more information about the nuances of students' vocabulary knowledge than current approaches offer. Finally, we need a better understanding of how vocabulary relates to other individual differences, such as executive functioning, metalinguistic awareness, and motivation—combined with the development and evaluation of new instructional approaches that account for these relations.

Ultimately, to improve vocabulary instruction in classrooms, we will need more than basic research and controlled instructional experiments on these questions. We will also need concerted efforts to engage educators in learning more about the complexities of their students' individual differences in vocabulary and how to address them in thoughtful ways. Although researchers do not agree on many of the specifics—including some important specifics—they concur in rejecting a reductive notion of vocabulary knowledge as the ability to match lists of isolated words to their definitions. Yet, the instructional and assessment practices that we observe in schools all too often continue to operate on this discredited, reductive notion of vocabulary. So there is much work left to be done in building teachers' capacity to provide multifaceted, thoughtful, and responsive vocabulary instruction.

## References

Anderson, R. C., & Freebody, P. (1981). Vocabulary knowledge. In J. T. Guthrie (Ed.), *Comprehension and teaching: Research reviews* (pp. 77–117). Newark, DE: International Reading Association.

Beck, I. L., McKeown, M. G., & Kucan, L. (2002). *Bringing words to life.* New York: Guilford Press.

Beck, I. L., McKeown, M. G., & Omanson, R. C. (1987). The effects and uses of diverse vocabulary instructional techniques. In M. G. McKeown & M. E. Curtis (Eds.), *The nature of vocabulary acquisition* (pp. 147–163). Hillsdale, NJ: Lawrence Erlbaum Associates.

Beck, I. L., Perfetti, C. A., & McKeown, M. G. (1982). Effects of long-term vocabulary instruction on lexical access and reading comprehension. *Journal of Educational Psychology, 74*(4), 506.

Blair, C., & Razza, R. P. (2007). Relating effortful control, executive function, and false belief understanding to emerging math and literacy ability in kindergarten. *Child Development, 78*, 647–663.

Bowers, P. N., Kirby, J. R., & Deacon, S. H. (2010). The effects of morphological instruction on literacy skills: A systematic review of the literature. *Review of Educational Research, 80*, 144–179.

Bravo, M. A., & Cervetti, G. N. (2008). Teaching vocabulary through text and experience. In A. E. Farstrup & S. Samuels (Eds.), *What research has to say about vocabulary instruction* (pp. 130–149). Newark, DE: International Reading Association.

Bravo, M. A., Cervetti, G. N., Hiebert, E. H., & Pearson, P. D. (2008). From passive to active control of science vocabulary. *Fifty-sixth yearbook of the National Reading Conference* (pp.122–135). Chicago, IL: The National Reading Conference.

Carlisle, J. F. (1995). Morphological awareness and early reading achievement. In L. Feldman (Ed.), *Morphological aspects of language processing* (pp. 189–209). Mahwah, NJ: Lawrence Erlbaum Associates.

Carlisle, J. F. (2000). Awareness of the structure and meaning of morphologically complex words: Impact on reading. *Reading and Writing: An Interdisciplinary Journal, 12*, 169–190.

Carlisle, J. F. (2010). Effects of instruction in morphological awareness on literacy achievement: An integrative review. *Reading Research Quarterly, 45*(4), 464–487.

Carlisle, J. F., Kelcey, B., & Berebitsky, D. (2013). Teachers' support of students' vocabulary learning during literacy instruction in high poverty elementary schools. *American Educational Research Journal, 50*(6), 1360–1391.

Coxhead, A. (2000). A new academic word list. *TESOL Quarterly, 34*(2), 213–238.

Cutting, L. E., Materek, A., Cole, C. A. S., Levine, T. M., & Mahone, E. M. (2009). Effects of fluency, oral language, and executive function on reading comprehension performance. *Annals of Dyslexia, 59*, 34–54.

Durkin, D. (1978/1979). What classroom observations reveal about reading comprehension instruction. *Reading Research Quarterly, 14*, 481–533.

Elleman, A. M., Lindo, E. J., Morphy, P., & Compton, D. L. (2009). The impact of vocabulary instruction on passage-level comprehension of school-age children: A meta-analysis. *Journal of Research on Educational Effectiveness, 2*(1), 1–44.

Flavell, J. H. (1979). Metacognition and cognitive monitoring: A new area of cognitive–developmental inquiry. *American Psychologist, 34*(10), 906–911.

Fukkink, R. G., & de Glopper, K. (1998). Effects of instruction in deriving word meaning from context: A meta-analysis. *Review of Educational Research, 68*(4), 450–469.

Gamse, B. C., Jacob, R. T., Horst, M., Boulay, B., & Unlu, F. (2008). *Reading First Impact Study final Report* (NCEE 2009–4038). Washington, DC: National Center for Education Evaluation and Regional Assistance, Institute of Education Sciences, U.S. Department of Education.

Goerss, B. L., Beck, I. L., & McKeown, M. G. (1999). Increasing remedial students' ability to derive word meaning from context. *Reading Psychology, 20*(2), 151–175.

Graves, M. F. (2006). *The vocabulary book: Learning and instruction.* New York: Teachers College Press.

Hart, B., & Risley, T. R. (1995). *Meaningful differences in the everyday experience of young American children.* Baltimore, MD: Paul H. Brookes Publishing.

Hoover, W. A., & Gough, P. B. (1990). The simple view of reading. *Reading and Writing: An Interdisciplinary Journal, 2*, 127–160.

Kieffer, M. J., & Lesaux, N. K. (2012). Knowledge of words, knowledge about words: Dimensions of vocabulary in first and second language learners in sixth grade. *Reading and Writing: An Interdisciplinary Journal, 25*, 347–373.

Kieffer, M. J., Vukovic, R. K., & Berry, D. J. (2013). Roles of attention shifting and inhibitory control in fourth-grade reading comprehension. *Reading Research Quarterly, 48*, 333–348.

Kuhn, M. R., & Stahl, S. A. (1998). Teaching children to learn word meanings from context: A synthesis and some questions. *Journal of Literacy Research, 30*(1), 119–138.

Landauer, T. K., & Dumais, S. K. (1997). A solution to Plato's problem: The Latent Semantic Analysis theory of the acquisition, induction, and representation of knowledge. *Psychological Review, 104*, 211–240.

Lesaux, N. K., Kieffer, M. J., Faller, S. E., & Kelley, J. (2010). The effectiveness and ease of implementation of an academic vocabulary intervention for linguistically diverse students in urban middle schools. *Reading Research Quarterly, 45*, 198–230.

Loftus, S. M., & Coyne, M. D. (2013). Vocabulary instruction within a multi-tier approach. *Reading & Writing Quarterly, 29*(1), 4–19.

McKeown, M. G., & Beck, I. L. (2006). Issues in the advancement of vocabulary instruction: Response to Stahl and Fairbanks's meta-analysis. In K. A. Dougherty Stahl & M. C. McKenna (Eds.), *Reading research at work: Foundations of effective practice* (pp. 262–271). New York: Guilford Press.

Mazuka, R., Jincho, N., & Oishi, H. (2009). Development of executive control and language processing. *Language and Linguistics Compass, 3*, 59–89.

Miller, T., Gage-Serio, O., & Scott, J. (2010). Word consciousness in practice: Illustrations from a fourth-grade teacher's classroom. In R. Jimenez, V. Risko, M. Hundley, & D. Rowe (Eds.), *59th annual yearbook of the National Reading Conference* (pp. 171–186). Oak Creek, WI: National Reading Conference.

Miyake, A., Friedman, N. P., Emerson, M. J., Witzki, A. H., & Howerter, A. (2000). The unity and diversity of executive functions and their contributions to complex "frontal lobe" tasks: A latent variable analysis. *Cognitive Psychology, 41*, 49–100.

Nagy, W. (2007). Metalinguistic awareness and the vocabulary–comprehension connection. In R. K. Wagner, A. E Muse, & K. R. Tannenbaum (Eds.), *Vocabulary acquisition: Implications for reading comprehension* (pp. 52–77). New York: Guilford Press.

Nagy, W. E., Berninger, V. W., & Abbott, R. D. (2006). Contributions of morphology beyond phonology to literacy outcomes of upper elementary and middle-school students. *Journal of Educational Psychology, 98*, 134–147.

Nagy, W. E., & Hiebert, E. H. (2011). Toward a theory of word selection. In M. L. Kamil, P. D. Pearson, E. B. Moje, & P. P. Afflerbach (Eds.), *Handbook of reading research* (Vol. IV, pp. 388–404). New York: Routledge.

Nagy, W. E., & Scott, J. (2000) Vocabulary processes. In M. L. Kamil, P. B. Mosenthal, P. D. Pearson, & R. Barr (Eds.), *Handbook of reading research* (Vol. III, pp. 269–283). Mahwah, NJ: Erlbaum.

Nagy, W., & Townsend, D. (2012). Words as tools: Learning academic vocabulary as language acquisition. *Reading Research Quarterly, 47*(1), 91–108.

National Institute of Child Health and Human Development (US) (2000). *Report of the National Reading Panel: Teaching children to read: An evidence-based assessment of the scientific research literature on reading and its implications for reading instruction: Reports of the subgroups.* Washington, DC: National Institute of Child Health and Human Development, National Institutes of Health.

Neuman, S. B., Newman, E. H., & Dwyer, J. (2011). Educational effects of a vocabulary intervention on preschoolers' word knowledge and conceptual development: A cluster randomized trial. *Reading Research Quarterly, 46*(3), 249–272.

NICHD Early Child Care Research Network (Ed.) (2005). *Child care and child development: Results from the NICHD study of early child care and youth development.* New York: Guilford Press.

Paris, S. G. (2005). Reinterpreting the development of reading skills. *Reading Research Quarterly, 40*(2), 184–202.

Pearson, P. D., Hiebert, E. H., & Kamil, M. L. (2007). Vocabulary assessment: What we know and what we need to learn. *Reading Research Quarterly, 42*(2), 282–296.

Pennington, B. F., & Ozonoff, S. (1996). Executive functions and developmental psychopathology. *Journal of Child Psychology and Psychiatry, 37*, 51–87.

Penno, J. F., Wilkinson, I. A., & Moore, D. W. (2002). Vocabulary acquisition from teacher explanation and repeated listening to stories: Do they overcome the Matthew effect? *Journal of Educational Psychology*, *94*(1), 23.

RAND Reading Study Group (2002). *Reading for understanding: Toward an R&D program in reading*. Arlington, VA: RAND.

Read, J. (2000). *Assessing vocabulary*. Cambridge, UK: Cambridge University Press.

Scott, J. A., Hoover, M., Flinspach, S., & Vevea, J. (2008). A multiple-level vocabulary assessment tool: Measuring word knowledge based on grade-level materials. In Y. Kim, V. Risko, D. Compton, D. Dickinson, M. Hundley, R. Jimenez, . . . D. Rowe (Eds.), *57th Annual Yearbook of the National Reading Conference* (pp. 325–340). Oak Creek, WI: National Reading Conference.

Scott, J. A., & Nagy, W. E. (1997). Understanding the definitions of unfamiliar verbs. *Reading Research Quarterly*, *32*(2), 184–200.

Scott, J. A., & Nagy, W. E. (2004). Developing word consciousness. In J. F. Baumann & J. Kame'enui (Eds.), *Vocabulary instruction: Research to practice* (pp. 201–217). New York: Guilford Press.

Snow, C. (1994). What is so hard about learning to read? A pragmatic analysis. In J. Dunchan, L. Hewitt, & R. Sonnenmeier (Eds.), *Pragmatics: From theory to practice* (pp. 164–184). Englewood Cliffs, NJ: Prentice-Hall.

Snow, C. E., Burns, M. S., & Griffin, P. (Eds.) (1998). *Preventing reading difficulties in young children*. Washington, DC: National Academies Press.

Snow, C. E., & Kim, Y. S. (2007). Large problem spaces: The challenge of vocabulary for English language learners. In R. K. Wagner, A. E. Muse, & K. R. Tannenbaum (Eds.), *Vocabulary acquisition: Implications for reading comprehension* (pp. 123–139). New York: Guilford Press.

Snow, C. E., Lawrence, J. F., & White, C. (2009). Generating knowledge of academic language among urban middle school students. *Journal of Research on Educational Effectiveness*, *2*(4), 325–344.

Stahl, K. A. D. (2008). The effects of three instructional methods on the reading comprehension and content acquisition of novice readers. *Journal of Literacy Research*, *40*, 359–393.

Stahl, K. A. D., & Bravo, M. A. (2010). Contemporary classroom vocabulary assessment for content areas. *Reading Teacher*, *63*, 566–579.

Stahl, S. A., & Fairbanks, M. M. (1986). The effects of vocabulary instruction: A model-based meta-analysis. *Review of Educational Research*, *56*(1), 72–110.

Stahl, S. A., & Nagy, W. E. (2006). *Teaching word meanings*. Mahwah, NJ: Erlbaum.

Stanovich, K. E. (1986). Matthew effects in reading: Some consequences of individual differences in the acquisition of literacy. *Reading Research Quarterly*, *22*, 360–407.

Swanson, H. L., & Siegel, L. (2001). Learning disabilities as a working memory deficit. *Issues in Education*, *7*(1), 1–48.

Tannenbaum, K. R., Torgesen, J. K., & Wagner, R. K. (2006). Relationships between word knowledge and reading comprehension in third-grade children. *Scientific Studies of Reading*, *10*, 381–398.

Terman, L. M., Kohs, S. C., Chamberlain, M. B., Anderson, M., & Henry, B. (1918). The vocabulary test as a measure of intelligence. *Journal of Educational Psychology*, *9*(8), 452–466.

Tunmer, W. E., Herriman, M. L., & Nesdale, A. R. (1988). Metalinguistic abilities and beginning reading. *Reading Research Quarterly*, *23*(2), 134–158.

Vygotsky, L. L. S. (1978). *Mind in society: The development of higher psychological processes*. Cambridge, MA: Harvard University Press.

Wagner, A. E., Muse, A. E., & Tannenbaum, K. R. (2007). Promising avenues for better understanding implications of vocabulary development for reading comprehension. In R. K. Wagner, A. E. Muse, & K. R. Tannenbaum (Eds.), *Vocabulary acquisition: Implications for reading comprehension* (pp. 276–292), New York: Guilford Press.

Wesche, T., & Paribakht, T. S. (1996). Assessing second language vocabulary knowledge: Depth versus breadth. *Canadian Modern Language Review*, *53*, 13–40.

Wixson, K. K. (1986). Vocabulary instruction and children's comprehension of basal stories. *Reading Research Quarterly*, *21*(3), 317–329.

# 11

# Individual Differences in Reading Comprehension

*Paul van den Broek, Jolien M. Mouw, and Astrid Kraal*

---

People read texts for many different purposes. We read for pleasure or esthetic enjoyment, to learn for school, to understand phenomena, to obtain instructions, and so on. For all of these purposes, it is essential that the reader *comprehends* the text. However, individuals differ tremendously in their ability to do so and, hence, in their ability to attain their purposes. In this chapter, we discuss sources of individual differences in reading comprehension abilities. The chapter consists of three sections. In the first section we discuss what it means to comprehend a text and what cognitive processes occur during reading for comprehension. In the second section we highlight sources of individual differences in executing these processes. In the third section we discuss the development of the skills and abilities necessary for successful reading comprehension and possible ways in which comprehension and comprehension skills may be fostered by instructions and interventions.

Comprehension of a text can be defined in various ways. It may refer to the ability to reproduce (parts of) the text, the ability to analyze the information in the text, to use or apply the information, as well as a range of other abilities. For example, Bloom's taxonomy of learning objectives describes levels of processing of texts and other learning materials that range from memory for the text to critical evaluation and even the production of information (Airasian et al., 2001; Bloom, 1956). Likewise, the PISA reports define *Reading Literacy* as "understanding, using, and reflecting on written texts, in order to achieve one's goals, to develop one's knowledge and potential, and to participate in society" (PISA report, OECD, 2004, p. 272). In all these conceptualizations, a crucial step in comprehending a text is that the reader first creates a mental representation of the meaning of the text. Individual differences in the representation of a text reverberate through all other comprehension-related activities. In this chapter we focus on the meaning-representation aspects of comprehension.

## Comprehension: Inferences and the Construction of a Coherent Representation

Comprehension of a text involves the construction of a mental representation of the meaning of the text. To understand individual differences in reading comprehension, it is useful to consider both the *product* of reading, the mental representation, and the *process* by which such a representation is constructed. The Landscape Model of Reading Comprehension (van den Broek, Risden, Fletcher, & Thurlow, 1996; Helder, van den Broek, Van Leijenhorst, & Beker, 2013) captures both product and process in an integrative account of reading comprehension, by combining research findings from many investigators. We summarize the model here.

## The Reader's Representation of a Text

With regard to the product, in a successful representation the reader combines parts from the text with information from background knowledge that he or she has recruited during reading. Together, these elements do not simply form a list—a crucial aspect of text comprehension is that the elements in the mental representation are interconnected by means of meaningful relations, thereby resulting in a *coherent* representation (Coté, Goldman, & Saul, 1998; Graesser & Clark, 1985; Kintsch & Van Dijk, 1978; McNamara, Kintsch, Bulter Songer, & Kintsch, 1996; Trabasso, Secco, & van den Broek, 1984). Meaningful relations occur between individual text and background knowledge elements but also between larger text units, such as paragraphs, sections, and chapters. For example, textbooks may elaborate on a newly introduced concept by explaining components of the concept in separate paragraphs. To grasp the concept, the reader must recognize the relations between the components across paragraphs.

There are various kinds of meaningful relations that provide coherence to texts. For most texts, the most crucial relations are *referential* relations, which identify who is who and what is what in the text (e.g., that a pronoun "she" in a sentence refers to a particular female character in the preceding text), and *causal* and *logical* relations, which explain events or facts depicted in the text (e.g., that the damage on a tropical island described in a text is the result of the frequent storms mentioned earlier in the text). Other types of relations, such as spatial, emotional, and temporal, may also contribute to the overall coherence of the representation of the text.

The elements from the text and from background knowledge, together with their relations, form a network of interconnected and mutually dependent events and facts. Some events and facts feature prominently in the network by having many connections to other parts of the representation. These highly connected elements are *structurally central* to the meaningful representation of the text. Proficient readers tend to judge these elements as more important, and remember or include them in summaries of the text more often than elements with few connections (Graesser & Clark, 1985; Trabasso & van den Broek, 1985). Struggling comprehenders may fail to identify all important relations and, as a result, arrive at an impoverished representation and compromised ability to utilize the textual information. This is because readers draw on their representation when they perform tasks based on their reading. These tasks include experimental tasks such as recall or judgments tasks, but also everyday life tasks such as retelling to others what they have read, applying the knowledge gained from reading, and comparing information across multiple texts or multiple media.

## Comprehension Processes: Inferring Relations

The construction of a mental representation of the text is the result of a rich set of coherence-building processes by which the reader identifies relations between textual elements and between elements and his or her background knowledge. The study of these processes is not only theoretically interesting, but also has profound implications for educational practice. The processes are the mechanisms by which representations are constructed and, therefore, determine success and failure of comprehension. To be effective, interventions aimed at improving comprehension must impact the processes that take place *during* reading—a point to which we will return in the third section.

There are several factors that limit a reader's ability to identify the relations in a text. One major factor is that most semantic relations are not explicitly marked in the text and therefore need to be inferred by the reader. For example, texts frequently have sentence pairs such as "The inhabitants suffer from frequent torrential rain falls. Farming is a challenge," in which the causal relation between the two facts is not explicitly stated. To comprehend, the reader must *infer* the relation. A second major factor is the fact that readers have limited attentional or working-memory capacities and, therefore, can only maintain a subset of all potentially relevant events and facts from the text as they proceed to subsequent sentences. The likelihood that the relation between two events or facts will indeed be recognized by the reader is increased when the two are presented closely together in the text or when the earlier event/fact is repeated. A third limiting factor is that, even when a semantic relation is marked and working memory is not overextended, the background knowledge necessary for the inference may be lacking (in the above example: Repeated heavy rain fall may wash crops off farmland). We will return to these and other limitations in the next section.

As a reader progresses through a text, each new sentence elicits a new reading cycle with automatic processes and, possibly, strategic processes. With respect to the *automatic* processes, the concepts in the sentence trigger a passive, spread-of-activation process that activates additional concepts from the reader's memory for the preceding sentences and from his or her general background knowledge. The latter involves individual facts and events, but also the "filling in" of conceptual gaps through activation of schemes or scripts (Anderson & Pearson, 1984). These activations are "for free" in that they do not require effort or conscious processing by the reader. Together with concepts, events, and facts processed in the preceding reading cycle and those in the currently read sentence, these activated concepts allow the reader to make coherence-building (and other) inferences (van den Broek, Risden, et al., 1996; Helder et al., 2013).

In addition to the automatic processes, a reader may engage in *strategic* coherence-based processes. These processes are initiated by the reader to establish coherence. They may involve the preceding text (such as looking back or searching in memory for information from the preceding text), background knowledge (e.g., searching for an explanation for an event or fact), or other sources of information altogether (e.g., Internet, other texts). Strategic processes are acquired through experience or instruction, and some may become relatively automatized as a child becomes proficient in reading. Readers differ in their "toolbox" of strategic processes. The strategic processes enable inference making beyond those already available through the automatic processes.

The degree to which a reader will engage in strategic processes, in addition to the automatic ones, is to a large extent determined by the reader's *standards of coherence*: For each reading situation (i.e., reading a particular text in a particular context), a reader implicitly or explicitly adopts a set of standards of coherence (McCrudden & Schraw, 2007; van den Broek, Bohn-Gettler, Kendeou, Carlson, & White, 2011). These standards reflect the type (e.g., causal, referential, temporal, etc.) and strength of coherence the reader considers desirable. Standards of coherence have a family resemblance to comprehension monitoring, but an important difference is that standards often are implicit and operate without the reader's conscious awareness (much like validation processes that have received considerable attention recently; see Isberner & Richter, 2013). A reader's standards depend on the reading situation (e.g., the reading task, instructions, presence of competing tasks), on the reader (e.g., reading goals, motivation, reading skills), and on the text (e.g., text genre, presence of text signals such as headers and connectives, and perceived source credibility; see van den Broek, Risden et al., 1996, van den Broek, Bohn-Gettler, et al., 2011a, for reviews).

Thus, the reader is likely to draw on the coherence-building strategic processes in his or her repertoire when the automatic processes described above do not establish sufficient coherence between a newly read sentence and the reader's representation of the preceding text to meet the reader's standards. This is particularly likely when the text is difficult or the reader has a particularly challenging goal for reading.

As the reader proceeds through the text, every new sentence elicits anew a combination of automatic and, possibly, strategic processes. The combinations change as a function of the properties of each newly read sentence and, thereby, create an unfolding landscape of inferential processes and fluctuating activations of concepts, events, and facts. Thus, the reading process is dynamic, with different combinations of processes taking place at different moments during reading, much like a cross-country runner whose body adjusts with every step to the unique combination of properties of the ground he is running on.

The reading process is dynamic in the sense that comprehension of a sentence and the gradual emergence of a mental representation continually interact with each other as the reader moves through the text. As each newly read sentence is processed and comprehended, the meaning derived from the sentence modifies the representation the reader has built of the text read so far. In turn, as we have seen, the representation built so far influences the processing of the next sentence. This reciprocal processing of sentence and text continues until the reader has finished reading the entire text.

## Individual Differences in Inference Generation and Comprehension

The summary of the processes and products of comprehending a text in the preceding section provides a description of the modal reader but in reality individuals differ considerably in the extent to which they execute the various processes and, hence, in the representation they have created by the time their reading is completed. Several sources of individual differences already have been mentioned; here we elaborate on these and others. The sources of individual variation roughly fall into three categories: *general cognitive* factors, *comprehension* factors, and *text-specific* factors (for detailed reviews see Cain & Oakhill, 2007; van den Broek & Espin, 2012; Helder et al., 2013).

### General Cognitive Factors

As described, reading comprehension depends on a complex set of interacting processes. Not surprisingly, several general cognitive factors have been found to influence an individual's comprehension abilities and, hence, to cause individual differences. An important factor in determining a reader's ability to arrive at correct and deep understanding is his or her *background knowledge* about the information presented in the text. The inferential processes that allow a reader to identify semantic relations draw heavily on his/her prior knowledge. This is the case for both automatic and strategic processes. As a result, differences in background knowledge strongly influence the reader's comprehension and representation of a text: generally, the more knowledge the reader possesses on topics in the text, the richer and more interconnected his or her representation will be (Anderson & Pitchert, 1978; McNamara et al., 1996; Voss, Vesonder, & Spilich, 1980). In addition to the amount and depth of a reader's knowledge, the accuracy of knowledge plays an important role. For example, misconceptions influence the representation of a text just as accurate knowledge does (e.g., Doyle & Smith, 1989; Kendeou & van den Broek, 2005; Mason, Gava, & Boldrin, 2008).

A second important source of individual differences concerns *working memory*. Differences in the capacity and efficacy of working memory have been found to affect comprehension in adults (Whitney, Ritchie, & Matthew, 1991; Just & Carpenter, 1992; Linderholm & van den Broek, 2002; Virtue, van den Broek, & Linderholm, 2006) as well as children (Cain & Oakhill, 2007; Reynolds, this volume). A greater working memory facilitates the maintenance and processing of more information from the text and background knowledge, thus supporting the generation of inferences and construction of a coherent representation. Working memory is one component of the broader class of *executive functions*, which include *inhibition*, *shifting*, and *updating* (Miyaki et al., 2000). These generally concern the individual's ability to effectively *allocate attention*, thereby influencing the content of working memory. Although these have received less attention from researchers than working memory, they too have been found to affect comprehension of text (e.g., Sesma, Mahone, Levine, Eason, & Cutting, 2009).

## General Comprehension Skills

Individual differences occur in the execution of comprehension processes that occur in all modalities, including but not limited to, reading. One important individual difference pertains to one's *standards of coherence*. Individuals may differ systematically in the type and degree of coherence they maintain while reading texts or processing information in other modalities (van den Broek, White, Kendeou, & Carlson, 2009). They may also differ in their ability to adjust their standards to fit the particular (reading) situation. For example, readers with weak comprehension adjust their reading processes less effectively to variations in reading goals than do good comprehenders (Cain & Oakhill, 2007; Linderholm & van den Broek, 2002).

A second important source of individual differences in comprehension skills concerns the degree to which individuals allocate attention to information that is important for the semantic structure of the text. Differences in this *sensitivity to structural centrality* result in differences in what information is selected from new text input for further processing. Selective attention has been investigated most extensively in developmental studies (see van den Broek, Helder, & van Leijenhorst, 2013, for a review; see also Reynolds, current volume).

For example, the attention of younger children tends to be more attracted to information that is visually interesting and less to semantically central information than that of older children (van den Broek, Lorch, & Thurlow, 1996). Similarly, within an age group, children with attentional difficulties experience more problems focussing on central information (e.g., Lorch, Diener, et al., 1999; Lorch, Sanchez, et al., 1999) than children without attentional difficulties.

A third source of individual differences in comprehension concerns *inferential skills*. The information that is available to the reader at a particular point in reading needs to be connected by the reader by constructing, actively or passively, a particular semantic relation. Differences in the ability to do so also have been studied with respect to children. We discuss these in the context of text-processing in the following subsection.

## Text-Specific Skills

The processes described in the preceding section apply to all comprehension contexts, whether in reading, listening, or another medium. There also are cognitive factors that are particular to the reading context. One concerns the reader's knowledge about *text genres*. Different genres are structured around different types of coherence relations. The reader's ability to adjust his or her reading to the genre of a text influences the depth of knowledge gained from reading (Oakhill & Cain, 2011).

A second source of individual differences pertains to a reader's knowledge of and ability to process *textual cues*. Texts contains "instructions for processing" such as headers for (sub)sections and connectives that promote the reader to engage in particular semantic processing (Lemarié, Lorch, Eyrolle, & Virbel, 2008). Through experience and instruction, developing readers acquire knowledge of these and other semantic cues. Together these cues also contribute to a reader's skill in recognizing the broader structure within a text. For example, in expository texts headers that signal (sub)sections may create a hierarchical organization of parts of the text (Lorch, 1989; Lorch, Lemarié, & Grant, 2011; Surber & Schroeder, 2007).

A third source of individual differences in text-specific factors concerns *inference-making* skills. Although these skills apply to any comprehension situation (which is why they were mentioned in the preceding section also), their implementation may be partially specific to the reading context. For example, evidence from eye-tracking and think–aloud studies shows that poorly comprehending readers often engage in suboptimal inferential processing during reading (Rapp, van den Broek, McMaster, Kendeou, & Espin, 2007; see also Oakhill & Cain, 2011). Interestingly, it appears that these poorly comprehending readers fall into at least two distinct subgroups (McMaster et al., 2012): those who generate relatively few inferences that connect text elements and those who *do* generate such inferences but often to irrelevant information. A second example of individual differences in inference-making skills concerns differences in reading-specific strategies that a reader may have available to establish coherence when reading a text, such as knowledge about when and how to reread, how to interpret a table of contents, and so on.

A fourth source of individual differences concerns variation in *motivation for reading*. The amount of motivation that a reader brings to a reading situation determines how much mental energy he or she is willing to expend, his or her standards of coherence, and so on. Motivation can be intrinsic (Guthrie & Wigfield, 2000; Wang & Guthrie, 2004; Clinton & van den Broek, 2012) or extrinsic (dependent on incentives; e.g., Konheim-Kalkstein & van den Broek, 2008). Intrinsic motivation for reading revolves around reading for enjoyment and for interest (Guthrie & Wigfield, 2000). It has been found to lead to both higher exposure (more frequent reading) and higher reading performance (Baker & Wigfield, 1999). With regard to processing, it leads to more frequent use of (adequate) strategies and deeper level learning (Schiefele, 1999).The role of extrinsic motivation for reading has been investigated less extensively. The results are mixed. For example, presenting student readers with incentives to read a text has been found to improve comprehension, at least in immediate tests (Konheim-Kalkstein & van den Broek, 2008). But the effect of external reinforcement may be detrimental in the long run: Becker, McElvany, and Kortenbruck (2010) observed that, over time, providing extrinsic reading motivation may have a negative effect on performance, even when they controlled for children's frequency of reading and previous reading performance.

## Individual Differences in the Representation of Texts

These and other potential factors that influence the processes that occur *during* reading result in differences in the mental representation of a text in a reader's memory and, hence, in differences in higher levels of comprehension that take this representation as input. Thus, problems in comprehension processes at the representational level likely reverberate in a reader's ability to engage in other comprehension activities such as reflecting on and evaluating the text, and integrating it with information from other texts or media.

With respect to the *product* of comprehension, there are considerable individual differences in the quality of representation and the sensitivity to structural centrality, in adults and in children.

For example, strong comprehenders consistently recall or judge as important events from a text that have many connections to other elements of the text, but struggling or less experienced (younger) readers show a much weaker tendency to do so (Bourg, Bauer, & van den Broek, 1997). This difference in sensitivity to structural centrality suggests that the latter group identifies and represents fewer (or different) connections than good comprehenders. Likewise, differences in background knowledge that the reader has recruited during reading result in differences in the richness and / or accuracy of the information that is included in the representation (Kendeou, Rapp, & van den Broek, 2004). Thus, considerable individual differences in both the quality and content of the representation of texts exist.

## Acquiring Reading Comprehension Skills: Development and Education

### Reading Comprehension Development

Children gradually develop the skills and strategies involved in reading comprehension, through experience, instruction, and maturation of the underlying cognitive functions. For some cognitive factors described above the developmental trajectories are fairly well mapped out. This is the case, for example, for working-memory capacity and other executive functions such as suppression of irrelevant information and attention shifting (Demetriou, Christiou, Spanoudis, & Platsidou, 2002; Gathercole, Pickering, Ambridge, & Wearing, 2004).

With respect to the development of reading-specific skills, several patterns have been clearly established. With age and schooling children's inference-making processes improve, and their repertoire of strategies (e.g., for repairing inconsistencies, for searching texts for relevant information) expands dramatically. As a result, they become increasingly able to identify semantic relations between text elements that are distal in the text as well as relations that are abstract (e.g., about characters' emotional and motivational states, about themes) rather than concrete and physical (Diergarten & Nieding, 2013; Lynch & van den Broek, 2007; van den Broek, Lynch, Naslund, Ievers-Landis, & Verduin, 2003; Williams, 1993). In addition, relations can become more complex, involving crossing episodic boundaries, or depending on integration of multiple pieces of information (Linderholm, Therriault, & Kwon, 2014).

As these skills and processes develop, individual differences remain fairly stable. The results of several longitudinal investigations indicate that comprehension and inference-making skills as described above already form a stable cluster of skills at an early age—as young as 4 years— and that this cluster predicts comprehension many years later, when the children are well into elementary school (e.g., Oakhill & Cain, 2011; van den Broek et al., 2009; Kendeou, van den Broek, Whit, & Lynch, 2009). Thus, children that comprehend well at a young age are likely to remain good comprehenders as they grow older, whereas children who struggle with comprehension when young are at risk of struggling with continued difficulties later in their lives. Importantly, this cluster of skills develops relatively independently from a second cluster of skills, those concerning letter and word identification. The longitudinal results show that these two clusters come together once the child starts to read for comprehension, with each cluster contributing uniquely to reading comprehension performance (e.g., Gough, & Tunmer, 1986; Kendeou et al., 2009).

### Educational Implications

As mentioned, many of the skills used to comprehend a text are *acquired*, through experience and learning. As a consequence, understanding what processes are particularly important for comprehension has potential implications for educational practice. Insights can be used to help optimize comprehension for all children—for struggling, regular, and talented comprehenders.

One set of implications concerns the fostering of inferential skills and strategies. For example, we already mentioned that there appear to be subgroups of struggling comprehenders, each with a distinct profile of processes—that differs from the profiles of both good and other struggling comprehenders (Rapp et al., 2007). One subgroup, labeled *paraphrasers*, engages in little inference generation beyond the sentence; the other subgroup, labeled *elaborators*, engages in relation-building activities but often to irrelevant pieces of information. It would be useful to develop diagnostic tools for identifying these subgroups and to design targeted interventions. For instance, McMaster and colleagues (McMaster et al., 2012; McMaster, Espin, & van den Broek, 2014) have developed targeted questioning techniques that are designed to elicit beyond-the-sentence inferences in the paraphrasers subgroup, and causally focused inferences in the elaborators subgroup. Originally designed and tested in a lab environment, the questioning methods have been scaled up for delivery in classroom settings, using peer-assisted learning systems (Fuchs, Fuchs, & Burish, 2000). The results suggest that paraphrasers indeed benefit from being encouraged to go beyond the sentence in their comprehension, whereas elaborators benefit from being encouraged to focus selectively on inferences that *explain* the current sentence (McMaster et al., 2014).

In general, questioning techniques that encourage coherence-building inferences can be used to improve comprehension in children K through 12 (Pressley & McCormick, 1995; Wood, Pressley, Turnure, & Walton, 1987). Such techniques are particularly effective in improving comprehension when they are implemented *during* reading, because they change the processing. However, potential benefits must be balanced with potential risks: beginning readers may have to devote considerable attention to deciphering the sentences, so for them the added burden of processing and answering questions may interfere rather than support (e.g., van den Broek, Tzeng, Risden, Trabasso, & Basche, 2001).

Because comprehension skills already start to develop in the preschool years, it is possible that inferential skills can be fostered at an early age. Indeed, questioning techniques with age-appropriate materials and in an auditory modality have been found to improve memory for simple narratives in preschool children (van den Broek, Kendeou, Lousberg, & Visser, 2011b). In general, comprehension skills and strategies can be fostered and practiced at an early age and in non-reading contexts. Interactive reading that includes practicing explanations and making connections is likely to foster the development of inferential skills.

A second set of implications for education concerns the design of texts. Here it is important to distinguish between two usages of texts. One usage is aimed at transferring knowledge to the child (or adult), the other usage is aimed at teaching the child strategies for comprehension that can be applied to *other* texts. With regard to the first usage, the child's ability to process and represent the textual information can be improved by designing the text such that the processes described in the section "Comprehension" are optimized. To-be-related information can be presented close together or reinstated when needed, coherence breaks can be clearly signaled, and the order of presentation can be designed to facilitate processing. Note that optimizing a text is not the same as simplifying. Comprehenders perform optimally with texts that are appropriate but somewhat challenging to their skill level; motivation declines when the text is considered too simple (van den Broek, 2010). With regard to the second usage, the aim would be to present children with suboptimal texts, in a way that is carefully calibrated with their developing skill, to foster the gradual emergence of the skills necessary to independently process and comprehend texts. There has been very little research on this usage of texts.

A final set of implications that we discuss here concerns the development of diagnostics for identification of individual differences in reading comprehension. There has been much debate on the quality and validity of currently available assessment tools (Francis, Snow, August, Carlson, Miller, & Iglesias, 2006; Keenan & Betjemann, 2006; Nation & Snowling, 1997; van den Broek, 2012) and on the importance of assessing the full range of reading for meaning (e.g., Afflerbach, 2012; Afflerbach, Cho, Kim, Crassas, & Doyle, 2013). It would be useful to develop assessment tools that capture the full range of comprehension activities that comprise reading literacy, and that allow the identification of subgroups of (struggling) readers that have unique profiles of processing.

## Concluding Remarks

Individuals differ in their ability to comprehend the texts they read. Even among those who arrive at a solid understanding, there are differences in the profiles of processes they recruit to achieve that goal. Similarly, struggling readers who arrive at inadequate understanding may do so because of problems in different processes, leading to distinct subgroups of struggling readers. In this chapter, we have attempted to provide an overview of the automatic and strategic processes that are involved in the comprehension of a text, and of the gradual emergence of a coherent, meaningful representation of the text in the reader's mind. This representation is the basis for other comprehension processes, such as analyzing and evaluating the text, comparing its content to that of other texts or non-texts, and so on. The content, quality, and form of the final representation are determined by the processes during reading of the text.

Understanding the dynamics of reading comprehension, with respect to both process and product, has implications for instruction and assessment. Methods can be developed to foster inferential skills—even at a young age, texts can be designed to foster learning or strategy development, diagnostic tools can be developed to capture overall comprehension skill but also to help identify subgroups of (struggling) readers—which, in turn, may lead to interventions targeted at subgroups.

We have focused on implications of understanding reading for educational practice, but applications in educational settings also have an important role to play in the development of theoretical accounts of reading. Educational practice poses important questions that theories and models need to address and also is in many respects the "ultimate testing ground" for such theories. Thus, the relation between theoretical accounts of reading comprehension and educational practice is reciprocal and mutually beneficial.

## Acknowledgments

The work reported in this chapter has been made possible by the support of the Leiden Brain, & Education Lab (www.brainandeducationlab.nl), the Leiden Institute for Brain and Cognition (www.libc-leiden.nl), and the Center for Cognitive Sciences at the University of Minnesota (www.cogsci.umn.edu).

## References

Afflerbach, P. (2012). *Understanding and using reading assessment, K–12* (2nd ed.). Newark, DE: International Reading Association.
Afflerbach, P., Cho, B.-Y., Kim, J.-Y., Crassas, M. E., & Doyle, B. (2013). Reading: What else matters besides strategies and skills? *The Reading Teacher, 66*, 1936–2714.

Airasian, P. W., Cruikshank, K. A., Mayer, R. E., Pintrich, P. R., Raths, J., & Wittrock, M. C. (2001). *A taxonomy for learning, teaching, and assessing: A revision of Bloom's Taxonomy of Educational Objectives* (Complete edition). New York, NY: Longman.

Anderson, R. C., & Pearson, P. D. (1984). *A schema-theoretic view of basic processes in reading comprehension* (Report No. 306). Champaign, IL: University of Illinois.

Anderson, R. C., & Pitchert, J. W. (1978). Recall of previously unrecallable information following a shift in perspective. *Journal of Verbal Learning and Verbal Behavior, 17,* 1–12.

Baker, L., & Wigfield, A. (1999). Dimensions of children's motivation for reading and their relations to reading activity and reading achievement. *Reading Research Quarterly, 34,* 452–477.

Becker, M., McElvany, N., & Kortenbruck, M. (2010). Intrinsic and extrinsic reading motivation as predictors of reading literacy: A longitudinal study. *Journal of Educational Psychology, 102,* 773–785.

Bloom, B. S. (1956). *Taxonomy of educational objectives: The classification of educational goals. Handbook I: Cognitive domain.* New York: Longmans.

Bourg, T., Bauer, P. J., & van den Broek, P. (1997). Event comprehension and representation. In P. W. van den Broek, T. Bourg, & P. J. Bauer (Eds.), *Developmental spans in event comprehension and representation: Bridging fictional and actual events* (pp. 385–407). New York, NY: Lawrence Erlbaum Associates.

Cain, K., & Oakhill, J. (2007). Reading comprehension difficulties: Correlates, causes, and consequences. In K. Cain & J. Oakhill (Eds.), *Children's comprehension problems in oral and written language: A cognitive perspective* (pp. 41–75). New York, NY: Guilford.

Clinton, V., & van den Broek, P. (2012). Interest, inferences, and learning from texts. *Learning and Individual Differences, 22,* 650–663.

Coté, N., Goldman, S. R., & Saul, E. U. (1998). Students making sense of informational text: Relations between processing and representation, *Discourse Processes, 25*(1), 1–53.

Demetriou, A., Christou, C., Spanoudis, G., & Platsidou, M. (2002). The development of mental processing: Efficiency, working memory, and thinking. *Monographs of the Society for Research in Child Development, 67,* 1–155.

Diergarten, A. K., & Nieding, G. (2013). Children's and adults' ability to build online emotional inferences during comprehension of audiovisual and auditory texts. *Journal of Cognition and Development,* 1–61. doi:10.1080/15248372.2013.848871

Doyle, J., & Smith, E. (1989). Prior knowledge and learning from science text: An instructional study. In S. McCormick & J. Zutell (Eds.), *Cognitive and social perspectives for literacy research and instruction* (pp. 345–352). Chicago, IL: NRC.

Francis, D. J., Snow, C. E., August, D., Carlson, C. D., Miller, J., & Iglesias, A. (2006). Measures of reading comprehension: A latent variable analysis of the diagnostic assessment of reading comprehension. *Scientific Studies of Reading, 10,* 301–322.

Fuchs, D., Fuchs, L. S., & Burish, P. (2000). Peer-assisted learning strategies: An evidence-based practice to promote reading achievement. *Learning Disabilities Research & Practice, 15*(2), 85–91.

Gathercole, S. E., Pickering, S. J., Ambridge, B., & Wearing, H. (2004). The structure of working memory from 4 to 15 years of age. *Developmental Psychology, 40,* 177–190.

Gough, P. B., & Tunmer, W. E. (1986). Decoding, reading, and reading disability. *Remedial and Special Education, 7*(1), 6–10.

Graesser, A. C., & Clark, L. C. (1985). *Structures and procedures of implicit knowledge.* Norwood, NJ: Ablex.

Guthrie, J. T., & Wigfield, A. (2000). Engagement and motivation in reading. In M. L. Kamil, P. B. Mosenthal, P. D. Pearson, & R. Barr (Eds.), *Handbook of reading research* (pp. 403–424). Mahwah, NJ: Lawrence Erlbaum Associates.

Helder, A., van den Broek, P., van Leijenhorst, L., & Beker, K. (2013). Sources of comprehension problems during reading. In B. Miller, L. Cutting, & P. McCardle (Eds.), *Unraveling reading comprehension: Behavioral, neurobiological, and genetic components* (pp. 43–53). Baltimore, MD: Paul H. Brookes Publishing.

Isberner, M., & Richter, T. (2013). Can readers ignore implausibility? Evidence for nonstrategic monitoring of event-based plausibility in language comprehension. *Acta Psychologica, 142*(1), 15–22.

Just, M. A., & Carpenter, P. A. (1992). A capacity theory of comprehension: Individual differences in working memory. *Psychological Review, 99*(1), 122–149.

Keenan, J. M., & Betjemann, R. S. (2006). Comprehending the Gray Oral Reading Test without reading it: Why comprehension tests should not include passage-independent items. *Scientific Studies of Reading, 10,* 363–380.

Kendeou, P., Rapp, D. N., & van den Broek, P. (2004). The influence of readers' prior knowledge on text comprehension and learning from text. In R. Nata (Ed.), *Progress in education* (pp. 189–210). New York, NY: Nova Science Publishers.

Kendeou, P., & van den Broek, P. (2005). The effects of readers' misconceptions on comprehension of scientific text. *Journal of Educational Psychology, 97*, 235–245.

Kendeou, P., van den Broek, P., White, M. J., & Lynch, J. S. (2009). Predicting reading comprehension in early elementary school: The independent contributions of oral language and decoding skills. *Journal of Educational Psychology, 101*, 765–778.

Kintsch, W., & Van Dijk, T. A. (1978). Toward a model of text comprehension and production. *Psychological Review, 85*, 363–394.

Konheim-Kalkstein, Y. L., & van den Broek, P. (2008). The effect of incentives on cognitive processing of text. *Discourse Processes, 45*, 180–194.

Lemarié, J., Lorch, R. F., Jr., Eyrolle, H., & Virbel, J. (2008). A text-based and reader-based theory of signaling. *Educational Psychologist, 43*, 27–48.

Linderholm, T., Therriault, D. J., & Kwon, H. (2014). Multiple science text processing: Building comprehension skills for college student readers. *Reading Psychology, 35*(4), 332–356.

Linderholm, T., & van den Broek, P. (2002). The effects of reading purpose and working memory capacity on the processing of expository text. *Journal of Educational Psychology, 94*, 778–784.

Lorch, E. P., Diener, M. B., Sanchez, R. P., Milich, R., Welsh, R., & van den Broek, P. (1999). The effects of story structure on the recall of stories in children with Attention Deficit Hyperactivity Disorder. *Journal of Educational Psychology, 91*, 273–283.

Lorch, E. P., Sanchez, R. P., van den Broek, P., Milich, R., Murphy, E. L., Lorch, R. F., Jr., & Welsh, R. (1999). The relation of story structure properties to recall of television stories in young children with attention-deficit hyperactivity disorder and nonreferred peers. *Journal of Abnormal Child Psychology, 27*, 293–309.

Lorch, R. F., Jr. (1989). Text signaling devices and their effects on reading and memory processes. *Educational Psychology Review, 1*, 209–234.

Lorch, R. F., Jr., Lemarié, J., & Grant, R. A. (2011). Signaling hierarchical and sequential organization in expository text. *Scientific Studies of Reading, 15*, 267–284.

Lynch, J. S., & van den Broek, P. (2007). Understanding the glue of narrative structure: Children's on- and off-line inferences about characters' goals. *Cognitive Development, 22*, 323–340.

McCrudden, M. T., & Schraw, G. (2007). Relevance and goal-focusing in text processing. *Educational Psychology Review, 19*, 113–139.

McMaster, K. L., Espin, C. A., & van den Broek, P. (2014). Making connections: Linking cognitive psychology and intervention research to improve comprehension of struggling readers. *Learning Disabilities Research & Practice, 29*(1), 17–24.

McMaster, K. L., van den Broek, P., Espin, C. A., White, M. J., Rapp, D. N., Kendeou, P., . . . Carlson, S. (2012). Making the right connections: Differential effects of reading intervention for subgroups of comprehenders. *Learning and Individual Differences, 22*(1), 100–111.

McNamara, D. S., Kintsch, E., Bulter Songer, N., & Kintsch, W. (1996). Are good texts always better? Interactions of text coherence, background knowledge, and levels of understanding in learning from text. *Cognition and Instruction, 14*, 1–43.

Mason, L., Gava, M., & Boldrin, A. (2008). On warm conceptual change: The interplay of text, epistemological beliefs, and topic interest. *Journal of Educational Psychology, 100*, 291–309.

Miyaki, A., Friedman, N. P., Emerson, M. J., Witzki, A. H., Howerter, A., & Wagner, T. D. (2000). The unity and diversity of executive functions and their contributions to complex "frontal lobe" tasks: A latent variable analysis. *Cognitive Psychology, 41*(1), 49–100.

Nation, K., & Snowling. M. J. (1997). Assessing reading difficulties: The validity and utility of current measures of reading skill. *British Journal of Educational Psychology, 67*, 359–370

Oakhill, J., & Cain, K. (2011). The precursors of reading ability in young readers: Evidence from a four-year longitudinal study. *Scientific Studies of Reading, 16*(2), 91–121.

Organisation for Economic Co-Operation and Development (2004). *Learning for tomorrow's world: First results from PISA 2003*. Paris, France: OECD Publications. Retrieved from http://www.oecd.org/edu/school/programmeforinternationalstudentassessmentpisa/learningfortomorrowsworldfirstresultsfrom pisa2003.htm.

Pressley, M., & McCormick, C. B. (1995). *Advanced educational psychology for educators, researchers, and policymakers*. New York, NY: HarperCollins.

Rapp, D. N., van den Broek, P., McMaster, K. L., Kendeou, P., & Espin, C. A. (2007). Higher-order comprehension processes in struggling readers: A perspective for research and intervention. *Scientific Studies of Reading, 11*, 289–312.

Schiefele, U. (1999). Interest and learning from text. *Scientific Studies of Reading, 3*, 257–279.

Sesma, H. W., Mahone, E. M., Levine, T., Eason, S. H., & Cutting, L. E. (2009). The contribution of executive skills to reading comprehension. *Child Neuropsychology, 15*, 232–246.

Surber, J. R., & Schroeder, M. (2007). Effect of prior domain knowledge and headings on processing of informative text. *Contemporary Educational Psychology, 32*, 485–498.

Trabasso, T., Secco, T., & van den Broek, P. W. (1984). Causal cohesion and story coherence. In H. Mandl, N. L. Stein, & T. Trabasso (Eds.), *Learning and comprehension of text* (pp. 83–111). Hillsdale, NJ: Lawrence Erlbaum Associates.

Trabasso, T., & van den Broek, P. (1985). Causal thinking and the representation of narrative events. *Journal of Memory and Language, 24*, 612–630.

van den Broek, P. (2010). Using texts in science education: Cognitive processes and knowledge representation. *Science, 328*, 453–456.

van den Broek, P. (2012). Individual and developmental differences in reading comprehension: Assessing cognitive processes and outcomes. In J. P. Sabatini, E. R. Albro, & T. O'Reilly (Eds.), *Measuring up: Advances in how we assess reading ability* (pp. 39–58). Lanham, MD: Rowman & Littlefield Education.

van den Broek, P., Bohn-Gettler, C., Kendeou, P., Carlson, S., & White, M. J. (2011a). When a reader meets a text: The role of standards of coherence in reading comprehension. In M. T. McCrudden, J. Magliano, & G. Schraw (Eds.), *Relevance instructions and goal-focusing in text learning* (pp. 123–140). Greenwich, CT: Information Age Publishing.

van den Broek, P., & Espin, C. A. (2012). Connecting cognitive theory and assessment: Measuring individual differences in reading comprehension. *School Psychology Review, 41*, 315–325.

van den Broek, P., Helder, A., & van Leijenhorst, L. (2013). Sensitivity to structural centrality: Developmental and individual differences in reading comprehension skills. In M. A. Britt, S. R. Goldman, & J.-F. Rouet (Eds.), *Reading: From words to multiple texts* (pp. 132–146). New York, NY: Routledge.

van den Broek, P., Kendeou, P., Lousberg, S., & Visser, G. (2011b). Preparing for reading comprehension: Fostering text comprehension skills in preschool and early elementary school children. *International Electronic Journal of Elementary Education, 4*, 259–268.

van den Broek, P., Lorch, E. P., & Thurlow, R. (1996). Children's and adults' memory for television stories: The role of causal factors, story-grammar categories and hierarchical level. *Child Development, 67*, 3010–3029.

van den Broek, P., Lynch, J. S., Naslund, J., Ievers-Landis, C. E., & Verduin, C. (2003). The development of comprehension of main ideas in narratives: Evidence from the selection of titles. *Journal of Educational Psychology, 95*, 707–718. doi:10.1037/0022-0663.95.4.707

van den Broek, P., Risden, K., Fletcher, C. R., & Thurlow, R. (1996). A "landscape" view of reading. Fluctuating patterns of activation and the construction of a stable memory representation. In B. K. Britton & A. C. Greasser (Eds.), *Models of understanding text* (pp. 165–187). Hillsdale, NJ: Lawrence Erlbaum Associates.

van den Broek, P., Tzeng, Y., Risden, K., Trabasso, T., & Basche, P. (2001). Inferential questioning: Effects on comprehension of narrative texts as a function of grade and timing. *Journal of Educational Psychology, 93*, 521–529.

van den Broek, P., White, M. J., Kendeou, P., & Carlson, S. (2009). Reading between the lines: Developmental and individual differences in cognitive processes in reading comprehension. In R. Wagner, C. Schatschneider, & C. Phythian-Sence (Eds.), *Beyond decoding: The behavioral and biological foundations of reading comprehension* (pp. 107–123). New York, NY: Guilford Press.

Virtue, S., van den Broek, P., & Linderholm, T. (2006). Hemispheric processing of inferences: The effects of textual constraint and working memory capacity. *Memory & Cognition, 34*, 1341–1354.

Voss, J. F., Vesonder, G. T., & Spilich, G. J. (1980). Text generation and recall by high-knowledge and low-knowledge individuals. *Journal of Verbal Learning and Verbal Behavior, 19*, 651–667.

Wang, J. H. Y., & Guthrie, J. T. (2004). Modeling the effects of intrinsic motivation, extrinsic motivation, amount of reading, and past reading achievement on text comprehension between U.S. and Chinese students. *Reading Research Quarterly, 39*, 162–186.

Whitney, P., Ritchie, B. G., & Matthew, C. B. (1991). Working-memory capacity and the use of elaborative inferences in text comprehension. *Discourse Processes, 14*, 133–145.

149

Williams, J. P. (1993). Comprehension of students with and without learning disabilities: Identification of narrative themes and idiosyncratic text representations. *Journal of Educational Psychology*, *85*, 631–641.

Wood, E., Pressley, M., Turnure, J. E., & Walton, R. (1987). Enriching children's recall of picture-dictionary definitions with interrogation and elaborated pictures. *Educational Communication and Technology Journal*, *35*, 43–52.

# 12

# Prior Knowledge

## Acquisition and Revision

*Panayiota Kendeou and Edward J. O'Brien*

## Introduction

Learning is frequently based on our ability to acquire information from what we read. Perhaps the most critical factor in the ability to acquire new information from texts is a reader's prior knowledge. Indeed, both the amount of knowledge an individual has, and the accuracy of that knowledge are important factors influencing the success of the learning process. For this chapter, we have been tasked with the goal to discuss individual differences in readers' prior knowledge in relation to the learning that occurs during reading. Thus, we review individual differences in prior knowledge and do so in a manner that would contribute to a deeper understanding of how the many faces of this construct influence reading comprehension. For that reason, we first discuss the nature, representation, and characteristics of prior knowledge. We then discuss the influences of prior knowledge on reading comprehension, highlighting processes and mechanisms that support both knowledge acquisition and knowledge revision. We conclude with a discussion of specific theoretical and practical implications for reading research, curriculum, and instruction.

## Knowledge Representation

Knowledge has been the subject of philosophy, psychology, and education (Murphy, Alexander, & Muis, 2012); however, it is still not totally understood. To aid our discussion in the role of individual differences in prior knowledge in relation to reading, we restrict our definition of knowledge in the context of psychology and education. Still, even within these domains, prior knowledge is considered a broad and multidimensional construct. We restrict our definition of knowledge as the theoretical or practical understanding of information and the representation of that understanding in memory.

Knowledge representation (i.e., how knowledge is organized or structured in memory) is central to any discussion about knowledge. There are various theories of how knowledge is represented and organized in memory: in the form of concepts, categories, propositions, prototypes, schemas or scripts (for a review, see Wyer, 1995). There are also various theories of the nature of knowledge representation: coherent versus fragmented (for reviews, see diSessa,

2013; Vosniadou, 2013). Independent of the unit of analysis or grain size, the widely adopted view is that knowledge is represented in the form of interconnected networks of information or *semantic networks* (Collins & Quillian, 1969). These networks represent knowledge as a system of interconnections between concepts in memory. Knowledge networks are typically represented as diagrams of nodes (i.e., concepts) and links (i.e., relations) often depicting complex relations that comprise the knowledge base (Goldman, Varma, & Coté, 1996). Typically, within these network representations the greater the degree of interconnectedness (i.e., relations among concepts), the greater the accessibility of that information, both in terms of speed of retrieval and probability of retrieval. Thus, to the extent that new knowledge can be linked to pre-existing knowledge that new knowledge takes advantage of already existing interconnections. This, in turn, increases the likelihood that the new knowledge will be accessible and usable at a later point in time; for example, it would facilitate the ability to answer a question, solve a problem, or guide the understanding of new information.

We adopt the view that prior knowledge becomes active and available during reading via passive activation processes derived from more global models of memory (e.g., Gillund & Shiffrin, 1984; Hintzman, 1986; Kintsch, 1988; Ratcliff, 1978; Ratcliff & McKoon, 1988). One instantiation of a model that captures this activation process during reading is the *Resonance Model* (Myers & O'Brien, 1998; O'Brien & Myers, 1999). The core assumption of the Resonance Model is that newly encoded information, in combination with the current contents of working memory, serves as a signal to all of long-term memory, including both earlier portions of the text representation as well as prior knowledge (e.g., Cook & Guéraud, 2005; Gerrig & O'Brien, 2005; O'Brien & Albrecht, 1991; O'Brien, Lorch, & Myers, 1998; Rizzella & O'Brien, 2002). The strength of the signal will depend on the level of attention a reader focuses on specific information currently in active memory. Nevertheless, the activation emanating from the signal proceeds autonomously and is unrestricted. Concepts from inactive portions of the text representation, as well as information from prior knowledge, *resonate* as a function of the degree of match to information in the signal. The match depends primarily on the overlap of semantic features. Concepts that are contacted by the initial signal in turn signal other elements in memory. During this resonance process, activation builds, and when the process stabilizes, information at the highest levels of activation enter working memory. That information will ultimately facilitate or hinder further processing and, hence, learning from text.

## Characteristics of Prior Knowledge

In the context of reading comprehension three forms of prior knowledge are particularly relevant: domain knowledge, topic knowledge, and general world knowledge (Alexander & Murphy, 1998). Domain knowledge refers to knowledge in a specific domain, field, or area of study (e.g., physics, psychology, earth science). Topic knowledge refers to knowledge relevant to a specific discourse (e.g., text, lecture, activity), and thus by definition is a subset of domain knowledge. General world knowledge is a broader level of knowledge that captures information assumed to be known by the general population. Although this level of knowledge is assumed to be the most stable, it does change over time. For example, according to general world knowledge norms in the 1980s (Nelson & Narens, 1980), very few people knew that Baghdad is the capital of Iraq. However, new norms (Tauber, Dunlosky, Rawson, Rhodes, & Sitzman, 2013) have shown increased general world knowledge in that respect because of the Iraq war.

When discussing individual differences in prior knowledge, one important characteristic is the distinction between the quality and quantity of knowledge. Quantity refers to the amount or extent of knowledge an individual has, whereas quality refers to the accuracy or structure (i.e., degree of interconnectedness) of that knowledge (Kendeou, Rapp, & van den Broek, 2004). Consideration of both quantity and quality is important because the quantity of prior knowledge a reader possesses is not indicative of the quality or validity of that knowledge. Conversely, the quality of knowledge may be unrelated to the quantity of that knowledge. Thus, the relation between quantity and quality dimensions has the potential to be orthogonal. For example, as the knowledge base of an individual grows, so does the structure and interconnectedness of that knowledge (high quantity–high quality). Higher quality is characterized by better organization, integration, and consolidation of knowledge. It is possible, however, for the knowledge base to increase but with inappropriate or invalid relations (high quantity–low quality). It is also possible to have a limited knowledge base but with appropriate and valid relations (low quantity–high quality) or a knowledge base that is both limited and invalid (low quantity–low quality).

Another important characteristic is the accuracy of prior knowledge, specifically whether knowledge is correct or incorrect according to an objective standard. This characteristic is especially important in educational settings in which students possess incorrect prior knowledge. For example, Lipson (1982) found that students demonstrated more successful learning when they lacked prior knowledge of a topic than when they possessed incorrect prior knowledge. The inaccurate prior knowledge provided a framework for the encoding and understanding of the new information; this made it especially difficult for these students to gain an accurate understanding of the new information, leading to greater interference during learning. With respect to the quantity and quality of prior knowledge, any increases in either of these when knowledge is incorrect would only exacerbate this interference.

## Influences of Prior Knowledge on the Acquisition of New Knowledge

Perhaps the most impressive influence of prior knowledge during reading is that it can both facilitate and interfere with the acquisition of new knowledge from text. Knowledge acquisition in this context is the process of encoding new information (included in texts) in memory, the success of which is often gauged by how well the information can later be retrieved from memory.

### Facilitation

The facilitative influences of prior knowledge on text comprehension can be traced to the work of schemas and scripts. This work demonstrated the tendency of readers to understand and interpret new information based on pre-existing structures in memory (e.g., Anderson & Pichert, 1978; Bransford & Johnson, 1972; Bower, Black, & Turner, 1979). Early models of reading comprehension were designed to capture the dynamic interaction between prior knowledge structures and text (Kintsch & van Dijk, 1978; van Dijk & Kintsch, 1983; Kintsch, 1988). In this context, the effects of prior knowledge have been shown to influence the time necessary to comprehend a text, the generation of inferences, and the final mental representation of the text which reflects a reader's understanding (e.g., Bower & Morrow, 1990; Just & Carpenter, 1980; McKoon & Ratcliff, 1992; O'Brien, 1995). In particular, a large body of work has considered differences between more or less knowledgeable readers (Afflerbach, 1990; Alexander, Murphy, Woods, Duhon, & Parker, 1997; Alexander & Murphy, 1998; Alexander & Jetton, 2000) and expert–novice differences in the comprehension of texts (Chiesi, Spilich, & Voss, 1979; Means & Voss, 1985; Voss & Bisanz, 1985). Experts excel in recalling information from their domain of expertise; they are better, faster, and more accurate than novices (Chi, Feltovich,

& Glaser, 1981; Chi, 2006). Expert–novice differences have also been observed with respect to the processes of inference generation. For example, prior knowledge was critical in determining whether an inference would be generated (Noordman & Vonk, 1992). Similarly, other studies have also shown that specific inferences are often constructed on the basis of readers' prior knowledge for the topics mentioned in texts (Graesser & Bertus, 1998; Millis & Graesser, 1994; McNamara & Kintsch, 1996; Millis, Morgan, & Graesser, 1990). These inferences, when accurate and correctly placed, result in a deeper understanding of the text and a richer representation in a reader's memory. It is this representation that is subsequently accessed and utilized to answer questions, solve problems, or apply in new contexts.

## Interference

The interference of prior knowledge can be traced to work in education highlighting that students often possess alternative frameworks, preconceptions, commonsense beliefs or misconceptions that are very robust and hinder the acquisition of new knowledge (e.g., Ariasi & Mason, 2011; Clement, 1989; Driver & Easley, 1978; McCloskey, 1982; Posner, Strike, Hewson, & Gertzog, 1982). There is extensive literature demonstrating the pervasive disruption in comprehension and learning arising from common misconceptions (Carey, 2009; Chi, 2005; Rapp, 2008; Vosniadou & Brewer, 1994; van den Broek, 2010). This research is important in terms of what it reveals about the effects of the accuracy of one's knowledge during reading comprehension. There is direct evidence that incorrect prior knowledge influences the actual cognitive processes during reading as well as the content of those processes (Kendeou & van den Broek, 2005, 2007; Kendeou, Muis, & Fulton, 2011). Specifically, readers with misconceptions proceed through texts at the same rate and with the same types of processes as do readers without misconceptions or inaccuracies. When the text calls for it, the readers with misconceptions activate and integrate their incorrect, prior knowledge with the textual information as frequently as do readers without misconceptions. Consequently, the content of their knowledge-based inferences (e.g., explanatory, predictive, and other inferences) reflects these misconceptions and inaccuracies, resulting in more incorrect inferences and fewer correct ones. These inferences, when inaccurate and incorrectly placed, also result in a richer representation in a reader's memory (in a manner similar to accurate inferences). Unfortunately, when this representation is subsequently accessed and utilized it only compounds the problem. This highlights the need for an understanding of the processes and mechanisms necessary to overcome the pervasive influence of inaccurate prior knowledge.

## Knowledge Revision when Prior Knowledge and New Knowledge Conflict

In this chapter, we restrict our discussion of knowledge revision to those situations that involve the modification of pre-existing, incorrect knowledge base in memory that must be revised to accommodate newly acquired information. A core assumption is that the knowledge revision process can only occur when newly acquired information makes contact with, and activates, the pre-existing knowledge so that both pieces of information are in working memory at the same time (Kendeou & van den Broek, 2007; van den Broek & Kendeou, 2008). We conceptualize the knowledge revision process as incremental, conservative, and slow. As new information is encoded it is integrated into, and becomes a part of, the pre-existing knowledge base. Thus, by definition, in the early stage of the knowledge revision process, the knowledge base will be dominated by pre-existing knowledge; evidence that any sort of knowledge revision has occurred will be subtle and difficult to measure. It is only after the amount, and quality, of new information integrated into the knowledge base crosses some threshold that overt evidence of knowledge revision will become evident.

## Knowledge Revision Components (KReC) Framework

Recently, Kendeou and O'Brien (2014) put forward the Knowledge Revision Components (KReC) framework that encompasses five key principles that guide this knowledge revision process during reading. These principles are: (1) encoding; (2) passive activation; (3) co-activation; (4) integration; and (5) competing activation. According to the *Encoding Principle*, once information has been encoded into long-term memory, it becomes a permanent part of long-term memory and cannot be "deleted." Information is subject to interference and decay, consistent with most models of memory (e.g., Gillund & Shiffrin, 1984; Hintzman, 1986; Kintsch, 1988; Ratcliff, 1978; Ratcliff & McKoon, 1988). However, the main premise is that once information becomes part of memory, it cannot be erased; and there is always the potential that it can be reactivated, even when it interferes with learning and/or comprehension. This interference from previously acquired incorrect information can occur even if the reader/learner already understands that the information is no longer correct (e.g., O'Brien, Rizzella, Albrecht, & Halleran, 1998; O'Brien, Cook, & Peracchi, 2004; O'Brien, Cook, & Guéraud, 2010). According to the *Passive Activation Principle*, inactive information in long-term memory becomes active and available via passive activation processes derived from global models of memory. Because this process is both passive and unrestricted, any information that is related to the current contents of working memory has the potential to become activated, independent of whether it facilitates or interferes with learning and/or comprehension. According to the *Co-Activation Principle*, co-activation is a necessary condition for knowledge revision because it is the only way that new information can come in contact with, and be integrated with, previously-acquired-but-no-longer-correct information. This principle is best captured by the co-activation hypothesis proposed by Kendeou and colleagues (Kendeou et al., 2011; Kendeou & van den Broek, 2007; van den Broek & Kendeou, 2008). The *Integration Principle* follows directly from the co-activation principle: Knowledge revision can only occur when newly encoded information is integrated with previously acquired information. Any time new information is integrated with previously acquired information (independent of whether the previously acquired information is correct or not), the long-term memory representation of that information is revised to take into account the new information (e.g., Kendeou, Smith, & O'Brien, 2013; Kendeou, Walsh, Smith, & O'Brien, 2014; O'Brien et al., 1998, 2004, 2010). If newly acquired information neither makes contact with, nor becomes integrated with previously acquired information, knowledge revision has not occurred. According to the *Competing Activation Principle*, as the amount of newly acquired, correct, information is increased, it will begin to dominate the integrated network of information. As this occurs, the newly encoded, correct information will begin to draw increasing amounts of activation to itself, and at the same time, draw activation away from the previously acquired-but-incorrect information. As activation is drawn away from incorrect information, the amount of interference from that information decreases accordingly. Kendeou et al. demonstrated that newly acquired information is most effective at eliminating any interference from previously acquired-but-no-longer-correct information when that newly encoded information provides causal explanations. However, it is important to note that it is not merely the causal explanations per se, but a function of the interconnections that they provide. Causal information inherently provides a rich set of interconnections (O'Brien & Myers, 1987; Trabasso & Suh, 1993; Trabasso & van den Broek,

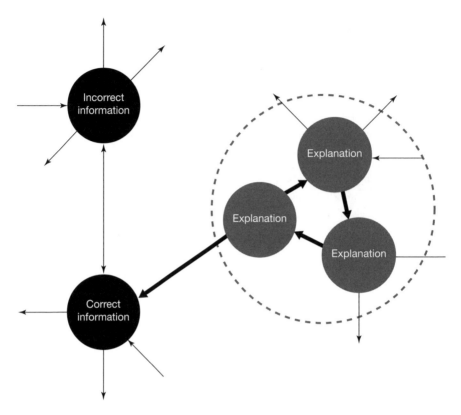

*Figure 12.1* Causal network demonstrating the competing activation mechanism assumed in the KReC framework

1985) and therefore provides an efficient and effective means of creating a network that will compete for activation, and draw sufficient activation so that any interference from previously-acquired-but-incorrect information is reduced and/or eliminated.

To illustrate the basic mechanism outline in the KReC framework, consider the causal network in Figure 12.1. In the context of KReC, when new correct information is processed, it sends a signal to all of memory and other information connected with it also get activated. In the example network, both the incorrect information and the correct explanation will get activated through this process. But the rich and recursive causal network of the correct explanation draws increasing amounts of the activation to itself, thereby reducing and/or eliminating activation reaching the incorrect information. The corresponding reduction in the amount of activation reaching the incorrect information then reduces and/or eliminates the impact of the incorrect information on subsequent processing. As the richness of the correct explanation increases, the potential for interference from the incorrect information is reduced and eventually eliminated. For example, one common incorrect piece of information the reader of this writing may hold is that meteors that land on earth are really hot. In the context of KReC one can potentially reduce or eliminate the impact this information can have on subsequent learning and memory by (1) presenting the correct information (i.e., meteors that make it to Earth are not hot, in fact some of them are found covered in frost), and (2) linking that correct information with a highly interconnected causal explanation (i.e., explaining that the high speed of the meteor when it enters the atmosphere causes it to melt or vaporize its outermost layer; its inside does not have time to heat up again before passing through the atmosphere because meteors are poor conductors of heat). In subsequent learning experiences when information about meteors gets activated, this highly, interconnected network that was created using the causal explanation will draw most of the activation to itself; as a result, there will not be sufficient activation left for the previously-acquired-but-incorrect information and its influence will be reduced and/or eliminated.

It is important to note that the KReC framework is one process account for knowledge revision. Indeed, there are many ways individuals can be enticed into knowledge revision as reflected by the number of existing models and theories in the conceptual change literature (e.g., Carey, 2009; Chi, 2008; Chinn & Brewer, 1998; Clark, 2006; diSessa, 2013; Dole & Sinatra, 1998; Hynd & Guzzetti, 1998; Posner et al., 1982; Sinatra & Pintrich, 2003; Thagard, 2008; Vosniadou, 2008, 2013) and research on persuasion (e.g., Alexander, Sperl, & Buehl, 2001; Petty & Cacioppo, 1986; Murphy & Alexander, 2004, 2008). What the KReC framework contributes to the existing literature is the fundamental underpinnings of knowledge revision at the level of basic processes and mechanisms, independent of the grain size or coherence level of the representation of prior knowledge. Specifically, KReC outlines basic comprehension processes and text factors that can be accentuated to increase the potential for successful knowledge revision during reading, by systematically mitigating the interference from prior incorrect knowledge.

## Theoretical Implications

What we have learned about knowledge acquisition and revision in the context of reading comprehension has important theoretical implications for models aiming to capture the reading comprehension processes. Because of the complexity of these processes, current models and theories of reading comprehension have focused primarily on the typical reader (see McNamara & Magliano, 2009). Examples of these models include the construction-integration model (Kintsch, 1998), structure-building theory (Gernsbacher, 1990), the event-indexing model (Zwaan, Magliano, & Graesser, 1995), the capacity-constrained construction-integration model (Goldman & Varma, 1995), the resonance model (Myers & O'Brien, 1998; O'Brien & Myers, 1999; O'Brien, Rizzella, et al., 1998), the causal network model (Langston & Trabasso, 1998; van den Broek, 1990), and the landscape model (van den Broek, Young, Tzeng, & Linderholm, 1999). There is also a model aiming to account for multiple text comprehension, the documents model (Perfetti, Rouet, & Britt, 1999). Despite apparent differences among these different theoretical positions, there is convergence with respect to the reading process itself, in that it is assumed that while reading, readers attempt to construct a coherent representation of what the text is about (i.e., a situation model). Furthermore, each of these models has attempted to account for the role of prior knowledge on text comprehension to some extent as a function of the strategic access of information from long-term memory, the automatic activation of information during moment-by-moment reading, or some combination of these two processes (but see Frank, Koppen, Noordman, & Vonk, 2003). As these models more closely approximate the reading comprehension process, it will become increasingly important and necessary to also explain how individual differences in prior knowledge influence reading processes and outcomes. In many of the current models this remains a promissory note.

## Educational Implications

What we have learned about knowledge acquisition and revision in the context of reading comprehension also has important educational implications. One set of implications pertains to the kinds of texts that could be used to facilitate knowledge acquisition and revision. This is particularly important in the context of the Common Core State Standards Initiative (CCSS Initiative, 2010). The CCSS explicitly aim to increase students' reading comprehension of complex informational texts (including history/social studies, science, and technical texts) at or above their grade level. Aligning teacher instruction and curriculum materials to meet these standards, however, remains an ongoing challenge. For example, one teaching strategy that has been proposed in the context of the CCSS is "cold reading." Cold reading involves asking students to read complex, unfamiliar text without any scaffolding or support. This approach has raised a number of questions because it requires students to respond independently and proficiently to a very demanding reading task. At the same time, this is a real expectation for the competent reader of the twenty-first century. The KReC framework can provide some guidance for the design of appropriate textual materials for "cold reading," so that both knowledge acquisition and revision are supported by the text (in the absence of teacher scaffolding or support). These textual materials can be used to develop and "internalize" in readers the necessary skills that support independent learning from texts.

With respect to knowledge acquisition, such texts should be written so that they take advantage of pre-existing knowledge. Several examples are: including explicit references in the text that serve to re-activate relevant, pre-existing knowledge; putting important information that needs to be connected in close proximity in the text; and making implicit connections explicit (McNamara, Ozuru, & Floyd, 2011). These approaches serve to increase network connectivity, which can facilitate learning even for less-skilled readers (Espin, Cevasco, van den Broek, Baker, & Gersten, 2007; Smith, 2013). In addition, textual markers such as headers (Lemarié, Lorch Jr., Eyrolle, & Virbel, 2008) and sub-headers (Lorch Jr., Lorch, & Mogan, 1987) can also serve to activate relevant, pre-existing knowledge and help readers create a coherent mental representation of the text with less effort (Naumann, Richter, Flender, Christmann, & Groeben, 2007). The activation of pre-existing knowledge can facilitate integration of textual information with prior knowledge and, as a result, knowledge acquisition.

With respect to knowledge revision, texts should be written so that they enable co-activation of correct and incorrect knowledge, as well as integration. Consider for example, an individual who believes that ostriches bury their heads in the sand to hide from their enemies. One way to assist readers in revising such commonsense beliefs is by presenting them with refutation texts (Guzzetti, Snyder, Glass, & Gamas, 1993; Sinatra & Broughton, 2011; Tippett, 2010). In the context of the ostrich example, such a text would include a refutation sentence that states that ostriches do not bury their heads. This would be followed by a causal explanation stating that people often think that ostriches bury their heads because they can regularly be seen positioning their heads near the ground, but the real reason they do this is to listen for enemies. According to the KReC framework (Kendeou & O'Brien, 2014) when the reader comes across a refutation text that states that ostriches do not bury their heads in the sand, the incorrect information will be activated via passive activation processes derived from global models of memory (Passive Activation Principle). These passive activation processes produce the co-activation of previously acquired and newly encoded information, a necessary condition for knowledge revision (Co-activation Principle). The refutation would be followed by a causal explanation stating that people often think that ostriches bury their heads because they can be seen positioning their heads near the ground, but the real reason they do this is to listen for enemies. When this new information is integrated with the previously acquired information, knowledge revision has occurred (Integration Principle). As the amount of newly acquired, correct information is increased, for example by strengthening the explanation even more, it will begin to dominate the integrated network of information. As this occurs, the newly encoded, correct information that ostriches do not bury their heads will begin to draw increasing amounts of activation to itself, and at the same time, draw activation away from the previously-acquired-but-incorrect information so that any interference from previously-acquired-but-incorrect information is reduced and/or eliminated (Competing Activation Principle).

## Concluding Remarks

In this chapter, our goal was to discuss the influences of prior knowledge on reading comprehension, highlighting processes and mechanisms that support both knowledge acquisition and knowledge revision.

The main point we wish to make is that comprehension during reading is always subject to the interaction between individual differences in prior knowledge and the text. Neither comprehension nor learning can occur without such an interaction. That is, if a text does not make contact with prior knowledge is impossible for a reader to develop an understanding or learn from text. At best, a reader would have a representation of a text in isolation from prior knowledge, thus making any newly acquired information in this representation virtually inaccessible at a later point in time.

This prior knowledge by text interaction can manifest itself in various ways. For example, if the reader possesses a rich and correct knowledge base, then the text can be written to build on that. Alternatively, if the knowledge base contains inaccurate information or misconceptions, then the text must contain information that addresses that in a manner that decreases its future influence. Alternatively, if the knowledge base is accurate but weak, then it is important for the text to be written in a manner that reduces the reader's reliance on their knowledge and allows for increased reliance on the text. In each of these situations, both comprehension and learning can be influenced with the use of appropriate text-based manipulations that match a reader's prior knowledge accordingly. In this context, the KReC framework outlines basic comprehension processes and text factors that can be accentuated to increase the potential for successful knowledge acquisition and revision during reading without making any assumptions about the grain size or level of coherence of knowledge representation. Thus, KReC can not only provide teachers and reading specialists with an interdisciplinary view of the impact of prior knowledge on reading comprehension, but can also inspire the design of effective instructional approaches and materials that align with the framework's key processes and mechanisms.

## References

Afflerbach, P. (1990). The influence of prior knowledge on expert readers' main idea construction strategies. *Reading Research Quarterly, 25*, 31–46.

Alexander, P. A., Sperl, C. T., & Buehl, M. M. (2001). The persuasiveness of persuasive discourse. *International Journal of Educational Research, 35*, 651–674.

Alexander, P. A., & Jetton, T. L. (2000). Learning from text: A multidimensional and developmental perspective. In M. L. Kamil, P. B. Mosenthal, P. D. Pearson, & R. Barr (Eds.), *Handbook of reading research* (Vol. 3, pp. 285–310). Mahwah, NJ: Erlbaum.

Alexander, P. A., & Murphy, P. K. (1998). Profiling the differences in students' knowledge, interest, and strategic processing. *Journal of Educational Psychology, 90*, 435–447.

Alexander, P. A., Murphy, P. K., Woods, B. S., Duhon, K. E., & Parker, D. (1997). College instruction and concomitant changes in students' knowledge, interest, and strategy use: A study of domain learning. *Contemporary Educational Psychology, 22*, 125–146.

Anderson, J. R., & Pichert, J. W. (1978). Recall of previously unrecallable information following a shift in perspective. *Journal of Verbal Learning and Verbal Behavior, 17*, 1–12.

Ariasi, N., & Mason, L. (2011). Uncovering the effect of text structure in learning from a science text: An eye-tracking study. *Instructional Science, 39*, 581–601.

Bower, G. H., & Morrow. D. G. (1990). Mental models in narrative comprehension. *Science, 247*, 44–48.

Bower, G. H., Black, J. B., & Turner, T. J. (1979). Scripts in memory for text. *Cognitive Psychology, 11*, 177–220.

Bransford, J. D., & Johnson, M. K. (1972). Contextual prerequisites for understanding: Some investigations of comprehension and recall. *Journal of Verbal Learning and Verbal Behavior, 11*, 717–726.

Carey, S. (2009). *The origin of concepts.* Oxford: Oxford University Press.

Chi, M. T. H., Feltovich, P., & Glaser, R. (1981). Categorization and representation of physics problems by experts and novices. *Cognitive Science, 5*, 121–152.

Chi, M. T. H. (2005). Commonsense concepts of emergent processes: Why some misconceptions are robust. *Journal of the Learning Sciences, 14*, 161–199.

Chi, M. T. H. (2006). Methods to assess the representations of experts' and novices' knowledge. In K. A. Ericsson, N. Charness, P. Feltovich, & R. Hoffman (Eds.), *Cambridge handbook of expertise and expert performance* (pp. 167–184). Cambridge, UK: Cambridge University Press.

Chi, M. T. H. (2008). Three types of conceptual change: Belief revision, mental model transformation, and categorical shift. In S. Vosniadou (Ed.), *International handbook of research on conceptual change* (pp. 61–82). New York: Taylor, & Francis.

Chiesi, H. L., Spilich, G. J., & Voss, J. F. (1979). Acquisition of domain-related information in relation to high and low domain knowledge. *Journal of Verbal Learning and Verbal Behavior, 18*, 257–273.

Chinn, C. A., & Brewer, W. F. (1998). An empirical test of a taxonomy of responses to anomalous data in science. *Journal of Research in Science Teaching, 35*(6), 623–654.

Clark, D. B. (2006). Longitudinal conceptual change in students' understanding of thermal equilibrium: An examination of the process of conceptual restructuring. *Cognition and Instruction, 24*(4), 467–563.

Clement, J. (1989). The concept of variation and misconceptions in Cartesian graphing. *Focus on Learning of Mathematics, 9*(30), 26–30.

Collins, A. M., & Quillian, M. R. (1969). Retrieval time from semantic memory. *Journal of Learning and Verbal Behavior, 8*, 240–247.

Common Core State Standards Initiative (2010). *Common Core State Standards for English language arts & literacy in history/social studies, science, and technical subjects.* Washington, DC: CCSSO and National Governors Association.

Cook, A. E., & Guéraud, S. (2005). What have we been missing? The role of general world knowledge in discourse processing. *Discourse Processes, 39*(2–3), 265–278.

diSessa, A. A. (1988). Knowledge in pieces. In G. Foreman, & P. Pufall (Eds.), *Constructivism in the computer age* (pp. 49–70). Mahwah, NJ: Lawrence Erlbaum Associates.

Dole, J. A., & Sinatra, G. M. (1998). Reconceptualizing change in cognitive construction of knowledge. *Educational Psychologist, 33*, 109–128.

Driver, R., & Easley, J. (1978). Pupils and paradigms: A review of literature related to conceptual development in adolescent science students. *Studies in Science Education, 5*, 61–84.

Espin, C. A., Cevasco, Y., van den Broek, P., Baker, S., & Gersten, R. (2007). History as narrative: The nature and quality of historical understanding for students with learning disabilities. *Journal of Learning Disabilities, 40*, 174–182.

Frank, S. L., Koppen, M., Noordman, L. G. M., & Vonk, W. (2003). Modeling knowledge-based inferences in story comprehension. *Cognitive Science, 27*, 875–910.

Gernsbacher, M. A. (1990). *Language comprehension as structure building.* Hillsdale, NJ: Lawrence Erlbaum.

Gerrig, R. J., & O'Brien, E. J. (2005). The scope of memory-based processing. *Discourse Processes, 39*(2–3), 225–242.

Gillund, G., & Shiffrin, R. M. (1984). A retrieval model for both recognition and recall. *Psychological Review, 91*(1), 1–67.

Goldman, S. R., & Varma, S. (1995). Capping the construction-integration model of discourse comprehension. In C. Weaver, S. Mannes, & C. Fletcher (Eds.), *Discourse comprehension: Essays in honor of Walter Kintsch* (pp. 337–358). Hillsdale, NJ: Erlbaum.

Goldman, S. R., Varma, S., & Coté, N. (1996). Extending capacity constrained construction integration: Toward "smarter" and flexible models of text comprehension. In B. K. Britton & A. C. Graesser (Eds.), *Models of text comprehension* (pp. 73–113). Hillsdale, NJ: Erlbaum.

Graesser, A. C., & Bertus, E. L. (1998). The construction of causal inferences while reading expository texts on science and technology. *Scientific Studies of Reading, 2*, 247–269.

Guzzetti, B. J., Snyder, T. E., Glass, G. V., & Gamas, W. S. (1993). Promoting conceptual change in science: A comparative meta-analysis of instructional interventions from reading education and science education. *Reading Research Quarterly, 28*(2), 117–159.

Hintzman, D. L. (1986). "Schema abstraction" in a multiple-trace memory model. *Psychological Review, 93*(4), 411–428.

Hynd, C., & Guzzetti, B. J. (1998). When knowledge contradicts intuition: Conceptual change. In Hynd, C. (Ed.), *Learning from text across conceptual domains* (pp. 139–163). Mahwah, NJ: Lawrence Erlbaum Associates.

Just, M. A., & Carpenter, P. A. (1980). A theory of reading: From eye fixations to comprehension. *Psychological Review, 87*(4), 329–354.

Kendeou, P., Muis, K., & Fulton, S. (2011). Reader and text factors in reading comprehension. *Journal of Research in Reading, 34*, 365–383.

Kendeou, P., & O'Brien, E. J. (2014). Knowledge revision: Processes and mechanisms. In D. N. Rapp & J. L. G. Braasch (Eds.), *Processing inaccurate information: Theoretical and applied perspectives from cognitive science and the educational sciences* (pp. 353–378). Cambridge, MA: MIT Press.

Kendeou, P., Rapp, D. N., & van den Broek, P. (2004). The influence of reader's prior knowledge on text comprehension and learning from text. In R. Nata (Ed.), *Progress in Education, Vol. 13* (pp. 189–209). New York: Nova Science Publishers.

Kendeou, P., Smith, E. R., & O'Brien, E. J. (2013). Updating during reading comprehension: Why causality matters. *Journal of Experimental Psychology: Learning, Memory, and Cognition, 39*, 854–865.

Kendeou, P., & van den Broek, P. (2005). The effects of readers' misconceptions on comprehension of scientific text. *Journal of Educational Psychology, 97*(2), 235–245.

Kendeou, P., & van den Broek, P. (2007). Interactions between prior knowledge and text structure during comprehension of scientific texts. *Memory & Cognition, 35*, 1567–1577.

Kendeou, P., Walsh, E., Smith, E. R., & O'Brien, E. J. (2014). Knowledge revision processes in refutation texts, *Discourse Processes, 51*, 374–397.

Kintsch, W. (1988). The role of knowledge in discourse comprehension: A construction-integration model. *Psychological Review, 95*, 163–182.

Kintsch, W. (1998) *Comprehension: A paradigm for cognition.* New York: Cambridge University Press.

Kintsch, W., & van Dijk, T. A. (1978). Toward a model of text comprehension and production. *Psychological Review, 85*, 363–394.

Langston, M. C., & Trabasso, T. (1998). Modeling causal integration and availability of information during comprehension of narrative texts. In H. van Oostendorp & S. Goldman (Eds.), *The construction of mental representations during reading* (pp. 29–69). Mahwah, NJ: Erlbaum.

Lemarié, J., Lorch Jr., R. F., Eyrolle, H., & Virbel, J. (2008). SARA: A text-based and reader-based theory of signaling. *Educational Psychologist, 43*(1), 27–48.

Lipson, M. Y. (1982). Learning new information from text: The role of prior knowledge and reading ability. *Journal of Reading Behavior, 14*, 243–261.

Lorch Jr., R. F., Lorch, E. P., & Mogan, A. M. (1987). Task effects and individual differences in on-line processing of the topic structure of a text. *Discourse Processes, 10*(1), 63–80.

McCloskey, M. (1982). *Naïve conceptions of motion.* Baltimore, MD: Johns Hopkins University, Department of Psychology.

McKoon, G., & Ratcliff, R. (1992). Inference during reading. *Psychological Review, 99*, 440–466.

McNamara, D. S., & Kintsch, W. (1996). Learning from text: Effects of prior knowledge and text coherence. *Discourse Processes, 22*, 247–288.

McNamara, D. S., & Magliano, J. P. (2009). Towards a comprehensive model of comprehension. In B. Ross (Ed.), *The psychology of learning and motivation* (pp. 297–384). New York: Academic Press.

McNamara, D. S., Ozuru, Y., & Floyd, R. G. (2011). Comprehension challenges in the fourth grade: The roles of text cohesion, text genre, and readers' prior knowledge. *International Electronic Journal of Elementary Education, 4*(1), 229–257.

Means, M. L., & Voss, J. F. (1985). Star Wars: A developmental study of expert and novice knowledge structures. *Journal of Memory and Language, 24*, 746–757.

Millis, K., & Graesser, A. C. (1994). The time-course of constructing knowledge-based inferences for scientific texts. *Journal of Memory and Language, 33,* 583–599.

Millis, K. K., Morgan, D., & Graesser, A. C. (1990). The influence of knowledge-based inferences on reading time for expository text. In A. C. Graesser & G. H. Bower (Eds.), *The psychology of learning and motivation: Inferences and text comprehension.* New York: Academic Press.

Murphy, P. K., & Alexander, P. A. (2004). Persuasion as a dynamic, multidimensional process: A viewfinder for individual and intraindividual differences. *American Educational Research Journal, 41,* 337–363.

Murphy, P. K., & Alexander, P. A. (2008). The role of knowledge, beliefs, and interest in the conceptual change process: A meta-analysis and synthesis of the research. In S. Vosniadou (Ed.), *International handbook of research on conceptual change* (pp. 583–616). New York: Routledge.

Murphy, P. K., Alexander, P. A., & Muis, K. R. (2012). Knowledge and knowing: The journey from philosophy and psychology to human learning. In K. R. Harris, S. Graham, & T. Urdan (Eds.), *Educational psychology handbook: Vol. 1. Theories, constructs, and critical issues* (pp. 189–226). Washington, DC: American Psychological Association.

Myers, J. L., & O'Brien, E. J. (1998). Accessing the discourse representation during reading. *Discourse Processes, 26*(2–3), 131–157.

Nelson, T. O., & Narens, L. (1980). Norms of 300 general-information questions: Accuracy of recall, latency of recall, and feeling-of-knowing ratings. *Journal of Verbal Learning and Verbal Behavior, 19,* 338–368.

Naumann, J., Richter, T., Flender, J., Christmann, U., & Groeben, N. (2007). Signaling in expository hypertexts compensates for deficits in reading skill. *Journal of Educational Psychology, 99*(4), 791–807.

Noordman, L. G. M., & Vonk, W. (1992). Readers' knowledge and the control of inferences in reading. *Language and Cognitive Processes, 7,* 373–391.

Novak, J. D. (1988). Learning science and the science of learning. *Studies in Science Education, 15,* 77–101.

O'Brien, E. J. (1995). Automatic components of discourse comprehension. In R. F. Lorch & E. J. O'Brien (Eds.), *Sources of coherence in reading* (pp. 159–176). Hillsdale, NJ: Erlbaum.

O'Brien, E. J., & Albrecht, J. E. (1991). The role of context in accessing antecedents in text. *Journal of Experimental Psychology: Learning, Memory, and Cognition, 17,* 94–102.

O'Brien, E. J., Cook, A. E., & Guéraud, S. (2010). Accessibility of outdated information. *Journal of Experimental Psychology: Learning, Memory, and Cognition, 36,* 979–991.

O'Brien, E. J., Cook, A. E., & Peracchi, K. A. (2004). Updating a situation model: A reply to Zwaan and Madden (2004). *Journal of Experimental Psychology: Learning, Memory, and Cognition, 30,* 289–291.

O'Brien, E. J., Lorch, R. F., & Myers, J. L. (1998). Memory-based text processing: Preface. Special issue. *Discourse Processes, 26,* 63–66.

O'Brien, E. J., & Myers, J. L. (1987). The role of causal connections in the retrieval of text. *Memory & Cognition, 15,* 419–427.

O'Brien, E. J., & Myers, J. L. (1999). Text comprehension: A view from the bottom up. In S. R. Goldman, A. C. Graesser, & P. van den Broek (Eds.), *Narrative comprehension, causality, and coherence: Essays in honor of Tom Trabasso* (pp. 36–53). Mahwah, NJ: Erlbaum.

O'Brien, E. J., Rizzella, M. L., Albrecht, J. E., & Halleran, J. G. (1998). Updating a situation model: A memory-based text processing view. *Journal of Experimental Psychology: Learning, Memory, and Cognition, 24*(5), 1200–1210.

Perfetti, C. A., Rouet, J.-F., & Britt, M. A. (1999). Towards a theory of documents representation. In H. van Oostendorp & S. R. Goldman (Eds.), *The construction of mental representations during reading* (pp. 99–122). Mahwah, NJ: Lawrence Erlbaum Associates.

Petty, R. E., & Cacioppo, J. T. (1986). *Communication and persuasion: Central and peripheral routes to attitude change.* New York: Springer-Verlag.

Posner, G. J., Strike, K. A., Hewson, P. W., & Gertzog, W. A. (1982). Accommodation of a scientific conception: Toward a theory of conceptual change. *Science Education, 66*(2), 211–227.

Rapp, D. N. (2008). How do readers handle incorrect information during reading? *Memory & Cognition, 36,* 688–701.

Ratcliff, R. (1978). A theory of memory retrieval. *Psychological Review, 85*(2), 59–108.

Ratcliff, R., & McKoon, G. (1988). A retrieval theory of priming in memory. *Psychological Review, 95,* 385–408.

Rizzella, M. L., & O'Brien, E. J. (2002). Retrieval of concepts in script-based texts and narratives: The influence of general world knowledge. *Journal of Experimental Psychology: Learning, Memory, and Cognition*, *28*(4), 780–790.

Sinatra, G. M., & Broughton, S. H. (2011). Bridging comprehension and conceptual change in science education: The promise of refutational text. *Reading Research Quarterly*, *46*(4), 369–388.

Sinatra, G. M., & Pintrich, P. R. (Eds.) (2003). *Intentional conceptual change*. Mahwah, NJ: Lawrence Erlbaum Associates.

Smith, E. R. (2013). *Enhancing memory access for less-skilled readers*. Paper presented at the Annual Meeting of the Society for Text and Discourse, Valencia, Spain.

Tauber, S. K., Dunlosky, J., Rawson, K. A., Rhodes, M. G., & Sitzman, D. M. (2013). General knowledge norms: Updated and expanded from the Nelson and Narens (1980) norms. *Behavior Research Methods*, *45*(4), 1115–1143.

Thagard, P. (2008). Conceptual change in the history of science: Life, mind, and disease. In S. Vosniadou (Ed.), *International handbook of research on conceptual change* (pp. 374–387). London: Routledge.

Tippett, C. D. (2010). Refutational text in science education: A review of two decades of research. *International Journal of Science and Mathematics Education*, *8*, 951–970.

Trabasso, T., & Suh, S. (1993). Understanding text: Achieving explanatory coherence through on-line inferences and mental operations in working memory. *Discourse Processes*, *16*(1–2), 3–34.

Trabasso, T., & van den Broek, P. (1985). Causal thinking and the representation of narrative events. *Journal of Memory and Language*, *24*(5), 612–630.

van den Broek, P. W. (1990). The causal inference maker: Towards a process model of inference generation in text comprehension. In D. A. Balota, G. B. Flores d'Arcais, & K. Rayner (Eds.), *Comprehension processes in reading* (pp. 423–446). Hillsdale, NJ: Lawrence Erlbaum Associates.

van den Broek, P. (2010). Using texts in science education: Cognitive processes and knowledge representation. *Science*, *328*, 453–456.

van den Broek, P., & Kendeou, P. (2008). Cognitive processes in comprehension of science texts: The role of co-activation in confronting misconceptions. *Applied Cognitive Psychology*, *22*(3), 335–351.

van den Broek, P., Young, M., Tzeng, Y., & Linderholm, T.(1999). The landscape model of reading: Inferences and the on-line construction of a memory representation. In H. van Oostendorp & S. R. Goldman (Eds.), *The construction of mental representations during reading* (pp. 71–98). Mahwah, NJ: Lawrence Erlbaum Associates.

Van Dijk, T. A., & Kintsch, W. (1983). *Strategies of discourse comprehension*. New York: Academic Press.

Voss, J. F., & Bisanz, G. L. (1985). Knowledge and the processing of narrative and expository texts. In B. K. Britton & J. B. Black (Eds.), *Understanding expository text: A theoretical and practical handbook for analyzing explanatory text* (pp. 173–198). Hillsdale, NJ: Lawrence Erlbaum Associates.

Vosniadou, S., & Brewer, W. F. (1994). Mental models of the day/night cycle. *Cognitive Science*, *18*, 123–183.

Vosniadou S. (Ed.). (2008). *International handbook of research on conceptual change*. New York: Routledge.

Vosniadou S. (2013). Conceptual change in learning and instruction: The framework theory approach. In S. Vosniadou (Ed.), *International handbook of research on conceptual change* (pp. 11–30). New York: Routledge.

Wyer, R. S. (Ed.) (1995). *Knowledge and memory: The real story*. Hillsdale, NJ: Erlbaum.

Zwaan, R. A., Magliano, J. P., & Graesser, A. C. (1995). Dimensions of situation model construction in narrative comprehension. *Journal of Experimental Psychology: Learning, Memory, and Cognition*, *21*, 386–397.

# 13

# Higher Order Thinking in Comprehension

*Danielle S. McNamara, Matthew E. Jacovina, and Laura K. Allen*

Reading is a pervasive activity in the classroom, as well as in everyday activities: comprehending text and discourse is crucial to success and survival in the modern world. Nonetheless, many students struggle to understand text at even a basic level, and even more fail to construct deep level understandings of content. Particularly for complex academic texts, students may understand individual words and sentences; yet, they frequently fail to comprehend the underlying meaning of the material, have little memory for the content, and struggle to learn from the texts. As a result, one goal of educators and reading researchers has been to optimize conditions such that readers engage in the higher level cognitive processes that aid in the construction of coherent, interconnected, and elaborated mental representations of content material. At the heart of this objective is the notion that students should engage in higher order thinking in order to understand material at deep levels (which is conducive to learning).

In this chapter, we discuss the role of higher order thinking in the context of text comprehension. We first describe a sample of frameworks that have been proposed to delineate lower and higher level processes leading to higher order processing. We then discuss some of the challenges faced by educators and researchers in defining and distinguishing lower and higher level processes, processes versus outcomes, as well as issues arising from individual differences among students. Ultimately, we suggest theoretical and educational implications of these concepts, emphasizing the importance of considering the needs of individual readers through sensitivity to the interactions among tasks, processes, and individual differences among students.

## Frameworks for Higher Order Thinking

### The Bloom Taxonomy

As a starting point, we should define the concept of *higher order thinking*. Consider the results of a Google search (the ultimate higher level answer to all questions), which yielded the following definition:

> Higher-order thinking, also known as higher order thinking skills, is a concept of Education reform based on learning taxonomies such as Bloom's Taxonomy. The idea is that some

types of learning require more cognitive processing than others, but also have more generalized benefits.

(http://en.wikipedia.org/wiki/Higher-order_thinking)

Indeed, one of the most commonly used frameworks to describe the distinction between different levels of processing, and in particular higher order thinking, is the Bloom Taxonomy (e.g., Bloom, 1956; Krathwohl, Bloom, & Masia, 1964; Simpson, 1972). This framework is used across a wide variety of contexts, most often in educational settings (e.g., Granello, 2001; Hanna, 2007). The Bloom Taxonomy, named after Benjamin Bloom, was developed in the 1950s to distinguish between different types of educational objectives. The taxonomy includes three types of processes: cognitive (knowledge, comprehension, application, analysis, synthesis, evaluation), affective (receiving, responding, valuing, organizing, characterizing), and psychomotor (perception, set, guided response, mechanism, complex overt response, adaptation, origination).

The most common use of the Bloom Taxonomy has been to distinguish between cognitive processes. The underlying notion is that students must acquire and master the skills at lower levels in order to advance to higher levels on the spectrum. The taxonomy has been used frequently in the development of educational standards to distinguish between types of processes or understanding that would be expected from students at different levels of development. For example, in the context of understanding text, readers would move from being able to describe, and then to evaluating and analyzing concepts within a text. Hence, a student at a lower level within a set of standards might be expected to use knowledge to describe the ideas, whereas students at more advanced levels may be expected to evaluate or analyze the ideas. In turn, rendering judgments based on criteria or evidence (evaluation) goes beyond and partially depends on breaking down ideas into parts (analysis). Hence there is a hierarchical organization wherein processes expected at more advanced levels depend on those at lower levels as the student moves toward higher order thinking. In this sense, higher order thinking comprises cognitive processes such as analysis, synthesis, and ultimately evaluation, in contrast to the use of knowledge, comprehending, and applying information. In turn, activities that call on higher order thinking are assumed to lead to a better, deeper understanding of the material: evaluating an idea is expected to lead to better learning than is describing an idea.

## The ICAP Framework

The Bloom Taxonomy has been widely used within the field of education. Another similar approach recently proposed by Michelene Chi (2009), the ICAP (Interactive, Constructive, Active, Passive) framework, focuses on ranking the relative value of learning tasks according to their overt, observable activities and their potential underling cognitive processes. Activities are considered *passive* when students are not visibly doing anything. Thus, watching videos or reading texts would both be considered passive learning activities. Students are defined as *active* when they are overtly doing something during a learning task, such as sliding beads on an abacus or highlighting key themes in a short story. *Constructive* activities require students to produce something that extends beyond the educational material. This could involve writing down novel uses for various objects or verbally self-explaining sentences in a science text. Finally, students are considered *interactive* when they engage with another person or computer system through dialogue or another joint activity. Some interactive activities may not provide learning benefits above other *constructive* tasks, such as when one student simply provides another student with information, rather than engaging them in conversation. Other interactions, however, that require students to more thoughtfully construct responses and explanations, to formulate their own questions, and to consider someone else's perspective can be more beneficial than basic constructive activities.

This framework primarily relies on information about students' overt behaviors to classify learning activities; however, it also suggests potential cognitive processes that may underlie these activities. For instance, active tasks engage students' attentional processes, which can help them to incorporate new information from the instructional materials with their prior knowledge, while simultaneously reinforcing that prior knowledge. Constructive tasks require students to engage in inferential processes, which allow them to develop a deeper understanding of the material. According to the framework, interactive processes are similar to constructive processes. However, when students engage in dialogue, they may more easily develop an understanding of complex concepts, thanks to the contributions of an interlocutor.

In contrast to the Bloom Taxonomy, the ICAP framework focuses more on the learning activities rather than on the processes or the outcomes. For example, whereas the Bloom Taxonomy might focus on a student's ability to explain a text (usually after having read it), the ICAP framework would consider the reading process itself to be inherently passive, and focus more on whether the student had explained the text while reading it (which might be *active* or *constructive*). Hence, one focuses more on the assumed processes and outcomes, whereas the other focuses primarily on the overt learning task.

Importantly, both the Bloom Taxonomy and the ICAP framework have strong potential to inspire insights about how individual differences influence higher order thinking for readers. For example, these frameworks may encourage researchers and educators to consider the types of cognitive processes that differ from person to person, or the particular tasks that might allow different readers to thrive. Unfortunately, however, considerations for individual differences are not built into these two frameworks. Therefore, educators and researchers who utilize these frameworks are at risk of making assumptions of homogeneity among learners. Not all readers will progress through Bloom's hierarchy in the same manner, nor will a task lead to the same cognitive processes and ultimate learning benefits for all participants. Thus the frameworks would greatly benefit from the addition of direct guidance that can aid educators in better understanding how individual differences among students may interact with various task demands to influence comprehension and learning.

## Comprehension Models

In contrast to frameworks such as the Bloom Taxonomy and the ICAP model, most contemporary models of text and discourse comprehension focus on *the stuff in the middle*: the processes associated with understanding. Most pertinent to higher order thinking, comprehension models differentiate between multiple levels of text understanding (e.g., Kintsch, 1998; McNamara & Magliano, 2009), most notably, the *surface*, *textbase*, and *situation model* levels of understanding (Kintsch & van Dijk, 1978; van Dijk & Kintsch, 1983).

Accordingly, a reader forms a mental representation of a text. This representation is generally considered in connectionist terms to comprise concepts (nodes) and relations (links) and includes spreading activation between concepts that are explicitly stated within the text as well as to concepts that are unstated in the text, but available in prior knowledge. The surface understanding comprises the explicit words and their relations in the text. The textbase essentially refers to the aspect of the mental representation reflecting understanding and memory for content that occurs within the text. The situation model refers to the aspect of the mental representation that reflects deeper understanding, or the integration and elaboration of ideas in the text and concepts from outside of the text (e.g., prior knowledge, a separate source). Hence, the situation model is most strongly associated with higher order thinking.

Deep understanding of a text is conceptualized in terms of the coherence of the reader's mental representation. The degree to which this representation has strong, appropriate connections between concepts within the text and connections to unstated knowledge is the degree to which the representation is coherent and stable. In turn, the coherence and stability of the representation predicts outcomes such as comprehension and memory for the text. Accordingly, the mental representation of the text comprises various aspects, including a textbase and a situation model. Notably, these are not assumed to be hierarchically organized or dissectible from the representation, but rather qualities, much like colors in a painting.

In contrast to educationally oriented approaches to higher order thinking, comprehension models focus on the quality of the mental representation constructed by the reader or comprehender. In turn, different types of assessments are assumed to pick up on these qualities of a reader's mental representation. Just as standing at a different angle or distance affords different perceptions of a painting, the objective in comprehension assessment is to collect various views and angles in order to infer the reader's mental representation. The textbase level of understanding might be inferred from multiple-choice questions, cloze tasks, questions about individual sentences, or paraphrasing. The quality of a reader's situation model is inferred from tasks that rely on the reader having made connections between concepts in the text (e.g., bridging inference questions) or to prior knowledge (e.g., elaboration questions). For example, if a participant were to perform well on questions focused on textbase level information and poorly on situation model questions, then it would likely be deduced that the reader had formed a coherent textbase but had not generated the kinds of inferences necessary to understand the text at a deep level (e.g., McNamara & Kintsch, 1996).

Most models of comprehension assume that prior knowledge is a critical factor in influencing the extent to which individuals construct deep understandings of text. When readers attempt to comprehend a text, they can either be limited or supported by what they already know. Thus, individual differences in prior knowledge for a particular text topic can play a crucial role in a student's comprehension. Outside of prior knowledge, however, most comprehension models tend to place little emphasis on the role of other individual differences among readers, such as motivation or strategy knowledge. Moreover, they rarely focus on the interactions between these individual differences and the various properties of texts that students are attempting to comprehend (e.g., cohesion, topic knowledge, audience, etc.)—in other words, how different readers might engage in different processes for different types of texts. Given the acknowledgement of these interactions, a challenge for researchers is to work towards the development of more comprehensive models of the comprehension process, more specifically incorporating components of both the text and the reader (McNamara & Magliano, 2009).

In relation to the concept of higher order thinking, models of comprehension make a number of predictions. First, assessments that require higher order thinking are more likely to reveal the quality of a reader's situation model (i.e., the extent to which the reader incorporated prior knowledge and constructed a coherent mental model of the text). Second, having a reader engage in activities associated with higher order thinking (e.g., explaining, evaluating) while learning from text is more likely to enhance comprehension. These predictions have been well supported in the literature (e.g., Coté, Goldman, & Saul, 1998; Eason, Goldberg, Young, Geist, & Cutting, 2012; Kintsch, 1998; van der Schoot, Horsley, & van Lieshout, 2010). Nonetheless, there are multiple caveats to these predictions, as we describe in the following sections.

## Important Caveats

### *Lower versus Higher Level Processing*

Higher order thinking implies that it involves higher level processing. One important consideration is how to delineate the line between what is considered *lower* and what is considered *higher*. Lower level processes are generally assumed to be computationally easier than higher level processes, requiring less explicit attention and effort, and relying less on unstated information or knowledge. For example, reading a word is considered to be relatively automatic for a developed reader, and familiar words are read more automatically (e.g., the, a, of, cat, dog), without conscious attention, than are less familiar words (e.g., terricolous, idyll, soporific). Such assumptions lead to definitions of lower and higher level processes as being more or less *automatic* versus *controlled* or *bottom-up* versus *top-down*. As such, across a number of fields, labeling processes as lower or higher level affords relatively quick and easy distinctions about the cognitive resources or knowledge required to complete a task. Such distinctions are appealing and are often quite useful to understanding cognition and learning.

One problem that emerges, however, regards the lack of specificity concerning what processes are considered higher level and the diversity of definitions for lower and higher level processing across disciplines and domains. The intended meaning of lower and higher level cognitive processes depends heavily on the particular domain, the research topic, and the context. For example, a vision researcher might consider the perception of color to be a lower level process whereas perceiving a word would be considered a higher level process. By contrast, some cognitive scientists classify all vision processes as lower level and all language processes as higher level (König, Kühnberger, & Kietzmann, 2013). Similarly, for some reading researchers, lexical decoding might be classified as a lower level process and sentence understanding as a higher level process, whereas for other reading researchers, sentence understanding exemplifies lower level processes and inferencing and elaboration involve higher level processes. Within their respective contexts, these distinctions often make sense. However, across domains, disciplines, and contexts, these terms lose definitional precision. Most importantly, where the line is drawn between lower and higher levels of processing depends on the range of processes under consideration. Hence, the task of delineating a universal definition of higher order thinking seems daunting at best. Moreover, given the utility of these distinctions within domains, regardless of the variance across domains, many researchers would not *want* to adopt a global, all-encompassing definition. They like their own definition.

Unfortunately, inconsistent distinctions made between lower and higher level processes are not always innocuous. For example, conclusions about higher level processing in visual research are unlikely to map onto conclusions about higher level processing in reading research. Education researchers and educators often have different perceptions of what higher level implies. "Higher order thinking" in the education domain often refers to specific objectives, such as the ability to evaluate texts using particular criteria (Anderson et al., 2001). By design, higher order thinking skills are meant to align with higher level cognitive processes, but because there is no standard definition of what those are, the intended alignment can be misleading.

A related concern is that attempts to import findings on higher level processing from one field to another might lead to costly incompatibilities. Consider a fledgling educator who reads an interesting finding that rereading a text allows readers to focus on higher level reading processes (e.g., Millis, Simon, & tenBroek, 1998). The educator, knowing that an objective of his English class is to encourage the higher order task of analyzing conceptual information from texts, adds a rereading task to his curriculum. The rereading task *might* lead to learning gains, but such a result would not be predicted from the findings in the Millis et al. rereading study, which operationalized the higher level reading process in terms of text-level integration. That is, the conceptual overlap is tenuous between the higher level reading processes described by Millis and colleagues and the higher order reading objectives of the (albeit fictional) educator. While this is a clearly cartoon example, similar misinterpretations are plausible and have likely been committed on much larger scales.

## Processes versus Outcomes

Another caveat to a discussion on higher order thinking, and in turn higher level processes, is the importance of clearly distinguishing between processes and outcomes. For decades, researchers have acknowledged the importance of distinguishing between learning processes and outcome measures (e.g., Kolers & Roediger, 1984). Within the context of reading comprehension research, this distinction between higher level processes and deep comprehension is crucial. The outcome of comprehension or learning processes (through tasks) is the primary variable that is observed through assessments. Typically, a participant is presented with a text (ranging from a sentence to a multi-paragraph passage), and during or after the exposure to the text, various dependent measures might be collected. In the classroom and other educational settings, these assessments often take the form of scores on classroom and standardized tests, and ultimately course grades. In a laboratory setting, these assessments may include reaction time measurements on various reading-related tasks (e.g., reading time, lexical decision-making, word naming) or questions explicitly aimed at assessing a student's comprehension of a passage (e.g., cloze tasks, true–false sentence recognition, sentence verification, multiple choice, open-ended; Cain & Oakhill, 2006; Pearson & Hamm, 2005).

These assessments are used in various ways to infer the state or quality of a reader's understanding. Online measures of comprehension, such as reaction time, cloze tests, or think aloud provide perhaps the closest assessment of the cognitive processes of a particular reader. Reaction time measures can be used to infer, for example, whether the reader makes inferences while reading, is challenged by the difficulty of the text, reads using more automatic processes, or at the least, is paying attention to the task. In particular, word and sentence reaction times are often used for fine-grained deductions regarding the effects of various manipulations such as word ambiguity, cohesion, sentence difficulty, and so on. Indeed, at fine-grained levels, reading times can be quite useful in assessing the effects of manipulations in text and discourse.

At more coarse-grained levels, however, their utility is sometimes lost in the limitless processes that readers might have engaged during extended reading. When the reader's task is to process and comprehend a 1,000-word text, with as many differences between each sentence as between a Manet and a Monet painting, the inferences that can be deduced from a long or short reading time can be lost in a sea of variance. Moreover, given reading times alone, it can be impossible to deduce what they mean: long reading times may indicate that the reader generated inferences, stumbled through the text, or daydreamed. For example, readers with less knowledge about a topic might take more time to read a challenging text (compared to a less challenging text) in one situation and less time in another (McNamara & Kintsch, 1996). Each result is equally facile to explain: The readers attempted to generate inferences to resolve conceptual challenges in the first situation, and the readers did not do so (and ultimately *gave up*) in the second.

Online measures also typically assess lower level cognitive processes. For example, cloze tasks omit certain words in a text and ask the reader to fill in or choose the appropriate word. Ideally, the omitted words and the foils are chosen such that the task requires the reader to have a full understanding of the sentences and their relations, rather than a superficial understanding of the sentence. Nonetheless, the task by its very nature is correlated most highly with readers' knowledge of words and their ability to understand individual sentences. Hence, readability measures such as the Flesch Kincaid correlate very highly with performance on cloze tasks (see McNamara, Graesser, McCarthy, & Cai, 2014, for a discussion).

By contrast, think aloud measures come the closest to assessing multiple aspects of a reader's comprehension and in particular, readers' deep level comprehension. However, few researchers and even fewer educators turn to think aloud as a measure of comprehension. An exception is the work by Keith Millis and Joe Magliano (Gilliam, Magliano, Millis, Levinstein, & Boonthum, 2007; Magliano, Millis, Levinstein, & Boonthum, 2011) who have leveraged think aloud and question asking during reading within an automated assessment called RSAT (Reading Strategy Assessment Tool). This tool asks students both indirect questions (e.g., what are you thinking now?) and direct questions (e.g., why does a tumor develop?) while reading. The reader's answers are scored automatically by comparing the words used in the answers to benchmark sets of words. The scores have been shown to correlate highly with standardized measures of reading as well as measures of post-reading comprehension.

While online measures may come closest to assessing both surface and deep comprehension processes, their use is also quite rare. Offline, or post-reading comprehension questions are more commonly used to infer how well a reader has understood a text. Typically, a set of questions is constructed about the text and the average correct is assumed to reflect how well a student understood the text, and in turn the degree to which the reader had deeply processed the text. These questions are usually multiple-choice or true–false questions because these types of questions can be most easily scored. In some cases, open-ended questions are used, requiring the reader to construct the answer without cues. These are less commonly used, both in research studies and educational settings, primarily because of the time to score the answers. Nonetheless, it is generally assumed that open-ended questions are more likely to reveal readers' deep comprehension because they call upon recall for the information in the text rather than recognition, which can be based on a reader's textbase representation (McNamara & Kintsch, 1996).

Whether the assessment is online or offline, the performance is used as a reflection of the processes engaged while reading. For instance, researchers can vary the difficulty of a particular text passage or they can change the instructions to reflect more or less difficult processes. If a student performs well on the assessment for a particularly challenging task, it may be assumed that this student engaged in higher level processes during the task. On the other hand, if the comprehension task is less difficult, performance on the assessment may be assumed to provide information about and relate to lower level processing. A notable issue, however, emerges when the results from outcome measures are conflated with the processes engaged while reading. Importantly, comprehension assessments do not provide *direct* information about the processes engaged by the learner during the given task. Rather, these processes are inferred based on assessment performance. Admittedly, researchers have made attempts to distinguish between the comprehension processes and outcomes from their research studies. More often than not, however, this distinction is dropped and the results become conflated over time.

Many researchers (ourselves included) describe performance based on the outcome of a particular assessment as if it were a direct reflection of the processes engaged by the learner during comprehension. Obviously, there are examples of processes and outcomes corresponding with each other. For example, McNamara, O'Reilly, Best, and Ozuru (2006) examined the benefits of engaging in various cognitive processes while self-explaining complex science text (i.e., after training and practice in using reading strategies while self-explaining). They then examined how those processes corresponded to outcomes on a post-training comprehension test. As expected, there was correspondence between paraphrasing and performance on textbase questions and between generating bridging inferences and performance on bridging inference questions. The field is full of examples similar to this one. Thus, we do not want to suggest that processes and outcomes cannot be related—that is certainly not the case. Our principal argument is that researchers and educators should be aware of the distinctions between these two concepts and remain sensitive to the differential effects of certain processes on learning outcomes (i.e., O'Reilly & McNamara, 2007).

By more carefully considering the distinction between processes and outcomes, and the relations between the two, researchers will be better able to detect and understand individual differences among students, and in turn, individual students' particular strengths and weaknesses. Knowing that one student scored 20 percent lower than another on a comprehension test tells us very little about *why* this particular student struggled or what individual differences may have contributed to comprehension difficulties. Considering both processes and outcomes, as well as nuanced differences in outcomes will move us toward more informed and useful assessment. For example, if we were able to analyze the performance *outcomes* from this struggling student's assessment score more closely and discern that this 20 percent difference was specifically driven by performance on, for example, deep comprehension questions (and these types of questions comprised some portion of the assessment), a more informed plan for individualized instruction might emerge. Similarly, assessing students' *processes*—perhaps through reading and questing answering times or think aloud protocols—would inform the areas in the text or specific time points where students engage in different cognitive processes, and where and how they may gain from instruction or scaffolding. While it is clearly useful and necessary to identify a student's overall levels of comprehension ability, summative assessments do little to inform instruction. If the ultimate goal is formative, to individualize and guide student instruction, greater attention must be turned to understanding the relations between processes and outcomes, and individual differences.

## Processes versus Tasks

Another distinction to be highlighted is between processes and the tasks in which students engage. Let's consider a few examples. First consider a task such as evaluation, considered to essentially be the epitome of higher order thinking within the Bloom Taxonomy. The process of evaluation can and should involve a great deal of higher order thinking. However, if the material to be evaluated is relatively simple, or the student is highly familiar with the material, the processes may merely comprise the use of knowledge (Kunen, Cohen, & Solman, 1966). For example, the student may be asked to evaluate the quality of an argument within an extended text. If the student has already been exposed to the text, as well as information about its quality, this turns into a memory task (i.e., recalling a prior evaluation). Such cases are unavoidable perhaps. Nonetheless, the familiarity of the materials plays an important role in what cognitive processes will be involved. Along the same line, the assessment used will also plan an important role. Many assessments may rely on multiple choice, where the student chooses the best evaluation (e.g., standardized tests such as the SAT). Such measures might tap into higher order processing (e.g., VanderVeen et al., 2007), but notably less so than open ended questions or think aloud (Magliano, Millis, Ozuru, & McNamara, 2007). On the surface, the Bloom Taxonomy makes good sense; clearly *evaluation* is better than *analysis*. Yet, in practice, using the taxonomy to distinguish between the value of various educational activities or outcomes can be more challenging.

Consider further a simple task such as a student repeating a list of words aloud. According to the ICAP framework, a literal interpretation would lead to classifying this behavior as *active* because it involves an overt response. However, the overt observation of an individual repeating words often has little correspondence with the cognitive processes engaged: The learner may be passively and rotely repeating the word or by contrast, the individual might be using complex mnemonics. Hence there is little correlation between word repetition and memory (Craik & Watkins, 1973; McNamara & Scott, 2001). Of course there is some correspondence between the processes inherent to tasks and the underlying processes engaged by individuals. How could we infer cognition otherwise? However, there is a strong tendency to conflate one with the other, with too little consideration of what might be required of the individual for a particular task.

Another consideration regards the tendency to treat frameworks as developmentally hierarchical. For example, the use of the Bloom Taxonomy can lead to assumptions that mastery at lower levels is required prior to advancing to higher levels. An educator (or researcher) may therefore focus on fully developing a learner's lower level skill such as word decoding before tackling a skill that is expected to involve higher level skills, such as comprehension. This poses a problem because developing students can make advances at higher levels before mastering those that came before (Resnick, 1987; Zohar & Dori, 2003). And, some skills that seem hierarchical in nature may best develop in tandem, such as decoding and comprehension (e.g., Kendeou, van den Broek, White, & Lynch, 2009).

Moreover, outcomes are often conflated with processes, as we have already discussed. Thus, poor performance may be assumed to indicate an insufficiency in one skill, but actually be caused by a very different underlying problem (Rapp, van den Broek, McMaster, Panayiota, & Espin, 2007). A student who seems to have an undeveloped skill may actually be engaging in appropriate cognitive processes, but not showing observable evidence of that skill. Relatedly, students might not engage with tasks and questions as originally conceived by educators. Gierl (1997) examined the relationship between the cognitive processes students were intended to engage while solving math problems (as defined using Bloom's Taxonomy) and the cognitive processes students actually engaged (as measured through think aloud protocols). He found alignment only 54 percent of the time, with slightly higher agreement for students with higher math ability. This result highlights the concern that educational intentions will frequently mismatch students' cognitive engagement, even when a thoughtfully formulated framework is intelligently implemented.

With regard to the Bloom Taxonomy in particular, some researchers and educators have developed revised versions that aim to make the taxonomy more comprehensive and flexible. For example, the Bloom's Revised Taxonomy (Anderson et al., 2001), spearheaded by Lorin Anderson, a former student of Bloom's, divides the cognitive process level into two dimensions: the cognitive process dimension (remember, understand, apply, analyze, evaluate, create) and the knowledge dimension (factual, conceptual, procedural, metacognitive). By filling in the resulting two-dimensional taxonomy table with lessons and goals, educators can review the number of higher level categories their curriculum manages. Educators might then modify their plans in order to move from lower to higher levels. Likewise, in the area of reading, Afflerbach, Cho, and Kim (2011) proposed a metacognition level to the taxonomy, which they convincingly argue is crucial because students must be able to recognize comprehension errors and make adjustments to their reading strategies in addition to possessing fundamental reading skills.

These enhanced frameworks can be quite useful as pedagogical tools when used appropriately. Appropriate usage cannot be taken as a given, however. Consider that North Carolina Public Schools' Common Core State and NC Essential Standards' home page invites educators to use the Revised Bloom's Taxonomy by providing the seemingly simple two-dimensional taxonomy table, and a brief explanation of the four types of knowledge and the six cognitive processes (http://www.ncpublicschools.org/acre/standards/). Educators (who are from North Carolina or who find the site through search engines) may not use the framework with nearly the full array of information provided by the authors. This is not to criticize North Carolina's Public Schools; they have consulted with Lorin Anderson in the development of their standards, and provide additional information throughout their website. Still, providing such a simplified version of a complex tool is a large-scale manifestation of the concern that the concept of higher level processing might be misinterpreted. A primary concern is that educators will mistake tasks or assessments designed to promote or measure higher level cognitive processes as definitively doing so.

## Interactions among Processes, Tasks, and the Reader

Thus far, we have discussed issues regarding differentiating between lower and higher level processes as well as guarding against conflating processes, tasks, and outcomes. A layer on top of these concerns is the importance of individual differences and interactions between the various factors that influence comprehension. Within the last few decades, a good deal of attention has turned toward the complex dependencies between factors such as the task, the context, the measures, and individual differences. One of the most pervasive problems in education and learning sciences is developing a more thorough understanding of how the same task can do very different things for different learners. For example, Voss and Silfies (1996) reported inter-actions between prior knowledge, reading ability, and text structure. McNamara, Kintsch, Songer, and Kintsch (1996) demonstrated a three-way interaction between prior knowledge, text cohesion, and the type of outcome measure (or level of understanding). These types of studies point toward the importance of recognizing that how an individual processes a certain text or task depends on the mental processes that may or may not be afforded by abilities such as knowledge and reading skill (among others). Although frameworks designed to describe stages of processing provide a basic delineation of higher and lower level processes, this distinction often falls apart for individual readers in specific contexts. This is primarily attributable to a conflation of the *task* assigned to the student and the actual cognitive *processes* engaged by that student as well as the success of those processes. It is commonly assumed that all tasks or stimuli have the same effects on all learners, and serve to induce the same internal processes. However, this is clearly not the case.

Take, for example, the task of paraphrasing a text passage. For a young child, this task may be highly complex, requiring the child to engage in the activation of knowledge about words, syntax, as well as the domain of the passage. For an adult, on the other hand, paraphrasing may be much more of a passive task. Of course, this is further complicated by the properties of the text passage itself. Even for adults, paraphrasing can be a challenging *higher level* process if the text is difficult enough or if they do not have sufficient prior knowledge of the domain. Current frameworks tend to operate under the assumption that a learner's outward behavior defines their learning outcomes, which is simply not true. Therefore, these frameworks frequently fail to capture the differences that arise from the reader and the nature of the task.

## Conclusions

Within the context of comprehension and education, there has been a heavy emphasis placed on an individual's ability to construct a coherent and elaborated mental representation of text content. To this end, research has aimed to establish the theoretical basis behind the comprehension process (e.g., Kintsch, 1998; Pressley & Afflerbach, 1995; Zwaan & Radvansky, 1998), as well as the most effective interventions for improving comprehension skills and strategies (McNamara, 2007; Pressley, 2000). A major problem lies in the task of operationally defining the component processes that contribute to the comprehension of text. A number of frameworks have been proposed to delineate the differences between lower and higher level cognitive processes (Bloom, 1956; Chi, 2009) and to map these various levels of thinking onto the task of reading comprehension (Afflerbach et al., 2011; Paris, 2005). However, the task of mapping such frameworks on to the reading comprehension process proves difficult, given the influences of various domains as well as the stages of development (Afflerbach et al., 2011).

One particularly salient aspect of implementations of hierarchical frameworks, such as the Bloom Taxonomy or the ICAP framework, is that they are primarily based on overt behaviors, tasks, and performance assessments. This allows educators to directly observe these behaviors and then intervene when students are not engaging in the desired behaviors. It provides tractable goals for encouraging higher level learning, whereas it would likely be futile to monitor and modify students' *actual* cognitive processes during classroom activities. Researchers and educators should be cautious, however, when assuming that certain cognitive processes consistently underlie particular types of learning activities, as overt behaviors do not always reliably indicate the processes in which students are engaged. A student may engage in a task considered to be lower level, but engage in higher level processing, and, vice versa, a student may engage in a higher level task, but engage in superficial processing. At the same time, a student who has engaged in higher level processing may manifest the benefits of this processing only at lower levels (which is likely the zone of proximal development for that student). These interactions between reader, task, and outcomes complicate simplistic interpretations of higher level processing.

Given the potential hazards of labeling cognitive processes or learning objectives as lower and higher level, one solution would be to throw out the terminology entirely. However, successful reading comprises a multitude of skills and strategies from the basic (letter recognition) to the complex (self-monitoring of comprehension), such that having hierarchically defined distinctions is clearly useful when building comprehension models (Kintsch & van Dijk, 1978), developing assessments (Magliano et al., 2011), and designing and evaluating classroom activities (Fisher & Hiebert, 1990). Hence, terminology related to higher order thinking is useful on various levels. Nonetheless, one of the primary goals of this chapter is to convince readers to avoid or temper the conflation between learning processes, tasks, and outcomes—particularly if the ultimate research objective is to understand the optimal conditions for enhancing student comprehension and learning. Ultimately, greater consideration must be turned to individual differences among students, and how students' abilities, goals, and dispositions differentially affect comprehension. Clearly the last few decades of research in the area of comprehension have elucidated a good deal in this respect (and much of that progress is described within this volume of work). But we can do better; there remain a multitude of questions to answer, particularly in regard to how to foster and how to scaffold students toward higher order thinking.

## Acknowledgments

This work was supported by the Institute of Education Sciences (IES), U.S. Department of Education, through grants R305A120707 and R305A130124 to Arizona State University. The opinions, findings, and conclusions or recommendations expressed are those of the authors and do not necessarily represent views of the IES.

# References

Afflerbach, P., Cho, B., & Kim, J. (2011). The assessment of higher order thinking skills in reading. In G. Schraw (Ed.), *Current perspectives on cognition, learning, and instruction: Assessment of higher order thinking skills* (pp. 185–215). Omaha, NE: Information Age Publishing.

Anderson, L. W., Krathwohl, D. R., Airasian, P. W., Cruikshank, K. A., Mayer, R. E., Pintrich, P. R., . . . Wittrock, M. C. (2001). *A taxonomy for learning, teaching, and assessing: A revision of Bloom's Taxonomy of Educational Objectives (Complete edition)*. New York: Longman.

Bloom, B. (1956). *Taxonomy of educational objectives, Handbook I: The cognitive domain*. New York: David McKay Co.

Cain, K., & Oakhill, J. (2006). Assessment matters: Issues in the measurement of reading comprehension. *British Journal of Educational Psychology*, *76*, 697–708.

Chi, M. T. H. (2009). Active–constructive–interactive: A conceptual framework for differentiating learning activities. *Topics in Cognitive Science*, *1*, 73–105.

Coté, N., Goldman, S. R., & Saul, E. U. (1998). Students making sense of informational text: Relations between processing and representation. *Discourse Processes*, *25*, 1–53.

Craik, F., & Watkins, M. (1973). The role of rehearsal in short-term memory. *Journal of Verbal Learning and Verbal Behavior*, *12*, 599–607.

Eason, S. H., Goldberg, L. F., Young, K. M., Geist, M. C., & Cutting, L. E. (2012). Reader–text interactions: How differential text and question types influence cognitive skills needed for reading comprehension. *Journal of Educational Psychology*, *104*, 515–528.

Fisher, C. W., & Hiebert, E. H. (1990). Characteristics of tasks in two approaches to literacy instruction. *The Elementary School Journal*, *91*, 3–18.

Gierl, M. J. (1997). Comparing cognitive representations of test developers and students on a mathematics test with Bloom's Taxonomy. *The Journal of Educational Research*, *91*, 26–32.

Gilliam, S., Magliano, J. P., Millis, K. K., Levinstein, I., & Boonthum, C. (2007). Assessing the format of the presentation of text in developing a Reading Strategy Assessment Tool (RSAT). *Behavior Research Methods*, *39*, 199–204

Granello, D. H. (2001). Promoting cognitive complexity in graduate written work: Using Bloom's Taxonomy as a pedagogical tool to improve literature reviews. *Counselor Education and Supervision*, *40*, 292–307.

Hanna, W. (2007). The New Bloom's Taxonomy: Implications for music education. *Arts Education Policy Review*, *108*, 7–16.

Kendeou, P., van den Broek, P., White, M. J., & Lynch, J. (2009). Predicting reading comprehension in early elementary school: The independent contributions of oral language and decoding skills. *Journal of Educational Psychology*, *101*, 765–778.

Kintsch, W. (1998). *Comprehension: A paradigm for cognition*. Cambridge, UK: Cambridge University Press.

Kintsch, W., & van Dijk, T. (1978). Toward a model of text comprehension and production. *Psychological Review*, *5*, 363–394.

Kolers, P. A., & Roediger, H. L. (1984). Procedures of mind. *Journal of Verbal Learning and Verbal Behavior*, *23*, 425–449.

König P, Kühnberger K. U., & Kietzmann T. C. (2013). A unifying approach to high- and low-level cognition. In U. V. Gähde, S. Hartmann, & J. H. Wolf (Eds.), *Models, simulations, and the reduction of complexity* (pp. 117–139). Berlin: De Gruyter.

Krathwohl, D. R., Bloom, B. S., & Masia, B. B. (1964). *Taxonomy of Educational Objectives: Handbook 2: The affective domain*. New York: David McKay Co.

Kunen, S., Cohen, R., & Solman, R. (1966). A levels-of-processing analysis of Bloom's Taxonomy, *Journal of Educational Psychology*, *73*, 202–211.

McNamara, D. S. (Ed.). (2007). *Reading comprehension strategies: Theory, interventions, and technologies*. Mahwah, NJ: Erlbaum.

McNamara, D. S., Graesser, A. C., McCarthy, P., & Cai, Z. (2014). *Automated evaluation of text and discourse with Coh-Metrix*. Cambridge, UK: Cambridge University Press.

McNamara, D. S., & Kintsch, W. (1996). Learning from text: Effects of prior knowledge and text coherence. *Discourse Processes*, *22*, 247–288.

McNamara, D. S., Kintsch, E., Songer, N. B., & Kintsch, W. (1996). Are good texts always better? Interactions of text coherence, background knowledge, and levels of understanding in learning from text. *Cognition and Instruction*, *14*, 1–43.

McNamara, D. S., & Magliano, J. P. (2009). Towards a comprehensive model of comprehension. In B. Ross (Ed.), *The psychology of learning and motivation* (Vol. 51, pp. 297–384). New York: Elsevier Science.

McNamara, D. S., O'Reilly, T. P., Best, R. M., & Ozuru, Y. (2006). Improving adolescent students' reading comprehension with iSTART. *Journal of Educational Computing Research*, *34*, 147–171.

McNamara, D. S., & Scott, J. L. (2001). Working memory capacity and strategy use. *Memory & Cognition*, *29*, 10–17.

Magliano, J. P., Millis, K. K., Levinstein, I., & Boonthum, C. (2011). Assessing comprehension during reading with the Reading Strategy Assessment Tool (RSAT). *Metacognition and Learning*, *6*, 131–154.

Magliano, J. P., Millis, K. K., Ozuru, Y., & McNamara, D. S. (2007). A multidimensional framework to evaluate reading assessment tools. In D. S. McNamara (Ed.), *Reading comprehension strategies: Theories, interventions, and technologies* (pp. 107–136). Mahwah, NJ: Erlbaum.

Millis, K. K., Simon, S., & tenBroek, N. S. (1998). Resource allocation during the rereading of scientific texts. *Memory & Cognition*, *26*, 232–246.

O'Reilly, T., & McNamara, D. S. (2007). Reversing the reverse cohesion effect: good texts can be better for strategic, high-knowledge readers. *Discourse Processes*, *43*, 121–152.

Paris, S. G. (2005). Reinterpreting the development of reading skills. *Reading Research Quarterly*, *40*, 184–202.

Pearson, P. D., & Hamm, D. N. (2005). The assessment of reading comprehension: A review of practices—Past, present, and future. In S. G. Paris & S. A. Stahl (Eds.), *Children's reading comprehension and assessment* (pp. 13–69). Mahwah, NJ: Lawrence Erlbaum Associates.

Pressley, M. (2000). What should comprehension instruction be the instruction of? In M. L. Kamil, P. B. Mosenthal, P. D. Pearson, & R. Barr (Eds.), *Handbook of reading research: Volume III* (pp. 545–561). Mahwah NJ: Erlbaum.

Pressley, M., & Afflerbach, P. (1995). *Verbal protocols of reading: The nature of constructively responsive reading*. Hillsdale, NJ: Lawrence Earlbaum.

Rapp, D. N., van den Broek, P., McMaster, K. L., Panayiota, K., & Espin, C. A. (2007). Higher-order comprehension processes in struggling readers: A perspective for research and intervention. *Scientific Studies of Reading*, *11*, 289–312.

Resnick, L. (1987). *Education and learning to think*. Washington, DC: National Academy Press.

Simpson, E. (1972). *The classification of educational objectives in the psychomotor domain: The psychomotor domain. Vol. 3*. Washington, DC: Gryphon House.

van der Schoot, M., Horsley, T. M., & van Lieshout, E. C. D. M. (2010). The effects of instruction on situation model construction: An eye fixation study on text comprehension in primary school children. *Educational Psychology*, *30*, 817–835.

van Dijk, T., & Kintsch, W. (1983). *Strategies of discourse comprehension*. New York: Academic Press.

VanderVeen, A., Huff, K., Gierl, M., McNamara, D. S., Louwerse, M., & Graesser, A. C. (2007). Developing and validating instructionally relevant reading competency profiles measured by the critical reading sections of the SAT. In D. S. McNamara (Ed.), *Reading comprehension strategies: Theories, interventions, and technologies* (pp. 137–172). Mahwah, NJ: Erlbaum.

Voss, J., & Silfies, L. (1996). Learning from history text: The interaction of knowledge and comprehension skill with text structure. *Cognition and Instruction*, *14*, 45–68.

Zohar, A., & Dori, Y. J. (2003). Higher order thinking skills and low-achieving students: Are they mutually exclusive? *Journal of Learning Sciences*, *12*, 145–181.

Zwaan, R. A., & Radvansky, G. A. (1998). Situation models in language comprehension and memory. *Psychological Bulletin*, *123*, 162–185.

# 14

# School Contexts and the Production of Individual Differences

*Julie E. Learned and Elizabeth Birr Moje*

What is the role of context in learning? What is the role of context in learning to read? Perhaps the most important question of all: What is the role of context in *successful* reading and learning? Where does context stop and the individual reader start? How might we reconsider what are seen as struggles of a given student to be products of textual and human interactions and relationships in learning contexts?

Our task in this chapter is to examine how individual differences are manifested in, mediated by, and challenged across in and out of school spaces and contexts that are produced or constructed in those spaces. In particular, we explore the question of why some youth who appear to be powerful readers (and writers) of myriad—and often cognitively and linguistically complex— texts *outside of school* seem to struggle when reading in school spaces and contexts. Some research has even shown that "struggling" youth readers demonstrated varying reading practices and skills across different school spaces and contexts (Dillon, 1989; Hall, 2007; Ivey, 1999). In particular, successful reading skills that individual youth exhibit in one school space and context do not always appear to transfer with those same youth to other contexts of school spaces. It stands to reason, given these empirical findings, that if youth skills, struggles, and successes change across contexts, then skill, struggle, and success must not inhere in individuals. That said, many children and youth do seem able to navigate the multiple contexts they traverse on a daily basis. What makes it possible for some youth to move easily across contexts and others to employ their skills to varying degrees in different contexts? To what extent can the explanation be a matter of individual differences, how much are the differences a matter of cultural practices, and when are the differences manifested in and even produced by the contexts themselves?

To address these questions, we review theory and research that demonstrates the context-dependent nature of what appear to be fixed and within-person, or individual, differences in reading and learning (see Stone & Learned, 2013). We ground our review of these studies in two case studies of ninth graders identified as struggling readers in their high school. In the cases, we document variability in the students' demonstrations of reading proficiency and struggle and demonstrate how their interactions in multiple school contexts appeared to construct the students as having individual differences—or, more specifically, individual *struggles*—in reading. We examine the institutional arrangements that influenced how these secondary school contexts were organized and consider how these contexts help create and maintain the appearance of individual differences in ways that constrain some learners and support others. Ultimately, we argue that literacy skill should not be thought of as an artifact of either individual or cultural differences, but that all kinds of differences in skill are taken up and mediated by the many different contexts in which children and youth learn. We close the chapter by discussing implications of this argument for improving four aspects of school contexts: the nature of reading interventions, the tools of reading interventions, the scheduling practices of secondary schools, and the school discourses around reading (difficulty).

## How Contexts Matter to Individual Differences: Theoretical and Empirical Review

As individuals interact across space and time, they form and re-form contexts, and so contexts are always under construction (Erickson & Schultz, 1997). In schools, classrooms are spaces; classroom contexts can be, for instance, student–teacher relationships, an instructional activity, a classroom management approach, or a class scheduling process. Spaces, then, are separate from the contexts that are constructed within and across spaces; spaces are containers in which contexts are built, maintained, challenged, and restructured minute by minute. These ever-evolving school contexts contribute to the production of what appear to be individual differences in reading. For example, incoming ninth graders typically take standardized reading assessments. Based on assessment outcomes, students are categorized into groups of different kinds of readers such as highly proficient, proficient, basic, and below basic. Based on these groupings, secondary teachers or administrators often assign students a label (e.g., proficient reader, struggling reader) and a particular class schedule, which may include, for example, literacy enrichment in an honors English Language Arts class or intervention support in a Read 180 class. Individual differences are not merely revealed through this process, they are constructed. Assessment cut scores vary, which means a student might be considered a struggling reader in one high school but a proficient reader in another. Teacher allocation varies, which influences the number and kind of reading interventions a high school offers. These kinds of institutional contexts—identification, categorization, labeling, and scheduling—help produce individual differences in reading.

Many contexts and factors influence the appearance of individual differences in reading and learning. We focus on school contexts and ways they mediate individual differences not only to delimit our examination, but also because schools are arenas in which teachers, administrators, and researchers have a powerful role in the production of contexts that, in turn, have a role in producing identifications of youth as struggling or successful. The effects of homelessness, poverty, or lack of resources are also important in the production of struggling reader identities, but such effects can be difficult for any one teacher or one school to mitigate. Similarly, cognitive and neurological differences exist among individuals, but such differences alone cannot account for the large number of students identified as struggling readers. Differences in home language, culture, and literacy can also contribute to the appearance of individual differences in school reading. We argue that linguistic and cultural differences can be positive sources of knowledge and identity for young people (cf., Heath, 1983; Moll & González, 1994; Moll & Greenberg, 1990). Schools and teachers can learn how to help students learn to draw on these resources to help build positive school contexts that advance school literacy learning.

Numerous scholars have examined how contexts—whether cultural, social, and/or virtual—shape language and literacy development and practice (Gumperz, 1981; Heath, 1983; Holland, Lachicotte, Skinner, & Cain, 1998; Hymes, 1994; Mead, 1934; Street, 1984; Vygotsky, 1986). In the late 1980s and early 1990s, armed with the power of these social and cultural theories, a number of scholars began to study the social contexts of school classrooms with the goal of documenting and analyzing the ways that learning literacy and language were socially situated and mediated. Detailing the particulars of the many studies related to literacy and social context is beyond the scope of this chapter, so we present representative studies that call into question assumptions about a divide between explanations of individual *or* cultural difference. These studies make evident how differences in people can be interpreted, cast, and recast in and by dynamic and co-constructed contexts that are produced in the physical and social spaces of school classrooms (Cazden, 1985; McDermott & Varenne, 1995).

## Studies of Elementary School Contexts

Cazden argued that learning to read is a "triangular relationship between a reader, a text being read, and the participation of teacher and peers" (p. 605). These studies suggest that any analysis of individual difference that does not take into account the relational or interactional dimensions of reading, writing, and learning to read and write—whether in school classrooms or between children and their parents (e.g., Purcell-Gates, 1995)—is at best a partial analysis. Equally important is the point that such relationships and interactions are always situated in relations of power, culture, and social class and that those relations of power, culture, and class are marked in particular ways in the spaces of school and classroom. In school spaces, where many people of different backgrounds come together, naming individuals as *different* can serve the interests of some groups and deny the interests of others, regardless of whether those differences are thought to be individually or culturally mediated.

For example, McDermott and Varenne (1995) analyzed how in school spaces, one child could be seen as having a learning disability by virtue of his teachers' views of what constitutes difference. Specifically, his teachers' views of skills and behaviors as a function of his individual cognition, together with their failure to understand and fully support his learning practices, produced a student whose differences were disabilities in the teachers' eyes. By examining the child from multiple angles, McDermott and Varenne documented strengths that he brought to the classroom, together with moments when those strengths were not taken up by the teacher or his fellow students. As a result, McDermott and Varenne argued for a view of "culture as disability," suggesting that how cultures view people, whether as individuals or as members of groups that do not fit the culture's practices, can consign those people to the status of disabled, or even of "pariah" (McDermott, 1993).

In an analysis of leveled reading group instruction in one elementary school classroom space, Golden (1988) provided evidence that the same text might be read and discussed quite differently by different groups of children, resulting, in effect, in a substantively different reading— and learning to read—experience for the children in the various groups. In particular, Golden noted that the teacher asked higher-order questions of the children whose decoding and word recognition skills appeared to be stronger and focused more on decoding skill development, to the virtual exclusion of comprehension instruction or even simple discussion of the stories, for less proficient decoders (Golden, 1988). These different interactions and readings dramatically shaped not only children's learning opportunities and perspectives on reading, but also the meanings that they made from the text (see also Bennett, 1991; Cazden, 1985).

## Research on Secondary School Contexts

Studies of how the social contexts of classrooms shape literacy learning have not been confined to young children just learning to read. Researchers of adolescent literacy learning in school examined the social interactions of middle and high school classrooms (e.g., Bloome & Egan-Robertson, 1993; Moje, 1996). Of particular interest in the study of individual differences as a function of classroom contexts, is a focus on how secondary school students understood the reading (and other learning tasks) they were asked to enact in various school content areas (Nicholson, 1984, 1985). Nicholson's study clearly showed many students were confused by the work they were asked to do in their high school classrooms because they could not make sense of the texts they were to read as part of their activities; Nicholson, however, did not link students' confusion explicitly to the myriad dimensions of classroom context, but saw confusion strictly as a matter of instruction.

Dressman, Wilder, and Connor (2005) engaged in narrative case study analyses and produced an etiology of struggle across eight students. After examining the effects of social class differences and race, Dressman et al. documented a unifying theme across the eight cases: Each of the youth had experienced trauma or hardship at young ages. However, because the researchers did not identify classroom contexts as key to the youths' struggles, they did not examine the youth moving across such contexts and thus could not speak to whether these youth struggled in uniform ways across school contexts. Important here is the question of to what extent classroom contexts either exacerbated past traumas or supported these youth in managing the effects of past traumatic experiences.

Even when classroom research has examined the role of social context on literacy learning, much of the research has focused on how social contexts—particularly instructional moves between teachers and students—shaped the construction of reading and writing practices at the classroom level, rather than at the level of the individual. Some notable exceptions include Ivey's (1999) and Hall's (2007) classroom-based case studies of middle-school readers. Ivey used classroom observation, interviews, and reading assessments to document that three middle-school students identified as struggling, average, and skilled readers respectively all appeared at different times to be skilled, average, and struggling readers, depending on the contexts in which they were reading. Ivey's sampling of three students who appeared to be differently skilled made a powerful challenge to assumptions about literacy skill as stable and immutable because each student looked different in different contexts.

Hall, by contrast, studied only youth identified as struggling readers but varied her sampling on multiple dimensions, including working with students from three grade levels (sixth, seventh, and eighth) and moving across different content areas and different teachers. She examined how students took up the literacy strategy instruction their teachers offered. According to Hall, the students who saw themselves as struggling wanted to protect their identities from exposure and resisted their teachers' attempts to scaffold their reading (see also Brozo, 1990). The teachers, in turn, positioned the students not only as struggling learners, but also as resistant ones. Hall, however, did not follow students across multiple school contexts to explain how differences in contexts may have contributed to producing participants' enacted identities as readers. Moreover, Hall's study, which focused on the students' identities as readers and learners, did not explicitly address how the teachers' instruction in the various classes she studied made a difference in the students' identifications and resistant practices.

## Studies of Contexts that Support Student Learning

In general, studies of struggling readers in secondary school classroom contexts have presented findings about how youth struggled to achieve or how they developed negative reader identities. By contrast, a number of scholars have shown how instructional contexts can facilitate achievement and positive identity development. Dillon (1989), for example, offered a microethnography of a "remedial" (the school's label) high school English class and documented how the teacher's practice of reading classic novels supported students' access to text even as it constrained their possibilities for learning to read independently. Dillon analyzed how and why the teacher privileged students' access to cultural literacy (Hirsch, Kett, & Trefil, 1987) and to experiencing a powerful reading of text over teaching youth the skills they needed to read independently. In effect, the teacher's well-intended practice positioned the youth as forever and always struggling readers by assuming that they could not improve their reading skill. Still, Dillon's study made clear the power of this practice as students described their teacher's supportive practices. Indeed, Dillon documented how some students, when followed to other classes, seemed to be very different kinds of learners in the sense that they were more invested in English class and seemingly less engaged in others.

O'Brien (1998) presented a very different kind of case of the power of classroom contexts. His research focused on students' use of digital tools (albeit rudimentary ones given the timing of the study) in a high school literacy lab designated for struggling adolescent readers. O'Brien found that teachers' willingness to allow the students to choose their reading and writing foci and tasks, coupled with the possibility of working with digital media, seemed to support the students' positive sense of selves as readers and writers in the lab environment. Lewis (2008) has demonstrated similar findings among marginalized youth in high school English classrooms that make digital media and new literacy practices the core of their work.

## Studies of Literacy Practices Outside of School

Motivated by contrasts in young people's school-based and non-school-based literacy practice within school spaces (e.g., Camitta, 1990; Lewis, 2008; O'Brien, 1998; Shuman, 1986), researchers of adolescent literacy took the study of literacy outside of school and into young people's everyday literacy lives—lives of reading magazines, novels, letters and notes from friends, and fanfiction (see Phelps, 2005). Drawing from this body of work, we offer exemplars of research that questioned representations of individual students' reading identities, motivations, and struggles as stable (see Franzak, 2006 for a review of the studies of youth positioned as marginalized—or struggling—in school). These studies document youth taking responsibility for and engaging in sophisticated and powerful literacy practices that have often gone unrecognized in school. The studies present findings of youth as savvy, strategic, and skilled in their work with literacy and text when they were operating in meaningful social contexts where purposes for reading and writing were clear, attainable, and socially motivated.

Finders (1996), for example, followed middle-school girls into afterschool and weekend gatherings of cliques, discovering that young women who appeared not to be interested in reading school texts while in their school classrooms read those same texts avidly in the privacy of their homes. Finders documented that these young women used their literate practices—and the texts that accompanied them—to position themselves as certain kinds of people, usually with the goal of fitting in with certain groups or, alternatively, of not being excluded from those groups. In many cases, the young women did not want to be seen as liking school texts. Most importantly, at times these positionings communicated to their teachers that they were uninterested in school and schooled literacies. Mahiri's (1994) study of youth who participated in afterschool game activities (basketball and videogaming, in particular) similarly demonstrated important literacy practices that were part of gaming and athletic pursuits. Mahiri's findings convincingly demonstrated that the same youths who appeared to resist and struggle in school were highly motivated and capable in settings that offered purpose, opportunities to network, and supports to improve their skills.

In her study of youth in or connected to street gangs, Moje (2000) analyzed what young people could do with the literacies, albeit *unsanctioned* literacies, they learned and practiced outside of school in powerful social worlds. Moje documented sophisticated metadiscursive and metalinguistic practices on the part of these "gangsta" (as they and their teachers identified them) youth and illustrated how the practices were motivated by and situated in social networks that mattered to the youth (see also Moje, Overby, Tysvaer, & Morris, 2008 for similar findings). The findings also demonstrated that their teachers did not recognize the sophistication of the youth literacy practices. Instead, their teachers typically saw these youth as weak or resistant readers and writers, at best, and as troublemakers, at worst.

Finally, although not intending to examine individual differences, Leander and Lovvorn (2006) followed one young man in and out school, examining how his literacy practices differed across the contexts of videogaming in the spaces of his home and in the spaces of his school English and history classrooms. Their study yielded important findings about how this young man's literate prowess differed dramatically in and across the three contexts. For example, Brian, the focal participant in the study, skillfully read and used a vast lexicon of challenging terms and proper nouns related to the specifics of the fantasy war game he played, but appeared uninterested in and unfamiliar with learning the lexicon of his history classroom. The findings pointed to the student's degree of engagement with the content and practices of the various spaces and to the role that the various spaces (and teachers or game-makers) played in constructing learning environments that promoted or did not promote both participation and continual learning.

Other researchers of youths' socially networked literacy practices outside of school have found similar results (e.g., Bitz, 2008; Black, 2006; Chandler-Olcott & Mahar, 2003; Cowan, 2005; Gustavson, 2007; Lam, 2009; Lewis & Fabos, 2005), raising questions regarding assumptions about individual difference in reading and writing success and struggle. This body of research helps identify the features of out-of-school contexts in which youth use texts and other tools to engage in literacy that might support youth reading and writing in ways that school classrooms do not. The studies also reveal the ways contexts get constructed through the use of out-of-school texts and tools.

The classroom-based studies outlined previously drew attention to the realities of reading and writing in secondary school settings by highlighting the challenges students faced and the moves teachers, students, or teachers and students together made as they navigated these challenges. These studies did not, however, examine how school and classroom contexts themselves may have produced the challenges students appeared to have in the classroom. Although research on out-of-school contexts has called into question the easy labeling of youth as either struggling or successful in regard to literate practice, little school-based social context research has attempted to discern the precise mechanisms by which social interactions and relationships shaped literacy learning or identities as struggling or successful in the adolescent years. Namely, what is it about school and classroom contexts that support some students in deploying their skills across multiple contexts, whereas others struggle to read and write to learn with power and proficiency?

In an attempt to address the last question, we offer the following two case studies of adolescent youth moving through and across several different physical and social spaces of a public high school as a way of examining how teachers and youth co-construct classroom learning contexts and institutional contexts in ways that position youth as either struggling or successful in school literacy learning.

## Difference as Contextual: Two Cases of Reading in Multiple School Contexts

We present two case studies of ninth-grade students identified as having reading difficulty. Data come from a school-year long qualitative study in which Learned shadowed eight youths identified as struggling readers and focused particularly on students' experiences as readers in US history, algebra, and reading intervention classes. Learned observed students across multiple school spaces and contexts; conducted ethnographic open-ended and semi-structured interviews with students and teachers; and collected school records (e.g., reading assessment scores, class grades, school attendance, and behavior referrals). These case studies demonstrate ways in which school contexts complexly evolved and how students' interactions with these ever-changing contexts contributed to the construction of students' individual differences in reading. Specifically, we document how three interdependent contexts—(1) institutional contexts (e.g., identification as a struggling reader and/or behavior problem, tracking); (b) instructional contexts (e.g., the extent to which reading assignments are supported with appropriate literacy instruction, the extent to which instruction is appropriately scaffolded); and (3) social contexts (e.g., the nature of student–teacher interactions, class climate)—mediated two students' demonstration of reading-related skills, practices, and identities and ultimately the manifestation (or perception) of individual reading differences. The findings presented derive from a long-term study of multiple students and teachers. For the purposes of this chapter, we focus on two students whose experiences document the power of supportive or constraining classroom contexts. We also provide details of one teacher who represents the possibilities for building classroom contexts that provide students powerful opportunities to learn.

### *Limiting School Contexts: The Case of Mark*

Mark began the 2012–2013 school year as an optimistic ninth-grade student at Moore High School. Mark could be thought of as "school identified" because he saw himself as liking and doing well in school. For example, he reported, "I came (to Moore High) for the academic program." In a different interview, he said "learning at high school could be fun if we could do stuff that's educational . . . (and they) give us a better learning experience." Mark came from a public middle school within the district. He was 14 years old and self-identified as African American and Native American. Outside of school he was a dancer involved as a choreographer in a community center breakdance group. He reported being interested in books about World War II, "Japanese comics all the way up to Chinese comics all the way up to (books about) American criminals. And, I read an English book from, like, the 1700s." At the end of eighth grade, middle school teachers identified Mark as needing high school reading intervention. Being scheduled into ninth-grade Read 180 not only afforded supplementary literacy instruction, it also ascribed an institutional label of struggling reader and clustered Mark with other students identified as struggling readers across content area classes. Moreover, Read 180 did not support Mark's disciplinary literacy learning. As a comprehensive reading curriculum purchased by the district, Read 180 did not align with the literacy or knowledge demands of ninth-grade coursework. Although Mark performed well across Read 180's three main components—computer-based instruction, teacher-led small group instruction, and independent reading—he experienced difficulty with disciplinary reading and writing in his other classes. Both the labeling and the scheduling served as key school contexts that mediated the construction of Mark's reading as a product of his individual struggle to read complex texts.

Mark's identification as a struggling ninth-grade reader is somewhat curious because his eighth-grade reading assessment data painted an ambiguous picture of his reading skill and because he reported reading frequently. Mark scored in the proficient range on the eighth-grade state standardized test for reading, but he scored below the district's benchmark on the district-administered standardized test (ACT, Inc., 2014). His Scholastic Reading Inventory (SRI) Lexile measure was 820. Despite the fact that SRI indicates a typical eighth-grader scores between an 805 Lexile (L) and 1100L depending on various factors such as the text being read (Scholastic, 2008), the school's literacy coach explained that Lexiles under 1000, in conjunction with other data, indicated an incoming ninth grader's need for reading support.

In early fall of his ninth-grade year, Mark scored a 1262L on the SRI, well above the 1000L benchmark used by the school to identify struggling readers, and he scored in the average range on the Test of Reading Comprehension (TORC) (Brown, Wiederholt, & Hammill, 2009). In addition, he read grade-level Read 180 texts with ease and motivation. Assessment data on Mark's literacy skill painted a picture of an average ninth-grade reader and called into question his placement in the Read 180 course.

The high school's reading intervention classes, among other classes targeted at specific populations (e.g., orchestra, band), contributed to de facto tracking. Clusters of students who were similar on one or more dimensions (e.g., identified as struggling readers, experienced musicians) often shared similar schedules. Mr. Robin, a history teacher, and Ms. Schmidt, a math teacher, independently described what they thought were the negative effects of de facto tracking. Ms. Schmidt explained:

> Like in my morning classes . . . it is very functional because there are a lot of leaders . . . We've switched some students from the afternoon classes into the morning classes and their behaviors just disappear because it's so out of the ordinary of what's happening in the room . . . They can't act out or everyone else in the room just looks at them like, "Why is this happening? This is not what class looks like." . . . I think the classes need to be more balanced because the afternoon class scores consistently lower on almost every test. I don't think it's necessarily ability, I think it's everything else in the room that brings everybody else down.

This kind of de facto tracking, in addition to institutionalized tracking (i.e., honors and regular classes), helped create classes in which literacy skills—what counted as proficient or struggling and who demonstrated proficiency or struggle—appeared to vary. Thus these skills did not derive solely from the individual but instead were mediated—brought forward or constrained—by tracked contexts. Tracked classes also segregated students by race and ethnicity. Youth of color were over represented in 13 lower-track classes included in the study (i.e., three intervention classes and ten core content classes in which students identified as struggling readers were clustered), constituting on average 67 percent of class enrollment for 56 percent of the school population. This disproportionately high enrollment of youth of color raises important questions about the role of race, ethnicity, and culture in struggling reading identification.

Mark's ninth-grade schedule included both de facto low-track classes and officially tracked classes (i.e., reading class, "regular" content area classes). Mark's US history and algebra teachers, both of whom were mid-career, white, middle class, and had spent the vast majority of their teaching years at Moore High, described the class periods in which Mark was scheduled as having students who appeared, on average, to be lower skilled, less academically confident, and more likely to have "behavior problems" than students in other periods. The algebra teacher, Ms. Malloy, described Mark's math class as the "single worst class . . . in my 16 years of teaching."

The extent to which the teachers' perceptions were accurate or fair, why and how their perceptions were formed, and the consequences that those perceptions had for students' learning are important questions that we will begin to take up, but equally important are ways that those perceptions shaped their interactions with the students in the classes. Also contributing to student–teacher interactions and classroom climate were contexts beyond the classroom (e.g., large class sizes, students' middle school preparation, poor building/classroom facilities), and Mark's teachers expressed frustration about these factors that they explained hindered students' learning but that were outside the scope of teachers' immediate influence. Mark's interaction among these tracked and often-strained classes mediated the extent to which he developed and/or was viewed as having strong or weak skills in reading and content area learning.

Mark's teachers were not the only ones who experienced their classes as challenging. In an interview, Mark identified what he perceived to be some of the challenges in US history and suggested that to improve the class, the teacher, Mr. Robin, could

> try to keep (the reading) in our mid-range of reading instead of how he thinks that we'll be able to read . . . try to let us do the work instead of sitting and watching him do it for us most of the time because that's mostly what the problem is . . . He's doing the work for us and he could teach us how to do it and then we could get like in groups or partners . . . we'll be able to talk and we'll do the work.

Field observations corroborated Mark's account. Mr. Robin tended to lecture, dominate class discussions, and assign highly complex texts (e.g., primary sources) with little scaffolding. Contrary to notions that struggling readers/students are unmotivated or work avoidant, Mark expressed a desire to do more work, take charge of his learning, collaborate with peers, and read accessible history texts. According to Mark, students "completely go off-task because we feel what we're doing is just completely meaningless." Mark experienced the instructional context of the class as one that limited students' learning and thus resulted in off-task behavior.

Whereas Mark attributed off-task behavior to lack of meaningful learning opportunities, Mr. Robin attributed it to student "ringleaders" who chose to instigate disruption in order to avoid work. Mr. Robin viewed Mark as "one of those kids in that class . . . who are not necessarily ringleaders, but who are kids who are perfectly willing to let things spiral out of control and help it spiral so they don't have to do stuff." In history class, Mark was constructed as having not only individual learning challenges, but also behavior problems. Similarly, the math teacher Ms. Malloy said that at times Mark could be disengaged and obstinate with an "I'm-not-going-to-do-this-because-you-might-want-me-to sort of attitude." Field observations failed to support the sweeping nature of these accounts. In approximately 21 history class observations and nine math class observations, Mark demonstrated engaged behaviors (e.g., reading aloud and silently, volunteering to answer a question, taking notes) and disengaged behaviors (e.g., head down on his desk, laughing at another student's joke, having a "side conversation"), but did not engage in highly disruptive or defiant behavior that helped classes "spiral out of control."

Perhaps perceptions of behavior problems and learning problems were so intertwined that when asked what would most help Mark's reading and learning in history class, Mr. Robin said "behavior expectations of, you know, you need to be in your seat, you need to not be engaged in a side conversation." When asked what would help Mark's math learning, Ms. Malloy said possibly "a different teacher . . . a different time of day . . . another year of maturity." These behavior- and context-focused recommendations may have proved helpful for Mark's learning. However, it is striking that neither teacher mentioned instruction as a way to bolster Mark's content area and literacy learning. This focus on behavior remediation over instruction illustrates the extent to which Mark had come to be viewed as a "behavior" problem as much as, or perhaps even more than, he was viewed as a student.

When asked about Mark's academic strengths and areas for growth in midyear interviews, both Mr. Robin and Ms. Malloy reported knowing relatively little about Mark as a reader and learner of history/math. Mr. Robin said:

> if I had to hazard a guess I would say he's probably on the lower side of things and that maybe (reading) comprehension is a place he might struggle with a little bit. I wouldn't also be surprised if it just takes more to process things at times as well, I mean he just kind of has some of those, you know, markers of a kid who takes a while to get through those things.

Mr. Robin suggested that Mark had weaknesses in reading comprehension and overall cognitive processing, but he was unable to speak with certainty or specificity about Mark's differences. Moreover, Mr. Robin did not seem to realize that Mark was capable of reading at least some secondary texts with proficiency and motivation, that Mark reported being interested in historical topics taught in US history such as Native Americans, slavery, and World War II, or that Mark had voluntarily been reading some books on historical topics that year. When asked about Mark's strengths, both Ms. Malloy and Mr. Robin said that Mark occasionally asked insightful questions that synthesized important points from a discussion or lesson. Ms. Malloy called these, "flashes of brilliance," and explained they happened rarely and if Mark "decided to," he could probably have them more often, locating the responsibility for Mark to have these flashes inside Mark himself, rather than as a dimension of the interactions among activity, texts read or written, and the participants in the teaching–learning process.

As the year progressed and Mark continued to read proficiently and earn A grades in Read 180, he experienced difficulty across his content area classes. His Grade Point Average (GPA) at the end first semester was 1.43. Field observations and interviews with teachers and Mark showed that many factors contributed to Mark's low school achievement (e.g., being scheduled into some low-track less-than-optimal classes, being positioned as a behavior problem, having poor organization skills, and low work completion). Another factor contributing to Mark's low achievement was under-developed disciplinary literacy knowledge and skills. During reading process interviews conducted with a history text and math text used in Mark's classes as well as a Read 180 narrative text that Mark chose, Mark read the expository school texts less strategically and with less background knowledge than the narrative text. It appeared that Read 180 was neither identifying nor addressing Mark's disciplinary literacy needs as they related to his school coursework.

By midyear Mark seemed less enthusiastic and motivated about high school than he was in the fall. Field observations indicated that he was more socially distant from teachers and peers and less engaged in classroom activities than in the fall. In a January interview, Mark talked about his first semester experiences and grades. Mark said, "Moore isn't helping me . . . I hear Lincoln High has a stronger (academic) program." Though Mark appeared disillusioned, he had the social acumen and the agency to articulate that much of the problem lay in the school. Despite the setbacks of his ninth-grade year, Mark still identified with school and continued to look for solutions as he wondered if the rival high school across town would be a better place for him.

Mark's case illustrates how being identified as struggling with reading can trigger a chain of events and involve students in a host of school contexts that, to varying degrees, construct and/or maintain the very challenges and behaviors that identification as a "struggling reader" is supposed to help remediate. Although Mark was an active participant in creating and maintaining contexts across school spaces, he had less institutional power than the school organization or adult actors to fundamentally change these contexts. For example, Mark could not opt out of reading intervention or change the nature of tracked classes at Moore High. Nevertheless, Mark often demonstrated agency and resilience as he navigated and helped construct school contexts; he remained largely school-identified, continued to read, and reported enjoying reading. By the end of the year, although disillusioned with Moore High, Mark did not consider himself a poor reader or a disruptive student. He remained hopeful that tenth grade could be different. Our question for researchers, school administrators, and teachers—and the purpose of this chapter—is how can we shift secondary school contexts to support literacy learning for students like Mark. What would it take for Mark's tenth-grade year to be different?

## Promising School Contexts: The Case of Keisha

Keisha was a highly social 14-year-old African American ninth grader. She nurtured her many friendships during school time and cultivated an active online network via Facebook and Twitter. She reported reading regularly outside of school and liking L. Divine's *Drama High* series and other young adult fiction by Sharon Draper. Keisha said that she and her mother enjoyed reading the same books and "on Sundays, I . . . stay in the house and just be reading. Me and my momma."

In addition, during her elementary school years, Keisha lived in Metropolitana, a major American city three hours away from Jonestown. Keisha explained that her family moved to Jonestown to get away from Metropolitana's escalating street violence, "Yeah, everybody's tired of Metropolitana, tired of shootings, tired of their kids dying all the time. Stuff like that. My auntie's daughter just died. She was my age." Jonestown offered safer streets and schools, but violence continued to be a part of Keisha's life as she traveled between the two cities and became affiliated with a Jonestown area gang. One of her teachers noted that Keisha had some demanding life circumstances that were "competing against her being academic." The teacher's comment illustrates how an academic identity could be viewed as being at odds with a student's life circumstances or other identities (e.g., gang member). Although there were instances when gang-related interactions distracted Keisha from school learning, there also were instances when she demonstrated engaged, skillful learning. Regardless sometimes of this variability, teachers' perceptions of Keisha and the extent to which she was "academic" mediated how teachers positioned her in classrooms.

Although Keisha engaged socially at school, she often demonstrated less interest and less facility with classroom learning than she did with her social engagements with other students. Her GPA at the end of first quarter during ninth grade was 0.50. At the beginning of ninth grade, Keisha scored in the poor range on the TORC but in the average range on the SRI with a Lexile of 852. According to the eighth-grade state standardized reading assessment, Keisha was a basic reader, which meant she demonstrated partial mastery of the knowledge and skills required for proficient reading. Despite the variability in Keisha's assessment scores, the district had placed Keisha in Read 180 since the sixth grade even though Read 180 is designed to be a one-year intervention for students without identified disabilities such as Keisha. Moore High School, limited perhaps by the district-adopted interventions and the rigidity of the master schedule, scheduled Keisha for a fourth year of Read 180, which surprised and deeply upset Keisha. The following interview excerpt shows how the intervention placement dimmed her excitement about ninth grade and began to undermine her identity as a learner.

> I've been in Read 180 since sixth grade and I need to get out . . . I was so happy to come up in this school but then as soon as I got my schedule and I found out I had Read 180, I just like, I just stopped . . . this is not fair, like, why am I in Read 180 . . . I don't keep needing practice because I read at home . . . I think I have the vocabulary in my mind, I can sound out words, I can read, I can spell, like I don't know why I need the extra help . . . I be feeling like I'm slow because I'm in this class.

The Read 180 placement sent Keisha a negative message that she had reading deficits. She countered that notion by identifying her reading strengths such as reading at home, knowing some vocabulary, and decoding well. Although Keisha appeared to shrug off a poor reader identity, she reported feeling "slow" because she was placed in the class. That is, being scheduled into Read 180 for a fourth time put Keisha in a tenuous position as a learner at the beginning of ninth grade because she began to internalize a sense of struggle or "feeling slow."

Keisha was not simply "unmotivated" (the school's term for identifying students like Keisha) to be in reading class. In the next excerpt she acknowledged how the program initially helped her, but after three-going-on-four years of enrollment, being in the Read 180 placement was demotivating:

> (Read 180) helped me in the beginning in sixth and seventh and eighth grade . . . but I already know what to do . . . Reading is boring. Reading is boring. Small group is boring to me. It used to be so fun . . . I don't want to do it.

At Moore High, teachers often discussed the low motivation of many reading intervention students like Keisha, treating engagement as a within-person fixed trait. Indeed, during the high school scheduling process, high school personnel used eighth-grade reports (e.g., middle school behavior records and eighth-grade teachers' end-of-year evaluations) and literacy assessment scores to sort incoming ninth graders into groups that the administration and teachers labeled "engaged" and "unengaged." Those identified as in need of extra reading support were subsequently scheduled into "engaged" and "unengaged" reading classes. Keisha, however, offered an alternative explanation of her own lack of engagement by attributing her decreased interest in reading not to an internal or personal state but rather to experiences with a particular curriculum. She articulated how instructional contexts (i.e., reading intervention) and institutional scheduling practices (i.e., Read 180 for a fourth time) had dampened her motivation over time.

Observing Keisha in reading, history, and math classes throughout the school year produced evidence that Keisha's level of engagement in learning activities was indeed not uniform or fixed. Her participation and interest in classroom learning varied dramatically across different spaces and times. As instructional and social contexts shifted, Keisha's interactions with those contexts contributed to her construction as a struggling reader and learner, or a productive reader and learner with potential. These differences were most noticeable when comparing how Keisha appeared to read and learn in her algebra class and how she appeared to read and learn in her other classes (i.e., history and reading).

In history and reading classes, teachers reported that Keisha was "unengaged," a "behavior problem," and even "dangerous." Although I never observed or heard any report that Keisha engaged in dangerous behavior in school, she frequently disregarded the history and reading teachers' requests to participate in classroom activities and to follow class norms (e.g., put away cell phones). Indeed, upon walking into those classes, Keisha's initial interaction with teachers was often negative. For example, one day before the bell rang to begin reading class, Ms. French said, "Keisha put the cell phone away. I'm not going to deal with it today. I'm serious. Put it away." On that particular day, three other students walked into the room using their cell phones, but the teacher only called out Keisha. When negative student–teacher interactions like this occurred—interactions that positioned Keisha as a behavior problem particularly at the beginning of a class period—they set a tone for the remainder of class in which Keisha appeared to feel defensive and annoyed, and she was less likely to participate. Ultimately, in Read 180 and US history periods, Keisha's interaction with classroom social contexts (e.g., teacher–student interactions) and instructional contexts (e.g., Read 180 curriculum, predominance of teacher lecture) in addition to institutional contexts (e.g., intervention placement processes, behavior policies) contributed to her construction as a struggling reader and a behavior problem.

Conversely, the contexts that occurred during Keisha's math class—and the ways she participated in and helped construct those contexts—mediated her reading practices, skills, and identities in more productive ways. First, the institutional processes that shaped math class were quite different from the ones that shaped the history and reading classes. In the 2012–2013 school year, the math department offered an intervention algebra class for incoming ninth graders who demonstrated difficulty with math but who were not identified as having behavior problems in eighth grade. Although algebra was a low-track class similar to Read 180 and US history, unlike those classes, algebra met for two class periods everyday and enrolled only 15 students. Rather than "ending up" with a low-track class as was the history teacher's experience, Mr. Henry, the algebra teacher, volunteered to teach this class and felt strongly about building class community, helping students feel "safe to take risks in math," and supporting students to "experience more success in math than they had in previous years."

Mr. Henry's math class was successful on several dimensions. According to Mr. Henry, the majority of students showed significant gains on the ACT EXPLORE standardized test for math (ACT, 2014) and demonstrated increased confidence and autonomy in their math learning throughout the year, which was corroborated by field observations. Mr. Henry attributed the effectiveness of the class to institutional factors such as having a double block to provide two hours of daily math instruction, having a low student–teacher ratio, and vetting student enrollment with eighth-grade teachers to avoid scheduling students with a history of behavior problems. Keisha echoed Mr. Henry's point about the double block when she said "having math for two hours, that's good. Like, it really did help."

The social and instructional classroom contexts cultivated by Mr. Henry and the students also appeared to contribute to the productivity of the class and to Keisha's positive student identity in algebra class. Whereas the history and reading teachers described her as "unengaged," "a behavior problem," and "dangerous," Mr. Henry described her in the following way:

> She actually learns things pretty quickly. I think that she's been in a circumstance in the past where again, somehow she was allowed to quit on things. Because when we really like get her, when we get her linked into what we're doing, she is an all star, but if she is disengaged, then you get just nothing, it's like trying to squeeze water out of a rock.

Mr. Henry was the only teacher (of three teachers interviewed) who identified a learning strength for Keisha. He acknowledged that she struggled with motivation, but by acknowledging past "circumstance" in which Keisha was "allowed to quit on things" and by using the word *disengaged* instead of *unengaged*, Mr. Henry recognized engagement as a temporary/changeable state for Keisha, not a permanent aspect of her constitution. He also recognized his role ("when we get her linked into what we're doing") in building a context of engagement, connection ("linked in") and success ("she is an all star").

189

In terms of student–teacher interactions, Mr. Henry regularly praised students for doing well more often than he disciplined or redirected students for being off task. In one representative class, he praised students eight times (e.g., "Excellent, yes good connection") and redirected students five times (e.g., "You guys have to pay attention right now"). Mr. Henry's use of praise and redirection stood in stark contrast to that of Keisha's history teacher who praised students two times and redirected 19 times during one representative class period. During field observations Mr. Henry regularly demonstrated curiosity about students' thinking, made positive assumptions about students' intentions, and treated students with respect. In an interview, he explained that building trusting and caring relationships with students was important in supporting their learning: "I think if you have kids that have a teacher that they feel like they have an honest relationship with and that there is trust and genuine care both ways, that they try harder, that they're more engaged."

Students reported feeling understood by Mr. Henry. One young woman said, "He gets us, and we get him." Several students said that they appreciated that Mr. Henry listened to what they had to say and that he joked around with students. Notably, both the students and Mr. Henry discussed positive social contexts in connection to positive instructional contexts. Keisha said, "We do math and then we have like our little fun time talking to each other and then we get right back to math. It's like a little thing—but, we still get our work done." The fact that Mr. Henry brought students "right back to math" and did not solely focus on fostering interpersonal connections was important to Keisha. In interviews, she reported learning math more effectively in ninth grade than in previous years. Similarly, Mr. Henry discussed the importance of trusting, caring relationships in connection to academic learning. He explained:

> I've had situations, like with the stuff we're doing on systems, honestly I had to tell them, "I know that this is super boring right now, but can you trust me that you just need to know this?" and they're like, "Yeah, Mr. Henry. Okay," and they'll do it, and I think that's because of the relationship that I've built with them. They know that I'm not going to make them do something just to do it. If I'm asking them to do it, they must really need to because I've built that trust that I don't waste their time.

Mr. Henry's social and instructional goals were intertwined. His goal was not to be friends with students or simply to have students feel good about themselves. He cared about students as young people *and* as math learners. Students responded positively to this teacher stance that respected both their personhood and their student identities, and together participants in the class constructed supportive social and instructional contexts for learning.

Moreover, Mr. Henry enacted highly effective instruction with a focus on mathematical literacy and carefully scaffolded teaching. To facilitate mathematical literacy, Mr. Henry explicitly taught students to use mathematical language, navigate multiple representations of mathematical concepts, think symbolically, read and write different symbol systems, interpret mathematical sentences, and defend mathematical answers. In observations, Mr. Henry consistently organized instruction around these aspects of mathematical literacy. In addition, he systematically scaffolded instruction and gradually transferred responsibility for learning to students.

For example, in a lesson on coordinate planes, Mr. Henry began by drawing an x- and y-axis on the board and asked, "What do you remember or know about coordinate planes?" One student pointed to the center of the graph and said, "That point is like zero zero." Mr. Henry confirmed this and asked what "that point" is called. No one responded, and so Mr. Henry said, "It starts with 'o'." A chorus of students yelled out words that began with "o," and one student said "origin." Mr. Henry said, "Origin, right! Let's say it together." The students collectively responded, "origin." Mr. Henry then taught the oral language conventions associated with mathematical terms "point" and "origin," and how to discuss (0, 0) on a coordinate plane. He said to say "point," is not wrong, but "origin is more precise." To help students understand, he said saying "origin" is like saying formally "hello" and "goodbye" in an interview situation, and saying "point" is like saying informally "hey" and "see ya" to friends. Neither was wrong, he explained, but in mathematics, "we want to use formal mathematical terms," so calling (0, 0) "the origin" is more appropriate than "point."

Throughout the lesson, Mr. Henry continued to draw out students' prior knowledge and synthesize students' responses. With statements such as, "According to Amber, this section of the graph is negative," he emphasized students' voices and publicly valued their ideas. Mr. Henry built on Amber's comment by asking, "Why is this section of the graph negative?" Questions such as this helped the instruction go beyond a step-by-step guide to plotting points on a graph and instead situated skill-building in a substantive discussion about the intellectual problems involved with interpreting and manipulating coordinate planes in mathematics. After the large group discussion, Mr. Henry scaffolded students by forming small groups and encouraging them to ask and answer each other's questions during an activity reading and producing coordinate planes.

Keisha explained that math was her favorite class because "I can get my work done, like a lot easier because Mr. Henry breaks it down." Two other students also noted that Mr. Henry "breaks it down" or "shows them the steps" for how to approach mathematical problems. Regarding vocabulary, Keisha explained that in math class "We just learn the words, you know. (Mr. Henry) wasn't there yesterday, so we had a substitute teacher and that's when we reviewed the word, but (the substitute) didn't really show us. Probably will tomorrow, (Mr. Henry) will show us." Keisha differentiated between showing and reviewing words. By "showing" words and mathematical concepts through extended discussion, multiple examples, and student participation, instead of superficially "reviewing" math terms, Mr. Henry helped students build mathematical knowledge.

Keisha participated more actively in math than in history and reading. She volunteered to answer questions, asked questions when she was confused, went to the board to solve problems, and worked collaboratively in groups. She tackled mathematical texts and appeared motivated to read and interpret them. Using her cell phone was an issue, but when Mr. Henry would ask Keisha to put it away or give it to him, the interaction rarely resulted in a heated debate or Keisha exiting class, which happened multiple times in both history and reading classes. Thus, the interacting institutional, social, and instructional contexts of the math class mediated Keisha's mathematical literacy learning, and she demonstrated productive reader/learner skills, practices, and identities more often than she did in other classes. Equally important is the point that through her active engagement, Keisha helped to construct the positive algebra classroom context even as she experienced it.

Keisha's mathematical literacy (and mathematics) learning was not simply a matter of a set of individual skills Keisha possessed (or did not possess). Nor can her learning experience be explained by a single contextual factor such as a good relationship with the teacher, good instruction, or small class size. Rather, it was the complex interaction of multiple contexts—and her participation in creating these contexts—that made the algebra class a positive and productive space for Keisha in the midst of a ninth-grade experience in which she was often constructed as a behavior and learning problem. Although it is true that Keisha participated in this construction of herself as a "behavior" in many classes, it is also true that Keisha participated in constructing her potential as a learner in Mr. Henry's class. Students do co-construct their identities, but they are not full participants in the institutional authority of classrooms, where teachers and other school personnel hold the power to invite students into positive learning experiences (as Mr. Henry did) or to exclude and even dismiss them from learning and learning spaces altogether. That Keisha's reading-related skills, practices, and identities varied across school spaces and times demonstrates the mediated nature of her reading and learning (difficulty) and suggests ways that school contexts might be shifted to support her literacy learning and social development across multiple content areas.

## Implications of Understanding Students' Literacy Skills as Individually, Culturally, and Contextually Mediated

These cases suggest the need not only to attend to school contexts in considerations of individual students' reading challenges and successes, but also to rethink four key aspects of school contexts. These four aspects include school discourses around reading (difficulty), the nature of reading interventions, the tools of reading interventions, and the scheduling practices of secondary schools or how we "do" secondary school.

As illustrated in these two representative cases, Mark's and Keisha's positioning as a result of their placement in the Read 180 course appear to have had a dramatic impact on both their self-identifications as good or poor readers and on their sense of self as students more generally. Students who saw themselves as good readers when they left eighth grade—as both Mark and Keisha did—responded in one of two ways to their positioning as in need of specialized instruction. They either accepted the identification and position as struggling (as Mark appeared to do over the course of the semester) or they rejected that identification and position but appeared to act out their frustration with being forced into a class they believed they did not need (as Keisha's case illustrates). In both cases, seemingly well-intended institutional moves such as offering special courses to support students' reading development appeared to have unintended negative consequences for both students and teachers. In part, the affordances made possible by offering extra instructional support for students who appeared to struggle were undermined by rigid adherence to cut scores on entrance assessments, a lack of multiple assessment measures, the separation of students into "engaged" and "unengaged" categorizations, and the de facto tracking that resulted from the assignment to the special reading support course.

These institutional moves produced a context in which teachers participated in negative positionings and identifications, describing students as weak, struggling, unengaged, problematic, or resistant. In some cases, the negative positioning was so strong that teachers actually began to conflate what they saw as students' negative and resistant behaviors with the students themselves, even referring to "problem" students as "behaviors" (as in, "I have a lot of the behaviors in my class"). Indeed, labeling—and the conflation of behavior labels and individual differences—was a kind of context that spanned across school spaces; in effect, as students moved from one physical space to another in the school, they carried with them these contextually derived and mediated labels as successful or struggling and resistant or compliant.

Mr. Henry, however, appeared able to maintain a positive view of the students' possibilities for engaged and productive reading and subject-matter learning even as he recognized differences in their skills, backgrounds, experiences, and attitudes. Notably, other institutional policies—block scheduling; a teacher-produced intervention (in contrast to a predetermined, prescribed intervention); and small class sizes for the special algebra class—appeared to support Mr. Henry's capacity for seeing the possibilities in his students. Finally, in regard to institutional contexts, the complex nature of high school scheduling arrangements can work against the potential for students to receive just-in-time—and not overly long or redundant—literacy support. In Mark's case, despite his Lexile score improving by approximately 400 points—well into the above-average range—he remained locked into a Read 180 class to which he probably should never have been assigned and, due to the nature of the generic reading material and assignments, which did not support his disciplinary literacy learning.

Instructional contexts also appeared to mediate how these youth exhibited individually mediated literacy skills and motivation. When Mark and Keisha felt supported by instruction, they were able to take up the classroom practices and demonstrate engaged, motivated, and often proficient reading and learning. Conversely, when they did not feel supported or when they felt that they were even being underserved instructionally, they retreated from the classroom, socially and academically, if not physically. The key point here is that strong instruction—not just friendly or caring teachers—mattered to the students. That said, these two youth, representative of a larger sample, acknowledged the value of a teacher who cared, who inspired trust, and who appeared to believe in the possibility that the youth could succeed.

The two case studies offered should remind literacy educators that even well-intended institutional or instructional moves can inadvertently produce identities that position youth as struggling, disengaged, and problematic. Together with the review of literacy-in-context studies presented previously, the cases of Mark and Keisha underscore Street's (1984) argument that the practice and learning of literacy skills can never be separated from the social contexts in which those skills are situated and motivated. Moreover, the analyses should serve as a reminder not to set up false divides between what appear to be individual differences and what appear to be cultural (which are intimately intertwined with class, race, ethnicity, and gender) differences. Indeed, for us, the question is not whether differences are individual or cultural, but instead how social interactions and power relationships produce positions or identities as struggling or successful in the various in-school and out-of-school contexts through which students move?

# References

ACT, Inc. (2014). It's time to EXPLORE. ACT EXPLORE. Retrieved from http://www.act.org/explorestudent/.

Bennett, K. (1991). Doing school in an urban Appalachian first grade. In C. E. Sleeter (Ed.), *Empowerment through multicultural education* (pp. 27–48). Albany, NY: State University of New York Press.

Bitz, M. (2008). The Comic Book Project: Literacy outside (and inside) the box. In J. Flood, S. B. Heath, & D. Lapp (Eds.), *Research on teaching litearcy through the communicative and visual arts* (Vol. II, pp. 229–236). New York: Lawrence Erlbaum Associates and the International Reading Association.

Black, R. W. (2006). Language, culture, and identity in online fanfiction. *E-Learning, 3*(2), 170–184.

Bloome, D., & Egan-Robertson, A. (1993). The social construction of intertextuality in classroom reading and writing lessons. *Reading Research Quarterly, 28*(4), 305–333. doi:10.2307/747928

Brown, V. L., Wiederholt, J. L., & Hammill, D. D. (2009). *Test of Reading Comprehension: TORC* (4th ed.). Austin, TX: Pro-Ed Inc.

Brozo, W. G. (1990). Hiding out in secondary content classrooms: Coping strategies of unsuccessful readers. *Journal of Reading, 33*(5), 324–328.

Camitta, M. (1990). Adolescent vernacular writing: Literacy reconsidered. In A. A. Lunsford, H. Moglen, & J. Slevin (Eds.), *The right to literacy* (pp. 262–267). New York: Modern Language Association.

Cazden, C. B. (1985). Social context of learning to read. In H. Singer & R. B. Ruddell (Eds.), *Theoretical models and processes of reading* (pp. 595–629). Newark, DE: International Reading Association.

Chandler-Olcott, K., & Mahar, D. (2003). "Tech-savviness" meets multiliteracies: Exploring adolescent girls' technology-mediated literacy practices. *Reading Research Quarterly, 38*(3), 356–385.

Cowan, P. M. (2005). Putting it out there: Revealing Latino visual discourse in the Hispanic academic summer program for middle school students. In B. V. Street (Ed.), *Literacies across educational contexts: Mediating learning and teaching* (pp. 145–169). Philadelphia, PA: Caslon Publishing.

Dillon, D. R. (1989). Showing them that I want them to learn and that I care about who they are: A microethnography of the social organization of a secondary low-track English-reading classroom. *American Educational Research Journal*, *26*(2), 227–259.

Dressman, M., Wilder, P., & Conner, J. C. (2005). Theories of failure and the failure of theories: A cognitive/sociocultural/macrostructural study of eight struggling students. *Research in the Teaching of English*, *40*, 8–61.

Erickson, F., & Schultz, J. (1997). When is a context? Some issues and methods in the analysis of social competence. In M. Cole, Y. Engeström, & O. Vaszquez (Eds.), *Mind, culture, and activity: Seminal papers from the Laboratory of Comparative Human Cognition* (pp. 1–21). Cambridge, UK: Cambridge University Press.

Finders, M. (1996). "Just girls": Literacy and allegiance in junior high school. *Written Communication*, *13*, 93–129.

Franzak, J. (2006). *Zoom*: A review of the literature on marginalized adolescent readers, literacy theory, and policy implications. In B. M. Gordon & J. E. King (Eds.), *Review of Educational Research* (Vol. 76, pp. 209–248). Washington DC: American Educational Research Association.

Golden, J. M. (1988). Structuring and restructuring text. In J. Green & J. Harker (Eds.), *Multiple perspective analysis of classroom discourse*. Nowood, NJ: Ablex.

Gumperz, J. J. (1981). Conversational inferences and classroom learning. In J. Green & C. Wallat (Eds.), *Ethnographic approaches to face-to-face interaction* (pp. 3–23). Norwood, NJ: Ablex.

Gustavson, L. (2007). *Youth learning on their own terms*. New York: Routledge.

Hall, L. A. (2007). Understanding the silence: Struggling readers discuss decisions about reading expository text. *Journal of Educational Research*, *100*(3), 132–141.

Heath, S. B. (1983). *Ways with words: Language, life, and work in communities and classrooms*. Cambridge, UK: Cambridge University Press.

Hirsch, E. D., Kett, J. F., & Trefil, J. S. (1987). *Cultural literacy: What every American needs to know*. Boston, MA: Houghton Mifflin.

Holland, D., Lachicotte, W., Skinner, D., & Cain, C. (1998). *Identity and agency in cultural worlds*. Cambridge, MA: Harvard University Press.

Hymes, D. (1994). Toward ethnographies of communication. In J. Maybin (Ed.), *Language and literacy in social practice* (pp. 11–22). Clevedon, UK: The Open University.

Ivey, G. (1999). A multicase study in the middle school: Complexities among young adolescent readers. *Reading Research Quarterly*, *34*(2), 172–193.

Lam, W. S. E. (2009). Multiliteracies on instant messaging in negotiating local, translocal, and transnational affiliations: A case of an adolescent immigrant. *Reading Research Quarterly*, *44*(4), 377–397.

Leander, K. M., & Lovvorn, J. F. (2006). Literacy networks: Following the circulation of texts, bodies, and objects in the schooling and online gaming of one youth. *Cognition and Instruction*, *24*(3), 291–340.

Lewis, C. (2008). Internet communication among youth: New practices and epistemologies. In J. Flood, S. B. Heath, & D. Lapp (Eds.), *Handbook of research on teaching literacy through the communicative and visual arts* (Vol. II, pp. 237–246). Newark, DE: International Reading Association.

Lewis, C., & Fabos, B. (2005). Instant messaging, literacies, and social identities. *Reading Research Quarterly*, *40*(4), 470–501.

McDermott, R. (1993). Acquisition of a child by a learning disability. In S. Chailklin & J. Lave (Eds.), *Understanding practice* (pp. 269–305). Cambridge: Cambridge University Press.

McDermott, R., & Varenne, H. (1995). Culture as disability. *Anthropology & Education Quarterly*, *26*(3), 324–348. doi:10.1525/aeq.1995.26.3.05x0936z

Mahiri, J. (1994). Reading rites and sports: Motivation for adaptive literacy of young African American males. In B. J. Moss (Ed.), *Literacy across communities* (pp. 121–146). Cresskill, NJ: Hampton Press.

Mead, G. H. (1934). *Mind, self, society*. Chicago, IL: University of Chicago Press.

Moje, E. B. (1996). "I teach students, not subjects": Teacher–student relationships as contexts for secondary literacy. *Reading Research Quarterly*, *31*, 172–195.

Moje, E. B. (2000). To be part of the story: The literacy practices of gangsta adolescents. *Teachers College Record*, *102*, 652–690.

Moje, E. B., Overby, M., Tysvaer, N., & Morris, K. (2008). The complex world of adolescent literacy: Myths, motivations, and mysteries. *Harvard Educational Review*, *78*, 107–154.

Moll, L. C., & González, N. (1994). Lessons from research with language-minority children. *Journal of Reading Behavior*, *26*(4), 439–456.

Moll, L. C., & Greenberg, J. (1990). Creating zones of possibilities: Combining social contexts for instruction. In L. C. Moll (Ed.), *Vygotsky and education* (pp. 319–348). New York: Cambridge University Press.

Nicholson, T. (1984). Experts and novices: A study of reading in the high school classroom. *Reading Research Quarterly*, *19*(4), 436–451.

Nicholson, T. (1985). The confusing world of high school reading. *Journal of Reading, 28*, 514–526.

O'Brien, D. G. (1998). Multiple literacies in a high school program for "at-risk" adolescents. In D. E. Alvermann, K. A. Hinchman, D. W. Moore, S. Phelps, & D. Waff (Eds.), *Reconceptualizing the literacies in adolescents' lives* (pp. 27–49). Mahwah, NJ: Lawrence Erlbaum Associates.

Phelps, S. F. (2005). *Ten years of research on adolescent literacy, 1994–2004: A review* (pp. 1–33). Naperville, IL: Learning Point Associates.

Purcell-Gates, V. (1995). *Other people's words: The cycle of low literacy*. Cambridge, MA: Harvard University Press.

Scholastic (2008). *The lexile framework for reading: A system for measuring reader ability and text complexity.* Available at http://teacher.scholastic.com/products/sri_reading_assessment/Lexile_Framework.htm.

Shuman, A. (1986). *Storytelling rights: The uses of oral and written texts by urban adolescents*. Cambridge, UK: Cambridge University Press.

Stone, C. A., & Learned, J. E. (2013). Atypical language and literacy development: An integrative perspective. In C. A. Stone, E. R. Silliman, B. J. Ehren, & G. P. Wallach (Eds.), *Handbook of language and literacy: Development and disorders* (2nd ed., pp. 5–25). New York: Guilford Press.

Street, B. V. (1984). *Literacy in theory and practice*. Cambridge, UK: Cambridge University Press.

Vygotsky, L. S. (1986). *Thought and language* (A. Kozulin, Trans.). Cambridge, MA: Massachusetts Institute of Technology.

# 15

# Classroom Influences on Individual Differences

*Richard L. Allington and Rachael Gabriel*

Classroom-level influences on individual reading development in US public schools have consistently been a topic of study since the early 1900s (e.g., Fulton, 1914; Betts, 1937), in part because of the differential impact of various factors of classroom instruction on individuals (e.g., Stanovich, 1986; Allington, 1977). Though conceptualizations and methodologies have evolved over time, two principles have remained consistent across sets of findings: texts matter, and tasks matter for individuals' reading development. Each is explored here in turn.

## Texts Matter

Texts matter for reading development for two central reasons. First, as part of an interaction between student, text and task, the content and difficulty of the text is central to the success of the experience and therefore volume of practice. Second, texts matter because individuals differ in their interests and background knowledge. Both of these differences influence student engagement when reading and when attempting to read.

### Skills- versus Meaning-Emphasis Texts

The reading wars, as the debates have been called, are largely over the sorts of emphases that should guide beginning reading instruction. Two broad approaches have been argued as the best approach for beginning readers (Pressley & Allington, 2014). Skills-emphasis proponents argue vociferously for lessons focussed on phonemic segmentation, letter–sound relationships, and the use of decodable texts because "breaking the code" is the central task facing beginning readers. Meaning-emphasis proponents argue that understanding what is read should be the central focus on initial reading lessons if only because reading with understanding is the ultimate goal. What has been demonstrated is that children learning with either emphasis learn different things than had they been given lessons with the other emphasis (e.g., Barr, 1975) but these differences have not been linked to differences in reading achievement as commonly measured on standardized tests.

Barr (1975) contrasted the reading performances of children taught with either skills or meaning emphasis. The skills-emphasis program was organized around teaching basic decoding skills and reading decodable texts. The meaning-emphasis program was organized around developing both a large sight word vocabulary and reading natural language texts. Barr summarizes her findings, pupils taught with a skills-emphasis (decoding) approaches:

> come up with nonsense words, and their word substitutions do more violence to sentence meaning than do those of pupils using a sight word strategy. So we must conclude that even though children using a phonics strategy draw from natural language, they are not really treating reading as a natural language experience. However, children using a sight word strategy draw from natural language . . . in the sense that they do not make nonsense word responses; nevertheless they cannot treat reading as a general natural language experience because they are constrained by the set of previously learned reading words. (p. 581)

Juel and Roper/Schneider (1985) contrasted the performances of children taught with either a skills-emphasis or a meaning-emphasis reading program. While they found some differences in the abilities these groups of children displayed when asked to read words in isolation over the school year, by the end of the first grade year they noted that performances on a standardized reading achievement test did not differ between groups and concluded, "The interpretation of the results of this study do not constitute advocacy for any one specific approach to beginning reading instruction" (p. 150). Similar findings comparing the reading performances of children using either decodable or predictable texts were reported by Jenkins, Peyton, Sanders, and Vadasy (2004).

Mathes et al. (2005) contrasted two reading interventions for struggling first grade readers. One intervention offered an explicit focus on decoding and used decodable texts. The second intervention followed a more implicit framework for developing decoding proficiencies with standard scope and sequence of decoding skills to be taught. Children in this intervention read from predictable texts. The authors report that children in the explicit decoding treatment were better at single-word decoding but children in the implicit decoding treatment produced oral reading that was more fluent. There were no differences between the groups on the standardized test of reading achievement. They concluded that, "Perhaps the most important finding of this research is that supplemental intervention derived from different theoretical perspectives were both effective. These findings suggest to us that there is likely not 'one best approach' and not one right philosophy or theory for how to best meet the needs of struggling readers" (Mathes et al., 2005, p. 179).

It seems we can conclude that different approaches to beginning reading can and do produce different patterns of responses to texts. What is less clear, however, is how individual differences interact with instruction representing these varied perspectives, which is perhaps why a so-called "balanced approach" to literacy instruction, with a nod to each perspective, has come into favor as classrooms have become more diverse. In other words, instead of giving some children exactly the kind of instruction that will support their reading development, and giving some of their classmates instruction that amounts to nothing more than perseveration on a weakness, or extra help on a strength, teachers tend to vary their approaches as a form of differentiation (Cuban, 1993). What also seems clear is that some children need more expert and more intensive reading instruction if they are to acquire reading proficiency alongside their peers. This point is well made by the evidence from the Mathes et al. (2005) and the Vellutino et al. (1996) studies; in both only a very few students were not reading on level by the end of first grade.

## Text Difficulty

There is a long tradition of research on optimal text difficulty, beginning with Betts (1946) and continuing with renewed fervor in recent years with the development of the Common Core State Standards and their explicit references to text complexity (e.g., Hiebert & Mesmer, 2013). Methods for quantifying text difficulty and text complexity have changed significantly over time, but the core principle that engagement in reading tasks with near-perfect accuracy oral reading after the near-perfect phrase is necessary for the acceleration of reading ability has remained consistent (Allington, McCuiston, & Billen, 2015; Ehri, Dreyer, Flugman, & Gross, 2007; Morris et al., 2011; O'Connor et al., 2002). Since individual students have various rates of fluency and accuracy, classrooms where students generally read the same whole-class text, rather than spending significant time reading individually matched or self-selected texts, are likely to sustain and widen individual differences by limiting opportunities for high rates of accuracy among certain individuals.

## High Success Reading

Individual differences in current reading ability and reading fluency turn the same text into a different experience for each reader. Students who are reading at or above their current grade level with strong oral reading accuracy are engaging in successful practice and have the opportunity to be exposed to more words than those with less fluency as they move through texts with greater speed and accuracy. They are likely to be able to overcome ambiguous sentences and infer the meaning of unknown words because they understand the majority of the text. Students with reading achievement below their current grade level are likely exposed to less text because they read text more slowly, and are engaged in a low-success reading experience that isn't likely to lead to comprehension, engagement, or the disambiguation of syntax or vocabulary. So, fifteen minutes spent reading or listening to someone read aloud from a class text might constitute optimal practice for some, and useless—even frustrating—practice for others.

Similarly, allowing students to read books on their individual levels for the same amount of time can induce individual differences in trajectories of reading growth purely because differences in fluency create differences in the volume (and complexity) of text read in a given amount of time. This means some students are getting a high volume of successful reading, and exposure to new words and text structures, while some are getting a lower volume of each in the same amount of time. In order to overcome individual differences in reading level and fluency, students not only need the opportunity to read texts at optimal levels of difficulty, they also may need to do so for different amounts of time.

This phenomenon was theoretically explained by Stanovich (1986), whose description of the "Matthew effect," explained the differential outcomes for individuals with varying reading ability as akin to the biblically based "rich get richer, poor get poorer" effect. He posited that the causal connection between reading ability and the efficiency of a cognitive process was reciprocal. This means that those who read more and better will read increasingly more text more successfully because of the "environmental quality" of their practice. Another way to put this is that high success experiences with reading breed additional high success experiences, while frustration level reading experiences limit practice and undermine the potential for future successful experiences.

Even as Anderson, Wilson, and Fielding (1988) demonstrated that time spent reading outside of school was correlated with exponential growth in word exposure and academic achievement, Stanovich's (1986) work highlights the importance of the match between reader and text as well as the varied trajectories of progress different readers will make under similar conditions. Texts that will promote optimal practice vary by individuals and these variations can lead to different outcomes for different readers, especially if the lower-achieving readers read less text and read that text with lower levels of accuracy (Foorman, et al., 2006).

## Accuracy in Text Reading

The Beginning Teacher Education Study (BTES) scientists (Fisher et al., 1978) noted that oral reading errors are often used as one measure of text difficulty. They found that the average number of errors made while reading aloud correlated negatively with achievement (second grade $r = -.36$) and fifth grade ($r = -.20$). Oral reading error rates were considered along with time on task and total allocated time for reading instruction. While all three factors were related to achievement, the correlations between error rates and achievement were stronger than the correlations for the other two aspects considered.

Anderson, Evertson, and Brophy (1979) led an experimental study of first-grade reading instruction. The treatment teachers each received printed information on 22 principles that had been developed but that focussed more on management of groups than on actual instruction (e.g., use ordered turns rather than calling on volunteers). The control group teachers used the same core reading materials but were not provided with the written principles. They found that the treatment teachers used more of the principles during their reading lessons than did the control teachers. In addition, students in treatment classrooms had superior reading at the end of the school year. While none of the principles addressed oral reading error rate, Anderson and her colleagues found, similar to Fisher et al. (1978), that "A high rate of success may be especially important when students are asked to read a passage aloud. The more mistakes made during the average reading turn, the lower the achievement" (p. 216). Again, however, little attention was paid to error rates while reading in communicating the findings of the study. Nonetheless, for over 35 years we have had good evidence that text appropriateness, as judged in relation to oral reading errors, is related to academic learning, especially to reading growth.

More recently, text difficulty has been the focus of efforts to accelerate reading growth with intervention classes. Ehri et al. (2007) noted that the reading growth of first-grade struggling readers was related to the number of texts the students had read with 98 percent accuracy or higher. In other words, as with both the BTES study (Fisher et al., 1978) and the Anderson et al. (1979) study, the volume of high-accuracy reading struggling readers engaged in explained their accelerated reading growth. Similarly, O'Connor et al. (2002) studied the effects of providing tutoring for struggling readers in grade-level texts drawn from the classrooms the children were enrolled in with tutoring using reading level matched texts that the tutors located. These third through fifth grade-level struggling readers (over half were identified as students with a learning disability) participated in tutoring sessions for 30 minutes a day, four days a week for 18 weeks (or 36 hours of intervention instruction). Both treatment conditions produced greater growth in reading proficiency than was observed in control group children.

However, the reading level matched treatment produced statistically significant differences in fluency compared to the grade-level texts treatment and control group students. Treatments had differential effects depending on degree of reading difficulties students exhibited. When examining the progress of the poorest readers, tutoring with reading level matched texts produced significantly larger gains on word identification, word attack, and fluency than tutoring with grade-level texts.

Finally, Fuchs, Fuchs, and Deno (1982) also demonstrated support for the traditional 95 percent oral reading accuracy standard. They concluded, "Our results support the use of the traditional

IRI standard of 95 percent for accuracy of word recognition. This standard of instructional level, as well as several other criteria used in informal reading assessment, agree relatively well with teachers' placements and with performance on standardized achievement tests" (p. 20).

Thus, the evidence available indicates that text difficulty plays a substantial role in an individual's reading acquisition. Elementary school students develop reading proficiency in texts where levels of oral reading errors are minimized. The findings of these studies support the original argument made by Betts (1946) that selecting reading materials that can be read with a high level of accuracy is an important aspect of effective reading lessons.

Three studies indicate that reading instruction can be modified in ways that make progress while using more difficult texts possible. In two of these studies this was accomplished, however, by using a one-to-one assisted reading support for each struggling reader. The assisted reading support was provided by better readers in their classrooms in the Morgan, Wilcox, and Eldredge (2000) study. Here, students were placed in dyads with one student a proficient reader and the other student a struggling reader. The struggling readers were all assessed as performing at non-reader, pre-primer, or primer level readers. Texts were assigned that were two to four levels above the struggling readers' demonstrated reading level. The better reader read the story aloud with the struggling reader attempting to read along with the proficient reader for 15 minutes daily for 95 days. All groups made progress, but the greatest progress was made by struggling readers who read along while the proficient reading buddy read texts two levels above their reading level. Because none of the participants engaged in assisted reading of texts at their reading level the effects of such a treatment remain unknown.

O'Connor, Swanson, and Geraghty (2010) developed two treatment groups and a control group to evaluate the effects of text difficulty on reading development. Adult tutors provided second and fourth grade struggling readers 15 minutes of reading practice three days a week for 20 weeks in texts that students could read at either 92–100 percent accuracy or with 80–90 percent accuracy. Tutors simply pronounced any words that the readers could not read accurately. They found that both tutoring groups performed better after tutoring than did the control group students who were given no tutorial support. There were no significant differences on measures of reading rate, word recognition, or comprehension between the two groups that used texts of differing difficulty levels or between students from different grade levels. The authors note that the lack of any significant effects between students tutored in materials of differing difficulty levels may be due to the fact that the differences in text difficulty were not that large.

Stahl and Heubach (2005) used grade-level texts as per school district policy in their evaluation of Fluency Oriented Reading Instruction (FORI). Features of the reading lesson included use of Oral Recitation Lesson format with story map introduction, with teacher reading story aloud, repeated reading of basal story, partner reading of basal story, choice reading every day (20 minutes), and home rereading of basal story. Students who needed extra help were given echo reading or had one section of text targeted for fluency. Thus, students in this study read the basal reader selection up to ten times with varying formats of support. These struggling readers made over a year and one-half progress in reading growth in each of the two years they participated in the study.

Summarizing the findings of this study, as well as those of the other two studies noted above, suggests that Stahl and Heubach (2005) were correct when they noted, "The instructional reading level for a given child is inversely related to the degree of support given to the reader" (p. 55). In other words, when teachers provide massive amounts of support, individuals can benefit when texts are more difficult than Betts had established as optimum level of difficulty. Our view of the research on text difficulty is that working with materials that students can read with only minimal difficulties produces the better effect in classrooms. This may only be true because few classroom teachers know how to organize the sorts of instructional scaffolding that make using more difficult texts successful.

## Engaged Reading

The second reason that texts matter is that they provide a reason and vehicle for sustained practice. Recent studies of time spent reading come from investigations of the national, federally-funded Reading First program. These studies suggest that students read for about 20 percent of a 90-minute period, or an average of 18 minutes daily (Brenner, Hiebert, & Tompkins, 2009). This modest figure represents an improvement from earlier studies of time spent reading which estimate that the average time students spend reading is eight to 14 minutes per period (Gambrell, 1984; Foerstch, 1992). Still, it accounts for less than a quarter of time allocated for learning to read. And, as the saying goes "if they don't read much, how they ever gonna get good?" (Allington, 1977). In other words, without engaging highly successful reading experiences, how could students solidify and expand their repertoire of skill and strategies? Moreover, why would they ever bother reading?

As we have learned from decades of process–product research, it is not just the time allocated for reading text, it is the quality of the engagement with text that correlates with increased achievement. Text is as important as a reason for reading as it is an object for reading.

At the heart of engaged reading is text that an individual reader finds interesting. In the absence of interesting texts, time spent reading can have little or a negative impact on reading ability by diminishing motivation to read and the quality of practice. Thorndike (1934) warned us 80 years ago that "the worst, which unfortunately occurs in basic readers and supplementary reading, is to require children to read material which they cannot understand; or can understand, but do not enjoy; or cannot understand, and would not enjoy if they could understand" (p. 19). The impact of allowing student choice of reading materials was recently demonstrated in a meta-analysis (Lindsay, 2010). The effect sizes on reading achievement were almost twice as large ($d = 0.77$ versus 0.40) in studies where children chose which books they would read as opposed to studies where children were reading books they were assigned. But while choice improves reading achievement, in most classrooms in the US it is the teacher who selects the texts students will read. This is especially true for remedial readers who are not likely to run into texts they can and want to read in class throughout the school day, and more likely to spend time practicing skills or reading along with a computerized intervention program than self-selecting texts (Allington, 1980, 1984).

Similarly, Guthrie and Humenick (2004) provide a meta-analysis of studies designed to improve engaged reading and reading comprehension. They found huge effect sizes (1.15 and 0.95) for enhancing student access to interesting texts and for student self-selection of the texts to be read, respectively. Guthrie (2004) has noted that more highly engaged readers are more successful than less engaged readers, and these differences persist despite factors that usually impact reading performance like socioeconomic status or even age (Guthrie, Shafer, & Huang, 2001). Highly engaged readers from low-income backgrounds can read at higher levels than less engaged readers from high-income backgrounds. The importance of engagement cannot be overestimated, and interesting, appropriate text options are a key ingredient for creating engaging individual interactions with text.

Creating opportunities for engaged reading requires, at minimum, the presence of choices and a range of levels that includes something each reader can read successfully (Guthrie et al., 2006). Unfortunately, this sort of experience is not aligned with traditions of instruction that favor single class texts rather than individual and/or small group reading assignments. Though such differentiated instruction is possible, even in content areas (e.g., Guthrie, McRae, & Klauda, 2007), it is rare in school settings.

As Guthrie and Wigfield (2000) noted, "an engaged reader comprehends a text not only because she can do it but because she is motivated to do it." The relationship between engaged reading and motivation to read requires principles of motivation to be brought to bear on the design of instruction and other learning opportunities (e.g., independent reading and reading in out-of-school settings). Research on motivation to read consistently indicates a downward trend in motivation as students progress through school. Though motivation is multifaceted, and types of motivation will vary by reader, interest in and choice of texts to be read can contribute to motivation for reading as well as self-efficacy for reading (Guthrie, & Wigfield, 2000). Additionally, as Pressley et al. (2003) reported, highly effective primary grade teachers provide both such texts as well as abundant opportunities to read such texts in their classrooms.

Finally, Wolk (2010) and Gallagher (2009) both argue that texts of dismal quality, assigned to students in schools, especially in middle and high school schools, lead to the ever declining interest in reading. As Wolk noted, "Children are not born hating science or social studies or even reading. We create that dislike by how we teach and what we make students read" (p. 11). Likewise, Gallagher argues that read-i-cide, defined as "the systematic killing of the love of reading, often exacerbated by the inane, mind-numbing practices found in schools" (p. 2) is the central reason so few adolescents read voluntarily. He argues that that three factors contribute to readicide in schools: (1) the dearth of interesting reading materials in schools; (2) removal of novels and other longer texts from the curriculum; and (3) students doing little reading during the school day. Ivey and Johnston (2013) provide evidence that changing the types of texts available in middle schools can influence both student achievement as well as their identities as readers. But few, if any other, middle schools currently use the "edgy," apparently engaging young adult novels that were used in their study.

Texts do matter and while we have a long tradition of teachers (or some other adult or groups of adults) selecting the texts that students will read and a long tradition of designing lessons around the reading of a single text by every student, the mounting evidence suggests that much of this tradition inhibits the development of reading proficiencies and in developing readers. When teachers create opportunities to read texts that individual students want to read, and that can be read accurately, the research suggests those individuals will make greater progress than when texts match neither criteria.

## Tasks Matter

Research on instructional effectiveness in literacy spans more than a century and includes a range of theoretical and methodological approaches. In this section we describe the results of the largest-scale studies of classroom tasks from research designed to identify effective methods of literacy teaching. Though most research in this area has focussed on reading acquisition, thus limiting investigations to the elementary grades (K–4), some research has attended to the conditions that support high achievement in middle and high school English classes. The intersection of these two complementary bodies of research centers around the notion that tasks that promote engagement with text are central, and that such tasks necessarily take into account (1) the importance of a focus on meaning rather than isolated skills work and (2) the social nature of literacy and learning. Thus individual differences in achievement may maintain or increase depending on the volume of opportunities to read, write, and talk about engaging texts with others.

In 1967 Bond and Dykstra published their findings from one of the first large-scale comparative studies of instructional programs in reading. When combined with the findings of future studies, the importance of a focus on meaning, without excluding systematic instruction on foundational skills, emerged as the central theme of research on effective instruction (Allington & Johnston, 2002; Knapp, 1995; Langer, 2001; Pressley, Allington, Wharton-MacDonald, Collins-Block, & Morrow, 2001; Taylor, Pearson, Peterson, & Rodriguez, 2003). Unfortunately, there is little evidence that this kind of instruction is commonly available to students, especially to students at highest risk for academic difficulty. In fact, the higher an individual's risk for reading difficulty because of family income levels (Dudley-Marling & Paugh, 2005) or disability label (Allington & McGill-Franzen, 1993), the less likely they are to receive meaning-focussed instruction. Instead, the most vulnerable readers are too often subjected to repetitive low-level skills practice in the absence of a balancing force of meaning-focussed instruction.

Even in the 1960s, Bond and Dykstra noted: "To improve reading instruction, it is necessary to train better teachers of reading rather than to expect a panacea in the form of materials" (p. 416). Indeed teachers, not materials, are consistently viewed as the main lever for influencing the amount of meaning-focussed instruction children have the opportunity to engage with. The exemplary teacher studies of the 1990s similarly confirmed that teachers with access to similar materials (e.g., basal reader, other textbook series, phonics program) offered reading instruction that differed and that those teachers who maintained a focus on meaning-making were more supportive of individual student learning. Of course it is easier to design and execute instruction that is focussed on discrete and/or basic skills both from a lesson planning and classroom management perspective. Classrooms that are predicated on teacher control rarely have room to venture towards higher order questions about text meaning, multiple interpretations, or discussions. Indeed extended student–student discussions about texts are rare in classrooms at any grade level (Nystrand, 2006).

As Nystrand and colleagues have demonstrated (Applebee, Langer, Nystrand, & Gamoran, 2003; Nystrand, Wu, Gamoran, Zeiser, & Long, 2003) English classrooms that ask open-ended questions and allow time for students to talk with one another about texts are consistently associated with more engaged reading, motivation to read, and higher achievement. Using micro-level analysis of classroom observations, often involving a turn-by-turn discourse analysis of classroom talk, Nystrand and others have demonstrated that robust discussions in English classes are (1) possible with expert teacher facilitation; (2) uniquely supportive of engagement and achievement; and (3) rare.

Similarly, Taylor et al. (2003) report on more and less effective teachers' lessons in high-poverty elementary schools. A central difference between these two groups of teachers was the focus on meaning that more effective teachers provided during their reading lessons. They accomplished this in a variety of ways including asking a larger number of higher-order questions, asking students to write after reading, and fostering student discussion after reading. Quoting the authors:

> One consistent finding is that higher-level questioning matters. The more a teacher asked higher-level questions, the more growth the nine target students in her class experienced on a variety of measures. The teachers who asked more high-level questions appeared to understand the importance of challenging their students to think about what they had read. In the process of asking more high-level questions, at least two thirds of the [effective] teachers emphasized character interpretation and connections to experience, and they focussed on thematic elements and student leadership in discussions more than did the [less effective] teachers (p. 22).

Connor et al. (2011) provided a framework that first-grade teachers used to individualize reading instruction. Tasks could be child-managed (independent reading) or teacher-managed (guided reading) and could focus on code aspects of reading or on meaning aspects. Teachers were guided on how much time should be allocated to each of the tasks described in the $2 \times 2$ (mode of reading/focus of instruction) panel. Basically, low readiness entering first-grade students were allocated more teacher-managed and more code emphasis activities while first graders entering with better developed beginning reading skills were assigned more child-managed and meaning emphasis activities. Reading achievement of the children in classrooms where this scheme was implemented with fidelity scored significantly better than students in classrooms without the guidance for teachers. As the authors noted, "Early literacy instruction that is balanced between basic skill, or code-based instruction, and meaningful reading experiences has been shown to be more effective than instruction that focusses on one to the exclusion of the other" (p. 174).

Langer's (2001) study of effective middle- and high-school teachers found a similar pattern of differences between more and less effective teachers. "In the higher performing schools, at least 96 percent of the teachers helped students engage in the thoughtful dialogue we call shared cognition. Teachers expected their students to not merely work together, but to sharpen their understandings with, against, and from each other. In comparison, teachers in the more typical classes focussed on individual thinking. Even when their students worked together, the thinking was parallel as opposed to dialogic" (Langer, 2001, p. 872).

Across this set of studies it seems clear that Knapp (1995) was on the mark twenty years ago when he concluded in his study of effective teaching in high-poverty urban schools that the key characteristics of high-achieving classrooms included:

- maximized opportunities to read;
- integrated reading and writing with other subject areas;
- focus on meaning and means of constructing meaning; and
- providing opportunity to discuss what was read.

But while the research completed to date suggests that Knapp was correct, there is little evidence from American classrooms that students are reading more, that reading and writing instruction has been integrated with other subjects, or that reading lessons, especially lessons for struggling readers, are focussed on developing meaning and engaging students in discussions after the texts are read. In other words, we have the evidence that a balanced version of reading instruction provides the optimal environment for fostering reading development but we still have classrooms focussed more on individual skills mastery, oral reading speed, and the ability to locate the answers to low-level literal questions. Our question is: When will educational policies and classroom practices begin to reflect what the evidence shows is effective reading instruction?

## Conclusions

Variations in classroom contexts do influence individual student outcomes. At the grossest level the sheer number of children struggling with learning to read is linked to the expertise of the classroom teacher (Pianta, Belsky, & Morrison, 2007). We also have good evidence from randomized experimental studies (McGill-Franzen, Allington, Yokoi, & Brooks, 1999; Scanlon, Gelzheiser, Vellutino, Schatschneider, & Sweeney, 2008) that providing classroom teachers with opportunities for professional development can develop the expertise needed to provide more individualized reading lessons such that participating teachers become much more effective teachers. Nonetheless, while there is currently much emphasis on student outcomes as a measure of instructional effectiveness, we see no emphasis on providing the sorts of professional development that research has indicated is so effective in developing teacher expertise and thereby facilitating more opportunities for optimal practice, engaged reading, and individual instruction.

Variation in the texts that are used in classrooms also influences student outcomes. Beginning reading programs that emphasize different aspects of the reading process (skills-emphasis versus meaning-emphasis) produce different patterns of strengths and weaknesses in students (e.g., Barr, 1975). Teacher selected texts produce different student outcomes than do texts that students select to read (e.g., Ivey & Johnston, 2013; Guthrie & Humenick, 2004; Lindsay, 2010). The difficulty of the texts children are given to read during their reading lessons also influences outcomes, with too difficult texts undermining both motivation to read and reading development (e.g., Allington, 1983; Ehri et al., 2007; Guthrie, 2008; O'Connor et al., 2002). At least for the elementary school grades, research indicates that texts that can be read with 95 percent oral reading accuracy are of an appropriate level of difficulty for fostering reading development (e.g., Allington et al., 2015; Fuchs et al., 1982; Morris et al., 2011). However, current emphases (as epitomized by the Common Core State Standards for reading and language arts) focus more on increasing text complexity and on texts selected by someone other than the student. Neither emphasis is supported by the available research on how individual students develop as readers.

Finally, the sorts of tasks that children complete day after day in school are also important aspects in what individuals are likely to learn. Summarizing the findings from the National Assessment of Educational Progress for reading, Applebee, Langer, and Mullis (1988) noted that while American students performed reasonably well on multiple-choice test items that focussed on recall of what had been read, their performance on test items (tasks) that required synthesis or analysis was dreadful. Quoting the authors, "These findings are disturbing . . . students in American schools can read with surface understanding, but have difficulty when asked to think more deeply about what they have read, to defend or elaborate upon their ideas, and to communicate them in writing" (p. 25). However, study after study has indicated that little class time and few assignments ever focus on thinking deeply or require students to defend or elaborate their arguments (e.g., Durkin, 1978; Nystrand, 2006; Taylor et al., 2003). In a similar fashion, studies indicate that attention to individual differences among students—in reading proficiencies and in personal interests—are largely ignored in favor of a one-size-fits-all batch-processing model for organizing reading instruction and intervention.

We have learned much about classroom factors that influence the development of reading proficiency. Much of what we know is largely absent from the classrooms American students attend every day. Cuban (1993) argued that a teacher from the 1800s would find modern classrooms quite comfortable places to work, if only because so little has changed since the 1800s in American classrooms. While industries as disparate as medicine and manufacturing have changed enormously since the 1800s, education and evangelism have remained largely the same. Provoking change such that all classrooms exhibit key characteristics of the various research studies remains an elusive goal. We worry that current practices in teaching children to read continues to ignore what the research tells us about the importance of attending to individual differences. We can hope that more progress will be made in the future than has been made in the past.

## References

Allington, R. L. (1977). If they don't read much, how they ever gonna get good? *Journal of Reading*, *21*(1), 57–61.

Allington, R. L. (1980). Teaching reading in compensatory classes: A descriptive summary. *Reading Teacher*, *34*, 178–183.

Allington, R. L. (1983). The reading instruction provided readers of differing abilities. *Elementary School Journal, 83*, 548–559.

Allington, R. L. (1984). Content coverage and contextual reading in reading groups. *Journal of Reading Behavior, 16*(1), 85–96.

Allington, R. L., & Johnston, P. H. (Eds.). (2002). *Reading to learn: Lessons from exemplary 4th grade classrooms.* New York: Guilford.

Allington, R. L., McCuiston, K., & Billen, M. (2015). What the research says about text complexity and learning to read. *Reading Teacher, 68*(7), 491–501.

Allington, R. L., & McGill-Franzen, A. (1993). Placing children at risk: Schools respond to reading problems. In R. Donmeyer & R. Kos (Eds.), *At-risk students: Portraits, policies, programs, and practices* (pp. 197–218). Albany, NY: SUNY Press.

Anderson, L. M., Evertson, C. M., & Brophy, J. E. (1979). An experimental study of effective teaching in first-grade reading groups. *Elementary School Journal, 79*(4), 193–223.

Anderson, R. C., Wilson, P. T., & Fielding, L. G. (1988). Growth in reading and how children spend their time outside of school. *Reading Research Quarterly, 23*, 285–303.

Applebee, A. N., Langer, J. A., & Mullis, I. V. S. (1988). *Who reads best? Factors related to reading achievement in grades 3, 7, and 11.* Princeton, NJ: Educational Testing Service.

Applebee, A. N., Langer, J. A., Nystrand, M., & Gamoran, A. (2003). Discussion-based approaches to developing understanding: Classroom instruction and student performance in middle and high school English. *American Educational Research Journal, 40*(3), 685–730.

Barr, R. (1975). The effect of instruction on pupil reading strategies. *Reading Research Quarterly, 10*(4), 555–582.

Betts, E. A. (1937). Teacher analysis of reading disabilities. Reprinted in R. D. Robinson (Ed.), *Readings in reading instruction: Its history, theory, and development* (pp. 207–211). Boston, MA: Pearson.

Betts, E. A. (1946). *Foundations of reading instruction: With emphasis on differentiated guidance* (4th ed.). New York: American Book Co.

Bond, G. L., & Dykstra, R. (1967). The cooperative research program in first-grade reading instruction. *Reading Research Quarterly, 2*(4), 5–142.

Brenner, D., Hiebert, E. H., & Tompkins, R. (2009). How much and what are third graders reading? In E. H. Hiebert (Ed.), *Read more, read better* (pp. 118–140). New York: Guilford.

Connor, C. M., Morrison, F. J., Schatschneider, C., Toste, J., Lundblom, E., Crowe, E., & Fishman, B. (2011). Effective classroom instruction: Implications of child characteristics by reading instruction interactions on first graders' word reading achievement. *Journal of Research in Educational Effectiveness, 4*(3), 173–207.

Cuban, L. (1993). *How teachers taught: Constancy and change in American classrooms, 1880–1990* (2nd ed.). New York: Longmans.

Dudley-Marling, C., & Paugh, P. (2005). The rich get richer, the poor get direct instruction. In B. Altwerger (Ed.), *Reading for profit: How the bottom line leaves children behind* (pp. 156–171). Portsmouth, NH: Heinemann.

Durkin, D. (1978). What classroom observations reveal about reading comprehension instruction. *Reading Research Quarterly, 14*, 481–533.

Ehri, L. C., Dreyer, L. G., Flugman, B., & Gross, A. (2007). Reading Rescue: An effective tutoring intervention model for language minority students who are struggling readers in first grade. *American Educational Research Journal, 44*(2), 414–448.

Fisher, C. W., Filby, N. N., Marliave, R., Cahen, L. S., Dishaw, M. M., Moore, J. E., et al. (1978). *Teaching behaviors, academic learning time, and student achievement: Final report of Phase III-B, beginning teacher evaluation study.* San Francisco, CA: Far West Laboratory for Educational Research and Development.

Foertsch, M. A. (1992). *Reading in and out of school: Achievement of American students in grades 4, 8, and 12 in 1989–90.* Washington, DC: National Center for Educational Statistics, US Government Printing Office.

Foorman, B. R., Schatschneider, C., Eakins, M. N., Fletcher, J. M., Moats, L., & Francis, D. J. (2006). The impact of instructional practices in grades 1 and 2 on reading and spelling achievement in high poverty schools. *Contemporary Educational Psychology, 31*(1), 1–29.

Fuchs, L. S., Fuchs, D., & Deno, S. (1982). Reliability and validity of curriculum-based informational reading inventories. *Reading Research Quarterly, 18*(1), 6–25.

Fulton, M. (1914). An experiment in teaching spelling. Reprinted in R. D. Robinson (Ed.), *Readings in reading instruction: Its history, theory, and development* (pp. 123–126). Boston, MA: Pearson.

Gallagher, K. (2009). *Readicide: How schools are killing reading and what you can do about it*. Portland, ME: Stenhouse.

Gambrell, L. (1984). How much time do children spend reading during reading instruction? In G. A. Niles & L. A. Harris (Eds.), *Changing perspectives on research in reading/language processing and instruction* (pp. 193–198). Rochester, NY: National Reading Conference.

Guthrie, J. T. (2004). Teaching for literacy engagement. *Journal of Literacy Research*, *36*(1), 1–28.

Guthrie, J. T. (2008). Growing motivation: How students develop. In J. T. Guthrie (Ed.), *Engaging adolescents in reading* (pp. 99–113). Thousand Oaks, CA: Corwin Press.

Guthrie, J. T., & Humenick, N. M. (2004). Motivating students to read: Evidence for classroom practices that increase motivation and achievement. In P. McCardle & V. Chhabra (Eds.), *The voice of evidence in reading research* (pp. 329–354). Baltimore: Paul Brookes Publishing.

Guthrie, J. T., McRae, A., & Klauda, S. L. (2007). Contributions of Concept-Oriented Reading Instruction to knowledge about interventions for motivations in reading. *Educational Psychologist*, *42*(4), 237–250.

Guthrie, J. T., Schafer, W. D., & Huang, C. (2001). Benefits of opportunity to read and balanced instruction on NAEP. *Journal of Educational Research*, *94*(3), 145–162.

Guthrie, J. T., & Wigfield, A. (2000). Engagement and motivation in reading. In P. M. M. Kamil, P. D. Pearson, & R. Barr (Ed.), *Handbook of reading research* (vol. III, pp. 403–422). Mahwah, NJ: Lawrence Erlbaum.

Guthrie, J. T., Wigfield, A., Humenick, N. M., Perencevich, K. C., Taboada, A., & Barbosa, P. (2006). Influences of stimulating tasks on reading motivation and comprehension. *Journal of Educational Research*, *99*, 232–245.

Hiebert, E. H., & Mesmer, H. A. E. (2013). Upping the ante of text complexity in the Common Core State Standards: Examining its potential impact on young readers. *Educational Researcher*, *42*(1), 44–51.

Ivey, G., & Johnston, P. H. (2013). Engagement with young adult literature: Outcomes and processes. *Reading Research Quarterly*, *48*(3), 255–275.

Jenkins, J. R., Peyton, J. A., Sanders, E. A., & Vadasy, P. F. (2004). Effects of reading decodable texts in supplemental first-grade tutoring. *Scientific Studies of Reading*, *8*(1), 53–85.

Juel, C., & Roper/Schneider, D. (1985). The influence of basal readers on first grade reading. *Reading Research Quarterly*, *20*(2), 134–152.

Knapp, M. S. (1995). *Teaching for meaning in high-poverty classrooms*. New York: Teachers College Press.

Langer, J. A. (2001). Beating the odds: Teaching middle and high school students to read and write well. *American Educational Research Journal*, *38*(4), 837–880.

Lindsay, J. J. (2010). *Children's access to print material and education-related outcomes: Findings from a meta-analytic review*. Naperville, IL: Learning Point Associates.

McGill-Franzen, A., Allington, R. L., Yokoi, L., & Brooks, G. (1999). Putting books in the classroom seems necessary but not sufficient. *Journal of Educational Research*, *93*(2), 67–74.

Mathes, P. G., Denton, C. A., Fletcher, J. M., Anthony, J. L., Francis, D. J., & Schatschneider, C. (2005). The effects of theoretically different instruction and student characteristics on the skills of struggling readers. *Reading Research Quarterly*, *40*(2), 148–182.

Morgan, A., Wilcox, B. R., & Eldredge, J. L. (2000). Effect of difficulty levels on second-grade delayed readers using dyad reading. *Journal of Educational Research*, *94*(2), 113–119.

Morris, D., Bloodgood, J. W., Perney, J., Frye, E. M., Kucan, L., Trathen, W., . . . Schlagal, R. (2011). Validating craft knowledge: An empirical examination of elementary-grade students' performance on an informal reading assessment. *Elementary School Journal*, *112*(2), 205–233.

Nystrand, M., Wu, L. L., Gamoran, A., Zeiser, S., & Long, D. A. (2003). Questions in time: Investigating the structure and dynamics of unfolding classroom discourse. *Discourse Processes*, *35*(2), 135–198.

Nystrand, M. (2006). Research on the role of classroom discourse as it effects reading comprehension. *Research in the Teaching of English*, *40*, 392–412.

O'Connor, R. E., Bell, K. M., Harty, K. R., Larkin, L. K., Sackor, S. M., & Zigmond, N. (2002). Teaching reading to poor readers in the intermediate grades: A comparison of text difficulty. *Journal of Educational Psychology*, *94*(3), 474–485.

O'Connor, R. E., Swanson, H. L., & Geraghty, C. (2010). Improvement in reading rate under independent and difficult text levels: Influences on word and comprehension skills. *Journal of Educational Psychology*, *102*(1), 1–19.

Pianta, R. C., Belsky, J., Houts, R., & Morrison, F. (2007). Opportunities to learn in America's elementary classrooms. *Science*, *315*(5820), 1795–1796.

Pressley, M., & Allington (2014). *Reading instruction that works: The case for balanced teaching* (4th ed.). New York: Guilford.

Pressley, M., Allington, R. L., Wharton-MacDonald, R., Collins-Block, C., & Morrow, L. (2001). *Learning to read: Lessons from exemplary first-grade classrooms*. New York: Guilford.

Pressley, M., Dolezal, S. E., Raphael, L. M., Mohan, L., Roehrig, A. D., & Bogner, K. (2003). *Motivating primary grade students*. New York: Guilford.

Scanlon, D. M., Gelzheiser, L. M., Vellutino, F. R., Schatschneider, C., & Sweeney, J. M. (2008). Reducing the incidence of early reading difficulties: Professional development for classroom teachers versus direct interventions for children. *Learning and Individual Differences*, *18*(3), 346–359.

Stahl, S. A., & Heubach, K. (2005). Fluency oriented reading instruction. *Journal of Literacy Research*, *37*(1), 25–60.

Stanovich, K. E. (1986). Matthew effects in reading: Some consequences of individual differences in the acquisition of literacy. *Reading Research Quarterly*, *21*, 360–407.

Taylor, B. M., Pearson, P. D., Peterson, D. S., & Rodriguez, M. C. (2003). Reading growth in high-poverty classrooms: The influences of teacher practices that encourage cognitive engagement in literacy learning. *Elementary School Journal*, *104*(1), 4–28.

Thorndike, E. L. (1934). Improving the ability to read. *Teachers College Record*, *36*(1), 1–19.

Vellutino, F. R., Scanlon, D. M., Sipay, E. R., Small, S. G., Pratt, A., Chen, R., & Denckla, M. B. (1996). Cognitive profiles of difficult-to-remediate and readily remediated poor readers: Early intervention as a vehicle for distinguishing between cognitive and experiential deficits as basic causes of specific reading disability. *Journal of Educational Psychology*, *88*(4), 601–638.

Wolk, S. (2010). What should students read? *Phi Delta Kappan*, *91*(7), 9–16.

# 16

# Discursive Contexts, Reading, and Individual Differences

*Peter Johnston and Gay Ivey*

Children are apprenticed into reading practices in their classrooms, immersed in particular forms of talk and particular kinds of texts. They bring to these engagements a wide range of individual differences, and the significance of these differences for their participation in reading practices is determined in large part by classroom context. In this chapter, we focus on the ways in which classroom talk and individual differences are linked to students' reading and to their development, particularly in the context of the texts they read. For example, in some classrooms, talk and activities focus on certain individual differences and project them onto a linear scale of competence through language like, "That's what good readers do," or "You're a really good writer," and through language invoking "levels" of competence. The question underlying such classroom discourse is, "Who is capable and who is not?" and children construct literate identities and relationships from those made available within that discursive structure. On the other hand, some classroom contexts foreground individual differences in perspective and experience, rather than differences in skill, because they make dialogic interaction possible and frame the differences as expanding the resources available for meaning making. The underlying question is, "How can we understand this more deeply?" Classrooms focused on making sense create relationally different literate communities and invite different literate identities than those focused on finding out who is most and least capable. In other words, individual differences become meaningful in the context in which they find themselves.

Consider fourth grade student, Sean. When asked whether there are different kinds of readers in his class, he observed that, "There's ones like the people who's not good and the people who are good" (Johnston, 1999). When asked to imagine he had a penpal in another class and wanted to find out about him as a reader—what kind of questions he would ask—he responded, "Maybe ask them what reading level you read at." As for whether he likes to contribute to class discussions, he commented, "Not really. 'Cause I think that what Mrs. Wilson does is right. She sort of starts off easy and then she gets real hard with the questions." Notice that this is about the construction of self and the construction of other, with important relational implications. It is also about the interpretation of difference—which differences are significant and in which ways. In another classroom (Johnston, Jiron, & Day, 2001, pp. 228–229), Henry, when asked the same question about different kinds of readers, populates his world very differently: "Steve, he reads longer books than other people. And Dan. When he gets into a book, you're not going to stop him, like if you say, 'Hey, Dan, listen to this sentence.' He's . . . not going to come out of that book. Jenny, she reads hard books like Steve. But, umm she finishes books, like, really fast . . . Priscilla. She really likes to read mysteries." He goes on describing differences at some length. Consistent with these descriptors, he would ask a penpal, "What kind of books do you like? Who's your favorite author? What book are you reading now? . . . Have you read any good books lately?" In other words, the individual differences Sean and Henry notice, and the significance they attribute to those differences, are worlds apart. Sean's world is populated by readers with fixed properties, good and bad. Henry's is populated by readers who are different in ways that are more dynamic, interesting, and non-hierarchical.

These constructions of self and other are composed from the materials made available in classroom talk. Classroom talk influences the ways students engage with texts, with each other, and with themselves by changing the significance of particular individual differences and literate events. These different constructions have consequences for a range of patterns of learning behavior including students' responses to failure (Diener & Dweck, 1978, 1980), their likelihood of choosing challenging tasks in the interests of learning (Mueller & Dweck, 1998), and their likelihood of asking for help when they run into difficulty. These implications extend into students' social and moral lives, influencing, for example, their propensity to stereotype (Levy & Dweck, 1999), and their views of morality and punishment (Chiu, Dweck, Tong, & Fu, 1997). As we shall see, these latter are not independent of views of reading or of academic learning. For example, when people who are learning something together disagree, if they enter Sean's good–bad, right–wrong world, they will likely turn the disagreement into a relational conflict and diminish their view of their partner's competence (Darnon, Doll, & Butera, 2007). If they are operating within Henry's more dynamic world, they are likely to focus instead on resolving the disagreement, merging the two perspectives, and in the process actually come to view their partner as more competent.

## Texts and Individual Differences

Text complexity and personal relevance both have implications for the kind of classroom talk invoked. There is no question that individual children bring very different interests to reading and that often those interests are not served by the text opportunities they find in schools (Ivey & Broaddus, 2001; Worthy, Moorman, & Turner, 1999). When children get to choose the texts they read, the discursive dynamics of the classroom change (Ivey, & Johnston, 2013; Wigfield et al., 2008). Choice commonly invites a sense of autonomy and personal relevance, provided the choices are meaningful, which in turn increases the likelihood of engagement and puts the child in control of the reading. Engagement has powerful consequences for children's development as readers and as human beings (Ivey, & Johnston, 2013; Wigfield, et al., 2008) in part because when students are fully engaged in reading, they develop different forms of talk.

Text complexity, in the abstract, also has implications for classroom talk, though these implications depend on the context. When children read texts that are well within their automatic processing repertoire, either offering no new information or failing to create interesting points of confusion, or are beyond their available strategic repertoire, opportunities for agentive narratives arise less frequently than if the text is at the outer edge of their repertoire. Similarly, readers encountering very challenging personally relevant texts are more likely to continue to act strategically than if the text is not personally relevant (Guthrie, Wigfield, & You, 2012). Likewise, children reading alone can only draw on their internalized repertoire of strategies or independently generate new strategies. By contrast, in a context where others (peers, teacher, family) are available, readers can solicit or collaboratively generate new strategies—provided the relational properties of the community enable help-seeking.

For example, consider the following description by eighth-grade student Ileana:

> Like I talk to Magdelena about what happens in the books. The books she hasn't read I give her a little bit of info about it. She can read it when she's done with her book. And some parts I have to get off my mind and talk through with her. And she helps me get through parts I'm stuck at. I'm either confused or it's bugging me. Like, then I'll go back to the book and I figure out what has happened, then I go back and tell her about it.

This student's comment describes a relationship in which each student brings something different to the practice of reading, and each contributes to the development of both readers and also to their personal relationship. Ileana gets support when she runs into difficulty and an attentive ear when she needs help to think through the issues that arise in the text. Magdelena also gets a responsive ear along with book recommendations. It is their differences within the context of their reading relationship that fuel their interactions.

These relational properties are generated by and evident in the discursive life of the class. In other words, the nature and context of the texts children read are more or less likely to invite and sustain children's construction of agentive narratives—narratives that represent them as individuals whose actions have intentional effects. Ileana can make her agentive claim about figuring things out and helping a peer because the classroom talk makes it possible to generate such narratives—talk in which individual differences can be taken up collaboratively to produce knowledge and strategic problem-solving (Ivey & Johnston, 2013).

## Capitalizing on Individual Differences

In the remainder of this chapter, as with the example of Ileana and Magdelena (above), illustrations of student and classroom talk come from eighth-grade classes in which students choose the books they read and discuss those books with and without the teacher. Only one to three copies of any book exist in the school, and instruction occurs in teacher-led read alouds and conversations between the teacher and individuals, small groups, or the whole class, and among students themselves without the teacher. Because the teachers are focused centrally on getting students engaged, the books are young adult novels that include personally relevant issues (e.g., relationships, racism, gangs, cultural difference, gender, drugs, suicide, and sexuality).

As a way to make individual differences concrete, consider two students: Lana, an honors student, and Rashad, a student whose less than stellar school career was coupled with experience with gang life. Introduced to the book, *My Bloody Life: The Making of a Latin King* (Sanchez, 2000), Rashad experienced fully engaged reading for the first time. Within the pages of this autobiography, Rashad took up Reymundo Sanchez's life as a Latin King and lived it as a potential future, putting himself in dialogic relationships with the book characters and with himself. He then set out to convince his classmates to experience the same powerful experience. Lana, however, was not keen on reading books about gang life. Indeed, Rashad had reported early in the year that there was no way people like her would ever read such books and that "Lana hates gang members." However, Lana found Rashad's fascination with the book compelling, so she tried it herself. She was deeply troubled by the narrator's confessions of the disturbing things he had done as a gang member, and she could not see eye to eye with him since it was completely outside of her experience. She made her perspective clear to Rashad who, with his peers Maurice and Emilio, talked her through why, as they understood from the text, the author did the things he had done—what his motives might have been. Lana said that Rashad talked her through it as if he were the author. She said she was able to see other possibilities from the author's perspective, and because of that she observed, "Me and that book will always have a better relationship." This also changed her relationship with Rashad as they took up conversations about other books. In this context, individual differences matter in terms of reading and the repositioning of expertise and relationships. Individual differences can be a source of growth, particularly in the context of personally meaningful texts and relationships.

On the other hand, there are many individual differences among students that are never capitalized on because other differences obscure the important ones. For example, in middle and high schools it is common for the "skaters" not to talk with the "Goths" or the cheerleaders, and vice versa. Student differences are visibly marked as statements of identity. In order for these students to actually engage and benefit from their differences, they need to be involved in conversations. In our research (Ivey & Johnston, 2013), we have found that students who are engaged in a book that they find disquieting, discover that they have to talk to someone about it. If there are only a couple of copies of the book in circulation, students will talk with whoever has read the book, regardless of group identity, as one girl asserted:

> It's like ok there's this thing where I like dress different from other people and then if ... like I wear like band T's and everything and then the girl will wear like Aeropostale and the cheerleaders clothes or whatever and I found myself talking to them about books. Whoa! They're actually cool to talk to about books and everything.

As a consequence of these exchanges, the relational properties of the classroom change, including an increase in trust, producing a cascade of additional changes in the ways in which students engage their reading, a change in students' social imaginations, their agency in reading, their critical reading, their reading mechanics, the breadth of their reading and their book knowledge, not to mention their reading test scores (Ivey & Johnston, 2013). In other words, in a context in which students are engaged with personally meaningful texts, individual differences can become an engine for growth in readers along many dimensions.

Individual differences in perspective and framing, if actively engaged in classroom reading conversations, as they are in dialogic classes, also stand to make readings more meaningful and more memorable (Nystrand, 2006). This aligns with research on mindfulness in which critical learner characteristics (and thus, discursive characteristics) include openness to novelty, alertness to distinction, sensitivity to different contexts, and implicit (if not explicit) awareness of multiple perspectives (Langer, 1997). In that context, it is not surprising that in discussions in which classroom conversations encourage students to think of things in different ways, and to notice different elements—a core feature of dialogic classrooms—students remember their readings better (Nystrand, 2006), or that the process is more engaging (Ivey & Johnston, 2013). It is also likely that the process is less frustrating.

## Identities: Who Are We?

A person's identities are certainly a dimension of individual difference, and identities have been linked to classroom discourse in multiple ways. Riessman (1993) has observed that "individuals become the autobiographical narratives by which they tell about their lives," and conversations that take place in classroom life offer students opportunities to place themselves in academic narratives in which they are particular kinds of people. For example, a student observed: "I feel like I used to be a very social person, and I'm not a very academic person, but I can actually like have conversations about books, now, which is kind of weird for me" (Ivey & Johnston, 2013). This observation reveals a clash of identities developed over different timescales (Wortham, 2005)—the current classroom life in the context of a history of schooling over many years. This sort of shift has been referred to as "restorying" (Worthy, Consalvo, Bogard, & Russell, 2012). The example, also reflects Wortham's (2004) conclusion that the academic and social are thoroughly intertwined and that within the academic talk of the classroom, students are not only learning subject matter, they are becoming "identified as recognizable types of people" (p. 715).

However, it is also important that students not view these identities as fixed but as ones over which they have some choice. Whether or not they view identities as malleable depends on classroom talk. When a student or students accomplish a literate task, the narrative a teacher attaches to that event is important—both how it is represented and the suggested causal process through which it was accomplished. Naming the nature of the event as "your expression that made us imagine what it was like to be Angel [the protagonist]" would be different from naming the event as getting all the words right, because these different responses name "what we are doing here" (Johnston, 2004). Attributing an outcome to good reader status has different implications from attributing it to the strategic actions taken by the reader. These distinctions offer narratives that explain what kind of people are involved—people who are good or not good at something (a fixed characteristic) versus people who act strategically (a dynamic characteristic). Furthermore, because the feedback is offered publicly, the strategic information in the dynamic framing becomes available to all children within earshot.

In other words, classroom talk can maximize and minimize the significance and the valence of particular individual differences, in the process influencing the identities students develop about selves and other. For example, when a student expresses an idea that is particularly divergent from what was expected, whether the teacher chooses to judge the accuracy of the response or to value the participation and the possibility that the response might cause new thinking, is consequential. Worthy and her colleagues (Worthy et al., 2012) provide just such an example when a second-grade student makes a claim about fairies and her teacher, Mae, responds as follows:

*Mae*: Lydia, thank you for waiting.
*Lydia*: Um, I have a fairy named Violet, and she's—purple. She's like—I read about that kind, it's like this kind of fairy, that protects your, you from bad dreams. She's actually real [inaudible].
[Lydia turns to a student next to her and says, "It *is* real."]
*Mae*: And you know you started a little draft in your WW [writer's notebook] about Violet.
*Lydia*: Yeah you can get [inaudible].
*Mae*: Really? Do you think you might like to add on to Violet's story? Maybe? Because the words that you just said? Those would be the words you would write down in your WW. And that would be your story.

Mae's response to Lydia publicly positions Lydia as a person who is to be respected ("thank you for waiting") and who has interesting things to say—things that should be written in her writer's notebook. At the same time, she demonstrates what will be valued in the community and how not to rush to judge peer differences in beliefs and experience. She represents Lydia and her ideas as valued both by listening to her and by showing she is familiar with, and interested in, her writing projects. Persistent interactions of this sort result in changing the identities of the students, as Worthy and her colleagues point out.

Classroom teachers play a key role in orchestrating the discourse within which these identities are constructed (Johnston, 2012; Moje, 1997; Wortham, 2003), but the identities are mutually negotiated, and the individual differences students bring to the negotiation include identity work performed over the months and years of previous school life along with their links to historically available identities such as those associated with race, gender, and (dis)ability including those offered by characters in the literature being read (Wigfield et al., 2008).

The ways students experience reading, individually and collaboratively, alter the relational properties of the classroom in reciprocal ways and alter the course of student development. Consider the following example. In November, Deandra, a female African American student in the class, made the following observation about Angela (her teacher and the orchestrator of the above classroom interactions): "She helps me to understand books more. It makes me think more educated in my mind when I read because of how she talks to me." Notice that she is not saying her teacher tells her she is more educated, rather, she is noticing a change in the way she herself thinks and talks, and attributing the change to her teacher. As a way of situating her observation, consider a conversation that took place that same month when Angela was reading aloud a chapter from *Jumping Off Swings* (Knowles, 2009), in which it is clear that the main female character, who is pregnant, suspects that the mother of one of her friends will be an adult she can trust with her secret. Deandra raises her hand and asks a question based on an intertextual connection which would be an unlikely event in a classroom in which everyone reads the same text, minimizing individual differences:

*Deandra*: Would that be like the person that the counselor was to Sonia [a character in *The Secret Story of Sonia Rodriguez* (Sitomer, 2010)]?

*Angela*: I can understand the connection you're making. I'd like us to help each other think deeper and broader. Can you think of similar relationships in other books the way Deandra did?

*Saul*: I think that woman police officer was trying to do that in *Living Dead Girl*.

*Lionel*: *Gym Candy*—he had someone like that . . .

*Dereanna*: He needed one in *A Child Called It* [Pelzer, 1995].

[Two other students add examples from *I Heart You, You Haunt Me* (Schroeder, 2008) and *Something Like Hope* (Goodman, 2010).]

*Angela*: I love how Deandra made us think about the word for that—confidante.

Notice how Angela has positioned Deandra as a person who initiates academic conversations using academic language. Later in the year, Deandra comments about aspects of a new role she has taken up: "Jennifer and Natalia, they show me books that they've read, and if they didn't like a book I'll try it out and see what they struggled with and try to help them." At the end of the year, when asked whether her family sees her differently, she adds: "They think I'm more educated because I read more. They always tell me to put down the book because I'm always reading."

These ways of talking suggest major shifts in identity, supported by the ways in which Deandra is positioned and then positions herself. She is supported in her new identity by others both inside and outside the classroom community. At the same time, Angela has shown the students how valuable difference is to their learning, and how listening to each other's contributions can benefit them. This has relational implications as well as learning implications.

## Talk Around Texts

We offer here an example from one of the eighth-grade classes described earlier. The example unfolds over a period of 15 minutes during a read aloud of a young adult novel *What Happened to Cass McBride?* (Giles, 2007)*,* a psychological thriller told in shifting perspectives and complicated further by frequent flashbacks. Their previous read aloud, *Jumping Off Swings* (Knowles, 2009) was also told from multiple perspectives, providing a point of reference for the complexities in *Cass McBride*. Students are highly engaged in the book and Angela, the teacher, quotes a student from another of her classes, saying that "The worst part of the book is getting to the end." In line with this, she notes that Conner, a student in the present class, said that he is slowing down in his reading because he doesn't want his book *Leverage* (Cohen, 2012) to end, indicating to students that reading speed is not an indicator of ability. The interaction then proceeds as follows.

The word "premeditation" occurs in the first sentence, and Angela pauses to ask what the class thinks the word means. A student breaks up the word into roots, and Angela writes those parts on the board (pre, meditate, -tion) and says: "Sometimes when we use roots to figure out the meaning of the word, we have to start at the end of the word and move to the front to define it. The act (-tion) of thinking (meditate) before (pre)."

The concept of premeditation is essential to the book, which deals with the crime of abduction, which is why Angela chooses the word as an opportunity to briefly draw students' attention to using affixes as a tool for sense-making. A student offers the initial analysis and Angela merely builds on it with two sentences. The actual definition is not provided, requiring active construction from the students. This is a typical "lesson" in this class in that it is offered conversationally at a point of high engagement for maximal meaningfulness, and it is deliberately brief both not to lose engagement and because some students already know this information (an individual difference she cannot ignore).

Angela reads that the character gives the victim drugs. She responds to the students' sharp reaction:

> Why are you freaking out? I think I know why. She's already taken some drugs before. We know that because we know her perspective. She's already taken two Xanax, but we learned that in her chapter. He doesn't know that, so he gives her more drugs. We react because we have multiple perspectives, but the characters don't know each other's experiences.

Capitalizing on the students' intense reaction, Angela briefly explains multiple perspectives by showing the significance of their knowing that one character knows something that another does not. In the process, she expands their social imaginations, the consequences of which include improved comprehension of narrative, but also improved self-regulation, social behavior (Kaufman & Libby, 2012; Lysaker, Tonge, Gauson, & Miller, 2011) and friendship networks (Ivey & Johnston, 2013). and their possible selves (Markus, & Nurius, 1986). These are changes in individual differences that have substantial reach not only into reading competence, but also into human development. Angela also reminds them to hold multiple perspectives in mind at the same time, sustaining the dialogicality of the reading. That is, she asks them to concurrently embrace multiple individual differences.

Next, a student expresses confusion about whether the narration is in the past or present. That the student is comfortable doing so is crucial because it enables on-demand teaching. It is also an indicator of the condition of the learning community in the classroom, which operates from a dynamic model in which students are focused on making sense rather than finding out who is the most capable (Dweck, 2000). When the student chooses to admit to lack of understanding, he is offering what, from his perspective, might be an individual difference—a difference that in another context might be taken as an indication of incompetence. Angela's reaction to his admission is exactly what makes the admission possible (Johnston, 2012). She points out that such confusions are to be expected. They're normal and are a result of the structure of the book. Confusions are not indicators of inability but expected indicators of learning: "That's not surprising, the confusion, because there are so many flashbacks that help us get to what the character is thinking." Angela not only makes the student's confusion normal, but reminds the class of the significance of characters' thinking, and of the literary terminology. She then reads an example of a flashback—another instance of explicit instruction. The flashback example involves the narrator, the older brother, who is remembering when he taught the younger brother how to climb trees. Angela stops suddenly:

*Angela*: This is settling heavy on my heart (pauses for a few seconds)
*Student*: If he hadn't taught him how to climb trees, maybe he wouldn't be dead.
*Student*: Wait a minute. He hung himself from a tree.
*Student*: Maybe he feels guilty for him hanging himself.
*Student*: He can't feel guilty for that.
*Angela*: Doesn't grief cause you to think in irrational ways?
*Student*: Didn't the girl do something to make him kill himself though?
*Student*: Maybe they went on a date and she didn't like him.
*Angela*: We don't know yet, do we? The author is leaving these huge gaps. And it's up to us to infer.
*Student*: I like that. It makes you think, and it makes you want to get into the book more. You don't want all the answers on one page. You want to think.
*Angela*: Do you remember in *The Secret Story of Sonia Rodriguez* [Sitomer, 2010] how the inferences we made initially were wrong. We learned that when we kept reading. We were surprised at the end, and that was fun. We don't know yet.

In a different classroom, the teacher would have taken the opportunity to explain the story more. Angela chooses instead to invite dialogic engagement with two different moves. First, she talks about what is going on in her mind, again expanding students' social imaginations. Second, rather than ask a question and control the conversation, she pauses and leaves space for students to say something—a move that allows more entry points to the conversation, accommodating a wider range of individual differences. Had she asked a question, she would have taken a step toward controlling the conversation. Instead, each of the subsequent student responses is marked by uncertainty or disagreement, encouraging further contributions from other students. Angela's only comment, "Doesn't grief cause you to think in irrational ways?" simply complicates the disagreement, preserving the dialogicality of the conversation and the uncertainty.

Angela's "We don't know yet . . ." again emphasizes the uncertainty, and points out the roles of author and reader, incidentally making it clear that reading and writing are social practices. This prompts a student to point out that s/he likes the uncertainty requiring filling in the gaps because the process produces thinking and engagement. Angela does not judge the student's response but reinforces the comment by reminding them of their positive experience in an earlier book when their attempts to resolve the uncertainty were misplaced, producing a more exciting and satisfying conclusion. Her aim is to help the students relish working with uncertainty and different perspectives in books (and perhaps in life), and to position all the students as engaged in collaborative knowledge construction, not as people who are confused and thus incompetent.

Throughout this sequence of exchanges, there is no rush to closure. On the contrary, there is a careful maintenance of openness and multiple perspectives which not only extends engagement but also likely reduces the students' need for closure which in turn influences the ways in which students will perceive and interact with each other (Kruglanski, Pierro, Mannetti, & Grada, 2006). In addition, at no point does Angela call on particular people to respond or take turns. The class offers a symmetrical power space in which everyone, including the teacher, is positioned equally. The message is that everyone present is a thinking person engaged in and trying to make sense of people's actions as an author has portrayed them. In other words, the characteristics of texts are, in part, mediated by the conversational context within which they are read. In particular, sustaining uncertainty invites inquiry and engagement (Johnston, 2012; Langer, 1989) and teachers can mark uncertainty by adding "perhaps," "maybe," or "I wonder" to their conversational contributions. When a teacher suggests that the answer to a question is uncertain, or that there are likely multiple answers, students are inclined to take up the issue. By contrast, eliminating uncertainty by, for example, asking known-answer questions and using the definite article asking for *the* main idea, would shift control of the conversation to the teacher, produce a monological arrangement, and remove the sense of autonomy from the students.

## Implicit Theories of People and Knowledge

One way in which language gains additional leverage is by invoking theories of how the world operates. For example, students can take up a dynamic theory of human characteristics theorizing human beings as being able to change, or a fixed model in which human beings are made up of rather immutable characteristics. Experimental research suggests that when people take up a dynamic theory in which intellect, personality, and other individual differences are malleable, they value trying hard, and attend closely to the processes through which people accomplish things. Relative to those who take up a fixed theory, they are also more likely to disagree productively (Darnon, et al., 2007), slower to judge and form stereotypes (Plaks, Dweck, Stroessner, & Sherman, 2001), more likely to avoid tasks that are too easy and to choose novel and challenging tasks in the interests of learning (Mueller, & Dweck, 1998), more likely to value collaboration, and more likely to manage social transgressions by trying to understand the thinking and context that produced the transgression and to forgive rather than seek retribution (Chiu et al., 1997). Within a dynamic theory, students gain a sense that they can choose who they will become.

Classroom talk can foreground either a fixed or a dynamic theory through quite small differences in language. A common way to invoke a fixed theory is to use person-oriented praise (or criticism), such as "good girl" or "you're really good at this" (Kamins & Dweck, 1999). But consider how Angela foregrounds a dynamic theory in the following interactions in read alouds:

*Angela*: See this is where I know she is a dynamic character . . . this is the point where I know she is changing. This is a big moment for her. . .she does something a different way.

At the end of reading the book *The Secret Story of Sonia Rodriguez* (Sitomer, 2010), Sonia and her mother had not resolved their issues. Angela again takes the opportunity to point to the possibility of character change:

*Student 1*: I think the mother was probably sad.

*Student 2*: I think she was just sad for losing her TV, not about her relationship with Sonia.

*Angela*: That's possible, that she's sad only about the TV, given what we know about her character typically. But suppose she's changed. Could she be more than a static character?

Similarly, in discussing *Jumping Off Swings* (Knowles, 2009), Angela again points to a dynamic view of human nature:

*Angela*: Her mom has such an amazing opportunity to change. Do you know who that reminds me of?

*Natalia*: Sonia's mother [from *The Secret Story of Sonia Rodriquez* (Sitomer, 2010)].

In each case, Angela directs students' attention to a dynamic model of human nature foregrounding the possibility of personal change and possibility. This same language begins to show up in students' language as they talk about books, as in this example about character in *Jumping Off Swings* (Knowles, 2009):

*Fahima*: Do you think she'll ever change, be a dynamic character by speaking out or something like that? I can see her doing that.

*Angela*: So, your decision is, as soon as she has the baby, what will make her change is the fact that she'll stand up for her baby? I see what you mean.

This language shows up in students' speech even when the students are talking with each other about books without the teacher present, as when they are discussing *Yummy* (Neri & Duburke, 2010), a nonfiction book about a boy in a gang who was killed at age 12:

*Rashad*: If Yummy had lived, I think he would have changed his life.

As we noted earlier, the fact that teacher and students sustain a dynamic model of human characteristics as they discuss characters in books, rather than one that invokes character traits, has important implications for the ways they deal with success and failure, the narratives they tell about themselves, and the ways in which they relate to each other and to themselves.

There are parallel epistemological theories linked to the type of classroom talk (Johnston, 2012; Johnston et al., 2001). Epistemologically, we can view knowledge as fixed—certain, context- and perspective-free facts—or as dynamic—contextualized, always tentative, and linked to perspectives (Johnston, 2012). As with the theories about characteristics of people, these theories about knowledge have consequences (Bråten & Strømsø, 2005). In particular, the valuing of uncertainty and difference and the lack of pressure to get to a singular answer are associated with a reduced need for closure which in turn is associated with greater tolerance for and interest in diversity, increased efforts to understand and engage individual differences, reduced tendency to stereotype, and resistance to autocratic interactions (Kruglanski, Pierro, Mannetti, & Shah, 2002; Pierro, Mannetti, De Grada, Livi, & Kruglanski, 2003; Shah, Kruglanski, & Thompson, 1998) .

Indeed, within the kind of talk evident in Angela's classroom, students report a preponderance of exactly these characteristics, often providing the causal logic. Consider this illustrative interaction in which Audrey and Sapphire are introducing a new student to potentially interesting books:

*Audrey*: [Introducing books to a new girl in school, notes that girls like *Twisted* (Anderson, 2007)] . . . because it goes into the boy's psyche.
*Sapphire*: These books go to all sorts of points of view. It will help you understand things.

Here, Sapphire recognizes the value of multiple points of view—individual difference in perspective—for her own development. In the following example a student's response to Angela's comments about uncertainty in a book indicate he is not interested in simple answers, nor is he in a rush to get to the bottom of things:

*Angela*: We don't know yet, do we? The author is leaving these huge gaps. And it's up to us to infer.
*Student*: I like that. It makes you think, and it makes you want to get into the book more. You don't want all the answers on one page. You want to think.

This student recognizes the engaging value of uncertainty and welcomes continued lack of closure for that reason.

In other words, classroom talk contains implicit theories about knowledge and about people, theories that can be evoked by the language choices the teacher makes. These theories have consequences for students' views of self and other and for their relationships that go well beyond what might be expected. In terms of students' reading, these theories affect the possible interactions they can have around texts, whether they can disagree productively, whether they can admit to having difficulty and ask for help, how they react when they run into difficulty, and how they experience confusion in their reading.

## Conclusions

In reading research, "individual differences" commonly refers to differences in constructs such as genetic makeup (Eicher & Gruen, 2013), ability to allocate attention (Kieffer, Vukovic, & Berry, 2013), phonological processing (Maïonchi-Pino, Magnan, & Ecalle, 2010) or sensitivity to speech rhythm (Holliman et al., 2008). As other chapters in this volume demonstrate, such differences certainly exist among children and are likely to influence the processes of reading and learning to read. Much of the research focusing on individual differences frames them in terms of potential deficits and as fixed capacities. It is easy to view them this way when reading is seen as merely a psychological process of decoding standard texts accurately. Our approach has been to assume that reading and learning to read are fundamentally social practices rather than merely psychological (Rowe, 2010; Street, 1995), that there are many kinds of differences among individual human beings, most of which are more dynamic than fixed, and that the significance of individual differences for reading and learning to read is determined by the social context—the positioning, the relationships, and the implicit theories about people, knowledge, and reading.

When reading is viewed as a fully dialogic social practice, individual differences in perspective and history can become particularly salient because they invite productive dialogic interaction (Ivey & Johnston, 2013). In that context, students asserting that they need a different perspective on a text, in order to understand it better, constitutes an important step in their literate development. These dialogic engagements, at the very least, open up the possibility of expanding comprehension beyond what is likely in the context of interactions between the reader and text alone (I. G. Wilkinson, & Son, 2011). We have also argued that this recognition of the value of difference is an important step in students' epistemological development—indeed, their human development. When children approach each other for new perspectives on an event from a book, or prominently display a book they are reading in order to attract conversations about it, these are reading strategies—strategies that occur in some classroom contexts and not in others.

Individual difference is what makes the dialogical possible, and the uncertainties produced make the learning engaging because they offer the possibility of agency in the production of knowledge. However, the realization of individual differences as significant in this way is only likely to occur in classrooms that frame individual differences in constructive ways. Similarly, the texts that are made available in classrooms, and how they are made available have consequences for children's engagement and their talk around texts, which in turn, influences their development. Individual choice in reading material fosters a sense of autonomy and relevance (Guthrie & Wigfield, 2000), both of which alter the discursive nature of the classroom by expanding the diversity of experience—the range of individual differences that can be capitalized on (Ivey & Johnston, 2013). As students recognize the value of others' experiences for their own understanding, "ability," as announced by individual differences in text processing at the word level and below, does not translate to status, so power is distributed symmetrically rather than asymmetrically in the community. This is the circumstance in which heterogeneous grouping is productive—when ability is not cast in terms of status (C. Wilkinson & Silliman, 2000). This is also why engagement matters, because when students are fully engaged, they are normally at the edge of their capabilities (Csikszentmihalyi, 1990), which is when they find that they need others to enable them to move forward.

We have also argued that classroom talk contains implicit theories about people and knowledge that have important consequences for children's literate development, and these theories are invoked by rather small differences in the ways language is used and taken up by students in significant ways. Teachers are normally in a discursively powerful positions in classrooms. They have a controlling voice in establishing which theories of people, knowledge, and reading are in play, with all that implies for the intellectual life of the classroom and thus for children's development. For this reason we need to take seriously conditions that affect the likelihood that teachers will take up language that makes the best use of individual differences in classroom life. For example, we know that people under pressure do not deal well with individual differences (Kruglanski et al., 2006). Similarly, assessment systems that represent reading as a cognitive decoding process with a premium on speed are likely to have an adverse effect on teachers' ability to use classroom talk that embraces a dialogic view of reading and places a positive value on individual differences.

## Young Adult Literature References

Anderson, L. H. (2007). *Twisted*. New York: Viking.

Cohen, J. (2012). *Leverage*. New York: Dutton.

Deuker, C. (2007). *Gym Candy*. New York: Houghton-Mifflin.

Giles, G. (2007). *What Happened to Cass McBride?* Boston, MA: Little, Brown.

Goodman, S. (2010). *Something Like Hope*. New York: Delacorte.

Knowles, J. (2009). *Jumping Off Swings*. Somerville, MA: Candlewick.

Neri, D., & Duburke, R. (2010). *Yummy: The Last Days of a Southside Shorty*. New York: Lee & Low.

Pelzer, D. (1995). *A Child Called It*. Deerfield Beach, FL: HCI.

Sanchez, R. (2000). *My Bloody Life: The Making of a Latin King*. Chicago, IL: Chicago Review Press.

Schroeder, L. (2008). *I Heart You, You Haunt Me*. New York: Simon Pulse.

Scott, E. (2008). *Living Dead Girl*. New York: Simon Pulse.

Sitomer, A. (2010). *The Secret Story of Sonia Rodriguez*. New York: Hyperion.

# References

Bråten, I., & Strømsø, H. I. (2005). The relationship between epistemological beliefs, implicit theories of intelligence, and self-regulated learning among Norwegian postsecondary students. *British Journal of Educational Psychology, 75*(4), 539–565.

Chiu, C., Dweck, C. S., Tong, J. Y., & Fu, J. H. (1997). Implicit theories and conceptions of morality. *Journal of Personality and Social Psychology, 73*(5), 923–940.

Csikszentmihalyi, M. (1990). *Flow: The psychology of optimal experience.* New York: HarperCollins.

Darnon, C. L., Doll, S. B., & Butera, F. (2007). Dealing with a disagreeing partner: Relational and epistemic conflict elaboration. *European Journal of Psychology of Education, 22*(3), 227–242.

Diener, C. I., & Dweck, C. S. (1978). An analysis of learned helplessness: Continuous changes in performance, strategy, and achievement cognitions following failure. *Journal of Personality and Social Psychology, 36*(5), 451–462.

Diener, C. I., & Dweck, C. S. (1980). An analysis of learned helplessness: II. The processing of success. *Journal of Personality and Social Psychology, 39*(5), 940–952.

Dweck, C. S. (2000). *Self-theories: Their role in motivation, personality, and development.* Philadelphia, PA: Psychology Press.

Eicher, J. D., & Gruen, J. R. (2013). Imaging-genetics in dyslexia: Connecting risk genetic variants to brain neuroimaging and ultimately to reading impairments. *Molecular Genetics & Metabolism, 110(3),* 201–212. doi: 10.1016/j.ymgme.2013.07.001

Guthrie, J. T., & Wigfield, A. (2000). Engagement and motivation in reading. In M. L. Kamil, P. B. Mosenthal, P. D. Pearson, & R. Barr (Eds.), *Handbook of reading research, Vol. III* (pp. 403–422). Mahwah, NJ: Erlbaum.

Guthrie, J. T., Wigfield, A., & You, W. (2012). Instructional contexts for engagement and achievement in reading. In S. Christensen, C. Wylie, & A. Reschly (Eds.), *Handbook of research on student engagement* (pp. 675–694). New York: Springer.

Holliman, A. J., Wood, C., & Sheehy, K. (2008). Sensitivity to speech rhythm explains individual differences in reading ability independently of phonological awareness. *British Journal of Developmental Psychology, 26(3),* 357–367.

Ivey, G., & Broaddus, K. (2001). "Just plain reading": A survey of what makes students want to read in middle school classrooms. *Reading Research Quarterly, 36*(4), 350–377.

Ivey, G., & Johnston, P. H. (2013). Engagement with young adult literature: Outcomes and processes. *Reading Research Quarterly, 48*(3), 255–275.

Johnston, P. H. (1999). Unpacking literate "achievement". In J. Gaffney & B. Askew (Eds.), *Stirring the waters: A tribute to Marie Clay* (pp. 27–46). Portsmouth, NH: Heinemann.

Johnston, P. H. (2004). *Choice words: How our language affects children's learning.* Portland, ME: Stenhouse.

Johnston, P. H. (2012). *Opening minds: Using language to change lives.* Portland, ME: Stenhouse.

Johnston, P. H., Jiron, H. W., & Day, J. P. (2001). Teaching and learning literate epistemologies. *Journal of Educational Psychology, 93*(1), 223–233.

Kamins, M. L., & Dweck, C. S. (1999). Person versus process praise and criticism: Implications for contingent self-worth and coping. *Developmental Psychology, 35*(3), 835–847.

Kaufman, G. F., & Libby, L. K. (2012). Changing beliefs and behavior through experience-taking. *Journal of Personality and Social Psychology, 103*(1), 1–19.

Kieffer, M. J., Vukovic, R. K. & Berry, D. (2013). Roles of attention shifting and inhibitory control in fourth-grade reading comprehension. *Reading Research Quarterly, 48(4),* 333–348.

Kruglanski, A. W., Pierro, A., Mannetti, L., & Grada, E. D. (2006). Groups as epistemic providers: Need for closure and the unfolding of group-centrism. *Psychological Review, 113*(1), 84–100.

Kruglanski, A. W., Pierro, A., Mannetti, L., & Shah, J. Y. (2002). When similarity breeds content: Need for closure and the allure of homogeneous and self-resembling groups. *Journal of Personality and Social Psychology, 83*(3), 648–662.

Langer, E. J. (1989). *Mindfulness.* Reading, MA: Addison-Wesley.

Langer, E. J. (1997). *The power of mindful learning.* Reading, MA: Addison-Wesley.

Levy, S. R., & Dweck, C. S. (1999). The impact of children's static versus dynamic conceptions of people on stereotype formation. *Child Development, 70*(5), 1163–1180.

Lysaker, J. T., Tonge, C., Gauson, D., & Miller, A. (2011). Reading and social imagination: What relationally oriented reading instruction can do for children. *Reading Psychology, 32*(6), 520–566.

Maïonchi-Pino, N., Magnan, A., & Écalle, J. (2010). The nature of the phonological processing in French dyslexic children: evidence for the phonological syllable and linguistic features' role in silent reading and speech discrimination. *Annals of Dyslexia, 60(2)*, 123–150. doi: 10.1007/s11881–010–0036–7

Markus, H., & Nurius, P. (1986). Possible selves. *American Psychologist, 41*, 954–969.

Moje, E. B. (1997). Exploring discourse, subjectivity, and knowledge in chemistry class. *Journal of Classroom Interaction, 32*(2), 35–44.

Mueller, C. M., & Dweck, C. S. (1998). Praise for intelligence can undermine children's motivation and performance. *Journal of Personality and Social Psychology, 75*(1), 33–52.

Nystrand, M. (2006). Research on the role of classroom discourse as it affects reading comprehension. *Research in the Teaching of English, 40*(4), 393–412.

Pierro, A., Mannetti, L., De Grada, E., Livi, S., & Kruglanski, A. W. (2003). Autocracy bias in informal groups under need for closure. *Personality and Social Psychology Bulletin, 29*, 405–417.

Plaks, J. E., Dweck, C. S., Stroessner, S. J., & Sherman, J. W. (2001). Person theories and attention allocation: Preferences for stereotypic versus counterstereotypic information. *Journal of Personality and Social Psychology, 80*(6), 876–893.

Riessman, C. K. (1993). *Narrative analysis* (Vol. 30). Newbury Park, CA: Sage Publications.

Rowe, D. W. (2010). Directions for studying early literacy as social practice. *Language Arts, 88*(2), 134–143.

Shah, J. Y., Kruglanski, A. W., & Thompson, E. P. (1998). Membership has its (epistemic) rewards: Need for closure effects on in-group bias. *Journal of Personality and Social Psychology Bulletin, 75*, 383–393.

Street, B. (1995). *Social literacies: Critical approaches to literacy in development, ethnography, and education.* New York: Longman.

Wigfield, A., Guthrie, J. T., Perencevich, K. C., Taboada, A., Klauda, S. L., McRae, A., & Barbosa, P. (2008). Role of reading engagement in mediating effects of reading comprehension instruction on reading outcomes. *Psychology in the Schools, 45*(5), 432–445.

Wilkinson, I. G., & Son, E. H. (2011). A dialogic turn in research on learning and teaching to comprehend. In M. L. Kamil, P. D. Pearson, E. B. Moje, & P. P. Afflerbach (Eds.), *Handbook of reading research* (Vol. 4, pp. 359–387). New York: Routledge.

Wilkinson, L. C., & Silliman, E. R. (2000). Classroom language and literacy learning. In M. L. Kamil, P. B. Mosenthal, P. D. Pearson, & R. Barr (Eds.), *Handbook of reading research* (Vol. 3, pp. 337–360). Mahwah, NJ: Lawrence Erlbaum.

Wortham, S. (2003). Curriculum as a resource for the development of social identity. *Sociology of Education, 76*, 228–246.

Wortham, S. (2004). The interdependence of social identification and learning. *American Educational Research Journal, 41*, 715–750.

Wortham, S. (2005). *Learning identity: The joint emergence of social identification and academic learning.* Cambridge: Cambridge University Press.

Worthy, J., Consalvo, A. L., Bogard, T., & Russell, K. W. (2012). Fostering academic and social growth in a primary literacy workshop classroom: "Restorying" students with negative reputations. *Elementary School Journal, 112*(4), 568–589.

Worthy, J., Moorman, M., & Turner, M. (1999). What Johnny likes to read is hard to find in school. *Reading Research Quarterly, 34*(1), 12–27.

# 17

# Language Differences that Influence Reading Development

## Instructional Implications of Alternative Interpretations of the Research Evidence

*Jim Cummins*

## Introduction

During the past decade, four major syntheses of research evidence have been published regarding the academic achievement of students whose home language (L1) is different from the dominant language of instruction at school (henceforth termed *linguistically diverse students*). Three of these syntheses have focused primarily on research and policy issues in the United States and one has focused on the performance of immigrant-background students on the Organisation for Economic Co-operation and Development's (OECD) Programme for International Student Assessment (PISA). The most comprehensive review carried out in the United States context was the report of the National Literacy Panel on Language-Minority Children and Youth entitled *Developing Literacy in Second-Language Learners* (August & Shanahan, 2006, 2008a). This report appeared in the same year as a volume edited by Genesee, Lindholm-Leary, Saunders, and Christian (2006) entitled *Educating English Language Learners: A Synthesis of Research Evidence*. More recently, the California Department of Education (2010) published *Improving Education for English Learners: Research-Based Approaches*, which highlighted the instructional implications and applications of the research evidence. Dolson and Burnham-Massey (2011) addressed similar issues in an adjunct monograph entitled *Redesigning English-Medium Classrooms: Using Research to Enhance English Learner Achievement* published by the California Association for Bilingual Education.

The synthesis of research provided by the OECD's PISA research program differs from those outlined above insofar as the findings derive entirely from the PISA's own dataset, which includes the academic performance of hundreds of thousands of 15-year-old students in countries around the world. The program, which reported initial results in 2000 and several times since then, focusses primarily on reading, mathematics, and science achievement and has identified a number of background and school-based predictors of achievement. PISA is intended to provide member countries with a "report card" on the effectiveness of their educational systems, including the relative success of students from immigrant backgrounds. The findings have highlighted the extent of immigrant-background students' underachievement in many affluent countries and also the considerable variability across countries in the extent to which these students succeed academically (Christensen & Segeritz, 2008; Christensen & Stanat, 2007; OECD, 2010a, 2010b, 2010c, 2010d, 2012; Stanat & Christensen, 2006).

These four syntheses of the empirical research regarding the role of linguistic differences in reading development and other aspects of academic achievement are invaluable in compiling and critically analyzing the research findings. However, all four syntheses (with the exception of the Dolson & Burnham-Massey (2011) monograph) suffer from significant limitations in the ways in which the research has been interpreted and linked to educational policy and classroom instruction. In this chapter, I propose an alternative interpretation of the research relating language differences to reading and highlight a very different set of implications for policy and practice. Briefly stated, the three research syntheses carried out in the United States context acknowledge the legitimacy both of students' L1 as a cognitive resource and bilingual education as a policy option but largely ignore the extensive empirical evidence highlighting the centrality of literacy engagement in the development of reading comprehension. These reports also focus primarily on *linguistic mismatch* as a cause of underachievement that can be addressed by more effective teaching of language and literacy. By focusing on linguistic variables in isolation from the ways in which language differences between home and school intersect with socioeconomic status (SES) and patterns of societal power relations in the wider society, they fail to identify instructional interventions that are of central importance for students' academic achievement.

By contrast, the PISA reports highlight the strong statistical relationship between reading engagement and reading achievement but, for the most part, position students' L1s as part of the problem rather than as part of the solution to the achievement gap experienced by immigrant-background students in many countries. Linguistic mismatch and presumed lack of exposure to the dominant language are posited as independent causal variables in some of the PISA reports despite the fact that we have known for more than 30 years that linguistic mismatch, by itself, cannot explain the empirical data (Cummins, 1979, 1986). None of the major research syntheses (again, with the exception of Dolson & Burnham-Massey (2011)) adequately examines data relating to the role of societal power relations and their manifestation in patterns of teacher–student identity negotiation as factors relevant to understanding patterns of academic outcomes. The alternative interpretation of the data, which I elaborate in this chapter, proposes *literacy engagement* and *identity affirmation* as central components of effective literacy instruction for linguistically diverse students who are learning the language of instruction.

The following sections map out important dimensions of individual differences associated with language and school achievement among linguistically diverse students. These individual differences are not fixed or static; language and literacy development are always nested within social contexts from birth and within educational contexts from the onset of schooling. Children's opportunities for language and literacy development are significantly affected by the interactions they experience with adults within these contexts. Thus, individual differences associated with language and literacy development are in a dynamic relationship with clusters of social variables such as SES and the extent of marginalization/discrimination in the wider society experienced by different communities. Similarly, the extent to which school instruction responds in an evidence-based way to the learning needs of linguistically diverse students will significantly affect their opportunities to learn and succeed academically. Thus, individual differences are not fixed invariant attributes of the individual but are shifting constantly in response to social and educational interactions.

## Dimensions of Difference

The international research literature on "educational disadvantage" typically identifies three categories of students who are at risk of educational difficulties: (1) linguistically diverse students whose L1 is different from the dominant language of school and society, (2) students from low-SES backgrounds, and (3) students from communities that have been marginalized or excluded from educational and social opportunities (often over generations) as a result of discrimination in the wider society. Although these three groups frequently overlap, they are conceptually distinct. Some students may fall into all three categories of potential disadvantage (e.g., Roma students in Europe, many Latino/a students in the United States), others may fall into two categories (e.g., English-L1 low-SES Native American students), while some may be characterized by only one dimension (e.g., Romanian-L1 students from highly educated parents learning English in the United States). Although the major focus of the present chapter is on differences in achievement associated with language, these differences cannot be isolated from potential disadvantages associated with socioeconomic variables and long-term discrimination in the wider society.

It is important to note that, in a similar way to individual differences in general, "disadvantage" is not a fixed or static construct; significant components of the background experiences of the three groups specified above are transformed into actual educational disadvantages only when the school fails to respond appropriately to these background experiences. For example, a home–school language switch becomes an educational disadvantage only when the school fails to provide effective support to enable students to learn the school language (Cummins, 1986, 2001; Dolson & Burnham-Massey, 2011). Effective educational responses can also reduce some of the negative consequences associated with SES (e.g., provision of breakfast programs or free/reduced lunches can at least partially offset nutritional inadequacies at home caused by poverty). Similarly, the effects of racism in the wider society can be significantly ameliorated when the school implements instruction that actively challenges the devaluation of students and communities in the wider society. These forms of instruction build on the "funds of knowledge" (González, Moll, & Amanti, 2005) within students' communities and have been variously labeled culturally relevant (Ladson-Billings, 1994, 1995), culturally responsive (Gay, 2010), and culturally sustaining (Paris, 2012). Thus, the creation of actual educational disadvantage is not socially determined by the realities outside of school. Rather, it is a dynamic process which is socially constituted within the structures of schooling and the interactions between teachers and students.

The major interpretative problem with the four syntheses of research outlined previously is that they focus on *language* differences between home and school, and students' consequent need to learn the school language, in isolation from the social context within which these language differences are embedded. As a result, their instructional prescriptions focus on more effective ways to develop students' academic language proficiency without integrating these instructional responses with those that are implied by the research on SES and marginalized group status. As noted above, only Dolson and Burnham-Massey (2011) highlight in a substantive way the relevance of societal power relations to student academic outcomes. They point out that stigmatized minority groups such as Native Americans, African Americans, and Hispanics have been historically subordinated through forms of violence such as war, slavery, forced relocation, and genocide. These historical realities and their current vestiges must be taken into account in the design of effective instruction for linguistically diverse learners.

The research literature documenting how home–school language difference, family income/educational status, and social marginalization/exclusion intersect with educational variables is summarized in Table 17.1 and in the following sections.

*Table 17.1* Dynamic relationships between dimensions of students' background and educational responses

| Student background | Linguistically diverse | Low-SES | Marginalized status |
|---|---|---|---|
| Sources of potential disadvantage | • Failure to understand instruction due to home–school language difference | • Inadequate prenatal care<br>• Inadequate nutrition<br>• Lead exposure<br>• Housing segregation<br>• Lack of cultural and material resources in the home due to poverty<br>• Range of language interaction<br>• Inadequate access to print in home and school<br>• Overall school quality; etc. | • Societal discrimination<br>• Low teacher expectations<br>• Stereotype threat<br>• Identity devaluation |
| Evidence-based instructional response | • Scaffold comprehension and production of language across the curriculum<br>• Reinforce academic language across the curriculum | • Maximize literacy engagement<br>• Reinforce academic language across the curriculum | • Connect instruction to students' lives<br>• Create contexts of student empowerment and identity affirmation thorough culturally sustaining instruction |

The evidence-based instructional responses listed in Table 17.1 are relevant for students from all three categories, as well as for dominant-group students who are native speakers of the school language. However, the specific instructional responses specified for each group are those that respond directly to the causal chain implied by the sources of potential disadvantage.

## Literacy Achievement among Linguistically Diverse Students

### Patterns of Performance

Labels such as "linguistically diverse," "English learner" (EL), or "English language learner" (ELL) are somewhat misleading because they imply homogeneity within the category based on the fact that students are required to learn the language of instruction in order to succeed academically. In fact, there is major variation both in the life circumstances and academic outcomes of linguistically diverse students both within and across countries.

The variation across countries is illustrated in the performance of first- and second-generation immigrant students in the PISA 2003 and 2006 Reading Literacy measure for Australia, Canada, Denmark, Germany, and the United States (Table 17.2). First-generation students (and their parents) were born outside the host country while second-generation students are of immigrant background but were born in the host country.

*Table 17.2* PISA Reading scores for 2003 and 2006 assessments*

|  | PISA 2003 Gen 1 | PISA 2003 Gen 2 | PISA 2006 Gen 1 | PISA 2006 Gen 2 |
|---|---|---|---|---|
| Australia | −12 | −4 | 1 | 7 |
| Canada | −19 | 10 | −19 | 0 |
| Denmark | −42 | −57 | −79 | −64 |
| Germany | −86 | −96 | −70 | −83 |
| United States | −50 | −22 |  |  |

* The scores for the five countries are extracted from the broader dataset presented in Christensen and Segeritz (2008); Gen 1 = first-generation students, Gen 2 = second-generation students; negative scores indicate performance below country mean, positive scores indicate performance above country mean. The United States did not participate in the 2006 Reading assessment.

Christensen and Segeritz (2008) highlight as particularly problematic the poor performance of second-generation students in many European countries: "Of particular concern, especially for policy-makers, should be the fact that second-generation immigrant students in many countries continue to lag significantly behind their native peers despite spending all of their schooling in the receiving country" (p. 18). In some cases (Denmark and Germany in 2003; Austria and Germany in 2006) second-generation students who received all their schooling in the host country performed more poorly than first-generation students who arrived as newcomers and would likely have had less time and opportunity to learn the host country language. These data clearly suggest that factors other than simply opportunity to learn the host country language are operating to limit achievement among second-generation students in these countries.

Students' performance tends to be better in countries such as Canada and Australia that have encouraged immigration during the past 40 years and that have a coherent infrastructure designed to integrate immigrants into the society (e.g., free adult language classes, language support services for students in schools, rapid qualification for full citizenship, etc.). Additionally, both Canada and Australia have explicitly endorsed multicultural philosophies at the national level aimed at promoting respect across communities and expediting the integration of newcomers into the broader society. In Canada (2003 assessment) and Australia (2006 assessment), second-generation students performed slightly *better* academically than native speakers of the school language. By contrast, second-generation students tend to perform very poorly in countries that have been characterized by highly negative attitudes towards immigrants (e.g., Austria, Belgium, Denmark, Germany).

Some of the positive results for Australia and Canada can be attributed to selective immigration that favors immigrants with strong educational qualifications. In both countries, the educational attainments of adult immigrants are as high, on average, as those of the general population. However, the OECD (2010a) points out that differences in immigrant-background students' reading performance both within and across countries cannot be fully explained by SES.

## L2 Learning Trajectories

There is extensive evidence that linguistically diverse students typically require at least four to five years to catch up to native speakers in academic language proficiency (e.g., Collier, 1987; Cummins, 1981; Hakuta, Butler, & Witt, 2000). By contrast, it usually takes only about one to two years for students to become reasonably fluent in everyday conversational language. Some students never catch up academically and become "long term English learners" (Olsen, 2010).

Data from California after the implementation of Proposition 227 in 1998, which mandated English-only instruction for a large majority of students, show that after three years of English-only instruction, only 12 percent of English learners had acquired sufficient academic English to be redesignated as fluent English-proficient. The probability of being redesignated as English proficient after ten years in California was less than 40 percent (Parrish et al., 2006).

The longer catch-up trajectory for academic as compared to conversational language proficiency reflects both the increased linguistic complexity of academic language and the fact that linguistically diverse learners are attempting to catch up to a moving target. Every year, native speakers of the school language are increasing their literacy and academic language skills and thus L2 learners have to "run faster" in order to catch up to grade expectations. The complexity of academic language reflects (1) the vocabulary in texts that, in English, include many Latin and Greek-origin low-frequency and technical words that we almost never use in everyday conversation (e.g., predict, photosynthesis, sequence, revolution, etc.), and (2) increasingly sophisticated lexical patterns (e.g., nominalization) and grammatical constructions (e.g., passive voice) that again are almost never used in everyday conversation. Students are not only required to read this language, but also to use it use it in an accurate and coherent way in their own writing.

It remains to be seen how the advent of the Common Core State Standards (CCSS) in the United States will affect the academic catch-up trajectories of English learners. The CCSS include a strong emphasis on building a focus on both task and text complexity into the curriculum from the earliest grades. If schools respond effectively to this challenge, they could potentially accelerate academic language learning among English learners. However, an effective response will require a major reorientation in policy and practice to ensure that *all* teachers are prepared to integrate the teaching of language and content across the curriculum. It will also require an instructional realignment to address causes of underachievement associated with low–SES and marginalized group status in addition to those associated with home–school language differences, as outlined in Table 17.1.

## Two Instructional Implications of Academic Language Trajectories

The extended trajectory for academic language catch-up clearly implies that teaching linguistically diverse learners is not the responsibility only of the language specialist teacher. Classroom teachers also need to know how to scaffold instruction to make academic content accessible to students who are still in the process of catching up academically. They also need to see themselves as *language* teachers with the expertise to integrate language objectives with content objectives in their teaching (e.g., California Department of Education, 2010).

A second instructional implication derives from the fact that we find academic language predominantly in two places: classroom discourse and printed texts. Consequently, students who read extensively both inside and outside the school have far greater opportunities to acquire academic language than those whose reading is limited. This logical inference is supported by a wide range of empirical research (e.g., Brozo, Shiel, & Topping, 2007; Guthrie, 2004; Krashen, 2004; Lindsay, 2010; OECD, 2004, 2010b; Sullivan & Brown, 2013), which, unfortunately, has been largely ignored by researchers and policy-makers in the United States. Research carried out specifically with L2 learners is consistent with the overall pattern of strong relationships between literacy engagement and academic language learning. Elley and Mangubhai (1983), for example, demonstrated that fourth- and fifth-grade students in Fiji exposed to a "book flood" program during their 30-minute daily English (L2) class in which they simply read books either alone or with the guidance of their teacher, performed significantly better over a two-year period than students taught through more traditional methods. Elley (1991, 2001) similarly documented the superiority of book-based English language teaching programs among elementary school students in a variety of other international contexts.

## Students' Use of L1 in the Home: What Role Does it Play in L2 Acquisition?

It is clear from the variation in group performance both within and across countries that far more than simply a home–school language switch is influencing patterns of literacy attainment. However, the PISA data also show that, on average, immigrant-background students who use their L1 at home perform significantly lower in reading than immigrant-background students who use L2 at home. This pattern of findings has led some OECD researchers (e.g., Christensen & Stanat, 2007; OECD, 2012) and others (Esser, 2006) to interpret the negative correlations between L1 use at home and academic performance in L2 as reflecting a causal relationship. Christensen and Stanat (2007), for example, concluded: "These large differences in performance suggest that students have insufficient opportunities to learn the language of instruction" (p. 3). Esser (2006) is more explicit in arguing on the basis of PISA data that "the use of the native language in the family context has a (clearly) negative effect" (p. 64). He further argued that retention of the home language by immigrant children will reduce both motivation and success in learning the host country language (2006, p. 34).

There are persuasive grounds to call into question this interpretation of the PISA data. In the first place, no relationship was found between home language use and achievement in the two countries where immigrant students were most successful (Australia and Canada). If L1 use at home were an independent causal factor, its negative effect should be evident across multiple contexts. Furthermore, the relationship disappeared for a large majority (10 out of 14) of OECD-member countries when socioeconomic status and other background variables (e.g., age on arrival/length of residence) were controlled (Stanat & Christensen, 2006, Table 3.5, pp. 200–202). The disappearance of the relationship in a large majority of countries suggests that language spoken at home does not exert any independent effect on achievement but is rather a proxy for a variety of interacting variables such as SES, marginalized group status, and, for first-generation students, length of residence in the host country. Students who have been in the host country for only a short amount of time (and have consequently had less opportunity to learn L2) are much more likely to use their L1 at home than students who have had all their schooling in L2.

The literature review carried out by Goldenberg, Rueda, and August (2006) as part of the National Literacy Panel report found inconsistent effects associated with students' L1 use at home. They conclude that because of "conflicting and inconclusive findings, no strong practice or policy recommendations are possible with respect to language use at home" (p. 314).

My interpretation of the data is somewhat different. I would argue that the data show clearly that linguistically diverse parents who interact consistently with their children in L1 as a means of promoting bilingualism and biliteracy can do so with no concern that this will impede their children's acquisition of the school language. This interpretation is based on data showing that short-term negative associations between L1 use at home and L2 achievement disappear as students' exposure to L2 increases. Over the short term, there will inevitably be strong associations between exposure to L2 (in the home, preschool, or elementary school) and attainment in that language. A child who is minimally exposed to English at home or at preschool will show considerably less knowledge of English when tested in kindergarten than a child who has had extensive exposure to English. However, the more relevant question relates to

Jim Cummins

the longer-term effects of language choice and input in the home. There is considerable evidence with respect to this issue that use of L1 in the home entails no long-term deficits in L2 development (e.g., Bankston & Zhou, 1985; Dolson, 1985; Oller & Eilers, 2002).

## Summary

The research shows clearly that linguistically diverse students exhibit considerable variation in academic performance both within and across countries. This variation in performance reflects specific factors related to students' exposure to and opportunity to learn the host country language (e.g., length of residence in the host country) as well as the quality of educational provision they experience in host country schools. The quality of educational provision is also likely to vary according to linguistically diverse students' SES and the extent to which their communities occupy marginalized positions in the wider society. The ways in which SES and societal marginalization intersect with educational provision are examined in the following sections.

## Literacy Achievement among Low-SES Students

### SES-Related Discrepencies in Achievement

The ways in which SES exerts its negative effects on achievement have been well documented, and the factors listed in Table 17.1 illustrate just some of these effects. Among the SES-related factors that have been highlighted in the United States context as directly affecting students' educational prospects are less access to maternal prenatal care, lower quality nutrition, exposure to lead, less overall linguistic input in the home, less access to books and computers, attendance at schools with (1) less qualified teachers, (2) greater concentrations of low-SES students, and (3) significantly less funding than schools serving more affluent students (Berliner, 2009; Kozol, 2005; Orfield, 2013; Rothstein, 2013). Further evidence of the impact of socioeconomic variables is seen in the fact that interventions to address these factors produce educational benefits. Detailed reviews (e.g., Berliner, 2009) highlight extensive evidence that nonschool interventions such as increasing family income, ensuring adequate nutrition, provision of prenatal and general health care were associated with increased cognitive ability and/or academic achievement among low-income students.

The effects of SES on students' reading performance were also evident in the OECD's PISA studies: "On average across OECD countries, 14% of the differences in student reading performance within each country is associated with differences in students' socio-economic background" (OECD, 2010c, p. 14). However, this report also noted that

> Regardless of their own socio-economic background, students attending schools with a socio-economically advantaged intake tend to perform better than those attending schools with more disadvantaged peers. In the majority of OECD countries, the effect of the school's economic, social and cultural status on students' performance far outweighs the effects of the individual student's socio-economic background.
>
> (2010c, p. 14)

This finding points to the impact of societal factors related to discrimination and exclusion (as manifested, for example, in housing segregation) in determining student outcomes.

The PISA studies also show that the impact of SES on achievement varies widely between countries. For example, the relationship between SES and achievement was much stronger in countries such as Germany and the United States than it was in countries such as Canada and Norway. Despite the strong overall relationship between SES and academic performance, some countries do succeed in promoting both equity (low-SES students perform relatively well) and excellence (overall performance is strong). In fact, according to the OECD (2010c), the "best performing school systems manage to provide high-quality education to all students . . . regardless of their own background or the school they attend" (p. 13).

## Potential Impact of Evidence-Based Intervention

Some of the sources of potential educational disadvantage associated with SES are beyond the capacity of individual schools to address (e.g. housing segregation) but, as pointed out previously, the potential negative effects of other factors can be ameliorated by school policies and instructional practices. The two sources of potential disadvantage that are most relevant to the present chapter are the limited access to print that many low-SES students experience in their homes (and schools) (Duke, 2000; Neuman & Celano, 2001) and the more limited range of language interaction that has been documented in many low-SES families as compared to more affluent families (e.g., Hart & Risley, 1995). As noted in a previous section, the logical inference that derives from the differences in print access and language interaction characteristic of different SES groups is that in order to address these realities, schools serving low-SES students should (1) immerse them in a print-rich environment in order to promote literacy engagement across the curriculum and (2) focus in a sustained way on how academic language works and enable students to take ownership of academic language by using it for powerful (i.e., identity-affirming) purposes.

The potential impact of addressing these causal factors in an evidence-based way is illustrated in the fact that successive PISA studies have reported a strong relationship between reading engagement and reading achievement among 15-year-old students. The 2000 PISA study (OECD, 2004) reported that the level of a student's reading engagement was a better predictor of literacy performance than his or her SES. The report pointed out that "engagement in reading can be a consequence, as well as a cause, of higher reading skill, but the evidence suggests that these two factors are mutually reinforcing" (OECD, 2004, p. 8). In more recent PISA studies, the OECD (2010b) reported that approximately one-third of the association between reading performance and students' SES was mediated by reading engagement. The implication is that schools can potentially "push back" about one-third of the negative effects of socioeconomic disadvantage by ensuring that students have access to a rich print environment and become actively engaged with literacy.

Unfortunately, the roles of print access and literacy engagement were not identified as particularly significant in either the National Reading Panel (NRP) (2000) or National Literacy Panel (NLP) (August & Shanahan, 2006, 2008a) reports in the United States and consequently these variables have been largely omitted from policy consideration. The problematic nature of this omission is considered in a later section together with a more detailed review of research supporting the central role of literacy engagement in determining literacy outcomes.

## Literacy Achievement among Marginalized Group Students

There is extensive research, primarily from the disciplines of sociology and anthropology, that documents how societal power relations influence educational achievement (e.g., Bishop & Berryman, 2006; Carter, 2013; Ladson-Billings, 1995; Ogbu, 1978, 1992). As noted previously, groups that experience long-term educational underachievement have frequently been excluded

| Structural/societal | Structural/educational | Interpersonal |
|---|---|---|

*Figure 17.1* Continuum representing the operation of societal power relations in education

from educational and social opportunities over generations. The historical and current operation of these power structures is a direct determinant of the current low SES of many of these groups. Educators who understand how societal power relations operate to limit students' literacy development are in a position, individually and collectively, to institute school policies and instructional practices aimed at challenging this process.

As outlined in Figure 17.1, we can locate the operation of societal power relations that affect marginalized group students' academic achievement along a continuum ranging from *structural/ societal*, through *structural/educational*, to *interpersonal*. Structural/societal factors reflect societal policies and social realities over which educators have minimal control. These include unequal funding for schools serving low- and high-income communities and school segregation that derives from patterns of housing segregation (Darling-Hammond, 2010, 2013; Kozol, 2005).

Structural/educational factors include aspects of the organization of schooling such as curriculum standards and textbooks, assessment/accountability provisions, tracking and ability grouping policies, and language-of-instruction mandates. Educators within schools, both individually and collectively, can resist or attempt to mitigate the negative effects of policies that they see as detrimental to their students' academic progress.

Finally, interpersonal factors reflect the ways in which identities are negotiated between teachers and students in schools (Cummins, 2001). As an example, consider the very different messages communicated to linguistically diverse students in a school that prohibits any use of students' L1s in the classrooms or corridors compared to a school that acknowledges students' multilingualism as an intellectual and personal accomplishment and encourages them to use the totality of their linguistic skills as cognitive tools to succeed academically.

Representation of these dimensions along a continuum rather than as totally distinct categories is appropriate because, as Carter (2013) points out, "structured school practices become cultural" (p. 149). She points out that educators transmit messages to children when they categorize by ability and this practice in some schools "is highly correlated to racial and ethnic background" (p. 149).

Obviously, educators have minimal ability to influence most structural/societal dimensions of societal power relations, and only partial influence over structural/educational realities but, in principle, they have considerable control over the ways in which identities are negotiated within their schools and classrooms. The ways in which structural/societal, structural/educational, and interpersonal dimensions of societal power relations influence student engagement and achievement are sketched in the following sections.

## Structural/Societal Dimensions

In the United States, one of the most obvious examples of how societal power relations influence the academic achievement of marginalized group students is the re-segregation of schools that has occurred during the past 20 years—what Kozol (2005) has termed *the restoration of apartheid schooling*. Currently, African American and Latino/a students increasingly attend schools with high concentrations of students from similar backgrounds (Berliner, 2009; Orfield, 2013). Neighbourhood schools reflect the prevailing patterns of housing segregation. Orfield (2013) expresses the consequences of these patterns of school segregation as follows:

Schools with high concentrations of students needing strong academic support are often staffed largely by inexperienced teachers who are not yet effective educators, and some do not want to be there. The combination of weaker teachers and less-prepared classmates exposes many children in disadvantaged schools to less-challenging instruction . . . The cumulative effect is a profoundly unequal educational experience, even when there is no overt discrimination (p. 41).

Darling-Hammond (2013) summarized the US data regarding differential educational experiences according to income and racial/ethnic background as follows: "By every measure of qualifications—certification, subject matter background, pedagogical training, selectivity of college attended, test scores, or experience—less qualified teachers are found in schools serving greater numbers of low-income and minority students" (p. 87).

These realities reflect what I have termed *coercive relations of power* where power is exercised by a dominant individual, group, or country to the detriment of a subordinated individual, group, or country (Cummins, 2001). A similar pattern of housing, and consequently school, segregation is evident in many European countries, with large numbers of underachieving immigrant-background students (e.g., Belgium, Denmark, France, Germany).

## Structural/Educational Dimensions

The influence of these factors can be illustrated with reference to Sleeter's (2002, 2011) documentation of the ways in which societal power relations influence the composition of textbooks and curriculum frameworks. Her analysis of the *History-Social Science Framework for California Public Schools* (California Department of Education 2001) revealed that of the 96 Americans who were named for study, 77 percent were White, 18 percent African American, 4 percent Native American, 1 percent Latino, and 0 percent Asian American. She concluded that "racial and ethnic minorities are added consistently in a 'contributions' fashion to the predominantly Euro-American narrative of textbooks" (2011, p. 3). Her 2012 review of the impact of culturally responsive curricula that attempted to connect instruction to students' lives and cultural backgrounds found a variety of positive outcomes. She interpreted these findings as indicating that when curriculum focuses on the realities of students' lives, including racism and poverty, and gives them tools to understand and act on those realities, they become "insiders" whose background knowledge is valued and constructed as useful for academic learning. Under these conditions, students become intellectually engaged and see themselves as intellectually capable.

In short, the curriculum projects reviewed by Sleeter (2011) illustrate how schools can enhance the academic engagement of students from marginalized social groups by challenging the exclusion of students' languages, cultural histories, and current realities from the curriculum.

## Interpersonal Dimensions

Coercive relations of power also operate in the interactions marginalized group students experience with educators at school. Schools generally reflect the societies that fund them and thus devaluation of the language and culture of particular communities in the wider society is likely to be mirrored in many schools serving students from those communities. Ladson-Billings (1994, 1995) clearly expressed this relationship in arguing that "[t]he problem that African-American students face is the constant devaluation of their culture both in school and in the larger society" (1995, p. 485). She also expressed the logical implication of this reality: "When students are treated as competent they are likely to demonstrate competence" (1994, p. 123).

The impact of teacher–student identity negotiation and its relationship to broader patterns of power relationships is illustrated in the research of Bishop and Berryman (2006) who explored patterns of educational engagement among Maori youth in New Zealand. Very different perspectives on causes of students' academic disengagement emerged from interviews with educators, the students themselves, and community members. According to Bishop and Berryman (2006), many teachers explained Maori students' lack of educational achievement in deficit terms, whereas the students themselves and members of their families viewed the issue in terms of relationships and interactions. They point out that this latter perspective highlights the power differentials and imbalances between the various participants in the relationships and puts the focus on how these power differentials can and must be managed better. On the basis of interventions they helped initiate in collaboration with educators, they argue that in order to be effective, instruction must challenge the devaluation of Maori identity in the school and wider society. This type of instruction involves "the teacher creating a culturally appropriate and responsive learning context, where young people can engage in learning by bringing their prior cultural knowledge and experiences to classroom interactions, which legitimate these, instead of ignoring or rejecting them" (pp. 264–265).

The well-documented phenomenon of *stereotype threat* (Steele, 1997) also highlights the relationships between societal power relations, identity negotiation, and task performance. Stereotype threat refers to the deterioration of individuals' task performance in contexts where negative stereotypes about their social group are communicated to them. For example, negative attitudes on the part of teachers towards the variety of English spoken by many low-SES African American students have frequently been communicated to students with predictable results (e.g., Baugh, 1999). A direct implication is that in order to reverse this pattern of underachievement, educators, both individually and collectively, must challenge the devaluation of students' language, culture, and identity in the wider society by implementing instructional strategies that enable students to develop "identities of competence" (Manyak, 2004) in the school context. These instructional strategies will communicate high expectations to students regarding their ability to succeed academically and support them in meeting these academic demands by affirming their identities and connecting curriculum to their lives (i.e., their communities' funds of knowledge).

In summary, much more than language differences between home and school are involved in the underachievement of linguistically diverse students in different educational contexts. Underachievement is observed predominantly among linguistically diverse students who are also experiencing the effects of low-SES and/or marginalized group status in the host country. Thus, in educating linguistically diverse students, schools need to take account of more than simply students' need to learn the host country language. Instruction must also address the sources of potential disadvantage that characterize low-SES and marginalized group students. As documented in the next section, previous syntheses of the research literature on the achievement of linguistically diverse students have largely failed to take account of the broader set of causal factors that determine achievement, and consequently they have also failed to identify crucial components of effective instruction for these students.

## A Critique of Previous Research Syntheses and their Instructional Recommendations

It is beyond the scope of this chapter to critique previous syntheses of the research on linguistically diverse learners in detail. A variety of problematic aspects of these reports have been identified elsewhere (e.g., Cummins, 2007a, 2007b, 2008, 2009a). For example, the NRP's blanket conclusion that "systematic phonics instruction" promotes reading development ignores the important qualification that after Grade 1, systematic phonics instruction showed no positive impact on reading comprehension among normally achieving and low-achieving students (Ehri, Nunes, Stahl, & Willows, 2001). My focus in this section, however, is on points of consensus in the reports with respect to the implications of the research for educational policies and classroom instruction. Subsequently, I will highlight some omissions and problematic interpretations that have major consequences for policy and practice.

## Areas of Consensus

All of the reports agree on the need for schools to modify instruction in order to support students in learning the school language. The most complete elaboration of evidence-based instructional practices for linguistically diverse learners is included in the California Department of Education (2010) research synthesis volume. These can be summarized under four overlapping categories:

- Scaffold instruction to support students' language comprehension and production.
- Activate students' existing background knowledge and build new background knowledge as needed.
- Teach academic language explicitly.
- Enable students to use their L1 as a cognitive resource either through bilingual education programs or within English-medium programs.

Each of these instructional mandates is briefly sketched below.

### Scaffold Instruction

The term *scaffolding* refers to the provision of instructional supports that enable learners to carry out tasks and perform academically at a higher level than they would be capable of without these supports. Dolson and Burnham-Massey (2011) summarize scaffolding (or "sheltered") instructional strategies as follows: "In sheltered settings, teachers make content comprehensible through a variety of techniques that include the use of visual aids, modeling, demonstrations, graphic organizers, vocabulary previews, predictions, adapted texts, cooperative learning, peer tutoring, multicultural content, and native language support" (p. 41). The best-known and most widely used comprehensive instructional system developed for linguistically diverse students is the Sheltered Instruction Observation Protocol (SIOP) Model (Echevarria & Short, 2010).

### Activate and Build Background Knowledge

There is virtually universal agreement among reading and learning theorists that effective instruction for all students activates their background knowledge and builds on it as needed (e.g., Bransford et al., 2000). Snow, Burns, and Griffin (1998) expressed the centrality of background knowledge as follows: "Every opportunity should be taken to extend and enrich children's background knowledge and understanding in every way possible, for the ultimate significance and memorability of any word or text depends on whether children possess the background knowledge and conceptual sophistication to understand its meaning" (p. 219). Consistent with this perspective, SIOP emphasizes the importance of linking new concepts explicitly to students' background experiences and past learning. Both Lindholm-Leary and Genesee (2010) and Dolson and Burnham-Massey (2011) interpret background knowledge in relation to the construct of "funds of knowledge" (González et al., 2005), which implies a much broader connection to students' lives and cultural realities than narrower conceptions of background knowledge that might focus only on content learned in previous lessons. Obviously, the research (reviewed above) which addresses the academic achievement of marginalized group students supports the instructional relevance of the broader rather than the narrower conception of "background knowledge".

## Teach Academic Language Explicitly

All of the research syntheses endorse the necessity of teaching academic language explicitly and consistently across the curriculum. Echevarria and Short (2010), for example, highlight the importance of articulating clearly defined content and language objectives in all subject areas. Dutro and Kinsella (2010) provide detailed strategies for expanding secondary EL students' vocabulary knowledge throughout the school day. The OECD (2010d) has also argued for an explicit and consistent focus on developing students' awareness of how academic language works in the different content areas in order to support struggling learners in catching up academically. This focus is also explicitly built into the recently implemented Common Core State Standards in the United States (see, for example, Wong Fillmore & Fillmore, 2012).

## Use Students' L1 as Scaffold and Cognitive Resource

As noted in a previous section, some OECD authors have inappropriately interpreted correlational data as causal and argued that immigrant-background students' use of L1 at home contributes to underachievement. However, other OECD publications have advocated more affirmative (and evidence-based) school policies that would welcome students' L1 as a tool for learning and understanding (OECD, 2010a, p. 49).

The research syntheses carried out in the US consistently endorse both bilingual education as a legitimate program option for linguistically diverse students and the inclusion of students' L1 as an instructional option within the English-medium classroom. Snow and Katz (2010), for example, cite the Lucas and Katz (1994) study which found that, in exemplary programs, a wide variety of L1/primary language uses were observed. Classroom uses included students using L1 to assist and tutor one another, writing in L1, and using bilingual dictionaries. In the larger school context, exemplary schools provided instruction in students' culture and history, libraries maintained multilingual collections, and teachers encouraged parents to read to their children in the L1.

August and Shanahan (2010) also highlight the fact that "effective literacy instruction for English learners is respectful of the home language" (p. 235). As examples of successfully implemented practices, they list (1) providing books in students' L1 during school reading time, (2) preview and review storybook reading in students' L1, (3) allowing students to converse and write in L1 as well as L2, (4) allowing some use of L1 in instructional conversations, (5) providing L1 vocabulary support through targeted translation of passages and individual vocabulary items, including building awareness of cognate connections.

It is clear from these examples that opening up the instructional space to include students' home languages as resources for learning can (1) scaffold both comprehension and production of L2, (2) more effectively activate students' background knowledge, much of which is likely to be encoded in L1, and (3) develop awareness of how academic language operates and how L1 and L2 connect with each other. Showing respect for students' L1 in these ways also clearly communicates a positive message to students and their families with respect to the value of bilingualism in their lives and its legitimacy as a cognitive and personal resource. In addition, these forms of identity affirmation represent an instructional challenge to historical (and current) societal power relations that have devalued marginalized students' cultures and languages.

## Limitations in the Research Syntheses

There are several major limitations in the way the research findings have been interpreted in the three US syntheses. In addition to exaggerating the impact of systematic phonics instruction in the development of reading comprehension, the reports have ignored or largely dismissed the research supporting the roles of (1) print access/literacy engagement and (2) identity affirmation. By contrast, as outlined previously, the OECD PISA studies highlight the central role that reading engagement plays in predicting reading achievement among 15-year-old students in countries around the world. PISA says very little about identity issues, presumably because constructs such as "identity" were not amenable to quantitative measurement. The following sections briefly outline the ways in which research relating to literacy engagement and identity affirmation were interpreted in the NLP report (August & Shanahan, 2006). These issues received minimal consideration in the Genesee et al. (2006) and California Department of Education (2010) publications apart from the endorsement of bilingual education programs and L1-inclusion strategies. In contrast to chapters in the California Department of Education (2010) volume, Dolson and Burnham-Massey (2011) do include consideration of culturally sustaining pedagogies that focus on identity and social justice issues in their discussion of effective practices for linguistically diverse learners (e.g., the autobiographical writing strategies documented in Ada and Campoy's (2003) *Authors in the Classroom*, and the *Bridging Multiple Worlds* program developed by Bhattacharya, Quiroga, and Olsen (2007)).

### Print Access/Literacy Engagement

Print access and literacy engagement are obviously two sides of the same coin since without access to print, literacy engagement is unlikely. Shanahan and Beck's (2006) review of studies that encouraged reading and writing or involved adults reading to children could identify only nine such studies that they deemed worthy of inclusion. By contrast, Lindsay's (2010) meta-analysis of 108 studies of "print access" (a more limited construct) identified 44 "rigorous" studies that employed experimental or quasi-experimental designs. Shanahan and Beck reviewed only one of the nine research studies compiled by Elley (1991, 2001). They focused on the Fiji "book flood" experiment (Elley & Mangubhai, 1983; Mangubhai, 2001) which Elley (1991) summarized. They largely dismiss the findings because of what they claim are reporting flaws in the study. For example, they claim that it was not possible to tell whether the pre-test was in the students' native language or English and the author (Elley) did not document what was done to account for attrition over the two years of the study (Grades 4 and 5).

These claims suggest that Shanahan and Beck (2006) may not have consulted the original study (Elley & Mangubhai, 1983), which they did not reference, or Mangubhai's (2001) later account of it, relying instead on Elley's (1991) summary. It is clear from Elley and Mangubhai (1983) that all testing was carried out in English including the pre-test measures. Mangubhai (2001) is also explicit on this point: "In February, 1980, pupils in Grades 4 and 5 in 15 rural schools were tested using a specially prepared ESL reading test and 12 schools were selected and matched to produce three equivalent groups" (p. 149). Attrition was also not an issue because the study was not a longitudinal study. Grade 4 and 5 classes in 1980 and Grade 5 and 6 classes in 1981 were tested as independent units, and results reported by grade level, with the result that any attrition of students between the 1980 and 1981 assessments would have been irrelevant to the results. In fact, the Elley and Mangubhai study is one of the most robustly designed of all of those considered in the NLP research synthesis. It involved random assignment of schools to treatments, relatively large sample sizes within each treatment, statistical controls for Grade 4 pre-test differences that were not resolved through random assignment, and replication of the original Grade 4 and 5 results through a second year of Grade 5 and 6 testing.

More recent findings reinforce the conclusion that engaged reading exerts a significant positive impact on academic achievement. In an ongoing British longitudinal study involving a nationally representative sample of several thousand students, Sullivan and Brown (2013) reported that children who were read to regularly by their parents at age 5 demonstrated significantly stronger performance on vocabulary, spelling, and math tests given at age 16 than those who did not have this early exposure to books. Furthermore, the amount of pleasure reading students reported at age 10 significantly predicted later scores at age 16. The authors were able to demonstrate a causal relationship between reading engagement and reading achievement that was not dependent either on the SES background of the parents or on cognitive or academic ability. Indices of childhood reading accounted for a gain of 14.54 percentage points in vocabulary, 10.0 percentage points in math, and 8.6 percentage points in spelling, far greater than the impact of SES (as reflected in parental educational level) which amounted to 4.4 percentage points for vocabulary, 3.2 percentage points for math, and 1.7 percentage points for spelling. The authors go on to point out that when they

> controlled for the child's test scores at age five and ten, the influence of the child's own reading [at age 16] remained highly significant, suggesting that the positive link between leisure reading and cognitive outcomes is not purely due to more able children being more likely to read a lot, but that reading is actually linked to increased cognitive progress over time (p. 37).

In summary, there is persuasive evidence from multiple sources that engaging students actively in literacy activities, both in school and in out-of-school contexts, promotes literacy attainment. This evidence includes both L1 and L2 contexts. Although most of the research has focused on *reading*, it seems appropriate to broaden the focus from simply *reading engagement* to *literacy engagement* in light of the fact that there is considerable research documenting the role of extensive writing not only in developing writing expertise but also in improving reading comprehension (Graham & Herbert, 2010).

## Identity Affirmation

The NLP panel concluded that "there is surprisingly little evidence for the impact of sociocultural variables on literacy learning" (August & Shanahan, 2008b, p. 8). They acknowledged that a significant number of ethnographic and case studies provide examples of teachers giving legitimacy to students' personal, communal, or cultural backgrounds in the classroom but did not find rigorous evidence that sociocultural validation in the school benefited students' literacy outcomes. This conclusion appears to reflect the excessively narrow criteria the NLP adopted with respect to adequacy of research design and the need to isolate variables so that their separate impact could be assessed. This is rarely possible in field research where multiple variables overlap and interact. In order to establish the credibility of different hypotheses, it is necessary to adopt a broader frame of analysis where empirical observations cumulatively contribute to the development of rigorous predictive models (Cummins, 1999, 2007a).

Certainly, many sociologists and anthropologists would take issue with the claim that their disciplines have contributed no credible evidence regarding the sociocultural and educational conditions that influence students' achievement. They might also point to some obvious omissions in the NLP of quantitative studies that point to the influence of sociocultural factors.

For example, Portes and Rumbaut (2001) concluded on the basis of their large-scale study of second-generation immigrant students that maintaining links to the home culture and language is associated with higher educational achievement. Bankston and Zhou (1995) similarly point out that "identification with Vietnamese ethnicity, Vietnamese reading and writing abilities, attitudes toward future education, and current study habits all have significant [positive] effects on current educational outcome" (p. 14). In addition, the many experimental studies that have documented the influence of stereotype threat (Steele, 1997) have highlighted how societal power relations influence task performance.

It is noteworthy that the conclusions of the NLP in relation to sociocultural factors (Goldenberg et al., 2006) are not even accepted by the policy-makers who coordinated the California Department of Education (2010) volume to which two of the authors contributed. In her Introduction to that volume, Aguila (2010) points to the "substantial and compelling research to support the notion that powerful sociocultural factors strongly influence the outcomes of programs for English learners and other minority students and students of low socioeconomic class" (p. 12). She goes on to endorse culturally responsive pedagogy (Gay, 2010) aimed at countering "the racism, prejudice, and discrimination [these students] experience in schools and society" (p. 13). However, as noted above, with the exception of the fact that they endorse the educational legitimacy of students' bilingualism, other chapters in the California Department of Education volume make little attempt to integrate their prescriptions for academic language instruction with culturally responsive pedagogy.

In the following section, the research evidence that has been presented to this point is integrated into a theoretical framework that specifies the major instructional implications of the findings.

## The Literacy Engagement Framework

As noted in previous sections, there is virtually universal consensus about the importance of scaffolding instruction, activating/building background knowledge, and extending students' knowledge of academic language across the curriculum as instructional strategies to enable linguistically diverse students to succeed academically. Most researchers also endorse both bilingual education (where feasible) and judicious instructional use of students' L1 as a means of enhancing students' access to the curriculum, activating their background knowledge, and increasing their awareness of how academic language works. However, researchers and policy-makers have been largely silent about the roles of literacy engagement and identity affirmation in promoting academic success for linguistically diverse students. The Literacy Engagement framework (Figure 17.2) integrates all of these components in a way that explicitly acknowledges the fact that a large proportion of linguistically diverse learners in the United States (and in many other countries) come from low-SES backgrounds and are members of socially marginalized communities. Print access/literacy engagement is posited as a direct determinant of literacy achievement. Linguistically diverse students will engage actively with literacy only to the extent that instruction scaffolds meaning, connects to their lives, affirms their identities, and extends their knowledge of academic language.

The distinctions captured in the framework are frequently fused in classroom practice. For example, connecting instruction to students' lives and activating their background knowledge simultaneously affirms the legitimacy of their experience and, by extension, the legitimacy of their identities. Bilingual students' identities are also affirmed when they are encouraged to use their L1 writing abilities as a stepping-stone or scaffold to writing in L2 (see Cummins & Early (2011) for multiple examples). It is important to note that the construct of *identity affirmation* is integrated directly into an analysis of how societal power relations affect academic engagement

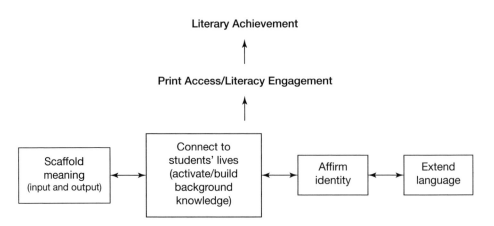

*Figure 17.2* The Literacy Engagement Framework

and achievement (Cummins, 1986, 2001; Cummins & Early, 2011). Instructional practices that affirm the identities of marginalized group students and communities are, by definition, challenging coercive power relations in the wider community. This perspective is largely absent from the research syntheses reviewed in this chapter apart from the Dolson and Burnham-Massey (2011) monograph.

## Conclusion

I have argued that current attempts in the United States to synthesize the research regarding effective instruction for linguistically diverse students have only partially accounted for the relevant data. The problematic interpretations of the research that have guided policy initiatives in the areas of reading and the education of linguistically diverse students have had major consequences as illustrated in the failure of the Reading First initiative, implemented under the Bush administration's No Child Left Behind (2001) legislation, to show any impact on reading comprehension, reading engagement, or spelling (Gamse, Jacob, Horst, Boulay, & Unlu, 2008). This $6-billion program aimed at low-income students required school systems to implement intensive phonics instruction and refused funding to many proposals that included any vestiges of "balanced" approaches to literacy (e.g., an emphasis on reading children's literature or on authentic writing—see Cummins (2007a) for documentation). This outcome should not have been a surprise to anyone who paid attention to the NRP finding that systematic phonics instruction was unrelated to reading comprehension after Grade 1 for normally achieving and low-achieving students (Ehri et al., 2001). Had literacy engagement been recognized as a powerful determinant of reading comprehension by researchers and policy-makers, a much wider variety of early literacy programs would have been funded and a very different set of outcomes might have been realized.

The failure of researchers and policy-makers to recognize variables related to teacher–student identity negotiation as relevant to linguistically diverse students' academic engagement and achievement has similarly resulted in ineffective policies and sterile instruction that fails to connect to students' lives. The literature is replete with case studies and evaluations that document the potentially powerful impact of culturally sustaining pedagogies that connect with students' lives and affirm their identities (e.g., Cummins, Brown, & Sayers, 2007; Cummins & Early, 2011; Sleeter, 2011). Yet these have been largely ignored in mainstream policies where high-stakes standardized testing has narrowed the curriculum for low-income and socially marginalized students (Afflerbach, 2005; Cummins, 2007a). Likewise, instructional prescriptions directed specifically at linguistically diverse students designed to make academic content accessible and extend their command over academic language (e.g., California Department of Education, 2010) have not explicitly recognized that engagement with language and literacy is a prerequisite for the success of these strategies.

The Literacy Engagement framework (Figure 17.2) is intended not just as a broad representation of the research evidence regarding effective instruction for linguistically diverse students but also as a heuristic tool to facilitate discussion at the level of the school in regard to the development of school-based language and literacy policies. Educators who engage in this school-based policy development process are reclaiming agency that (in the United States) has been significantly undermined by top-down mandates in relation to curriculum and assessment that have been largely evidence-free.

# References

Afflerbach, P. (2005). High stakes testing and reading assessment. *Journal of Literacy Research*, *37*, 151–162.

Ada, A. F., & Campoy, I. (2003). *Authors in the classroom: A transformative education process.* Boston, MA: Allyn & Bacon.

Aguila, V. (2010). Schooling English learners: Contexts and challenges. In California Department of Education, *Improving education for English learners: Research-based approaches* (pp. 1–18). Sacramento, CA: California Department of Education.

August, D., & Shanahan, T. (Eds.) (2006). *Developing literacy in second-language learners: Report of the National Literacy Panel on Language-Minority Children and Youth.* Mahwah, NJ: Lawrence Erlbaum.

August, D., & Shanahan, T. (Eds.) (2008a). *Developing reading and writing in second-language learners: Lessons from the Report of the National Literacy Panel on Language-Minority Children and Youth.* Mahwah, NJ: Lawrence Erlbaum.

August, D., & Shanahan, T. (2008b). Introduction and methodology. In D. August & T. Shanahan (Eds.), *Developing reading and writing in second-langue learners: Lessons from the Report of the National Literacy Panel on Language-Minority Children and Youth* (pp. 1–17). Mahwah, NJ: Lawrence Erlbaum.

August, D., & Shanahan, T. (2010). Effective English literacy instruction for English learners. In California Department of Education, *Improving education for English learners: Research-based approaches* (pp. 209–249). Sacramento, CA: California Department of Education.

Bankston, C. L., & Zhou, M. (1995). Effects of achievement of Vietnamese youths in New Orleans. *Sociology of Education*, *68*, 1–17.

Baugh, J. (1999). *Out of the mouths of slaves: African American language and educational malpractice.* Austin, TX: University of Texas Press.

Berliner, D. C. (2009). *Poverty and potential: Out-of-school factors and school success.* Boulder and Tempe: Education and the Public Interest Center & Education Policy Research Unit. Retrieved from http://epicpolicy.org/publication/poverty-and-potential.

Bhattacharya, J., Quiroga, J., & Olsen, L. (2007). *Bridging multiple worlds: Creating affirming environments for young people to thrive.* Oakland, CA: California Tomorrow.

Bishop, R., & Berryman, M. (2006). *Culture speaks: Cultural relationships and classroom learning.* Wellington, NZ: Huia Publishers.

Bransford, J. D., Brown, A. L., & Cocking, R. R. (2000). *How people learn: Brain, mind, experience, and school.* Washington, DC: National Academy Press.

Brozo, W., Shiel, G., & Topping, K. (2007). Engagement in reading: Lessons learned from three PISA countries. *Journal of Adolescent & Adult Literacy*, *51*, 304–315.

California Department of Education (2001). *History-Social Science framework for California Public Schools.* Sacramento: California Department of Education.

California Department of Education (2010). *Improving education for English learners: Research-based approaches.* Sacramento: California Department of Education.

Carter, P. L. (2013). Student and school cultures and the opportunity gap: Paying attention to academic engagement and achievement. In P. L. Carter & K. G. Welner (Eds.), *Closing the opportunity gap: What America must do to give every child an even chance* (pp. 143–155). New York: Oxford University Press.

Christensen, G., & Segeritz, M. (2008). An international perspective on student achievement. In Bertelsmann Stiftung (Ed.), *Immigrant students can succeed: Lessons from around the globe* (pp. 11–33). Gütersloh, Germany: Bertelsmann Stiftung.

Christensen, G., & Stanat, P. (2007). *Language policies and practices for helping immigrant second-generation students succeed.* The Transatlantic Task Force on Immigration and Integration convened by the Migration Policy Institute and Bertlesmann Stiftung. Retrieved from http://www.migrationinformation.org/transatlantic/.

Collier, V. P. (1987). Age and rate of acquisition of second language for academic purposes. *TESOL Quarterly, 21,* 617–641.

Cummins, J. (1979). Linguistic interdependence and the educational development of bilingual children. *Review of Educational Research, 49,* 222–251.

Cummins, J. (1981). Age on arrival and immigrant second language learning in Canada: A reassessment. *Applied Linguistics, 1,* 132–149.

Cummins, J. (1986). Empowering minority students: A framework for intervention. *Harvard Educational Review, 56,* 18–36.

Cummins, J. (1999). Alternative paradigms in bilingual education research: Does theory have a place? *Educational Researcher, 28*(7), 26–32.

Cummins, J. (2001). *Negotiating identities: Education for empowerment in a diverse society* (2nd ed.). Los Angeles: California Association for Bilingual Education.

Cummins, J. (2007a). Pedagogies for the poor? Re-aligning reading instruction for low-income students with scientifically based reading research. *Educational Researcher, 36,* 564–572.

Cummins, J. (2007b). Review of F. Genesee, K. Lindholm-Leary, W. M. Saunders, and D. Christian (Eds.), *Educating English language learners: A synthesis of research evidence.* New York: Cambridge University Press. *Language and Education, 21*(1), 87–92.

Cummins, J. (2008). Review of P. Stanat & G. Christensen (Eds.), *Where immigrant students succeed: A comparative review of performance and engagement in PISA 2003.* Paris: OECD, 2006. *Curriculum Inquiry, 30,* 493–499.

Cummins, J. (2009a). Literacy and English-language learners: A shifting landscape for students, teachers, researchers, and policy makers. Review of D. August & T. Shanahan (Eds.), *Developing reading and writing in second-language learners: Lessons from the Report of the National Literacy Panel on Language-Minority Children and Youth.* New York: Routledge, 2008. *Educational Researcher, 38,* 382–384.

Cummins, J., Brown, K., & Sayers, D. (2007). *Literacy, technology, and diversity: Teaching for success in changing times.* Boston, MA: Pearson Education.

Cummins, J,. & Early, M. (Eds.) (2011). *Identity texts: The collaborative creation of power in multilingual schools.* Stoke-on-Trent, UK: Trentham Books.

Darling-Hammond, L. (2010). *The flat world and education. How America's commitment to equity will determine our future.* New York: Teachers College Press.

Darling-Hammond, L. (2013). Inequality and school resources: What it will take to close the opportunity gap. In P. L. Carter & K. G. Welner (Eds.), *Closing the opportunity gap: What America must do to give every child an even chance* (pp. 77–97). New York: Oxford University Press.

Dolson, D. (1985). The effects of Spanish home language use on the scholastic performance of Hispanic pupils. *Journal of Multilingual and Multicultural Development, 6,* 135–156.

Dolson, D., & Burnham-Massey, L. (2011). *Redesigning English-medium classrooms: Using research to enhance English learner achievement.* Covina, CA: California Association for Bilingual Education.

Duke, N. (2000). For the rich it's richer: Print experiences and environments offered to children in very low and very high-socioeconomic status first-grade classrooms. *American Educational Research Journal, 37,* 441–478.

Dutro, S., & Kinsella, K. (2010). English language development: Issues and implementation. In kindergarten through grade 5. In California Department of Education, *Improving education for English learners: Research-based approaches* (pp. 151–207). Sacramento, CA: California Department of Education.

Echevarria, J., & Short, D. (2010). Programs and practices for effective sheltered content instruction. In California Department of Education, *Improving education for English learners: Research-based approaches* (pp. 251–321). Sacramento, CA: California Department of Education.

Ehri, L. C., Nunes, S., Stahl, S., & Willows, D. (2001). Systematic phonics instruction helps students learn to read: Evidence from the National Reading Panel's meta-analysis. *Review of Educational Research, 71,* 393–447.

Elley, W. B. (1991). Acquiring literacy in a second language: The effect of book-based programs. *Language Learning, 41*, 375–411.

Elley, W. B. (2001). Guest editor's introduction. *International Journal of Educational Research, 35*, 127–135.

Elley, W. B., & Mangubhai, F. (1983). The impact of reading on second language learning. *Reading Research Quarterly, 19*, 53–67.

Esser, H. (2006). *Migration, language, and integration.* AKI Research Review 4. Berlin: Programme on Intercultural Conflicts and Societal Integration (AKI), Social Science Research Center. Retrieved from http://www.wzb.eu/zkd/aki/files/aki_research_review_4.

Gamse, B. C., Jacob, R. T., Horst, M., Boulay, B., & Unlu, F. (2008) *Reading First Impact Study final report (NCEE 2009–4038).* Washington, DC: National Center for Education Evaluation and Regional Assistance, Institute of Education Sciences, US Department of Education.

Gay, G. (2010). *Culturally responsive teaching.* New York: Teachers College Press.

Genesee, F., Lindholm-Leary, K., Saunders, W., & Christian, D. (Eds.) (2006). *Educating English language learners: A synthesis of research evidence.* New York: Cambridge University Press.

Goldenberg, C., Rueda, R., & August, D. (2006). Sociocultural influences on the literacy attainment of language-minority children and youth. In D. August & T. Shanahan (Eds.), *Developing literacy in second-language learners: Report of the National Literacy Panel on Language-Minority Children and Youth* (pp. 269–318). Mahwah, NJ: Lawrence Erlbaum.

González, N., Moll, L. C., & Amanti, C. (2005). *Funds of knowledge: Theorizing practices in households, communities and classrooms.* Mahwah, NJ: Lawrence Erlbaum.

Graham, S., & Herbert, M. (2010). *Writing to read: Evidence for how writing can improve reading.* New York: Carnegie Corporation.

Guthrie, J. T. (2004). Teaching for literacy engagement. *Journal of Literacy Research, 36*, 1–30.

Hakuta, K., Butler, Y. G., & Witt, D. (2000). *How long does it take English learners to attain proficiency?* Santa Barbara, CA: University of California Linguistic Minority Research Institute.

Hart, B., & Risley, T. R. (1995) *Meaningful differences in the everyday experience of young American children.* Baltimore, MD: Paul H. Brookes Publishing.

Kozol, J. (2005). *The shame of the nation: The restoration of apartheid schooling in America.* New York: Crown.

Krashen, S. D. (2004). *The power of reading: Insights from the research.* 2nd ed. Portsmouth, NH: Heinemann.

Ladson-Billings, G. (1994). *The dreamkeepers: Successful teachers of African American children.* San Francisco, CA: Jossey-Bass.

Ladson-Billings, G. (1995). Toward a theory of culturally relevant pedagogy. *American Educational Research Journal, 32*, 465–491.

Lindholm-Leary, K., & Genesee, F. (2010). Alternative educational programs for English learners. In California Department of Education, *Improving education for English learners: Research-based approaches* (pp. 323–382). Sacramento, CA: California Department of Education.

Lindsay, J. (2010). *Children's access to print material and education-related outcomes: Findings from a meta-analytic review.* Naperville, IL: Learning Point Associates.

Lucas, T., & Katz, A. (1994). Reframing the debate: The roles of native languages in English-only programs for language minority students. *TESOL Quarterly, 28*, 537–562.

Mangubhai, F. (2001). Book floods and comprehensible input floods: Providing ideal conditions for second language acquisition. *International Journal of Educational Research, 35*, 147–156.

Manyak, P. C. (2004). "What did she say?" Translation in a primary-grade English immersion class. *Multicultural Perspectives, 6*, 12–18.

National Reading Panel (2000). *Teaching children to read: An evidence-based assessment of the scientific research literature on reading and its implications for reading instruction.* Washington, DC: National Institute of Child Health and Human Development.

Neuman, S. B., & Celano, D. (2001). Access to print in low-income and middle-income communities: An ecological study of four neighbourhoods. *Reading Research Quarterly, 36*, 8–26.

No Child Left Behind Act of 2001, Pub. L. No. 107–110 (2001).

OECD (2004). *Messages from PISA 2000.* Paris: OECD.

OECD (2010a). *Closing the gap for immigrant students: Policies, practice and performance.* OECD Reviews of Migrant Education. Paris: OECD.

OECD (2010b). *PISA 2009 results: Learning to learn—Student engagement, strategies and practices (Volume III).* Paris: OECD. Retrieved from http://www.oecd.org/dataoecd/11/17/48852630.pdf.

OECD (2010c). *PISA 2009 results: Overcoming social background—Equity in learning opportunities and outcomes (Volume II).* Paris: OECD. Retrieved from http://www.oecd.org/pisa/pisaproducts/48852584.pdf.

OECD (2010d). *Strong performers and successful reformers in education: Lessons from PISA for the United States.* Paris: OECD. Retrieved from http://www.oecd.org/dataoecd/32/50/46623978.pdf.

OECD (2012). *Untapped skills: Realising the potential of immigrant students.* Paris: OECD. Retrieved from http://www.oecd.org/edu/Untapped%20Skills.pdf.

Ogbu, J. U. (1978). *Minority education and caste.* New York: Academic Press.

Ogbu, J. U. (1992). Understanding cultural diversity and learning. *Educational Researcher, 21*(8), 5–14, 24.

Oller, D. K., & Eilers, R. E. (Eds.) (2002). *Language and literacy in bilingual children.* Clevedon, UK: Multilingual Matters.

Olsen, L. (2010). *Reparable harm: Fulfilling the unkept promise of educational opportunity for California's long term English learners.* San Francisco, CA: Californians Together. Retrieved from www.californians together.org.

Orfield, G. (2013). Housing segregation produces unequal schools. In P. L. Carter & K. G. Welner (Eds.), *Closing the opportunity gap: What America must do to give every child and even chance* (pp. 40–60). New York: Oxford University Press.

Paris, D. (2012). Culturally sustaining pedagogy: A needed change in stance, terminology, and practice. *Educational Researcher, 41*(3), 93–97. doi:10.3102/0013189X12441244

Parrish, T., Merickel, A., Pérez, M., Linquanti, R., Socías M., Spain, A. . . . DeLancey, D. (2006). *Effects of the implementation of Proposition 227 on the education of English learners, K–12: Findings from a five-year evaluation (Final Report).* Palo Alto and San Francisco: American Institutes for Research and WestEd.

Portes, A., & Rumbaut, R. G. (2001). *Legacies: The story of the immigrant second generation.* Berkeley: University of California Press.

Rothstein, R. (2013). Why children for lower socioeconomic classes, on average, have lower academic achievement than middle-class children. In P. L. Carter & K. G. Welner (Eds.), *Closing the opportunity gap: What America must do to give every child and even chance* (pp. 61–74). New York: Oxford University Press.

Shanahan, T., & Beck, I. (2006). Effective literacy teaching for English-language learners. In D. August & T. Shanahan (Eds.), *Developing literacy in second-language learners: Report of the National Literacy Panel on Language-Minority Children and Youth* (pp. 415–488). Mahwah, NJ: Lawrence Erlbaum.

Sleeter, C. E. (2002). State curriculum standards and student consciousness. *Social Justice, 29*(4), 8–25.

Sleeter, C. E. (2011). *The academic and social value of Ethnic Studies: A research review.* Washington, DC: The National Education Association.

Snow, C. E., Burns, M. S., & Griffin, P. (Eds.) (1998). *Preventing reading difficulties in young children.* Washington, DC: National Academy Press.

Snow, M. A., & Katz, A. (2010). English language development. Foundations and implementation in kindergarten through grade five. In California Department of Education, *Improving education for English learners: Research-based approaches* (pp. 83–149). Sacramento, CA: California Department of Education.

Stanat, P., & Christensen, G. (2006) *Where immigrant students succeed: A comparative review of performance and engagement in PISA 2003.* Paris: OECD. Retrieved from http://www.oecd.org/pisa/pisaproducts/pisa2003/36664934.pdf.

Steele, C. M. (1997). A threat in the air: How stereotypes shape intellectual identity and performance. *American Psychologist, 52*, 613–629.

Sullivan, A., & Brown, M. (2013). *Social inequalities in cognitive scores at age 16: The role of reading.* London: Centre for Longitudinal Studies, Institute of Education, University of London. Retrieved from www.cls.ioe.ac.uk.

Wong Fillmore, L. W., & Fillmore, C. J. (2012). What does text complexity mean for English learners and language minority students? Retrieved from www.ell.stanford.edu.

# 18

# Individual Differences in Reading History

*Bruce VanSledright*

---

> History is fundamentally an interpretive domain. We can talk about history as a subject or a textual object. However, for my purposes here, it will make sense to speak of it more as a practice, that is, as a practice of reading the past to see what it might tell us here in the present about how things were, how people back then thought about their worlds. As the argument often goes, this helps us understand ourselves better. So, as a practice, history is all about reading, reading ourselves and reading the world of the past together in an inextricable combination.
>
> (Scholes, 1989, p. 10)

To say that history is about reading therefore invokes a reader. The reader reads objects from the past—texts, maps, photographs, artifacts, paintings, and the like—in search of the past's meaning, partly to understand it on its own terms but also to render the present more intelligible if possible. Consequently, the reader is an interpreter of the past. If this is an apt enough description, then it might follow that who that reader is could not be more important.

In this chapter, my task is to lay out the ways in which that reader matters. This is the focus: how individual differences among readers influence the nature of reading, the historical interpretations readers produce, the subsequent understandings of the past those entail, and to what end. Knowing about these differences is useful for history education in general, and the teaching of and reading in history in particular. After a brief discussion about my assumptions, I begin with an illustration of three readers reading objects from the past. It sets a context that enables me to show how the reader matters. Then I tease out these differences and show how crucial they are in determining how readers make sense of the past and themselves. I draw from the research literature specific to history and history education in order to show how that research has sought to clarify the relationship between reader, text, and context. I conclude by drawing research-based implications for improving the quality of a history education and the lives of readers who are invited to engage in it.

Because my task is tied to reading in history, I purposely focus on research in that domain, leaving the rich, more generic literature on the nature of individual differences in reading aside. I do that to conserve space here but also to avoid repetition, since there are many references to that broader literature in other chapters in this volume.

## Making Assumptions

A word is in order on assumptions I will make as I proceed. Understanding the past is enabled by careful, thoughtful reading. Although other domains share in similar types of reading practices, there are ways of reading in history that are unique. Making sense of the past is challenging for several reasons. It involves a transaction between reader, text, and the context in which the reader is historicized. As I will show, readers cannot step outside themselves and the story they tell about *who they are* in order to fully read the past independent of that story. Readers impose the story (a text) in their heads on the past as they read (see again, Scholes, 1989). Readers have identities, consisting of prior ideas and experiences that are formed by spoken language before they learn to read. Therefore, reading the past is always already intertextual.

Reading the past is also hypertextual in the sense that multiple stories or texts are constantly in play, from the standard textbook that draws synthetically on many previous stories humans have told about themselves, to the proliferation of stories on the Internet and other media, to narratives and stores of prior ideas pre-existing in readers' heads. There is no one text or story that can definitively trump other stories in order to silence the hypertextual (intertextual) "noise." By noise here I mean the mental play of differing stories/texts that vie for believability, sometimes competing and conflicting with one another, creating a metaphorical racket in a reader's head that seeks reconciliation (e.g., VanSledright, 2012).

To understand the past well in ways that permit a deeper understanding of self requires considerable reading expertise. I assume that that expertise is epitomized in the way historians read, that the practices of those historians can be looked to for benchmarks on what it means to read with deep understanding. I draw from what the research in history education teaches us about the substance of reading expertise and apply it to a consideration of what it might mean to analyze novice readers' practices. This, I hope, will allow for suppositioning about how novice readers with individual differences can be helped toward becoming more expert readers of the past. This will suggest ideas about teaching approaches that promote historical thinking and understanding.

Understanding the past, I assume, depends upon being able to think in historical ways. This thinking begins by asking questions of the past. Reading well is a subspecies of that thinking practice; reading/thinking enables answering questions. Learning to think and question (to read) historically is complicated by the problem of limited access to the past. All we have is the past's *residua*. These come to us in the present in the form of objects (e.g., diary excerpt) that typically were never created to address the questions we are now asking (Lee, 2005). This problem raises the intellectual, cognitive demand on readers. It is compounded by our additional difficulty of being unable to recreate the past as it was in order to observe it and say, "See, that's how things were."

Interpretation can be a high-inference activity plagued by all sorts of opportunities to misread. Individual differences, as we will see, heavily influence the nature of readers' inferencing activity. Thus, we could argue that some sort of mental discipline must be developed so as to avoid reading in an anything-goes manner. Reading well in history consequently can be thought of as a bounded space, governed by criteria, specifically reading and inferencing protocols (rules). We find guidance about those criteria by looking to what expert readers in history do.

## Three Readers and Five Texts

Ben, Brittney, and Alexandra are each on-grade-level readers who are reasonably accomplished. They sit together with a series of short texts spread in front of them. The texts deal with conflicting interpretations of what has become known as the Battle of Lexington Green. This battle in the minds of many signaled the opening volleys in what is referred to in American textbooks as the American Revolutionary War. Most agree that it occurred in April of 1775 and involved a skirmish between a group of armed Massachusetts Minutemen and a regiment of British regulars in the village of Lexington (Massachusetts colony), on the open green at the center of that village. What is in dispute is who fired the first shots, or, put differently, who should be considered the aggressors. This question animates their investigative efforts. The teacher, Ms. Katz, has instructed them to carefully read and analyze the texts to see if they can ferret out an answer.

One of the texts is a short summary of the skirmish drawn from the students' fifth-grade US history textbook. The book's authors intimated that the British marched in formation onto the green in Lexington, took up a confrontational position, raised their muskets, and very likely let go the first volley at the Minutemen crouched behind rocks at the edge of the green. This volley signaled that the British were in charge and would suppress any aggression by the American rebels. The Americans returned fire and the Revolutionary War began.

There were two other longer texts. The first was a modified excerpt from testimony 34 Massachusetts Minutemen gave under oath six days following the battle. The Minutemen argued in a consistent voice that the British had marched into Lexington and began firing on them as they drew up to protect the village. The second of these primary sources came from Ensign Jeremy Lister, a member of the British regiment that marched into Lexington. His account was reversed. He contended that the Minutemen had fired first on the British column and that the troops had no recourse but to return fire. It was the rebel Americans who had started the war. Lister's account surfaced in 1782, seven years after the battle.

Extending the intertextual/hypertextual noise were two additional paragraph-long texts, one from the *Salem Gazette* (Massachusetts colony) dated the same day as the Minutemen testimony, and the other from the *London Gazette*, dated 46 days later (news took roughly 40 days to travel across the ocean). As might be expected, the newspaper excerpts put their partisanship on full display. The Salem paper blamed the British for starting a full-scale war. The London paper blamed the unrepentant Americans for fomenting the conflict by firing the first shots. Both resorted to reporting hyperbole.

The three readers pored over the accounts. They cycled them around the table until each of them had time to read each one. Then a conversation ensued as each attempted to address the question, who fired the first shots and therefore initiated the war? Brittney began the discussion. She started by noting how puzzling it was to address the question; all the conflicting ideas made it difficult to understand what actually happened. She then said that she was leery of the textbook account because it provided so few details relative to the other sources. She also observed how concerned she was about the newspaper accounts because the way they were written was designed to agitate people, rather than report out evenly. She was drawn to the two first-person accounts.

Ben partially agreed with her. But he wondered if they could trust Lister's telling because he was offering his story seven years after the battle. Was his memory that good? Did he mess around with the details, and frame them to support his own position as a British soldier? Was this the "company line" he was retelling? Alexandra balked at all the skepticism registered by Brittney and Ben. She appeared to be uncomfortable with all the textual noise the accounts had created. She said she thought that this exercise was too complicated, and they needed to answer Ms. Katz's question. She gravitated to the simplicity and directness of the textbook. She pleaded her case that textbooks get it right. They held the definitive account; it's why schools issue kids textbooks after all. She was going with the textbook and was ready to tell Ms. Katz that they had reached a conclusion.

Brittney told Alexandra not to go so fast. What was she going to do with the conflicting accounts: the Minutemen versus Lister? Alexandra said that both were deeply biased, simply tried to blame the other side, and so couldn't be trusted at all. The same was true of the newspaper accounts. All these different biased stories made answering the question too difficult. They should be ignored. That left the textbook.

Brittney protested. She said that any account would have some bias. "People can't help it," she said. "People try to argue for their side, to support the people they care about, just like in a fight on the playground at recess." Alexandra insisted that the textbook was the only story that could really be trusted. Ben sat and watched. He then noted that he saw the bias also, but he wondered why Alexandra was so quick to trust the textbook, especially if Brittney was right that all accounts hold some sort of bias. He wondered if the textbook was simply biased toward the American side because it was a textbook made in the United States for American kids. Alexandra remained convinced that the British were in the wrong to begin with and were trying to limit the right to freedom that the American colonists were anxious to obtain. Their discussion ended in an interpretive stalemate.

## Exploring Differences

Each reader reads the same five historical accounts differently. As a result, each reader draws different interpretations and understandings from them as s/he attempts to answer a difficult historical question. Addressing the question is difficult because the accounts do not provide a definitive answer. There isn't one. It turns out that this is common in practicing history, especially if students are invited to wrestle with the past's intertextual and hypertextual noise. Even if in school students such as these do not get opportunities to do that wrestling, the noise is still very much a part of the environment in which these children live. Brittney makes an allusion to it in her analogy about the playground fight.

## Three Reading Protocols in History

Alexandra is uncomfortable with all the textual noise these conflicting accounts generate. It confuses her and makes her anxious. She thinks it derails her from the real task: to answer Ms. Katz's question as conclusively as possible. No waffling allowed. She wants to silence the noise because it gets in her way.

She apparently enters the task with the preconceived idea that, when it comes to freedom seeking, no one should be allowed to stand in the way. People are entitled. She would be entitled; it's built into the way of life in the United States. The British sought to deny by force the colonists' right to freedom and the colonists justifiably fought back. The British were the aggressors; it could hardly have been any other way. The textbook reinforces this point. Why would anyone need to go much beyond it? It presents the story concisely and its task is to tell the truth. It therefore rises to elevated epistemological status and trumps the other accounts.

Brittney is far more skeptical than Alexandra. Her reading protocol—or approach to reading history, which, like Alexandra's, includes criteria for judging the believability of texts—oozes with this skepticism. It does seem healthy, rooted as it appears to be in the sense that words can mean different things depending on context and who the speaker and listener (reader) are. Getting to the bottom of things can be elusive. You need to pay close attention and read carefully. She seems to be saying during the discussion that authors can have agenda that affect how they see, hear, read, and write.

As a result, she finds all the accounts intriguing. They play to her curiosity. She wants to dig into them to see if she can find some clarity below the surface. She seems to welcome the textual noisiness. She pushes back at Alexandra for her reticence in the face of that noise. Instead of opting for the simplicity of the textbook account, she appears to lean in the direction of Lister's retelling because of the richness of its detail. Her reading protocol appears to contain a criterion relative to the question in play. It hinges on the requirement that a strong answer will depend on rich detail and ample evidence. If this is accurate, she has two choices: the Lister account or the one by the Minutemen. The former, by her lights, appears stronger than the latter even though it appeared seven years after the fact.

Ben tends to side with Brittney. However, he seems uncertain, perhaps more uncertain than necessarily skeptical in the way Brittney is. He appears to be waiting to see how these two girls argue out their cases, as though he wishes to listen to their interpretive, spoken texts in order to decide which one is stronger. He waits to be persuaded by one of them. All we can tell is that he is reluctant to accept Alexandra's position on its face. He tilts to the strength of Brittney's argument. Yet, he does register doubt about Brittney's choice of the Lister account. In the end, he seems to quietly waffle.

It is possible that Ben possesses few strong criteria in his reading protocol that allow him to address Ms. Katz's question with confidence. If she asked him to provide an answer to the question, we might surmise that he would say that he could not give one, that the accounts did not allow for drawing a clear conclusion. In this sense, he would be at an interpretive impasse, cognitively handcuffed in the face of conflicting historical accounts. Impasses of this nature are not uncommon among novice history readers (e.g., Ashby, Lee, & Shemilt, 2005; VanSledright & Afflerbach, 2005).

## Differing Protocols

Based on this brief analysis, we can say that these three readers hold different history reading protocols for making sense of the past (e.g., Derrida, 1967; Scholes, 1989). Those differing protocols produce different interpretive understandings. Alexandra selects the textbook account and makes it her own. Brittney leans toward the Lister account. One attributes first shots and by extension responsibility for initiating the war to the British. The other does the same to the colonists. Ben seems to remain stuck and indecisive, caught somewhere in between the two arguments.

If we accept the premise that reading in history operates from personal reading protocols (or the lack of ones with strong criteria for judging the veracity of accounts), then we can further say that the protocols will produce differing histories—in this case, of what happened at Lexington Green. The question I explore next in detail is what accounts for these differing protocols? Speaking to this question might tell us something about the different kinds of histories that could be produced, say, in a classroom. The reason that might be important in history hinges on the idea that for more than a century in the United States school history courses and the teachers who teach them have expended considerable effort in trying to help children all produce the same historical story about the birth and development of the nation (Foster & Crawford, 2006). Given the foregoing illustration, we might ask: Is that really possible? Or is it even a good goal? This is contested space to which I return by way of conclusion.

For clarity, I divide the discussion of reader differences, and what may explain them, into three categories that are illustrative rather than definitive. They include (1) sociocultural positionalities, (2) epistemic beliefs, and (3) prior historical ideas. These three categories are interconnected, overlapping, and mutually dependent, but, as I will show, distinctive in their implications for what teachers might work on in history education.

They are also important to history education because they impact the way educators and policymakers might think about the history curriculum and the ways it could be taught. Embedded here is a tension that traverses a continuum between accepting the idea that each reader is very likely to develop his or her own interpretations/stories/histories of the past and the desire to afford considerable discipline to them in order to avoid a corrosive relativism—that any old historical narrative will do. Therefore, understanding different reading protocols in history and their sources can go some distance toward bringing about disciplined reading protocols structured around strong text-evaluation criteria. This may be one of history education's chief purposes in K–12 schooling.

## Sociocultural Positionalities

Sociocultural positionality is a significant factor in how children read the past. By positionality I am referring to the social class and ethnoracial locations of children in society. To the extent that social class and ethnicity influence and are influenced by language metaphors, gender also would be considered part of one's positionality. Social class, ethnoracial, and gendered positionalities shape the texts we tell ourselves about who we are. Positionalities hold ontological, epistemic, and existential textual power. These texts of self in turn shape and reshape reading protocols, enabling some ways of reading and disenabling others, especially when it comes to reading in school and in the history classroom (e.g., Cherryholmes, 1999; Wineburg, 1991).

Ben is a brown-skinned Latino-American male, born of working-class parents who voluntarily emigrated to the US from Mexico. His first language was Spanish but he also learned English early and is fluently bilingual. His parents think of history in a different way than European Americans do. The latter form an ethnoracial group that traces lineage and history from east to west, from Europe across the Atlantic and then across North America. Ben's parents form a group that traces its history, generally speaking, in the opposite direction. Ben is often considered an outsider, despite the fact that he was born in the US.

Alexandra, by contrast, is an upper-middle-class female, born of European-American parents. Unlike Ben and Brittney, she has travelled widely and learned to read very early because she began at home and in preschool when she was only 3 years old. Her parents are conservative, believe very much in the textbook version of the American dream, and subscribe to the American sociocultural idea that, if you work hard, you can succeed at almost anything to which you set your mind. Ben's parents believe in the same thing, but to date have not been rewarded with the same benefits that Alexandra's parents have experienced.

Brittney is an African-American female. Her parents are also working class. Brittney traces her lineage and history through forced emigration from Africa and up through slavery, although she does not know of any of her slave ancestors because the records of that past have long been lost. Her parents also endorse the American dream, but, given their history, are far more skeptical of how and when that dream might be fully realized by black people. She has heard stories about slavery and involuntary immigration at the dinner table, in the community, and at church. She has also heard many stories of past civil rights struggles among black Americans, of marches on Washington, Dr. Martin Luther King and Malcolm X, of sacrifice, setbacks, and successes.

Research studies in history education have shown repeatedly that the historicized sociocultural positionalities of learners deeply influence how they read, investigate, and interpret the past (e.g., Epstein, 2009; Levstik, 2000; Seixas, 1993; Wineburg, Mosborg, Porat, & Duncan, 2007).

In one study, for example, conducted in Detroit schools, African-American students demonstrated strong reservations about trusting textbook and teacher accounts of American history (Epstein, 2009). They claimed that they had difficulty finding themselves in such treatments other than as victims of slavery and subsequent Jim Crow laws and Black Codes, or as victors during the civil rights movement. Many of the stories they had heard and learned in church and in the community did not coincide with what they heard and read in school, prompting considerable skepticism and occasional downright distrust. The African-American students in this study appeared to read from protocols that were similar to Brittney's.

European-American students interviewed as a part of this same study expressed considerable faith in their teachers' and the textbook's narratives. They were often selected first as definitive accounts of the past worth believing. The textbook and teacher stories tended to align with the texts the white students had constructed at home and in their community before they entered school. Textual skepticism for them was hardly necessary, since school texts corresponded with home and community texts, and, above all, tended to reinforce their existing sociocultural positionalities. Textbook and teacher texts could be read (and trusted)—as Alexandra appears to—as extensions of previously existing texts.

The textbook story that students often encounter in school history turns on a literary theme of relentless progress in America (e.g., Foner, 2002; Foster & Crawford, 2006; VanSledright, 2008). Life in the nation almost always improves. Democratic participation is widened to include more people. Technology advances making things easier. Wars allow for the US to vanquish threats to its freedom. The standard of living rises. This is the American dream: work hard and life gets better.

As pervasive as this theme might be, it remains questionable. Working-class people, the parents of Ben and Brittney, have witnessed the promises of this thematic register wane for them over the past several decades in particular (e.g., Stiglitz, 2012). Skepticism about believing in the textbook account might be a reasonable response to the demise of the American dream's promise. Alexandra, the child of upper-middle-class parents, is unlikely to harbor any reduction in her sense that the textbook accurately describes the thematic register of American life. Differences in social class moorings thus influence how these students read the past.

In some cases, social class appears to matter more than race/ethnicity in the ways in which students read history. In a study of upper-middle-class Cuban-American adolescents, researchers found that, despite their minority status, the adolescents read and interpreted US history much as European-American Alexandra did (Terzian & Yeager, 2007). The students considered the textbook narrative they encountered at school to be believable, and an accurate account of an American past that aligned with their experiences.

Gender is another influence. In history education, and with regard to reading history texts specifically, this is an under-researched area. Some speculation and inference are necessary in order to understand how gender influences reading and interpreting history texts. The illustration of the three readers provided gives us little insight into differences. However, we can see that the two girls are much more animated about what they have read and much more interested in discussing it. This coheres with general studies that indicate more interest in and frequency of reading coupled with greater verbal facility among girls (e.g., Logan & Johnston, 2009). But what influence does gender have on differences in reading and making meaning from history texts?

One exploratory study considered this question tangentially by asking groups of fifth- and seventh-grade boys and girls to draw pictures of pilgrims, settlers, and hippies after reading short texts about each group (Wineburg & Fournier, 1997). Both boys and girls showed a tendency to draw pictures of pilgrims and settlers as males. When it came to hippies, the boys tended to draw males, but the girls tended to draw females. The researchers speculated that drawings were influenced in the case of the hippies by the propensity children have to create images that reflect their own gender (e.g., Koppitz, 1968; Richey, 1965). But that did not explain what happened when they drew images of settlers and pilgrims. The researchers conjectured that the ways children have read history in school, especially through traditional textbook accounts, shaped a view of the past that placed males in positions of accomplishment, whereas females receded into the background. Textbooks typically tell long stories about pilgrims and settlers, but are relatively silent about hippies. In the former two cases, gendered reading (understood via drawings) reflected school socialization, whereas in the other case, children responded outside that shaping force in ways more consistent with research on how children draw gender-centric images.

Differences in positionalities shape reading practices in distinctive ways. However, they also can be *shaped by* the cultural texts in which reading protocols, and the interpretations of the past they generate, are situated. It is a delicate dance that cannot help but surface in any history class (and outside those classes). Focusing history readers' attention on that ubiquitous school task of finding the main idea in a paragraph, for example, all but ignores this fundamental reading issue.

## Epistemic Beliefs

By epistemic beliefs I mean the often taken-for-granted assumptions people hold about where knowledge comes from, how it gets produced, and how it is warranted as knowledge (Buehl & Alexander, 2001). Alexandra appears to hold rather rigid epistemic beliefs. She trusts the "knowledge" in the textbook as right, trustworthy, and ultimately most warranted. The other accounts are too biased to be believed. She dismisses them. Alexandra appears to say that the textbook's objective and straightforward treatment of the battle rendered in an omniscient tone by the almost invisible textbook authors is unassailable. Why can't Brittney and Ben see that?

Brittney and Ben are more suspicious, refusing to immediately trust the textbook as an object of warranted truth. They wish to explore the other textual objects in front of them. Here again, differing positionality-infused skepticism influences what they are willing to trust, what their epistemic beliefs will allow. They appear to trust themselves and their own judgments before they trust the objects. They want to retain the decision-making power over the texts, even if it means they have difficulty arriving at a singular interpretation.

Epistemic beliefs represent a specific manifestation of the influences of sociocultural positionalities. The epistemic problem among our case readers is deciding on what to trust from among several different possibilities. Alexandra defers to an object of ostensible veneration— the textbook story. It solves her epistemic problem. Brittney and Ben demur, preferring to wrestle longer with the problem, perhaps seeking to trust themselves in the end. As we saw, Alexandra has good reason to trust the textbook as an object of truth; Brittney and Ben less so. But neither fully trusting the textbook account or trusting one's own judgment seems to resolve the epistemic impasse.

Research work on epistemic beliefs in history and their influence on reading protocols and subsequent historical interpretations is ongoing. For now, researchers and theorists appear to cast the issue as a tension much like I have just suggested it—between objects from the past that can be known and the role of the knower in knowing them (e.g., Hofer & Pintrich, 2002; Maggioni, Alexander, & VanSledright, 2004; Maggioni, VanSledright, & Alexander, 2009; Tabak & Weinstock, 2011).

Epistemically speaking, objects from the past—histories of whatever stripe including a textbook—are not entirely trustworthy for a variety of reasons, the least of which is that they so often do not speak accurately about the past. They are authored interpretations of that past (Olneck, 1989). There are many ways to under or over-interpret them. History authors cannot overcome their own enculturated positionalities and are compelled to write from their perspective. That perspective must be interrogated. Alexandra is probably naive and misguided in her easy willingness to trust the textbook.

Yet trusting one's own judgment as Brittney and Ben seem to desire can be equally naive and misguided, especially among young readers who are investigating the battle at Lexington Green for the first time. Over-trusting self in this type of reading context can create unsupported interpretations. Young readers in history class are notorious for their lack of disciplined, history-specific reading and interpretive protocols (e.g., Afflerbach & VanSledright, 2001; Seixas, 1994; VanSledright & Brophy, 1992; Wineburg, 1991). They become beguiled by the idea that it is an interpretive free for all, in which any opinion will do because we are entitled to our opinions after all. What our three readers have yet to learn is how to apply sound criteria to their reading and interpretive protocols that *coordinate* what readers might defensibly conclude about the past with what can be known, gleaned analytically from its residual objects. Unexamined position-alities underpin unexamined epistemic beliefs that in turn influence reading and interpretation protocols in quite variable and unpredictable ways.

## Prior Historical Ideas

Social classed, gendered, and ethnoracialized positionalities also play a powerful role in the sorts of ideas readers bring to the history reading experience. This role has received considerable research attention. It has spawned at least four literature reviews specific to historical understanding (Barton, 2008, VanSledright & Limon, 2006; Voss, 1998; Wineburg, 1996). There is also a voluminous literature in reading research that speaks to the importance of prior ideas.

What children and adolescents have learned about the past, at school and away from it, forms a set of stories they carry in their minds, as I have noted. Those stories become woven into their positionalities. Even though our three readers may not know much if anything about Lexington Green, they do possess ideas about conflict, choosing sides, weapons, war, freedom, rights, varying opinions, everyday empathy, nations, patriotism, fear, and the like. These ideas and understandings might be naive, ill-formed, presentist (as opposed to historicized), and filled with unwarranted assumptions. But the ideas are embedded in stories children tell about who they are in the world in their efforts to make sense of it. Children and adolescents bring these stories to the classroom. The stories make up sizable portions of how children define themselves.

To the extent that positionalities vary as I have described them, the stories and their accompanying prior ideas and experiences children bring also vary. Alexandra's effort to silence intertextual/hypertextual noise likely stems from an unexamined belief that American colonists were fighting for their freedom, the right to live according to their own rules (on the power of this theme among Americans, see Wertsch & O'Connor, 1991). The British soldiers were intent on trying to abridge this inalienable right. The British therefore were the aggressors. It would make sense that they would charge onto Lexington Green, form a battle position, and begin to abridge the rights of the colonists to obtain their freedom. The textbook only confirms her prior ideas.

By contrast, Brittney's uneasiness about Alexandra's reading move may well come from a story she has learned to tell herself that the right to freedom in America has not been one to be granted equally. It was not every American's birthright and the right to life, liberty, and the pursuit of happiness often has been more rhetoric than reality for her African-American ancestors. Those ideas influence the interpretive and evaluative criteria that frame her reading protocol, her desire to read more closely, and to locate where rhetoric and reality converge and diverge. The story and its ideas and meanings are different for Brittney, and quite possibly for Ben as well. Making sense of the past is affected by the different prior ideas, meanings and metaphors these three readers bring to the classroom task.

## Addressing Reading Differences in History

The individual differences in reading and interpreting history that I have described suggest that children and adolescents approach their study of the past from distinctively personal and parochial positions. They impose those positions on the past as they read and make sense. This is their starting point; they cannot help but draw from their positionalities, epistemic beliefs, and prior ideas as they encounter that past. If we stand back and permit personal and parochial impositions to constitute the ways students achieve a history education, we might wish to ask whether or not this is sufficient. Do such impositions teach a deep understanding of the past, or of history, or of the shared culture? If a culture, such as that of the United States, prides itself on the democratic traditions it has built—traditions that require a civic mindfulness characterized by an embrace of the commonweal, tolerance for difference and pluralism, and the ability to exercise judgments that go well beyond personal and parochial interests—then the answer would be no.

If we agree with this answer, then learning to read and interpret the past, understand it deeply, and know how history works would need to be the centerpiece of a history education worthy of its name. However, this raises questions about how history students might learn to read and interpret. In other words, what reading protocols might they be taught in such a history education? This is a question that gets at the matter of mental discipline, of using cognitive strategies, tools, and criteria in learning to read.

School history—especially the course of study in United States history—has been used as a tool to teach a form of allegiance to a particular interpretation of that history. The common textbook has served as the primary purveyor of that storyline. Those who designed the school-history exercise pivoted it around what Gunner Myrdal calls the American creed (Schlesinger, 1991): believing in freedom, rugged individualism, a powerful work ethic, exceptionalism, boundless progress, and Manifest Destiny. Teaching the creed demands a reading protocol that is designed to supplant personal and parochial interests with nationalistic ones. Instead of allegiance to self and one's vernacular stories, the reading protocol cultivates allegiance to the state and its storyline (common in many countries; see Foster & Crawford, 2006).

However, as we saw, only one of our readers appears to accept this form of reading-protocol discipline. The other two resist. Historian Michael Frisch (1989) observes: "students cannot be bullied into attention or retention; that [type of] intimidation is likely to be met with further and more rapid retreat" (p. 1154). If Frisch is right that the type of reading protocol so common to school history misses its mark with many students, as Brittney's and Ben's history reading protocols suggest, then what other reading protocols and interpretive strategies might be an improvement? This has been the subject of a recent thought about disciplinary literacies (Moje, 2008; Shanahan & Shanahan, 2008).

In history education, researchers have been looking at how professional historians read the past in search of protocol strategies, criteria, and tools that enable them to more expertly make deep sense of the past and learn to check their parochial and personally narrow sentiments (e.g., Levisohn, 2010). Historians' ways of reading are then thought of as learning targets toward which young readers can be pointed (Ashby et al., 2005; VanSledright, 2002; Wineburg, Martin,

- Reading with textual skepticism (e.g., texts from or about the past cannot be fully trusted to mean exactly what they say)
- Asking questions, and interrogating texts from the past with them
- Identifying what a text is, where it comes from, and when
- Attributing the text to a historically situated author
- Assessing the author's perspective (e.g., possible agenda, subtext)
- Judging the reliability of a text for producing evidence used in addressing questions being asked
- Placing/reading texts within their historical context
- Deriving evidence from the texts (if possible) to address questions
- Corroborating evidence across multiple accounts in building interpretations
- Attempting to constrain the way the investigator imposes her own positionality on what is read

*Figure 18.1* Protocol criteria for reading expertise in learning history

& Monte-Sano, 2011). Not all researchers use exactly the same vocabulary to describe these forms of reading expertise; but the list might look like what appears in Figure 18.1.

These strategies form a type of history-specific reading protocol that is honored within the community of historians. The specific contours and criteria of the protocol are still debated. However, the protocol is honored because it (1) leads to deeper understandings of the past, (2) produces evidence-based interpretations that are considered defensible epistemologically, (3) leavens narrow interest meddling and parochialism, and (4) teaches tolerance for particularity and sociocultural and historic difference. The latter two outcomes seem especially welcome in cultures that pride themselves on their democratic traditions.

We can see that our three readers have much to learn if they are to reach this type of reading expertise, Alexandra most pointedly. Yet that is precisely what a history classroom experience might teach if it was configured to help such readers become more skillful and strategic. Rather than press readers to replace trust in vernacular self-stories with allegiance to an officialized nation-state story, it encourages a way of reading that seeks to provide a measure of coordination and balance between the two.

## Strategic and Skillful Literacy in History Class

By way of a conclusion, I briefly sketch out what a history classroom might look like that moves students toward attaining the types of literacy capabilities just described. This description will sit in sharp contrast to what we have typically done. Instead of pursuing the quixotic quest of compelling all students regardless of sociocultural difference to come, say, to one official interpretation of the past, the one found in the traditional textbook, the goal of a history course experience shifts to one in which students learn to read the past, *and themselves as a result*, much more closely and carefully.

The classroom is centered around rich historical questions. Students become historical investigators. They dig into accounts from the past (e.g., original and synthetic/secondary ones) clustered around particular watershed events and decisions. Knowledgeable history teachers use this occasion to teach young investigators how to read along the lines of the strategies described in Figure 18.1. Students apply those strategies to *build their own* interpretations of the past, but ones that are only acceptable because they can be defended by preponderating evidence drawn from accounts while also taking into consideration competing interpretations. Students learn that evidence-backed interpretations take precedence. Reading protocols are comprised of criteria that produce them.

Individual differences in interpretive outcomes are tolerated within this type of community. However, it becomes a matter of checking naive subjectivism, or arresting a corrosive relativism that concludes that any old personal opinion about the past is as good as any other. Drawing such conclusions breeds intolerance, feeds narrow parochial interests, defies an attitude of support for the commonweal, and ironically, tends to erode the glue that binds together the nation-state (see Kimlicka, 2001; Merry, 2003).

Reading in history configured on these literacy principles would tilt toward teaching respect for particularity and individual differences, but at the same time help to reverse some of their more troubling ramifications, such as the propensity to let narrow parochial and/or partisan interpretations stand unconstrained by an evidentiary basis. This is a type of reading that provides individual readers with a means of more skillfully navigating a multifaceted world while simultaneously respecting difference. It seems worth pursuing for just these reasons.

## References

Afflerbach, P., & VanSledright, B. A. (2001). Hath! Doth! What? Middle graders reading innovative history text. *Journal of Adolescent & Adult Literacy, 44*, 696–707.

Ashby, R., Lee, P. J., & Shemilt, D. (2005). Putting principles into practice: Teaching and planning. In S. Donovan & J. Bransford (Eds.), *How students learn: History in the classroom* (pp. 79–178). Washington, DC: National Academies Press.

Barton, K. C. (2008). Research on students' ideas about history. In L. Levstik & C. Tyson (Eds.), *Handbook of research in social studies education* (pp. 239–258). New York: Routledge.

Buehl, M., & Alexander, P. (2001). Beliefs about academic knowledge. *Educational Psychology Review, 13*, 385–418.

Cherryholmes, C. H. (1999). *Reading pragmatism*. New York: Teachers College Press.

Derrida, J. (1967). *Of grammatology*. Baltimore, MD: Johns Hopkins University Press.

Epstein, T. (2009). *Interpreting national history: Race, identity, and pedagogy in classrooms and communities*. New York: Routledge.

Foner, E. (2002). *Who owns history? Rethinking the past in a changing world*. New York: Hill and Wang.

Foster, S. J., & Crawford, K. (Eds.) (2006). *What shall we tell the children? International perspectives on school history textbooks*. Greenwich, CT: Information Age.

Frisch, M. (1989). American history and the structures of collective memory: A modest exercise in empirical iconography. *Journal of American History, 75*, 1130–1155.

Hofer, B., & Pintrich, P. (Eds.) (2002). *Personal epistemology: The psychology of beliefs of learning and knowing*. Mahwah, NJ: Lawrence Erlbaum Associates.

Kimlicka, W. (2001). *Politics in the vernacular: Nationalism, multiculturalism, and citizenship*. Oxford: Oxford University Press.

Koppitz, E. (1968). *Psychological evaluation of human figure drawings by middle school pupils*. Boston, MA: Pearson Allyn & Bacon.

Lee, P. J. (2005). Putting principles into practice: Understanding history. In S. Donovan & J. Bransford (Eds.), *How students learn: History in the classroom* (pp. 31–78). Washington, DC: National Academies Press.

Levisohn, J. (2010). Negotiating historical narratives: An epistemology of history for history education. *Journal of Philosophy of Education, 44*, 1–21.

Levstik, L. S. (2000). Articulating the silences: Teachers' and adolescents' conceptions of historical significance. In P. Stearns, P. Seixas, & S. Wineburg (Eds.), *Knowing, teaching, and learning history: National and International Perspectives* (pp. 284–305). New York: New York University Press.

Logan, S., & Johnston, R. (2009). Gender differences in reading ability and attitudes: Examining where these differences lie. *Journal of Research in Reading, 32*, 199–214.

Maggioni, L., Alexander, P., & VanSledright, B. (2004). At the crossroads: The development of epistemological beliefs and historical thinking. *European Journal of School Psychology, 2*, 169–197

Maggioni, L., VanSledright, B., & Alexander, P. (2009). Walking on the borders: A measure of epistemic cognition in history. *Journal of Experimental Education, 77*, 187–213.

Merry, M. S. (2003). Patriotism, history, and the legitimate aims of American education. *Educational Philosophy and Theory, 41*, 378–398.

Moje, E. B. (2008). Foregrounding the disciplines in secondary literacy teaching and learning. *Journal of Adolescent & Adult Literacy, 52*, 97–107

Olneck, M. (1989). Americanization and the education of immigrants, 1900–1925: An analysis of symbolic action. *American Journal of Education, 92*, 398–423.

Richey, M. (1965). Qualitative superiority of the "self" figure in children's drawings. *Journal of Clinical Psychology, 21*, 59–61.

Schlesinger, Jr., A. (1991). *The disuniting of America: Reflections on a multicultural society.* New York: Whittle Communications.

Scholes, R. (1989). *Protocols of reading.* New Haven: Yale University Press.

Seixas, P. (1993). Historical understanding among adolescents in a multicultural setting. *Curriculum Inquiry, 23*, 301–327.

Seixas, P. (1994). Confronting the moral frames of popular film: Young people respond to historical revisionism. *American Journal of Education, 102*, 261–285.

Shanahan, T., & Shanahan, C. (2008). Teaching disciplinary literacy to adolescents: Rethinking content-area literacy. *Harvard Educational Review, 78*, 40–59.

Stiglitz, J. (2012). *The price of inequality: How today's divided society endangers our future.* New York: W. W. Norton.

Tabak, I., & Weinstock, M. (2011). If there is no one right answer? The epistemological implications of classroom interactions. In J. Brownlee, G. Shraw, & D. Berthelson (Eds.), *Personal epistemology and teacher education* (pp. 180–194). New York: Routledge.

Terzian, S. G., & Yeager, E. A. (2007). "That's when we became a nation": Urban Latino adolescents and the designation of historical significance. *Urban Education, 42*, 52–81.

VanSledright, B. A. (2002). *In search of America's past: Learning to read history in elementary school.* New York: Teachers College Press.

VanSledright, B. (2008). Narratives of nation state, historical knowledge, and school history education. *Review of Research in Education, 32*, 109–146.

VanSledright, B. (2012). Learning with history texts: Protocols for reading and practical strategies. In T. Jetton & C. Shanahan (Eds.), *Adolescent literacy within disciplines: General principles and practical strategies* (pp. 199–226). New York: Guilford.

VanSledright, B., & Afflerbach, P. (2005). Assessing the status of historical sources: An exploratory study of eight elementary students reading documents. In P. Lee. (Ed.), *Children and teachers' ideas about history*, International Research in History Education, Vol. 4 (pp. 1–20). London: Routledge/Falmer.

VanSledright, B., & Brophy, J. (1992). Storytelling, imagination, and fanciful elaboration in children's reconstructions of history. *American Educational Research Journal, 29*, 837–859.

VanSledright, B. A., & Limon, M. (2006). Learning and teaching in social studies: Cognitive research on history and geography. In P. Alexander & P. Winne (Eds.), *The handbook of educational psychology*, 2nd ed. (pp. 545–570). Mahwaeh, NJ: Lawrence Erlbaum Associates.

Voss, J. (1998). Issues in the learning of history. *Issues in Education: Contributions from Educational Psychology, 4*, 163–209.

Wertsch J., & O'Connor, K. (1991). Multi-voicedness in historical representation: American college students accounts of the origin of the US. *Journal of Narrative and Life History, 4*, 295–310.

Wineburg, S. S. (1991). On the reading of historical texts: Notes on the breach between school and academy. *American Educational Research Journal, 28*, 495–519.

Wineburg, S. S. (1996). The psychology of teaching and learning history. In R. Calfee & D. Berliner (Eds.), *Handbook of educational psychology* (pp. 423–437). New York: Macmillan Reference.

Wineburg, S., & Fournier, J. E. (1997). Picturing the past: Gender differences in the depiction of historical figures. *American Journal of Education, 105,* 160–185.

Wineburg, S., Martin, D., & Monte-Sano, C. (2011). *Reading like a historian: Teaching literacy in middle and high school history classrooms.* New York: Teachers College Press.

Wineburg, S., Mosborg, S., Porat, D., & Duncan, A., (2007). Common belief and the cultural curriculum: An intergenerational study of historical consciousness. *American Educational Research Journal, 44,* 40–76.

# 19

# Individual Differences in the New Literacies of Online Research and Comprehension

*Donald J. Leu, Carita Kiili, and Elena Forzani*

Knowledge-based societies require citizens to be skilled in the effective use of online information for inquiry and communication (OECD, 2010; Rouet et al., 2009). The ability to conduct online research, comprehend, and learn has become an important aspect of online information use (Goldman, Braasch, Wiley, Graesser, & Brodowinska, 2012). Research into the individual differences of online research and comprehension is important so that educational systems can better support the diversity that defines us, especially as the Internet is now central to both literacy and life.

We face an important challenge, however. As reading shifts from page to screen, new literacies emerge from the new online texts, technologies, affordances, and social practices that become possible (Lankshear & Knobel, 2006; Kist, 2005). As a result, we are unable to simply apply what we know about individual differences from offline reading to online reading; the two are not necessarily isomorphic (Leu et al., 2007).

There is also another challenge; new literacies are not just new today, they are new every day as even newer technologies are regularly distributed online (Leu, Kinzer, Coiro, Castek, & Henry, 2013). Each contains new affordances, requiring additional new literacies. This also complicates our understanding. Do the individual differences in online research and comprehension that we know about today apply tomorrow, when even newer technologies for literacy appear?

This chapter explores an emerging understanding of individual differences in online research and comprehension. We begin by defining online research and comprehension and exploring several measurement issues that present challenges to the analysis of individual differences in this area. Then we discuss what we know about individual differences in online research and comprehension in a number of areas. We conclude by connecting these issues to the development of a broader theory of New Literacies.

Donald J. Leu et al.

## Defining Online Research and Comprehension

Initially, online reading comprehension was the term used to describe what happens when we read online to identify a question, and then locate, critically evaluate, synthesize, and communicate online information. This construct informed several earlier studies into online reading (Castek, 2008; Coiro, 2011; Coiro & Dobler, 2007; Leu, Castek, & Hartman, 2006) often framed within an emerging new literacies theory (Leu, Kinzer, Coiro, & Cammack, 2004). Unfortunately, the term online reading comprehension, connected to a theory of new literacies, has led to some confusion about whether or not anything is really "new" when we read online, perhaps because people first encountering the construct assumed a limited online reading activity such as the reading of a single web page.

There are many situations in which we might read online, such as when we read an email message, an online newspaper, or a single web page. Isolated reading acts, such as these, do not differ from offline reading comprehension except for the online context; there is little that is "new." Usually, however, online reading does not take place within isolated contexts. Instead, it occurs within a rich and complex process of inquiry as we seek answers to questions, large and small, and use the Internet to learn.

Recently, a more precisely descriptive term, the new literacies of online research and comprehension, has been used to capture the rich and complex nature of this inquiry process with greater precision and accuracy (Leu et al., 2013). In addition, one can more easily understand how this term might not be identical to offline reading comprehension since online research requires technologies that are not used during offline reading (e.g., text messaging and note-taking tools) and online comprehension requires additional strategies (e.g., using a search engine to locate information about the creator of a website to help determine the reliability of the information).

Online research and comprehension is a process of problem-based inquiry using information on the Internet. It includes the skills, strategies, dispositions, and social practices that take place as we read online information to learn (Leu et al., 2013). During online research and comprehension, readers construct texts, meaning, and knowledge while engaged in several online reading practices: reading to identify important problems, reading to locate information, reading to critically evaluate information, reading to synthesize information, and reading to communicate information.

Online research and comprehension is not limited to lengthy and formal research projects. It also includes shorter tasks when one needs to know the answer to a question such as "When was Abraham Lincoln born?" or "What is the easiest way to get to downtown London from Heathrow?" Information queries, both large and small, initiate online research and require the use of new technologies to read, comprehend, and learn.

## Differences between Offline Comprehension and Online Research and Comprehension

Does the nature of reading and writing change during online research and comprehension? What individual differences are important to this process? We are just discovering answers to these questions (Afflerbach & Cho, 2010). Preliminary evidence suggests that online research and comprehension may include additional, somewhat distinctive, skills and strategies compared to offline reading comprehension (Coiro, 2011; Coiro & Dobler, 2007; Leu et al., 2007).

Both offline and online elements of comprehension are layered in complex ways during online research and comprehension, and the nature of this commingling is yet to be fully understood

260

(Leu et al., 2013). Much like offline comprehension, online research and comprehension includes meaning construction. It appears to differ, though, from offline reading comprehension in several respects.

First, online research and comprehension take place within a problem-solving task (Castek, Coiro, Guzniczak, & Bradshaw, 2012); a question or other informational need activates and informs the reading of online information. This results in a complex sampling process, as readers only select portions of text, often from multiple sources, to inform the solution of the problem. While this can happen with offline reading comprehension, it always happens during online research and comprehension.

Second, while readers construct meaning during both offline comprehension and online research and comprehension, they also physically construct the texts that they read online. They construct these texts through the sampling choices that they make and the links that they follow (Coiro & Dobler, 2007). Again, this can happen offline but always happens during online research and comprehension.

Third, online research and comprehension take place in a complex and unrestricted information space that may be poorly structured and ill-defined—the Internet. Typically, offline reading takes place within a more restricted, well structured, and more clearly defined information space.

A fourth difference is that new technologies such as browsers, search engines, wikis, blogs, email, and others are required, each containing affordances that differ from those found offline. Thus, additional skills and strategies appear to be needed in order to read, write, and interact with each of these technologies effectively.

Fifth, online research and comprehension also become tightly intertwined with writing as we communicate with others to learn more about the problems we seek to solve, and this often includes writing and communication as important parts of the meaning construction processes. For example, readers might take notes or seek others' opinions on Twitter, with text messaging, or on many other communication tools available on the Internet. During offline reading this may occur with writing, but not always, and typically not in such easily accessible, collaborative, and socially constructed ways.

Finally, while both offline comprehension and online research and comprehension require higher-level, critical thinking, this might be needed even more often online (Forzani, & Maykel, 2013). In a context in which anyone may publish anything, higher-level thinking skills, such as the critical evaluation of source material, are required with particular frequency. Again, this happens offline, of course (cf. Bråten, Strømsø, & Britt, 2009), but it becomes especially urgent and important online.

This brief discussion of the distinctive nature of online research and comprehension suggests a number of areas where individual differences are likely to appear. The precise nature of these individual differences as well as the extent to which they may differ from offline reading comprehension are not completely understood, however. This is at least partly true because we have yet to fully solve several measurement issues.

## Measurement Issues

### The Unique Nature of Readers' Text Constructions

During online research and comprehension, readers construct their own texts as they select different links, follow different paths, and connect different texts to solve a problem. Seldom will two readers read the same texts; each constructs a unique text from choices that are made during the location, evaluation, and synthesis of information (Leu et al., 2007). Even when two students have an identical problem to solve, they may use different keywords to locate information, evaluate and select different links from a set of search results, explore links on a web page in distinctive ways, and connect the results in a unique fashion (Coiro & Dobler, 2007; Leu et al., 2013).

The unique nature of readers' text construction processes presents a central challenge for measuring individual differences. This is not to indicate that larger patterns cannot be identified, but that any conclusions about comprehension, drawn from multiple individuals who read the same text, are not possible. On the other hand, the unique nature of readers' text construction processes presents a special opportunity to explore an additional layer of individual differences by studying differences in text construction processing. To date, there have been no systematic studies of this area.

## The Limited Number of Stable Assessments that Capture the Complex and Integrated Aspect of Online Research and Comprehension

The first assessments used in this area (Leu et al., 2006) took place within the dynamic environment of the Internet, presenting a problem with stability. Simply put, the reading context changed from day to day, making comparability difficult, if not impossible, for any single reader, or groups of readers, over time. This also presented important challenges when trying to compare the performance of different individuals at different times, or when growth curve analyses (Duncan, Duncan, & Strycker, 2013) are conducted.

Recently, several assessments have been developed that measure elements of online research and comprehension in more stable environments: PISA's Digital Reading Assessment (OECD, 2011), PIAAC's Problem Solving in Technology-Rich Environments (Rouet et al., 2009), Global Integrated Scenario-Based Assessments, or GISA (Sabatini, O'Reilly, Halderman, & Bruce, 2014), and Online Research and Comprehension Assessments, or ORCAs (Leu, Kulikowich, Sedransk, & Coiro, 2009).

The PISA Digital Reading and PIAAC assessments sampled performance with isolated tasks within separate and restricted information spaces for items. As a result, they may not capture the full complexity and complex interdependencies that appear between elements of online research and comprehension tasks. Many items, for example, appear within a multiple-choice format and/or take place at a single website. Somewhat surprisingly, there are a far greater percentage of multiple-choice items, restricting the information space for responses, that appear in the PISA Digital Reading Assessment (72 percent) than appear in the PISA assessment of print reading (47 percent).

The lack of a connected and more integrated sequence of tasks in the first two assessments fails to capture the more complex and integrated nature of online research and comprehension. Thus, any analysis of individual differences based on these measures may be limited. The GISA approach uses scenario-based assessments to attempt to measure more integrated skills associated with higher-level comprehension during online research and comprehension in a stable environment. This is an important improvement on previous attempts.

Another recent attempt to capture the complexity of online research and comprehension in a stable environment is the ORCA project (Leu et al., 2009). This project has developed performance-based assessments that include online research and problem-solving tasks in science within a stable but complex information space, a representation of the actual Internet. This includes a social network, a search engine, websites imported from the Internet, text messaging, a notepad, a wiki, and email. Students conduct an online research project on topics in human body systems and their performance on 16 different aspects of the task are evaluated. A video overview appears at http://youtu.be/aXxrR2wBR5Y and a video of one assessment appears at http://neag.uconn.edu/orcavideo-ira/. Approaches such as GISA and ORCA may be more likely to give us a better understanding of individual differences in online research and comprehension by using an assessment context that is both rich and complex as well as stable.

## Individual Differences: The Components of Online Research and Comprehension and the Monitoring and Regulation of these Practices

### Component Areas

A number of studies (e.g., Coiro, 2011; Coiro & Dobler, 2007; Goldman et al., 2012) have explored various contexts of online research and comprehension. Most have tended to focus on the cognitive practices and the relative difficulty of these skills for students, in general, rather than systematically examining individual differences in component skills. There are, however, several small-scale studies that have tried to capture individual differences in component skills.

Kiili, Laurinen, and Marttunen (2008, 2009) found considerable inter-individual differences among 25 upper secondary school students in their ability to locate relevant information on the web. The students who located relevant information effectively were able to spend much of their time reading useful online sources. On the other end of the continuum, students less skilled at locating information online spent more time trying to locate useful information and, as a result, had less time available for reading relevant information.

In addition to individual differences with locating information, several studies have found that students generally lack skills in critically evaluating online information (e.g., Grimes & Boening, 2001; Walraven, Brand-Gruwel, & Boshuizen, 2008). However, only a few studies have reported findings related to individual differences in this area. Kiili et al. (2008) found five evaluation profiles among 25 upper secondary schools students, using several dimensions of evaluation: *versatile evaluators* considered both the relevance and credibility of information by applying various evaluation strategies; *relevance-oriented evaluators* paid attention to the relevance of information but, compared to versatile evaluators, gave less attention to the credibility of information, and their strategic repertoire was also not very diverse; *limited evaluators* seldom evaluated the credibility of information, and their evaluation of relevance was less active compared to the previously mentioned groups of students; *disoriented readers* had difficulty in locating relevant information on the Internet; and *uncritical readers* differed from the other groups in the quality of the web pages they selected to read.

Synthesizing information during online reading may be the least understood online reading practice. There are some studies that have explored synthesizing information with pre-selected online texts (e.g., van Strien, Brand-Gruwel, & Boshuizen, 2014; Wiley et al., 2009) but few studies (Barzilai & Zohar, 2012; Kiili, Hirvonen, & Leu, 2013) have explored the synthesis of multiple online sources within a dynamic, Internet environment. Barzilai and Zohar (2012) investigated sixth-graders' epistemologies and their relation to online reading practices. They found considerable variability in students' epistemic thinking which, in turn, was found to play an important role in the way in which the students integrated online sources. Students who viewed knowledge as complex and developing made comparisons between websites and used multiple websites to construct an argument more often than the students who viewed knowledge as absolute.

## Metacognition

The Internet is a complex information environment that requires readers to orchestrate several, often intertwined, cognitive processes. As such, it is likely to demand substantial amounts of metacognitive processing (Kiili, 2012; Quintana, Zhang, & Krajcik, 2005). Quintana et al. (2005) suggest that problems in metacognitive processing may appear as inadequate planning of search tasks, poor time allocation between searching and other online reading practices, and an inability to change one's ineffective behavior. Kiili et al. (2009; see also Kiili, 2012) found differences among upper secondary school students in how they planned, monitored, and regulated their activities on the web. While some students seemed to work on the web in a forward-looking, proactive fashion, adjusting their strategies to the task's demands, others largely monitored and regulated their immediate actions in a reactive fashion. The way of working seemed to be associated with success in locating relevant information, the evaluation of information relevance, and with elaborative processing of content.

Some research describes attempts to support students' metacognitive processes during online reading with verbal scaffolds (Li & Lim, 2008). Online reading also has been supported with software tools that prompt readers to monitor their activities, making students more aware of online reading processes (Stadtler & Bromme, 2008; Zhang & Quintana, 2012). Research still needs to clarify how students with differing skills, epistemological beliefs, and learning problems benefit from metacognitive support, and how metacognition develops for online readers.

## Individual Differences: Gender, Domain Knowledge, and Economics

### Gender

There is little research on gender differences specifically related to online research and comprehension. The primary international source, the PISA study of digital reading (2011) shows a gender gap among 15-year-olds in 19 nations, favoring girls who scored, on average, 24 points higher than boys. This gender gap was larger with offline reading (39 score points) compared to online reading (24 score points), suggesting that girls perform better than boys, overall, but that the gap is larger for offline reading than for online reading. The smallest gap in online reading (3 score points) appeared in Colombia; the largest gap (40 points) appeared in New Zealand. Thus, gender differences may be somewhat related to culture.

Studies of gender differences in attitudes towards the Internet provide somewhat mixed findings and may suggest that gender differences in attitudes are changing. Earlier studies showed that men and boys had more positive attitudes about the Internet (e.g., Jackson, Ervin, Gardner, & Schmitt, 2001; Schumacher & Morahan-Martin, 2001). Other, more recent, studies have shown no difference in attitudes between boys and girls (e.g., Kim, Lehto, & Morrison, 2007; Koohang & Durante, 2003). Few direct studies exist, however, of gender differences in attitudes specific to online research and comprehension.

## Domain Knowledge

Domain knowledge of a topic is a major contributor to reading comprehension with offline texts (Kintsch, 2000; Spilich, Vesonder, Chiesi, & Voss, 1979). Domain knowledge also appears to be important during online research and comprehension, but perhaps in different ways. One of the few studies to evaluate the role of domain knowledge during online research and comprehension was conducted by Coiro (2011). Surprisingly, Coiro found that prior knowledge of the domain did not significantly contribute to predicting online research and comprehension performance among 13-year-olds when offline reading comprehension ability was controlled. Coiro speculated that students with lower levels of domain knowledge could acquire it through the texts they selected during the online research and comprehension task, thus developing necessary prior knowledge along the way. No data were provided to support this hypothesis, however, and studies have yet to replicate this finding. Thus, we will need to establish the precise role of domain knowledge and how it differs among individual students during online research and comprehension.

## Economics

According to the National Assessment of Educational Progress, the offline reading achievement gap based on wealth is not only substantial but is increasing in the US, while the gaps based on ethnicity are decreasing (Bailey & Dynarski, 2011; Reardon, 2011). Leu et al. (2012) controlled for offline reading comprehension differences and found a separate and independent achievement gap in online research and comprehension between seventh grade students attending economically advantaged and challenged 5 school districts. This suggests that achievement gaps may actually be greater than those found in offline reading.

Given the expense of computers and online access, advantages are likely to accrue to students from wealthier households as they are more likely to have opportunities to conduct online research and comprehend online information at home. Data from the US Census indicate that 35.6 percent of households with income less than $25,000 have no computer at home and no Internet access anywhere, while only 2.8 percent of households with income of $150,000 or greater report the same (US Census Bureau, 2013).

Internationally, the PISA assessment of digital reading found, on average, a significant difference in scores between students who used a computer at home and those who did not use a computer at home (OECD, 2011). Another recent study found there was both an offline reading achievement gap and a separate and independent online research and comprehension achievement gap between seventh grade students attending a richer school district and a poorer district in the US (Leu et al., 2012). These results suggest there may be important equity issues, in many nations, with online research and comprehension.

# Individual Differences: Younger Children, Older Adults, and Struggling Readers

## Younger Children

Investigations into online research and comprehension have focused primarily on adolescents and college-age students (e.g., Coiro & Dobler, 2007; Goldman et al., 2012) while young children largely have been ignored. This is especially true in studies of broader digital literacy issues in young children's classrooms where there is little research (Burnett, 2009). Instead, most research with young children focuses on out-of-school digital literacy practices (e.g., Lieberman, Bates, & So, 2009). Many important questions that focus on school contexts have yet to be fully explored, such as "What type of instruction is needed for different types of young learners, and how should this instruction be implemented?" "Will different instructional models work better than others for particular types of readers?" Research that examines these issues would allow teachers to create more targeted instruction to better suit the needs of particular types of younger learners.

Several studies of young children's in-depth, online experiences have found that these experiences can greatly contribute to overall learning among young children (Black, 2010; Kafai, 2010; Marsh, 2011). Yet these studies have not looked specifically at online research and comprehension. Instead, they have focused more on online games and virtual worlds than on reading, specifically. One exception is a study by Zawilinski (2012) who compared fifth graders and first graders during a collaborative classroom research project requiring the use of a blog. Students in both classrooms taught one another important blog strategies but first graders required instruction in how to effectively teach one another. Generally, however, we are still developing an understanding of individual differences in online research and comprehension during young children's development.

## Older Adult Learners

Similarly, there are only limited data on individual differences among older, adult learners. We know that older adults (ages 60–83) perform less well than younger adults on well-defined search tasks (e.g., searching for a specific medical condition using a given medical term and its definition) but perform better than younger adults on less well-defined search tasks such as searching for information on pain symptoms (Chin, Fu, & Kannampallil, 2009). It also appears that older adults use qualitatively different search strategies while locating information, taking more of a conceptually-based, "top down" approach compared to younger adults (Fairweather, 2008). Thus, at both ends of the lifespan continuum there is a need for ongoing research that helps us better understand the nature of individual differences.

## Struggling Readers

We also know little about how struggling offline readers perform with online research and comprehension. The prevailing wisdom, often expressed in schools, is that students who are weak offline readers should wait until they are more skilled at offline reading before going online. However, there are several aspects of online research and comprehension that may actually facilitate reading for weaker offline readers.

First, the Internet is a multimedia context with video, audio, and animations that are likely to support weaker offline readers (Henry, Castek, O'Byrne, & Zawilinski, 2012). These supports may be easier to make meaning from than text for these readers. Second, online research and comprehension typically require the reading of shorter text units as short search result entries are read and as readers follow links to drill down to important information where they then skim a page to locate the relevant information. Having to read shorter units of text may be supportive since struggling readers typically struggle with fluency and longer text. Thus, those struggling readers who are skilled in locating information do not always have to labor with the fluency demands required to read extended text.

Third, readers direct their own reading paths during online research and comprehension through the links they select. Thus, it may be more likely that weaker readers can find information suitable to their interest, prior knowledge, and ability through the choices they make. All of these aspects may motivate weaker readers to continue to read online, since online text contains important supports. This may further develop their reading skills as students gain more and more practice. This, however, is speculation. We require systematic studies of struggling readers to fully evaluate individual differences among this population. We have little work in this area.

Goldman et al. (2012) found that better learners engaged in greater amounts of sense making, self-explanation, and comprehension monitoring on reliable sites than did poorer learners. These were college students, however, few of whom are likely to truly struggle with reading. This study reminds us that the Internet can pose unique challenges to struggling readers, as readers must contend with clickable and often moving advertisements, hyperlinks, and multimedia features, which can be distractions. It is clear that much more work is needed to ascertain the extent to which struggling readers offline are also struggling readers online, or if several unique affordances of online reading permit special opportunities for learning among struggling readers.

## Individual Differences: Collaborative Online Research and Comprehension

From more of a social practice perspective (Lankshear & Knobel, 2006), online research and comprehension seem to be enhanced when students engage in productive collaboration (Castek et al., 2012; Kiili et al., 2012). Kiili, Laurinen, Marttunen, and Leu (2012) conducted a study of Finnish upper secondary students who read online, in pairs, to gather information and write a short report about a controversial issue. Cluster analysis revealed five collaborative reading profiles ranging, in order, from the greatest to the least amount of collaboration: co-constructors, collaborators, blenders, individually oriented readers, and silent readers. Essay performance matched this sequence of profiles, with those who co-constructed meaning the most having the highest scores.

However, it seems that students differ considerably in their ability to engage in productive collaborative interaction during online inquiry (Castek et al., 2012; Kiili et al., 2012; Sormunen, Tanni, Alamettälä, & Heinström, 2013). While some students can take full advantage of the collaborative situation by engaging in productive co-construction of meaning, others may have a stronger preference for working alone (Kiili et al., 2012). What we do not know yet is how various individual (e.g., personality traits and epistemic beliefs), social (e.g., relationships between students), and cultural factors (e.g., culturally specific conversational conventions) are related to these differences.

Some direction may be provided by Davis and Neitzel (2010), who looked at students' reading orientations: strategy-oriented, experience-oriented, precision-oriented, or tactic-oriented. They found these reading orientations were related to interaction patterns while working together to construct meaning from four printed short texts. In addition, personality traits and individual approaches to studying may affect successful interaction patterns during online research and comprehension.

Gender differences may also influence collaborative interaction patterns when students read online together. Salminen, Marttunen, and Laurinen (2012) found gender differences in communication styles when students engaged in chat discussions after reading three offline texts on a controversial issue. Results from this study suggest that males' more adversarial communication style may support the critical exploration of issues during online inquiry, whereas females' more collaborative communication style may facilitate the sharing and elaboration of ideas.

Finally, there appear to be some cultural differences in the ways in which people talk about and learn from texts. For example, Weinberger, Marttunen, Laurinen, and Stegmann (2013) found cultural differences in communication styles when Finnish and German students tried to solve a problem in an online learning environment with the help of text material they read. Compared to Finnish students, the argumentative practices of German students were more conflict-oriented. German students expressed disagreements whereas Finnish students avoided them and often integrated arguments of learning partners into their own line of reasoning. Although the study found cultural differences that may frame the way people talk around text, there are also situational and personal differences within cultures as well.

## Individual Differences in Online Research and Comprehension: Theoretical Implications

This review of individual differences in online research and comprehension suggests that we have much work ahead. Part of the challenge is that we now read in continuously changing contexts online.

How can we develop adequate theory about individual differences in online research and comprehension when the very context for our study of these differences continuously changes? Our field has never before faced a challenge like this, since literacy has generally been static, permitting us, over time, to carefully study and understand it. One way out of this conundrum may be to think about theory on two different levels using a dual-level theory of New Literacies (Leu et al., 2013).

A dual-level theory of New Literacies conceptualizes literacy at lowercase (new literacies) and uppercase (New Literacies) levels. Lowercase conceptions of new literacy, such as the new literacies of online research and comprehension, are better able to keep up with the rapidly changing nature of literacy; they are closer to the specific types of changes that take place. There are many other lowercase conceptions of new literacies, driven by separate lines of research, such as studies of text messaging (Lewis & Fabos, 2005), the semiotics of multimodality in online media (Kress, 2003), or new literacy studies (Street, 2003). Multiple lowercase theories permit our field to maximize the perspectives we use and the technologies and contexts we study. This chapter has only focused on one of these lowercase theories, the new literacies of online research and comprehension, and we have described the limited knowledge we have of individual differences in this area. Similar limitations exist in the many other lowercase levels of new literacies.

New Literacies, the uppercase theory, includes the common principles that appear across most lowercase areas. These common principles define New Literacies and, as such, are likely to be more stable in a context in which the technologies of literacy rapidly change. While eight common principles have been identified (Leu et al., 2013), none speaks to the important issues of individual differences in online contexts. This review of work in one lowercase area of new literacies suggests that much work remains to be done, suggesting that the principles of New Literacies may need to be reframed around individual differences to bring greater attention to this important issue. This is a significant omission since nearly all of these lines of research explore performance with complex literacy tasks online, a context that should be rich with possibilities for individual variation and could inform an uppercase theory of New Literacies in important ways.

In today's knowledge-based society, where accessing and using online information is essential for full participation in both work and life, creating effective learning environments to teach online information skills is important. Understanding individual differences is essential for designing and creating these environments for learners of different genders, ages, ability levels, cultures, socioeconomic backgrounds, and developmental stages. Clearly, however, we have much work ahead of us before we can confidently create effective learning environments tailored to the needs of individual students, preparing them for a world that is increasingly defined by reading, writing, communicating, and learning online.

## Acknowledgments

Portions of this material are based on work supported by the US Department of Education under Award No. R305G050154 and R305A090608. Opinions expressed herein are solely those of the authors and do not necessarily represent the position of the US Department of Education, Institute of Educational Sciences.

We wish to express our appreciation to Nicole Timbrell who assisted with the research for this project and in the construction of the ORCA video.

## References

Afflerbach, P. A., & Cho, B. Y. (2010). Determining and describing reading strategies: Internet and traditional forms of reading. In H. S. Waters & W. Schneider (Eds.), *Metacognition, strategy use, and instruction* (pp. 201–255). New York: Guilford.

Bailey, M. J., & Dynarski, S. M. (2011). *Gains and gaps: Changing inequality in U.S. college entry and completion.* National Bureau of Economic Research Working Paper No. 17633. Cambridge, MA: National Bureau of Economic Research. Available at: http://www.nber.org/papers/w17633.pdf.

Barzilai, S., & Zohar, A. (2012). Epistemic thinking in action: Evaluating and integrating online sources. *Cognition and Instruction, 30*(1), 39–85.

Black, R. W. (2010). The language of Webkinz: Early childhood literacy in an online virtual world. *Digital Culture & Education, 2*(1), 7–24.

Bråten, I., Strømsø, H. I., & Britt, M. A. (2009). Trust matters: Examining the role of source evaluation in students' construction of meaning within and across multiple texts. *Reading Research Quarterly, 44*, 6–28.

Burnett, C. (2009). Research into literacy and technology in primary classrooms: An exploration of understandings generated by recent studies. *Journal of Research in Reading, 32*(1), 22–37.

Castek, J. (2008). *How do 4th and 5th grade students acquire the new literacies of online reading comprehension? Exploring the contexts that facilitate learning.* Unpublished doctoral dissertation, University of Connecticut, Storrs, CT.

Castek, J., Coiro, J., Guzniczak, L., & Bradshaw, C. (2012). Examining peer collaboration in online inquiry. *Educational Forum, 76*(4), 479–496.

Chin, J., Fu, W. T., & Kannampallil, T. (2009). Adaptive information search: Age-dependent interactions between cognitive profiles and strategies. In *Proceedings of the SIGCHI Conference on Human Factors in Computing Systems* (pp. 1683–1692). ACM.

Coiro, J. (2011). Predicting reading comprehension on the Internet contributions of offline reading skills, online reading skills, and prior knowledge. *Journal of Literacy Research, 43*(4), 352–392.

Coiro, J., & Dobler, E. (2007). Exploring the online reading comprehension strategies used by sixth-grade skilled readers to search for and locate information on the Internet. *Reading Research Quarterly, 42*(2), 214–257.

Davis, D. S., & Neitzel, C. (2010). The relationship between students' reading orientations and their strategic activity during a collaborative reading task. *Reading Psychology, 31*(6), 546–579.

Duncan, T. E., Duncan, S. C., & Strycker, L. A. (2013). *An introduction to latent variable growth curve modeling: Concepts, issues, and application.* New York: Routledge Academic.

Fairweather, P. (2008). How older and younger adults differ in their approach to problem solving on a complex Website. In *Proceedings of the 10th international ACM SIGACCESS conference on computers and accessibility*. Halifax, Nova Scotia, Canada: ACM.

Forzani, E., & Maykel, C. (2013). Teaching digital literacies for the Common Core: What results from new assessments tell us. *Connecticut Reading Association Journal*, *1*(4), 12–17.

Goldman, S., Braasch, J., Wiley, J., Graesser, A., & Brodowinska, K. (2012). Comprehending and learning from Internet sources: Processing patterns of better and poorer learners. *Reading Research Quarterly*, *47*, 356–381. doi:10.1002/RRQ.027

Grimes, D. J., & Boening, C. H. (2001). Worries with the web: A look at student use of web resources. *College & Research Libraries*, *62*(1), 11–23.

Henry, L. A., Castek, J., O'Byrne, W. I., & Zawilinski, L. (2012). Using peer collaboration to support online reading, writing, and communication: An empowerment model for struggling readers. *Reading & Writing Quarterly*, *28*(3), 279–306.

Jackson, L. A., Ervin, K. S., Gardner, P. D., & Schmitt, N. (2001). Gender and the Internet: Women communicating and men searching. *Sex Roles*, *44*(5–6), 363–379.

Kafai, Y. B. (2010). World of Whyville: An introduction to tween virtual life. *Games and Culture*, *5*(1), 3–22. doi:10.1177/1555 412009351264

Kiili, C. (2012). *Online reading as an individual and social practice*. Jyväskylä, Finland: University of Jyväskylä. Jyväskylä studies in education, psychology and social research, 441, http://dissertations.jyu.fi/studeduc/ 9789513947958.pdf.

Kiili, C., Hirvonen, S., & Leu, D. J. (2013). *Synthesizing information during online reading and writing a joint argumentative essay*. Paper presented at the 15th Biennial EARLI Conference for Research on Learning and Instruction, August 27, Munich, Germany.

Kiili, C., Laurinen, L., & Marttunen, M. (2008). Students evaluating Internet sources: From versatile evaluators to uncritical readers. *Journal of Educational Computing Research*, *39*(1), 75–95.

Kiili, C., Laurinen, L., & Marttunen, M. (2009). Skillful internet reader is metacognitively competent. In L. T. W. Hin & R. Subramaniam (Eds.), *Handbook of research on new media literacy at the K–12 Level: Issues and challenges* (pp. 654–668). Hershey, PA: IGI Global.

Kiili, C., Laurinen, L., Marttunen, M., & Leu, D. J. (2012). Working on understanding during collaborative online reading. *Journal of Literacy Research*, *44*(4), 448–483.

Kim, D. Y., Lehto, X. Y., & Morrison, A. M. (2007). Gender differences in online travel information search: Implications for marketing communications on the internet. *Tourism Management*, *28*(2), 423–433.

Kintsch, W. (2000). Discourse comprehension. In W. J. Perrig & A. Grob (Eds.), *Control of human behavior, mental processes, and consciousness: Essays in honor of the 60th birthday of August Flammer* pp. 137–146, Mahwah, NJ: Lawrence Erlbaum.

Kist, W. (2005). *New literacies in action: Teaching and learning in multiple media*. New York: Teachers College Press.

Koohang, A., & Durante, A. (2003). Learners' perceptions toward the web-based distance learning activities/assignments portion of an undergraduate hybrid instructional model. *Journal of Information Technology Education: Research*, *2*(1), 105–113.

Kress, G. (2003). *Literacy in the new media age*. London: Routledge.

Lankshear, C., & Knobel, M. (2006). *New literacies: Changing knowledge in the classroom*. (2nd ed.). Maidenhead, UK: Open University Press.

Leu, D. Castek, J., & Hartman, D. (2006). *Evaluating the development of scientific knowledge and new forms of reading comprehension during online learning*. Final Report to North Central Regional Educational Laboratory/Learning Point Associates. Chicago, IL.

Leu, D. J., Forzani, E., Kulikowich, J., Sedransk, N., Coiro, J., McVerry, G.,... Everett-Cacopardo, H. (2012, April). Performance Patterns of Common Core State Standards in New Literacies Within Rich and Poor School Districts: Are the Rich Getting Richer and the Poor Getting Poorer? Paper presented at the annual meeting of the American Educational Research Association, Vancouver, BC, Canada.

Leu, D.J., Forzani, E., Rhoads, C., Maykel, C., Kennedy, C., & Timbrell, N. (2015). *The new literacies of online research and comprehension: Rethinking the reading achievement gap*. Reading Research Quarterly, 50(1). 1–23. Newark, DE: International Literacy Association. doi: 10.1002/rrq.85. Available at: http://www.edweek.org/media/leu%20online%20reading%20study.pdf

Leu D. J., Kinzer, C. K., Coiro, J., Castek, J., & Henry, L. A. (2013). New literacies and the new literacies of online reading comprehension: A dual level theory. In N. Unrau & D. Alvermann (Eds.),

*Theoretical models and process of reading*, 6th ed. (pp. 1150–1181). Newark, DE: International Reading Association.

Leu, D. J., Kinzer, C. K., Coiro, J., & Cammack, D. (2004). Toward a theory of new literacies emerging from the Internet and other information and communication technologies. In R. B. Ruddell & N. Unrau (Eds.), *Theoretical models and processes of reading*, 5th ed. (pp. 1568–1611). Newark, DE: International Reading Association.

Leu, D. J., Kulikowich, J., Sedransk, N., & Coiro, J. (2009). Assessing online reading comprehension: The ORCA project. Research grant funded by the US Department of Education, Institute of Education Sciences.

Leu, D. J., Zawilinski, L., Castek, J., Banerjee, M., Housand, B., Liu, Y., & O'Neil, M. (2007). What is new about the new literacies of online reading comprehension? In L. Rush, J. Eakle, & A. Berger (Eds.), *Secondary school literacy: What research reveals for classroom practices* (pp. 37–68). Urbana, IL: National Council of Teachers of English.

Lewis, C., & Fabos, B. (2005). Instant messaging, literacies, and social identities. *Reading Research Quarterly*, *40*, 470–501.

Li, D. D., & Lim, C. P. (2008). Scaffolding online historical inquiry tasks: A case study of two secondary school classrooms. *Computers & Education*, *50*(4), 1394–1410.

Lieberman, D. A., Bates, C. H., & So, J. (2009). Young children's learning with digital media. *Computers in the Schools*, *26*(4), 271–283. doi:10.1080/07380560903360194

Marsh, J. (2011). Young children's literacy practices in a virtual world: Establishing an online interaction order. *Reading Research Quarterly*, *46*(2), 101–118.

OECD and Centre for Educational Research and Innovation (2010). *Trends shaping education 2010*. Paris: OECD.

OECD (2011). *PISA 2009 results: Students on line: Digital technologies and performance (Volume VI)*. Paris: OECD, available at http://dx.doi.org/10.1787/9789264112995-en.

Quintana, C., Zhang, M., & Krajcik, J. (2005). A framework for supporting metacognitive aspects of online inquiry through software-based scaffolding. *Educational Psychologist*, *40*(4), 235–244.

Reardon, S. F. (2011). The widening academic achievement gap between the rich and the poor: New evidence and possible explanations. In R. Murnane & G. Duncan (Eds.), *Whither opportunity? Rising inequality and the uncertain life chances of low-income children* (pp. 91–115). New York: Russell Sage Foundation Press.

Rouet, J. F., Bétrancourt, M., Britt, M. A., Bromme, R., Graesser, A. C., Kulikowich, J. M. . . . van Oostendorp, H. (2009). *PIAAC problem solving in technology-rich environments: A conceptual framework*. OECD Education Working Papers, No. 36. Paris: OECD.

Sabatini, J. P., O'Reilly, T., Halderman, L. K., & Bruce, K. (2014). Integrating scenario-based and component reading skill measures to understand the reading behavior of struggling readers. *Learning Disabilities Research & Practice*, *29*(1), 36–43.

Salminen, T., Marttunen, M., & Laurinen, L. (2012). Argumentation in secondary school students' structured and unstructured chat discussions. *Journal of Educational Computing Research*, *47*(2), 175–208.

Schumacher, P., & Morahan-Martin, J. (2001). Gender, Internet and computer attitudes and experiences. *Computers in Human Behavior*, *17*(1), 95–110.

Sormunen, E., Tanni, M., Alamettälä, T., & Heinström, J. (2013). Students' group work strategies in source-based writing assignments. *Journal of the American Society for Information Science and Technology*, *65*(6), 1217–1231.

Spilich, G. J., Vesonder, G. T., Chiesi, H. L., & Voss, J. F. (1979). Text processing of domain-related information for individuals with high and low domain knowledge. *Journal of Verbal Learning and Verbal Behavior*, *18*(3), 275–290.

Stadtler, M., & Bromme, R. (2008). Effects of the metacognitive computer-tool met.a.ware on the web search of laypersons. *Computers in Human Behavior*, *24*, 716–737.

Street, B. (2003). What's new in new literacy studies? *Current Issues in Comparative Education*, *5*(2), 1–14.

US Census Bureau (2013). *Computer and Internet use in the United States*. Washington, DC: US Department of Commerce. Available at http://www.census.gov/prod/2013pubs/p20-569.pdf.

van Strien, J. L., Brand-Gruwel, S., & Boshuizen, H. (2014). Dealing with conflicting information from multiple nonlinear texts: Effects of prior attitudes. *Computers in Human Behavior*, *32*, 101–111.

Walraven, A., Brand-Gruwel, S., & Boshuizen, H. P. A. (2008). Information-problem solving: A review of problems students encounter and instructional solutions. *Computers in Human Behavior*, *24*(3), 623–648.

271

Weinberger A., Marttunen, M., Laurinen, L., & Stegmann, K. (2013). Inducing socio-cognitive conflict in Finnish and German groups of online learners by CSCL script. *International Journal of Computer-Supported Collaborative Learning, 8,* 333–349.

Wiley, J., Goldman, S. R., Graesser, A. C., Sanchez, C. A., Ash, I. K., & Hemmerich, J. A. (2009). Source evaluation, comprehension, and learning in Internet science inquiry tasks. *American Educational Research Journal, 46*(4), 1060–1106.

Zawilinski, L. (2012). *An exploration of a collaborative blogging approach to literacy and learning: A mixed method study.* Unpublished doctoral dissertation, University of Connecticut, Storrs, CT.

Zhang, M., & Quintana, C. (2012) Scaffolding strategies for supporting middle school students' online inquiry processes. *Computers & Education, 58,* 181–196.

# 20

# Family Matters

## Home Influences and Individual Differences in Children's Reading Development

*Jennifer D. Turner, Maria E. Crassas, and Pamela H. Segal*

[T]he home environment is a powerful context for shaping children's early-literacy foundations. The experiences in this realm that each child has or does not have greatly affects the creation of the knowledge sources of oral language, book and print concepts, and attitudes about learning and literacy that will ultimately be available for use during reading comprehension.

(Tracey & Morrow, 2002, p. 224)

Tracey and Morrow's words remind us that children's development as readers and writers begins long before they arrive at the schoolhouse door. Parents are their child's first and most influential teachers (Edwards & Turner, 2009), and the home literacy environments that they orchestrate provide the literacy and language foundation that children will build upon throughout their schooling years and their adult lives.

Research has revealed a number of demographic factors that are critical to the ways that families enact literacy in their homes. Family structures have significantly changed over the past 50 years, such that the term "family" now includes a broad range of primary caregivers who create home literacy environments, including two-parent households, single-parent households, unmarried partners, grandparents raising their grandchildren, older siblings, and foster families. Cultural and linguistic diversity are also key demographic factors that have implications for children's literacy learning at home. More than half of US children are projected to be children of color, and more specifically, 36 percent of US children are projected to be Hispanic by 2050 (America's Children, 2013). Children of immigrants "comprise the fastest-growing segment of the U.S. youth population—one out of every five children is born to immigrant parents" (Váldez & Callahan, 2011, p. 5). Families are becoming more linguistically diverse as well: approximately 63 percent of school-age Asian children and 64 percent of school-age Hispanic children spoke a language other than English at home in 2011 (America's Children, 2013).

Today's families are also facing difficult economic circumstances. According to the America's Children Report (2013), 22 percent of all children ages 0–17 (16.1 million) lived in poverty in 2011, up from 16 percent in 2001. Racial disparities compound issues of poverty, as 13 percent of White children lived in poverty in 2011, compared with 39 percent of Black, non-Hispanic children and 34 percent of Hispanic children. Poverty can pose a significant risk in the literacy lives and learning of children. To illustrate, Hart and Risley (2003) estimated that over the first four years of childhood, children from families on welfare experience approximately 13 million spoken words, while children from professional families experience approximately 45 million spoken words, a vocabulary gap which creates a significant disadvantage for children of poverty as they enter school.

Taken together, these demographic factors strongly suggest that different families provide different literacy experiences to their children. As Sonnenschein, Brody, and Munsterman (1996) explain, "virtually all children in a literate society such as ours have numerous experiences with [literacy] and written language before they enter school. There are, however, both qualitative and quantitative differences in the ways that children from different cultural groups experience literacy" (p. 3). Parents orchestrate home literacy environments where the relationships, activities, and events typically reflect the family's cultural background, heritage, and traditions (Edwards & Turner, 2009). As a result, families expose their children to varying literate and language practices, and "the influence of these differential experiences during the preschool years may extend into the school years" (Sonnenschien et al., 1996, p. 3). A growing body of evidence shows that children with limited language and literacy deployment in the early years are less likely to be successful readers in kindergarten and first grade, and their struggles to achieve are likely to persist throughout their academic careers (Snow, Burns, & Griffin, 1998; Strickland & Riley-Ayers, 2006).

Differences in children's home literacy experiences can be viewed in two ways. Deficit-oriented perspectives view families from diverse backgrounds as *villains* (Edwards, McMillon, & Turner, 2010), positioning caregivers as "bad parents" (e.g., neglectful, uncaring), "illiterate," or "disadvantaged," and blaming them for what are often characterized as deficiencies in their home literacy lives (Edwards & Turner, 2009; Paratore & Yaden, 2011). In contrast, strengths-based perspectives on family acknowledge that parents and other caregivers have important funds of knowledge (Moll, Amanti, & Gonzalez, 2005) that support children's early literacy and language experiences. Drawing on their funds of knowledge, diverse families serve as *villages* for their children (Edwards et al. 2010), facilitating daily encounters with a wide range of texts (e.g., coupons, newspapers, websites, recipes, religious texts), using reading and writing for varied purposes (e.g., cooking, entertainment, spirituality), and promoting literate competencies in multiple dimensions (Anderson, & Stokes, 1984). Importantly, strengths-based perspectives acknowledge that diverse families' funds of knowledge may include literacies that embody cultural practices and discourses that are very different from those enacted by White, middle class families and from those valued in schools (Compton-Lilly, Rogers, & Lewis, 2012).

In our chapter, we adopt a strengths-based approach, framing our understanding of how the family influences children's reading development through the term *literacy practices*. We conceptualize literacy, not as a set of decontextualized, technical skills, but rather as instances of reading, writing, and language "embedded in and shaped by social and cultural contexts . . . [constituting] the ways that people interact with texts along with the assumptions, values, feelings, and social processes that underpin these interactions" (Manyak & Dantas, 2010, p. 12). More specifically, we highlight four key categories of familial practices that shape individual differences in children's literacy development: (1) *print-based home practices*; (2) *oral language-based home practices*; (3) *bilingual-based home practices*; and (4) *technology-based home practices*. We conclude with thoughts about how we might support the literacy and language development of children, especially in diverse families, by connecting home and school literacy practices.

# Print-Based Home Literacy Practices and Children's Reading Development

Research on parent/family influences has consistently demonstrated that "the quality of a child's home environment exerts an extremely powerful effect on his or her literacy development" (Tracey & Morrow, 2002, p. 222). Home literacy environmental factors that generally enrich children's literacy and language development include parental characteristics (e.g., educational attainment, beliefs about and orientation towards reading) as well as the amount of books and reading materials in the home, purposeful uses of print in the home (e.g., cooking with recipes, reading newspapers for information), and the frequency of reading and discussing books, completing homework, visiting bookstores and libraries, and other literacy events (Anderson & Stokes, 1984; Purcell-Gates, 1996; Tracey & Morrow, 2002; Wasik, 2012). In what follows, we review research that demonstrates the influences of two familial print-based literacy practices on children's early development as readers and writers: (1) parent–child book-reading; and (2) family writing activities.

## Parent–Child Book-Reading

Perhaps the most highly recommended practice for supporting children's reading growth is parent–child storybook reading (Snow et al., 1998). According to the National Commission on Reading, "the single most important activity for building the knowledge required for eventual success in reading is reading aloud to children" (Anderson, Hiebert, Scott, & Wilkinson, 1985, p. 23). Consequently, this literacy event has historically been one of the most studied topics related to children's home literacy environments (Tracey & Morrow, 2002).

Research exploring book-reading activities at home has typically examined two factors that have an impact on children's language and literacy development: frequency of book-reading and quality of parent–child interactions during book-reading. In a meta-analysis of studies that examined frequency of parent–child reading with preschoolers, Bus, van Ijzendoorn, and Pelligrini (1995) determined that frequency of parent–child reading (i.e., how many times per week parents read to children) was related to children's language growth (e.g., vocabulary) and reading achievement. When combined with other components of parent–child reading experiences, such as duration of shared reading between the parent and child, and the age of the child when shared reading began, frequency significantly predicted early literacy skills, such as receptive vocabulary and story and print concepts (Bracken & Fischel, 2008). Moreover, Sénéchal, Lefevre, Thomas, & Daley (1998) found that more frequent exposure to storybooks, measured by assessing parent knowledge of popular children's book titles and authors, correlated to kindergarteners' oral language skills, including vocabulary, listening comprehension, and phonological awareness.

Studies have also determined that parent–child interactions during book-reading, which (1) support children's reading with key comprehension strategies, (2) foster positive affect about reading, (3) encourage parental talk about meaning rather than decoding talk, and (4) demonstrate parents' interest in reading, help facilitate children's literacy growth. Parents who made reading with their children a regular part of their lives, and who used key comprehension strategies such as asking questions, attending to illustrations and text, and making predictions, enhanced their children's print knowledge, alphabetic knowledge, and reading comprehension (Barnyak, 2011; Strickland & Riley-Ayers, 2006; Wasik, 2012). Parents who facilitate positive affect during book-reading interactions by involving their children during reading, being sensitive to their children's needs, and connecting physically with their children are likely to raise resilient readers who take on more challenging texts (Baker, Mackler, Sonnenschein, & Serpell, 2001) and who are highly motivated (Sonnenschein & Munsterman, 2002). Additionally, the type and amount of parent talk is crucial to successful parent–child book-reading interactions. Parent talk focussed on text meaning rather than decoding and error corrections fosters more positive interactions with books, enhances children's vocabulary knowledge, and contributes to increased reading achievement (Baker et al., 2001; Neuman & Dickinson, 2011). Tracey and Young (2002), for example, found that mothers of advanced readers and struggling readers used similar error correction strategies (i.e., supplying words, modeling, and indicating an error) when reading with their children; however, mothers of advanced readers used them less frequently than mothers of struggling readers. As a result, the advanced readers talked significantly more to their mothers about the books, which contributed to positive affect about reading, and improved comprehension. In contrast, parent talk focussed on negative child behaviors during storybook reading significantly mitigates children's reading comprehension (Leseman & de Jong, 1998). Finally, parents who demonstrate their interest in reading serve as literacy role models and motivational forces in their children's lives. Klauda and Wigfield (2012), for example, reported that fourth- and fifth-grade readers who perceived more parental support in reading (e.g., reading together, provision of reading materials, having reading models, and receiving encouragement to read) had more positive reading achievement, habits, and attitudes. Relatedly, children's motivation to read is optimized in home environments where parents read for pleasure and view reading as a source of entertainment rather than a skill set to be learned (Baker, Sonnenschein, & Serpell, 1999; Neuman & Dickinson, 2011).

## Family Writing Activities

Family writing activities, though less studied than family reading activities, can influence children's literacy development. Parental graphophonemic support (i.e., support in helping their children address letter-sound correspondences) during writing activities is predictive of children's decoding skills and phonological awareness, and parental print support (i.e., letter formation) predicts children's decoding skills (Skibbe, Bindman, Hindman, Aram, & Morrison, 2013). Moreover, children who learn to print words from their parents also tend to have more advanced early written language skills, such as print concepts and invented spelling (Sénéchal et al., 1998). The home, then, serves as an important context where parents can model writing in various ways, including journaling, completing job applications, writing letters and notes, writing lists and reminders (Heath, 1983; Taylor & Dorsey-Gaines, 1988; Wasik, 2012), and children can experiment with written sign systems (Aram & Levin, 2011). Activities such as family message journals, in which students and parents communicate about daily events (Valerie & Foss-Swanson, 2012), and community and family profile writing, in which students interview family and community members and write expository texts about them (Werderich, 2008), can also enhance children's writing motivation and skills.

## Oral Language-Based Home Literacy Practices and Children's Reading Development

Oral language practices, including verbal expression, listening comprehension, and oral vocabulary, are foundational to literacy development (Strickland & Riley-Ayers, 2006). In this section, we focus on two critical oral language practices: storytelling and sociodramatic play.

## Storytelling

Oral storytelling is a cultural tradition enacted by Appalachian families (McIntyre, 2010; Purcell-Gates, 1995), African American families (Heath, 1983; Wasik, 2012), European American families (Langellier & Peterson, 2004), and American Indian and Alaskan Native families (Wasik, 2012), among others. Research suggests that parental storytelling can enhance children's vocabulary development, build content knowledge, develop phonological awareness, and support narrative competence (Neuman, & Dickinson, 2011; Sonnenschein et al., 1996). However, storytelling is not only a literate practice enacted by adults; children can be empowered to "take ownership" of language through the telling of their own narratives. To illustrate, Reese (2012) found that oral narratives, such as *consejos* (advice), and *dichos* (sayings), were highly valued in working-class and middle-class Mexican homes, and children were strongly encouraged to engage in these narrative practices by listening to and retelling family stories. Similarly, the African American children in Trackton, a working-class community in the Piedmont Carolinas, were inspired by family and neighbors to master the art of storytelling by using creative, engaging, and witty language to capture the audience's attention (Heath, 1983).

## Sociodramatic Play

Play serves as a key context for oral language development at home, because in the early years, children spend between 3 percent and 20 percent of their day engaged in play (Burghardt, 2005 cited in Pinkham & Neuman, 2012). Pinkham and Neuman (2012) identified three types of play that children engage in at home: (1) object play, which can enhance reading and writing development when it centers on materials such as crayons, pencils, and plastic letters; (2) guided play, in which adults focus the play on particular themes (e.g., going to the beach), topics (e.g., farm animals), and props (e.g., dolls, toys) that build children's background knowledge and develop content vocabulary and conceptual understandings; and (3) pretend play, through which children can develop sophisticated narrative storylines by envisioning and enacting literate practices in imagined contexts (e.g., "playing school"). Parents, and especially siblings, are central to all three types of play, as these close familial relationships create meaningful contexts for children to demonstrate language acquisition, learn new vocabulary, and discover new interests (Gregory, 2005; Long & Volk, 2010; Neuman & Dickinson, 2011).

## Bilingual-Based Home Literacy Practices and Children's Reading Development

The number of children who speak more than one language at home has grown exponentially in recent years and is expected to continue rising (America's Children, 2013). According to the National Literacy Panel on Language-Minority Children and Youth (August, & Shanahan, 2006), children benefit from developing specific language and literacy skills, including phonological and phonemic awareness, phonics, fluency, vocabulary, and text comprehension, in both English and their heritage language. In this section, we feature two prominent bilingual practices that facilitate children's literacy learning and language development: (1) biliterate activities and (2) language brokering.

## Biliterate Activities

Biliteracy is defined as "the acquisition and learning of the decoding and encoding of and around print using two linguistic and cultural systems in order to convey messages in a variety of contexts"

(Perez & Torres-Guzman cited in Reyes, Kenner, Moll, & Orellana, 2012, p. 308). Biliteracy can support reading and writing in powerful ways because children "who are most likely to succeed in school are those with strong academic language skills in their native language and in English, [and] who have the benefit of rich home literacy practices" (Fránquiz & Ortiz, 2012, p. 253). For example, bilingual, Pentecostal families used literacy-based religious rituals, such as daily Bible readings, praying, and discussing psalms and other scriptures, as a means for providing opportunities for their children (1) to practice reading as they read Biblical passages with their parents, (2) to foster comprehension through discussions of literary and spiritual meanings, and (3) to draw on their linguistic capital in Spanish and English as literate resources (Long & Volk, 2010). In addition to family engagements with religious texts, biliterate practices include letter and word recognition, writing and spelling, and general language ability, which can enhance positive transfer from Spanish to English (Paez, Bock, & Pizzo, 2011). Children who speak heritage languages other than Spanish can also benefit from biliterate practices in their homes; Bauer (2004), for example, found that young children were able to use their linguistic knowledge of German and English to code-switch as writers and as readers when both languages were spoken at home.

## Language Brokering

Within some multilingual homes, children take up roles as language brokers because "translating and interpreting are chores that children do to contribute to the family's well-being" (Reyes et al., 2012, p. 318). Ethnographic portraits of Latino families (Mónzo, 2010; Orellena, 2006; Vásquez, Pease-Alvarez, & Shannon, 1994), Vietnamese families (Li, 2010), and Sudanese refugees (Perry, 2010) have demonstrated how immigrant children help their parents to negotiate meaning from a wide range of English texts, including school-issued correspondence, financial statements and bills, medicine bottles and appointment reminders, legal documents, and religious materials. By providing children with opportunities to engage with real-world texts, to meaningfully practice their English language and literacy skills, and to reinforce their connections to their home language(s) and cultural heritage, language brokering can (1) facilitate young emergent bilinguals' proficiency in English reading and writing; (2) promote vocabulary development (e.g., articulating meanings through word choice); (3) enhance genre knowledge (e.g., differences between medical forms and fictional stories); (4) support comprehension and critical interpretation skills (e.g., knowing what particular forms and texts "mean"); (5) facilitate understanding of audience and purpose for literacy; and (6) expose them to finance, governmental/legal information, education, health, and other subject matter (Orellena, 2006).

## Technology-Based Home Literacy Practices and Children's Reading Development

Over the past decade, there has been an increase in Internet use and a rise in mobile connectivity in family life (Zickuhr, & Smith, 2012). The digital divide still exists when it comes to high-speed broadband Internet access at home, with 84 percent of white families and 80 percent of Asian American families having broadband compared to 72 percent of African American families and 65 percent of Latinos (Lopez, Gonzalez-Barrera, & Pattern, 2013; Rainie, 2011; Smith, 2013). However, the divide has closed significantly for daily Internet usage (e.g., 97 percent of Whites, 96 percent Latinos, 92 percent of African Americans, 89 percent Asian Americans), and smartphone ownership and mobile connectivity, with more than half of

Asian Americans, African Americans, Whites, and Latinos using phones for Internet access (Lopez et al., 2013; Rainie, 2011; Smith, 2013). As a result of this increased online connectivity, families are engaging with technology, and with digital texts, more than ever before. In this section, we highlight two technology-based home literacy practices that can impact a child's early reading development: (1) parent–child engagement with digital texts and (2) parental support of online literacy.

## Parent–Child Engagement with Digital Texts

Recent studies have demonstrated that parents can facilitate their children's vocabulary development, comprehension, engagement, and critical thinking skills by enacting literacy practices in their homes with digital texts (Bittman, Rutherford, Brown, & Unsworth, 2011; Davidson, 2009; Hillman & Marshall, 2009). To illustrate, Kim and Anderson (2008) explored the benefits of mother–child interactions during readings of print and digital texts, noting that while reading digital texts, children and their mothers talked 10 percent more (e.g., making inferences, predictions, or personal connections), were 25 percent more engaged in the text, and frequently explored and raised questions using the hyperlinks with the digital format (i.e., e-books). Increased parent–child interaction when reading a variety of digital texts (i.e., e-books, emails, instant messages) helped children learn to embrace the texts and become motivated readers because digital media offers "unique opportunities for parents and children to read together" (Rasinski & Padak, 2008, p. 584). Digital literacies also afford opportunities for children to improve their vocabulary, learn new content, and communicate their new knowledge to others; Korat and Or's (2010) study of 49 socioeconomically diverse kindergarten families determined that the use of digital books facilitated statistically significant more child-initiated talk, elicited sophisticated responses from the mothers to their children, and sparked conversations about word meanings and textual interpretations. Taken together, this empirical work suggests that access to technology alone is not sufficient to enhance children's literacy development; rather, parents' and children's close interactions, and the talk generated between them as they read online texts, are most integral to children's oral language growth and literacy skill acquisition.

## Parental Support of Online Literacy

As children develop into more mature readers, technology, and specifically digital texts, can influence the cognitive and affective quality of their literacy experiences. Kindles and other digital readers, for example, provide opportunities for children to practice comprehension strategies, such as taking notes in the margins, looking up words in the online dictionary, and formulating questions (Larson, 2010), and some children, especially struggling readers from diverse backgrounds, report feeling more confident and competent reading digital texts (Levy, 2009; Mitchell, 2013). Yet research suggests that children still benefit from their parents' support when reading and writing online. Parental interactions and discussions are key supports; children whose parents read with them on the Internet reported higher levels of comfort and comprehension with digital texts compared to print texts (Levy, 2009). Coupled with good discussions, parents also modeled research strategies and posed questions to enhance children's content knowledge, vocabulary, and literacy skill development. To illustrate, the parents in Davidson's (2009) study encouraged their children to learn more about lizards by (1) modeling how to locate information in print and online texts; (2) helping their children navigate informational websites; (3) asking purposeful questions related to the topics that their children were researching; and (4) discussing with their children what they were learning as the children completed their research. Parental support can also facilitate their children's biliterate development; McTavish (2009), for example, demonstrated how one immigrant family read the online newspaper in English and the home language with their child, and used those current events as the basis of family discussions. Collectively, these studies indicate that parental behaviors (e.g., interacting and discussing, modeling research strategies, questioning, and reading bilingual newspapers) that facilitate online literacy can strengthen children's online reading strategies (e.g., comprehension, locating, and synthesizing information), technological knowledge (e.g., conducting research, navigating websites), and linguistic competencies (e.g., reading and communicating in their home language and English).

## Concluding Thoughts: Positive Home–School Connections Strengthen Children's Reading Development

Our chapter highlights four main categories of literacy practices that families take up in their homes: (1) print-based literacy practices; (2) oral language-based practices; (3) bilingual-based practices; and (4) technology-based practices. Through these literate practices, parents and other family members (e.g., siblings, grandparents, cousins) significantly shape children's reading histories, provide exposure to print and digital texts, build foundational reading skills (e.g., phonological awareness), develop their vocabularies, enhance their print knowledge and comprehension, and guide their interests in reading and writing. Families not only influence their children's early literacy lives, but their entire academic careers; young adults have reported that the activities in their home environments, and their parents' views of and expectations for literacy, continued to impact how they saw themselves as readers in college (Segal, 2013).

In light of the sustained effects that home literacy environments have on children's reading, writing, and language development, we believe that strengthening connections between families and schools is critical for supporting their literacy achievement. To this end, we offer two recommendations. First, schools and teachers need to implement curriculum and pedagogy in ways that are responsive to and respectful of the literacy and language practices enacted in diverse families. Children enter classrooms with multiple funds of knowledge (Moll et al., 2005) from their families; unfortunately, too few teachers know how to utilize this experiential knowledge as a learning resource at school. Research has shown that when teachers create classroom communities which draw on children's cultural and linguistic assets (Manyak & Dantas, 2010; Turner & Kim, 2005), and "purposefully connect instruction with students' [family] backgrounds while assisting them in developing fluency, comprehension, and vocabulary skills in reading and . . . writing" (McIntyre & Turner, 2013, p. 146), these children successfully learn the academic literacies valued and needed in schools. Enacting culturally responsive literacy pedagogies in schools require teachers to get to know students and their families using a number of tools, including parent stories (Edwards & Turner, 2009), home visits (Dantas & Coleman, 2010), photography documenting home literacy experiences (Allen et al., 2002), and journaling about family literacy events (Turner & Hoeltzel, 2010; Werderich, 2008), and then to use that information to build bridges to the formal reading and writing skills and knowledge necessary for school success.

Second, it is important to provide families, particularly those from diverse backgrounds, with greater exposure and access to the codes of power validated by mainstream society (Delpit, 2006). We are not advocating for homes to become replicas of schools, nor are we suggesting that families must learn more "researcher-approved" or "appropriate" ways to support their children's literacy development and schooling. However, scholars (Crassas, 2013; Edwards & Turner, 2009, 2010) have found that many culturally and linguistically diverse parents *want* to know more about the literacy practices affirmed in schools; they see the value in "adding" mainstream literacy practices to their familial repertories because they want their children to acquire the cultural capital required for success in American society (Delpit, 2006). For example, school-based events, such as Family Nights, provide families with opportunities to work with their children on particular curriculum topics and engage in literacy activities, which in turn helps them to feel welcomed into the school, become comfortable with school personnel, and have greater knowledge about curricular expectations and demands (Edwards & Turner, 2009, 2010; McIntyre & Turner, 2013).

Furthermore, family literacy programs also support families' knowledge about and acquisition of mainstream literacy practices. Because storybook reading is a significant contributor to children's future literacy achievement, family literacy programs have often centered on shared book-reading experiences. Successful national initiatives like *Reading is Fundamental* and *Reach Out and Read* have aimed to increase book-reading experiences in the home by providing families with books (Strickland & Riley-Ayers, 2006).

Local programs in various communities can also positively impact family literacy practices. For example, programs focused on dialogic reading, an interactive shared reading method that empowers children to become active storytellers as adults serve as supportive listeners, reported improved expressive vocabulary, phonological awareness, and oral narrative construction for participating children (Chow & McBride-Chang, 2003; Edwards & Turner, 2009; Hargrave & Sénéchal, 2000; Huebner & Payne, 2010). Relatedly, research describes family programs with interactive parent–child reading components that enhanced children's reading comprehension and supported positive attitudes towards book-reading (Morrow & Young, 1997; Roberts, 2013). In family literacy programs for older elementary children and their parents, researchers reported vocabulary gains from programs that targeted specific vocabulary and supported extended conversations, wide reading, and interactive word activities (Jordan, Snow, & Porsche, 2000) and with programs that focused on interactive reading and writing experiences (Cairney & Munsie, 1995). Importantly, there is a growing body of evidence that family literacy programs can help families acquire mainstream literacy practices and language skills in ways that are responsive and respectful of their diverse home literacy practices. Project FLAME (*Family Literacy: Aprendiendo, Mejorando, Educando*), for example, provided opportunities for working-class Latino parents to strengthen their literacy skills in both Spanish and English while simultaneously working with them to increase the literacy materials and experiences in their homes, and to improve their confidence in their ability to read and write with their children (Rodriguez-Brown, 2004). In her work with homeless families living in a transitional home, Crassas (2013) implemented a series of workshops focused on book-reading, phonics, and vocabulary, using parents' perspectives on literacy and their perceptions of their family's literacy strengths as a springboard.

In closing, we believe that for children from diverse families, "the most promising approach to facilitating . . . reading . . . success is to develop a strong, broad, and rich . . . literacy foundation" (Tracey & Morrow, 2002, p. 231). Toward this end, parents need a wide repertoire of literate practices that help children to not only comprehend multiple texts—whether they are orally narrated, digital, or print based, in English or their heritage language—but to also meaningfully use literacy to achieve their own purposes and goals. We hope that future research on family literacy will provide new insights into the collaborative efforts that parents, educators, and scholars can promote to help *all* children become competent readers.

## References

Allen, J., Fabregas, V., Hankins, K. H., Hull, G., Labbo, L., Lawson, H. S. . . . Urdanivia-English, C. (2002). PhOLKS Lore: Learning from photographs, families, and children. *Language Arts, 79*(4), 312–322.

America's Children (2013). *America's Children: Key national indicators of well-being.* Retrieved from http://www.childstats.gov/americaschildren/famsoc1.asp.

Anderson, A. B., & Stokes, S. J. (1984). Social and institutional influences on the development and practice of literacy. In H. Goelman, A. Oberg, & F. Smith (Eds.), *Awakening to literacy* (pp. 24–37). Exeter, NH: Heinemann.

Anderson, R. C., Hiebert, C. H., Scott, J. A., & Wilkinson, I. A. G. (1985). *Becoming a nation of readers: The report of the Commission on Reading.* Washington, DC: National Institute of Education.

Aram, D., & Levin, I. (2011). Home support of children in the writing process: Contributions to early literacy. In S. B. Neuman & D. K. Dickinson (Eds.), *Handbook of early literacy research* (3rd ed., pp. 189–199). New York: Guilford.

August, D., & Shanahan, T. (2006). Developing literacy in second-language learners. *Report of the National Literacy Panel on Language-Minority Children and Youth.* Mahwah, NJ: Lawrence Erlbaum.

Baker, L., Mackler, K., Sonnenschein, S., & Serpell, R. (2001). Parents' interactions with their first-grade children during storybook reading and relations with subsequent home reading activity and reading achievement. *Journal of School Psychology, 39*(5), 415–438.

Baker, L., Sonnenschein, S., & Serpell, R. (1999). *A five-year comparison of actual and recommended parent practices for promoting children's literacy development.* Paper presented at the Annual Meeting of the American Educational Research Association, Montreal, Canada.

Barnyak, N. C. (2011). A qualitative study in a rural community: Investigating the attitudes, beliefs, and interactions of young children and their parents regarding storybook read alouds. *Early Childhood Educational Journal, 39*, 149–159.

Bauer, E. B. (2004). Parallel development of writing in English and German. In F. B. Boyd & C. H. Brock (Eds.), *Multicultural and multilingual literacy and language: Contexts and practices* (pp. 207–217). New York: Guilford.

Bittman, M., Rutherford, L., Brown, J., & Unsworth, L. (2011). Digital natives? New and old media and children's outcomes. *Australian Journal of Education, 55*(2), 161–175.

Bracken, S. S., & Fischel, J. E. (2008). Family reading behavior and early literacy skills in preschool children from low-income backgrounds. *Early Education and Development, 19*(1), 45–67.

Bus, A. G., van Ijzendoorn, M. H., & Pelligrini, A. D. (1995). Joint book reading makes for success in learning to read: A meta-analysis on intergenerational transmission of literacy. *Review of Educational Research, 65*(1), 1–21.

Cairney, T. H., & Munsie, L. (1995). Parent participation in literacy learning. *Reading Teacher, 48*(5), 392–403.

Chow, B. W., & McBride-Chang, C. (2003). Promoting language and literacy development through parent–child reading in Hong Kong preschoolers. *Early Education and Development, 14*(2), 233–248.

Compton-Lilly, C., Rogers, R., & Lewis, T. (2012). Analyzing epistemological considerations related to diversity: An integrative critical literature review of family literacy scholarship. *Reading Research Quarterly, 47*(1), 33–60.

Crassas, M. E. (2013). *A book reading workshop in a transitional home: Parental experiences, self-efficacy, and practices when taught codes of the culture of power.* Unpublished doctoral dissertation, University of Maryland, College Park, MD.

Dantas, M., & Coleman, M. (2010). Home visits: Learning from students and families. In M. L. Dantas & P. C. Manyak (Eds.), *Home–school connections in a multicultural society: Learning from and with culturally and linguistically diverse families* (pp. 156–176). New York: Routledge.

Davidson, C. (2009). Young children's engagement with digital texts and literacies in the home: Pressing matters for the teaching of English in the early years of school. *English Teaching: Practice and Critique, 8*(3), 36–54.

Delpit, L. D. (2006). *Other people's children: Cultural conflict in the classroom.* 2nd ed. New York: New Press Publishers.

Edwards, P. A., McMillon, G. M. T., & Turner, J. D. (2010). *Change is gonna come: Transforming literacy education for African American students.* New York: Teachers College Press.

Edwards, P. A., & Turner, J. D. (2009). Family literacy and comprehension. In S. Israel & G. Duffy (Eds.), *Handbook of research on reading comprehension* (pp. 622–641). New York: Routledge.

Edwards, P. A., & Turner, J. D. (2010). Do you hear what I hear? Using the parent story approach to listen to and learn from African American parents. In M. L. Dantas & P. C. Manyak (Eds.), *Home–school connections in a multicultural society: Learning from and with culturally and linguistically diverse families* (pp. 137–155). New York: Routledge.

Fránquiz, M. E., & Ortiz, A. A. (2012). Coeditors' introduction: Home, school, and program influences on bilingualism and biliteracy. *Bilingual Research Journal*, *35*(3), 253–257.

Gregory, E. (2005). Guiding lights: Siblings as literacy teachers in a multilingual community. In J. Anderson, M. Kendrick, T. Rogers, & S. Smythe (Eds.), *Portraits of literacy across families, communities, and schools* (pp. 21–40). Mahwah, NJ: Lawrence Erlbaum.

Hargrave, A. C., & Sénéchal, M. (2000). A book reading intervention with preschool children who have limited vocabulary: The benefits of regular reading and dialogic reading. *Early Childhood Research Quarterly*, *15*(1), 79–90.

Hart, B., & Risley, T. R. (2003). The early catastrophe. *Education Review*, *17*(1), 110–118.

Heath, S. B. (1983). *Ways with words: Language, life, and work in communities and classrooms*. New York: Cambridge University Press.

Hillman, M., & Marshall, J. (2009). Evaluation of digital media for emergent literacy. *Computers in the Schools*, *26*, 256–270.

Huebner, C. E., & Payne, K. P. (2010). Home support for emergent literacy: Follow-up of a community-based implementation of dialogic reading. *Journal of Applied Developmental Psychology*, *31*, 195–201.

Jordan, G. E., Snow, C. E., & Porsche, M. V. (2000). Project EASE: The effect of a family literacy project on kindergarten students' early literacy skills. *Reading Research Quarterly*, *35*, 524–546.

Kim, J. E., & Anderson, J. (2008). Mother–child shared reading with print and digital texts. *Journal of Early Childhood Literacy*, *8*(2), 213–245.

Klauda, S. L., & Wigfield, A. (2012). Relations of perceived parent and friend support for recreational reading with children's reading motivations. *Journal of Literacy Research*, *44*(1), 3–44.

Korat, O., & Or, T. (2010). How new technology influence parent–child interaction: The case of e-book reading. *First Language*, *30*, 139–154.

Langellier, K. M., & Peterson, E. E. (2004). *Storytelling in daily life: Performing narrative*. Philadelphia, PA: Temple University Press.

Larson, L. (2010). Digital readers: The next chapter in e-book reading and response. *Reading Teacher*, *64*(1), 15–22.

Leseman, P. P., & de Jong, P. F. (1998). Home literacy: Opportunity, instruction, cooperation and social-emotional quality predicting early reading achievement. *Reading Research Quality*, *33*(3), 294–381.

Levy, R. (2009). 'You have to understand words . . . but not read them': Young children becoming readers in a digital age. *Journal of Research in Reading*, *32*(1), 75–91.

Li, G. (2010). Learning from Asian families. In M. L. Dantas, & P. C. Manyak (Eds.), *Home–school connections in a multicultural society: Learning from and with culturally and linguistically diverse families* (pp. 41–58). New York: Routledge.

Long, S., & Volk, D. (2010). Networks of support: Learning from the other teachers in children's lives. In M. L. Dantas & P. C. Manyak (Eds.), *Home–school connections in a multicultural society: Learning from and with culturally and linguistically diverse families* (pp. 177–200). New York: Routledge.

Lopez, M. H., Gonzalez-Barrera, A., & Pattern, E. (2013). *Closing the digital divide: Latinos and technology Adoption*. Retrieved from http://www.pewhispanic.org/2013/03/07/ii-internet-use-3/.

McIntyre, E. (2010). Issues in funds of knowledge teaching and research: Key concepts from a study of Appalachian families and schooling. In M. L. Dantas & P. C. Manyak (Eds.), *Home–school connections in a multicultural society: Learning from and with culturally and linguistically diverse families* (pp. 201–217). New York: Routledge.

McIntyre, E., & Turner, J. D. (2013). Culturally responsive literacy instruction. In B. M. Taylor & N. K. Duke (Eds.), *Handbook of effective literacy instruction: Research-based practice K–8* (pp. 137–161). New York: Guilford Press.

McTavish, M. (2009). 'I get my facts from the Internet': A case study of the teaching and learning of information literacy in in-school and out-of-school contexts. *Journal of Early Childhood Literacy*, *9*(1), 3–28.

Manyak, P. C., & Dantas, M. L. (2010). Introduction. In M. L. Dantas & P. C. Manyak (Eds.), *Home–school connections in a multicultural society: Learning from and with culturally and linguistically diverse families* (pp. 1–15). New York: Routledge.

Mitchell, C. C. (2013). *Technology in their hands: Students' voices from a Nook summer reading program for non-proficient fifth grade students.* Unpublished doctoral dissertation, University of Maryland, College Park, MD.

Moll, L., Amanti, C., & Gonzalez, N. (2005). *Funds of knowledge: Theorizing practices in households and classrooms.* Mahwah, NJ: Lawrence Erlbaum Publishing.

Mónzo, L. D. (2010). Fostering academic identities amongst Latino immigrant students: Contexualizing parents' role. In M. L. Dantas, & P. C. Manyak (Eds.), *Home–school connections in a multicultural society: Learning from and with culturally and linguistically diverse families* (pp. 112–130). New York: Routledge.

Morrow, L. M., & Young, J. (1997). A family literacy program connecting school and home: Effects on attitude, motivation, and literacy achievement. *Journal of Educational Psychology, 89,* 736–742.

Neuman, S. B., & Dickinson, D. K. (Eds.). (2011). *Handbook of early literacy research,* Vol. 3. New York: Guilford.

Orellena, M. F. (2006). *¿Que Dice Aqui?* Building on the translating experiences of immigrant youth for academic literacies. In R. Jimenez & V. O. Pang (Eds.), *Race, ethnicity, and education: Language and literacy in schools,* Vol. 2 (pp. 115–132). Westport, CT: Praeger.

Paez, M. M., Bock, K. P., & Pizzo, L. (2011). Supporting the language and early literacy skills of english language learners: Effective practices and future directions. In S. B. Neuman & D. K. Dickinson (Eds.), *Handbook of early literacy research* (3rd ed., pp. 136–152). New York: Guilford.

Paratore, J. R., & Yaden, D. B. (2011). Family literacy on the defensive: The defunding of Even Start— Omen or opportunity? In D. Lapp & D. Fisher (Eds.), *Handbook of research on teaching the English Language Arts* (3rd ed., pp. 90–96). New York: Routledge.

Perry, K. (2010). "Lost Boys," cousins, and aunties: Using Sudanese refugee relationships to complicate definitions of "family." In M. L. Dantas, & P. C. Manyak (Eds.), *Home–school connections in a multicultural society: Learning from and with culturally and linguistically diverse families* (pp. 19–40). New York: Routledge.

Pinkham, A., & Neuman, S. B. (2012). Early literacy development. In B. H. Wasik (Ed.), *Handbook of family literacy* (2nd ed., pp. 23–37). New York: Routledge.

Purcell-Gates, V. (1995). *Other people's words: The cycle of low literacy.* Cambridge, MA: Harvard University Press.

Purcell-Gates, V. (1996). Stories, coupons, and the TV guide; Relationships between home literacy experiences and emergent literacy knowledge. *Reading Research Quarterly, 31,* 406–428.

Rainie, L. (2011). *Asian-Americans and technology.* Retrieved from http://www.pewinternet.org/~/media// Files/Presentations/2011/Jan/2011%20-%20pdf%20-%20Asian%20Americans%20-%20DC.pdf.

Rasinski, T., & Padak, N. (2008). Beyond stories. *Reading Teacher, 6*(7), 582–584.

Reese, L. (2012). Storytelling in Mexican homes: Connections between oral and literacy practices. *Bilingual Research Journal, 35*(3), 277–293.

Reyes, I., Kenner, C., Moll, L. C., & Orellana, M. F. (2012). Biliteracy among children and youth. *Reading Research Quarterly, 47*(3), 307–327.

Roberts, K. L. (2013). Comprehension strategy instruction during parent–child shared reading: An intervention study. *Literacy Research and Instruction, 52,* 106–129.

Rodriguez-Brown, F. (2004). Project FLAME: A parent support family literacy model. In B. H. Wasik (Ed.), *Handbook of family literacy* (pp. 213–229). Mahwah, NJ: Erlbaum.

Segal, P. H. (2013). *Reading the defense: Conceptualizations of literacy by college football student-athletes.* Doctoral dissertation. Retrieved from ProQuest Dissertations & Theses. (3590670).

Sénéchal, M., Lefevre, J., Thomas, E. M., & Daley, K. E. (1998). Differential effects of home literacy experiences on the development of oral and written language. *Reading Research Quarterly, 33*(1), 96–116.

Skibbe, L. E., Bindman, S. W., Hindman, A. H., Aram, D., & Morrison, F. J. (2013). Longitudinal relations between parental writing support and preschoolers' language and literacy skills. *Reading Research Quarterly, 48*(4), 387–401.

Smith, A. (2013). *African Americans and technology use: A demographic portrait.* Retrieved from http://pewinternet.org/Reports/2014/African-American-Tech-Use/Main-Findings.aspx.

Snow, C. E., Burns, M. S., & Griffin, P. (Eds.). (1998). *Preventing reading difficulties in young children.* Washington, DC: National Academy Press.

Sonnenschein, S., Brody, G., & Munsterman, K. (1996). The influence of family beliefs and practices on children's early reading development. In L. Baker, P. Afflerbach, & D. Reinking (Eds.), *Developing engaged readers in school and home communities* (pp. 3–20). Mahwah, NJ: Lawrence Erlbaum.

Sonnenschein, S., & Munsterman, K. (2002). The influence of home-based reading interactions on 5-year-olds' reading motivations and early literacy development. *Early Childhood Research Quarterly, 17,* 318–337.

---

Strickland, D. S., & Riley-Ayers, S. (2006). *Early literacy: Policy and practice in the preschool years*. New Brunswick, NJ: National Institute for Early Education Research.

Taylor, D., & Dorsey-Gaines, C. (1988). *Growing up literate: Learning from inner-city families*. Portsmouth, NH: Heinemann.

Tracey, D. H., & Morrow, L. M. (2002). Preparing young learners for successful reading comprehension: Laying the foundation. In C. C. Block & M. Pressley (Eds.), *Comprehension instruction: Research-based best practices* (pp. 219–233). New York: Guilford.

Tracey, D. H., & Young, J. W. (2002). Mother's helping behaviors during children's at-home oral-reading practices: Effects of children's reading ability, children's gender, and mothers' educational level. *Journal of Educational Psychology*, *94*(4), 729–737.

Turner, J. D., & Hoeltzel, C. C. (2010). Assessing every child: Using purposeful language arts assessments in diverse classrooms. In D. Lapp & D. Fisher (Eds.), *Handbook of research on teaching English Language Arts* (3rd ed., pp. 329–335). New York: Routledge.

Turner, J. D., & Kim, Y. (2005). Learning about building literacy communities in multicultural and multilingual communities from effective elementary teachers. *Literacy Teaching and Learning*, *10*, 21–42.

Váldez, V. E., & Callahan, R. M. (2011). Who is learning language(s) in today's schools? In D. Lapp & D. Fisher (Eds.), *Handbook of research on teaching the English Language Arts* (3rd ed., pp. 3–9). New York: Routledge.

Valerie, L. M., & Foss-Swanson, S. (2012). Hey! Guess what I did in school today: Using family message journals to improve student writing and strengthen the school–home partnership. *Teaching Exceptional Children*, *44*(3), 40–48.

Vásquez, O., Pease-Alvarez, L., & Shannon, S. (1994). *Pushing boundaries: Language and culture in a Mexicano community*. New York: Cambridge University Press.

Wasik, B. H. (Ed.). (2012). *Handbook of family literacy*, 2nd ed. New York: Routledge.

Werderich, D. E. (2008). Bringing family and community into the writing curriculum. *Middle School Journal*, *39*(3), 34–39.

Zickuhr, K., & Smith, A. (2012). *Digital differences*. Pew Research Center, April 13, 2012. Retrieved from http://www.pewinternet.org/2012/04/13/digital-differences/.

# 21

# Influences of the Experience of Race as a Lens for Understanding Variation in Displays of Competence in Reading Comprehension

*Carol D. Lee*

This chapter examines the interconnected ways that experiences with positioning around race play out in displays of competence in reading comprehension. In reviewing relevant research literatures, it is important initially to make explicit two fundamental propositions that guide this review. First, race is a social and political construction, not a biological reality (DuBois, 1996; Long & Kittles, 2003). Differences at the level of the genome among human communities are insignificant. It is important to note that constructions of the idea of race are historical and have not always existed. The history of such constructions is fraught with conundrums: using physical characteristics such as color and hair texture to distinguish among presumed racial groups; attributing inferiority and superiority along multiple dimensions to presumed racial groupings; shifting classifications as to different racial groups; shifts in the meaning of race in different parts of the world and at different points in history (e.g., meaning of race in the United States versus across Latin America) (Gould, 1981; Mills, 1997). In the western world, especially in the United States, conceptions of race have historically been correlated with opportunity within and across multiple levels of the ecological system. Bronfenbrenner and Morris (1998) describes an ecological system as consisting of the macro-level (broad societal beliefs and institutional practices), the micro-level (the local settings in which individuals participate), the meso-level (relationships across the various settings in which a person participates), and the exo-system (with regard to children's development, the places where parents and other adult caregivers participate). I reference these multiple levels of an ecological system as opportunities associated with race, at least in the United States, that have been associated with societal racial stereotypes, political ideologies, and the structuring of economic opportunities. At the level of micro-systems, the quality of local schools serving predominantly racial minorities and the poor, the availability of quality housing, the availability of youth serving organizations and green space also create challenging contexts for racial minorities and the poor. The construct of a meso-system is important because it highlights the concentration of challenge in neighborhoods that are both racially segregated and poor. And the construct of an exo-system provides leverage for thinking about the range of social capital that adult caregivers may accrue based on their experiences in terms of schooling, participation in the job market, etc. I will argue that these constraints at every level of the ecological system must be understood in terms of affording both risk and protective factors (Muschinske, 1977; Tucker, 1994; Carruthers, 1995). Thus, in this chapter I examine the influences of racial positioning on displays of competence in reading comprehension as having to do with the experience of race, rather than with race as an uncontested given, or a deterministic categorization. The second basic proposition reflected in the title is displays of competence with regard to reading comprehension. So much of the data we have to measure reading comprehension focuses on assessments in schools which do not address the question of what people read and do with texts—broadly speaking—outside of school. Thus, I am positioning competence as related to the contexts under which we attempt to determine what people know and can do.

## What Reading Outcome Data Suggest about Race and Opportunity to Learn

National Assessment of Educational Progress (NAEP) data indicate a persistent achievement gap on NAEP reading outcomes in relation to race and ethnicity (National Center for Education Statistics, 2013). However, there are several interesting caveats related to this persistent pattern. While we have seen progress since the 1970s for 9 and 13-year-olds, the average reading scores for 17-year-olds have remained relatively flat. The gap between whites and blacks, and whites and Hispanics has narrowed largely because gains for white students have not been as great. These racial gaps narrow primarily when compared to data trends before 2008. However, since 2008, on the whole the gap has not changed (except for 13-year-old Hispanics). These data suggest that the tasks of reading comprehension change substantively from elementary to middle to high school. These data also suggest, at least, that there may be differences in the experience of middle and high school that are related to positioning with regard to race. There is evidence that academic tracking, enrollment in Advanced Placement courses, and the general rigor of the curriculum are associated with students' race, where African American, Latino, American Indian, and certain Asian American groups are significantly less likely to experience optimal opportunities to learn (Darling-Hammond, 2010) than white students, although this is complicated by socioeconomic status (SES). The lack of equal access is further complicated by the fact that schools in the US remain largely segregated with regard to race and class (Orfield, Kucsera, & Siegel-Hawley, 2012) and as a consequence schools with majority minority populations are likely to have less per pupil funding, more teachers who are not certified in the subjects they teach, more teachers who lack experience, and less access to information technologies (Darling-Hammond, 2010). All of these influence the quality of students' school experiences, including reading comprehension instruction. And throughout the school years, but especially in middle and high school, the ability to comprehend texts is among the most critical variables affecting success in school across the curriculum, certainly creating challenging contexts that racialized young people have to navigate.

## Impacts of a Racialized Ecological System on Opportunity to Learn

This experience of race in the US manifests itself at all levels of the ecological system, from family life to resource availability in neighborhoods to broader societal stereotypes that play out in institutional configurations in schools, in the media, and the workplace. While the challenges are most intense in segregated black and brown communities living in poverty, the prevalence of racism remains a challenge for the middle class as well (Patillo, 1999). For example, there are persistent achievement gaps, based on students' race, even in more affluent suburban schools, especially high schools (Oakes, 1985, 1990). Ferguson (2003, 2007) has identified a myriad of social network issues and perceptions on the part of teachers and students in these schools that may well contribute to these gaps. Thus the social territories the black and brown youth in these middle-class suburban schools must navigate are complex and complicated by positioning with regard to race. And while the focus in this chapter is largely on black and brown youth, it is important to note that poor white youth face similar ecological challenges (e.g., dropout rates in Appalachia and the Mississippi Delta; Purcell-Gates, 1995; Hicks, 2002; Teets, 2006). It is interesting to note that when thinking about race and educational outcomes, we tend to focus on black and brown youth and to not address poor white youth. Thus, there are interesting intersections between positioning with regard to race/ethnicity and SES. Black and brown youth in integrated middle-class schools face constraints in opportunity to learn where SES is not the predictor; and yet poor white youth in schools of concentrated poverty also experience restricted opportunities to learn.

Describing the experience of race, especially for black and brown youth, demonstrates that learning to navigate these challenges (e.g., subject to stereotyping, restrictive school environments, neighborhood poverty, etc.) is part of the life course socialization required for these youth (Spencer et al., 2006). As a consequence, learning to read—in school and out—is situated within ecological spaces that extend beyond the individual classroom. The array of resources that must be recruited and coordinated as youth learn to read and comprehend texts— knowledge structures, motivation, persistence, relationship building—are socialized and supported both within and beyond the walls of an individual classroom or school building (Lee, 2002, 2007).

The coordination of the complex psychological system to support student reading development must focus on individuals and their interactions with other people as well as artifacts available within and across settings (Bronfenbrenner & Morris, 1998; Cole, 1998; Fischer & Bidell, 1998; Rogoff, 2003). This psychological system includes the work of identity building as a reader and a participant in the practices that especially school based reading can invite. This identity work for students includes perceptions of the self in terms of individuality, race and ethnicity, gender, class, ability, and abilities to do particular kinds of tasks (Spencer, 2006)— including reading intently and critically in school and out, for particular reasons, with particular kinds of texts. It includes perceptions of school tasks, including reading, as a meaning-making endeavor or something of an artificial task that one does or not for the purposes of getting a grade; perceptions of school as a place that is supportive or threatening to the ego; of teachers as persons who intend to help one or hurt one. These perceptions arise out of the history of students' participation, to a large degree, in the practices of the particular kind of schooling they experience over time. Experiences with texts outside of school matter, including being read to as a child, having copious reading materials in the home, and participating in social networks that entail reading particular kinds of texts. However, considering the amount of time young people spend in school, the experiences of reading in school are critically important. The issue here is that while we may have less opportunity to influence literacy experiences of youth outside of school, especially within the home, we certainly have significant opportunities to influence those literacy experiences in schools. And as argued earlier, these school-based, and for that matter neighborhood-based, experiences around literacy are influenced by positioning with regard to race.

## Psycho-Social and Ecological Models of Learning Influencing Reading Comprehension

Psycho-social and ecological models of learning help us understand how students' identities and perceptions influence learning, and suggest implications for how meaning making around race is entailed in how and what people learn. The models I discuss are Eccles' Achievement Motivation Model (Eccles, Wigfield, & Schiefele, 1998) and Spencer's Phenomenological Variant of Ecological Systems Theory (PVEST; Spencer, 2006). I will argue that while these two models do not address reading comprehension as a domain of learning, they are sufficiently comprehensive as to provide explanatory power as to why race matters for learners, no matter what the domain. Both models have been empirically validated.

Eccles argues that motivation to pursue and persist toward academic goals is not simply an outgrowth of traits of the individual. Rather, she argues, achievement-related choices are an outgrowth of dynamic relations among ten factors identified in Table 21.1.

From the student's perspective, subjective task value includes perceptions regarding interest in the task, the value of attaining competence, the utility of the task, and the relative costs entailed in pursuing the task. Consider the task of learning to read and comprehend texts in the contexts of schooling. What matters includes what the student believes the teacher thinks of her or him; what the student believes is the point of making sense of texts, especially in later grades where reading in the disciplines is the norm; what the student believes about his or her ability to comprehend, especially complex and discipline-specific texts; and how the student interprets success or failure to comprehend—all matter for goals and effort. These perceptions are colored by the experience of positioning with regard to race, for students, for teachers, for parents and other socializers. As a consequence, if students spend their K–12 experiences in schools with a culture of low expectations, with scripted curricula that focus on a narrow conceptualization of what students need to develop into engaged readers, with limited exposure to reading purposefully across genres within school subject matters, developing the grit to pursue rigorous academic tasks is made more complex and challenging. The fact of the matter is that black and brown youth living in poverty—and for that matter poor white youth—are more likely to attend schools of this sort than their middle-class white peers. Lest we think these conditions are solely an outgrowth of poverty (see Chapter 22 on poverty), the data on tracking and enrollment in advanced placement classes associated with race in middle class,

*Table 21.1* Eccles Subject Task value model

| | |
|---|---|
| 1. | Cultural milieu (including prevalence of stereotypes) |
| 2. | Socializers' beliefs and behaviors (which can include both parents and teachers) |
| 3. | Stable child characteristics |
| 4. | Previous achievement related experiences |
| 5. | Child's perceptions of socializer's beliefs, of gender roles, of the demands of academic tasks |
| 6. | Child's interpretation of his or her experiences |
| 7. | Child's goals and general self-schemes (including perceptions of ability, of goals, and the social milieu) |
| 8. | Child's affective reactions and memories |
| 9. | Expectations of success |
| 10. | The subjective value of a task. |

often suburban school districts, suggest these challenges are not merely class based (Ferguson, 2003).

One important point to emphasize is that the impacts of exposure to the conditions of racism and poverty are not deterministic. For example, we do have examples of schools that "beat the odds," serving majority black and brown youth living in poverty, where students excel on measures of reading comprehension (Langer, 2001). Even in schools where a majority of black and brown students are struggling readers, there are still students who excel as readers. And there are powerful examples of black and brown youth living in poverty who excel in rich literacy practices in out-of-school environments (Ball, 1995; Morrell, 2002; Fisher, 2003; Kirkland & Jackson, 2009; Kinloch, 2010). Spencer (2006) argues that resilience in the face of challenge is an outgrowth of the relationship between the nature of the risks and the nature of the supports available. For example, in schools reported as "beating the odds" in literacy outcomes, schools are organized around robust pedagogical practices. Documentation of rich literacy learning in informal community-based settings in low-income neighborhoods highlights the importance of nurturing relationships between adults and youth, structuring reading and writing tasks to connect both with students' interests, and also of addressing community needs. Often both the relationship building and the articulation of literacy tasks and supports for developing competence in such tasks address the range of risks with which these youth wrestle as a consequence of their positioning with regard to race and class (Lee, 2007; Ball, 2009; Gutiérrez, Morales, & Martinez, 2009; Paris, 2012).

Spencer's PVEST situates understanding academic challenges with regard to race centrally in the model. It also posits a powerful and often overlooked proposition, namely that to be human is to be at risk. This premise is important to the discussion in this chapter because sometimes our attention to the risks associated with race blinds us to the risks that all of our youth face over the life course, and shifts our attention from focusing on sources of resilience in black and brown communities. Again, I argue, learning to read and comprehend texts is not accomplished in isolation, but is situated in a wide array of experiences with literacy that are not restricted to the home and school alone. Rich literacy learning depends on relationship building within and across multiple settings, and is sensitive to how meaning-making processes are influenced by where in the life course learners are. This developmental dimension is another important contribution of Spencer's model. For example, classroom culture in primary-level classrooms tends to be more nurturing than in high schools. Young children are more likely to be able to move around the classroom, to make choices about what to read, to demonstrate their understanding through multiple modalities including speaking and drawing, and to experience personal connections with their teacher. Older youth in high school are more likely to have an opposite set of experiences. Additionally, high school students are at a point where social comparisons with regard to ability are more pronounced. They have more complex cognitive capacities for making inferences and attributions related to ability, relevance, and utility (American Psychological Association, 2002; American Psychological Association Task Force on Resilience and Strength in Black Children and Adolescents, 2008). Youth at both levels are going through important life course transitions that can influence what significance they place on what they are asked to read and write about in school. The prevalence of learning to read through stories in primary grades offers more opportunities for personal meaning making than the informational text genres that are prevalent in middle and high school. In early grades, the focus on skill acquisition in decoding increases the likelihood that students experience some measure of success in reading. However, this contrasts with what may be a lack of attention to teaching strategies for comprehension in discipline-specific classes in high school, especially for struggling readers (Snow & Biancarosa, 2003; Heller & Greenleaf, 2007; Lee & Spratley, 2009;

Carnegie Council on Advancing Adolescent Literacy, 2010). In addition, primary grade teachers have a much broader and richer array of resources to support reading instruction, especially with regard to decoding, than middle and high school teachers, particularly with regard to reading in the disciplines. Just this distinction alone illustrates one of the core principles of PVEST: understanding outcomes in terms of relations between risks and supports. In the examples I have provided, risks of poor reading outcomes associated with racial positioning and SES can be buffered with the nature of relationship building more typical in primary classrooms, access to reading narrative texts that invite personal meaning making, and availability of professional supports for teachers (e.g., diagnostic tools, professional development, curricular materials explicitly focussing on skill development in reading) that are more characteristic of primary-level classrooms. By contrast, the risks associated with race and SES for negative reading outcomes in adolescence differ from childhood and can be exacerbated by how reading comprehension is taught (or not) and experienced in middle and high school (e.g., disciplinary texts decontextualized from personally relevant purposes; the psychological demands of navigating multiple-subject-matter teachers who require that students read and comprehend, but typically do not teach students, especially struggling readers, how to tackle such tasks; lack of availability of diagnostic tools and rich curriculum to support comprehension in content areas). While these are my hypotheses, the decline in reading achievement the longer students stay in school at least suggests possible warrants for such ideas.

The PVEST model includes five dynamically connected dimensions represented in Table 21.2. This model has interesting implications for how we can approach understanding outcomes in reading comprehension for black and brown youth, and generally youth living in poverty. The developmental lens of PVEST helps us appreciate that it is important to understand that these youth must wrestle with both the normative challenges of where they are in the life course (e.g., the differences in the need for attachments among young children and among adolescents who are entering sexual maturation where the meaning of peer relationships is highly consequential) along with the additional challenges of wrestling with positionings around race (e.g., stereotypes around ability, conceptions of beauty, gender, etc.). Again, I reiterate that learning to read and comprehend complex texts in the contexts of schooling is not an isolated, purely within the individual, cognitive process. The net vulnerabilities of black and brown youth, especially those living in poverty, are populated by the historical and contemporary vestiges of racism that include residential segregation, lack of inter-generational wealth, placement in schools with limited resources and cultures of low expectations, health care disparities, as well as negative

*Table 21.2* Dimensions of risk and resilience in Spencer's Phenomenological Variant of Ecological Systems Theory (PVEST)

| | |
|---|---|
| 1. | Net vulnerability (the objective nature of risks faced and protective factors available) |
| 2. | Net stress (how the individual experiences those vulnerabilities as an outgrowth of the relationship between challenges and supports) |
| 3. | Reactive coping processes (how the individual copes with challenges, which can be adaptive or maladaptive) |
| 4. | Emergent identities (the kinds of ways of coping that emerge over time, across the life course, that become part of the meaning making repertoires upon which one draws, which can be negative or positive) |
| 5. | Stage-specific coping outcomes (productive or unproductive outcomes in early childhood, adolescence, adulthood, etc.). |

societal stereotypes. An interesting perspective on the question of curriculum content—what students are expected to read and read about—is to what extent such content can play a role in helping black and brown students, and indeed all students, to wrestle with understanding these political, economic, and social conditions, on the assumption that having more complex understandings of these macro-level issues may serve a buffering function in expanding the conceptual resources available to them to make sense of race-related negative experiences. (Boykin & Toms, 1985; Miller & MacIntosh, 1999). Research on racial socialization documents positive academic outcomes associated with positive racial socialization, although this has not been documented with respect to reading outcomes particularly (Hughes, 2003; Mandara, 2006).

The focus on reactive coping processes and emergent identities is useful in several ways (Spencer et al., 2006) . Particularly in middle and high school, it is important to realize that students accumulate a long history of experiences in this place called school (Spencer et al., 2006). And because reading is so central to learning across domains in school, they come to middle and high school with histories of imputing salience to what it means to read in school. This distinction between the salience of reading in school and reading out of school is important as studies have documented discontinuities between how often and for what purposes students read outside of school versus in school (Mahiri, 2000/2001; O'Brien, Moje, & Stewart, 2001; Fisher, 2004; Alvermann, Hinchman, Moore, Phelps, & Waff, 2006; Kirkland & Jackson, 2009; Moje & Tysvaer, 2010). These young people have developed routinized ways of coping with the experiences of failure in reading, as indicated by low test scores and grades; of being asked to read and knowing they do not understand; or of being able to comprehend but not seeing the point of working to deeply understand the texts they are being expected to "cover" in content area classes. These routine coping processes include criteria for perceiving when the reading experience is likely to be threatening. Behavior problems, especially in middle and high school, can often be attributed to such perceptions and coping responses, especially for youth with histories of low achievement (Spencer, 1999; Spencer, Fegley, Harpalani, & Seaton, 2004). Perhaps the most central question to emerge from using the PVEST model to examine the question of this chapter is what kinds of supports will be most relevant to the challenges that black and brown youth and youth living in poverty face with regard to learning to become successful, critical readers. I will address this question at the end of this chapter, but will explore next how some of these challenges are situated in terms of the demands of reading comprehension.

In Box 21.1, I offer the story of Mykelle Wheeler (http://www.wbez.org/story/news/education/keeping-mykelle-class; http://www.wbez.org/episode-segments/5050-grading-mykelle). His story was reported in 2008 on WBEZ (Chicago's National Public Radio station) as part of their 50–50 Series: The Odds of Graduating. The series focused on the dilemmas in Chicago high schools where at the time of this story 12,000 students had dropped out, the majority black and brown males. I present this case to illustrate the challenges many black and brown students living in poverty face in urban school districts and the challenges their teachers and administrators face. I then offer an example of how researchers and practitioners might employ ecological, cultural, and human development perspectives to figure out what generative questions to ask. I argue that posing the appropriate questions is the first step in avoiding what is the dominant deficit orientation that dominates how in both practice and research we typically address the achievement gap, with the gap in reading comprehension as just one area where the gap persists. As I will explore in the next section, it is interesting that in the United States we have made greater gains in mathematics than in reading comprehension.

## Box 21.1 The story of Mykelle Wheeler

### The Challenge

Mykelle Wheeler is a young African American male enrolled in 2008 as a freshman in Robeson High School in the Chicago public schools. He lives in a low-income community and is enrolled in a low-performing public school. He lives in a two-parent working-class household, in the home in which his father grew up. His English Language Arts (ELA) instructor, Ms. Ring, is a first-year teacher. She is facing pressures from the school administration to try to make sure that most of her freshmen students pass the course. Mykelle is failing English and other courses. His ELA teacher initially begins the school year teaching novels, but finds many students are not reading, not bringing the books to class, and not completing assignments. She then reverts to using work sheets. She creates time for students to complete missing assignments. The reporter covering the story observes Mykelle in the back of the class copying from the worksheet of another student.

### From the Transcript of the Program

Like a lot of 9th grade teachers, Mykelle's English teacher is new to Robeson. Caitlin Ring came straight from Barnard College, where she studied English and writing. At the beginning of the year, Ring issued Mykelle and his classmates two brand-new novels, She was going to help them find meaning in those pages. It wasn't long before she'd collected the books again.

*Ring*: Whoever thought that giving freshmen two novels that they need to carry around, bring to class, read on their own, it's just not gonna happen. By the second or third class there were only like six people who actually knew where their books were.
*Ambi*: So it's a red day sheet, a blue-purple day sheet, a bright yellow day sheet, and a green day sheet.

Now, instead of essays and discussions, Ring makes color-coded worksheets, a different color for every day. She says it's helped students focus. And instead of assigning students to read she tried that initially she now reads aloud to them.

*Ring*: My standards have gone down so much since working here. Part of me, when the kids show up and they sit down and write anything, whether it's right or wrong I want to pass them. Which is really unfair to them, because most of them can't do the work.
*Mykelle*: Can I get my stamp?
*Ring*: Mostly the reasons that I fail people is because they don't come to school.
*Reporter*: So basically if you just show up and . . .What? Do anything?
*Ring*: Uh huh.
*Reporter*: You get a D at least?
*Ring*: Yeah.

Ring and other teachers at Robeson say students don't comprehend what they're reading. But 70 percent of Ring's students passed the semester and earned their credit toward graduation. CPS has no uniform policy or philosophy on grading. And it's not an easy issue, especially in a school system that includes the best and worst schools in the state. Should kids who are poorly prepared for high school be held to the same standards as other kids in the city who are well prepared? Robeson's principal says it's impossible.

(www.wbez.org/episode-segments/5050-grading-mykelle)

### Understanding Mykelle's Challenge from an Ecological and Human Development Framework

Rather than interrogating Mykelle's dilemma simply through the cognitive lens of his skill set for reading comprehension as an individual capacity or trait, or his motivation from a deficit perspective, I offer a more comprehensive set of questions to examine, informed by what studies in ecological systems and human development pose:

1. What perceptions of the task of reading in school does Mykelle bring from his prior experiences in school? (Note: Mykelle says he is bored.)
2. What perceptions does he have of his ability to do the comprehension work he is being asked to do, and the relevance of such work for his immediate and distal goals?
3. What perceptions does he bring of the school as a supportive or threatening environment?
4. With what challenges is he wrestling, what challenges is he attempting to balance that derive from the fact that he is a teenager, from the fact that he is a black male (not just in America but especially in Chicago where the high school graduation rate for black males in 2009–2010 was 39 percent, where the discipline referral and suspension rates for black males far outweighs that of whites, where the murder rate in 2012 was the highest in the nation) (Boykin, 1986; Noguera, 2003; Toldson, 2008; Schott Foundation for Public Education, 2012)?
5. What resources are available to him to navigate these multiple challenges (e.g., in his ELA class, in his other classes, in the school, in his neighborhood, in his family, in his peer social network)?
6. What resources are available to his ELA teacher (and other content area teachers) to understand:

   (a) what skills and dispositions he brings as a reader
   (b) how to understand Mykelle's resistance
   (c) how to structure instruction in such a way as to position Mykelle as competent and efficacious
   (d) how to scaffold the relevant knowledge and dispositions that Mykelle has developed from his everyday practices outside of school
   (e) and how these resources are constrained by the state of our knowledge base for instruction and the uptake and interrogation of that knowledge base inside practice.

## Demands of Reading Comprehension

In this section I examine how processes of learning to comprehend written texts as cognitive may be connected to positioning with regard to race. I am defining "cognitive" broadly to include thinking processes within individuals, but also as intertwined with people's participation in an array of cultural practices within and across settings. To do so, let me first articulate what we know from the extant research base about what is entailed in comprehension.

All learning involves some recruitment of prior knowledge—whether simple recall or constructing new knowledge. This is certainly true of acts of comprehending texts. For the purposes of text comprehension, relevant prior knowledge includes knowledge of the following (Snow, 2002; Anderson, 2004):

- topics
- text structures
- syntactical structures of language
- phonology
- vocabulary
- pragmatic goals that genres and disciplines may typically examine
- strategies for constructing literal and inferential meanings from the language and structure of texts.

The terrain of relevant prior knowledge for text comprehension has been contested territory for many decades with regard to black and brown students who speak a non-standard dialect of English as well as black and brown students for whom English is a second language (Lee, 2005). Prior knowledge required for reading comprehension is tied to linguistic knowledge, including knowledge of topics, text structures, vocabulary, and syntax. These are all embedded in language and, with regard to reading in school, embedded in academic language.

Thus the language question has most typically been the root of debates (Farr, 1991; Ball, 2002). For example, African American English (AAE) and African American English Vernacular (AAEV) (an important distinction) have been the most widely studied and debated variety of English studied in relation to literacy teaching and learning (Smitherman, 1977). The origins of Direct Instruction (DI) in early reading were based on research which proposed that children who were speakers of non-standard dialects had linguistic deficits that had to be explicitly addressed in early reading instruction (Bereiter & Engelmann, 1966). Even today, DI is commonly used in primary grades in schools serving largely black and brown youth living in poverty. In fact, at one point the state of California required DI. Even before this, there were programs of research examining the impact of what were called dialect readers, written in such a way as to reflect morphological features of AAEV to determine if they improved reading comprehension for AAEV-speaking children (Baratz, 1969; Johnson & Simons, 1973; Piestrup, 1973; Culinan, 1974; Hall & Guthrie, 1980; Rickford & Rickford, 1995). The hypothesis was that phonetic features of AAEV would interfere with pronunciation and comprehension (e.g., distinction between told and toll, four and foe); or syntactic features such as the use of the copula be in AAEV (e.g., he be instead of he is; he be doing it). Findings from these studies showed no significant impact of dialect readers, suggesting that dialect interference was not a major factor influencing comprehension. Other studies that attempted to teach standard English phonology were also found to have no impact on comprehension (Melmed, 1971; Rentel & Kennedy, 1971). This hypothesis was further refuted in comparative studies of comprehension of stories written in AAEV and standard English (Johnson & Simons, 1973; Sims, 1972).

Political debates have surrounded the uses of AAEV in literacy instruction, from the King case from Ann Arbor, Michigan to the highly politicized debates over the decision of the Oakland, California school board to address AAE directly in instruction (Smitherman, 2000). These political debates over the function and relevance of AAE in literacy instruction abound despite repeated declarations from the American Society of Linguistics and an abundance of research in sociolinguistics that AAE and AAEV are not inferior versions of English and have systematic features that serve important pragmatic functions (Labov, 1972; American Association for Applied

Linguistics, 1997). While the focus of this chapter is on reading comprehension, it is useful to note an important study by Smitherman (1994), who did a post hoc analysis of NAEP writing samples from 1984 to 1988 to examine how the presence of what she called AAE rhetorical features were correlated with quality determinations by the original raters. She found, interestingly, that the presence of these features was positively correlated with quality of writing. While the logic and systematicity of AAE has been well established in linguistic research, attitudes toward its status and attributions made about its use in school contexts have been and remain problematic. Other studies have documented the challenges teachers face in evaluating children's knowledge displays around oral storytelling in AAEV despite research documenting the complex structures, rhetoric, and pragmatic functions of AAEV-speaking children's linguistic repertoires (DeMeis & Turner, 1978; Michaels, 1981; Gee, 1989).

Another dimension of these debates over language repertoires entailed in comprehension has focused explicitly on the question of vocabulary and access to books in the home. In early reading there has been a wealth of research arguing that poor children typically come to school with limited vocabulary knowledge compared to their middle-class counterparts. Again because race and class are so deeply correlated in the US, these claims are relevant to understanding how achievement in reading comprehension may be influenced by race. The most widely cited study is that of Hart and Risley (1995), which found that by the age of 3, middle-class children had experienced 30 million more words than their peers whose families lived on welfare. Beyond exposure, they documented more complex verbal interactions between children and adults in middle-class families. In addition, studies have documented that there are fewer books available in the homes of children living in poverty and less regularity of parents reading to their children. I do not call the validity of these studies into question, but rather the implications that have been taken up widely. The implicit assumption is that there is a singular pathway through which children learn to read and comprehend. On the other hand, the research on the rich oral narrative repertoires of children who speak non-standard English dialects (Gee, 1989; Bloome, Champion, Katz, Morton, & Muldrow, 2001; Champion, 2003) and empirical studies of literacy interventions that draw upon these repertoires suggest that multiple pathways for learning to read and comprehend are possible (Stahl & Miller, 1989). The institutional infrastructures to bring such a range of instruction into wide use is limited (e.g., teacher training, commercially available curricular materials, assessments). And while this chapter has discussed dialect variation in English, there is a similar breadth of research on the intellective repertoires made possible through the availability of use of multiple national languages in literacy instruction, including research on the ways that students for whom English is a second language navigate, cognitively and affectively, through multiple languages in their sense-making processes while comprehending and communicating their understandings (Langer, Bartolome, Vasquez, & Lucas, 1990; Valdes, 1996; Garcia, 1998; Orellana & Reynolds, 2008; Gutiérrez et al., 2009).

Overall, the disconnects among the range of variation in American English dialects across the country, the empirical base in linguistics documenting the complex structures of these dialects, and the breadth of knowledge about language processing in both oral reading and reading comprehension contribute to the challenges that black and brown youth face when instructed in classroom environments where teachers' knowledge in these domains is limited (Wolfram, 1981; Wolfram, Adger, & Christian, 1999).

The role of content area prior knowledge has been well documented in the research on text comprehension. Starting with Barlett's (1932) early work on what has come to be referred to as cultural schemata to schema studies from the Center for the Study of Reading (Steffensen, Joag-Dev, & Anderson, 1979; Reynolds, Taylor, Steffenson, Shirey, & Anderson, 1982; Delain,

Pearson, & Anderson, 1985), research documents how prior knowledge, including culturally situated prior knowledge, can impact what readers come to understand from texts. This question of prior knowledge and comprehension is complicated and consequential along multiple dimensions. First, as students move into middle and high school, texts become discipline-specific (e.g., reading in literature, in history, in science, in mathematics). Whether these are textbooks, literary works, or largely expository primary source documents, the requirements of prior knowledge increase substantively (Lee & Spratley, 2009), or what we can call content area prior knowledge. This aspect of text comprehension can play out in several ways with regard to black and brown youth living in poverty. First, the broader stereotype that the life experiences of these young people work against them in school decreases the likelihood that instruction will be structured in ways that draw upon these experiences. These are youth who are more likely to be enrolled in schools with scripted curriculum and limited exposure to being expected to read across genres beyond textbooks in their academic classes. They are also less likely to experience literacy instruction where building requisite content prior knowledge in preparation for reading across multiple texts is the norm. And they are less likely to be in schools with sufficient assessment tools and instructional capacity to disentangle how insufficient prior knowledge may impede comprehension. I make this case because, particularly with the kinds of accountability measures that have been in place in recent years across districts for moving from elementary to high school, low-achieving students entering high school are less likely to have problems with decoding (e.g., reading the words on the page). This suggests that their problems with comprehension are more likely related to prior knowledge of content, vocabulary, or strategies.

Earlier I raised the question that PVEST (Spencer, 2006) implies: What supports are needed to address the challenges related to the role of schools in developing high levels of competence in reading comprehension for black and brown youth and youth living in poverty generally? While there are many examples of work being done in out-of-school settings to address these challenges, I will focus attention on schooling. I will address reading in the disciplines in middle and high school because NAEP data trends suggest this is where black and brown students face the greatest challenges in reading achievement. While the challenges of reading comprehension at this level are great for all students, in part because of our limited infrastructure at this level, they are greatest for black and brown youth because of the multiple ecological factors I have described across this chapter, including the dual demands of wrestling with the normative challenges of adolescent development along with the additional challenges posed by poverty and racism (including the greater likelihood of being in schools with restrictive curriculum and pedagogy in reading comprehension).

## Specialized Demands of Reading in the Disciplines in Middle and High School

Reading in middle and high school is focussed on the content areas (Heller & Greenleaf, 2007). Generic strategies for comprehension, such as determining main ideas or making predictions of text content, are necessary but insufficient for discipline-specific comprehension. Textbooks are the dominant texts used in middle and especially high school (Lee, & Spratley, 2009). Textbooks have generic structures that can be explicitly taught (e.g., headings, illustrations, margin notes, indexes, and use of prototypical text structures such as compare/contrast, problem/solution), but the language and conceptual density of textbooks become more complex over the grades (Snow & Biancarosa, 2003). Illustrations in science, history, and mathematics serve explicit functions and have explicit structures that can be taught. However, rich understandings of the problems of the disciplines require reading beyond textbooks. Primary source documents in history and science include specific genres, genres that can also include illustrations and graphic representations (Wineburg, 1991; Levin & Mayer, 1993). The tasks go beyond recall of facts to interpreting and making judgments, drawing on accepted criteria in the disciplines. Constructing arguments based on data from across multiple texts is what is required for college readiness. Such arguments should be both oral and written. These are the foci of the Common Core State Standards and earlier College Readiness Standards. However, addressing these challenges is complicated, especially in high school, when students are struggling readers. Teachers have few tools available to help them assess sources of text complexity in disciplinary texts. While Lexiles and other readability measures are useful, they can be deceiving because they do not measure conceptual complexity (Goldman, & Lee, 2014; Graesser, McNamara, Louwerse, & Cai, 2004). In addition, there are virtually no measures available to high schools to assess discipline-specific reading skills. Finally, these conundrums are complicated by stereotypes suggesting that everyday repertoires of black and brown youth and youth living in poverty are not relevant to the tasks of disciplinary comprehension. These complexities of disciplinary comprehension confounded by the insufficient professional infrastructure for addressing them, especially for struggling readers, poses a significant challenge for black and brown students living in poverty and for white students living in poverty.

There are a number of interventions and programs of research that take on these kinds of complex reading challenges for adolescents, particularly black and brown youth. I offer several as illustrations of possibilities. The first is Cultural Modeling, focussing on literary reasoning (Lee, 1993, 1995, 2007). The second is the Migrant Youth Program, focussing on reading as a tool of ideological meaning making (Gutiérrez, 2008; Gutiérrez et al., 2009).

Cultural Modeling (CM) identifies specific interpretive problems that readers will meet across genres and literary traditions, and strategies expert readers bring to detecting and examining these problems (e.g., symbolism, problems of narration, satire, irony; criteria for examining archetypal themes and character types; Lee, 2011). It articulates specific criteria for examining sources of text complexity. Similar to the focus on processes for reasoning in mathematics, CM specifies processes for reasoning about interpretive problems, characterization, and themes in literature. CM has documented how youth from black and brown communities tacitly employ these strategies and epistemic orientations toward language in their everyday lives. CM curricula pose cultural data sets from students' everyday practices as objects of study to make public knowledge of strategies that is typically tacit. Texts are selected by the nature of the interpretive problems they pose and sequenced so that students' prior knowledge of themes and character types can initially support their emerging explicit knowledge of strategies. Classroom discourse invites everyday interactional patterns and instruction positions students from the very beginning as competent. Thus CM seeks to leverage everyday knowledge, scaffold disciplinary specific reading, and leverage students' perceptions of their competencies and the potential relevance of the reading tasks to their lives. Box 21.2 gives an example of CM in practice.

The Migrant Student Leadership Institute at UCLA was a summer program started in 2000 for high school students whose families were migrant workers. Gutiérrez (2008) describes the goals of the program as follows:

> Within the learning ecology of the MSLI at the University of California, Los Angeles, a collective Third Space is interactionally constituted, in which traditional conceptions of academic literacy and instruction for students from nondominant communities are contested and replaced with forms of literacy that privilege and are contingent upon students' socio-historical lives both proximally and distally. Within the MSLI, hybrid language practices;

---

*Box 21.2* **An example of Cultural Modeling in practice**

In an instructional unit on symbolism and coming of age, texts set are organized to begin with cultural data sets and then move on to novels, short stories, and poems in which both symbolism and the theme of coming of age are prominent. Initial canonical texts are ones in which we presume that students will bring significant prior knowledge with regard to theme, characterization, and setting. Students then go on to read texts which pose the same technical challenges but where the characters and settings are further removed from their experiences. Cultural data sets include such rap lyrics as "The Mask" by the Fugees and a five-minute film replete with symbolism called "Subway Stories," directed by Julie Dash who made the acclaimed film "Daughters of the Dust." Toni Morrison's novel *Beloved* serves as the anchor novel in one such unit. Students read historical texts to provide background knowledge about the African Holocaust of Enslavement and view the film Sankofa directed by Haile Gerima. Sankofa provides both a visualization of the experience of enslavement, but also has a recurring symbol (the image of a bird flying overhead, referring back to the Akan Adinkra symbol of the Sankofa bird, conveying the proverb "in order to know where you are going you must know from whence you came"). Stories and poems that follow include William Faulker's "Rose for Emily," Stephen Crane's "The Open Boat," selections from Amy Tan's *The Joy Luck Club* ("Rice Husband" and "Ying Ying"), Robert Frost's "The Road Not Taken," and Emily Dickinson's "Because I Could Not Stop for Death."

See Lee (2001, 2007) for detailed descriptions of the enactments and outcome data.

---

the conscious use of social theory, play, and imagination; and historicizing literacy practices link the past, the present, and an imagined future (p. 148).

Students were brought to the UCLA campus and were supported in reading complex sociological texts through which to examine the social, political, and economic factors that shaped the challenges they faced (Espinoza, 2009; Pacheco & Nao, 2009). The use of multiple languages was encouraged as a resource for meaning making. A central goal was to help these young people see themselves as members, contributors to the UCLA campus (Gildersleeve, 2010), but equally important as empowered to pursue their dreams and to interrogate the political and economic forces that shaped their life conditions, and to resist these forces. The curriculum was designed to use literacy as a tool for personal and community empowerment. A systematic study of differences in outcomes for equivalent groups of students who applied for the program but did not attend and students who attended shows significant impact on college applications and acceptance rates. Eighty–eight percent of participants who applied to UC schools were admitted (Nunez, 2009).

## Conclusion

In this chapter, I have attempted to integrate the implications of psycho-social frameworks for understanding academic motivation as well as mechanisms underlying risk and resiliency to place the persistence of the achievement gap in reading associated with race and ethnicity in a broader context. I have further situated the challenges that black and brown youth, especially black, brown, and white youth living in poverty, in a broader ecological context, beyond viewing pedagogy inside schools as the sole resource available to address this persistent gap. Fundamentally, the argument is that academic motivation and persistence are influenced by students' perceptions of themselves as learners, of the tasks they are asked to carry out (in this case around reading in schools), of their teachers and caretakers in schools, and of their school environments as supportive or threatening. These perceptions are influenced certainly by individual differences in temperament, knowledge, and personal goals. However, these perceptions are also influenced by the broader ecological contexts in which the students live (societal beliefs, institutional practices, neighborhood resources, social networks, etc.). I have argued that these ecological contexts, including the organization of schools and instruction, can offer both sources of risk and protection.

I have further argued that these ecological contexts are again complicated for black, brown, and white youth living in poverty by the state of knowledge and practice with regard to teaching reading comprehension, especially in middle and high school grades (Lee, 2014).

## References

Alvermann, D., Hinchman, K. A., Moore, D., Phelps, S., & Waff, D. (2006). *Reconceptualizing the literacies in adolescents' lives*. Mahwah, NJ: Lawrence Erlbaum.

American Association for Applied Linguistics (1997). American Association for Applied Linguistics: Resolution on application of dialect knowledge to education. *AAAL Letter: The Newsletter of the American Association for Applied Linguistics*, *19*(1), 7–8.

American Psychological Association (2002). *Developing adolescents: A reference for professionals*. Washington, DC: APA.

American Psychological Association Task Force on Resilience and Strength in Black Children and Adolescents (2008). *Resilience in African American children and adolescents: A vision for optimal development*. Washington, DC: American Psychological Association.

Anderson, R. (2004). Role of the reader's schema in comprehension, learning, and memory. In R. B. Ruddell & N. J. Unrau (Eds.), *Theoretical models and processes of reading*. Newark, DE: International Reading Association.

Ball, A. (1995). Community based learning in an urban setting as a model for educational reform. *Applied Behavioral Science Review*, *3*, 127–146.

Ball, A. (2002). Three decades of research on classroom life: Illuminating the classroom communicative lives of America's at-risk students. *Review of Reseach in Education*, *2*(6), 71–112.

Ball, A. (2009). Toward a theory of generative change in culturally and linguistically complex classrooms. *American Educational Research Journal*, *46*(1), 45–72.

Baratz, J. (1969). A bidialectical task for determining language proficiency in economically disadvantaged children. *Child Development*, *40*(8), 889–901.

Bartlett, F. C. (1932). *Remembering: A study in experimental and social psychology*. Cambridge, UK: Cambridge University Press.

Bereiter, C., & S. Engelmann (1966). *Teaching disadvantaged children in pre-school*. Englewood Cliffs, NJ: Prentice Hall.

Bloome, D., Champion, T., Katz, L., Morton, M. B., & Muldrow, R. (2001). Spoken and written narrative development: African American preschoolers as storytellers and storymakers. In J. Harris, A. Kamhi, & K. Pollock (Eds.), *Literacy in African American communities*. Mahwah, NJ: Lawrence Erlbaum, pp. 45–76.

Boykin, A. W. (1986). The triple quandary and the schooling of Afro-American children. In U. Neisser (Ed.), *The school achievement of minority children*. Hillsdale, NJ: Lawrence Erlbaum, pp. 57–92.

Boykin, A. W., & Toms, F. D. (1985). Black child socialization: A conceptual framework. In H. P. McAdoom & J. L. McAdoo (Eds.), *Black children: Social, educational, and parental environments*. Newbury Park, CA: Sage, pp. 33–52.

Bronfenbrenner, U., & Morris, P. A. (1998). The ecology of developmental processes. In W. Damon & R. M. Lerner (Eds.), *Handbook of child psychology: Theoretical models of human development*. New York: Wiley & Sons, vol. 1, pp. 993–1028.

Carnegie Council on Advancing Adolescent Literacy (2010). *Time to act: An agenda for advancing adolescent literacy for college and career success*. New York: Carnegie Corporation of New York.

Carruthers, J. H. (1995). Science and oppression. In D. A. Azibo (Ed.), *African psychology in historical perspective and related commentary*. Trenton, NJ: Africa World Press.

Champion, T. (2003). *Understanding storytelling among African American children: A journey from Africa to America*. Mahwah, NJ: Lawrence Erlbaum Associates.

Cole, M. (1998). Can cultural psychology help us think about diversity? *Mind, Culture and Activity*, *5*(4), 291–304.

Culinan, B. E. (1974). *Black dialects and reading*. Urbana, IL: National Council of Teachers of English.

Darling-Hammond, L. (2010). *The flat world and education: How America's commitment to equity will determine our future*. New York: Teachers College Press.

Delain, M., Pearson, P. D., & Anderson, R. (1985). Reading comprehension and creativity in Black language use: You stand to gain by playing the sounding game. *American Educational Research Journal*, *22*(2), 155–173.

DeMeis, D. K., & Turner, R. R. (1978). Effects of students' race, physical attractiveness and dialect on teachers' evaluations. *Contemporary Educational Psychology*, *3*, 77–86.

DuBois, W. E. B. (1996). The concept of race. In M. K. Asante, & A. S. Abarry (Eds.), *African intellectual heritage: A book of sources*. Philadelphia: Temple University Press, pp. 409–417.

Eccles, J., Wigfield, A., & Schiefele, U. (1998). Motivation to succeed. In W. Damon & N. Eisenberg (Eds.), *Handbook of child psychology*. New York: Wiley, vol. 3, pp. 1017–1095.

Espinoza, M. (2009). A case study of the production of educational sanctuary in one migrant classroom. *Pedagogies*, *4*(1), 44–62.

Farr, M. (1991). Dialects, culture and teaching the English language arts. In J. Flood, J. Jenson, D. Lapp, & J. Squire (Eds.), *Handbook of research on teaching the English Language Arts*. New York: Macmillan, pp. 365–371.

Ferguson, R. (2003). Teachers' perceptions and expectations and the black–white test score gap. *Urban Education*, *38*(4), 460–507.

Ferguson, R. (2007). *Toward excellence with equity: An emerging vision for closing the achievement gap*. Boston, MA: Harvard Education Press.

Fischer, K. W., & Bidell, T. R. (1998). Dynamic development of psychological structures in action and thought. In W. Damon, & R. M. Lerner (Eds.), *Handbook of child psychology: Theoretical models of human development*. New York: Wiley, vol. 1, pp. 467–562.

Fisher, M. T. (2003). Open mics and open minds: Spoken word poetry in African diaspora participatory literacy communities. *Harvard Education Review*, *73*(3), 362–389.

Fisher, M. T. (2004). "The song is unfinished": The New Literate and the Literary and their institutions. *Written Communication*, *21*(3), 290–312.

Garcia, G. E. (1998). Mexican-American bilingual students' metacognitive reading strategies: What's transferred, unique, problematic? *National Reading Conference Yearbook*, *47*, 253–263.

Gee, J. P. (1989). The narrativization of experience in the oral style. *Journal of Education*, *171*(1), 75–96.

Gildersleeve, R. E. (2010). *Fracturing opportunity: Mexican migrant students and college-going literacy*. New York: Peter Lang Publishers.

Goldman, S. R., & Lee, C. D. (2014). Text complexity. *Elementary School Journal*, *115*(2), 290–300.

Gould, S. J. (1981). *The mismeasure of man*. New York: Norton.

Graesser, A. C., McNamara, D. S., Louwerse, M. M., & Cai, A. (2004). Coh-Metrix: Analysis of text on cohesion and language. *Behavioral Research Methods, Instruments and Computers*, *36*, 193–202.

Gutiérrez, K. (2008). Developing a sociocritical literacy in the third space. *Reading Research Quarterly*, *43*(2), 148–164.

Gutiérrez, K., Morales, P. L., & Martinez, D. (2009). Re-mediating literacy: Culture, difference, and learning for students from non-dominant communities. *Review of Research in Educational Research*, *33*, 212–245.

Hall, W., & L. Guthrie (1980). On the dialect question and reading. In R. Spiro, B. Bruce, & W. Brewer (Eds.), *Theoretical issues in reading comprehension: Perspectives from cognitive psychology, linguistics, artificial intellligence and education*. Hillsdale, NJ: Lawrence Erlbaum, pp. 221–244.

Hart, B., & Risley, R. T. (1995). *Meaningful differences in the everyday experience of young American children*. Baltimore, MD: Paul H. Brookes.

Heller, R., & Greenleaf, C. (2007). *Literacy instruction in the content areas: Getting to the heart of middle and high school improvement*. Washington, DC: Alliance for Excellent Education.

Hicks, D. (2002). *Reading lives: Working-class children and literacy learning*. New York: Teachers College Press.

Hughes, D. (2003). Correlates of African American and Latino parents' messages to children about ethnicity and race: A comparative study of racial socialization. *American Journal of Community Psychology, 31*(1/2), 15–33.

Johnson, K. R., & Simons, H. D. (1973). *Black children's reading of dialect and standard texts.* East Lansing, MI: National Center for Research on Teacher Learning.

Kinloch, V. (2010). *Harlem on our minds: Place, race, and the literacies of urban youth.* New York: Teachers College Press

Kirkland, D., & Jackson, A. (2009). "We real cool": Toward a theory of Black masculine literacies. *Reading Research Quarterly, 44*(3), 278–297.

Labov, W. (1972). *Language in the inner city: Studies in the Black English vernacular.* Philadelphia, PA: University of Pennsylvania Press.

Langer, J. A. (2001). Beating the odds: Teaching middle and high school students to read and write well. *American Educational Research Journal, 38*(4), 837–880.

Langer, J., Bartolome, L., Vasquez, O., & Lucas, T. (1990). Meaning construction in school literacy tasks: A study of bilingual students. *American Educational Research Journal, 27*(3), 427–471.

Lee, C. (2011). Education and the study of literature. *Scientific Study of Literature, 1*(1), 49–58.

Lee, C. (2014). Reading gaps and complications of scientific studies of learning. In S. Harper (Ed.), *The elusive quest for civil rights in education: Evidence-based perspectives from leading scholars on the 50th anniversary of the Civil Rights Act.* Philadelphia, PA: Center for the Study of Race and Equity in Education, University of Pennsylvania.

Lee, C. D. (1993). *Signifying as a scaffold for literary interpretation: The pedagogical implications of an African American discourse genre.* Urbana, IL: National Council of Teachers of English.

Lee, C. D. (1995). A culturally based cognitive apprenticeship: Teaching African American high school students skills in literary interpretation. *Reading Research Quarterly, 30*(4), 608–631.

Lee, C. D. (2002). Interrogating race and ethnicity as constructs in the examination of cultural processes in developmental research. *Human Development, 45*(4), 282–290.

Lee, C. D. (2005). Culture and language: Bi-dialectical issues in literacy. In P. L. Anders & J. Flood (Eds.), *Culture and language: Bi-dialectical issues in literacy.* Newark, DE: International Reading Association.

Lee, C. D. (2007). *Culture, literacy and learning: Taking bloom in the midst of the whirlwind.* New York: Teachers College Press.

Lee, C. D., & Spratley, A. (2009). *Reading in the disciplines and the challenges of adolescent literacy.* New York: Carnegie Foundation of New York.

Levin, J. R., & Mayer, R. E. (1993). Understanding illustrations in text. In B. K. Britton, A. Woodward, & M. Binkley (Eds.), *Learning from textbooks: Theory and practice.* Hillsdale, NJ: Lawrence Erlbaum, pp. 95–114.

Long, J. C., & Kittles, R. (2003). Human genetic diversity and the non-existence of biological races. *Human Biology, 74*(4), 449–471.

Mahiri, J. (2000/2001). Pop culture pedagogy and the end(s) of school. *Journal of Adolescent & Adult Literacy, 44*(4), 382–386.

Mandara, J. (2006). The impact of family functioning on African American males' academic achievement: A review and clarification of the empirical literature. *Teachers College Record, 108*(2), 206–223.

Melmed, P. J. (1973). Black english phonology: The question of reading interference. In J. L. Laffey & R. Shuy (Eds.), *Language differences: Do they interfere?* (pp. 70–85). Newark, DE: International Reading Association.

Michaels, S. (1981). "Sharing time": Children's narrative styles and differential access to literacy. *Language in Society, 10*, 423–442.

Miller, D. B., & MacIntosh, R. (1999). Promoting resilience in urban African American adolescents: Racial socialization and identity as protective factors. *Social Work Research, 23*(3), 159–269.

Mills, C. W. (1997). *The racial contract.* Ithaca, NY: Cornell University Press.

Moje, E. B., & Tysvaer, N. (2010). *Adolescent literacy development in out-of-school time: A practitioner's guide.* New York: Carnegie Corporation of New York.

Morrell, E. (2002). Toward a critical pedagogy of popular culture: Literacy development among urban youth. *Journal of Adolescent & Adult Literacy, 46*(1), 72–78.

Muschinske, D. (1977). The nonwhite as child: G. Stanley Hall on the education of nonwhite peoples. *Journal of the History of the Behavioral Sciences, 13*(4), 328–336.

National Center for Education Statistics (2013). *The Nation's Report Card: Trends in Academic Progress* (NCES 2013 456). Washington, DC: Institute of Education Sciences. Department of Education.

Noguera, P. (2003). The trouble with black boys: The role and influence of environmental and cultural factors on the academic performance of African American males. *Urban Education, 38,* 431–459.

Nunez, A. (2009). Creating pathways to college for migrant students: Assessing a migrant outreach program. *Journal of Education for Students Placed at Risk, 14*(3), 226–237.

O'Brien, D. G., Moje, E. B., & Stewart, R. (2001). Exploring the context of secondary literacy: Literacy in people's everyday school lives. In E. B. Moje & D. G. O'Brien (Eds.), *Constructions of literacy: Studies of teaching and learning in and out of secondary schools.* Mahwah, NJ: Lawrence Erlbaum, pp. 24–42.

Oakes, J. (1985). *Keeping track: How schools structure inequality.* New Haven, CT: Yale University Press.

Oakes, J. (1990). *Multiplying inequalities: The effects of race, social class and teaching.* Santa Monica, CA: Rand.

Orellana, M., & Reynolds, J. (2008). Cultural modeling: Leveraging bilingual skills for school paraphrasing tasks. *Reading Research Quarterly, 43*(1), 48–65.

Orfield, G., Kucsera, J., & Siegel-Hawley, G. (2012). *E pluribus . . . separation: Deepening double segregation for more students.* Los Angeles: Civil Rights Project, University of California, Los Angeles

Pacheco, M., & Nao, K. (2009). Rewriting identities: Using historicized writing to promote migrant students' writing. *Pedagogies, 4*(1), 24–43.

Paris, D. (2012). Culturally sustaining pedagogy: A needed change in stance, terminology, and practice. *Educational Researcher,* 41(3), 93–97.

Patillo, M. (1999). *Black picket fences: Privilege and peril among the black middle class.* Chicago, IL: University of Chicago Press.

Piestrup, A. M. (1973). *Black dialect interference and accomodation of reading instruction in first grade.* Monographs of the Language-Behavior Research Laboratory 4. Berkeley, CA: University of California.

Purcell-Gates, V. (1995). *Other people's words: The cycle of low literacy.* Cambridge, MA: Harvard University Press.

Rentel, V., & Kennedy, J. (1972). Effects of pattern drill on the phonology, syntax, and reading achievement of rural Appalachian children. *American Educational Research Journal, 9,* 87–100.

Reynolds, R., Taylor, M. Steffensen, M., Shirey, L., & Anderson, R. (1982). Cultural schemata and reading comprehension. *Reading Research Quarterly, 17*(3), 353–365.

Rickford, J., & Rickford, A. (1995). Dialect readers revisited. *Linguistics and Education, 7,* 107–128.

Rogoff, B. (2003). *The cultural nature of human development.* New York: Oxford University Press.

Schott Foundation for Public Education (2012). *The Schott 50 state report on public education and black males.* Cambridge, MA: Schott Foundation for Public Education.

Sims, R. (1972). *A psycholinguistic description of miscues created by selected young reders during oral reding of text in black dialect and standard English.* Unpublished doctoral dissertation, Wayne State University, Detroit, MI.

Smitherman, G. (1977). *Talkin and testifyin: The language of Black America.* Boston, MA: Houghton Mifflin.

Smitherman, G. (1994). "The Blacker the berry, the sweeter the juice": African American student writers and the NAEP. In A. H. Dyson & C. Genishi (Eds.), *The need for story: Cultural diversity in classroom and community.* Urbana, IL: National Council of Teachers of English.

Smitherman, G. (2000). Ebonics, King, and Oakland: Some folks don't believe fat meat is greasy. In G. Smitherman (Ed.), *Talkin that talk: Language, culture and education in African America.* New York: Routledge, pp. 150–162.

Snow, C. (2002). *Reading for understanding: Toward an R&D program in reading comprehension.* Arlington, VA: Rand Reading Study Group.

Snow, C., & Biancarosa, G. (2003). *Adolescent literacy and the achievement gap: What do we know and where do we go from here?* New York: Carnegie Foundation of New York.

Spencer, M. B. (1999). Social and cultural influences on school adjustment: The application of an identity-focused cultural ecological perspective. *Educational Psychologist, 34*(1), 43–57.

Spencer, M. B. (2006). Phenomenology and ecological systems theory: Development of diverse groups. In W. Damon & R. M. Lerner (Eds.), *Handbook of child psychology.* New York, Wiley, vol. 1, pp. 829–893.

Spencer, M. B., Fegley, S., Harpalani, V., & Seaton, G. (2004). Understanding hypermasculinity in context: A theory-driven analysis of urban adolescent males' coping responses. *Research in Human Development, 1*(4), 229–257.

Spencer, M. B., Harpalani, V., Cassidy, E., Jacobs, C., Donde, S., & Goss, T. N. (2006). Understanding vulnerability and resilience from a normative development perspective: Implications for racially and ethnically diverse youth. In D. Chicchetti & E. Cohen (Eds.), *Handbook of developmental psychopathology.* Hoboken, NJ: Wiley, pp. 627–672.

Stahl, S., & Miller, P. (1989). Whole language and language experience approaches for beginning reading: A quantitative research synthesis. *Review of Educational Research, 59*, 87–116.

Steffensen, M., Joag-Dev, C., & Anderson, R. (1979). A cross-cultural perspective on reading comprehension. *Reading Research Quarterly, 15*(1), 10–29.

Teets, S. (2006). Education in Appalachia. In G. T. Edwards, J. A. Asbury, & R. L. Cox (Eds.), *A handbook to Appalachia: An introduction to the region.* Knoxville, TN: University of Tennessee Press

Toldson, I. A. (2008). *Breaking barriers: Plotting the path to academic success for school-age African-American males.* Washington, DC: Congressional Black Caucus Foundation.

Tucker, W. H. (1994). *The science and politics of racial research.* Chicago, IL: University of Chicago Press.

Valdes, G. (1996). *Con respeto: Bridging the distances between culturally diverse families and schools.* New York: Teachers College Press.

Wineburg, S. (1991). Historical problem solving: A study of the cognitive processes used in evaluating documentary and pictorial evidence. *Journal of Educational Psychology, 83*(1), 73–87.

Wolfram, W. (1981). Varieties of American English. In C. Ferguson & S. B. Heath (Eds.), *Language in the USA.* New York: Cambridge University Press, pp. 44–68.

Wolfram, W., Adger, C., & Christian, D. (1999). *Dialects in schools and communities.* Mahwah, NJ: Lawrence Erlbaum.

# 22

# The Influence of Poverty on Individual Differences in Reading

*Alpana Bhattacharya*

## Introduction

According to the 2012 US Census Bureau report, 16.1 million or 21.6 percent of children under the age of 18 lived in poverty. Children represented 23.7 percent of the total population and 34.6 percent of the people in poverty, and about 1 in 4 of these children were in poverty in 2012. Overall, the child poverty rate has increased from 16.9 percent in 2001 to 21.8 percent in 2012, and currently is higher than the rates for people aged 18 to 64 and those aged 65 and older (DeNavas-Walt, Proctor, & Smith, 2013). The consistent rise in the child poverty rate is crucial because it is likely to have an adverse impact on the cognitive development and social-emotional functioning of poor children (Duncan, Ziol-Guest, & Kalil, 2010; Lichter, 1997).

The implications of poverty for the reading development of children are considerable, contributing to differences in children's reading achievement at an early age. In addition, for children who experience poverty at an early age there may be more long-lasting negative effects such as low educational attainment and high school dropout rates than for children who experience poverty later in life (Brooks-Gunn & Duncan, 1997; Duncan, Yeung, Brooks-Gunn, & Smith, 1998).

## Perspective on Childhood Poverty

Poverty is a dynamic process, with some families entering and exiting from poverty in a relatively short time and others experiencing a chronic cycle of poverty across generations (Cuthrell, Stapleton, & Ledford, 2010). Although all circumstances of poverty negatively affect the reading ability of children, the duration of poverty is of significance, with persistent poverty exerting more substantial influences on children's reading ability than transient poverty (Rayer, Blair, & Willoughby, 2013). The effects of persistent poverty often are more debilitating than transient poverty, because individuals can respond to short spells of poverty by reducing expenditures, borrowing, or spending savings that usually are not viable strategies for dealing with recurring poverty (Kicrnan & Mensah, 2011). Moreover, persistent poverty contributes to the division of the general population into distinct subgroups: those with access to economic resources such as education, employment, and health care and those without. Persistent poverty often is a trap wherein certain consequences of poverty, such as low educational outcomes, diminished health, and homelessness jeopardize individuals' subsistence (Worts, Sacker, & McDonough, 2010). Given that persistent poverty generates a long-term effect on individuals, discussion in this chapter is limited to influences of persistent poverty on children's reading differences.

## Pathways of Poverty: Impact on Reading Development

Some theories examine the effects of poverty by focussing on the family and community contexts within which children are developing. The quality of the home environment, the quality of parent–child interactions, the quality of early learning, and community environment are considered in determining the impact of poverty on children's readiness to learn (Hilferty, Redmond, & Katz, 2010). Two models, the Family Investment Model (Haveman & Wolfe, 1994) and the Family Stress Model (Conger & Elder, 1994), one involving the quality of home environment and the other involving the quality of parent–child interactions, are referenced in this section to examine the effects of poverty on children's reading development.

According to the Family Investment Model (Haveman & Wolfe, 1994), many of the negative effects of poverty on children's educational development such as low exam scores, chronic absenteeism, and high school dropout rates result from parents' inability to purchase educational materials (e.g., books, toys, and computers), provide particular educational experiences (e.g., museums, theatres, and sports), and get services (e.g., tutors, therapists, and childcare) in relation to their children's schooling. In a study conducted with children from poverty, Eamon (2005) found that children whose parents provided educational materials, discussed school-related issues, and engaged in less conflict over family rules had higher reading achievement. Conversely, Bradley, Corwyn, McAdoo, and Coll (2001) found that poor children who had limited access to educational materials and activities tended to have lower reading scores than their non-poor peers. Since poverty decreases the likelihood that children will be exposed to developmentally enriching materials and experiences both inside and outside of the home (Evans, 2004), the reading development of poor children is negatively affected (Engle & Black, 2008; McLoyd, 1998) because of increased parental distress and decreased parental involvement (Kainz, Willoughby, Vernon-Feagans, & Burchinal, 2012).

Cooper, Crosnoe, Suizzo, and Pituch (2010) posit that finances are not the only factor contributing to the educational gap between poor and non-poor children, and believe that parental involvement also plays a role in the reading development of poor children. Moreover, Cooper and her colleagues, like other researchers, have found that poor parents provide fewer educational materials for their children's development, engage their children in fewer organized activities, and are less involved in their children's schools than non-poor parents. Although poor parents often do engage their children in home-learning activities, their activities are not as frequently related to reading and do not appear to improve their children's reading.

The Family Stress Model (Conger & Elder, 1994) looks at parent–child relationships within the household to determine the impact of poverty on children's development and readiness to learn. Poverty generates psychological distress among adults within a household due to financial hardships, limited family resources, and familial responsibilities, which then interferes with their ability to provide adequate emotional support, sufficient parent–child interactions, and consistent involvement in their children's readiness to learn (Dubow & Ippolito, 1994; Evans & Kim, 2013). The economic pressure of poverty can lead to conflict between children and parents and impairs parent–child interactions because of parental irritability and depressive symptom, which in turn results in lower school grades for poor children (Duncan & Brooks-Gunn, 2000).

According to Bradley and his colleagues (2001), parents who experience economic hardship often display little verbal and physical affection, use more harsh punishment, and rarely monitor their children's behavior and growth. Thus, children who lack strong support systems, relationships, and role models tend to have a hard time overcoming the burden of poverty, and consequently their academic progress, including reading performances, are adversely affected by poverty (Payne, 2005). Conversely, parents who are able to provide supportive parenting by incorporating rich language and learning experiences in the home, despite economic hardships, tend to promote cognitive readiness for poor children (Hilferty et al., 2010).

Although parents' characteristics such as depression, irritability, and detachment affect children's educational development as a result of poverty, research findings indicate that children's characteristics also affect their development due to poverty. For example, children who are temperamentally difficult tend to exacerbate symptoms of depression and detachment amongst poor parents, thereby adversely affecting parents' ability to provide responsive caregiving and positive interactions. On the other hand, although in poverty, poor parents are more likely to invest in educational resources for their children who are academically talented and have an easy temperament. Thus, individual differences in reading have the potential of being propagated due to parents' ability or inability to meet the emotional, cognitive, and caregiving needs of their children due to the pressures of poverty (Engle & Black, 2008).

## Theoretical Framework of Poverty and Reading Differences

The dynamic processes of Bronfenbrenner's microsystem, mesosystem, and macrosystem (Eamon, 2001) are reviewed in this section to ascertain the influences of the home and school environments on poor children's reading development. Effects of poverty on reading development are examined through bidirectional interactions at the child, family, and school levels of Bronfenbrenner's *Ecological Theory of Human Development* (Bronfenbrenner, 1977).

According to Bronfenbrenner (1994), a child is involved in several interrelated contexts and processes, or microsystems. The home and school are two important microsystems for a developing child and these environments have the potential of influencing a child's reading development. The home environment exerts an important influence on a child's reading development (Hilferty et al., 2010). Because poor parents have to constantly handle the stress of meeting the needs of their family based on limited financial capital, they experience a sense of powerlessness, lower self-esteem, depression, low nurturance, uninvolved and inconsistent parenting, and harsh discipline, which then adversely affects their children's reading ability. The school environment, a second critical microsystem for children, also affects children's reading development: schools in high-poverty neighborhoods may be marked by fewer resources, poor classroom discipline, low-achieving peers, and less able teachers (Eamon, 2001).

Two poor children who enter kindergarten with similar literacy skills could exhibit differing reading development based on the kind of classroom setting they are placed in. One poor child who is placed in a kindergarten classroom where availability of printed materials is limited, opportunities for social interactions are sparse, and literacy activities are minimal may exhibit constrained reading development due to the lack of cognitively stimulating materials (e.g., books and computers) and interactive literacy activities (e.g., reading and writing) in the school. Another poor child who is placed in a kindergarten classroom where there is an abundance of literacy materials (e.g., alphabet charts and picture books), opportunities for language exchanges through social play, and engagement in interactive literacy activities (e.g., alphabet recognition and reading books) could show enhanced reading development due to the literacy-rich school environment (Kainz & Vernon-Feagans, 2007). Within the school microsystem, the nature and availability of cognitively stimulating materials and opportunity for interactive activities acts to enhance or constrain reading development.

Bronfenbrenner's mesosystems involve interrelationships between two or more microsystems (Bronfenbrenner, 1994). The relationship between a child's family and school would be a mesosystem (Hilferty et al., 2010). Parents who are less involved in their children's educational development due to economic hardships may also be uninvolved in their children's school activities. Lack of communication between home and school may diminish poor parents' ability to reinforce their children's learning at home due to absence of critical information about their children's performance and progress at school. Furthermore, lack of communication with school personnel could lessen poor parents' ability to support and shape the academic development of their children (Cooper et al., 2010). Similarly, fewer family resources would mean that the child would most likely not be able to engage in school activities such as athletic events, fieldtrips, and musical performances which would require parents to pay for clothing, supplies, and transportation (Bradley et al., 2001). Thus, mesosystem processes can impact children's achievement due to poverty (Eamon, 2001).

The relationship between the home and school, a mesosystem of the developing child, often negatively impacts reading development due to inadequacies within the home and school environments. For example, poor children who attend schools with a high concentration of peers whose mothers did not complete high school have lower reading scores than children in schools with a high concentration of mothers with a high school diploma (Fantuzzo, LeBoeuf, & Rouse, 2014). In addition to being poorly educated, often the financial constraints of poverty restrict poor parents' involvement in their children's education, and often schools also discourage parental involvement because of negative perceptions about poor parents' attitudes and values regarding their children's academic abilities (Cooper et al., 2010). Thus, families who are poorly educated and have minimal involvement in their children's education may have more difficulty protecting their children from the negative effects of poverty (Engle & Black, 2008).

Bronfenbrenner's (1994) macrosystems include economic resources, educational opportunities, and neighborhoods, which vary across high-poverty households. Children from high-poverty households tend to be vulnerable to the adversities contained within the macrosystems, which then affects their reading development (Eamon, 2001).

Resources at home influence poor children's ability to engage in literacy activities. Findings from large national studies indicate that children living in extreme poverty often do not have age-appropriate literacy materials and parental involvement in literacy activities is limited (Bradley et al., 2001; Eamon, 2005; Evans, 2004). Limited access to literacy materials and limited parental involvement in literacy activities often lowers reading achievement for poor children. Furthermore, absence of literacy materials and emotionally supportive home environments decreases academic achievement, and may also result in longstanding failure of poor children to place value on academic achievement (Dubow & Ippolito, 1994).

The school context is a critical component associated with children's reading outcomes, and a significant predictor of reading comprehension of poor children. School resources such as operating costs, costs per student, and student-to-teacher ratio make a significant contribution to differences in the reading achievement of poor children. Schools with a higher allocation of money per student and a better student-to-teacher ratio report higher reading achievement for poor children (Ransdell, 2012). Thus, experiences and resources within schools are associated with differences in children's reading development (Aikens & Barbarin, 2008). Children who perceive their school environment as positive (i.e., consisting of knowledgeable teachers, a safe school classroom, and interesting classes) tend to have higher levels of reading achievement (Eamon, 2005; McLoyd, 1998).

Kainz and Vernon-Feagans (2007) found that poor children attending schools with higher percentages of peers reading below grade level underperformed in reading despite comprehensive literacy instruction. The explanation for low reading performance according to the researchers may be that teachers adjust the nature and pace of instruction to meet the needs of the struggling readers, which then constrains the reading performance of the non-struggling readers as well. Similar results have also been reported by Aikens and Barbarin (2008), who found that the number of children reading below grade level and the presence of poor peers were consistently associated with differences in children's reading achievement. Thus, school characteristics propagate variations in children's reading.

## Indicators of Poverty and Individual Differences in Reading

Irrespective of the theoretical perspective on poverty, reading development and achievement of poor children is generally determined within the context of their home environment and school environment. In particular, variables at home and at school play a significant role in generating individual differences in poor children's reading development.

### *Influence of Poverty and Home Environment on Reading Achievement*

A wide range of factors within the home environment can influence children's reading. Bradley and his colleagues (2001) examined parental responsiveness, physical environment, and learning stimulation as dimensions of home environment to understand their influence on poor and non-poor children. Findings indicated that poverty decreases opportunities for children to be exposed to developmentally enriching materials and experiences, both inside and outside of the home. Children from poverty were more likely to have fewer than ten books, and few to no instances wherein a family member read to them, taught them school-related concepts, or took them to museums and theatres. Furthermore, poor parents were less responsive to their children (e.g., spontaneously speaking with children, responding verbally to children, and providing interesting activities for children), and less likely to show verbal and physical affection, often because of the stresses connected to the economic hardships experienced on a daily basis.

Although poverty has been found to adversely affect children's reading development, there can be differential impacts of household poverty on children's reading achievement. Drawing on Bronfenbrenner's ecological theory (Bronfenbrenner, 1977), Lee (2009) investigated the influence of poverty on children's reading development by examining poverty status (persistent poverty, transient poverty, and no poverty), child's reading outcomes as measured by a standardized reading test, home environment (maternal emotional and verbal responsiveness, maternal involvement and acceptance, learning materials, parental modeling, and variety of stimulation such as activities involving the child, books, and toys for learning), and child and family characteristics (gender, age, ethnicity, first language, and household size). The Lee investigation indicated that long-term poverty negatively affects children's reading development. Children who lived in poverty during early childhood had lower reading scores during preschool years and the negative effect on their reading development continued throughout childhood. Children who lived in poverty also had lower ratings on home environment factors that included availability of learning materials, maternal involvement in reading, and stimulation for reading.

The role of home environment in the development of reading skills has also been studied by Molfese, Modglin, and Molfese (2003). Socioeconomic status and home observations were used as measures of home environment. Family income, parental education, and parental occupation were included as measures of socioeconomic status. Home observations were conducted using a standardized inventory that focused on information about educational toys and games, family activities, and conversational events, encouragement for the development of academic skills, parental stimulation and assistance for the child's language and reading behaviors, and characteristics of the physical environment of the home. Reading achievement was measured by school-administered and laboratory-administered standardized reading tests. Results indicated that environment plays an important role in the development of reading abilities. Children's reading abilities were influenced by activities in the household and parenting practices. Although parental behaviors toward the child and opportunities available to the child within the home environment (educational toys, family activities, and conversational events) do not have to be extraordinary, the quality and quantity of child-centered activities, more than socioeconomic status, influence reading and language abilities of school-age children (Bhattacharya, 2010).

Effects of poverty on reading achievement of children have also been investigated by Eamon (2002). Cognitive home environment (physical quality of home, presence of educational materials, and reading activities) and emotional home environment (encouraging maturity, engaging in social activities, mother's disciplinary practices, and mother's emotional responsiveness) were considered in determining the impact of poverty on adolescents' reading achievement. Reading achievement was measured by adolescents' scores on standardized reading tests, including measures such as pronunciation, word recognition, silent reading of sentences, and determining the meaning of sentences. Other factors such as mother's years of education, poverty level, and parent-to-child ratio were also taken into account in studying the impact of home environment on reading.

Results from the Eamon (2002) investigation indicated that poverty was related to reading achievement through its associations with the cognitive and emotional home environments. Economic resources available within the home determined parents' ability to provide adolescents with cognitively stimulating activities, experiences, and materials. A less cognitively stimulating home environment was related to low reading achievement. Mothers with more intellectual resources were found to provide a more cognitively stimulating home environment, and a higher parent-to-child ratio resulted in a more emotionally supportive home environment. Stress resulting from economic hardship was associated with emotionally unsupportive and uninvolved parenting, which in turn resulted in lower reading achievement. Furthermore, adolescents who experienced less cognitively enriched and emotionally supportive home environments tended to exhibit lower reading achievement. In sum, poverty was indirectly related to reading achievement of adolescents, and directly related to less cognitively stimulating and emotionally supportive home environments, which in turn were related to lower reading achievement. Thus, among the in-home variables that influence the reading achievement of poor children and adolescents, the availability of cognitive stimulation and emotional support is primary (Bhattacharya, 2010; Eamon, 2005; McLoyd, 1998). These findings corroborate Dubow and Ippolito's (1994) conclusion that a cognitively stimulating and emotionally supportive home increases children's reading achievement, independent of poverty and other risk factors such as maternal education, mother's age at childbirth, and number of children in the family.

## Influence of Poverty and School Environment on Reading Achievement

The influence of school environment on the reading achievement of poor children has been investigated by several researchers. Parcel and Dufur (2001) investigated the influences of school environment on children's reading achievement. Data from the 1992 and 1994 National Longitudinal Survey of Youth were used to study the effects of school capital on the reading achievement of children from first through eighth grades. Weighted data were used to correct for oversampling of respondents from poverty. Factors such as social problems (gang activity, absenteeism, racial conflict, vandalism, and tardiness), physical environment (traffic, noise, loitering, and neighborhood crime), parent–teacher communication, and school-wide parental involvement (parent–teacher associations, parent advisory organization, parent–teacher conferences, fundraising, and volunteering in classroom) were part of the school social capital. School human capital included measures such as the number of teachers with master's degrees and teacher's teaching skill. School financial capital was measured in terms of learning resources (number of books, videos, and computers per student and per pupil expenditures).

Findings from the Parcel and Dufur (2001) investigation indicated that attending a school with a better physical environment enhanced reading achievement, while attending a troubled school negatively affected reading outcomes. Schools with higher per pupil expenditures and higher parent–teacher communication better supported reading development and achievement. Children's reading achievement benefitted from attending schools with greater parental involvement in school activities and better communication with parents. Thus, school environments that include learning resources, safer physical settings, and supportive and involved adults tend to enhance the reading achievement of poor children (Ransdell, 2012). Since poor children generally live in poor neighborhoods, they are more likely to attend poorly funded schools with low instructional expenditures, high teacher turnover, a large number of truants, and serious crime problems, which in turn have the potential of negatively affecting their reading achievement (Eamon, 2005; Evans & Kim, 2013).

The poverty research literature indicates that many schools serving poor children often are lacking in basic learning resources (i.e., computers, books, and dictionaries), are marked by a troubled school environment (i.e., large number of truants, high student absenteeism, and serious crime problems), and are populated by underprepared teachers, all of which adversely affect reading outcomes. Furthermore, teachers tend to have lower expectations of poor children and provide poor children with less positive attention, fewer learning opportunities, and less reinforcement for good performance. Schools also contribute towards the achievement gap between poor and non-poor children by stratifying classes by ability levels, thereby adding to the achievement differences (McLoyd, 1998). Moreover, children who attend schools with a high percentage of poor children, low instructional expenditure, and crime problems are more likely to have lower reading scores (Eamon, 2005). Thus, school environment affects reading achievement.

The association between school characteristics and reading achievement of poor and non-poor children has also been examined by Aikens and Barbarin (2008). Classroom teachers completed questionnaires related to school characteristics of kindergarten, first-grade, and third-grade children. Classroom teachers provided reports on children's classroom peers, classroom literacy instruction, teacher experience (i.e., number of years the teacher has taught at the school and grade level), and teacher preparation (i.e., number of courses taken on teaching reading and highest degree earned). Results of the investigation indicated that teachers' experience, preparation, and classroom literacy instruction were not related to children's reading achievement. Peers were found to be a critical part of the school environment as related to reading achievement. The presence of peers from poverty and peers with low reading skills were strongly related to reading achievement. Thus, the association between school characteristics and reading achievement indicated that the number of children from poverty and the number of children with reading difficulties determine overall reading achievement in elementary grades.

From the preceding discussion, it can be concluded that reading achievement of poor children is influenced by their home and school environments. Poverty adversely impacts upon poor children's reading achievement due to lack of learning materials and activities and supportive and involved parents and teachers.

## Individual Differences in Reading Achievement of Poor Children

While many of the research studies discussed above report detrimental effects of poverty on children's reading achievement, there are individual differences in the home and school environments of poor children that can advance their reading skills despite poverty. Individual differences in reading therefore can be noted amongst poor children due to resilience both within the home and school environments despite persistent financial hardships.

### Individual Differences in Reading within High-Poverty Homes

One such differential influence is showcased in the research of Purcell-Gates (1996), who documented the different ways in which literacy materials were used in 20 low-income families, with 24 children between the ages of 4 and 6, and the resultant differences in the emergent literacy knowledge of the children in the different homes. Although the selected families came from poverty, had limited educational resources, and were mainly functionally literate, the adults in the family engaged the children in reading and writing activities which advanced their literacy skills. For example, parents used printed materials such as utility bills, television guides, greeting cards, and magazines to engage children in reading, writing, talking, and drawing activities. However, there were individual differences across families in the use of printed materials for involving their children in literacy activities. Some families filled their home with posters, notebooks, and magnetic letters on refrigerators. The adults consistently engaged their children in reading and writing activities. The adults also engaged in reading newspapers, talking about current events, and writing letters, thereby serving as role models for their children to emulate. Other families, who were from similar socioeconomic backgrounds as the families that explicitly engaged their children in literacy activities, only vicariously engaged their children in literacy activities, mainly as a part of attending to their daily chores such as looking at advertisements, paying bills, watching televisions, and listening to music. Thus, differences in literacy practices and reading were noted amongst children from poverty across families. However, despite differences in literacy practices within poor families, findings from the Purcell-Gates study indicated that direct mother–child interactions around printed materials contributed to children's understanding of the functional nature of written language. Regardless of the frequency of the home literacy event, findings also indicated that explicit teaching of literacy concepts by the parents was significantly related to the literacy knowledge acquired by the children. In sum, parent–child literacy practices at home contributed to children's literacy development.

### Individual Differences in Reading within High-Poverty Schools

Research has consistently highlighted the difference between the reading achievements of poor and non-poor children, with poor children often exhibiting scores that are significantly below those of non-poor children. Despite considerable research that indicates low reading achievement amongst poor children, there is evidence suggesting that poor children can excel in reading, even in schools that have a high percentage of poor children. McGee (2004) examined the effectiveness of the Illinois' Golden Spike High-Poverty, High-Performing Schools in closing the achievement gap between poor children and their non-poor peers. Some noteworthy factors that contributed towards the high reading achievement of poor children in the Golden Spike High-Poverty, High-Performing Schools were: principals advocating high learning standards and emphasizing early literacy, teachers believing that every child can learn, large proportions of class time dedicated to reading and literacy activities, and consistent efforts to regularly involve parents in their children's education.

Although research has consistently indicated that poor children often do not progress well academically because of schools that are ridden with limited educational resources, low teacher retention rates, classroom discipline problems, and crowded classrooms (Eamon, 2005; McLoyd, 1998), there are schools that advance academic achievement of poor children through their emphasis on resilience. Doll, Jones, Osborn, Dooley, and Turner (2011) examined the school success of 34 elementary school children based on a resilience paradigm which focused on three indicators from the perspectives of their teachers, their parents, and the children themselves: active engagement in learning, homework problem (intensity and frequency of a child's problem completing homework), and effective peer friendships. Children were ethnically, economically, and linguistically diverse and a majority of them qualified for free or reduced breakfast and lunch. Results indicated that the majority of the poor children exhibited resilience through active engagement in learning, experiencing fewer homework problems, and forming effective peer friendships. The school success of the poor children was attributed to small class size and teachers who were committed to their students. Alternately, poor children's accommodation to the social and academic demands of schooling, despite limited family income, was explained through maturity-related increases in their capacities for self-regulation. Despite their struggles with poverty, poor children were successful due to a supportive school environment.

## Building School–Home Partnerships to Advance Reading Development

Research evidence describes the value of family involvement in children's reading development, yet advising parents to read to their children or to involve their children in reading activities may not be enough. Parents may need specific guidelines for participating in their children's reading development (Padak & Rasinski, 2006). Often the harsh social and economic circumstances of poverty limit parents' ability to participate in their children's reading development. Therefore, educational interventions should take into consideration the needs of individual families (Huebner, 2000), and utilize school resources for advancement of poor children's reading. This could be accomplished by forging school–home partnerships, wherein school resources could be utilized to support children's reading and advance parents' ability to engage their children in reading activities (Bhattacharya, 2010). The following section describes programs that advance the reading skills of poor children through school–home partnerships.

One way of building a school–home partnership is to ensure availability of learning resources for children to engage in reading. Koskinen et al. (1999) provided a closer look at a school–home program focused on sharing books to support children's reading. Through a two-pronged approach, *Enhancing book access in school* and *Enhancing book access at home*, teachers created interactive literacy environments in school and at home. The in-school component of the shared reading project involved setting up of classroom libraries containing more than 150 books for children to read. The children were then engaged in shared book reading via teacher read-aloud of books, teacher and children's choral reading of books, paired rereading of books by children, and independent rereading of books by children. The at-home component of the project involved teachers preparing school–home materials (i.e., checkout system and backpack for lending books), introducing home reading (i.e., modeling reading activities and parent participation), and assessing and maintaining home reading (i.e., observation of children reading to peers and reminder notes for parents). The school–home books program is an example of a collaboration that supported effective classroom instruction. The inclusion of home-based reading provided a way to extend reading into the home environment by supplementing the limited supply of literacy materials and opportunities for parental involvement in children's reading. The in-class shared reading with peers and at-home reading with parents provided scaffolding to facilitate children's reading with understanding and experience success.

The *Bridges to Literacy* project (Waldbart, Meyers, & Meyers, 2006) increases parent–child literacy interactions and school–home collaboration through three distinct phases. Phase 1 provides parents with an opportunity to share their concerns and interests about their children's literacy development, and to consider strategies for implementing at-home reading activities through focus-group discussions, in-class demonstrations of shared-reading instruction, and a lending library in which the teacher checks out books for the students and supplements them with assignments designed to support parents' use of literacy strategies. Phase 2 emphasizes at-home reading via two home visits in which a Bridges staff member works with the child and models shared-reading techniques; then the parent reads the book with the child and gets feedback from the staff member; and finally, the parent independently reads a book with the child, using the shared-reading strategies included in a tip sheet. Phase 3 involves three home visits focussed on modeling paired reading and conducting a semi-structured interview about the home literacy environment and ways to improve it. First, a Bridges staff member models paired reading and discusses the strategy with the parent. Subsequently, the parent and child engage in paired reading and discuss the process. Finally, the staff member engages the child in literacy-related assignments, such as drawing a picture about a favorite part of a book. Findings of the Bridges to Literacy program challenge the popular view that parents from poverty have low expectations for their children's reading development and that they refuse to be involved in their children's schooling. Instead, the Bridges project demonstrates that including poor families in the design and implementation of reading interventions can help parents recognize their own expertise in facilitating their children's reading development.

Promoting the reading development of poor children is the goal of the *Family Fluency Program* (Morrow, Kuhn, & Schwanenflugel, 2006), a program of reading activities that helps parents to participate in their children's reading. The Family Fluency Program involves parents in literacy activities at home to heighten their awareness of oral reading strategies. It does this through a two-pronged approach. Basal readers are sent home twice weekly for parent–child reading. Parents are asked to document their joint book reading behaviors with their children and to talk about their children's interactions with them during the joint reading activities. The second feature is three workshops designed to heighten parents' awareness of reading strategies to enhance children's reading fluency. The workshops demonstrate echo reading, choral reading, and partner reading strategies, and discuss the importance of oral reading concepts, such as decoding words, learning new vocabulary, and using intonation to correctly express the meaning of the text. Parents are given handouts, audiotapes, and videos that explain and demonstrate the strategies. They are also given opportunities to practice echo reading, choral reading, and partner reading with their children and other parents.

Although research has consistently indicated that parental involvement is positively associated with poor children's reading development (Ordonez-Jasis & Ortis, 2006), and that increased family involvement in school is associated with increased literacy performance (Dearing, Kreider, Simpkins, & Weiss, 2006; Ediger, 2008), parents will be able to play a critical role in their children's reading development provided parental involvement is not time consuming and complex (Baker, 2003; Breitborde & Swiniarski, 2002). Parental involvement in their children's reading development can be as simple as modeling literate behaviors, answering children's questions, and helping with homework through school–home partnerships (Padak & Rasinski, 2006).

## Summary

Research overwhelmingly suggests that children from persistent poverty face a multitude of challenges in their home and school environments, which then adversely affect their reading development. Scarcity of learning materials at home and lack of parental involvement in children's education often lower the reading achievement of poor children. The reading achievement of poor children is also lowered due to overcrowded classrooms, underprepared teachers, and limited literacy resources in the school environment. Although poverty at home and school lowers reading achievement of children, individual differences in reading have been reported amongst poor children due to their resilience towards the negative influences of poverty. Some poor children exhibit high reading outcomes on account of their parents' determination to invest money and time towards their education despite financial constraints. The reading development of poor children also tends to accelerate on account of school-based support systems, including structured reading instruction, parental involvement in reading instruction, and reading instruction by knowledgeable teachers. Poor children who have access to learning materials, parental involvement, supportive teachers, and reading instruction tend to have higher reading achievement, despite financial hardships, than other poor children who may be academically non-resilient.

Differences within the home and school environments of poor children therefore can produce individual differences in reading development and achievement. Despite of limited educational materials, underprepared teachers, and overcrowded classrooms, differences in reading can result from poor children's individualized reading experiences within their home and school environments. Poor children who are consistently exposed to interactive reading activities at home, individualized reading instruction at school, and age-appropriate reading materials through school–home partnerships show better reading development and achievement than other poor children who are not similarly engaged in reading activities, instruction, and materials at home and school. Overall, opportunities for interactive reading activities at home and individualized reading instruction at school, together with school–home exposure to appropriate reading materials, appear to mitigate the adverse effects of persistent poverty on poor children's reading development and achievement, thereby producing individual differences in reading.

## References

Aikens, N. L., & Barbarin, O. (2008). Socioeconomic differences in reading trajectories: The contribution of family, neighborhood, and school contexts. *Journal of Educational Psychology*, *100*, 235–251.

Baker, L. (2003). The role of parents in motivating struggling readers. *Reading & Writing Quarterly*, *19*, 87–106.

Bhattacharya, A. (2010). Children and adolescents from poverty and reading development: A research review. *Reading & Writing Quarterly*, *26*, 115–139.

Bradley, R. H., Corwyn, R. E., McAdoo, H. P., & Coll, C. G. (2001). The home environments of children in the United States Part I: Variations by age, ethnicity, and poverty status. *Child Development*, *72*, 1844–1867.

Breitborde, M., & Swiniarski, L. B. (2002). Family education and community power: New structures for new visions in the educational village. *Educational Studies*, *28*, 305–318.

Bronfenbrenner, U. (1977). Toward an experimental ecology of human development. *American Psychologist*, *32*, 513–531.

Bronfenbrenner, U. (1994). Ecological models of human development. In T. Husen & T. N. Postlethwaite (Eds.), *International encyclopedia of education* (2nd ed., pp. 1643–1647). New York: Elsevier Science.

Brooks-Gunn, J., & Duncan, G. J. (1997). The effects of poverty on children and youth. *Future of Children*, *7*, 55–71.

Conger, R. D., & Elder, G. H. (1994). *Families in troubled times: Adapting to change in rural America*. New York: Aldine de Gruyter.

Cooper, C. E., Crosnoe, R., Suizzo, M., & Pituch, K. A. (2010). Poverty, race, and parental involvement during the transition to elementary school. *Journal of Family Issues*, *31*, 859–883.

Cuthrell, K., Stapleton, J., & Ledford, C. (2010). Examining the culture of poverty: Promising practices. *Preventing School Failure*, *54*, 104–110.

DeNavas-Walt, C., Proctor, B. D., & Smith, J. C. (2013). *Income, poverty, and health insurance coverage in the United States: 2012*. Washington, DC: United States Census Bureau.

Dearing, E., Kreider, H., Simpkins, S., & Weiss, H. B. (2006). Family involvement in school and low-income children's literacy: Longitudinal associations between and within families. *Journal of Educational Psychology*, *98*, 653–664.

Doll, B., Jones, K., Osborn, A., Dooley, K., & Turner, A. (2011). The promise and the caution of resilience models for schools. *Psychology in the Schools*, *48*, 652–659.

Dubow, E. F., & Ippolito, M. F. (1994). Effects of poverty and quality of the home environment on changes in the academic and behavioral adjustment of elementary school-age children. *Journal of Clinical Child Psychology*, *23*, 401–412.

Duncan, G. J., & Brooks-Gunn, J. (2000). Family poverty, welfare reforms, and child development. *Child Development*, *71*, 188–196.

Duncan, G. J., Yeung, W. J., Brooks-Gunn, J., & Smith, J. R. (1998). How much does childhood poverty affect the life chance of children? *American Sociological Review*, *63*, 406–423.

Duncan, G. J., Ziol-Guest, K. M., & Kalil, A. (2010). Early-childhood poverty and adult attainment, behavior, and health. *Child Development*, *81*, 306–325.

Eamon, M. K. (2001). The effects of poverty on children's socioemotional development: An ecoecological systems analysis. *Social Work*, *46*, 256–266.

Eamon, M. K. (2002). Effects of poverty on mathematics and reading achievement of young adolescents. *Journal of Early Adolescence*, *22*, 49–74.

Eamon, M. K. (2005). Social-demographic, school, neighborhood, and parenting influences on the academic achievement of Latino young adolescents. *Journal of Youth and Adolescence*, *34*, 163–174.

Ediger, M. (2008). Psychology of parental involvement in reading. *Reading Improvement*, *45*, 46–52.

Engle, P. L., & Black, M. M. (2008). The effect of poverty on child development and educational outcomes. *Annals of the New York Academy of Sciences*, *1136*, 243–256.

Evans, G. W. (2004). The environment of childhood poverty. *American Psychologist*, *59*, 77–92.

Evans, G. W., & Kim, P. (2013). Childhood poverty, chronic stress, self-regulation, and coping. *Child Development Perspectives*, *7*, 43–48.

Fantuzzo, J. W., LeBoeuf, W. A., & Rouse, H. (2014). An investigation of the relations between school concentrations of student risk factors and student educational well-being. *Educational Researcher*, *43*, 25–36.

Haveman, R., & Wolfe, B. (1994). *Succeeding generations: On the effects of investments in children*. New York: Russell Sage Foundation.

Hilferty, F., Redmond, G., & Katz, I. (2010). The implications of poverty on children's readiness to learn. *Australian Journal of Early Childhood*, *35*, 63–71.

Huebner, C. E. (2000). Community-based support for preschool readiness among children in poverty. *Journal of Education for Students Placed at Risk*, *5*, 291–314.

Kainz, K., & Vernon-Feagans, L. (2007). The ecology of early reading development for children in poverty. *Elementary School Journal*, *107*, 407–427.

Kainz, K., Willoughby, M. T., Vernon-Feagans, L., & Burchinal, M. R. (2012). Modeling family economic conditions and young children's development in rural United States: Implications for poverty research. *Journal of Family Economic Issues*, *33*, 410–420.

Kiernan, K. E., & Mensah, F. K. (2011). Poverty, family resources and children's early educational attainment: The mediating role of parenting. *British Educational Research Journal*, *37*, 317–336.

Koskinen, P. S., Blum, I. H., Bisson, S. A., Phillips, S. M., Creamer, T. S., & Baker, T. K. (1999). Shared reading, books, and audiotapes: Supporting diverse students in school and at home. *Reading Teacher*, *52*, 430–444.

Lee, K. (2009). The bidirectional effects of early poverty on children's reading and home environment scores: Associations and ethnic differences. *Social Work Research*, *33*, 79–94.

Lichter, D. T. (1997). Poverty and inequality among children. *Annual Review of Sociology*, *23*, 121–145.

McGee, G. W. (2004). Closing the achievement gap: Lessons from Illinois' Golden Spike High-Poverty High-Performing Schools. *Journal of Education for Students Placed at Risk*, *9*, 97–125.

McLoyd, V. C. (1998). Socioeconomic disadvantage and child development. *American Psychologist*, *53*, 185–204.

Molfese, V. J., Modglin, A., & Molfese, D. L. (2003). The role of environment in the development of reading skills: A longitudinal study of preschool and school-age measures. *Journal of Learning Disabilities*, *36*, 59–67.

Morrow, L. M., Kuhn, M. R., & Schwanenflugel, P. J. (2006). The family fluency program. *Reading Teacher*, *60*, 322–333.

Ordonez-Jasis, R., & Ortis, R. W. (2006). Reading their worlds: Working with diverse families to enhance children's early literacy development. *Young Children*, *61*, 42–48.

Padak, N., & Rasinski, T. (2006). Home–school partnerships in literacy education: From rhetoric to reality. *Reading Teacher*, *60*, 292–296.

Parcel, T. L., & Dufur, M. J. (2001). Capital at home and at school: Effects on student achievement. *Social Forces*, *79*, 881–912.

Payne, R. K. (2005). *A framework for understanding poverty*, 4th ed. Highlands, TX: aha! Process.

Purcell-Gates, V. (1996). Stories, coupons, and the TV guide: Relationships between home literacy experiences and emergent literacy knowledge. *Reading Research Quarterly*, *31*, 406–428.

Ransdell, S. (2012). There's still no free lunch: Poverty as a composite of SES predicts school-level reading comprehension. *American Behavioral Scientist*, *56*, 908–925.

Rayer, C. C., Blair, C., & Willoughby, M. (2013). Poverty as a predictor of 4-year-olds' executive function: New perspectives on models of differential susceptibility. *Developmental Psychology*, *49*, 292–304.

Waldbart, A., Meyers, B., & Meyers, J. (2006). Invitation to families in an early literacy support program. *Reading Teacher*, *59*, 774–785.

Worts, D., Sacker, A., & McDonough, P. (2010). Falling short of the promise: Poverty vulnerability in the United States and Britain, 1993–2003. *American Journal of Sociology*, *116*, 232–271.

# 23

# Constructions of Difference

## How Reading First, Response to Intervention, and Common Core Policies Conceptualize Individual Differences

*Sarah L. Woulfin*

## Chapter Overview

The literature on individual differences in reading addresses cognitive skills and strategies but pays less attention to the broader forces, including policy, that contribute to the construction of individual differences. To broaden our view on the political and social construction of individual difference, I interrogate the messages within contemporary reading policy. This chapter explores the aims and ideas of reading policy in order to advance our understanding of the relationship between institutional forces and the construction of individual differences. I will compare how three waves of reading reform—Reading First, Response to Intervention, and Common Core State Standards—construct individual difference. First, I will briefly review the recent history of US education policy. Second, I will analyze policy documents to surface how these policies conceptualize reading and individual difference. Specifically, to illustrate how institutional forces shape the conceptualization of reading and individual difference, I martial evidence from policy documents from two large states: California and New York. I treat the policy documents as sources of data on the ways in which reading and individual differences are defined. The policy documents from three reading reforms showcase differences in how policymakers and reformers define the problem of reading instruction and construct various solutions. Throughout, I argue that education policy plays a vital role in the construction of students' individual difference in reading.

## Role of Policy and Nature of Implementation

Policies are imbued with ideas related to societal and political problems. Because policy has a loudspeaker to transmit its definition of problems and proposals for solutions, it exerts a strong influence on school systems, leaders, and teachers. Policymakers and policies address issues of reading instruction in various ways (Coburn, 2001; Coburn & Woulfin, 2012; Pearson,

2004, 2007). Some reading policies focus on accountability and assessment, while other policies mandate particular instructional methods (Coburn, Pearson, & Woulfin, 2010). Because policies carry ideas and influence actors at multiple levels of the education system, it is necessary to unpack how policies implicitly, as well as explicitly, conceptualize reading instruction and individual differences in reading. For example, Reading First emphasized the "Big 5" of phonemic awareness, phonics, fluency, vocabulary, and comprehension, thereby defining reading as a discrete set of skills and strategies (University of Oregon Center on Teaching and Learning, 2013). Many district and school level practices flowed from this policy's conceptualization of reading; the policy directed teachers to use particular instructional materials which addressed the Big 5 and to structure instruction to cover these specific elements of reading.

Research on the implementation of education policy has revealed the ways in which macro-level, institutional forces shape the conceptualization of issues and pervade schools. Federal and state policies are institutional forces emanating from the broader environment which have been shaped by historical, political, and social conditions. For instance, the political environment and economic conditions enabled No Child Left Behind to pass as a sweeping reform. Numerous studies reveal that policy reaches schools and can restructure educational practices. For example, Diamond's (2007) study of the implementation of accountability policy in urban schools found that both the *content*, including what a teacher addresses during lessons, and the *pedagogy*, or process, comprised of how the teacher structures and carries out teaching, of instruction can be altered by reform initiatives. In addition, this research indicates that certain dimensions of teachers' classroom practice are more subject to policy influence than others. In the field of reading, programs promoting different approaches to literacy instruction are associated with different patterns of instruction (Correnti & Rowan, 2007). Specifically, two Comprehensive School Reform models, Success for All and America's Choice, emphasized decoding and writing to differing degrees. Correnti and Rowan's (2007) findings indicate that schools implementing one or the other model had significantly different patterns of literacy instruction involving more—or less—decoding and writing instruction.

In the field of reading, policies aiming to change the nature of reading instruction and raise student achievement impact elementary schools in numerous—and profound—ways (Achinstein & Ogawa, 2006; Coburn et al., 2010; Kersten & Pardo, 2007). Waves of reform, from whole language to the basic skills, have shaped the field of reading (Coburn, 2001; Pearson, 2007). Scholars have provided insights into the way institutional forces, including policy and institutional *logics*, enable and constrain various ways of teaching reading (Coburn, 2001). *Logics* are the broad principles with the force to influence institutional structures and activities (Russell, 2011; Scott, 2001). A logic encourages particular practices within organizations. For example, a logic of the accountability movement is that all children can learn. This principle, in turn, guides activities, such as the adoption of specific programs to structure teaching and learning.

This chapter discusses how two institutional logics, Accountability First and Just Read, and their associated instructional initiatives are reflected in three waves of reading reform. The *Accountability First* logic emphasizes instruction in alignment with the demands of state standards and testing to meet externally developed goals (e.g., state benchmarks for proficiency on standardized tests) and raise student achievement. The Accountability First logic treats reading instruction as a lever for raising students' academic proficiency. It focuses on using standards-based reading instruction to improve standardized test scores to obtain legitimacy for schools. In this manner, its model of reading instruction is concerned with the relationship between federal, state, and district policy and student outcomes. It has a state-down theory of action in which pressure from the state influences schools and teachers to alter their practice.

With regard to individual differences, state legislatures and departments of education endorse particular instructional programs, such as Read 180, in an attempt to structure the remediation of below-grade level readers. The Accountability First logic tends to downplay the role or value of teachers' autonomy, as well as students' choice as readers. Thus, the initiatives aligned with this logic frequently pay less attention to meeting the needs of students with individual differences.

In contrast, the *Just Read* logic encourages instruction that uses authentic literature to instill a love of reading. Accountability First and Just Read espouse differing ideas about appropriate ways to teach reading, related teachers' roles, and how children learn to read. Just Read treats reading instruction as an interactive, or constructivist, process to develop children's lifelong love of books, reading, and learning. Lucy Calkins, the leader of the Teachers College Reading and Writing Project (TCRWP) and the author of several practitioner resource texts associated with TCRWP, underscored that "we [educators] must not only teach children how to read well; we must also teach children how to love reading." The Just Read logic concentrates on the needs of individual students and the role of books, as authentic literature, as a tool for instruction. It follows that this logic privileges authentic texts over core reading programs.

## Situating Education Reforms in their Historical and Political Contexts

Education reforms are situated in a particular sociocultural and historical context. As depicted in Figure 23.1, in the United States there exists a state-down model of reform. It is evident that the political environment influences the tenor of debates around improving US schools, the research privileged and martialed by policymakers and reformers, and, ultimately, the education bills passed at the state and federal levels. These bills, in turn, influence reading instruction and the conceptualization and construction of students' individual differences in reading.

Thus, I will situate Reading First, Response to Intervention (RtI), and Common Core State Standards (CCSS) historically and will link them to Accountability First and Just Read. These three reforms arose during a 12 year period, yet it is necessary to consider several key events from the preceding decade which influenced federal policymaking. By the late 1980s, politicians and business leaders had deep concerns about the state of the US education system, and the 1989 Charlottesville Governors Summit assembled political leaders (including future President Clinton) to discuss major national educational goals (Vinovskis, 1999). During this historical moment, the whole language approach to fostering students' reading growth was gaining traction, and it spread due to grassroots organizations, including Reading Recovery, and their work in developing educators on particular approaches to reading instruction (Coburn, 2001).

Several years later, the standards movement was born; reformers were confident that aligning standards, instruction, and assessment would raise student achievement. President G. W. Bush, inaugurated in January 2001, brought Texas-style accountability reforms to Washington. For example, these reforms relied on high stakes tests, in English language arts and mathematics to "prove" that schools were holding themselves accountable to the public. The passage of the No Child Left Behind Act in 2001 provided guidance and funding for Reading First (United States Department of Education, 2004). By 2003, many states, including California, New York, and Texas, were implementing Reading First. In 2004, Congress' reauthorization of the Individuals with Disabilities Education Act (IDEA) raised the prominence of RtI, an approach emanating from special education (Fletcher, 2013) as a favored model of instruction.

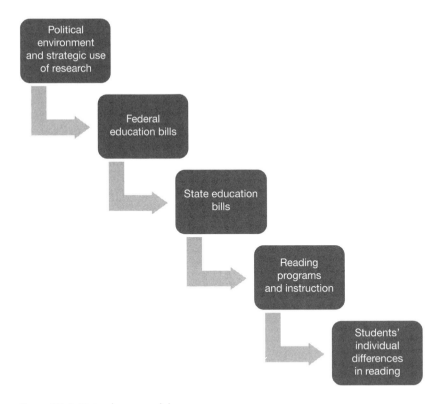

*Figure 23.1* State-down model

In 2009, President Obama and Secretary of Education Arne Duncan arrived in Washington. Importantly, Reading First funding had been discontinued, and states were coping with unprecedented budget cuts, affecting districts and schools in profound ways. Race to the Top was announced in 2009; this reform offered support for RtI and encouraged states to shift towards the CCSS. Aiming to improve the quality of teaching and learning across the United States, the CCSS initiative is an instructional reform that involved unprecedented cooperation among states. The National Governors Association and the Chief State School Officers Council worked together to develop these standards; leaders of these organizations asked a variety of stakeholders, including state educational leaders, administrators, teachers, and parents, for input. The relative influence of input from these groups varied widely, and it appears that teachers and parents were less central to the formulation and specification of Common Core. The new CCSS advance instructional goals that emphasize critical thinking skills and college and career readiness (ASCD, 2012; National Governors Association, 2009). By 2012, many states had designed implementation plans for the CCSS and new assessment systems. Reform proceeded with the selection and piloting of new assessments to monitor students' proficiency on the Common Core standards.

## Reading First: All Children Will Reach Proficiency

Reading First is a branch of No Child Left Behind (NCLB) legislation that focused on kindergarten to third-grade reading instruction in elementary schools (United States Department of Education, 2004). Reading First had a tightly defined goal of raising the reading achievement of poor and minority students, so that, by the end of third grade, all students in the United States would be proficient readers, as measured by standardized, norm-referenced reading tests (United States Department of Education, 2004). The US Department of Education funded states' individual plans, but each state constructed its own Reading First plan, mandating the adoption of particular instructional materials, monitoring assessments, and forms of professional development. For example, most states adopted core reading programs, such as Houghton Mifflin and Open Court Reading, as a way to shape or control teachers' approaches to reading instruction (Achinstein & Ogawa, 2006; Kersten & Pardo, 2007). These programs included texts for students to read, including decodable books with controlled vocabulary and phonetically regular words for students in kindergarten through third grade and anthologies with reading selections for students in first through fifth grade plus scripts to guide teachers' lessons and assessments to administer. By dictating the texts available to students and presuming that all students should use a single collection of texts, these programs associated with the Reading First policy conceptualize students' individual differences in reading as of secondary importance. These programs neglect to consider how different children—with different interests and ability levels—may benefit from reading different texts. Additionally, a federal investigation determined that federal officials strong armed state officials into selecting instructional materials, assessments, and consultants from preferred sources. The US Department of Education's Inspector General highlighted conflicts of interest because officials had "favorite" reading series. It became evident that federal officials were privileging particular resources of as well as forms of reading instruction based on financial considerations (US Department of Education, 2006)

In alignment with the Accountability First logic, Reading First conceptualizes reading instruction as a set of practices that could strengthen students' mastery of discrete skills in phonemic awareness, phonics, fluency, vocabulary, and comprehension. For instance, this policy defines appropriate and effective ways to teach and assess fluency. The three foundational principles of Reading First are: (1) systematic and explicit instruction; (2) mandated curricula; and (3) progress monitoring assessments and analysis of student data to drive instructional decision making (Coburn & Woulfin; 2012; United States Department of Education, 2004). These three principles are associated with the Accountability First logic. As summarized in Table 23.1, Reading First *mandated* that instruction would include direct strategy and skill instruction related to the "Big 5" and that teachers would follow instructions from core reading programs. Under this policy, certain core reading programs were favored. Additionally, states and districts developed progress monitoring assessments in order to gather and analyze data on student reading development. Some of these assessments involved students reading lists of nonsense words to gauge their proficiency in fluently decoding text. Reading First is tightly aligned with the Accountability First logic because they share the logic's principles regarding the value of systematic reading instruction to prepare students for testing. Furthermore, Reading First functioned as a top-down accountability policy. The federal guidelines for Reading First strongly influenced implementation across state and districts and even within schools. It appears that Reading First aimed to raise standardized test scores rather than develop engaged readers.

As a reform effort, Reading First backgrounds the role of individual difference. First, the policy does not address differentiation, such as how to support Special Education students and English Language Learners, or how to reach other students in a classroom with quite different

Table 23.1 How three reading reforms conceptualize reading and individual difference

| Policy or reform | Logics | Conceptualization of reading and reading instruction | Conceptualization of individual differences |
|---|---|---|---|
| *Reading First* | | | |
| A reading policy to restructure instruction for all students | Accountability First | • Teach the Big 5 of phonemic awareness, phonics, fluency, vocabulary, and comprehension<br>• Deliver scientifically based reading instruction (SBRI)<br>• Attention to systematic and explicit reading instruction<br>• Mandated curricula— focus on core reading programs as instructional materials that guide teaching and teachers' work | • Assess students to identify those with differences in reading skill<br>• All students need access to scientifically based reading instruction, involving systematic, explicit instruction on phonemic awareness, phonics, fluency, vocabulary, and comprehension<br>• Less attention to individual difference |
| *Response to Intervention* | | | |
| A reform to restructure instruction for students in need of intervention | Accountability First | • Identify student needs and differentiate instruction<br>• Provide research-based reading instruction to certain students<br>• Extends and applies the principles and practices of Reading First<br>• Attention to what to do with students at different levels | • Provide intervention services to students with individual differences in reading skills<br>• Primary focus is on meeting the needs of students in need of intervention. This policy defines differences as students who fail to specific reading benchmarks |
| *Common Core State Standards* | | | |
| A reform to restructure literacy instruction for all students | Just Read | • Across subject areas; close reading; students should read "just right" books<br>• Attention to nature of the book/text<br>• Attention to what reading skills to teach at one point | • Use different books/texts at different levels and related to different backgrounds<br>• "Staircase" of skills<br>• Individual difference not fully fleshed out |

instructional needs, in robust ways. By relying upon systematic and explicit instruction, this policy belies a theory of action that standardized instruction works for all students. Quite simply, Reading First's one-size-fits-all approach to teaching and learning neglects to consider how different children learn, including how some children would benefit from different forms of instruction. Second, this policy's strong emphasis on core reading programs negates the importance of student choice and engagement in reading and literacy activities. Instruction in many Reading First schools was steered by the lessons and "script" from core reading program's teachers' guide and by accompanying texts. As a result, there was little room or discretion for teacher or student choice of texts. Third, although several core reading programs (including Open Court Reading) recommended a workshop period to provide differentiated instruction, the policy commonly ignored individual differences. The policy recommended moving in lockstep through the program's lessons. Specifically, in many districts, teachers were not expected or allowed to veer from the content of lessons. Reformers and administrators leaned on a theory of action in which teachers' adherence to these types of curricula would raise achievement on standardized tests. Thus, state standardized tests pushed teachers towards strictly following these curricula.

## Response to Intervention: Curing Children's Deficiencies in Reading

Similar to Reading First, Response to Intervention (RtI) is a reform effort aligned with the principles, and logic, of Accountability First. Specifically, RtI used a state-down theory of action and leaned on programs, rather than teachers, to instruct reading skills. Rooted in the field of special education, RtI gained prominence because it was included in the 2004 reauthorization of IDEA. This instructional reform was included in IDEA because House and Senate Committees were influenced by research supporting instructional methods with the capacity to distinguish between children with learning disabilities and those who can be remediated with general education interventions (United States Department of Education, 2007). Simply stated, legislators were aiming to reduce the number of student referrals to Special Education and to decrease schools' use of pull-out programs to remediate students. Advocates for RtI declared that

> the formal incorporation of Response-to-Intervention (RTI) models in the 2004 reauthorization of the Individuals with Disabilities in Education Act (IDEA 2004; USDOE, 2004) signals a major change in approaches that schools may use to identify students as eligible for special education in the learning disability (LD) category.
>
> (Fletcher, 2013)

Specifically, RtI mandated that educators "identify children with learning disabilities, determine their eligibility for special education, and most importantly, develop effective intervention approaches" (Fletcher, 2013). In this manner, RtI was part of a sorting process for students with differences. Furthermore, RtI encouraged tiers of assessments and "treatments" that were based, in part, on the determination of individual differences. Yet RtI carried a narrow view of what counts as individual differences in reading. RtI primarily attended to individualized differences as they relate to the Big 5.

RtI has been defined as the practice of delivering instruction or intervention matched to each student's specific needs and basing instructional decision making around data on a student's rate of learning over time (IDEA Partnership, 2007). It follows that reformers associated with RtI emphasize the measurement and analysis of student progress in order to assign and design interventions for particular categories of students. At the school level, RtI specifies three tiers of instructional support. The first tier is comprised of general classroom instruction following a scientifically based curriculum. Within classrooms, RtI's hallmark for Tier 1

> is flexible, differentiated teaching. Teachers differentiate instruction by identifying students who may need further assistance or enrichment through the use of screening and/or formative assessments. As specific student needs are identified, teachers can re-teach in a variety of settings, including one-on-one, pairs, small groups, and whole groups.
>
> (Ventura County Office of Education, 2011, p. 16)

The second tier involves more intensive instruction using an alternate curriculum, while the third tier relies on individualized, intensive interventions, including pull-out services, to meet more severe needs (Fletcher, 2013).

RtI conceptualizes reading as a collection of strategies and skills. This reform contends that students in need of intervention can become proficient readers by engaging with core curricula or by completing intervention programs with corresponding computer programs or workbooks that attempt to raise their proficiency in individual skills. RtI's approach to reading instruction is imbued with the Accountability First logic. This reform privileges standardized instruction on discrete strategies and skills, and promotes the use of particular types of assessment. In particular, this reform's emphasis on progress monitoring assessments and the analysis of student outcomes is tightly coupled to Accountability First.

Yet, in comparison to Reading First, RtI is more attuned to individual difference. This is because RtI concentrates on how to meet the needs of intervention students through a series of escalating types of instructional services coupled with assessments to track student progress. A policy document from California explicates that, in an RtI school:

> students' social, behavioral, and academic competence are encouraged, promoted, monitored, and supported to foster expected progress. Highly qualified teachers are knowledgeable and seek on-going training to deliver culturally and linguistically responsive instruction for optimal student engagement. Access and engagement for all students are promoted through the use of differentiated instruction for students who require additional support or enrichment for those who are ready to move ahead.
>
> (Ventura County Office of Education, 2011, p. 14)

This progressive rhetoric from a school district reveals that RtI is concerned with providing tailored instruction that matches students' background and learning needs. At the same time, this reform conceives of individual difference as something to "fix." In this manner, RtI employs a medical model in which students are tested and then prescribed a dose of instruction to boost their skills. Finally, RtI is a more generalized reform than Reading First. RtI reforms are less targeted on issues of reading, providing fewer specific mandates on how to structure the content and pedagogy of reading instruction (California Department of Education, 2013). The RtI model is not subject specific, and in fact, is frequently applied to the subject area of mathematics. It is necessary to consider the relationship between assessment, policy, and practice. Assessment is a policy lever for Accountability First reforms. Assessment is a tool that serves a potent function in linking policy demands with changes in practice. In particular, assessment functions as the eyes through which policymakers and district leaders see educational goals, as well as movement (or lack of movement) towards those goals, and, at times, students' individual differences.

## Common Core: States Will Adopt Rigorous Standards

Twenty years after the initial efforts of the standards movement, the CCSS arose as a reform to raise the level of instructional rigor across the 50 states. The new standards "were developed with the aim of establishing common educational goals that states could share" (NEA Education Policy and Practice Department, 2013, p. 3). The new standards' overarching goals are to standardize practices across the country, raise the quality of instruction to prepare students for college and the workforce, and boost the achievement of all students. In certain ways, CCSS reform incorporates the logics of both Accountability First and Just Read. On the one hand, CCSS, in alignment with Accountability First, is another reform with a state-down model. On the other hand, CCSS is colored by Just Read because this reform acknowledges the relationship between students, books, engagement, and positive outcomes. These new standards were drafted to be: "focused, coherent, clear, and rigorous; internationally benchmarked; anchored in college and career readiness; and evidence and research-based" (NEA Education Policy and Practice Department, 2013, p. 3). By 2013, the majority of states adopted CCSS:

> to provide a clear and consistent framework to prepare our children for college and the workforce . . . The Common Core standards aspire to truly enable the next generation of U.S. students to succeed in college and in work by introducing new rigor and demanding new analytical and evidence-based argument skills.
>
> (Achieve 3000, 2013 p. 1)

Thus, this wave of reform sets a high bar for teaching and learning with a high degree of cognitive complexity. From 2009 to 2013, a variety of educational leaders heralded CCSS as a sea change. A White Paper on the arrival of CCSS asserts that these standards necessitate fundamental changes in teachers' instructional practice (Achieve 3000, 2013). In this manner, reformers are framing CCSS as an initiative that sets significantly higher standards and that necessitates fundamentally different ways of teaching.

As compared to Reading First or RtI, Common Core is much more closely aligned with Just Read because this latest wave of reform incorporates assumptions about the positive impact of matching students to appropriately leveled and engaging, or even *satisfying*, forms of text. Common Core's English Language Arts standards do value students reading engaging, appropriately leveled books. In these standards, "the role of text complexity is based on research indicating that students need to develop competency in dealing with increasingly complex texts if they are to be successful with the reading demands beyond high school" (NEA Education Policy and Practice Department, 2013, p. 4). This attention to text complexity matches the principles of the Just Read logic. For example, New York's state policy documents assert that:

> Students need opportunities to stretch their reading abilities but also to experience the satisfaction and pleasure of easy, fluent reading within them, both of which the Standards allow for . . . Such factors as students' motivation, knowledge, and experiences must also come into play in text selection. Students deeply interested in a given topic, for example, may engage with texts on that subject across a range of complexity.
>
> (Common Core State Standards Initiative, 2013, p. 9)

Although the formal policy mentions students' motivation, Common Core reform efforts rarely paid significant attention to motivation. This is because districts and schools were still being held accountable to the results of standardized tests of students' decoding and comprehension skill, and because factors such as motivation have been largely absent in relation to prior state-down program initiatives.

Additionally, there is evidence that Common Core policy attends to individual differences in reading development. New York's policy acknowledges that:

> Students reading well above and well below grade-band level need additional support. Students for whom texts within their text complexity grade band (or even from the next higher band) present insufficient challenge must be given the attention and resources necessary to develop their reading ability at an appropriately advanced pace. On the other hand, students who struggle greatly to read texts within (or even below) their text complexity grade band must be given the support needed to enable them to read at a grade-appropriate level of complexity.
>
> (Common Core State Standards Initiative, 2013, p. 9)

In this way, the CCSS reform effort is attuned to individual differences in students' reading level and expects teachers to provide support and resources to both high and low-achieving students. However, at this stage of implementation of the CCSS, issues of individual difference have not yet been fully fleshed out. Most policies on CCSS ignore issues of pedagogy, particularly for students with individual differences. It is left to districts, schools, and teachers to determine how (and if) individual differences are to be addressed within a curriculum that is tied to the CCSS. This wave of reform is accompanied by ambiguity about the most effective and appropriate methods for how to address students' individualized strengths and weaknesses as readers and learners. So current policies have much less specificity around *how* teachers should provide support to meet students' needs. For example, a White Paper asserted that "students who are receiving special education services are no exception. They, too, are expected to be challenged to excel within the general education curriculum based on the Common Core State Standards" (International Center for Leadership in Education, 2013, p. 4).

This points to the way in the way in which the reform presumes that all students would benefit from a standard curriculum. In addition, it matches the view that these common standards "provide an historic opportunity to improve access to rigorous academic content standards for students with disabilities" (Common Core State Standards, n.d., p. 1). However, there is little concrete advice around planning and delivering Common Core-aligned instruction to students with disabilities. In fact, the designers of New York's state policy noted that it is "beyond the scope of the Standards to define the full range of supports appropriate for English language learners and for students with special needs" (New York State Department of Education, 2011, p. 4). This state's policy refers to a "staircase" of skills, and implies that students should work their way up this continuum of reading skills.

Yet it is the key to note the challenges involved for all students to meet the new Common Core Standards. Currently, little attention is being paid to how lower performing children will be supported in order to gain access to and proficiency on the ambitious new standards. Policymakers appear to be acknowledging issues of individual difference while setting up CCSS reforms, but still tend to not provide guidance or support around how educators can effectively address these differences in order to raise students' reading proficiency. The ambiguity of Common Core policy around individual difference has implications for reform and instruction.

## Conclusion and Implications

This chapter compared how Reading First, Response to Intervention, and the Common Core State Standards conceptualized reading instruction and individual differences. First, I exposed how the three contemporary policies drew upon the logics of Accountability First and Just Read. The Accountability First logic gained prominence in the late 1990s and advocated the alignment of standards, instructional materials, and assessments to ensure that students received systematic reading instruction. The Just Read logic co-existed in the institutional environment, encouraging a very different model of reading instruction in which teachers guided students to select and read authentic literature. On the one hand, Reading First and RtI utilized the principles of Accountability First, which included frequent assessment of students' phonemic awareness skills. These policies were tightly coupled with other accountability policies and systems, such as state testing and district level monitoring of schools, teachers, and students. On the other hand, CCSS deployed the ideas and rules of Just Read and Accountability First. This reform treats reading instruction, teachers, and students in a different manner. However, Common Core reform remains relatively ambiguous about how educators should address individual differences; the reform paints the issues of individual difference in broad brushstrokes.

After explaining the history and rationale for these three reforms, I presented each reform's construction of reading and individual difference. Both Reading First and CCSS paid greater attention to the content and pedagogy of reading instruction than RtI. Furthermore, Reading First offered highly specified messages about how teachers should and must teach reading. However, RtI devoted the greatest attention to issues of individual difference, albeit difference in relation to cognitive skill and strategy, and, in particular, how to work with students who were not meeting grade-level expectations. The other two reading policies presented ambiguous messages about issues of individual difference. These policies' conceptualizations of individual differences were limited and were strongly reinforced by high stakes standardized tests.

Each of the three policies contained different conceptualizations of reading instruction and individual difference. These conceptualizations mattered for implementation because they directed attention towards particular elements of reading and certain aspects of instruction (Coburn, 2006; Spillane, Reiser, & Reimer, 2002). For example, Reading First privileged core reading programs over teacher discretion, contributing to district and school administrators providing professional development focused on these programs and monitoring how teachers followed core reading programs. Districts implemented testing systems to track student progress, and schools also administered state standardized tests for accountability purposes. Yet CCSS acknowledged the importance of students reading engaging text at their reading level; this encourages the adoption of leveled classroom libraries. Furthermore, each policy framed the problems and solutions of reading instruction and individual difference in different ways. Therefore, educators' sense making around how and why to shift their approaches to instruction was colored by these policy frames (Coburn, 2006). It follows that teachers constructed different understandings of individual difference during each of these waves of reform. At the same time, these policies influenced teachers' capacity, opportunity, and preference to address individual differences within their classrooms.

Given the histories of Reading First, RtI, and CCSS, I argue that policies could conceptualize individual differences in reading in an alternative way. Policies could more explicitly address issues of individual difference. Reading policies could include strands that conceptualize students with individual differences plus appropriate and effective ways to engage those students to further their development as readers. By explicitly addressing issues of individual difference, policies would send clearer messages to reformers, administrators, and teachers. These messages could support decision making around the selection of instructional materials and professional development, potentially steering teachers' classroom practice and benefitting students. In addition, these messages could elaborate on ways in which teachers could encourage students to develop as motivated readers. For instance, reforms could promote the practice of students selecting their own texts. Finally, the message that individual differences are of varied and complex nature could be forwarded.

We need additional research on the influence of institutional forces on the construction of the notion of individual differences in reading development. Researchers need to study how policies implicitly and explicitly conceptualize individual difference and, in turn, how these policies affect educational practice and educators' understandings of individual difference. First, how are policymakers, reformers, and educational leaders crafting and mediating reading policy? What influences policymakers' creation of policies specifying the nature of reading instruction and ways to approach individual difference? What sets of ideas, or logics, are drawn on during the policymaking process? It is necessary to consider what forms of research on students' development as readers are consulted during the policymaking process. By responding to these questions, we can gain a thorough understanding of the relationship between ideas from the environment, policy, and reading instruction to meet the challenges of individual difference. Second, scholars need to begin to analyze similarities and differences among reading policies. Researchers should consider how and why policies wield particular logics. By comparing policies from different contexts, we can surface the ways in which the content and structure of instructional policies affects implementation in schools. What accounts for similarities and differences among states' reading policies? To what extent are states, and even districts, replicating policies from other states and districts? The answers to these questions will extend our understanding of policy development and the spread of ideas that shape reform. Furthermore, this type of research could guide the design of more effective and feasible policies addressing reading instruction as well as issues of individual difference.

## References

Achieve 3000. (2013) *10 steps for migrating your curriculum to the common core*. Retrieved April 2, 2014, from http://www.achieve3000.com/literacy-solutions/pedagogy/common-core.

Achinstein, B., & Ogawa, R.T. (2006). (In)fidelity: What the resistance of new teachers reveals about professional principles and prescriptive educational policies. *Harvard Educational Review*, 76(1), 30–63.

ASCD (2012). *Fulfilling the promise of the common core state standards*. Alexandria, VA: ASCD.

California Department of Education (2013). Core components-RtI2. Retrieved August 20, 2013, from http://www.cde.ca.gov/ci/cr/ri/rticorecomponents.asp.

Coburn, C. E. (2001). *Making sense of reading: Logics of reading in the institutional environment and the classroom*. Unpublished Ph.D. dissertation, Stanford University, Stanford, CA.

Coburn, C. E. (2006). Framing the problem of reading instruction: Using frame analysis to uncover the microprocesses of policy implementation. *American Educational Research Journal*, 43(3), 343–349.

Coburn, C. E., Pearson, P. D., & Woulfin, S. L. (2010). Reading policy in an era of accountability. In M. Kamil, P. D. Pearson, E. Moje, & P. Afflerbach (Eds.), *Handbook of reading research* (vol. IV, pp. 561–592). Mahwah, NJ: Lawrence Erlbaum Associates.

Coburn, C. E., & Woulfin, S. L. (2012). Reading coaches and the relationship between policy and practice. *Reading Research Quarterly*, 47(1), 5–30.

Common Core State Standards Initiative (2013). *Application to students with disabilities*. Washington, DC: Common Core State Standards Initiative. Retrieved April 14, 2013, from http://www.corestandards.org/wp-content/uploads/Application-to-Students-with-Disabilities-again-for-merge.pdf.

Common Core State Standards Initiative (n.d.). *Common Core State Standards for English Language Arts and literacy: Appendix A*. Washington, DC: Common Core State Standards Initiative.

Correnti, R., & Rowan, B. (2007). Opening up the black box: Literacy instruction in schools participating in three comprehensive school reform programs. *American Educational Research Journal*, 44(2), 298–339.

Diamond, J. (2007). Where the rubber meets the road: Rethinking the connection between high-stakes testing policy and classroom instruction. *Sociology of Education, 80*(4), 285–313.

Dillon, S. (2006). Report says education officials violated rules. *New York Times*, September 23.

Fletcher, J. (2013). Identifying learning disabilities in the context of response to intervention: A hybrid model. New York: RTI Action Network. Retrieved August 20, 2013, from http://www.rtinetwork.org/learn/ld/identifyingld.

IDEA Partnership (2007). *Leaving no child behind: Response to intervention*. Alexandria, VA: IDEA Partnership. Retrieved April 2, 2014, from http://ideapartnership.org/index.php?option=com_content&view=article&id=263.

International Center for Leadership in Education (2013). Fewer, clearer, higher Common Core State Standards. Washington, DC: International Center for Leadership in Education. Retrieved April 22, 2015, from http://teacher.scholastic.com/products/scholastic-achievement-partners/downloads/SpecialED_CCSS.pdf.

Kersten, J., & Pardo, L. (2007). Finessing and hybridizing: Innovative literacy practices in reading first classrooms. *Reading Teacher, 61*(2), 146–154.

National Governors Association (2009). Fifty-one states and territories join Common Core State Standards initiative. Washington, DC: NGA. Retrieved May 15, 2013, from http://www.nga.org/cms/home/news-room/news-releases/page_2009/col2-content/main-content-list/title_fifty-one-states-and-territories-join-common-core-state-standards-initiative.html.

NEA Education Policy and Practice Department (2013). *Common Core State Standards: A tool for improving education*. Washington, DC: NEA. Retrieved August 27, 2013, from http://www.nea.org/assets/docs/HE/PB30_CommonCoreStandards10.pdf.

New York State Department of Education (2011). *New York State P-12 common core learning standards for English Language Arts & literacy*. New York: New York State Department of Education. Retrieved April 2, 2014, from http://www.p12.nysed.gov/ciai/common_core_standards/.

Pearson, P. D. (2004). The reading wars. *Educational Policy, 18*(1), 216–252.

Pearson, P. D. (2007). An endangered species act for literacy education. *Journal of Literacy Research, 39*(2), 145–162.

Russell, J. L. (2011). From child's garden to academic press: The role of shifting institutional logics in redefining kindergarten education. *American Educational Research Journal, 48*(2), 236–267.

Scott, W. R. (2001). *Institutions and organizations*. Thousand Oaks, CA: Sage Publications.

Spillane, J. P., Reiser, B. J., & Reimer, T. (2002). Policy implementation and cognition: Reframing and refocusing implementation research. *Review of Educational Research, 72*(3), 387–431.

United States Department of Education (2004). *Introduction and overview: Reading First*. Washington, DC: US Department of Education. Retrieved July 16, 2007, from http://www.ed.gov/programs/readingfirst/index.html.

United States Department of Education (2006). *The Reading First program's grant application process: Final inspection report*. Washington, DC: US Department of Education. Retrieved April 2, 2014, from http://www2.ed.gov/about/offices/list/oig/aireports/i13f0017.pdf.

United States Department of Education (2007). *Questions and answers on Response to Intervention (RTI) and Early Intervening Services (EIS)*. Washington, DC: US Department of Education. Retrieved August 27, 2013, from http://idea.ed.gov/explore/view/p/,root,dynamic,QaCorner,8,.

University of Oregon Center on Teaching and Learning (2013). Big ideas in beginning reading instruction. Eugene, OR: University of Oregon Center on Teaching and Learning. Retrieved August 27, 2013, from http://reading.uoregon.edu/big_ideas/.

Ventura County Office of Education (2011). *Response to instruction and intervention*. Ventura, CA: Ventura County Office of Education.

Vinovskis, M. (1999). *The road to Charlottesville*. Washington, DC: National Education Goals Panel.

# 24

# The Role of Individual Differences in Working Memory Capacity on Reading Comprehension Ability

*Chantel S. Prat, Roy Seo, and Brianna L. Yamasaki*

Skilled reading comprehension is incredibly cognitively demanding, requiring the coordination of multiple sub-component processes executed largely in parallel. The outputs of these processes are dynamically employed to update mental representations of the scenarios described in a text as they unfold in time. Thus, it is not surprising that individual differences in reading comprehension ability have been repeatedly linked to working memory capacity, which enables the "mental juggling" necessary for dynamically maintaining and manipulating information in a cognitive workspace (Daneman & Carpenter, 1980; Just & Carpenter, 1992; Long & Prat, 2008). In this chapter, we will repeatedly refer to juggling as an analogy for working memory, as it allows us to examine multiple models of how mental representations are maintained and manipulated in the mind of a reader.

The manifestations of individual differences in working memory capacity during reading are observable early in development (e.g., Gathercole & Baddeley, 1993), and continue to be pervasive even at the college level (e.g., Long & Prat, 2008). Thus, a complete understanding of individual differences in reading ability requires an understanding of how working memory constrains reading comprehension. This chapter will summarize the findings of over 30 years of research on this topic, in an attempt to facilitate such an understanding. This is not a trivial undertaking, however, as the construct of working memory capacity has evolved dramatically over that timeframe, and its precise nature remains controversial. Many of the leading theories adopt different views of the key limits on human information processing, and how differences in the experienced limitations are reflected in reading performance. Our goal is to synthesize and clarify the results herein.

## What is Working Memory Capacity?

Working memory is a construct that has been used to describe a system for maintaining information in a state that allows it to be accessible for current cognitive processes (Wilhelm,

Hildebrandt, & Oberauer, 2013). This construct has evolved from the notion of a short-term memory buffer that mediates the transfer of information to and from long-term memory (e.g., Miller, 1956), to one that describes a shared pool of resources used both for executing the required processes of a task, and for managing and maintaining activation of relevant intermediate and final products of such processes (Baddeley & Hitch, 1974). More contemporary theories of working memory vary in their depictions of its precise computational and neural underpinnings (e.g., Kane & Engle, 2002; Wilhelm et al., 2013); however, all theories converge on the understanding that *working memory* as a construct attempts to describe some key constraints on human information processing, and that *working memory capacity* is an index of how much a particular individual is limited by such constraints.

Multiple measures of working memory capacity have been developed as the construct has evolved, but *complex span tasks* are by far the most commonly used (see Conway, Kane, Bunting, Hambrick, & Engle, 2005 for a review). Complex span tasks measure the amount of information an individual can hold in memory while concurrently executing secondary "distractor" processes such as reading sentences (reading span: Daneman & Carpenter, 1980), computing mathematical equations (operation span: Turner & Engle, 1986), or counting the number of target items on a display (counting span: Case, Kurland, & Goldberg, 1982). A sample block from a computerized operation span task (Unsworth, Heitz, Schrock, & Engle, 2005) is illustrated in Figure 24.1. In this paradigm, participants are initially given mathematical equations to solve (A), and a prompt to verify that they have solved the equation correctly (B). They are then given a letter to hold

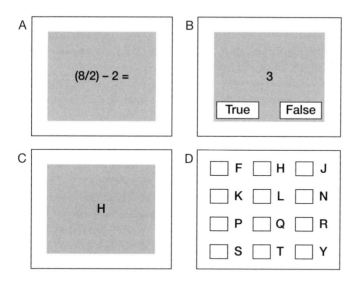

*Figure 24.1* Illustration of the Automated Operation Span Task (Unsworth, Heitz, Schrock, & Engle, 2005). On each trial, participants are presented with a math problem (A) for which they have to determine if a subsequently given digit (B) is the correct or incorrect solution. Following each math problem, participants are presented with a later to be remembered letter (C). After participants have complete a series of math problems and letter pairs ranging from 3 to 7, they are presented with an array of letters (D) and must select the letters in the order that they were presented in

in mind (C). These first three processes are repeated between three and seven times, after which participants are asked to recall the letters that they received on all trials in that block, in order (D). Such tasks have been widely employed, putting *working memory span* on the map as a key individual-difference variable that predicts general performance across a variety of complex cognitive tasks (e.g., Kyllonen & Christal, 1990).

One limitation of complex span tasks is that the ability they measure may be related to the ease or efficiency with which an individual can execute the concurrent "distractor" task, and/or by the more general information processing capacity of an individual. Returning to the mental juggling analogy, the number of items an individual can keep in the air at any given time can be viewed as their performance on complex span tasks. In this scenario, variability in the number of items juggled may result from the *efficiency* with which an individual can handle the items being juggled (skill or experience with distractor task) or from individual differences in the number of *mental hands* an individual has (capacity). A skilled juggler may be able to easily maintain six items in the air with only two hands; whereas even a person who has never juggled before can keep the same six items off the ground if he or she has six hands.

Therefore, if the goal is to figure out what an individual's working memory capacity (number of hands) is, multiple assessments of working memory capacity (or manual dexterity by analogy) should be employed (e.g., Wilhelm et al., 2013). Alternately, if the goal is to predict individual differences in a particular cognitive task such as reading comprehension, choosing the task that incorporates a distractor that most closely resembles the skill of interest will explain the most variance, as it will account for both experiential factors and more general indices of capacity (Kane, Conway, & Engle, 1999).

The vast majority of the research on individual differences in working memory capacity and reading comprehension ability has employed some version of the reading span task (Daneman & Carpenter, 1980). Unless otherwise specified, the terms *high-span* and *low-span* will be used throughout this chapter to refer to individuals whose working memory capacity is characterized by performance on the reading span task alone.[1] Thus, the possibility that increased *reading experience* contributes both to greater reading span (by increasing efficiency on the distractor task) and to better reading comprehension ability (by increasing practice) exists in much of the literature discussed herein. This potential confound will be considered further in the subsequent discussion of the various theoretical accounts of individual differences in working memory capacity and reading ability.

## How does Working Memory Capacity Relate to Reading Acquisition?

The impact of working memory capacity on reading ability is first observed during early reading acquisition. A number of investigations of children learning to read have linked indices of working memory capacity with subsequent measures of reading acquisition and skill (Baddeley, Gathercole, & Papagno, 1998; Gathercole & Baddeley, 1993; Leather & Henry, 1994). This research has primarily investigated the relevance of working memory capacity for phonological processes, which are fundamental to reading acquisition. Thus, the earliest investigations of the role of working memory capacity on reading acquisition relied largely on Baddeley and Hitch's (1974) original conceptualization of working memory capacity, which included a phonological (or articulatory) loop. In this model, the phonological loop is defined as a system dedicated to maintaining auditory (typically verbal) memory traces. The importance of such a system for learning novel phonological combinations during vocabulary acquisition (e.g., Baddeley et al.,

1998) and for learning to map speech sounds onto printed words (e.g., Gathercole & Baddeley 1989; Wagner & Torgesen, 1987) has thus been widely investigated. Interestingly, when indices of phonological *awareness* (such as those measured in rhyming tasks) are pitted against more general indices of working memory capacity (such as those obtained using complex span tasks), research suggests that each factor explains unique variance in reading acquisition (Cormier & Dea, 1997; Leather & Henry, 1994; Rohl & Pratt, 1995). The factors are not fully independent, however, as Oakhill and Kyle (2000) demonstrated that working memory capacity (as measured by complex span tasks) reliably predicted performance on tasks designed to measure phonological awareness, rather than phonological retention. To complicate the issue, learning to read in and of itself is likely to increase phonological awareness (see Wagner & Torgesen, 1987 for a review). Thus, the relation between working memory capacity and early reading acquisition is complex, with working memory capacity seeming to mediate the relation between phonological awareness and reading acquisition, and the causal relation between phonological awareness and reading ability being bidirectional. In the remainder of this chapter, we will shift our focus to the more widely investigated (and thus better understood) relation between working memory capacity and skilled reading comprehension in fluent readers.

## How does Working Memory Capacity Relate to Skilled Reading Comprehension?

Individual differences in working memory capacity remain pervasive in fluent readers, and can be observed at the word, sentence, and discourse levels. At the word level, the most frequently reported individual differences involve lexical ambiguity resolution, or the process by which a reader selects the contextually appropriate meaning of a word which has multiple possible meanings. Resolving ambiguity is costly in terms of working memory resources, as multiple word meanings are likely to be represented until the reader can select the contextually appropriate one. Behavioral research has shown that when an ambiguous word (i.e. a homograph such as *boxer*) is encountered, readers initially activate multiple possibilities of the meaning of the word, but then rapidly select only the contextually supported meaning (see Holbrook, Eiselt, Granger, & Matthei, 1988 for a review). If the context does not disambiguate between multiple meanings (e.g., in the sentence *She is a boxer*), readers typically default to the most frequently occurring sense of the word (i.e., *She is a pugilist who takes part in the sport of fighting*) rather than considering the less likely interpretation (i.e., *She is a medium-sized dog with a pug-like face*). In a series of reading time experiments, Miyake, Just, and Carpenter (1994) showed that while waiting for disambiguating context, high-span readers were more likely to maintain both senses of ambiguous words in mind for long periods of time. Thus, in sentences such as "Because she was a boxer, she was the most popular dog in the pet store," high-span readers were able to easily comprehend the words "dog in the pet store," whereas low-span readers had difficulty reading that section (as indexed by slower reading times) when the context resolved to the less-frequent interpretation of the word. Subsequent research on individual differences in lexical ambiguity resolution has focused on the ability to *select* appropriate meanings of words in the face of early disambiguating information (e.g., Gadsby, Arnott, & Copland, 2008; Gunter, Wagner, & Friederici, 2003). This research suggests that high-span readers are more successful than low-span readers at inhibiting the inappropriate meanings of ambiguous words. Taken together, these results suggest that high-span readers are able to maintain multiple meanings of ambiguous words strategically, selecting the appropriate meaning as soon as disambiguating context is provided.

At the sentence level, a plethora of research has shown that working memory capacity facilitates syntactic parsing. For instance, King and Just (1991) showed that high-span readers were faster and more accurate than low-span readers when comprehending syntactically complex, object-relative sentences. Additionally, sensitivity to syntactic ambiguity also varies as a function of individual working memory span (e.g., MacDonald, Just, & Carpenter, 1992). Specifically, high-span readers are more likely than low-span readers to slow down during regions of a sentence that are syntactically ambiguous (see Waters & Caplan, 1996 for a counter-example). MacDonald and colleagues (1992) argued that the slowed reading times observed in high-span readers reflected the cost placed on working memory when multiple possible sentence structures were constructed and maintained in parallel.

Multiple follow-up experiments have investigated differences in high- and low-span readers' sensitivity to probabilistic constraints during syntactic parsing (e.g., Long & Prat, 2008; Pearlmutter & MacDonald, 1995). In one such experiment, Long and Prat (2008) demonstrated that both high- and low-span readers have access to information about contextually based probabilities (e.g., as indexed by sentence completion tasks), but that only high-span individuals use such information during online sentence comprehension (e.g., as indexed by slowing reaction times during potentially ambiguous sentence regions). Thus, the results of individual differences in syntactic parsing converge with those investigating lexical processes. Specifically, high-span readers seem able to represent multiple possibilities when parsing syntactically ambiguous sentences, and at the same time, are able to more readily use contextual information online to flexibly decide which structure is more likely, given all of the information available.

Because discourse comprehension relies on the outputs of word- and sentence-level processes, it is not surprising that individual differences in working memory capacity are readily apparent at the discourse level (Prat, Mason, & Just, 2012). For instance, high-span readers are more likely to engage in optional, elaborative processes (such as inference generation) during discourse comprehension than are low-span readers (e.g., Barreyro, Cevasco, Burín, & Marotto, 2012; St. George, Mannes, & Hoffman, 1997). Additionally, high-span readers are better able than low-span readers at focussing on the key details of a passage during comprehension. For example, Sanchez and Wiley (2006) demonstrated that high-span readers are less susceptible than low-span readers to the *seductive details effect* (Harp & Mayer, 1997), or the reduction in comprehension that occurs when texts are accompanied by "seductive" distractors such as illustrations that are not central to the themes of the text. Using an eye-tracking paradigm, Sanchez and Wiley demonstrated that low-span readers spent almost as much time viewing illustrations as they did reading texts, and spent significantly more time viewing illustrations than did high-span individuals. Finally, a recent study by Unsworth and McMillan (2013) showed that individuals with higher working memory capacity (as indexed by a battery of complex span tasks) are less likely to *mind wander*, or shift attention away from the task at hand to internal thoughts or feelings that are unrelated to the task, while reading.

Taken together, this body of research demonstrates that differences in reading ability in high- and low-span individuals may reflect individual differences in the amount of cognitive resources available for completing a task (e.g., when maintaining multiple possible outcomes of an ambiguous situation or performing optional, elaborative processes). Alternately, these differences may arise because of variability in attentional control (e.g., when selecting only contextually supported meanings and resisting distraction). The attempts to explain these findings, described below, have been divided accordingly into two classes: (1) capacity theories, and (2) attention theories.

## Capacity Theories of Working Memory and Reading Ability

The original and most prominent theory relating working memory capacity to reading ability is Just and Carpenter's Capacity Theory of Comprehension (CTC; Just & Carpenter, 1992). The CTC's view of working memory resembles that of Baddeley and Hitch (1974), in which the resource limitations of working memory are distributed between storage and processing functions. According to Just and Carpenter, individuals differ in a "pool of resources" available both for executing language comprehension processes, and for maintaining activation of elements at levels that allow them to be utilized for such processes. In their discussion, they further specify that the CTC assumes that language comprehension processes including "lexical access, syntactic analysis, and referential processing" (p. 144) rely on the same resource pool, but that language production processes may draw from separate resources. Using a computational model of the CTC, Just and Carpenter replicated many of the key individual differences in reading performance exhibited by high- and low-span readers. Specifically, they showed that increased resource pool availability can lead to more efficient syntactic parsing, greater sensitivity to syntactic ambiguity, and greater reliance on contextual information during disambiguation. The authors acknowledge, however, that an individual's *resource availability* maps onto two dissociable components: (1) the efficiency (or skill) with which they can execute the various processes, and (2) the total size of the "resource pool" (or capacity) one has available for executing all comprehension processes. In the CTC, Just and Carpenter do not attempt to differentiate between the two factors. Returning to the juggling analogy, the CTC states that the key factor for reading ability is the total number of items one can juggle, irrespective of whether this is accomplished through an increase in the number of mental hands, or because of efficient item handling.

Alternate models of the relation between working memory capacity and reading ability have argued about the domain generality or specificity of the "pool of resources" measured by tests of working memory capacity. Drawing heavily on neuropsychological research (e.g., Waters, Caplan, & Hildebrandt, 1991), Waters and Caplan (1996) argued for a more restricted view of capacity constraints on comprehension, proposing that the "operations involved in assigning the syntactic structure of a sentence do not use the same working memory resource as that required for conscious, controlled verbally mediated processes" (p. 761). In what we will call the Offline Capacity Model (OCM), Waters and Caplan proposed that the processes involved in the initial interpretation of a sentence are not limited by working memory constraints. Instead, working memory comes into play when a reader uses the output of these initial comprehension processes to complete offline tasks such as tests of recall and meaning judgment. Importantly for this chapter, according to the OCM, individual variation is found only in this later manipulation of initial sentence comprehension processes. Returning to the juggler analogy, Waters and Caplan would propose that every juggler has a machine (e.g., syntax) that automatically launches a fixed number of items into the air. Individual differences are manifest by how well an individual can manipulate those items, keeping them in the air long enough to integrate them into a juggling routine.

Engle, Cantor, and Carullo (1992), on the other hand, argued for a *more general* characterization of the relation between working memory capacity and reading comprehension ability, which we will call the Global Capacity Theory (GCT). Using multiple measurements of working memory capacity, the authors reported that capacity is a stable characteristic of an individual that relates to the ability to perform multiple complex cognitive tasks including reading. Thus, returning to the juggler analogy, the GCT emphasizes the use of multiple tests of dexterity to determine how many "mental hands" an individual has (capacity) and the extended predictive utility that such information can have.

When debating the generality of the influence of working memory capacity on reading ability, one cannot ignore the role of *reading experience*. On the one hand, individual differences in reading experience are likely to relate to the efficiency with which one can execute comprehension processes, thus influencing the amount of resources available to an individual (e.g., CTC; Just & Carpenter, 1992), and also to the ease with which they can execute the distractor portion of the reading span task. On the other hand, certain theories emphasize the role of reading experience in building up the mental "database" used to determine the likelihood of various outcomes during comprehension (e.g., MacDonald & Christiansen, 2002). For example, the distributed-learning model (DLM) described by MacDonald and Christiansen (2002) proposes that during comprehension, readers draw on their own experience with language for determining probabilistic outcomes, and the extent to which their predictions are accurate is largely contingent on the amount of data that has gone into their estimate of the likely outcomes. Thus, for linguistic structures (such as reduced-relative clauses) that have a very low frequency of occurrence overall, a less-experienced reader will have *much less* familiarity, resulting in greater difficulty with comprehension (as is observed when low-capacity readers comprehend incredibly low-frequency object-relative sentences). In addition, when a word or sentence is ambiguous, but one of the possible meanings or structures is low frequency, a less-experienced reader will be unlikely to consider the low-frequency interpretation (thus treating the situation as unambiguous). Returning again to the juggling analogy, the DLM suggests that as experience increases, the juggler will have more sophisticated information to use (e.g., wind conditions) when predicting where and when the next item will fall, allowing him to position his hands accordingly.

Long and Prat (2008) explored the relation between reading experience and working memory capacity across a series of experiments aimed at understanding how readers use plausibility information during online comprehension. Initially, the authors demonstrated that high-span, but not low-span, readers showed differential reading times for verbs that were biased to main verb past-tense interpretations (e.g., *tossed*) over those biased to reduced-relative interpretations (e.g., *mixed*) in sentences that began with inanimate noun phrases and resolved to reduced-relative structures (e.g., *The salad tossed/mixed for the party looked delicious*). To examine the hypothesis that these results reflect less experience with reduced-relative structures in low-span individuals, the authors exposed both high- and low-span readers to ten training sessions (distributed across five weeks). The materials read during training consisted of multiple examples of sentences containing the less-frequent reduced-relative structures, as well as filler sentences, and sentences in which animate noun phrases were followed by main verb structures (e.g., *The dog tossed the ball into the air*). Thus, the authors manipulated a portion of the contents of the database used by readers when calculating probabilistic outcomes online. After training, low-span individuals showed the same sensitivity to the ambiguous verb region of the sentences that high-span individuals showed before training. Thus, most consistent with the DLM, Long and Prat's results demonstrated that systematic exposure to lower-frequency syntactic structures modulated the influence of working memory capacity on online syntactic parsing. These results are inconsistent with the OCM (Waters & Caplan, 1996), as individual differences in online reading times were observed even when no offline measures were used. The results may also be partially explained by the CTC, however, because low-span readers may have increased their processing efficiency through practice, thus making more resources available for maintaining multiple syntactic structures during ambiguity resolution. Thus, while the role of reading

*Table 24.1* Mapping theories of the nature of working memory constraints on reading to the mental juggling metaphor

| Theory | Key individual differences using the juggling analogy |
|---|---|
| *Capacity theories* | |
| Capacity Theory of Comprehension (CTC) Just & Carpenter, 1992 | The total number of items you can juggle (span) is the key individual differences feature, irrespective of how the juggling is accomplished. |
| Offline Capacity Model (OCM) Waters & Caplan, 1996 | Individual differences in juggling ability reflect how well a person can maintain, manipulate, and integrate a fixed number of items that are launched in the air automatically. |
| Global Capacity Theory (GCT) Engle, Cantor, & Carullo, 1992 | The key individual differences feature is how many hands an individual has. Emphasis is placed on using multiple measures of dexterity (not only juggling) to assess this. The predictive utility is extended to multiple tasks involving manipulating items with your hands. |
| Distributed Learning Model (DLM) MacDonald & Christiansen, 2002 | The emphasis is placed on how much experience an individual has with juggling. Increased practice can lead to better predictions of where the next item will fall, in a variety of conditions (e.g., accounting for wind factors) allowing a skilled juggler to position his hands accordingly. |
| *Attention-based theories* | |
| McVay & Kane, 2012 | The total number of items an individual can juggle will vary as a function of his ability to strategically allocate attention to the critical features of the task (e.g., the items that need to be caught next) while ignoring distracting information (e.g., from the other items or from a noisy audience member). |

experience is important, it is difficult to distinguish behaviorally whether this importance stems from an increased efficiency with increased reading experience (consistent with the CTC), or from an increased representation of probabilities with increased reading experience (consistent with the DLM).

To summarize, each of the capacity theories described herein proposes that readers differ in the amount of mental resources available during reading comprehension, and that this variability is manifest in differential abilities to process information during reading comprehension. The theories differ, however, in their mappings of individual resources to cognitive processes, and in their conceptualizations of what influences resources availability in an individual. We will now turn to the attention-based theories, which can be seen as more "skill" based than "resource" based.

## Attention-Based Theories of Working Memory and Reading Ability

Attention-based theories of working memory and reading ability differ fundamentally from capacity theories in their primary understanding of the nature of individual differences in working memory capacity. Specifically, Engle writes that working memory capacity "is not really about storage or memory *per se*, but about the capacity for controlled, sustained attention in the face of distraction" (Engle, Kane, & Tuholski, p. 104, cited in Wilhelm et al., 2013). Thus, although attentional theories often use the word "*capacity*" out of convention, they do not postulate that individual differences in working memory are related to processing or storage components, but rather to an *ability* to allocate attention flexibly and to resist distraction. Returning to the juggler analogy, attention-based theories would propose that the number of items an individual can juggle is related, in part, to their ability to strategically shift attention to the key items "in action" (e.g., those items that are about to be caught) while resisting distracting information (e.g., from those items that are ascending, or from an annoying heckler in the crowd). Although views of working memory capacity as attention allocation are not new, the application of this concept to theories of individual differences reading ability *is* relatively novel; thus resulting theories are few and not divisible into sub-categories.

Attention-based theories of working memory capacity as a whole can readily account for individual differences in reading ability that reflect a better ability to select the relevant or contextually supported pieces of information in a text (e.g., appropriate meanings of ambiguous words: Gadsby et al., 2008; Gunter et al., 2003), and to resist distracting information during comprehension (e.g., Sanchez & Wiley, 2006). They do not as readily explain research suggesting that high-span readers engage in *more* processing, whether exhibited by maintaining activation of multiple possible word or sentence structures (e.g., MacDonald et al., 1992; Miyake et al., 1994), or by engaging in optional, elaborative comprehension processes (e.g., St. George et al., 1997).

One possibility is that individual differences in both attention allocation *ability* and in processing and storage *capacity* relate to reading comprehension ability. For instance, McVay and Kane (2012) used a structural-equation-modeling approach to measure the relation between reading comprehension, attentional control, and working memory capacity. They found that *mind wandering*, which was related to attentional control, reliably mediated the effects of working memory capacity on reading comprehension ability (see also Unsworth & McMillan, 2013). Thus, some part of the observed correlation between working memory capacity and reading ability seems to be driven by attentional control differences.

We have described evidence so far suggesting that both attention allocation and reading experience contribute to working memory capacity indices. It follows then, that each of these individual differences measures relate to reading comprehension ability on top of any measure of "pure capacity." Thus, one way of integrating the various classes of theories discussed so far is that each emphasizes one of the factors that contribute working memory span (or the number of items an individual can juggle), and that these factors are not mutually exclusive. To summarize the emphases of the various theories, Table 24.1 organizes them using the juggling analogy referred to throughout this chapter.

## Using Neuroimaging Research to Inform Theories of Individual Differences in Working Memory and Reading Comprehension Ability

Contemporary neuroimaging research has much to contribute to our understanding of the relation between individual differences in working memory and reading ability. One of the obstacles outlined in this chapter is that both working memory capacity and reading comprehension ability are multifaceted concepts, thus affording multiple interpretations of the correlation between individual differences in the two. Neuroimaging research can critically inform this debate by characterizing the features of skilled reading comprehension (Prat, Keller, & Just, 2007), and by uncovering the shared neural mechanisms that underpin individual differences in working memory capacity and reading ability (Prat & Just, 2011; Prat, 2011).

### What Does Capacity Look Like in the Brain?

If the "pool of resources" first described by Just and Carpenter (1992) exists, how might it be manifest in the brain, and how might it be used during comprehension? The most straightforward expectation might be that higher-capacity individuals simply have more neurons in the key computational centers of interest. While working memory capacity *is* positively correlated with brain volume (e.g., Posthuma et al., 2003), the correlation explains 7 percent of the variance, at best. Thus, some additional facet of neural *functioning* must also contribute to working memory capacity. One such characteristic that has been investigated using reading comprehension paradigms is neural adaptability (Prat et al., 2007; Prat & Just, 2011). Human cognition, and in particular language comprehension, is characterized by dynamic processing demands; thus a cortical network performing a complex task must be able to adapt to changing task requirements (e.g., Garlick, 2002). With respect to language comprehension, adaptability can be conceived of as the dynamic recruitment of neural networks on an "as needed" basis with changing task demands. For example, prefrontal cortex becomes recruited at the precise moment of sentence comprehension that requires problem-solving processes (Newman, Just, & Carpenter, 2002).

Returning to our debate on the factors that influence resource availability, one might ask whether differences in neural adaptability merely result from differences in baseline neural efficiency. In other words, consistent with findings relating the influence of reading experience to capacity and comprehension, do high-span readers show greater neural adaptability when tasks become more complex because they use fewer neural resources when executing the easier tasks? Alternately, differences in adaptability may arise from some property of brain function (e.g., better plasticity, improved function of control regions) that underpins cortical dynamics and is separable from resource availability. This explanation maps more closely to either an attention-based view or to the Capacity Theory of Comprehension, provided that such adaptability is a general property of good brain functioning. Like the corresponding theories, these two accounts of neural dynamics are not mutually exclusive. In fact, research has demonstrated that both efficient resource utilization and resource allocation mechanisms are necessary for fluent neural adaptability (Prat & Just, 2011).

To examine the mechanism underpinning individual differences in neural adaptability, Prat and Just (2011) measured adaptability to syntactic demands by recording changes in activation for syntactically complex (object relative) – simple (active conjoined) sentences read under varying extrinsic working-memory conditions (reading sentences alone versus sentences preceded by to-be-remembered words or non-words) in readers with varying working memory spans. Their results showed that individual differences in adaptability were related *both* to the availability of

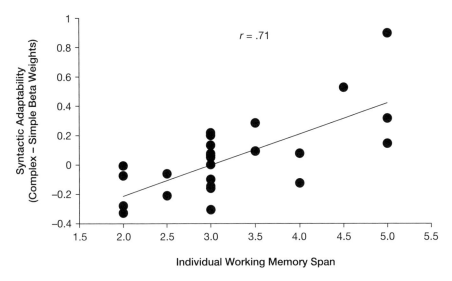

*Figure 24.2* Increased syntactic adaptability with increased individual working memory capacity

resources and to working memory span. In fact, reading span explained 50 percent of the variability in neural adaptability, even when vocabulary, a more direct index of reading experience (e.g., Stanovich & Cunningham, 1992), was controlled for (see Figure 24.2).

Thus, our results suggest that working memory capacity is related to individual differences in neural adaptability, a functional brain characteristic that underlies the dynamic coupling of neural resources to changing task demands.

## The Neural Basis of Reading Practice

One of the better understood links between brain function and individual differences in cognitive abilities is that more skilled, or practiced, individuals generally accomplish a task more efficiently, using fewer neural resources, than less skilled individuals (Haier et al., 1988; Maxwell, Fenwick, Fenton, & Dollimore, 1974). The assumption behind efficiency research is that the amount of "mental resource consumption" that is required to effectively perform a task is reflected by the amount of brain activation observed during the task. Neuroimaging research has shown that the regions of the brain in which individual differences in efficiency are observed correspond with those that are most central to the task at hand. For example, Reichle, Carpenter, and Just (2000) investigated individual differences when readers performed a sentence-verification task using different strategies. They found that participants with higher spans showed more efficient processing in typical left-lateralized language regions (e.g., Broca's area) than did participants with lower spans *when verbal strategies were used*. In contrast, individuals with higher visual-spatial skills showed more efficient processing in typical visual association regions (e.g., parietal cortex) than did individuals with lower visual-spatial skills *when spatial strategies were used*. In other words, the relation between skill and efficiency was observed only when the task evoked a particular skill, and only in the regions of the brain that executed the relevant computations.

With respect to reading comprehension, Prat and colleagues have found that vocabulary size, an index of reading experience, is correlated with increased neural efficiency (see Prat, 2011 for a review). This increased efficiency is manifest by decreased activation in the distributed cortical regions that support language comprehension processes, and in particular, in the right hemisphere homologues of left hemisphere language regions (Prat, Mason, & Just, 2011). Combining data from comparable baseline reading conditions across five neuroimaging investigations, Prat, Mason, and Just (2010) conducted a multiple regression analysis of neuroimaging data from 84 readers, using indices of vocabulary size, working memory capacity, age, handedness, and sex to predict patterns of activation. They found that the best predictor of neural efficiency was vocabulary size, with high-vocabulary readers showing reliably less activation (see Prat, 2011 for a complete discussion).

Taken together, the efficiency and adaptability research suggest a possible explanation for differences in the differential amount of maintenance and elaboration that high- and low-capacity readers engage in during reading comprehension. Specifically, it is possible that increased neural efficiency in baseline comprehension processes results in greater availability of cortical resources in the language network for the execution of non-essential, elaborative comprehension processes that characterize skilled reading.

## The Role of the Fronto-Striatal Loops in Attention and Control

One important implication of the neuroimaging literature not yet discussed centers on the key neural *regions* in which individual differences in adaptability are manifest as a function of working memory capacity. Specifically, Prat and colleagues have shown greater adaptability in a network of regions known to support cognitive control (i.e., the prefrontal cortex and striatal nuclei) in high-span individuals during reading (Prat et al., 2007; Prat & Just, 2011). Interestingly, these regions were among the first implicated in functional neuroimaging investigations of working memory demands (Rypma, Prabhakaran, Desmond, Glover, & Gabrieli, 1999), and have recently received increasing attention for their involvement in linguistic "control" (Buchweitz & Prat, 2013; Friederici, 2006; Prat & Just, 2011; Stocco, Yamasaki, Natalenko, & Prat, 2014).

To explain the nature of these differences, Prat and colleagues have used a contemporary computational model which proposes that the striatum functions as a gate to the prefrontal cortex, enabling flexible selection and routing of signals to the prefrontal cortex (e.g., Stocco, Lebiere, & Anderson, 2010). Specifically, they propose that the ability to flexibly select the pertinent information (e.g., a semantic or propositional representation) for a given language task and to route it to the prefrontal cortex for further processing facilitates "skilled" comprehension. The capacity of the striatum to control which signals are eventually directed to the prefrontal cortex provides the critical link between working memory capacity, attention allocation, and skilled comprehension. Critically, our model adds an important mechanism for selecting and prioritizing information that is missing in the previously discussed theories of the role of the prefrontal cortex in individual differences in executive attention and working memory capacity (Kane & Engle, 2002). We propose that by *altering the number of* (capacity) and by *prioritizing* (attentional selection) signals that are routed to the prefrontal cortex, the striatum can strategically allocate the most relevant information to the appropriate prefrontal processing centers. Although this research area is new and somewhat speculative, converging results suggest that not only are individual differences in working memory capacity during reading comprehension manifested in differences in fronto-striatal functioning, but the influence of different linguistic environments on measures of executive attention (e.g., in the bilingual advantage in executive functioning) are also associated with similar differences in fronto-striatal circuitry (Stocco et al., 2014; Buchweitz & Prat, 2013).

The neuroimaging research as a whole supports the idea that multiple factors account for both individual differences in reading span and reading comprehension ability. In particular, we propose that increased reading experience results in more efficient cortical processing, leaving additional resources available for maintaining multiple representations during periods of ambiguity as well as for engaging in additional, elaborative processes during comprehension. Additionally, more general executive abilities are reflected by changes in adaptability of the fronto-striatal network. The functioning of this network corresponds to the ability to flexibly route task relevant signals to the prefrontal cortex, while blocking representations that are either distracting or no longer relevant. We propose that this fronto-striatal functioning is an index of general executive information processing abilities, and that the combination of the two facets of brain functioning can explain a large amount of the covariance between individual differences in working memory capacity as measured by reading span tests and reading comprehension ability.

## Summary and Future Directions

This chapter summarizes the body of research investigating individual differences in working memory capacity and reading ability, with the goal of generating an understanding of the neural and behavioral factors that underlie the two. In doing so, we have outlined the numerous ways in which working memory constrains and enables reading comprehension during reading acquisition, and the ways in which working memory capacity interacts with reading practice to give rise to individual differences in reading ability. The implications of this research for education are broad, as the evidence for the ability to *train* working memory capacity is mounting (e.g., Jaeggi, Buschkuehl, Jonides, & Perrig, 2008; Jaeggi, Buschkuehl, Jonides, & Shah, 2011; Takeuchi et al., 2010).

Based on the well-established relation between working memory capacity and reading ability summarized herein, it is not surprising that several studies have demonstrated positive transfer effects from working memory training paradigms to measures of reading ability (e.g., Chein & Morrison, 2010; Dahlin, 2011; Horowitz-Kraus & Breznitz, 2013; Loosli, Buschkuehl, Perrig, & Jaeggi, 2011). For example, Loosli and colleagues (2011) investigated the impact of a brief, two-week-long working memory training intervention that was implemented in schools on several measures of reading ability in typically developing children. For the intervention, children completed an adaptive working memory task that consisted of a processing stage, where they had to decide on the orientation of a series of line-drawn animals presented on the screen one at a time, and a recall stage, where children had to recall, in the order that they were presented, the animals that were presented in that series. Despite the relatively brief period of training, a significant increase in working memory performance, as indexed by a larger final set-size on the last day of training as compared to the first day of training, was found for the training group. Importantly for this chapter, significant transfer effects were also observed in the training group, with improvements in performance on both word and text reading in being observed after working memory training.

The implications for training working memory capacity may be particularly important for individuals who experience additional demands during reading. For example, our research has demonstrated that bilingual individuals may experience increased difficulty when reading in their second language, resulting from interference that arises when their first language is automatically activated in the process (Yamasaki & Prat, 2014). Therefore, interventions that can improve resource availability, such as those that aim to improve working memory capacity, may be particularly beneficial for these second-language readers. In summary, working memory capacity is a core constraint that explains wide individual differences in reading comprehension ability and interacts with reading experience during skill acquisition. Thus, it is likely that the future of reading education will include an emphasis on cognitive trainings developed to extend working memory capacity, in combination with the more traditional practice-based approaches. Ultimately, such training in "mental juggling" abilities would enable individuals not only to become better comprehenders, but also to perform other complex cognitive tasks that require dynamic consideration of information (e.g., multi-tasking) more effectively..

## Notes

1    Although there are many ways of scoring the reading span task (Friedman & Miyake, 2005) and different mechanisms for deciding the cutoff point for "high" versus "low" capacity individuals (e.g., taking the top and bottom thirds of the distribution at hand versus using a predefined score to categorize "high" versus "low"), using the scoring method first outlined by Daneman and Carpenter (1980), the average young-adult reading span scores range from 3 to 3.5. Thus, it is fairly safe to assume that the term *high-span* will refer to individuals with reading span scores of 4.0 or above, and the term *low-span* will refer to individuals with a reading span score of 2.5 or below (e.g., Prat et al., 2007).

## References

Baddeley, A., Gathercole, S., & Papagno, C. (1998). The phonological loop as a language learning device. *Psychological Review, 105*(1), 158–173.

Baddeley, A. D., & Hitch, G. J. (1974). Working memory. In G. H. Bower (Ed.), *The psychology of learning and motivation: Advances in research and theory* (vol. 8, pp. 47–90). New York: Academic Press.

Barreyro, J. P., Cevasco, J., Burín, D., & Marotto, C. M. (2012). Working memory capacity and individual differences in the making of reinstatement and elaborative inferences. *The Spanish Journal of Psychology, 15*(2), 471–479.

Buchweitz, A., & Prat, C. S. (2013). The bilingual brain: Flexibility and control in the human cortex, *Physics of Life Reviews, 10*(4), 428–443.

Case, R., Kurland, D. M., & Goldberg, J. (1982). Operational efficiency and the growth of short-term memory span. *Journal of Experimental Child Psychology, 33*(3), 386–404.

Chein, J. M., & Morrison, A. B. (2010). Expanding the mind's workspace: Training and transfer effects with a complex working memory span task. *Psychonomic Bulletin & Review, 17*(2), 193–199.

Conway, A. R., Kane, M. J., Bunting, M. F., Hambrick, D. Z., Wilhelm, O., & Engle, R. W. (2005). Working memory span tasks: A methodological review and user's guide. *Psychonomic Bulletin & Review, 12*(5), 769–786.

Cormier, P., & Dea, S. (1997). Distinctive patterns of relationship of phonological awareness and working memory with reading development. *Reading and Writing, 9*(3), 193–206.

Dahlin, K. I. E. (2011). Effects of working memory training on reading in children with special needs. *Reading and Writing, 24*(4), 479–491.

Daneman, M., & Carpenter, P. A. (1980). Individual differences in working memory and reading. *Journal of Verbal Learning and Verbal Behavior, 19*(4), 450–466.

Engle, R. W., Cantor, J., & Carullo, J. J. (1992). Individual differences in working memory and comprehension: A test of four hypotheses. *Journal of Experimental Psychology: Learning, Memory, and Cognition, 18*, 972–992.

Engle, R. W., Kane, M. J., & Tuholski, S. W. (1999). Individual differences in working memory capacity and what they tell us about controlled attention, general fluid intelligence, and functions of the prefrontal cortex. In A. Miyake & P. Shah (Eds.), *Models of working memory: Mechanisms of active maintenance and executive control* (pp. 102–134). Cambridge: Cambridge University Press.

Friederici, A. D. (2006). What's in control of language? *Nature Neuroscience, 9*(8), 991–992.

Friedman, N. P., & Miyake, A. (2005). Comparison of four scoring methods for the reading span test. *Behavior Research Methods, 37*(4), 581–590.

Gadsby, N., Arnott, W., & Copland, D. A. (2008). An investigation of working memory influences on lexical ambiguity resolution. *Neuropsychology, 22*, 209–216.

Garlick, D. (2002). Understanding the nature of the general factor of intelligence: The role of individual differences in neural plasticity as an explanatory mechanism. *Psychological Review, 109*(1), 116–136.

Gathercole, S. E., & Baddeley, A. D. (1989). Evaluation of the role of phonological STM in the development of vocabulary in children: A longitudinal study. *Journal of Memory and Language, 28*, 200–213.

Gathercole, S. E., & Baddeley, A. D. (1993). Phonological working memory: A critical building block for reading development and vocabulary acquisition? *European Journal of Psychology of Education, 8*(3), 259–272.

Gunter, T. C., Wagner, S., & Friederici, A. D. (2003). Working memory and lexical ambiguity resolution as revealed by ERPs: A difficult case for activation theories. *Journal of Cognitive Neuroscience, 15*(5), 643–657.

Haier, R. J., Siegel Jr, B. V., Nuechterlein, K. H., Hazlett, E., Wu, J. C., Paek, J. . . . Buchsbaum, M. S. (1988). Cortical glucose metabolic rate correlates of abstract reasoning and attention studied with positron emission tomography. *Intelligence, 12*(2), 199–217.

Harp, S. F., & Mayer, R. E. (1997). The role of interest in learning from scientific text and illustrations: On the distinction between emotional interest and cognitive interest. *Journal of Educational Psychology, 89*(1), 92–102.

Holbrook, J. K., Eiselt, K. P., Granger, Jr., R. H., & Matthei, E. H. (1988). (Almost) never letting go: Inference retention during text understanding. In S. I. Small, G. W. Cottrell, & M. K. Tanenhaus, (Eds.), *Lexical ambiguity resolution: Perspectives from psycholinguistics, neuropsychology, & artificial intelligence* (pp. 383–410). San Mateo, CA: Morgan Kaufmann.

Horowitz–Kraus, T., & Breznitz, Z. (2013). Can reading rate acceleration improve error monitoring and cognitive abilities underlying reading in adolescents with reading difficulties and in typical readers? *Brain Research, 1544*, 1–14.

Jaeggi, S. M., Buschkuehl, M., Jonides, J., & Perrig, W. J. (2008). Improving fluid intelligence with training on working memory. *Proceedings of the National Academy of Sciences, 105*(19), 6829–6833.

Jaeggi, S. M., Buschkuehl, M., Jonides, J., & Shah, P. (2011). Short- and long-term benefits of cognitive training. *Proceedings of the National Academy of Sciences, 108*(25), 10081–10086.

Just, M. A., & Carpenter, P. A. (1992). A capacity theory of comprehension: Individual differences in working memory. *Psychological Review, 99*, 122–149.

Kane, M. J., Conway, A. R., & Engle, R. W. (1999). What do working-memory tests really measure? *Behavioral and Brain Sciences, 22*, 101–102.

Kane, M. J., & Engle, R. W. (2002). The role of prefrontal cortex in working-memory capacity, executive attention, and general fluid intelligence: An individual-differences perspective. *Psychonomic Bulletin & Review, 9*(4), 637–671.

King, J., & Just, M. A. (1991). Individual differences in syntactic processing: The role of working memory. *Journal of Memory and Language, 30*(5), 580–602.

Kyllonen, P. C., & Christal, R. E. (1990). Reasoning ability is (little more than) working memory capacity?! *Intelligence, 14*(4), 389–433.

Leather, C. V., & Henry, L. A. (1994). Working memory span and phonological awareness tasks as predictors of early reading ability. *Journal of Experimental Child Psychology, 58*(1), 88–111.

Loosli, S. V., Buschkuehl, M., Perrig, W. J., & Jaeggi, S. M. (2011). Working memory training improves reading processes in typically developing children. *Child Neuropsychology, 18*(1), 62–78.

Long, D. L., & Prat, C. S. (2008). Individual differences in syntactic ambiguity resolution: Readers vary in their use of plausibility information. *Memory & Cognition, 36*(2), 375–391.

MacDonald, M. C., & Christiansen, M. H. (2002). Reassessing working memory: Comment on Just and Carpenter (1992) and Waters and Caplan (1996). *Psychological Review, 109*(1), 35–54.

MacDonald, M. C., Just, M. A., & Carpenter, P. A. (1992). Working memory constraints on the processing of syntactic ambiguity. *Cognitive Psychology, 24*(1), 56–98.

McVay, J. C., & Kane, M. J. (2012). Why does working memory capacity predict variation in reading comprehension? On the influence of mind wandering and executive attention. *Journal of Experimental Psychology: General, 141*(2), 302.

Maxwell, A. E., Fenwick, P. B. C., Fenton, G. W., & Dollimore, J. (1974). Reading ability and brain function: A simple statistical model. *Psychological Medicine, 4*(3), 274–280.

Miller, G. A. (1956). The magical number seven, plus or minus two: Some limits on our capacity for processing information. *Psychological Review, 101*(2), 343–352

Miyake, A., Just, M. A., & Carpenter, P. A. (1994). Working memory constraints on the resolution of lexical ambiguity: Maintaining multiple interpretations in neutral contexts. *Journal of Memory and Language, 33*(2), 175–202.

Newman, S. D., Just, M. A., & Carpenter, P. A. (2002). Synchronization of the human cortical working memory network. *NeuroImage, 15*, 810–822.

Oakhill, J., & Kyle, F. (2000). The relation between phonological awareness and working memory. *Journal of Experimental Child Psychology*, *75*(2), 152–164.

Pearlmutter, N. J., & MacDonald, M. C. (1995). Individual differences and probabilistic constraints in syntactic ambiguity resolution. *Journal of Memory and Language*, *34*(4), 521–542.

Posthuma, D., Baaré, W. F., Pol, H., Hilleke, E., Kahn, R. S., Boomsma, D. I., & De Geus, E. J. (2003). Genetic correlations between brain volumes and the WAIS–III dimensions of verbal comprehension, working memory, perceptual organization, and processing speed. *Twin Research*, *6*(2), 131–139.

Prat, C. S. (2011). The brain basis of individual differences in language comprehension abilities. *Language and Linguistics Compass*, *5*(9), 635–649.

Prat, C. S., & Just, M. A. (2011). Exploring the neural dynamics underpinning individual differences in sentence comprehension. *Cerebral Cortex*, *21*(8), 1747–1760.

Prat, C. S., Keller, T. A., & Just, M. A. (2007). Individual differences in sentence comprehension: A functional magnetic resonance imaging investigation of syntactic and lexical processing demands. *Journal of Cognitive Neuroscience*, *19*(12), 1950–1963.

Prat, C. S., Mason, R. A., & Just, M. A. (2010). Right hemisphere contributions to reading: A multi-experiment individual differences investigation. Poster presented at the Organization for Human Brain Mapping, Barcelona, Spain.

Prat, C. S., Mason, R. A., & Just, M. A. (2011). Individual differences in the neural basis of causal inferencing. *Brain and Language*, *116*(1), 1–13.

Prat, C. S., Mason, R. A., & Just, M. A. (2012). An fMRI investigation of analogical mapping in metaphor comprehension: The influence of context and individual cognitive capacities on processing demands. *Journal of Experimental Psychology: Learning, Memory, and Cognition*, *38*, 282–294.

Reichle, E. D., Carpenter, P. A., & Just, M. A. (2000). The neural basis of strategy and skill in sentence–picture verification. *Cognitive Psychology*, *40*, 261–295.

Rohl, M., & Pratt, C. (1995). Phonological awareness, verbal working memory and the acquisition of literacy. *Reading and Writing*, *7*(4), 327–360.

Rypma, B., Prabhakaran, V., Desmond, J. E., Glover, G. H., & Gabrieli, J. D. (1999). Load-dependent roles of frontal brain regions in the maintenance of working memory. *NeuroImage*, *9*(2), 216–226.

Sanchez, C. A., & Wiley, J. (2006). An examination of the seductive details effect in terms of working memory capacity. *Memory & Cognition*, *34*(2), 344–355.

St. George, M. S., Mannes, S., & Hoffman, J. E. (1997). Individual differences in inference generation: An ERP analysis. *Journal of Cognitive Neuroscience*, *9*(6), 776–787.

Stanovich, K. E., & A. E. Cunningham. (1992). Studying the consequences of literacy within a literate society: The cognitive correlates of print exposure. *Memory & Cognition*, *20*(1), 51–68.

Stocco, A., Lebiere, C., & Anderson, J. R. (2010). Conditional routing of information to the cortex: A model of the basal ganglia's role in cognitive coordination. *Psychological Review*, *117*(2), 541–574.

Stocco, A., Yamasaki, B. L., Natalenko, R., & Prat, C. S. (2014). Bilingual brain training: A neurobiological framework of how bilingual experience improves executive function. *International Journal of Bilingualism*, *18*(1), 67–92.

Takeuchi, H., Sekiguchi, A., Taki, Y., Yokoyama, S., Yomogida, Y., Komuro, N. . . . Kawashima, R. (2010). Training of working memory impacts structural connectivity. *Journal of Neuroscience*, *30*(9), 3297–3303.

Turner, M. L., & Engle, R. W. (1986). Working memory. *Proceedings of the Human Factors Society*, *30*, 1273–1277.

Unsworth, N., Heitz, R. P., Schrock, J. C., & Engle, R. W. (2005). An automated version of the operation span task. *Behavior Research Methods*, *37*(3), 498–505.

Unsworth, N., & McMillan, B. D. (2013). Mind wandering and reading comprehension: Examining the roles of working memory capacity, interest, motivation, and topic experience. *Journal of Experimental Psychology: Learning, Memory, and Cognition*, *39*(3), 832–842.

Wagner, R. K., & Torgesen, J. K. (1987). The nature of phonological processing and its causal role in the acquisition of reading skills. *Psychological Bulletin*, *101*(2), 192–212.

Waters, G. S., & Caplan, D. (1996). The capacity theory of sentence comprehension: Critique of Just and Carpenter (1992). *Psychological Review*, *103*(4), 761–772.

Waters, G. S., Caplan, D., & Hildebrandt, N. (1991). On the structure of verbal short-term memory and its functional role in sentence comprehension: Evidence from neuropsychology. *Cognitive Neuropsychology*, *8*(2), 81–126.

Wilhelm, O., Hildebrandt, A., & Oberauer, K. (2013). What is working memory capacity, and how can we measure it? *Frontiers in Psychology*, *4*, 433.

Yamasaki, B. L., & Prat, C. S. (2014). The importance of managing interference for second language reading ability: An individual differences investigation. *Discourse Processes*, *51*(5–6), 446–467.

# 25

# Individual Differences in Perceptual Processing and Eye Movements in Reading

*Keith Rayner, Matthew J. Abbott, and Patrick Plummer*

Our primary concern in this chapter will be to examine the extent to which there are differences in perceptual processing and eye movements among individuals who are generally considered to be good readers. By good or "skilled" readers we refer to any individual with a normal, adult-sized vocabulary and sufficient command of their written language system. Noteworthy differences in speed notwithstanding, skilled readers are capable of comprehending normal written text with no external assistance and with little conscious effort. However, the categorization would not extend to individuals with language-specific deficits, general cognitive deficits, or those who are still acquiring critical aspects of literacy, such as grade school children who are still being taught to read. Skilled reading is often discussed as if the processes and strategies involved were very much the same for all readers. Is it possible that readers are doing somewhat different things and still coming out with the same end product, namely comprehension of the text? Our primary contention will be that perceptual processing in skilled readers is quite similar for both slow and fast readers (though some differences will be noted below). Thus, eye movement data which reflect relatively "low-level" perceptual processing will be not very different for such readers. However, "higher-level" cognitive processing, particularly processes that allow for varying strategies to come into play, may yield differences between readers and their eye movement data will therefore look somewhat different.

During reading, eye movements are very important in the sense that they serve as the means by which readers are able to acquire new information from the text. Indeed, new information is acquired only during eye *fixations* (the period of time when the eyes are relatively still) which typically last 200–250 ms. Between the fixations, the eyes move very rapidly to a new part of the text; these movements are called *saccades* and typically take 20–30 ms during reading. No new information is acquired from the text during saccades (see Rayner, 1998, 2009 for reviews). During reading, the eyes typically move seven to nine letter spaces during a saccade. However, the eyes do not move relentlessly forward from word to word. Around 25–33% of the words are skipped; skipping is highly related to word length, with shorter words skipped more than longer words. Given a constant word length, words that are more predictable from prior context are skipped more than words that are not predictable. In addition, about 10–15% of the saccades

*Table 25.1* Mean fixation duration (in ms), mean forward saccade length (in character spaces), proportion of fixations that were regressions, and words per minute (wpm) for ten good college-aged readers reading expository text

| Reader | Fixation duration | Saccade length | Regressions | WPM |
|---|---|---|---|---|
| 1 | 241 | 7.2 | 14 | 230 |
| 2 | 193 | 8.3 | 20 | 314 |
| 3 | 247 | 6.7 | 1 | 257 |
| 4 | 205 | 8.5 | 6 | 347 |
| 5 | 206 | 7.9 | 4 | 335 |
| 6 | 255 | 7.7 | 19 | 244 |
| 7 | 196 | 9.5 | 15 | 382 |
| 8 | 190 | 8.6 | 11 | 348 |
| 9 | 227 | 7.6 | 12 | 251 |
| 10 | 195 | 9.0 | 6 | 378 |
| Mean | 216 | 8.1 | 11 | 308 |

are *regressions* that move the eyes backwards in the text to previously read material. The values provided here are averages across readers, but there is considerable variability in all of these measures between readers (see Table 25.1). It is also important to note that there is considerable variability in all of these measures within any given reader. Specifically, for any given reader (see Figure 25.1), while the average fixation duration might be 250 ms, the range would actually be from under 100 ms to over 500 ms, and while the average forward saccade length might be eight letter spaces, the range would be from less than one letter to about 25 letter spaces (though such long saccades only really occur following a regression back in the text). In general, across all skilled readers, more difficult text leads to longer fixation durations, shorter saccade lengths, and more frequent regressions.

The reason we make eye movements so frequently during reading is because of limitations of visual acuity. Any given line of text that we read can be divided into three regions: foveal, parafoveal, and peripheral. The foveal region comprises the 2 degrees of visual angle in the center of vision. Here, acuity is best, and readers need to move their eyes so as to place the fovea over that part of the text they wish to process. However, information is also obtained from parafoveal vision (extending out to roughly 5 degrees from the point of the eye fixation) in reading (see Rayner, 1978, 1998, 2009; Schotter, Angele, & Rayner, 2012 for reviews). For normal sized text, three to four letters typically make up 1 degree of visual angle; thus, six to eight letters would typically fall in the foveal region (see Figure 25.2 for a graphical example).

## Individual Differences in Fixation Durations and Saccade Lengths

As indicated above, it is well known that there are individual differences in the eye movement characteristics of readers. From Table 25.1, which shows mean eye movement data during normal reading for ten skilled readers, it is obvious that some readers read fast because they make fewer fixations (including regressions) than readers who are not quite so fast, while others may read a bit faster by making shorter fixations. In fact, while reading rate can be increased by making either fewer fixations or shorter fixations (or both), most of the increase is generally due to making fewer fixations. Figure 25.1 shows distributions of fixation durations and saccade lengths

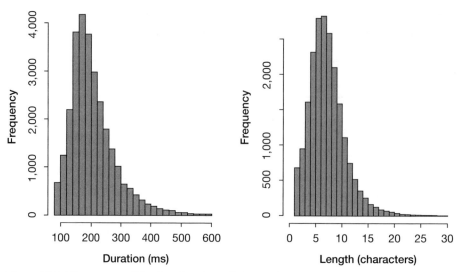

*Figure 25.1* Histograms of fixation durations (left panel) and forward saccade lengths (right panel) based on 60 readers

for 60 skilled readers (college students) as they read sentences. As is obvious in the figure, there is considerable variability in these two eye movement measures; much of this variability is related to cognitive processes associated with understanding text (Rayner, 1998, 2009). To more clearly document the individual differences, Figure 25.2 shows the fixation duration distributions for three of the readers whose data contribute to Figure 25.1. Each distribution includes every fixation recorded from an individual while reading the sentences. While the overall shape of each distribution is similar across the three readers, there are obviously differences. The average fixation duration for each reader roughly corresponds to the peak of the curve (along the x-axis). It is evident from Figure 25.2 that these readers differ not only in the placement of their fixation distribution's peak, but also in the height of the peak and the shape of the right tail. The height of the peak reflects the within-reader variability in fixation durations; higher peaks correspond to less variability. Whereas, the shape of the right tail reflects the frequency with which these readers make longer fixations. In addition to the variability across the different readers there is comparable variability within individuals. Taken together, the height of the peak and shape of the right tail (i.e., the rightward skew) correspond to the within-reader variability in fixation durations, these distributions clearly reveal differences both within and across individual readers in the duration of eye fixations during normal reading.

In a recent study of fixation duration distributions like those in Figures 25.1 and 25.2, Staub and Benatar (2013) performed a computational analysis examining the peak locations on the x-axis, overall curve shape, and right tail shape. They concluded that individual readers vary in the time required for normal perceptual and linguistic processing during eye fixations. Their analyses suggest that readers vary in the time needed for word recognition and sentence comprehension as well as the frequency with which they encounter disruption or difficulty during these processes. Furthermore, their research suggests that these distinct aspects of processing have independent contributions to individual differences, though more work must be done to address this. Interestingly, it is also the case that distributions very similar to those we have shown will also emerge in simple oculomotor reaction time tasks where subjects have to move their eyes from a central fixation point to a specific target when it appears in the

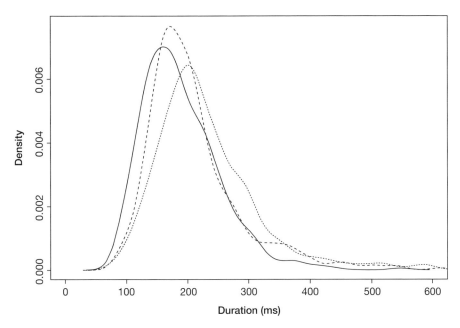

*Figure 25.2* Density plots for fixation duration distributions from three subjects

visual field. Importantly, a task such as this involves no language processing of any kind. Thus, overall speed of processing (independent of word processing) seems to vary across readers.

In light of the individual differences that are evident in Table 25.1 and Figures 25.1 and 25.2, (Rothkopf 1978; Rothkopf & Billington, 1979) suggested that such differences in eye movement patterns are extremely important. He reported what appear to be marked differences in readers in both their eye movement patterns and their responses to changes in reading task demands and goals (e.g., skimming, reading normally, or preparing for a recall question), and suggested that eye movement patterns of different individuals may not be sufficiently alike to warrant a single theoretical model of the reading process. In contrast, on the basis of a large scale examination of individual differences in eye movement patterns (as readers read easy and difficult text under six different experimental conditions), Fisher (1983) concluded that the extent of individual differences in reading is not sufficient to challenge the validity of a general model of reading. A general model of reading would assume that, aside from variability around central tendencies, there should be no qualitative differences in patterns of eye movement behavior during reading; whereas, an alternative account would predict apparent qualitative differences in patterns of behavior across different readers. Fisher argued that most individual differences in terms of eye movement behavior remain across conditions of different reading demands. So while there are differences between readers, the differences remain when the task is changed from careful reading to skimming. This suggests that variability across readers is driven by differences in processing speed rather than qualitative differences in the kinds perceptual and linguistic processes being executed (though see Wotschack & Kliegl, 2013 for recent evidence that task demands have an influence on eye movements during reading). On the other hand, Rayner, Li, Williams, Cave, and Well (2007) compared eye movement data for subjects while reading or while engaged in a visual search or scene perception task, and found that fixation durations and saccade lengths did not have high correlations across the tasks. It is also of interest that Rayner and McConkie (1976) reported that during reading there was no significant correlation between successive fixations (where regions of text are processed) and successive saccades (where new regions of text are brought into clear view). There are undoubtedly places in text where there will be long successive fixations (or a series of them), but across an entire text Rayner and McConkie found no such effect.

Our contention in this chapter is that, although there is clear variability within and across individuals with regard to eye movement patterns and characteristics among skilled readers, most skilled readers are pretty much doing the same thing in terms of eye movements and language comprehension. Specifically, eye movement characteristics and patterns for any skilled reader could be predicted by adopting a single model of how skilled readers coordinate low-level perceptual processing and higher-level language comprehension. Moreover, empirically observable individual differences can be explained by assuming that readers will vary in the speed and efficiency of higher-level language processes but much less so for the associated lower-level perceptual processes. By this account, as the reading situation allows for more strategic higher-level processing, individual differences will become more apparent (Hyönä, Lorch, & Kaakinen, 2002). For the most part, our observation that most skilled readers are doing similar things (and hence their eye movement behavior is quite similar for perceptual processing) derives from the large number of studies done in our lab using the *gaze-contingent moving window* and *boundary* paradigms (McConkie & Rayner, 1975; Rayner, 1975; Rayner & Bertera, 1979). In the moving window paradigm, as a subject reads, the amount of information available on each fixation is controlled by the experimenter (via a *moving window* of variable size). We will describe this paradigm (and the boundary paradigm) in much more detail below. But, to preview the results, in the moving window paradigm studies the presence of a restricted window affects all readers in pretty much the same way. That is, as small windows are presented, readers decrease saccade length (and make more fixations) and increase fixation duration in comparison to when larger windows are presented. Thus, while there are indeed individual differences in eye movement characteristics (and in the moving window studies, as we will document below), our sense

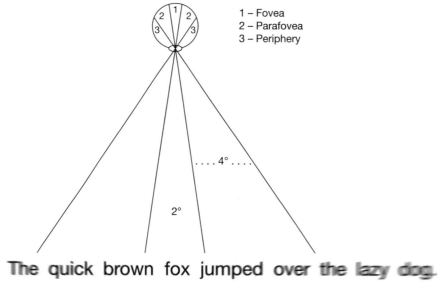

*Figure 25.3* An example showing the foveal, parafoveal, and peripheral regions when three characters make up 1° of visual angle. The point of fixation is centered on the "o" in "fox". Blurring outside of the fovea is done for graphical demonstration

is that they may not be particularly important in explaining perceptual processing in reading. In large part, this is because of the anatomy of the eye in which the distinction between foveal, parafoveal, and peripheral regions of text holds for all readers (see Figure 25.3). Prior to discussing the gaze-contingent moving window and boundary paradigms, we turn to other attempts to examine individual differences in perceptual processing in reading.

## Individual Differences in Information Processing Tasks Related to Reading

In an attempt to determine what differentiates a fast reader from a slower reader, Jackson and McClelland (1975) tested subjects on a number of information processing tasks. Prior to doing so, they had subjects read a passage of text and computed their reading speed and comprehension. On the basis of their reading speeds (words per minute, wpm), they divided the subjects into two groups: fast readers and slow readers. Comprehension scores were approximately 80% correct for both groups. The mean reading speed for the slow readers was 260 wpm (with the range being 206 wpm to 299 wpm), while the mean reading speed for the fast readers was 586 wpm (with all reading over 400 wpm). Jackson and McClelland also computed an effective reading rate by multiplying the reading rate by the comprehension score; the effective reading rate for the slow readers was 207 wpm and for the fast readers it was 490 wpm. Note that while the slow readers' reading speed was in the general range usually associated with college-aged readers (200–350 wpm), the fast readers were quite fast in comparison to typical averages.

In two tasks, sentences were presented to the subjects. In the free report task, sentences such as *Dan fixed the flat tire* were presented for 200 ms; all sentences contained short words such as in the example. Subjects fixated on a target point and then the sentence was presented around the fixation. After each exposure, they wrote down as much of the sentence as they could; they were also instructed to write down any letters they saw whenever they recognized letters without identifying the whole word. The slow readers reported 61% of the letters and the fast readers reported 87%; the slow readers reported 58% of the words and the fast readers reported 82%. In terms of reporting the entire sentence, the slow readers reported 16% of the sentences and the fast readers reported 39% of them. In the forced-choice test, subjects were shown a sentence such as *Kevin fired a new worker* for 200 ms and then asked to indicate if the word *fired* or *hired* was presented in the sentence. The slow readers were correct 71% of the time and the fast readers were correct 79% of the time. In both of these tasks, the exposure of the sentence was preceded and followed by a visual mask consisting of overlapping Os and Xs.

In a single letter threshold task, capital letters were presented starting at 20 ms and subjects were asked to report the letter. If they could not report the letter, the duration of the exposure was increased incrementally until they could report it. For the final 20 trials subjects were given in which they could identify the target letter, the exposure duration averaged 52.7 ms for the slow readers and 49.3 ms for the fast readers (a non-significant difference).

In an unrelated letter task, eight randomly chosen letters (all consonants) were presented for 200 ms (again preceded and followed by a mask). After each exposure, subjects wrote down eight letters in any order, guessing if necessary. The slow readers correctly reported 53% of the letters, while the fast readers reported 64% of the letters.

Finally, in a letter separation task, two letters were presented at different distances to the left and right of fixation for 200 ms (again with a mask preceding and following the stimulus); the spatial separation between the two letters was 2.3, 3.4, 4.8, or 5.9 degrees of visual angle. The subjects had to write down the letters. There was no difference between the fast and slow readers in terms of the number of correct letters reported at any of the spatial separations. On the basis of this result, Jackson and McClelland concluded that the overall processing span for letters in the visual field did not differ between the slow and fast readers. For a number of reasons that we will not document here (for further details see McConkie & Rayner, 1975; Rayner, 1975), their method of assessing the processing span (or perceptual span) is not nearly as precise as the gaze-contingent moving paradigm discussed in the next section.

Overall, Jackson and McClelland concluded that there were no differences between the fast and slow readers in the tasks described above which they termed sensory or low-level perceptual tasks. That is, on the single letter threshold task, thresholds for the two groups did not differ and on the letter separation task, there was no difference between the two groups. On all other tasks (e.g., the sentence report task), however, there was a difference in favor of the fast readers. Jackson and McClelland concluded that the breadth of field from which visual information can be utilized during an eye fixation was approximately the same for the fast and slow readers (but see our caveat at the end of the prior paragraph). What apparently distinguishes the two groups, Jackson and McClelland concluded, is that faster readers are able to encode more of the contents of each fixation, whether or not higher-order linguistic structure is present. The results of their study also suggested that differences in reading speed are not due to the reader's ability to infer or fill in missing information.

Jackson and McClelland's analysis that differences in reading speed are not due to basic sensory or low-level perceptual skills is consistent with a large number of other studies (Carr, 1981; Jackson & McClelland, 1979; Jackson, 1980; Daneman & Carpenter, 1980, 1983; Masson & Miller, 1983; Palmer, MacLeod, Hunt, & Davidson, 1985; Baddeley, Logie, Nimmo-Smith, & Brereton, 1985) which examined how relatively good readers differ from each other in component skills related to reading. The primary approach taken in these studies has been to present subjects with a large battery of tests (as per Jackson and McClelland) and then determine how the different tasks (and differences on these tasks) correlate with some measure of reading performance.

Rather than reviewing the outcome of each study, we will present the important points to be gleaned from this research. The tasks that have been used in these studies include tests of sensory functions (e.g., test of visual acuity), verbal and quantitative reasoning skills, memory span, listening comprehension, visual letter matching, lexical decision, naming ability, picture-sentence verification, semantic categorization, and so on. Among the important results that have emerged from this research are the following. First, reading performance correlates rather well with these various information processing tasks when words are used as stimuli, but not so well when letters are used (Palmer et al., 1985). Second, reading speed and comprehension have different correlations with the information processing measures (Palmer et al., 1985; Jackson & McClelland, 1979), again suggesting that factors that affect reading speed may differ somewhat from those factors that affect comprehension processes. Third, much of the variability in reading speed appears to be due to the speed with which subjects can access long-term memory codes for meaningful material as in word recognition (Jackson & McClelland, 1979; Jackson, 1980). Fourth, much of the variability in comprehension processes appears to be due to working memory differences between fast and average readers (Baddeley et al., 1985; Daneman & Carpenter, 1980, 1983; Masson & Miller, 1983). For example, the research tends to suggest that readers with small working memories devote so many resources to the decoding aspects of written text that they have less capacity for retaining earlier verbatim wording in working memory. Finally, while reading speed is only moderately correlated with listening comprehension, reading comprehension ability is apparently indistinguishable from listening comprehension ability (Palmer et al., 1985; Jackson & McClelland, 1979).

In essence, the evidence from these studies dealing with individual differences suggests that skilled readers do not differ at the basic sensory or perceptual level in terms of what they perceive in a fixation. Rather, the speed with which material can be encoded and accessed in memory appears to play a part in determining reading speed. Furthermore, working memory span appears to mediate comprehension processes. As such, these data do not imply that fast and slow readers (all of whom we would want to categorize as relatively good readers) are doing vastly different things. Readers may use sophisticated strategies that help them remember things that they have read, and some may be more adept than others in using these strategies. However, when we examine individual differences in terms of on-line and immediate processing of text, it appears that most skilled readers are doing essentially the same thing; some may do it a bit slower (hence their reading speed will be slower) and some may not have as good working memory abilities (hence their comprehension will not be quite as good) as others. Yet, the bottom line is that there are many more similarities than differences and, hence, it is justifiable to try and specify a general model of the reading process.

## Gaze-Contingent Moving Window and Boundary Paradigms

We now turn to a description of the moving window and boundary paradigms. In the moving window paradigm (McConkie & Rayner, 1975), a reader's eye movements are monitored by a high-speed computer as they read from a computer monitor. An experimenter-defined window of normal text is then presented on each fixation while outside of the window the text is distorted in some way (so that letters could be replaced by Xs or random letters). The size of the window is varied so that it could be either quite small (in the extreme it would only be a single character, forcing the reader to read letter-by-letter) or quite large (say, up to 15–19 letter spaces on each side of fixation). Whenever the reader moves his or her eyes, the window moves in synchrony with the eyes (exposing a new region of text, see Figure 25.4). The primary rationale associated with the paradigm is that when the window is large enough that readers can acquire all of the information that they typically would obtain on a fixation, the window size will not differ from a normal reading situation in which there is no window. Critically, denial of textual information outside of the window (relative to the point of fixation) can only have an influence on reading behavior when it is attended to in sequence. Hence, as the window size becomes smaller than the perceptual span, readers will be deprived of information they routinely utilize; normal processing will be disrupted and reading will be slowed.

In the boundary paradigm (Rayner, 1975), a target word in the text is initially replaced by a preview word or non-word letter string, and when the reader's saccade crosses an invisible boundary location, the preview word changes into the target word. The relationship between the preview word and the target word has been varied across a number of studies (see Rayner, 1998, 2009; Schotter et al., 2012 for reviews); the results of these studies clearly document that readers get a head start on processing characteristics of the target word (especially orthographic and phonological properties of the preview, and in some cases semantic properties, see Schotter, 2013). While the moving window paradigm provides information about the size of the perceptual span, the boundary paradigm provides information about the type of information acquired within the span relative to the point of fixation.

A large number of studies (originating with McConkie & Rayner, 1975, 1976) have demonstrated that for readers of alphabetic writing systems like English the perceptual span (or region from which readers can acquire useful information on an eye fixation) extends from three to four letter spaces to the left of fixation to about 14–15 letter spaces to the right of fixation. Thus, the span is asymmetric, being larger in the direction of reading (Rayner, Well,

| | |
|---|---|
| Normal: | primary concern in this chapter will be to examine the |
| | |
| 7-Letter window: | xxxxxxxxoncern in this xxxxxxxxxxxxxxxxxxxxxxxxxxx |
| | * |
| | xxxxxxxxxxxxxxxn this chapter wxxxxxxxxxxxxxxxxxx |
| | * |
| | xxxxxxxxxxxxxxxxxxxxxxxxpter will be toxxxxxxxxxxx |
| | * |
| | |
| Boundary Paradigm: | primary concern in this article  will be to examine the |
| | *          *          * |
| | primary concern in this chapter will be to examine the |
| | * |

Figure 25.4. Examples of the moving window paradigm and the boundary paradigm.

*Notes:*

a. For the moving window paradigm, the window is 7 character spaces to the left and right of fixation.  The asterisk marks the location of a fixation.  When the reader moves, the window moves in synchrony with the eyes (with successive fixations also illustrated via the asterisk).  In this particular example, the letters outside of the window are replaced by xs, but they are sometimes replaced by other letters (see Rayner et al., 1982).  Also, the spaces are filled in outside of the window in this particular example, but sometimes they are not.  And, in this example, the window is defined in terms of letter spaces, but it can be defined in terms of words (again, see Rayner et al., 1982).

b. For the boundary paradigm example, a preview word (in this case *article*) is initially presented in the target location, but when the readers' eyes cross an invisible boundary (typically located just after the last letter of the prior word), the preview changes to the target word (in this case *chapter*).

& Pollatsek, 1980). It is interesting in this context to note that the asymmetry is reversed for readers of Hebrew (which is read from right to left). It is also smaller (extending about 11–12 letters to the left of fixation) because information is more densely packed in Hebrew than in English (Pollatsek, Bolozky, Well, & Rayner, 1981). In Chinese, where information is even more densely packed, the perceptual span is roughly one character to the left of fixation to three characters to the right of fixation (Inhoff, & Liu, 1998). It is very important to note that while these cross-language differences might seem large, when one does the appropriate conversions it is the case that the perceptual span extends roughly two words beyond the currently fixated word (Rayner, Well, Pollatsek, & Bertera, 1982).

Some recent studies have used the moving window paradigm to examine differences between groups of readers. Rayner, Slattery, and Bélanger (2010; see also Ashby, Yang, Evans, & Rayner, 2012) found that slow readers have a smaller perceptual span than fast readers, though this probably has more to do with difficulties encoding the fixated word than differences in acuity. Veldre and Andrews (2013a) found that readers high on "lexical expertise" (defined by the combination of effective reading comprehension and accurate spelling) had a larger perceptual span than readers low on this variable. They concluded that readers with high-quality lexical representations (indexed by the combination of high reading and spelling ability) were more able to efficiently process parafoveal information. Finally, Bélanger, Slattery, Mayberry, and Rayner (2012) found that skilled deaf readers had a larger perceptual span than less skilled deaf readers and normal hearing control subjects. Apparently, skilled deaf readers are able to effectively process information further from the point of fixation than the other two groups.

It is important to note again, that across all of these studies, restricting the size of the window (i.e., making it smaller) led to corresponding decreases in reading rate and saccade size, and an increase in fixation durations. Thus, while it is undoubtedly the case that there are individual differences, perhaps along the lines suggested by Veldre and Andrews (2013b), virtually all readers react similarly to windows that are smaller than the size of the perceptual span, which appears to differ among readers, with more skilled readers obtaining information at least 15 character spaces to the right of fixation and less skilled readers obtaining less information.

Other studies have utilized the boundary paradigm to examine differences between groups of readers. Chace, Rayner, and Well (2005) examined whether differences in reading skill affect parafoveal word recognition processes during silent reading. In their study, the parafoveal preview was either an identical word (*beach–beach*), a homophone (*beech–beach*), an orthographic control (*bench–beach*), or a consonant string (*jfzrp*). They found that fixation times of the more skilled readers were comparable in the homophone and identical preview conditions, and shorter than in the control and consonant string conditions. In contrast, the less skilled readers had roughly comparable mean fixation times in all four conditions. Also, the fixation times of the two groups did not differ in the orthographic and consonant string conditions. Chace et al.'s data indicate that phonologically similar parafoveal previews reduced word recognition time for the better readers only, and that the poorer readers did not benefit from any parafoveal information. Likewise, Bélanger and Rayner (2013) found that skilled deaf readers effectively process orthographic information from the parafovea, but not phonological information. Finally, Veldre and Andrews (2013b) reported that the amount of parafoveal preview benefit depended on their lexical expertise variable; increased reading ability was associated with a larger preview benefit, particularly in difficult sentences, but only amongst good spellers. Taken together these data suggest that while the limitations of visual acuity and basic sensory perception are effectively indistinguishable across faster and slower skilled readers, differences in the size of the perceptual span and the amount of preview benefit obtained during reading are driven by linguistic processing speed and efficiency. Faster readers are able to obtain more information per eye fixation because of increased speed and efficiency of higher-level language processing such as accessing word meanings and comprehending sentences. Readers who have more robust or stable mental representations for words in long-term memory will access those representations more quickly and easily. Presumably, a considerable part of becoming a skilled reader depends on developing stable representations for the written word forms in one's vocabulary. As written word vocabulary and language skill increase, readers should be able to process more linguistic information per eye fixation. However, it is important to note that these generalizations may not apply to comparisons between skilled readers who are deaf and those who have developed with normal hearing.

## Eye Movements and Individual Differences

Finally, a handful of other studies have examined eye movements in the context of individual differences. Schilling, Rayner, and Chumbley (1998) found that subjects tended to rank themselves consistently in both overall speed and in the size of the word frequency effect across naming/lexical decision tasks and eye fixation time measures (though Kuperman, Drieghe, Keuleers, & Brysbaert, 2013 found smaller correlations overall). Several studies (see Clifton et al., 2003; Traxler, 2007; Traxler et al., 2012; Traxler, Williams, Blozis, & Morris, 2005) have examined sentence parsing and working memory abilities via the use of the Daneman and Carpenter (1980) sentence span task. Others (Azuma, Ikeda, Minamoto, Osaka, & Osaka, 2012; Kaakinen & Hyönä, 2007) have examined memory span influences on eye movements, but have generally dealt with higher-level processes (e.g., word memorization). The results of these studies have not been overly clear in terms of how working memory span differentiates speed and efficiency in parsing. Differences have emerged across the studies; however, these differences have generally appeared in eye movement measures capturing re-reading behavior (e.g., regression frequency, second-pass, and total reading times). These "later" measures are generally thought to reflect higher-level comprehension processes rather than initial perceptual and word recognition processes. These differences reported in the studies referenced above likely are indices of increased reading comprehension difficulty for low-span when compared to high-span readers. Kennison and Clifton (1995) examined whether differences in working memory capacity correlate with parafoveal preview and found no effect. While there is little evidence that working memory capacity influences initial encoding and word recognition, one of the problems with determining effects of working memory span is that working memory capacity correlates with other reading variables (e.g., reading speed, vocabulary size, and print exposure).

Kuperman and Van Dyke (2011) recently reported a study of how individual differences in reading-related tasks affect eye movements during reading. They used a sample of 16 to 24-year-old not-college-bound subjects and used a large battery of tests that they then related to their subjects' eye movements during reading. They found that across the various assessments, fixation durations during first-pass reading as well as re-reading were only reliably predicted by individual scores on a standardized word recognition test and the rapid automatic naming (RAN) test wherein subjects name aloud an array of letters, digits, color patches, or objects as fast and accurately as possible. In their analysis, they found that only two variations of the RAN test, letter and digit naming, reliably predicted patterns of eye fixations. They also found that the effect sizes of these two variables were larger in magnitude than established effects due to word length and word frequency. Finally, they found that poorer readers tended to fixate closer to the beginning of a word (see also Hawelka, Gagl, & Wimmer, 2010) when initially fixating the word during first-pass reading (for recent studies using the RAN test, eye movements, and dyslexia, see Jones, Ashby, & Branigan, 2013; Pan, Yan, Laubrock, Shu, & Kliegl, 2013).

Other studies have used scores on the Nelson–Denny test, which provides a standardized measure of reading comprehension, to identify individual differences in reading skill. Ashby, Rayner, and Clifton (2005) used this test in an investigation of highly skilled and average college readers' word recognition processes. They compared the eye movements of the two groups as they read high- and low-frequency words in predictable, unpredictable, and neutral contexts. In the neutral and predictable contexts, both groups of readers fixated low-frequency words longer than the high-frequency words (the typical, and highly reliable, word frequency effect). In unpredictable contexts, frequency effects appeared for the highly skilled readers but the average readers did not fixate the low-frequency words any longer than the high-frequency words. The re-reading patterns of the average readers indicated that their eyes left low-frequency predictable words before recognition was complete and re-read the sentence contexts, which suggests that they relied on context to recognize less familiar words. In contrast, finding comparable frequency effects across different predictability conditions for the highly skilled readers indicates that their automatic word recognition processes were resilient to changes in contextually based word predictability. Therefore, Ashby et al.'s study (2005) demonstrates that the best college readers maintain stable, automatic word recognition processes, although they may adjust their conscious reading strategies for different types of text.

Another study used the Nelson–Denny test to examine the phonological processing of high- and low-skilled college readers. Jared, Levy, and Rayner (1999) measured eye movements as good and poor readers read sentences that contained a correctly spelled target, a homophone of the target, or a misspelled control. They found that poor readers were less likely to notice homophone errors than the misspelled controls. In contrast, the good readers had comparable fixation times in the homophone and misspelled conditions—both of which were longer than for the correct target. Together, the findings from Jared et al. (1999) and Chace et al. (2005) suggest that more skilled readers primarily process phonological information parafoveally whereas less skilled readers are more susceptible to foveal phonological effects.

As a final discussion point concerning individual differences, let's consider beginning and (especially) older readers in comparison to young college-aged skilled readers. It is well known that beginning readers make more and longer fixations than skilled readers, and they also regress more frequently and their saccades are much shorter than skilled readers' (see Rayner, 1978, 1998, 2009 for reviews). It is also the case that beginning readers have a smaller perceptual span than older readers (Häikiö, Bertram, Hyönä, & Niemi, 2009; Rayner, 1986); while second graders have a smaller span than fourth graders, who start to approximate the span of adult readers for age-appropriate material, their span is asymmetric after only a year's worth of reading instruction (Rayner, 1986). Underwood and Zola (1986) reported no difference in the span of letter recognition between young children who were categorized as either good or poor readers. However, their finding seems to be a bit at odds with more recent findings (Veldre, & Andrews, 2013a, although the readers in this study were college students).

Older readers (65 to 85 years old) tend to read more slowly than younger readers; their fixation times are longer and they make more regressions (Rayner, Reichle, Stroud, Williams, & Pollatsek, 2006; Laubrock, Kliegl, & Engbert 2006). However, their reading comprehension is typically as good as or better than that of younger readers. Older readers have a smaller and more symmetric perceptual span (Rayner, Castelhano, & Yang, 2009) than younger readers and on some fixations they obtain less preview benefit (i.e., extracted less information from words to the right of the fixated word) than younger readers (Rayner, Castelhano, & Yang, 2010). However, the older readers apparently do not take longer to encode words than younger readers (Rayner, Yang, Castelhano, & Liversedge, 2010). This suggests that as individuals advance into older age, perceptual processing efficiency may decline, but language processing ability remains stable. The general conclusion from this research is that older readers tend to read more slowly than younger readers (presumably due to some type of general cognitive slowing). In order to circumvent the slower reading, the older readers engage in guessing strategies concerning what the next word is more frequently than younger readers. This results in longer average saccades for older readers (Rayner et al., 2006; Laubrock et al., 2006), but because they are wrong about their guess sometimes, it also results in them making more regressions than younger readers. The main point to be gleaned from this discussion is that while older readers are quite similar to younger readers in many ways, they engage in a more risky reading strategy to try to compensate for the fact that they read more slowly than they previously did.

## Summary

In this chapter, we have reviewed research on perceptual processing, eye movements, and individual differences in reading. While there is no doubt that there are large individual differences across readers in terms of fixation durations, saccade lengths, and frequency of regressions, our view is that at the level of perceptual processing and initial encoding of text during eye fixations most readers are doing pretty much the same thing. They are processing the fixated word to access its meaning and they also shift their attention to the word to the right of fixation prior to making a saccade to it. Sometimes readers can identify the word to the right of fixation while still on the fixated word; in such cases, they will typically then skip that next word. Also, when reading breaks down, readers tend to regress to look back in the text.

Each skilled reader must bring their own knowledge and experience to bear on the task of comprehending language. To the extent that individuals differ with regard to vocabulary size and general world knowledge one would expect to find differences in comprehension, especially when dealing with more difficult text. When readers encounter unfamiliar or difficult words they must decipher the meaning of the word using the sentence context, what they know about the world, and what they know about their language. When readers encounter complex, unfamiliar, or ambiguous grammatical structures normal comprehension processes are more likely to break down. Once readers recognize that comprehension has broken down they can choose from several strategies to resolve the difficulty. Under these circumstances it is likely that there will be more differences between readers than when reading is going smoothly (Frazier, & Rayner, 1982): Some readers will quickly regress back in the text to the point where they first encountered difficulty; some will hold their eyes in place while they try to resolve the breakdown mentally (without overtly looking back); and others will engage in more idiosyncratic re-reading strategies in which they resolve the problematic part of the text.

Eye movement data provide excellent measures associated with encoding of text and lexical access, but they are not so precise with respect to the impact of higher-level influences (other than the effect of contextual constraint and plausibility). Thus, when higher-level processes such as ambiguity resolution or complex reasoning are at play, the effect of an experimental manipulation is likely to be smeared across a number of fixations (Clifton, Staub, & Rayner, 2007; Staub & Rayner, 2007). Only recently have researchers rigorously investigated individual differences in reading. In many ways, this is not surprising because the primary goal has been to establish how important benchmark effects of linguistic variables are reflected in the eye movement record. Given that much research has been successful in doing this, it may well be that more investigations now focus on the role of individual differences.

Hypothetically, an account whereby individual differences across skilled readers are driven by the use of qualitatively different perceptual and comprehension processes would have difficulty accounting for the observed data. The vast majority of evidence suggests that the close coordination of attention, low-level perceptual processing, working memory, and high-level linguistic knowledge is achieved in much the same way across all skilled readers. Further, studies show that the variability in reading speed and eye movement patterns across faster and slower skilled readers are driven by differences in word processing and comprehension speed rather than qualitative differences in the architecture of linguistic representations or the order of processing stages during comprehension.

## Acknowledgments

Preparation of this chapter was supported by funds from the Microsoft Corporation and from the Atkinson Chair fund.

## References

Ashby, J., Rayner, K., & Clifton, C. (2005). Eye movements of highly skilled and average readers: Differential effects of frequency and predictability. *Quarterly Journal of Experimental Psychology, 58A*, 1065–1086.
Ashby, J., Yang, J., Evans, K. H. C., & Rayner, K. (2012). Eye movements and the perceptual span in silent and oral reading. *Attention, Perception, & Psychophysics, 74*, 634–640.
Azuma, M., Ikeda, T., Minamoto, T., Osaka, M., & Osaka, N. (2012). High working memory performers have efficient eye movement control systems under Reading Span Test. *Journal of Eye Movement Research, 5*(3), 1–10.

Baddeley, A., Logie, R., Nimmo-Smith, I., & Brereton, N. (1985). Components of fluent reading. *Journal of Memory and Language, 24,* 119–131.

Bélanger, N. N., & Rayner, K. (2013). Frequency and predictability effects in eye fixations for skilled and less-skilled deaf readers. *Visual Cognition, 21,* 477–496.

Bélanger, N. N., Slattery, T. J., Mayberry, R. I., & Rayner, K. (2012). Skilled deaf readers have an enhanced perceptual span in reading. *Psychological Science, 23,* 816–823.

Carr, T. H. (1981). Building theories of reading ability: On the relation between individual differences in cognitive skills and reading comprehension. *Cognition, 9,* 73–114.

Chace, K. H., Rayner, K., & Well, A. D. (2005). Eye movements and phonological parafoveal preview: Effects of reading skill. *Canadian Journal of Experimental Psychology, 59,* 209- 217.

Clifton, C., Staub, A., & Rayner, K. (2007). Eye movements in reading words and sentences. In R. van Gompel, M. H. Fischer, W. S. Murray, & R. L. Hill (Eds.), *Eye movements: A window on mind and brain* (pp. 341–372). Oxford: Elsevier.

Clifton, Jr., C., Traxler, M. J., Taha Mohamed, M., Williams, R. S., Morris, R. K., & Rayner, K. (2003). The use of thematic role information in parsing: Syntactic processing autonomy revisited. *Journal of Memory and Language, 49,* 317–334.

Daneman, M., & Carpenter, P. A. (1980). Individual differences in working memory and reading. *Journal of Verbal Learning and Verbal Behavior, 19,* 450–466.

Daneman, M., & Carpenter, P. A. (1983). Individual differences in integrating information between and within sentences. *Journal of Experimental Psychology: Learning, Memory, and Cognition, 9,* 561–584.

Fisher, D. G., (1983). An experimental study of eye movements during reading. Unpublished manuscript. Murray Hill, NJ: Bell Laboratories.

Frazier, L., & Rayner, K. (1982). Making and correcting errors during sentence comprehension: Eye movements in the analysis of structurally ambiguous sentences. *Cognitive Psychology, 14,* 178–210.

Häikiö, T., Bertram, R. Hyönä, J., & Niemi, P. (2009). Development of the letter identity span in reading: Evidence from the eye movement moving window paradigm. *Journal of Experimental Psychology, 102,* 167–181.

Hawelka, S., Gagl, B., & Wimmer, H. (2010). A dual-route perspective on eye movements of dyslexic readers. *Cognition, 115*(3), 367–379.

Hyönä, J., Lorch Jr, R. F., & Kaakinen, J. K. (2002). Individual differences in reading to summarize expository text: Evidence from eye fixation patterns. *Journal of Educational Psychology, 94,* 44–55.

Inhoff, A. W., & Liu, W. (1998). The perceptual span and oculomotor activity during the reading of Chinese sentences. *Journal of Experimental Psychology: Human Perception and Performance, 24,* 20–34.

Jackson, M. D. (1980). Further evidence for a relationship between memory access and reading ability. *Journal of Verbal Learning and Verbal Behavior, 19,* 683–694.

Jackson, M. D., & McClelland, J. L. (1975). Sensory and cognitive determinants of reading speed. *Journal of Verbal Learning and Verbal Behavior, 14,* 565–574.

Jackson, M. D., & McClelland, J. L. (1979). Processing determinants of reading speed. *Journal of Experimental Psychology: General, 108,* 151–181.

Jared, D., Levy, B. A., & Rayner, K. (1999). The role of phonology in the activation of word meanings during reading: Evidence from proofreading and eye movements. *Journal of Experimental Psychology: General, 128,* 219–264.

Jones, M. W., Ashby, J., & Branigan, H. P. (2013). Dyslexia and fluency: Parafoveal and foveal influences on rapid automatized naming. *Journal of Experimental Psychology: Human Perception and Performance, 39,* 554–567.

Kaakinen, J. K., & Hyönä, J. (2007). Strategy use in the reading span test: An analysis of eye movements and reported encoding strategies. *Memory, 15,* 634–646.

Kennison, S. M., & Clifton, C. (1995). Determinants of parafoveal preview benefit in high and low working memory capacity readers: Implications for eye movement control. *Journal of Experimental Psychology: Learning, Memory, and Cognition, 21,* 68–81.

Kuperman, V., Drieghe, D., Keuleers, E., & Brysbaert, M. (2013). How strongly do word reading times and lexical decision times correlate? Combining data from eye movement corpora and megastudies. *Quarterly Journal of Experimental Psychology, 66,* 563–580.

Kuperman, V., & Van Dyke, J. A. (2011). Effects of individual differences in verbal skills on eye-movement patterns during sentence reading. *Journal of Memory and Language, 65,* 42–73.

Laubrock, J., Kliegl, R., & Engbert, R. (2006). SWIFT explorations of age differences in eye movements during reading. *Neuroscience & Biobehavioral Reviews, 30,* 872–884.

McConkie, G. W., & Rayner, K. (1975). The span of the effective stimulus during a fixation in reading. *Perception & Psychophysics*, *17*, 578–586.

McConkie, G. W., & Rayner, K. (1976). Asymmetry of the perceptual span in reading. *Bulletin of the Psychonomic Society*, *8*, 365–368.

Masson, M. E., & Miller, J. A. (1983). Working memory and individual differences in comprehension and memory of text. *Journal of Educational Psychology*, *75*, 314–318.

Palmer, J., MacLeod, C. M., Hunt, E., & Davidson, J. E. (1985). Information processing correlates of reading. *Journal of Memory and Language*, *24*, 59–88.

Pan, J., Yan, M., Laubrock, J., Shu, H., & Kliegl, R. (2013). Eye–voice span during rapid automatized naming of digits and dice in Chinese normal and dyslexic children. *Developmental Science*, *16*, 967–979.

Pollatsek, A., Bolozky, S., Well, A. D., & Rayner, K. (1981). Asymmetries in the perceptual span for Israeli readers. *Brain and Language*, *14*, 174–180.

Rayner, K. (1975). The perceptual span and peripheral cues in reading. *Cognitive Psychology*, *7*, 65–81.

Rayner, K. (1978). Eye movements in reading and information processing. *Psychological Bulletin*, *85*, 618–660.

Rayner, K. (1986). Eye movements and the perceptual span in beginning and skilled readers. *Journal of Experimental Child Psychology*, *41*, 211–236.

Rayner, K. (1998). Eye movements in reading and information processing: 20 years of research. *Psychological Bulletin*, *124*, 372–422.

Rayner, K. (2009). The thirty-fifth Sir Frederick Barlett Lecture: Eye movements and attention in reading, scene perception, and visual search. *Quarterly Journal of Experimental Psychology*, *62*, 1457–1506.

Rayner, K., & Bertera, J. H. (1979). Reading without a fovea. *Science*, *206*, 468–469.

Rayner, K., Castelhano, M. S., & Yang, J. (2009). Eye movements and the perceptual span in older and younger readers. *Psychology and Aging*, *24*, 755–760.

Rayner, K., Castelhano, M. S., & Yang, J. (2010). Preview benefit during eye fixations in reading for older and younger readers. *Psychology and Aging*, *25*, 714–718.

Rayner, K., Li, X., Williams, C. C., Cave, K. R., & Well, A. D. (2007). Eye movements during information processing tasks: Individual differences and cultural effects. *Vision Research*, *47*, 2714–2726.

Rayner, K., & McConkie, G. W. (1976). What guides a reader's eye movements? *Vision Research*, *16*, 829–837.

Rayner, K., Reichle, E. D., Stroud, M. J., Williams, C. C., & Pollatsek, A. (2006). The effect of word frequency, word predictability, and font difficulty on the eye movements of young and older readers. *Psychology and Aging*, *21*, 448–465.

Rayner, K., Slattery, T. J., & Bélanger, N. N. (2010). Eye movements, the perceptual span, and reading speed. *Psychonomic Bulletin & Review*, *17*, 834–839.

Rayner, K, Well, A. D., & Pollatsek, A. (1980). Asymmetry of the effective visual field in reading. *Perception & Psychophysics*, *27*, 537–544.

Rayner, K., Well, A. D., Pollatsek, A., & Bertera, J. H. (1982). The availability of useful information to the right of fixation. *Perception & Psychophysics*, *31*, 537–550.

Rayner, K., Yang, J., Castelhano, M. S., & Liversedge, S. P. (2011). Eye movements of older and younger readers when reading disappearing text. *Psychology and Aging*, *26*, 214–223.

Rothkopf, E. Z. (1978). Analyzing eye movements to infer processing styles during learning from text. *Eye movements and the higher psychological functions*. Hillsdale, NJ: Lawrence Erlbaum Associates.

Rothkopf, E. Z., & Billington, M. J. (1979). Goal-guided learning from text: Inferring a descriptive processing model from inspection times and eye movements. *Journal of Educational Psychology*, *71*, 310–327.

Schilling, H. E., Rayner, K., & Chumbley, J. I. (1998). Comparing naming, lexical decision, and eye fixation times: Word frequency effects and individual differences. *Memory & Cognition*, *26*, 1270–1281.

Schotter, E. R. (2013). Synonyms provide semantic preview benefit in English. *Journal of Memory and Language*, *69*, 619–633.

Schotter, E. R., Angele, B., & Rayner, K. (2012). Parafoveal processing in reading. *Attention, Perception, & Psychophysics*, *74*, 5–35.

Staub, A., & Benatar, A. (2013). Individual differences in fixation duration distributions in reading. *Psychonomic Bulletin & Review*, *20*, 1304–1311.

Staub, A., & Rayner, K. (2007). Eye movements and on-line comprehension processes. In G. Gaskell (Ed.), *The Oxford handbook of psycholinguistics* (pp. 327–342). Oxford, UK: Oxford University Press.

Traxler, M. J. (2007). Working memory contributions to relative clause attachment processing: A hierarchical linear modeling analysis. *Memory & Cognition*, *35*, 1107–1121.

Traxler, M., Johns, C. L., Long, D. L., Zirnstein, M., Tooley, K. M., & Jonathan, E. (2012). Individual differences in eye-movements during reading: Working memory and speed-of-processing effects. *Journal of Eye Movement Research*, *5*(1), 1–16.

Traxler, M. J., Williams, R. S., Blozis, S. A., & Morris, R. K. (2005). Working memory, animacy, and verb class in the processing of relative clauses. *Journal of Memory and Language*, *53*, 204–224.

Underwood, N. R., & Zola, D. (1986). The span of letter recognition of good and poor readers. *Reading Research Quarterly*, *21*, 6–19.

Veldre, A., & Andrews, S. (2013a). Lexical quality and eye movements: Individual differences in the perceptual span of skilled adult readers. *Quarterly Journal of Experimental Psychology*, *67*(4), 703–727.

Veldre, A., & Andrews, S. (2013b). *Lexical expertise and parafoveal processing*. Presented at the European Conference on Eye Movements, Lund, Sweden.

Wotschack, C., & Kliegl, R. (2013). Reading strategy modulates parafoveal-on-foveal effects in sentence reading. *Quarterly Journal of Experimental Psychology*, *66*, 548–562.

# 26

# Cognitive Processing and Reading Comprehension

## Issues of Theory, Causality, and Individual Differences

*Ralph E. Reynolds, Byeong-Young Cho, and Amy Hutchison*

The topic of individual differences in reading performance has a long and robust history in the reading literatures of psychology, education, linguistics, and special education. Much of this research concerns how variations in children's skills in basic reading processes affect overall reading performance. There has been particular focus on research on the cognitive processes that make up word identification (Brady, Braze, & Fowler, 2011). Results from this research show that proficient readers tend to be fast and accurate at the process of word identification. Over time, more proficient readers become automatic at word identification processes, allowing them to be performed with minimal demand for the allocation of cognitive resources. Less proficient readers commonly have slower, less accurate, and more cognitive resources demanding word identification processes; thus, more proficient readers tend to have more cognitive resources remaining to attend to the more complex processes involved in reading comprehension (Just & Carpenter, 1992; Stanovich, 2000).

In contrast, less research has been done that explains exactly how more proficient readers use the cognitive resources they have conserved via automatic word identification to facilitate the processes involved in reading comprehension. A major purpose of this chapter is to add to the discussion of individual differences in reading ability by investigating whether variations in readers' selective cognitive resource allocation during reading comprehension affect reading performance. A second chapter purpose is to trace the theoretical and methodological insights that have moved understanding of the processes involved in reading toward a more integrated explanation of the interplay among basic and higher level cognitive processes.

Initially, the discussion will focus on the theoretical assumptions on which selective attention/reading comprehension research rests and the methodological and causal issues that have influenced the research. Providing the theoretical and methodological context is necessary for deeper understanding of the results of the studies presented and integrating them into the larger research and theory context. Subsequently, several selective attention studies will be outlined that provide specific information on potential individual differences in how readers use and allocate their cognitive resources to the implicit and explicit tasks of reading comprehension. A discussion of the potential of these ideas to add to current reading theory will conclude the chapter. For ease of communication, the terms "cognitive effort," "cognitive capacity," and "cognitive resources" will be used to refer to attention allocated to a task, attention capacity, and attention available, respectively. This is done in an effort to ease the integration of two different, but related, research literatures: selective attention and cognitive processes.

The theoretical basis for much of modern process-oriented reading research originated in the discipline of psychology during the 1960s and early 1970s—dates that coincide with the initial influences of the cognitive revolution on psychology. The cognitive revolution was also a watershed moment in the history of social science and education research because it freed scholars from the behaviorist restriction of explaining learning events only in terms of observable phenomena. Instead, cognitivists embraced the creation of theory and testable hypotheses, similar to the approaches of the so-called "hard sciences." Hawking (1993) elaborated on the straightforward view of the scientific method as follows:

> The theory always comes first, put forward from the desire to have an elegant, consistent . . . model. The theory makes predictions, which can be tested by observation. If the observations agree with the predictions, that doesn't prove the theory; but the theory survives to make further predictions, which again are tested against observation. If the observations don't agree with the predictions, one abandons the theory. Or rather that is what is supposed to happen (p. 42)

The cognitive revolution was initiated by two events: the publication of Chomsky's review of Skinner's book *Verbal Behavior* (Chomsky, 1959) and the creation of the Harvard Center for Cognitive Studies in 1960 by George Miller and Jerome Bruner (Hunt, 1993). Chomsky's review showed that behaviorist principles could not explain higher-order human learning such as language acquisition because the behaviorist system did not allow for more abstract theoretical explanations of observed phenomena, in this case the role of the inherent organizational aspects of the brain in language acquisition. Underpinning the cognitivist approach were three concepts not possible in behaviorism. These ideas were that: theory was essential for the advancement of knowledge in any science or social science, incoming information was processed (re-coded and integrated) and stored when people learned from text—sometimes called the computational hypothesis—and, information could be represented symbolically in memory. By extension, cognitivists suggested that students' abilities to acquire language were significantly more complex than the simple accretion of stimulus-response bonds as Skinner had implied (Skinner, 1957).

The International Reading Association published the first edition of *Theoretical Models and Processes of Reading* in 1970 to begin what has become an almost 50-year discussion of reading theories and models in conjunction with the new theoretical freedom allowed by the cognitive revolution. The second edition of this book appeared in 1976 and contained two seminal articles in reading research history: *Behind the Eye: What Happens in Reading* (Goodman, 1971) and *One Second of Reading* (Gough, 1971). Gough's model was an application of cognitive theory to explain the nature of reading processes. It was built on three key assumptions that remain relevant in research today: The process of reading is not a natural process, it must be learned; the foundation of successful reading is fast, accurate word identification processes; and reading comprehension flows almost automatically from fast, accurate word identification and knowledge of word meanings.

In contrast, Goodman's model was based on a psycholinguistic approach to understanding the reading process. The approach was also loosely based on Chomsky's ideas concerning the acquisition of spoken language and vocabulary (Chomsky, 1959) and was more concerned with text comprehension than word identification. Interestingly, both scholars suggested that individual differences in reading achievement would likely center on the processes involved in word identification; though, for very different reasons.

Most modern reading scholars now characterize themselves as supportive of more "balanced" or interactionist models of the reading process than either of the former views (Perfetti, 1985; Rayner & Pollatsek, 1989). These views contain aspects of previous models and theories, plus information gleaned from more recent research concerning the processes involved in reading comprehension (Just & Carpenter, 1992; Anderson, Reynolds, Schallert, & Goetz, 1977; Stanovich, 2000). Notions such as the idea that the cognitive processes involved in aspects of reading comprehension might be another cause of individual differences in reading performance can be comfortably contained within these interactionist theoretical frames.

## Theoretical Foundations

Several theoretical assumptions were made at the onset of the selective attention/reading comprehension work that continues to the present day. The first concerns the use of attention as an indicator of cognitive effort and how it operates in learning situations. Cognitive effort can be selective in that it can be focused on certain text information to the exclusion of other text information. Both volitional (intentional) and automatic processes play roles in the allocation of cognitive effort (Reynolds, 1992); however, the degree of each type of contribution is as yet not known. Research suggests that some reading processes begin as intentional, effortful processes and evolve into automatic processes with practice, making determining the exact degree of contribution difficult to ascertain at any given time (Bargh & Chartrand, 1999; Reynolds, 2000).

Additional theoretical assumptions involved in the cognitive effort/reading comprehension work are: individual's cognitive capacity is of adequate magnitude to address most of human cognitive activities; cognitive capacity is fixed, in that it cannot be increased beyond an individual's limit regardless of task demands; cognitive capacity is limited in that *certain cognitive tasks* might exceed available resources; significant differences are assumed to exist among individual readers concerning cognitive capacity; and these differences will likely affect reading comprehension performance. Indeed, differences in working memory capacity affect reading comprehension performance (Just & Carpenter, 1992).

Two different theories were proposed to explain how cognitive effort could be selective (focused on some information at the expense of other information). Broadbent (1958) suggested that cognitive effort "selectivity" was accomplished by rapid switching of all of the available cognitive capacity from one information source to another—one might watch TV and monitor the time by focusing all effort on the TV show, then focusing all effort on the clock, and then switching all effort back to the TV. Conversely, Kahneman (1973) suggested that congruent cognitive tasks would draw on the same reservoir of cognitive capacity at the same time—one could watch TV and monitor the time at the same time by unevenly allocating available cognitive effort between the two tasks—likely more effort to the TV and less effort to monitoring the time. The distinction is important because it explains the decreased performance on all cognitive tasks when cognitive effort demands exceed available cognitive capacity. Kahneman's theory has garnered the most empirical support; hence, it was used in the selective attention/reading comprehension research being discussed (Reynolds, 2000).

Perfetti (1985) introduced Verbal Efficiency Theory (VET) in an effort to create a general theory of reading ability that was more specific and more precisely predictive than previous models.

The primary focus of this theory was to explain the initial or basic aspects of the reading process; however, implications for comprehension were included as well. Stated simply, VET suggests that when the cognitive effort involved in word identification becomes minimal/automatic, cognitive capacity is conserved for use in higher-order comprehension processes. Perfetti stated:

> In the ideal case, these lexical and schematic processes can take place with little [cognitive] resource expenditure. That leaves resources for the work that needs them: (1) the encoding of propositions, especially the integration of propositions within and across sentences; some of the inference processes that are not automatic, i.e., the kind of memory search that is needed for recently backgrounded information . . . (3) the interpretive, inferential, and critical comprehension of a text that goes beyond the text itself. (pp. 103–104)

Implicit in Perfetti's model is the idea that using cognitive resources efficiently is the key to developing proficiency in reading. Stated another way, Perfetti predicted that more proficient readers would be more efficient at using available cognitive capacity to decode words and comprehend texts. Conversely, less proficient readers would be less efficient at using these same resources. A major purpose of the initial selective attention/reading comprehension studies described here was to begin to understand whether more proficient readers allocate their cognitive resources more efficiently during reading comprehension as well; hence, indicating possible sources of individual difference in comprehension processes.

## Measures and Procedures

### Indices of Cognitive Effort Use

Cognitive effort usage has been measured in numerous ways in various types of attention-related research (Reynolds, 2000). Two of the most commonly used indicators have been reading time used as a measure of effort duration and secondary task reaction time used as a measure of the intensity of the effort allocated to the primary cognitive task (Posner & Boies, 1971); however, other indicators have been used as well (Jacoby, 1983b). Four measures or indicators of selective cognitive effort use will be discussed here because they are used in the studies to be described later in the chapter.

*Effort duration* was measured by reading times (time spent reading individual text segments presented). In most studies, text segments or sentences were presented individually on a computer screen. Readers proceeded through each text display by pressing the spacebar on the computer keyboard. The text displayed on the screen would be replaced with a new text segment with each spacebar press. The computer recorded the time between spacebar presses to the nearest millisecond. Subjects continued this process until they had completed the entire text.

*Effort intensity* was measured using secondary task methodology. Cognitive effort can be allocated to a greater or lesser degree to any given text aspect. Secondary task methodology as used in the described experiments was based on a technique developed by Posner and Boies (1971). In the reading comprehension studies described later the primary task was reading and learning from the text. A secondary task was given to the subjects as well: that of monitoring for a tone that would sound occasionally while they were reading. The subjects were told to hit the spacebar on the computer as fast as they could when they heard the tone. The resulting reaction time (measured to the nearest millisecond) provided an indirect estimate of how intensely readers had been attending to their primary task, reading and learning. The longer the reaction time, the more cognitive effort was being applied to the primary task (Reynolds & Anderson, 1982).

*Effort focus* was measured using Jacoby's (1983a, 1983b) methodology. Jacoby suggested that readers were capable of allocating cognitive resources to different aspects of the reading process. Effort could be focused on the perceptual/structural aspects of words in a text, likely in the service of word identification, or resources could be focused on the conceptual/meaning aspects of words, likely in the service of comprehension. Jacoby named these two indices *perceptual effort* and *conceptual effort*, respectively. Jacoby reasoned that when readers focused on the perceptual aspects of words, they would be better able to identify those words when they were flashed on a computer screen at a very high rate of speed—so fast that subjects reported seeing only fleeting images on the screen. In contrast, when readers focused cognitive resources on the conceptual aspects of the words, they would better comprehend general word meaning, thus increasing overall comprehension. Jacoby suggested that more proficient readers would have a relatively high ratio of conceptual focus to perceptual focus as they read. Less proficient readers would have a lower or even an inverted ratio of effort focused on perceptual rather than conceptual word aspects. These two different foci of cognitive effort were thought to indicate aspects of individual differences between more and less proficient readers as a result of more proficient readers' more automatic word identification processes.

Studies were conducted using all of these indicators of cognitive effort use, sometimes in combination and sometimes alone. All were necessary in order to answer various questions about efficient allocation of cognitive resources during reading comprehension, particularly given the complexity and diversity of the cognitive processes likely involved. In addition, all of these measures seem to hold potential for revealing individual differences in readers at the reading comprehension level.

## Experimental Procedures

All of the studies discussed in this chapter used similar experimental procedures. Subjects were shown text presented on a computer screen to be read and learned. In some cases, text was presented a sentence at a time whereas other texts were presented in segments of about 33 words in length to better mimic the natural flow of printed text. Measures of effort duration and/or intensity would be collected unbeknownst to the reader. Subjects would then be asked to take a short test on the content of the text or write down everything they could remember from the text. The perceptual/conceptual effort studies used a slightly different approach. Subjects were given a passage to read and study. Then, for one group of subjects the passage content words, plus distractors, would be flashed on the computer screen at a high rate of speed. A second group of subjects read the same passage presented in the same way; however, they were asked to take a word recognition test after reading rather than a faster word identification task. It was hypothesized that readers who were able to do better at the word recognition task had allocated more effort to the conceptual (meaning) aspects of the passage words.

The relationship between information importance and learning from texts has been well established almost from the beginning of prose comprehension research (Reynolds, 2000). For that reason, many of the reviewed studies used relative text importance as an initial independent variable. There are many heavily researched ways to manipulate the relative importance of text items in reading tasks. Relative text element importance was manipulated in the reviewed studies by assigning readers tasks to accomplish, perspectives from which to read, or inserting questions into the text that asked about a consistent type of information—proper names or technical terms. It was important to predetermine text item importance in order to determine if cognitive effort was selectively focused on this information as a causal aspect of learning it (Reynolds, 1992).

## Causal Explanations

The primary goal of deductive, theory-based research is to test hypotheses made on the basis of theoretical expectation or prediction; however, all tests of these predictions are not of equal value. Of most value are causal explanations of why predictions are correct or incorrect. Plotkin (1998) states this point succinctly:

> One of the most remarkable features of most, or perhaps all, sciences is that they rely heavily upon causal explanations that invoke causal elements that are not part of normal life and everyday experience . . .What behaviorism did was forbid causal explanations if they did not lie within the limits of ordinary everyday experience. Scientifically, this is an extraordinarily bankrupting stance. Cognitivism rescued . . . [social scientists] from this cripplingly narrow vision. (p. 33)

Causal explanations are very difficult to obtain in reading research because many of the studies are conducted in real-life situations (classrooms) where adequate levels of random assignment to condition and tight experimental control are not normally available. Cognitive resource allocation studies are an exception to this generalization because the research is conducted in a laboratory setting where these conditions are possible. Even with these advantages, causality is difficult to prove when outcome data come from different groups of subjects with different outcome measures that must be compared.

Most cognitive resource allocation studies involve both measures of resource allocation and learning. Normally, two or more ANOVAs (analyses of variance) are performed, one for each outcome measure. From these ANOVAs one can ascertain that additional cognitive resources are allocated to important text information and that important information is better learned and recalled; however, one cannot tell if the additional cognitive resource allocation caused the increased learning because an alternative explanation cannot be eliminated. It might be that the additional cognitive effort was epiphenomenal in relation to the higher level of learning. Resource allocation and learning took place on or near the same text elements, but were not necessarily causally related (Reynolds, Trathen, Sawyer, & Shepard, 1993). Indeed, it is problematic when scholars assume causal relations exist among treatments or observations, mediating variables, and outcomes without actually proving causality through proper experimental or quasi-experimental designs or other logical or statistical means.

A possible solution to this problem was proposed by Reynolds and Anderson (1982). They suggested that data from experiments like those just described could be subjected to a rigorous test of logical causality. Many experiments, particularly in the field of education, are designed to prove hypotheses such as the following: *Variable A* (a certain type of instruction) causes changes in *Variable C* (normally post-test learning) because of changes in *Variable B* (a mediating variable such as interest, motivation, or allocation of additional cognitive effort). The research design suggested above could be described as follows: Variable A causes changes in Variable B which in turn causes changes in Variable C. Arrows represent causal relationships.

Variable A → Variable B → Variable C

369

The following example will illustrate that it follows logically that for the above formulation to be true, the following four entailments of the relationship must also be true—an entailment is a deduction or implication, that is, something that follows logically from or is implied by something else.

*Entailment I*    Variable A (instruction type) must be significantly related to Variable C (increased learning)

*Entailment II*    Variable A (instruction type) must be significantly related to Variable B (increased motivation)

*Entailment III*    Variable B (increased motivation) must be significantly related to Variable C (increased learning)

*Entailment IV*    After the relationship between Variable B and Variable C are removed, the relationship between Variable A and Variable C must be significantly decreased if the overall model is to be considered causal.

If the relationship between Variable A and Variable C still remains the same when Variable B is removed, then Variable B cannot be a causal variable in the relationship between Variables A and C. A non-significant result for any entailment ends the causal testing procedure. Proving the nature of the relationship between the cognitive effort variables and the outcome variable is a critical step in determining whether individual differences in readers' cognitive resource allocation patterns actually cause differences in reading comprehension.

## Cognitive Resource Use in Reading Comprehension

Reynolds (2000) reviewed numerous studies dealing with cognitive resource use in the service of reading comprehension. It is beyond the scope of the current chapter to replicate such a review. Instead, a series of three studies will be reviewed briefly with the purpose of explicating the processing differences among four grade/age levels of more proficient and less proficient readers; thus, identifying probable sources of individual differences in the use of selective cognitive resource allocation in reading comprehension. In all cases, readers' level of proficiency was determined using age-appropriate reading comprehension tests. Experimental subjects included more and less proficient fourth graders, sixth graders, tenth graders, and college students. Additionally, reviewing these studies will demonstrate the increased sophistication of the selective use of cognitive resources strategy as readers develop over time. Causal analyses using the four-entailment process just described were conducted using data from each study.

Reynolds and Anderson (1982) conducted a study of highly proficient college student readers' use of selective allocation of cognitive resources as an approach or strategy in increasing comprehension. The study had two primary goals: to demonstrate optimal use of selective cognitive resource allocation by readers of the highest level and to demonstrate that this approach or strategy was causally involved in proficient readers' comprehension processes. Text element importance was manipulated via inserted questions of two types—proper names and technical terms. Measures of cognitive effort duration (reading time) and intensity (secondary task reaction time) were collected as students read the computer-presented text. Causal entailment analysis showed that the extra cognitive effort duration and intensity that readers allocated to the important text elements played a causal role in the eventual learning and recall of this information. These results confirmed the initial notion that selective allocation of cognitive resources was a causal comprehension component employed by proficient comprehenders to improve the learning and recall of text information. This causal relationship was presented visually as follows:

Text Importance → Increased Cognitive Effort → Increased Learning
(duration and intensity)

Subsequent research efforts focused on determining when and how young readers begin to effectively use the selective allocation of cognitive resources to enhance comprehension once the causal use of the approach was established for highly proficient readers. Fourth grade is the year in which many public school curriculum plans refocus reading instruction away from learning to read to reading to learn; hence, there is more emphasis on reading comprehension than in previous grades. It is for this reason that fourth grade seemed a good starting point for work on attempting to identify exactly when and how causal use of the selective allocation approach would begin to emerge. More proficient and less proficient fourth graders were asked to read a simple two-page passage that concerned a trip to a grocery store where food items of different colors were purchased. More proficient readers comprehended and recalled significantly more overall text information than did less proficient readers. Causal entailment analysis showed that item importance was related to improved comprehension only for the more proficient readers. Less proficient readers showed no identifiable comprehension approach at all, suggesting that at least some of the more proficient readers' comprehension advantage accrued from their use of a simple comprehension strategy—learning and recalling more information made important by their assigned purpose for reading (Bliss, 1984). Note that establishing a positive relationship between text item importance and learning is the first step in developing a causal relationship among important, selective cognitive resources allocation, and learning.

A similar study was conducted using more and less proficient sixth graders as subjects and a similar text rewritten on the sixth grade level (Reynolds et al., 1993). Text element importance was manipulated using instructions: readers were told to try to remember all of the color or food items they could depending on group membership. Reading times and secondary task reaction times were collected as measures of cognitive resource duration and intensity. More proficient readers learned and recalled more general text information than did less proficient readers. Causal entailment analysis showed that more proficient readers' learning advantage over less proficient readers was in part due to learning more of the information made important by the initial instructions. In addition, more proficient readers allocated more effort duration to these same important text items. Again, less proficient sixth grade readers showed no discernible comprehension strategy or approach. These results suggest that more proficient readers are more sophisticated in using selective allocation of their cognitive resources to assist comprehension even in sixth grade; however, they still do not use the approach in a fully causal manner.

Failure to find causal use of the selective resource allocation approach in sixth graders motivated the next study in this series. Reynolds, Shepard, Lapan, Kreek, and Goetz (1990, Experiment 1) conducted a study using more proficient and less proficient tenth graders as subjects. They read an excerpt from Rachel Carson's *The Sea Around Us* (1951) as their experimental text. Text element importance was manipulated by using inserted questions that asked about two different categories of information: technical terms and proper names. This task is considerably more difficult than the method of determining text element importance for the fourth and sixth grade studies. In this task, readers must infer that the questions all ask about the same type of information and that this information is important. They are not told what text elements are important as they were in the studies with younger readers.

As usual, more proficient readers learned and recalled more information on the post-test than did less proficient readers. Causal entailment analyses were conducted for both levels of readers. The less proficient tenth grade readers showed the same pattern of results as had

Less proficient fourth and sixth grade readers show no significant relationships among any of entailments:

More proficient fourth grade readers' selective cognitive resource allocation pattern is as follows:

More proficient sixth grade readers' and less proficient tenth grade readers' selective cognitive resources allocation:

The selective resource allocation pattern for more proficient tenth grade readers is as follows:

Highly proficient adult readers show the entire or full causal use of the selective cognitive resources allocation model (duration and intensity).

Text Importance ⟶ Increased Cognitive Effect ⟶ Increased Learning

*Figure 26.1* Results from causal entailment analysis of resources allocation patterns across ages and level of reading proficiency

the more proficient sixth grade readers. They learned more important text items and they allocated more resource duration to these important text items. The more proficient readers showed the same patterns with one additional finding. More proficient tenth grade readers learned more of the information to which they had allocated effort duration. However, there was no reduction in the relationship between text element importance and learning when the effect for resource duration allocation was removed (Entailment 4). The results from these three studies are represented visually in Figure 26.1.

Figure 26.1 shows that efficient use of selective allocation of cognitive resources appears to improve over time and as reader age and reading skill increases. Both more and less proficient readers seem to be developing initial stages of causal use of the selective resource allocation approach; however, more proficient readers at every age/grade develop more quickly than less proficient readers. In addition, study results showed that at least a portion of more proficient readers' reading comprehension advantage at each age/grade level was due to their more effective use of their cognitive resources. Another interesting result was that no age/grade group made effective use of effort intensity, as the highly proficient adult readers did. These younger readers relied on extending effort duration only.

Jacoby (1983a, 1983b) suggested two measures of cognitive effort focus that might allow investigation of exactly how more and less proficient tenth-grade readers use the cognitive resources that they allocate to important text elements. Perceptual effort is defined as focusing on the structural/orthographic aspects of words; hence, it is used to facilitate word identification. Conceptual effort is focused on the semantic aspects of words; hence, it should enhance word recognition and ultimately text learning. It is not clear which, if either, of these processes requires additional duration and/or intensity of cognitive effort. Text element importance was manipulated by assigning different groups perspective from which to read. Measures of perceptual effort, conceptual effort, effort duration, and effort intensity were collected for all subjects.

Jacoby (1983b) had suggested that more proficient readers would allocate a higher percentage of conceptual effort to perceptual effort to the reading task because they would use their cognitive resources to support learning rather than to identify words. Conversely, less proficient comprehenders would allocate a lower ratio of conceptual effort to perceptual effort because their word identification processes were less efficient. The results supported Jacoby's hypothesis. More proficient comprehenders' conceptual to perceptual effort ratio was 1.70 to 1 when reading important text elements, while less proficient comprehenders had a comparable ratio of 1.04 to 1. A second important finding was that more proficient readers used more conceptual effort and less perceptual effort regardless of the importance of the text element learned. This was true even though the less proficient tenth-grade readers allocated more cognitive effort duration and effort intensity to the overall reading task (Reynolds et al., 1990, Experiment 2).

Taken together, the reviewed studies show some interesting differences among more and less proficient readers regardless of age/grade level. Less proficient readers at all levels read more slowly, work harder at the reading task (increased effort intensity), and learn less text information than do more proficient readers. More proficient readers' comprehension advantage likely accrues for many reasons; however, at least some of these reasons are related to the sophistication with which they selectively and efficiently allocate cognitive resources to important text items and the remaining text. Another way in which more proficient readers might gain a comprehension advantage over less proficient readers is to use their available cognitive resources in support of metacognitive activities that assist learning. Metacognitive activities are operationalized as readers' ability to become aware of high-level patterns and strategies as they read and comprehend text. Two studies concerning these issues will be reviewed in the next section.

## Metacognition and Cognitive Effort

The first study to be discussed used all of the standard methods and techniques employed in the studies already reported. More and less proficient college-age readers read a science-oriented text passage. Text element importance was manipulated using the previously discussed inserted question technique. Measures of selectively allocated effort duration and intensity were collected. Spectral analysis (Gottman, 1981) was used to detect hidden cognitive resource allocation patterns throughout the text and beyond the expected allocation to important text elements. The results showed the expected outcomes for cognitive resource allocation to important text element studies, increased learning of this information for both groups of readers, and more overall learning for the more proficient reader group. Spectral analysis detected two patterns in the effort duration allocation. Both more and less proficient readers evidenced a pattern that indicated high resource allocation to important text elements but much lower allocation to less important text elements. The more proficient readers showed an additional pattern, one of high effort duration resource allocation to the area in which each inserted question occurred and lower effort duration allocation but increased effort intensity allocation to the text that followed. This pattern repeated after each inserted question suggesting that the more proficient readers had understood (become aware) of the implicit purpose of the inserted questions and began using them as trigger points for implementing a strategy that involved increasing their effort intensity to the important text elements that followed (Lapan & Reynolds, 1994).

A recently completed study (Reynolds, Brown, Niederhauser, & Trathen, in submission) revealed another set of results that suggests more proficient readers' effective use of a meta-comprehension activity as another reason for their overall comprehension advantage over less proficient readers. The only major difference between this study and that of Lapan and Reynolds (1994) is that halfway through the long 48-page science text, the nature of the inserted questions changes. Subjects who had previously received questions concerning the proper names of scientists in the text now began receiving questions that asked about the technical terms used in the descriptions of their scientific advances. Conversely, subjects that had been receiving technical terms questions now received questions concerning proper names. The switch was unannounced, it just happened. The goal was to see which group of readers would become aware of the switch first. Further, would members of this group change their resource allocation approach once they became aware of the change in item importance? The results showed that the less proficient college-level readers never noticed the change in inserted question type and never changed their resource allocation approach. The more proficient readers did not notice the question switch immediately; however, by the last 25% of the text they had changed their cognitive resource allocation approach to reflect the new set of important text items.

The study revealed another interesting finding. More and less proficient readers seemed to begin reading with the same resource allocation approach—focus on text elements that were tentatively perceived as important because of the inserted questions. More proficient readers read about 25% faster and learned and retained about 79% more information than did the less proficient readers in the initial 25% of the text. More proficient readers increased their efficiency and learning advantage over the less proficient readers in the second 25% of the text. They read about 20% faster and learned almost 200% more information. The less proficient readers actually learned and retained more information than the more proficient readers in the third 25% of the text, just after the question type switched. More proficient readers' learning advantage was back to about 50% in the fourth 25% of the text.

These results suggest that more proficient readers are much more metacognitive in their approach to reading comprehension than are less proficient readers. The greatest comprehension advantages over less proficient comprehenders seems to exist when proficient readers are satisfied that they understand what is important to learn from the text. The more convinced they are that they understand what is important, the greater the learning advantage over less proficient readers becomes.

## Conclusions

One purpose of the current chapter was to establish the need for theory and causal explanations in social science research. Testing theoretical predictions and assumptions of the initial processing theories derived from the cognitive revolution demonstrated the value of this approach. Theory not only motivates new research, it allows for the results of studies to be explained in a coherent and meaningful ways while at the same time linking new results to an established body of literature. Causal explanations increase the value study results in supporting or improving theoretical predictions. They establish chains of events that lead to theoretically predicted outcomes; thus, adding to the explanatory power of the theory.

Perfetti's (1985) Verbal Efficiency Theory provided the framework from which the work concerning the use of cognitive resources in the comprehension process evolved. The idea that more proficient readers conserve cognitive resources for reading comprehension by becoming automatic word identifiers allowed speculation about how the more proficient readers used these resources in service of comprehension. In addition, beginning readers have evidenced individual differences in word identification skill; hence, it seemed possible that individual differences could exist in how those resources were employed in reading comprehension.

The reviewed studies revealed several differences between more and less proficient readers in terms of how cognitive resources are allocated to the comprehensions process. Some of the main individual differences follow:

1. More proficient readers begin to develop the first traces of a causal cognitive resource allocation strategy as early as fourth grade. Less proficient readers do not show similar development until about tenth grade.
2. Only highly proficient adult readers use the selective allocation of cognitive resources in a causal manner; however, more proficient readers show better use of resource allocation at every grade tested.
3. Only highly proficient readers use the selective allocation of cognitive intensity to support reading comprehension. Less proficient readers never seem to develop this ability.
4. Less proficient readers continue to allocate significant cognitive resources to the word identification process, while more proficient readers are able to focus their resources on the meaning aspects of words.
5. More proficient readers have adequate resources available to engage in metacognitive activities to improve what they learn and recall from text. Specifically, they are able to monitor the text for information that helps them better focus their cognitive resources on text information that it is important to learn.

In summary, reading comprehension is a complex cognitive activity that involves many aspects and components. The selective use of cognitive resources is just one of these many components and as such likely explains only a small portion of the variance in comprehension performance. Nevertheless, many other critical components of the comprehension process may rest on the idea that more proficient readers have adequate cognitive resources available to engage them.

## References

Anderson, R. C., Reynolds, R. E., Schallert, D. L., & Goetz, E. T. (1977). Frameworks for comprehending discourse. *American Educational Research Journal, 14*, 367–382.

Bargh, J. A., & Chartrand, T. L. (1999). The unbearable automaticity of being. *American Psychologist, 54*(7), 462–479.

Bliss, S. M. (1984). The effect of specificity of reading purpose on good and poor sixth grade readers' distribution of reading time. Unpublished Master's Thesis, University of Utah, Salt lake City, UT.

Brady, S., A., Braze, D., & Fowler, C. A. (2011). *Explaining individual differences in reading: Theory and evidence*. New York: Taylor & Francis.

Broadbent, D. (1958). *Perception and communication*. London: Pergamon Press.

Carson, R. I. (1951). *The sea around us*. New York: Oxford University Press.

Chomsky, N. (1959). Review of "Verbal Behavior" by B. F. Skinner. *Language, 35*, 26–58.

Goodman, K. (1971). Behind the eye: What happens in reading. In H. Singer & B. R. Ruddell (Eds.), *Theoretical models and processes of reading* (pp. 470–496). Newark, DE: International Reading Association.

Gottman, J. M. (1981). *Time series analysis*. Cambridge, MA: Cambridge University Press.

Gough, P. B. (1971). One second of reading. In H. Singer & B. R. Ruddell (Eds.), *Theoretical models and processes of reading* (pp. 470–496). Newark, DE: International Reading Association.

Hawking, S. (1993). *Black holes and baby universes and other essays*. New York: Bantam Books.

Hunt, M. (1993). *The story of psychology*. New York: Random House.

Jacoby, L. L. (1983a). Perceptual enhancement: Persistent effects of an experience. *Journal of Experimental Psychology: Learning, Memory, and Cognition, 9*, 21–38.

Jacoby, L. L. (1983b). Remembering the data: Analyzing interactive processes in reading. *Journal of Verbal Learning and Verbal Behavior, 22*, 485–508.

Just, M., A., & Carpenter, P., A. (1992). A capacity theory of comprehension. Individual differences in working memory. *Psychological Review, 99*, 122–149.

Kahneman, D. (1973). *Attention and effort*. Englewood Cliffs, NJ: Prentice-Hall.

Lapan, R., & Reynolds, R. E. (1994). The selective attention strategy as a time-dependent phenomenon. *Contemporary Educational Psychology, 19*(4), 379–398.

Perfetti, C. (1985). *Reading ability*. New York: Oxford University Press.

Plotkin, H. (1998). *Evolution in mind: an introduction to evolutionary psychology*. Cambridge, MA: Harvard University Press.

Posner, M. L., & Boies, S. J. (1971). Components of attention. *Psychological Review, 78*, 391–408.

Rayner, K., & Pollatsek, A. (1989). *The psychology of reading*. Englewood Cliffs, NJ: Prentice Hall.

Reynolds, R. E. (1992). Selective attention and prose learning: Theoretical and empirical research. *Educational Psychology Review, 4*(4), 1–48.

Reynolds, R. E. (2000). Attentional resource emancipation: Toward understanding the interaction of word identification and comprehension processes in reading. *Scientific Studies of Reading, 4*(3), 169–195.

Reynolds, R. E., & Anderson, R. C. (1982). Influence of questions on the allocation during reading. *Journal of Educational Psychology, 74*(5), 623–633.

Reynolds, R. E., Brown, K. J., Niederhauser, D. S., & Trathen, R. W. (2014, in submission). The attention advantages of proficient readers.

Reynolds, R. E., Shepard, C., Lapan, R., Kreek, C., & Goetz, E. T. (1990). Differences in the use of selective attention by more successful and less successful tenth grade readers. *Journal of Educational Psychology, 82*(4), 749–759.

Reynolds, R. E., Trathen, W., Sawyer, M., & Shepard, C. (1993). Causal and epiphenomenal use of the selective attention strategy in prose comprehension. *Contemporary Educational Psychology, 18*, 258–278.

Skinner, B. F. (1957). *Verbal learning*. New York: Appleton.

Stanovich, K. E. (2000). *Progress in understanding reading*. New York: Guilford Press.

# 27

# Individual Differences Relations and Interrelations

## Reconciling Issues of Definition, Dynamism, and Development

*Sandra M. Loughlin and Patricia A. Alexander*

> Behavior is serial, not a mere succession. It can be resolved—it must be—into discrete acts, but no act can be understood apart from the series to which it belongs.
>
> (John Dewey, 1930, p. 412)

Almost a century ago, Dewey (1930) argued that efforts to understand a behavior must take into account the series to which it belongs; that is, the complex and dynamic context in which it arises. This volume aims to illuminate a set of factors that contribute to the complexity and dynamism of reading comprehension: individual differences. An impressive panel of international scholars has identified a plethora of individual differences factors that require consideration, including differences in cognitive skills and strategies, motivation, self-efficacy, and epistemic beliefs. These scholars have also offered insights into how these individual differences influence the practice and development of reading. In this effort, the chapters in this volume have, perhaps necessarily, examined individual differences in relative isolation from one another. However, these individual differences do not and cannot stand alone. Decoding and comprehending text occurs in a complex and ever-changing composition of facets relating to the reader, the text, and the context. Moreover, these facets interact and give rise to one another in various and dynamic configurations across the developmental trajectory.

In this chapter, we take on Dewey's challenge of understanding individual differences in "the series to which [they] belong" (1930, p. 412). In effect, we discuss the nature and necessity of focusing on specific individual difference factors in reading while also considering those factors in interactive and dynamic contexts. Specifically, we highlight three issues to consider when determining and describing the relations and interactions of individual difference factors in the act of reading. These issues are definition, dynamism, and development. With regard to *definition*, we examine what seemingly constitutes a "true" individual difference, rather than group or cohort variability, in order to promote research that is focused and consistent. In this effort, we offer a two-tiered, nested configuration of the individual differences represented in this *Handbook*. We then address the issue of *dynamism* and argue that individual difference factors must be considered in relation to one another and in light of the ever-changing nature of what must be read, for what purpose, and in what context. In terms of *development*, we discuss the developmental nature of reading and degree to which individual difference individually and in conjunction unfold over the lifespan. For each of these issues, we identify implications for research.

Ultimately, we step back and consider what the issues of definition, dynamism, and development collectively imply for the study of individual differences in reading. In this effort, we reflect upon the distinction between *patterns of difference* and *differences of patterns* (Salomon, 2006) and offer the Model of Domain Learning (Alexander, 1997, 2003a, 2003b) as a prototype for examining the dynamic interdependence of individual differences factors. Through this focus on reading as a complex and dynamic system, we hope to raise critical issues about the nature and study of individual differences.

## Issues of Definition

In order to determine and describe how individual differences relate and interact with one another in the context of reading, we must know what one is. Thus, the first issue we address is one of definition: What counts as an individual difference in reading? Two possible sources to answer this question are evident: traditional conceptions of individual differences and those differences included in this *Handbook*. We address each of these sources and then seek to reconcile the conceptual quandary they represent.

### *Traditional Conceptions of Individual Differences*

There is a long and rich history to the study of individual differences in human learning and development, a history that traces back to Sir Frances Galton (1869). Drawn to the revolutionary work of his cousin, Charles Darwin, Galton set out to turn a general fascination with the human uniqueness into a scientific exploration. More specifically, Galton's investigations into human differences were first triggered when he realized that many of those who received honors at Cambridge University were offspring of previous winners; raising the prospect of inherited traits.

Based on the principles of evolution, Galton hypothesized that such familial successes were not chance occurrences but arose as a consequence of particular mental and physical capabilities and propensities passed from parent to child. Galton's obsession in trying to document the mental and physical characteristics that account for some individuals' successes and other individuals' struggles became the foundation of the science of individual differences. His methodical approach, while primitive by contemporary standards, gave credence to the argument that there are a range of rather stable mental and physical factors that play an unavoidable and significant role in human learning and development.

In contemporary literature, we find that the traditional focus on individual differences has often been reframed or augmented by more neurobiological studies of human performance (Byrnes, 2012; Geary, 2012). The rise of techniques and instruments that Galton could never have envisioned—from event-related potentials (ERPs) and functional magnetic resonance imaging (fMRIs) to eye-tracking and eye-gaze analyses—have permitted researchers to look into the mind and through the eyes of readers. The resulting literatures on executive functioning and physiological indicators afford an even more complex and intricate portrait of the capabilities and propensities that individual readers bring to each and every engagement with text.

In addition, there has been a growing realization that individuals' successes and struggles, be they in reading or any challenging domain, cannot be ascribed solely to mental acuity or physical attributes. Indeed, rather durable personality factors (e.g., Eysenck & Eysenck, 1985; Komarraju, Karau, Schmeck, & Avdic, 2011) and particular affective/motivational concerns (e.g., Jonassen & Grabowski, 2012) have been increasingly associated with the individuals' achievements both in school and out of school. Concomitantly, within the educational literature, there has been extended consideration of how the nature of the context in which individuals' live and learn exert undeniable influence on how specific mental, physical, personality, and motivational attributes configure to promote or hinder learning and performance, including in the domain of reading.

Whether we are looking at definitions of individual differences historically or within contemporary literature, there is the consistent notion that such factors have a relatively stable nature. Without such relative stability there would be no mechanism for building models of or programs for reading development that consider the nature of the reader in any meaningful way. That is not to say that changes do not occur within any of the cognitive, dispositional, and conative attributes that mark human variability. However, such changes do not occur easily or sporadically, but transform over time as a result of neurophysiological maturation as a consequence of dramatic or accumulated events and experiences.

## Instantiated Definitions of Individual Differences in Reading

Within the pages of this *Handbook*, there is the concerted effort to take the historical and contemporary literature on individual differences and position it within the domain of reading. In this effort, an impressive and diverse group of international reading researchers has contributed topics that they believe represent sources of difference in individuals' reading abilities. As such, this volume arguably represents the instantiation of general conceptions of individual differences into the domain of reading. Herein we consider whether this instantiation retains the central character of individual difference or whether the translation from general to domain-specific conceptions has discernible effects on what counts as an individual difference.

Specifically, in examining the *Handbook* for the purpose of determining what counts as an individual difference, we identified chapters that reflect the traditional conception of individual differences as relatively stable and inherited traits, including contributions on memory, perceptual processing, and attention. Other offerings, however, do not at first blush appear to be about individual differences as Galton envisioned it, or about the tendencies or capacities of interest to contemporary neuroscientists or neurobiologists. Rather, these consider the effects that broader sociocultural and educational contexts exert on students, individually and collectively. For instance, in her chapter on poverty, Bhattacharya (Chapter 22) highlights characteristics of children raised in a culture of poverty and the consequences of those poverty-induced outcomes on reading performance. Similarly, Learned and Moje (Chapter 14) address how school context can support or constrain readers in ways that can produce and maintain individual differences. Other topics addressed in the *Handbook* appear to fall somewhere in between. Prior knowledge, for example, one of the most studied influences on successful reading (Alexander, Schallert, & Hare, 1991), is neither an inherited individual difference nor a contextual influence.

Despite the diversity of the contributions, as a collective, this volume seeks to establish that the cognitive, dispositional, and conative attributes of individual readers are enacted in environments and in learning contexts that can moderate, mitigate, or exacerbate whatever differences exist at a given point and time. Moreover, these sociocultural and educational contexts can work to shift the learning trajectory for individuals or groups of individuals over time.

Thus, while the topics represented in the *Handbook* do not all adhere to the traditional conception of individual differences, they are nevertheless all essential to understanding differences among individuals.

As the editor of this volume, Afflerbach (Chapter 1), clearly acknowledges this conceptual quandary when he states that:

> The lack of comprehensive accounting of individual differences in reading is reflected in the nature of reading programs, the outcomes that are expected from successful teaching and learning, and the manner in which reading development is assessed. It is my hope that this volume contributes to a fuller accounting and appreciation of individual differences in reading, and better understanding of how individual differences matter in students' reading development.
>
> (Preface, p. xv)

## Definitional Mapping

How do we reconcile this seeming conceptual quandary: What counts as individual differences traditionally, and how such differences are conceptualized in reading? Our approach is to offer a conceptual model of individual differences that positions definitional elements within a two-tiered, nested system (Figure 27.1). Specifically, we suggest that individual differences in reading can be described as primary, extended, or contextual in nature. Tier 1 of the model is consistent with the traditional literature on individual differences, as well as the more contemporary studies of neurobiological factors. Specifically, these differences are those primary cognitive or

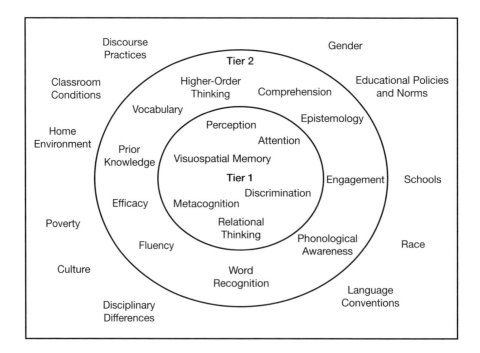

*Figure 27.1* A representation of Tier 1 and Tier 2 differences characteristics and their relation to broader sociocultural and educational contexts

neurophysiological characteristics of an individual that influence all human performance and development, including the development of reading. These primary, or what Afflerbach (Chapter 1) refers to as "basic" differences, include memory (Baddeley, 2003), attention (James, 1890; Wertheimer, 1923), relational thinking (Dumas, Alexander, & Grossnickle, 2013), and perceptual abilities (Gibson, 1994; Peirce, 1955).

By comparison, Tier 2 characteristics are those that grow out of primary capabilities and propensities, and that shape the nature of learning and development in specific arenas of human performance, including reading. Among such extended Tier 2 forces at work in reading are prior knowledge (Alexander & Judy, 1988), higher-order thinking (Schraw & Robinson, 2011), comprehension (McNamara & Kintsch, 1996), vocabulary (Nagy, Herman, & Anderson, 1985), and such motivational constructs as engagement (Guthrie & Wigfield, 1997) and self-efficacy (Bandura, 1982). What distinguishes these as Tier 2 attributes is that these individual-level factors are themselves influenced or shaped by even more basic and inherited Tier 1 abilities. For instance, readers' comprehension is predicated to some degree on their memory, attention, and perceptual processing (Reynolds, 1992). Further, while both Tier 1 and Tier 2 facets of individual differences are situated at the level of the individual and are potentially malleable, it is expected that elements within Tier 2 are more readily susceptible to endogenous and exogenous forces.

Finally, we nest Tier 1 and Tier 2 characteristics within broader sociocultural and educational contexts, and acknowledge that the attributes of the individual reader, be they primary or secondary in nature, reciprocally function in social, cultural, linguistic, and educational contexts that include society at large, homes, schools, classrooms, as well as the language and media systems in which reading occurs.

To illustrate better this conceptual mapping, let us turn to the specific contributions within this volume and position them within this two-tiered, nested model (see Figure 27.2). In so doing, we must acknowledge that our attempts at placement remain open to debate and discussion, but undertake this effort to serve to illuminate the definitional distinctions we seek to establish.

Easily positioned in Tier 1 are the chapters on attention (Reynolds et al., Chapter 26), perceptual processing (Rayner et al., Chapter 25), and memory (Prat et al., Chapter 24). Although the authors of these chapters have infused discussion of these basic attributes within contemporary theory and research, and have linked the findings directly to the domain of reading, their topics nonetheless would be familiar to traditional individual difference researchers.

Perhaps somewhat more contentious is our proposed positioning of metacognition within Tier 1. On the one hand, metacognition requires a level of awareness and effort that would seem to raise it to the realm of Tier 2. However, it could also be argued that humans, by their very nature, are inherently metacognitive—but not in a particularly sophisticated or well-honed manner. As John Flavell (e.g., Flavell & Wellman, 1977) has convincingly argued, individuals do not need to be taught to be metacognitive, and such capability in a rather rudimentary version seems to be evidenced in infancy. For that reason, we have also chosen to position Veenman's Chapter 3 on metacognition to this primary position, although it could well be that some manifestations of metacognition, as with self-regulation, have a more Tier 2 character, reflective of deeper contemplation and reflection (Stanovich, 2009).

Other contributions reflect the second tier of individual differences; that is, they consider aspects of individual differences that grow out of primary, Tier 1, differences. Among those contributions are the chapters on prior knowledge (Kendeou, & O'Brien, Chapter 12), epistemic beliefs (Bråten et al., Chapter 6), phonological awareness (Quinn et al., Chapter 7), comprehension (van den Broek et al., Chapter 11), higher-order thinking (McNamara et al., Chapter 13), engagement (Guthrie & Klauda, Chapter 4), phonological awareness (Schwanenflugel &

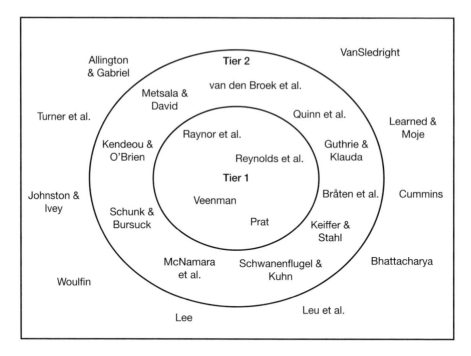

*Figure 27.2* Positioning of individual contributions to the *Handbook on Individual Differences in Reading* within a two-tiered socioculturally and educationally-nested system

Kuhn, Chapter 9), efficacy (Schunk, & Bursuck, Chapter 5), vocabulary (Kieffer & Stahl, Chapter 10), and word recognition (Metsala & David, Chapter 8). As this delineation conveys, many more of the contributions in the *Handbook* fall within Tier 2 of individual characteristics. This is perhaps not surprising given the domain-specific nature of this volume and the many interacting factors that give rise to reading performance.

Whereas Tier 1 and Tier 2 chapters attend to individual characteristics in basic or more extended ways, other chapters in this volume serve to position these characteristics in a wider sociocultural and educational context. For instance, contributions examine the effects of home (Turner et al., Chapter 20), schools (Learned & Moje, Chapter 14), and classroom characteristics (Allington, & Gabriel, Chapter 15) on students' reading, while others explore the relation between native language (Cummins, Chapter 17), classroom discourse (Johnston & Ivey, Chapter 16), and students' reading successes or struggles (Lee, Chapter 21). We have also positioned chapters in the broader context that focus on the influence of disciplinary (VanSledright, Chapter 18) and educational policies (Woulfin, Chapter 23) on individuals' reading.

## Implications for Research

In considering the issue of definition, particularly with respect to how it is defined in the *Handbook*, we see two broad implications for research on individual differences in reading. First, given the multi-level and nested nature of individual differences, it is essential that researchers strive for conceptual and methodological clarity. While there is some arguable benefit to broadening the traditional conception of individual difference, there is a concomitant burden to retain a clear understanding of the term. In essence, even as we seek to position discussion of individual differences within the domain of reading and thereby consider the effects of such an instantiation of these complex and relatively durable cognitive, dispositional, and conative factors on readers' engagement with and learning from text, care must be taken not to distort the inherent nature of individual differences in the process.

The second implication we see is a greater acknowledgment of the complex relation between context and primary and extended individual differences. This volume includes several insightful contributions regarding the ways in which individual differences play out in educational and sociocultural contexts. However, what typifies these contributions is a more one-directional rather than reciprocal consideration of the interplay between contextual forces and individual differences. Given the nature and scope of the *Handbook*, this approach is warranted. However, empirical research must move beyond a unidirectional approach to individual difference research and adopt more nuanced examinations of the manner in which cognitive, dispositional, and conative characteristics of learners play out differently in different contexts .

## Issues of Dynamism

The conceptual model presented in Figure 27.1 allows us to consider types of individual differences in reading, and to categorize each as primary, extended, or contextual in nature. As well, this representation foreshadows the complex and variable ways in which these differences relate and interact. As suggested by Figure 27.1, individual differences manifest in continuous and complicated orchestrations across and within Tiers 1 and 2, and are differentially enacted within broader educational and sociological contexts. Thus, the second issue we address here relates to the dynamism; specifically, the dynamic relations between and among individual differences and the evolving nature of what school and society consider text.

### Dynamism across and within Levels

Reading involves a transaction between a reader and an author through the text. The reader's individual attributes, both basic and extended, configure to shape the nature of that transaction even as the process of reading unfolds within a given context. For instance, the attention that the reader allocates and to what, as well as the perceptions that are formed about the message (Tier 1), are influenced by what that reader already knows about the topic, the vocabulary the authors has chosen, as well as the reader's beliefs about knowledge and knowing in the domain of reading (Tier 2). Further, what the student assumes to be the academic task at hand, the linguistic and discursive conventions within the classroom, the level of academic support or care communicated within the learning environment, and more (the sociocultural and educational contexts) continually conspire to shift reader attention or alter perceptions.

This across-level dynamism is well exemplified by the chapter on discursive practices in classrooms (Johnston & Ivey, Chapter 16). What Johnston and Ivey contend, for instance, is that positive discursive contexts can serve to promote students' social imagination, social self-regulation, their epistemic competence, and comprehension and recall of text, as well as other desirable outcomes. In essence, the influence of discursive practices in classrooms has deep and broad effects on more Tier 2 attributes of students.

The dynamism witnessed across the various levels of the two-tiered, nested model is mirrored, to some extent, within each of the designated levels. Indeed, the realization that unique characteristics of learners continuously interact in important ways is evident in many of the contributions to this volume. For instance, in their chapter on engagement, Guthrie and Klauda (Chapter 4) explicitly address the way in which factors of motivation, engagement, and achievement interrelate to forge an almost inseparable confluence within the Tier 2 system. Further, as Bråten et al. (Chapter 6) illustrate well in their examination of epistemic beliefs, readers' epistemic cognition and competence and the resulting actions they take become exponentially more complicated and challenging when there are multiple texts to process, a situation that occurs frequently within contemporary online reading environments.

Even at the level of the word, there is ample evidence of dynamism that must be acknowledged. Kieffer and Stahl (Chapter 10), for example, describe the "large problem space" (p. 122) created by vocabulary vis-à-vis other foundational reading components. Certainly, at a minimum, the word knowledge readers possess has long been a marker of their world knowledge as well as a predictor of academic success. In addition, phonological processing has a role to play in the words that readers come to recognize in oral and written language (Quinn et al., Chapter 7)—words that may eventually migrate into their oral or written vocabularies.

## Dynamism in Conceptions of Reading and Text

Another aspect of dynamism relates to evolving conceptions of reading and the ever-changing nature of what is ultimately read—that is, what constitutes *text*. Research on individual differences must take into account the multiplicity of symbol systems, sources, and contexts that make up the corpus of reading today.

Traditionally, reading has been associated with language, and involved decoding and comprehending words written on physical pages. However, contemporary conceptions of reading are shifting to include a variety of linguistic and non-linguistic symbol systems (e.g., mathematical symbols, musical notation, visual displays; Adams, 2003; Flood, Heath, & Lapp, 2008; Kress, 2008; Loughlin, 2013; New London Group, 1996; van Leeuwen, 1999). As Barton, Hamilton, and Ivanic (2000) observed, "people read times tables, maps, and music, as well as novels and academic articles . . . There is a great deal in common in the practices associated with these diverse texts" (p. 95). This expanded conception of reading has been reflected in recent and extensive education policy initiatives. Indeed, the new Common Core State Standards in Literacy specifically target the *reading* of non-text compositions. For instance, as described by Coleman (2013), the ninth and tenth grade Standards in Literacy require students to "analyze the representation of a subject or a key scene in two different artistic mediums, including what is emphasized or absent in each treatment" (p. 2).

Current conceptions of reading also increasingly acknowledge the critical need for readers to understand and integrate text from multiple sources (Anmarkrud, McCrudden, Bråten, & Strømsø, 2013; Braasch et al., 2009). VanSledright (Chapter 18), for instance, notes that historical thinking requires students to read and comprehend a variety of sources—many with competing or even conflicting accounts—and to integrate the many sources to form a coherent mental representation. The demands of multi-source reading occur both in print and online. Search engines present innumerable hits, which require the reader to navigate, select, comprehend, adjudicate, and integrate sources. Hypertexts, which are characterized by a nonlinear presentation of multiple sources of digital information, likewise have the benefits and burdens of multiple-source comprehension tasks. Indeed, multiplicity of sources is considered the defining characteristic of the *age of information* (Coiro & Dobler, 2007). In a similar vein, the ability to navigate and manage information in multiple sources is arguably an essential ability of competent readers (Alexander & the Disciplined Reading and Learning Research Laboratory [DRLRL], 2012). Unfortunately, research continues to document students' difficulties in understanding, integrating, and learning from multiple sources both in print and online (Bråten, Strømsø, & Ferguson, Chapter 6).

The rapid shift from print to screen (Leu et al., Chapter 19) underscores the dynamic nature of "text." As noted by these authors, the Internet reflects the diversity of what can be read and understood. Thus, reading online involves decoding and comprehending compositions encoded in a variety of symbol systems, navigating and synthesizing across multiple texts, and reading for pleasure as well as for purpose.

These evolving contexts for reading—the increasing prevalence of nonlinguistic, multi-sourced, and online texts—have ramifications for any number of Tier 1 and Tier 2 individual difference characteristics. For instance, when reading online there is a limitless number of texts that could be accessed—texts that vary by genre (e.g., blogs, articles, or books), symbol systems (e.g., pictures, music, language), and purpose (e.g., narrate, inform, or persuade). The diversity of this universe of texts puts readers' Tier 2 cognitive, dispositional, and conative characteristics (e.g., prior knowledge, epistemic judgments, higher-order thinking, or phonological awareness) to continual test and contributes to concomitant shifts in enactments of more basic processes (e.g., attention allocation, perceptual processing, or metacognitive monitoring).

## Implications for Research

Our understanding of how Tier 1 and Tier 2 characteristics differentially manifest in contexts is sorely limited. This limited understanding is not relegated solely to reading online, but extends to each of the sociocultural and educational settings acknowledged within this *Handbook* and in the extant literature. More research is needed that investigates how varying sociocultural and educational contexts affect students, individually and collectively. However, an equal emphasis should be given to a more systemic study of how the uniqueness of individual learners dynamically shapes what transpires within such contexts.

## Issues of Development

We have described reading as involving an exchange between reader and an often unseen and unknown author through the medium of a message (text)—a message engaged for *some* purpose within a *certain* time and *particular* place. Consequently, this exchange is inevitably developmental, as readers' ever-evolving understandings, affect, or motivations modulate from word to word, page to page, or text to text, and as the time and place of the reading act progresses. Thus, the final issue we raise here relates to the developmental nature of reading and the variable relation among individual differences that give rise to it. In particular, we argue that any effort to determine and describe relations and interactions of individual differences in reading must consider them—collectively and individually—over time.

## Developmental Nature of Reading

Reading is developmental; it is an ability acquired over time, which undergoes continual and complex changes across the lifespan. These changes occur as a consequence of individual differences and experiences, and the knowledge, beliefs, and processes that those differences and experiences afford (Alexander & DRLRL, 2012; Fox & Alexander, 2011). This developmental trajectory is also significantly influenced by the cognitive and metacognitive awareness and strategies that readers bring to bear with every reading act. In essence, readers' course of development is not set but remains somewhat in their own control (Bandura, 1986) and is shaped by the choices made (Deci & Ryan, 1985) and the efforts exerted (Dweck & Leggett, 1988).

Alternative perspectives on reading development exist within the literacy community. For instance, reading development is often conveyed in terms of the particular literacy skills that individuals acquire—skills that allow for the processing of more complex texts and tasks over time. This perspective of reading development is represented within curricular mappings or learning progressions such as frame the Common Core or related policies. In effect, students at grade X are expected to be able to perform task Y when reading text Z. One outcome of this orientation toward reading development is that it deals largely with the acquisition of foundational reading skills and processes and attends little to ideas of reading competence or expert reading (Fox, 2009) or the course of development that leads to those outcomes. Such an orientation toward reading development likewise emphasizes factors of reading amenable to interventions with early or struggling readers (e.g., phonemic awareness, phonics, or fluency). A significant rationale for the emphasis on early and struggling readers is the belief that reading is broken up into two distinct periods: learning to read and reading to learn. In this perspective, which is predicated an oversimplification of Chall's (1983) stages of reading development, young children must master the rudiments of decoding before they can tackle the challenge of understanding it. Regrettably, the bifurcation of reading and the concomitant emphasis on the early stage of its development is embedded in widely cited documents and entrenched in education policy (Alexander & DRLRL, 2012; Woulfin, Chapter 23).

In contrast, the second view of reading development extends well beyond emergent literacy, and considers reading to be a long-term process occurring across the lifespan, culminating in a proficient adult reader who easily reads a variety of materials—including those that are difficult or not intrinsically interesting—for varying purposes (Alexander, 2005; Alexander & DRLRL, 2012; RAND Reading Study Group, 2002). In their overview of individual differences in reading, Fox and Maggioni (Chapter 2) offer a thoughtful and detailed examination of the cognitive, dispositional, and conative factors at play in the processing of text at any time or over time. In so doing, they highlight the myriad ways in which individuals' abilities, capacities, dispositions, and inclinations change over the lifespan and as the demands of text evolve in purpose and complexity. While developmental models of reading have been offered (Alexander, 2005; Chall, 1983), popular perspectives and current policy initiatives often do not reflect this longer-term view of reading (Alexander & DRLRL, 2012).

Like Fox and Maggioni (Chapter 2), however, we promote this second, less emphasized perspective on reading development, and argue that considering reading—and the associated individual differences that give rise to it—within a lifespan developmental framework is both more accurate and more generative.

## Developmental Nature of Individual Differences

Just as reading develops in meaningful and predictable ways over the lifespan, there are changes that occur in the array of individual difference factors that help to fuel that development—changes that transpire as a result of the neurophysiological maturation or life events and experiences. Thus, even though we can speak about the relative stability of individual differences, we must do so with the acknowledgment that the "relative" disclaimer allows for the certain and essential variation and modulation evidenced over time. Let us take the case of working memory, a richly investigated factor in human variability, to illustrate what we are referring to as developmental change in individual difference factors.

It is often presumed that individuals manifest certain capacities in working memory early and that those capacities influence learning over time (Prat et al., Chapter 24). However, it is also understood that individuals' base capacity is not fixed but can be significantly influenced by the memory strategies they develop (e.g., chunking and elaboration) and the effort after remembering that they regularly exert. Thus, individuals can alter their ability to remember and those transformations can remain relatively stable pending dramatic or traumatic events.

What is also important to the theme of this chapter is that we can conceive of these developmental changes in individual differences as related or interrelated. In effect, if changes in one individual difference factor occur, there is the expectation that other factors can likewise be affected. Let us return to the case of working memory to explain this argument. Consider for a moment that a student has worked diligently to improve her ability to remember what she reads in text. She has learned to employ several effective memory strategies when confronted with what she judges to be challenging texts or demanding tasks. Consequently, she has begun to feel more efficacious about academic reading and has come to enjoy reading more. Thus, the rather enduring shifts in her working memory have influenced other individual differences including her metacognitive judgments, cognitive strategies, and self-efficacy beliefs. We will revisit this issue of the related and interrelated nature of individual difference factors in our consideration of a systems approach to the study individual differences in reading.

## Implications for Research

As we bring the issue of development to a close, critical implications for research rise to the fore. On the one hand, efforts to understand how the array of cognitive, dispositional, and conative individual difference factors plays out in the act of reading will be unavoidably hampered unless the developmental nature of reading is duly considered. Reading at age 5 is not the same as reading at age 15, 30, or 45. Thus, how individual differences contribute to and shape the act of reading at those varied ages must be systematically weighed. On the other hand, the same concern manifests in the study of individual difference factors. To delve deeply into any one of the individual difference factors that populate this volume without appreciating the effect that comes as the nature of reading per se transforms across the lifespan results in an incomplete and potentially misleading portrayal.

## A Systems Approach to the Study of Individual Differences

Up to this point, our intention has been to highlight three issues—definition, dynamism, and development—that arise in the study of individual differences in reading, and to identify what these issues imply for research. In so doing, we have described reading, and the individual differences that give rise to it, as being multidimensional and multicontextual, dynamically related, and developmental in nature. Here, we consider what these issues together imply for efforts to describe and determine relations and interrelations of individual difference factors in reading.

Given its multidimensionality, dynamism, and development, the study of individual differences in reading is necessarily the study of a complex system; that is, a whole composed of interconnected parts whose relations change over time (Bar-Yam, 2004). In the case of reading, the interconnected parts are the many individual difference factors—both basic and extended— that manifest and interact with one another in variable contexts across the lifespan. What is required for the study of a complex and ever-changing system? We argue that a more systems-focused research orientation is necessary. In making this case, we draw on Salomon's (1991, 2006) distinction between analytic and systemic research, which contrasts patterns of difference and differences of patterns. We also offer the Model of Domain Learning (Alexander, 1997, 2003a, 2003b) as a prototype of a bounded-systems approach to studying individual differences with implications for the domain of reading.

## Analytic vs. Systemic Research

Salomon (1991, 2006) differentiates between two categories of research orientations, what he terms the *analytic* and *systemic* approaches. According to Salomon, analytic research assumes that it is both possible and desirable to isolate and manipulate variables, leading to a better understanding of the whole system. Corollary assumptions of an analytic approach are that each variable or element in the system has meaning in and of itself, such that the variable's contribution can be observed and understood, and such that the manipulation of a variable in a system leaves the others unchanged. Hence, in analytic research, hypotheses pertain to individual variables and *patterns of difference* in mean outcomes.

In contrast, systemic research seeks to identify *difference of patterns* of groups of variables. Systems-focused research considers complex systems as wholes, under the assumption that variables occur in "clouds of interrelated events," which afford and define one another in a transactional manner. By extension, the systemic approach assumes that a complex system cannot be satisfactorily reduced to its component parts—variables cannot be meaningfully isolated or manipulated because a change in one necessarily implies a change in others. Thus, in the systemic approach, hypotheses pertain to complex systems as gestalts, rather than individual variables.

Both analytic and systemic approaches can and should be utilized in research addressing individual differences in reading. In some cases, one individual difference variable may be potentially more potent or salient than others, and research studies should examine the influence of that variable on reading outcomes. However, analytic research cannot fully account for the complex and dynamic relations among individual difference factors or capture how sociocultural and educational contexts modulate, amplify, or reconfigure them. Thus, systemic research is a necessary corollary.

The need for both analytic and system research can be elaborated by way of example. In this effort, we consider relational reasoning as an individual difference variable. Relational reasoning has been defined as the ability to discern pattern within any informational stream (Alexander, Dumas, Grossnickle, List, & Firetto, 2014; Dumas et al., 2013). Whenever individuals recognize the similarities or dissimilarities between ideas, objects, or experiences, they are reasoning relationally. The literature is replete with studies that have demonstrated how particular forms of relational reasoning, particularly analogical reasoning, are linked to human learning and performance (e.g., Holyoak, 2012). Due to its foundational nature, we position relational reasoning as a Tier 1 individual difference variable. Indeed, there is a growing body of analytic research studies illuminating the essential nature of relational reading for comprehension (e.g., Ivanova, Pickering, Branigan, McLean, & Costa, 2012). For instance, when the words on a page configure into a main idea or a specific structure for a paragraph or a passage is recognized, then relational reasoning is evidenced (Meyer & Poon, 2001). Likewise, when children recognize words based on orthographic similarities (Goswami, 1992; Savage, Deault, Daki, & Aouad, 2011), they are reasoning relationally.

Overall, the purpose of the aforementioned analytic studies was to determine the possible contribution of a single factor on a dependent variable. That is, such investigations attempted to estimate the net effect of relational reasoning on students' reading outcomes at the level of word or passage. The patterns of difference that emerged from these studies suggest that changes in relational reasoning ability are associated with differences in reading outcomes.

While research has established relational reasoning as an important source of variability in individuals' learning and development, including in the domain of reading, the ways in which relational reasoning relates to other individual difference factors remains underspecified. There are a number of likely relations yet to be investigated. A student's use of relational reasoning strategies in a reading task is likely influenced by a number of other Tier 1 and Tier 2 differences: interest in the topic, efficacy for reading, working memory capacity, vocabulary, and so on. As a result, given two comprehension tasks, a student may demonstrate differential patterns of relational reasoning strategies and apparent capabilities. However the patterns of relation among relational reasoning and other sources of individual difference—at a given time and over the lifespan—remain unclear. Moreover, the relational reasoning literature has only begun to investigate the developmental trajectory associated with this ability and its potential for malleability and intervention.

Relational reasoning is just one example of a broader problem plaguing the individual differences literature: a relative dearth of research acknowledging and investigating the complexities associated with how individuals' cognitive, dispositional, and conative features relate and interact in reading tasks across the lifespan. More research is needed to illuminate the pattern of relations among the variables or to describe how those patterns differ across reading tasks and across time.

## A Bounded-Systems Approach to Research

Given the myriad individual difference factors that impact reading outcomes, however, how can a systemic examination be accomplished? It is virtually impossible—both theoretically and empirically—to account for all of the individual difference variables in a single reading task, let alone the innumerable reading tasks that occur over a lifetime. How can individual difference researchers attempt to model these complex and dynamic relations? A number of solutions have been proposed. For instance, Bruner (1990) suggests that qualitative narrative can offer a nuanced and plausible description of a complex interrelation of factors. There are also quantitative approaches. Winne (2006), for example, recommends tracing many kinds of fine-grained events over time, and using computer trace data to describe whether and how learning changes and develops over time. Likewise, Salomon (1991) argues for the use of a Guttman-like Small Space Analysis protocol, which produces a static, spatial map of distances (i.e., correlations) between all variables in an analysis.

To these, we would like to add another suggestion that has proved fruitful for our research efforts, what we term here the *bounded-systems approach*. This conceptual approach seeks to identify and model a set of interrelated variables and examine their dynamic interaction over time. Key to this effort is identifying a composite of variables. A composite is not simply a collection or cluster of variables; rather, it is a configuration of variables that relate to one another in a way that is organized and discernible. The focus of bounded-systems research is articulating the structure—the pattern— of those relations in a given time point and over time.

The Model of Domain Learning (MDL; Alexander, 1997, 2003a, 2003b; Alexander, Jetton, & Kulikowich, 1995; Murphy & Alexander, 2002) provides a prototype for a bounded-systems approach. While the MDL can be applied to the development of expertise in any domain, it has most frequently been applied to expertise development in reading, as we do here. The MDL addresses six Tier 2 individual difference factors: domain and topic knowledge, situational and individual interest, and deep and surface strategic processing. Specifically, the MDL considers how these six factors manifest and interrelate across the lifespan. This relation is depicted in Figure 27.3. As seen in Figure 27.3, the MDL demonstrates that the six individual difference variables under examination change over time. For instance, students' use of deep-processing strategies, which involve the personalization or transformation of text, increase over time, while their surface-processing strategies, those that promote initial access to text, decrease.

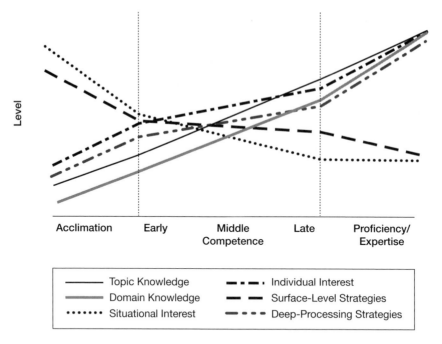

*Figure 27.3* The Model of Domain Learning and the concomitant interplay of knowledge, interest, and strategic processing in the path of development from acclimation to competence to proficiency/expertise in any academic domain

The power of the MDL, however, is not in its modeling of the six factors individually. Rather, the power of the MDL is in its ability to predict and explain configurations of all six factors by articulating *difference of patterns* across the lifespan of a reader. The first pattern is one of high levels of situational interest and a reliance on surface-processing strategies, combined with low levels of topic and domain knowledge, low individual interest, and infrequent use of deep-processing strategies. This pattern of variables is frequently seen in young readers and is described as acclimation. Proficient readers, in contrast, manifest a very different pattern of variables. Proficient readers have high levels of topic and domain knowledge, display individual interest in reading, and use deep rather than surface-processing strategies to comprehend text. By identifying differential patterns of knowledge, interest, and strategic processing over time, the MDL provides a window into the complexities of reading, reflecting a systemic approach to its study.

A similar bounded-systems approach may prove valuable for others seeking to determine and describe relations and interactions of individual differences in reading. For instance, we argued that the interplay between contextual forces and individual differences—the manner in which cognitive, dispositional, and conative characteristics of learners play out differently in different contexts—need elucidation. A bounded-systems approach could prove powerful for this effort. A researcher might, for example, consider how a set of Tier 1or Tier 2 factors (e.g., prior knowledge, higher-order thinking, and self-efficacy) are differentially manifest in reading comprehension activities for school or for personal interest, or consider how the pattern of variables changes when text is presented online instead of in print. Through the use of the bounded-systems approach and other systemic research efforts, researchers can identify *differences of pattern*, and better illuminate the manner and degree to which individual differences contribute to the complexity and dynamism of reading comprehension.

## Conclusion

We opened this contribution with a quote by Dewey (1930), who reminded us of the tension inherent in the study of any complex behavior. On the one hand, aspects of the behavior must be identified and isolated, resolved into "discrete acts," in an effort to study them in a systematic fashion (1930, p. 412). On the other hand, it is not possible to satisfactorily reduce a complex behavior to its component parts—this is the nature of complexity—and so the behavior must simultaneously be considered as a gestalt, in the "series to which it belongs" (1930, p. 412).

We have been honored here to consider the series to which individual difference in reading belong. In so doing, we identified reading comprehension as a complex behavior, marked by multiple dimensions and iterations of individual difference factors that manifest and interact in variable configurations by context and over time. In light of our finding and Dewey's (1930) insight, we have argued that the study of individual differences in reading requires a systems-focused research approach, one that sets out to identify and describe patterns in variables in order to consider how those patterns differentially manifest in sociocultural and educational contexts and over the lifespan of a reader.

Just as conceptions of text and reading evolve, so too must our approach to studying the myriad differences that individuals bring to a reading task. It is not enough to engage predominantly in analytic-focused research; analytic research is necessary but not sufficient to illuminate the role of individual difference factors in reading comprehension. Rather, an equal and concerted effort must be made to consider relations and interrelations of differences in the differing contexts and developmental stages that make up the life of a reader.

What our brief contribution suggests is that whatever the presumed profiles of individual students as readers or regardless of the typical course of actions that might unfold in a particular context, variation and modulation can occur for any number of reasons. Change any one of the factors that compromise that system of individual differences in some significant way, and the behaviors that manifest can be surprising in potentially positive or negative ways. It is this intricacy—the inherent juxtaposition of *relative stability* and *inevitable variability*—that makes the study of individual differences in reading so complex, yet so fascinating.

## References

Adams, T. L. (2003). Reading mathematics: More than words can say. *The Reading Teacher, 56*, 786–795.

Alexander, P. A. (1997). Mapping the multidimensional nature of domain learning: The interplay of cognitive, motivational, and strategic forces. In M. L. Maehr & P. R. Pintrich (Eds.), *Advances in Motivation and Achievement* (Vol. 10, pp. 213–250). Greenwich, CT: JAI Press.

Alexander, P. A. (2003a). The development of expertise: The journey from acclimation to proficiency. *Educational Researcher, 32*(8), 10–14.

Alexander, P. A. (2003b). Profiling the developing reader: The interplay of knowledge, interest, and strategic processing. In C. M. Fairbanks, J. Worthy, B. Maloch, J. V. Hoffman, & D. L. Schallert (Eds.), *The fifty-first yearbook of the National Reading Conference* (pp. 47–65). Oak Creek, WI: National Reading Conference.

Alexander, P. A. (2005). The path to competence: A lifespan developmental perspective on reading. *Journal of Literacy Research, 37*, 413–436.

Alexander, P. A., & the Disciplined Reading and Learning Research Laboratory (2012). Reading into the future: Competence for the 21st century. *Educational Psychologist, 47*(4), 1–22. doi:10.1080/00461520.2012.722511

Alexander, P. A., Dumas, D., Grossnickle, E. M., List, A., & Firetto, C. M. (2014). *Measuring relational reasoning*. Manuscript submitted for publication.

Alexander, P. A., Jetton, T. L., & Kulikowich, J. M. (1995). Interrelationship of knowledge, interest, and recall: Assessing a model of domain learning. *Journal of Educational Psychology, 87,* 559–575.

Alexander, P. A., & Judy, J. E. (1988). The interaction of domain-specific and strategic knowledge in academic performance. *Review of Educational Research, 58*(4), 375–404.

Alexander, P. A., Schallert, D. L., & Hare, V. C. (1991). Coming to terms: How researchers in learning and literacy talk about knowledge. *Review of Educational Research, 61,* 315–343.

Anmarkrud, Ø., McCrudden, M. T., Bråten, I., & Strømsø, H. I. (2013). Task-oriented reading of multiple documents: Online comprehension processes and offline products. *Instructional Science, 41*(5), 1–22.

Baddeley, A. (2003). Working memory: Looking back and looking forward. *Nature Reviews Neuroscience, 4*(10), 829–839. doi:10.1038/nrn1201

Bandura, A. (1982). Self-efficacy mechanism in human agency. *American Psychologist, 37,* 122–147.

Bandura, A. (1986). *Social foundations of thought and action: A social cognitive theory.* Englewood Cliffs, NJ: Prentice-Hall.

Bar-Yam, Y. (2004). *Making things work: Solving complex problems in a complex world.* Cambridge, MA: NECSI Knowledge Press.

Barton, D., Hamilton, M., & Ivanic, R. (2000). *Situated literacies: reading and writing in Context.* London: Routledge.

Braasch, J. L., Lawless, K. A., Goldman, S. R., Manning, F. H., Gomez, K. W., & MacLeod, S. M. (2009). Evaluating search results: An empirical analysis of middle school students' use of source attributes to select useful sources. *Journal of Educational Computing Research, 41*(1), 63–82.

Bruner, J. S. (1990). *Acts of meaning (the Jerusalem-Harvard Lectures).* Cambridge, MA: Harvard University Press.

Byrnes, J. P. (2012). How neuroscience contributes to our understanding of learning and development in typically developing and special-needs students. In K. R. Harris, S. Graham, & T. Urdan (Eds.), *Educational psychology handbook* (Vol. 1, pp. 561–595). Washington, DC: American Psychological Association.

Chall, J. S. (1983). *Stages of reading development.* New York: McGraw-Hill.

Coleman, D. (2013). *Guiding principles for the arts, Grades K–12.* New York State Education Department. Retrieved May 12, 2013 from http://usny.nysed.gov/rttt/docs/guidingprinciples-arts.pdf.

Coiro, J., & Dobler, E. (2007). Exploring the online reading comprehension strategies used by sixth-grade skilled readers to search for and locate information on the Internet. *Reading Research Quarterly, 42*(2), 214–257.

Deci, E. L., & Ryan, R. M. (1985). *Intrinsic motivation and self-determination in human behavior.* New York: Plenum Publishing.

Dewey, J. (1930). Conduct and experience. In C. Murchism (Ed.), *Psychologies of 1930* (pp. 410–429). Worchester, MA: Clark University Press.

Dumas, D., Alexander, P. A., & Grossnickle, E. M. (2013). Relational reasoning and its manifestations in the educational context: A systematic review of the literature. *Educational Psychology Review, 25,* 391–427. doi: 10.1007/s10648-013-9224-4

Dweck, C. S., & Leggett, E. L. (1988). A social-cognitivist approach to motivation and personality. *Psychological Review, 95,* 256–273.

Eysenck, H. J., & Eysenck, M. W. (1985). *Personality and individual differences.* New York: Plenum Press.

Flavell, J. H., & Wellman, H. M. (1977). Metamemory. In R. V. Kail & J. W. Hagen (Eds.), *Perspectives on the development of memory and cognition* (pp. 3–33). Hillsdale, NJ: Lawrence Erlbaum Associates.

Flood, J., Heath, S. B., & Lapp, D. (2008). *Handbook of research on teaching literacy through visual and communicative arts, volume II.* Newark, DE: International Reading Association.

Fox, E. (2009). The role of reader characteristics in processing and learning from informational text. *Review of Educational Research, 79,* 197–261.

Fox, E., & Alexander, P. A. (2011). Learning to read. In P. A. Alexander & R. Mayer (Eds.), *Handbook of research on learning and instruction* (pp. 7–31). New York: Routledge.

Galton, F. R. (1869). *Hereditary Genius.* London: Macmillan and Company.

Geary, D. C. (2012). Evolutionary educational psychology. In K. R. Harris, S. Graham, & T. Urdan (Eds.), *Educational psychology handbook* (Vol. 1, pp. 597–621). Washington, DC: American Psychological Association.

Gibson, J. J. (1994). The visual perception of objective motion and subjective movement. *Psychological Review*, *101*, 318–323.

Goswami, U. (1992). *Analogical reasoning in children*. Hillsdale, NJ: Lawrence Erlbaum Associates.

Guthrie, J. T., & Wigfield, A. (1997). *Reading engagement: Motivating readers through integrated instruction*. Newark, DE: International Reading Association.

Holyoak, K. J. (2012). Analogy and relational reasoning. In K. J. Holyoak & R. G. Morrison (Eds.), *The Oxford Handbook of Thinking and Reasoning* (pp. 234–259). New York: Oxford University Press.

Ivanova, I., Pickering, M. J., Branigan, H. P., McLean, J. F., & Costa, A. (2012). The comprehension of anomalous sentences: Evidence from structural priming. *Cognition*, *122*(2), 193–209. doi: 10.1016/j.cognition.2011.10.013

James, W. (1890). *The principles of psychology* (Vols. 1 & 2). New York: Literacy Classics of the United States. http://www.emory.edu/EDUCATION/mfp/james.html http://psychclassics.yorku.ca/James/Principles/index.htm.

Jonassen, D. H., & Grabowski, B. L. (2012). *Handbook of individual differences learning and instruction*. New York: Routledge.

Komarraju, M., Karau, S. J., Schmeck, R. R., & Avdic, A. (2011). The big five personality traits, learning styles, and academic achievement. *Personality and Individual Differences*, *51*(4), 472–477.

Kress, G. R. (2008). "Literacy" in a multimodal environment of communication. In J. Flood, S. B. Heath, & D. Lapp (Eds.), *Handbook of research on teaching literacy through visual and communicative arts, volume II*. Newark, DE: International Reading Association.

Loughlin, S. (2013). *Examining trans-symbolic and symbol-specific processes in poetry and painting*. Unpublished doctoral dissertation. University of Maryland, College Park.

McNamara, D. S., & Kintsch, W. (1996). Learning from texts: Effects of prior knowledge and text coherence. *Discourse Processes*, *22*(3), 247–288.

Meyer, B. J. F., & Poon, L. W. (2001). Effects of the structure strategy and signaling on recall of the text. *Journal of Educational Psychology*, *93*, 141–159.

Murphy, P. K., & Alexander, P. A. (2002). What counts? The predictive power of subject-matter knowledge, strategic processing, and interest in domain-specific performance. *Journal of Experimental Education*, *70*, 197–214.

Nagy, W. E., Herman, P. A., & Anderson, R. C. (1985). Learning words from context. *Reading Research Quarterly*, *20*(2), 233–253.

New London Group (1996). A pedagogy of multiliteracies: Designing social futures. *Harvard Educational Review*, *66*, 60–92.

Peirce, C. (1955). *Philosophical writings of Peirce*. Mineola, NY: Courier Dover.

RAND Reading Study Group (2002). *Reading for understanding: Toward an R&D program in reading comprehension*. Santa Monica, CA: RAND Corporation

Reynolds, R. E. (1992). Selective attention and prose learning: Theoretical and empirical research. *Educational Psychology Review*, *4*(4), 345–391.

Salomon, G. (1991). Transcending the qualitative-quantitative debate: The analytic and systemic approaches to educational research. *Educational Researcher*, *20*, 10–18.

Salomon, G. (2006). The systemic vs. analytic study of complex learning environments. In J. Ellen & R. E. Clark (Eds.), *Handling complexity in learning environments: Theory and research* (pp. 255–274). Amsterdam: Elsevier.

Savage, R. S., Deault, L., Daki, J., & Aouad, J. (2011). Orthographic analogies and early reading: Evidence from a multiple clue word paradigm. *Journal of Educational Psychology*, *103*, 190–205. doi: 10.1037/a0021621

Schraw, G., & Robinson, D. H. (2011). *Assessment of higher order thinking skills: Current perspectives on cognition, learning and instruction*. Charlotte, NC: Information Age Publishing.

Stanovich, K. E. (2009). Rational and irrational thought: The thinking that IQ tests miss. *Scientific American Mind*, *20*(6), 34–39.

van Leeuwen, T. (1999). *Speech, music, sound*. London: Macmillan.

Wertheimer, M. (1923). Principles of perceptual organization. Translated in D. C. Beardslee & M. Wertheimer (Eds.), *Readings in Perception* (pp. 115–135). New York: Van Nostrand.

Winne, P. H. (2006). Meeting challenges to researching learning from instruction by increasing the complexity of research. In J. Elen & R. E. Clark (Eds.), *Handling complexity in learning environments: Research and theory* (pp. 221–236). Amsterdam: Pergamon.

# List of Contributors

**Matthew J. Abbott**, University of California, San Diego, USA

**Peter Afflerbach**, University of Maryland, USA

**Patricia A. Alexander**, University of Maryland, USA

**Laura K. Allen**, Learning Sciences Institute, Arizona State University, USA

**Richard L. Allington**, University of Tennessee, USA

**Alpana Bhattacharya**, Queens College, CUNY, USA

**Ivar Bråten**, University of Oslo, Norway

**William D. Bursuck**, University of North Carolina at Greensboro, USA

**Byeong-Young Cho**, University of Pittsburgh, USA

**Maria E. Crassas**, University of Maryland, USA

**Jim Cummins**, The University of Toronto, Canada

**Anne E. Cunningham**, University of California, Berkeley, USA

**Margaret D. David**, Mount Saint Vincent University, Canada

**Leila E. Ferguson**, University of Oslo, Norway

**Elena Forzani**, University of Connecticut, USA

**Emily Fox**, University of Maryland College Park, USA

**Rachael Gabriel**, University of Connecticut, USA

**John T. Guthrie**, University of Maryland College Park, USA

**Amy Hutchison**, Iowa State University, USA

**Gay Ivey**, University of Wisconsin-Madison, USA

**Matthew Jacovina**, Learning Sciences Institute, Arizona State University, USA

**Peter Johnston**, The University at Albany, USA

**Panayiota Kendeou**, University of Minnesota, USA

**Michael J. Kieffer**, New York University, USA

**Carita Kiili**, University of Jyväskylä, Filand

**Susan Lutz Klauda**, University of Maryland College Park, USA

**Astrid Kraal**, Leiden University, the Netherlands

**Melanie R. Kuhn**, Purdue University, USA

**Julie E. Learned**, University at Albany, SUNY, USA

**Carol D. Lee**, Northwestern University, USA

**Donald J. Leu**, University of Connecticut, USA

**Sandra M. Loughlin**, University of Maryland, USA

**Danielle S. McNamara**, Learning Sciences Institute, Arizona State University, USA

**Liliana Maggioni**, The Catholic University of America, USA

**Jamie L. Metsala**, Mount Saint Vincent University, Canada

**Elizabeth Birr Moje**, University of Michigan, USA

**Jolien M. Mouw**, Leiden University, the Netherlands

**Edward J. O'Brien**, University of New Hampshire, USA

**Patrick Plummer**, University of California, San Diego, USA

**Chantel S. Prat**, University of Washington, USA

**Jamie M. Quinn**, Florida State University, USA

**Keith Rayner**, University of California, San Diego, USA

**Ralph E. Reynolds**, Iowa State University, USA

**Dale H. Schunk**, University of North Carolina at Greensboro, USA

**Paula J. Schwanenflugel**, University of Georgia, USA

**Pamela H. Segal**, University of Maryland, College Park, USA

**Roy Seo**, University of Washington, USA

**Mercedes Spencer**, Florida State University, USA

**Katherine D. Stahl**, New York University, USA

**Keith E. Stanovich**, University of Toronto, Canada

**Helge I. Strømsø**, University of Oslo, Norway

**Jennifer D. Turner**, University of Maryland, College Park, USA

**Paul van den Broek**, Leiden University, the Netherlands

**Bruce VanSledright**, University of North Carolina, Charlotte, USA

**Marcel V.J. Veenman**, Institute for Metacognition Research, The Netherlands / Leiden University, The Netherlands

Contributors

**Richard K. Wagner**, Florida State University, USA

**Sarah L. Woulfin**, University of Connecticut, USA

**Brianna L. Yamasaki**, University of Washington, USA

# Index

ability grouping 232
absolutist view of knowledge 68, 72
academic language; academic conversations 214; catch-up trajectories 227–228; compared with conversational language proficiency 228; development 225; linguistic complexity 228; linguistically diverse students 227; scaffolded instruction 228
academic tracking; institutionalized 184; negative effects 183–184, 232; opportunity to learn 287; reading intervention practices 183–184; relation to poverty and racism 289
academic vocabulary; assessment 131; breadth and depth 123; development 133; instruction 126, 128; tiers of words 125–126
accountability; Accountability First logic 319–328, *323*; political influences 319; relation to curriculum 297, 319; tests scores 9, 130; top-down policy 322
achievement 112, 180, 186, 265, 330, 366, 379, 384; classroom influences 196–204; factors 9; family influences 275–281; language differences 223–232, 234–240; motivation 41–51; policy 319–326; poverty 305–315; race 287–292, 296–299; self-efficacy 55, 59–60; word recognition 93–101, 103
achievement gap *see also* National Assessment of Educational Progress; immigrant students 224; online reading 265; race 287–292; socioeconomic status 265, 311, 313
achievement motivation 289
action control theory 57
activity theory 50
adequate yearly progress (AYP) 9
adolescent literacy; need for literacy instruction 291; social interactions 179–180
affect 1–12; academic achievement 289, 296; Bloom's Taxonomy 165; cognition 1–12; development 385; engagement and motivation 41–53; parent-child book reading 275–276; RAND report 16; self-efficacy, volition and agency 54–66; vocabulary learning 134

agentive narrative 210–211
agency 18, 54–66, 186–187, 212, 220, 241 *see also* self-efficacy, volition; definition 54; in models of reading 58–59; motivation 59–62; relation to self-efficacy and volition 57; social cognitive theory 56–57
allocating attention 219, 339; important information 142; working memory 142
analytic research 388, 391
assessment; accountability; comprehension 146; fluency 109, 113–115; higher-order thinking 167–174; influence on conceptualization of individual differences 7–10, 18, 178–192, 319–325, 328, 333; influence on curriculum 7–10; limitations 7–10, 287, 296–297; metacognition 34–35; motivation 45; new literacies 262–263; phonological awareness 88; qualitative measures and quantitative measures 21; self-efficacy 60; testing 7–10, 319–325; vocabulary 132–135; word recognition 99
attention 42, 49, 55, 59–60, 152, 156, 168–169, 215, 359–360; allocation 142, 218–219, 365, 385; regulation 132; resources 15–17; selective 27, 32, 142, 342, 364–367; shifting 132–133, 144, 335; theories 337–339
attitude 1–5, 20, 185, 192, 227, 234, 239, 256, 264, 273, 276, 281, 296, 308
attributions 6, 290, 296
automaticity 47; decoding 47; fluency 107–108, 112–114; rapid automatized naming (RAN) 114; relation to motivation and engagement 47; word recognition 93, 100–101
autonomy 56–57, 189, 210, 217, 220, 320; perceived 46; support 48

background knowledge *see also* domain knowledge; prior knowledge 15, 44, 69, 151–163, 186, 196, 277, 299; L2 235–236, 239–240; motivation 46–47; reading achievement 44; relation to comprehension 139–144; valuing 233
balanced approach to literacy instruction 197, 207, 240, 366